1 MONTH FREE READING

at

www.ForgottenBooks.com

By purchasing this book you are eligible for one month membership to ForgottenBooks.com, giving you unlimited access to our entire collection of over 1,000,000 titles via our web site and mobile apps.

To claim your free month visit: www.forgottenbooks.com/free278715

* Offer is valid for 45 days from date of purchase. Terms and conditions apply.

English
Français
Deutsche
Italiano
Español
Português

www.forgottenbooks.com

Mythology Photography **Fiction**
Fishing Christianity **Art** Cooking
Essays Buddhism Freemasonry
Medicine **Biology** Music **Ancient Egypt** Evolution Carpentry Physics
Dance Geology **Mathematics** Fitness
Shakespeare **Folklore** Yoga Marketing
Confidence Immortality Biographies
Poetry **Psychology** Witchcraft
Electronics Chemistry History **Law**
Accounting **Philosophy** Anthropology
Alchemy Drama Quantum Mechanics
Atheism Sexual Health **Ancient History**
Entrepreneurship Languages Sport
Paleontology Needlework Islam
Metaphysics Investment Archaeology
Parenting Statistics Criminology
Motivational

1,000,000 Books

are available to read at

www.ForgottenBooks.com

Read online
Download PDF
Purchase in print

ISBN 978-1-332-06306-2
PIBN 10278715

This book is a reproduction of an important historical work. Forgotten Books uses state-of-the-art technology to digitally reconstruct the work, preserving the original format whilst repairing imperfections present in the aged copy. In rare cases, an imperfection in the original, such as a blemish or missing page, may be replicated in our edition. We do, however, repair the vast majority of imperfections successfully; any imperfections that remain are intentionally left to preserve the state of such historical works.

Forgotten Books is a registered trademark of FB &c Ltd.
Copyright © 2018 FB &c Ltd.
FB &c Ltd, Dalton House, 60 Windsor Avenue, London, SW19 2RR.
Company number 08720141. Registered in England and Wales.

For support please visit www.forgottenbooks.com

PHENOMENA OF MATERIALISATION

A CONTRIBUTION TO THE INVESTIGATION OF MEDIUMISTIC TELEPLASTICS

BY

BARON VON SCHRENCK NOTZING
PRACTISING PHYSICIAN IN MUNICH

TRANSLATED BY

E. E. FOURNIER d'ALBE, D.Sc. (Lond. and Birm.)
Author of "The Electron Theory," "Two New Worlds,"
"New Light on Immortality," etc.

Reissue of the First English Edition

WITH 225 ILLUSTRATIONS

LONDON
KEGAN PAUL, TRENCH, TRUBNER & CO. Ltd.
NEW YORK: E. P. DUTTON & CO.
1923

BF1378
.S413

PRINTED IN GREAT BRITAIN BY
THE EDINBURGH PRESS, 9 AND 11 YOUNG STREET, EDINBURGH

Preface to the First German Edition

"Nothing is too wonderful to be true."—FARADAY.

IT is not without some misgiving that I publish in the present work the results of four years' observations of the medium Eva C. For the observations of mediumistic phenomena hitherto made, do not, up to now, in spite of their continuity and their independent agreement, and in spite of the high reputation of the authors whose names vouch for the facts stated, fulfil the requirements of an exact scientific method. This may, however, be due to the character of the occurrences themselves.

Any dealings with the discredited so-called "spiritistic" phenomena are attended, even now, by certain disadvantages to the investigator. Not only are his powers of observation, his critical judgment and his credibility brought into question, not only is he exposed to ridicule by the reproach of charlatanism—as, for example, was the famous criminal anthropologist, Lombroso—but he even incurs the danger of being regarded as mentally deficient, or even as insane, as was the case with the astronomer, Zöllner, and the English chemist, Crookes.

The open or secret opponents of scientific men thus discredited are in the habit of deriving some advantage from the destruction of their scientific authority. Recognising this fact, the well-known French psychologist, Charles Richet, has for the present entirely withdrawn from any dealings with the forbidden subject.

As to the means sometimes adopted by those who wish to prove the supposed fraud underlying mediumistic phenomena, the experience of the author furnishes an instructive contribution. Convinced that the author was the victim of expert deceptions practised by two women, *i.e.*, the medium Eva C. and her protectress Mme. Bisson, somebody secretly and without the author's knowledge instructed a well-known Parisian detective office to watch these two ladies. The employees of this firm, besides gathering the necessary information about the medium herself, also gained illegal possession of a number of photographic copies of the negatives obtained during the experiments, though these were the exclusive property of the author and his collaborator.

In spite of the unwelcome annoyances to which these two ladies were exposed by the tools of this anonymous agency, not only in the street but in their domestic and family life for eight months, the agency did not succeed in furnishing any proof of fraud or in finding the firm which supplied what they supposed to be the material required for the sittings, in the way of hand-shapes of all kinds, of veils, muslins, plaster casts of faces, or portrait drawings of four entire phantom images. One can hardly imagine a more miserable fiasco of this well-meant, but incorrect, method of serving the truth, if the alleged fraud had actually taken place. One remembers that in the case of the German flower medium, Anna Rothe, and the Australian, Charles Bailey, the purveyors of the objects required as "apports" during the sittings were easily found, even without spies. Clever detectives are in the habit of solving more difficult problems in a shorter time than was available in this case.

Though we may condemn the method here described, we must acknowledge that a healthy scepticism and an open, benevolent and reasoned opposition may contribute to the elucidation of mediumistic problems. For they lead to the subsequent testing of the objections brought forward, and thus often to an improvement in the methods of investigation.

The great astronomer, Johann Kepler, was right when he said "Only resistance awakens slumbering forces. The works of foolishness perish. They must further what they seem to hinder. But that which comes from the fountain-head is eternal." Since all honest investigation means a step forward in knowledge, the author has, in spite of all these hesitations, made up his mind, after a twenty-five years' experience on the subject of mediumship, that he will no longer withhold from the public the four years' observations with Eva C. For, possibly, we may succeed in again directing attention to a dark and unexplored side of human Soul Life, and in particular to certain problematical psycho-physical effects, and, furthermore, furnish an incitement towards further tests.

Whatever view we may take of this question, we cannot deny that the method of experiment employed in the observations with Eva C. and Stanislava P. marks a distinct step in advance in comparison with former similar investigations, so that further progress along the same road may yield even better results.

The present work records in as impartial a manner as possible, and with the avoidance of attempts at explanations which would, at present, be premature, observations and occurrences in the case of the medium Eva C., which were objectively recorded by free photography. The majority of the experiments took place in Paris, and the author has stayed there as often as possible in order to continue these studies.

PREFACE TO THE FIRST GERMAN EDITION

During his absences the sittings were regularly continued under the accepted conditions, and in this case his collaborator, Mme. Bisson, made considerable use of the author's photographic apparatus.

In order to give a continuous view of the development of the mediumistic phenomena during that time, nearly all the photographs taken by Mme. Bisson herself, dating from May 1909, are also published, as well as numerous personal observations made by her (*e.g.* on the spontaneous occurrences of the phenomena), which were facilitated by several years of her joint residence with the medium. These communications furnish a valuable and necessary supplement to the author's own experimental material. Besides, the reports could often be confirmed by a subsequent repetition in the author's presence of such occurrences as were, in the first instance, observed by Mme. Bisson alone, so that there is no occasion to doubt the correctness of these supplementary reports. The photographic plates were always inserted by the author himself during his experiments. They were developed also in his presence either by Barenne & Co. (Rue Duret 27 bis), or in Munich by the Photo-Chemical Institute of Dr Hauberrisser (Dienerstrasse 19).

The majority of the materialisation phenomena photographed were also taken as stereoscopic photographs, but these could not, from considerations of clearness and brevity, be reproduced in the present work.

Since in the first year, on account of the imperfect working of the flash-light apparatus, the photographs were often failures, certain situations of some apparent importance were reconstructed, according to the records, by the welcome assistance of the painter, Karl Gampenrieder. Such pictorial representations cannot, of course, be regarded as substitutes for photographs, and they only claim a relative value as graphic renderings of certain interesting moments.

In the present year (1913) the author had the unexpected opportunity of observing materialisation phenomena in the case of a young Pole, Stanislava P., whose mediumistic powers are not yet sufficiently developed. These observations took place at Munich under similar conditions as with Eva C., but in a less rigid and convincing form. The independent agreement of certain performances of the Polish medium with those of Eva C. is so striking, that certain selected photographs from these sittings, together with explanatory notes, are added to this work in a special chapter.

As regards the criticism of the occurrences related in the case of the medium Eva C., such men of science must be acknowledged as qualified in the first instance who command adequate knowledge and a special study of the subject of Physical Mediumship. He who has not read the works of Lombroso and Zöllner, nor is acquainted with the several years' investigations of Sir W. Crookes, will possibly arrive at an erroneous conception or even a denial of the results communicated. But new acquisitions of knowledge must not be judged according to their probability or improbability; they need not be swayed by temporarily dominant scientific dogmas or by popular opinion.

Even though, at the present moment, we cannot comprehend the strange capacities of mediums, we have not to deal with "miracles" in the religious sense, but with occurrences happening fairly regularly under certain conditions, though their causes and laws are at present unknown. As Richet justly observes: "Nothing is touched that belongs to the classical treasury of science."

Let the reader then approach without prejudice and with an open mind the study of the present work, and let him not be shaken in his judgment by prevalent opinion, nor by the numerous failures and disappointments hitherto encountered in the history of "Occultism."

As the author was guided in his experiments, so may also the reader be guided by the words of Frederick the Great: "I seek the truth everywhere, and respect it wherever I find it, and I submit to it whenever it is shown to me."

ALBERT VON SCHRENCK NOTZING.

MUNICH, 15*th October* 1913.

TRANSLATOR'S PREFACE

THIS first English version of Dr von Schrenck Notzing's *Materialisations-Phænomene* embodies not only the original volume but also the more important parts of the supplementary work entitled *Der Kampf um die Materialisations Phænomene*, published early in 1914, as well as certain subsidiary material accumulated since these researches were first made public. The English version has been prepared in consultation with the author and with Mme. Bisson, and it may be taken to represent their results and views as finally arrived at in 1920 and embodied in the forthcoming Second German Edition.

The English-speaking public has, therefore, now an opportunity of studying these remarkable results at first hand. The present work is unique, in that it gives a full scientific account of a set of strange occurrences observed under the strictest conditions of control, and as yet quite unexplained. With admirable candour the author takes us into his confidence, and publishes his results in full, regardless of the dangers of misinterpretation by superficial and prejudiced critics. It cannot be expected that the facts here stated will be readily accepted as presented. Nobody believes facts merely because they are true. They must also link up with other facts, they must fit into our prevailing habits of thought, they must be "useful" in the sense of leading to workable practical conclusions. But any intelligent man may safely be challenged to read through this work with an open mind, and then deny that the case for the reality of the phenomena, and for the novelty and abnormality of their mode of production, has been completely established; and once that point of view is attained, the new branch of knowledge will soon find its place in the intellectual inheritance of our race.

The translator is convinced of the authenticity of the phenomena, not only from the perusal of this work but from the opportunities he had, through the kindness of the Society for Psychical Research, of witnessing some of the phenomena presented by the medium Eva C. in London. He does not venture an explanation, but agrees in the main with the author in regarding them as a new, or rather a hitherto unexplored, function of certain human organisms. He also takes the author's view that a spiritistic interpretation has not, so far, become unavoidable.

In reading the reports of some of the Sittings one cannot help regretting that certain excessively severe precautions to eliminate the hypothesis of fraud should have been considered necessary, and hoping that the physical and emotional martyrdom undergone by the French medium should suffice to silence the most ruthless and exacting critic, and so pave the way for more humane methods of investigation. That the medium has retained her mental and moral equilibrium through so many years of experimentation is entirely due to the wisdom, patience and devotion of Mme. Bisson.

The world is now for the first time in possession of a Monograph on these mysterious and much-controverted phenomena, investigated by a trained observer, and recorded by him with the aid of great scientific resources. The work demands, and is entitled to, an unprejudiced and respectful hearing. The verdict as to its value in the advancement of knowledge can be safely left to an enlightened public opinion.

E. E. FOURNIER d'ALBE.

LONDON, *August* 1920.

CONTENTS

PART I.—1909-1913.

INTRODUCTION.

	PAGE
General and Historical	1
On Method in Mediumistic Investigations	14
Facts and Hypotheses	28

PHENOMENA WITH EVA C.

Sittings in May and June 1909 (Paris)	37
Sittings in November 1909 (Paris)	44
Sittings in May and June 1910 (Paris)	50
Observations in Biarritz	57
Sittings in October and November 1910 (Paris)	59
Sittings in December 1910 and January 1911 (Paris)	80
Sittings in March and April 1911 (Paris)	86
Sittings in May and June 1911 (Paris)	91
Further Observations in June and July 1911 (Paris)	97
Sittings in July and August 1911 (St Jean de Luz)	99
Further Observations in September 1911 (St Jean de Luz)	115
Sittings in October and November 1911 (Paris)	117
Observations in December 1911 (Paris)	134
Sittings in December 1911 and January 1912 (Paris)	137
Observations in March and April 1912 (Paris)	145
Sittings in April 1912 (Paris)	147
Psychical Phenomena	149
Sittings in May and June 1912 (Paris)	156
Observations in June and July 1912 (Paris)	169
Sittings in July, August and September 1912 (Munich)	171
Sittings in October and November 1912 (Paris)	207
Observations in December 1912 and January and February 1913 (Paris)	216
Sittings in February and March 1913 (Paris)	222
Observations in March, April and May 1913 (Paris)	228
Sittings in May and June 1913 (Paris)	231
Observations in June and July 1913 (Paris and La Baule)	243
Result of the Microscopic Examinations	246

CONTENTS

PHENOMENA WITH STANISLAVA P.

	PAGE
Introduction	251
Sittings in January and February 1913 (Munich)	252
Sittings in June and July 1913 (Munich)	257
Results of the Observations	259

RETROSPECT.

Negative Points and the Hypothesis of Fraud	260
Artistic and Technical Opinions	271
Method of Observation and Development of Teleplastic Structures	274
Head Fragments, Faces and Phantoms	279
Conclusion	283

PART II.—1913-1919.

Introduction	285
The Rumination Hypothesis	286
Front Page Illustrations from the Journal *Le Miroir*	292
Sittings with Eva C. in November and December 1913 and January 1914 (Paris)	306
Sittings with Eva C. in May and June 1914 (Paris)	311
Result of the Observations	320
Reports of French Investigators 1916 (Paris)	324
Dr V. Gustave Geley (Paris) on his Observations with Eva C. in 1918 (Paris)	327
Conclusion	336

PHENOMENA OF MATERIALISATION.

INTRODUCTION.

GENERAL AND HISTORICAL.

THE history of Science in the last few decades confirms, more perhaps than in any previous age, the justice of the words of the great mathematician Arago, that the word " impossible " should be very sparingly used outside mathematics. Among the " impossibilities " of former opinion we may enumerate the following:—free motor traction on ordinary roads; flying; the arbitrary production of psychic dependence of a human being (hypnotic suggestion); vision into closed spaces (Röntgen rays); colour photography; wireless telegraphy; and radio-activity; not to mention other facts of recent research.

Hypnotism, which encountered more opposition than anything else, is now the common property of psychology, and the cure of nervous disease. At all times new discoveries have encountered violent opposition. Facts were denied because they did not fit into the theories prevailing at the time, or because fantastic people drew unwarrantable conclusions from them.

A particularly instructive example of this kind is furnished by meteoric stones, whose actuality struggled long for recognition. Thus Chladni[1] complains in his work on " Fiery Meteors " of the treatment accorded to him by his colleagues : " When my work appeared, the majority of them declared the whole contents to be foolishness, as indeed I had expected. It was said in the General German Library that my assertions were unworthy of refutation." J. A. du Luc expressed himself in this sense, that if he had seen such a stone fall at his feet he would have said, " I have seen it, and yet I do not believe it."

But, as a rule, people make the matter easy for themselves by distorting the facts newly announced, or by simply denying them, instead of taking the trouble to make further investigations. Disbelief went so far that most of the meteorites which had been kept in public collections were simply thrown away by the Keepers, for fear of being made ridiculous and being regarded as uneducated if they admitted the possibility of the thing. This *a priori* resistance to new phenomena, an old inherited scientific sin, is seen more particularly in medicine, which owed originally to laymen so many of its present secure possessions. Let us remember the violent resistance opposed to

[1] Chladni, *Uber Feuermeteore*, Vienna, 1819.

Harvey's discovery of the circulation of the blood (this excellent investigator was even declared to be insane), also the opposition of the French Academy to vaccination for smallpox, as proposed by Jenner.

The history of Science offers numerous examples of this kind, which may be found enumerated in the writings of Flammarion, Zöllner, and Kemmerich.[1]

Our investigation of Nature is subject to change. We have no justification for condemning *a priori*, though a healthy scepticism can only contribute to the furtherance of truth. A recollection of the revolutionary results of investigation obtained in the last few decades may, however, have cleared the judgment of the present world of science. Thus our present time appears to be better disposed towards the reception and sober examination of new facts, however strange and absurd they may appear to be.

Another important advance is the abandonment of the materialistic conception of the universe which, even thirty years ago, was in sole possession. Modern physics regards matter as a form of motion, and is dominated by the idea of energy. Psychology also is gradually emancipating itself from the purely physiological conception of mental life; and under the leadership of the philosopher Bergson, it tends to acknowledge the superiority of the psychical over the physical. Thus the circumstances are much more favourable to the investigation of great new problems and facts than they were some decades ago.

Among the more important problems we may place the scientific investigation of the physical phenomena of mediumship which, up to now, has been entirely in the hands of superstitious spiritists.

In view of the improvement of our natural knowledge there is no *a priori* reason against the possibility of abnormal phenomena and effects which may have their origin in the wonderful human organism. Our knowledge of that which we call life is limited. The riddles of propagation, of growth, of the transmission of racial qualities, are entirely unsolved, although they take place daily before our eyes. Perhaps, as Kayserling[2] supposes, the individual is only a stage in the process of life. If that is so, the *real* in Nature is based upon something *ideal*. The principle of life is not exhaustively represented by its temporary appearance. According to this view we overestimate the importance of consciousness, which does not imply anything essential to life, and so we exaggerate the sense of personal existence.

Now we find abnormal phenomena of human nature, as presented by mediumistic processes, at all times in the history of civilisation, so that, for this reason alone, an examination of them is justified quite apart from any subsequent explanation. Is it only a matter of fraud, superstition and self-deception? Even if that were so, an investigation of the subject, and a re-education of the persons thus misled and deceived, would appear to be necessary.

But if, as has been asserted, we have to deal with genuine phenomena of an unknown, transcendental origin, then the study of these facts is one of the most important tasks ever imposed upon science. For

---

[1] Flammarion, *Les Forces Inconnues de la Nature*; Zöllner, *Wissenschaftliche Abhandlungen*, 1878, Leipzig; Kemmerich, *Kultur-Kuriosa*, Vol. II. (Langen, Munich, 1910).

[2] Kayserling, *Unsterblichkeit*, Munich, 1907.

INTRODUCTION

it must bring about an unexpected widening of the knowledge of the processes of human life.

The unprejudiced and sober examination of the records contributed to literature by well-known investigators familiar with the methods of scientific observation, shows that it is absolutely necessary to make further tests of their results if there is a suitable opportunity of doing so. The best known of such records are those made 1870 to 1874 by the late Sir William Crookes, the great English chemist and physicist, which were undertaken with the medium, Florence Cook, then fifteen years of age, and with Daniel Dunglas Home. The investigations of this savant were conducted with such care that it is difficult to deny him any credibility simply on account of his cursory and sometimes rather startling form of publication, as was done by Alfred Lehmann.[1] Crookes employed self-registering measuring apparatus and treated the medium as a sort of power-engine. He published the first record of certain phenomena in the case of Home in 1871, and eighteen years later further notes on the same sittings. In these we get a picture of some occurrences rather different from that presented in the original publication. Thus Lehmann, who exposes a few contradictions in the two publications, finds fault with the dependence of the experimenter on the wish of the medium, the defective illumination, the free movement of the medium during the experiments, and many inaccuracies in the records. According to him a conscientious investigator should only publish such results as he has repeatedly obtained under definite conditions, and the records should be published in full, together with a description of all accompanying circumstances.

Even if we admit certain faults in Crookes's records of his experiments, these do not impair the value of any single definite experiment, or of a self-contained single observation. Must these results, therefore, have been observed inaccurately and falsely, because they are not recorded as Lehmann justly desires it?

As regards the good-will of the medium, we may take it that all experiments are dependent on that, and the education of the mediums (who have a very imperfect understanding of the requirements of scientific method), so as to make them into useful subjects for research, is one of the most difficult problems which investigators, in this subject, have to solve.

As regards the famous materialisations of "Katie King," Podmore[2] showed that the decisive proofs were not obtained in Crookes's own house, but at the house of the Cook family in Hackney, where the bedroom of the medium was used as the cabinet.

The electric control of the medium proposed by Varley did not, according to Lehmann, exclude fraud. Yet this critic admits that Katie King was a living being! Must we take it that the circumstances of the medium's bedroom being used in some cases as a dark cabinet has anything to do with the value of the results obtained by Crookes, who, in the course of four years, made hundreds of experiments in his own laboratory? Decision can only rest with the conditions of the single experiment performed. The genuineness of the medium-

---

[1] Lehmann, *Aberglaube und Zauberei*, Enke, Stuttgart, 1908.
[2] Podmore, *Modern Spiritualism*, Vol. II., p. 155.

istic phenomenon should be considered as completely established by the generation and disappearance of a figure without any artificial means before the eyes of the experimenter, as was so often described by Crookes. That this phenomenon accompanied the medium, and was effected even better in the rooms in which she lived, is quite natural.

Lehmann says nothing about the photographs taken by Crookes, which proved that Katie King and Florence Cook were two different living beings. When, several years after the medium's marriage with Mr Corner, during a sitting of the 9th January 1880, the spirit "Mary" was seized and found to be the medium in a flannel dress and corsets, and when, later, six unsatisfactory sittings were held by Polish men of science, it was said everywhere that the celebrated medium of Professor Crookes was a fraud, and that she had deceived him during several years. Whether this exposure was really a case of " transfiguration," " transmutation," or pseudo-materialisation, such as often occurs, and has also been observed by the author, may be left aside for the moment. But the readers of Crookes's reports may remember the farewell sitting of Katie King, in which she declared that she would depart and would never return.

Possibly this termination was a hint of the close of Miss Cook's mediumship. We may find it humanly comprehensible that she made further attempts, and that, in spite of the failure of her mediumistic powers, she consented to sittings which came to a lamentable end.

But even this circumstance cannot diminish the importance of the facts which Crookes obtained with the medium at the height of her creative power. Of the whole of Lehmann's criticism of the English investigator only one justifiable objection remains, viz., that the record of these interesting phenomena might have been more complete and accurate.

Besides, the late Sir William Crookes, who was regarded as one of England's greatest chemists and physicists, never recanted a single one of his statements on this matter. In this connection he has made the following pronouncement :[1]

" Thirty years have passed since I published a report concerning experiments purporting to show that behind our scientific knowledge a power exists which differs from that common to all mortals. . . . To stop in an investigation which promises to open wide the gates of knowledge, to hesitate for fear of difficulties and hostile criticism, would mean exposing science to censure. The investigator has nothing to do but to go straight ahead, to gather information everywhere, to follow the light inch by inch with the aid of his reason, wherever the light may lead, even should it resemble a will-o'-the-wisp ! "

Among other mediums referred to in the literature of the latter part of the nineteenth century and the first years of the twentieth, a few may be mentioned here, whose performances furnish links and parallels with the statements contained in the present work.

The private medium, Mrs d'Esperance, born in London in 1852, is described by all who came in contact with her as an honest and credible person. In spite of her truthful character she was not spared

---

[1] Hyslop, *Enigmas of Psychical Research* (passage retranslated from the German).

an " exposure." While she was believed to be sleeping in the cabinet, her shadow friend " Yolande " was seized. On this she says : " The man who had seized her said it was I. This assertion appeared to me so extraordinary and incomprehensible that I could have laughed, if my utter helplessness and weakness had not rendered me incapable of thinking or even of moving." In consequence of this shock, this lady of unimpeachable character broke down completely, became seriously ill, retired from the world, and ceased to give any sittings for a long time. She had devoted herself to mediumistic studies solely from a love of the subject and from a thirst for knowledge. From these and other remarks Lehmann arrives at the reasonable conclusion that Mrs d'Esperance, during the exposure, played the part of Yolande automatically in a dream. In general, he adopts the view that the spirit forms are unconscious figments dramatically enacted by the materialising mediums.

Mrs d'Esperance was a dreamer even as a child. She had a lively imagination. At fourteen she believed herself to be insane, on account of numerous visual and auditory hallucinations. Under the influence of spiritists she commenced with table-tilting, psychography, and automatic drawing and writing. (She had been taught drawing and painting.) The genesis of her own materialisation phenomena she describes just as they are observed in other mediums : a white heap of muslin lying on the floor becomes animated and ascends in the form of white clouds, until, under the folds of the drapery, a living being in human shape appears. On p. 254 of her book [1] the same process is described as follows :—

" First a filmy, cloudy patch of something white is observed on the floor in front of the cabinet. It then gradually expands, visibly extending itself as if it were an animated patch of muslin, lying fold upon fold, on the floor, until extending about two and a half by three feet, and having a depth of a few inches—perhaps six or more. Presently it begins to rise slowly in or near the centre, as if a human head were underneath it, while the cloudy film on the floor begins to look more like muslin falling into folds about the portion so mysteriously rising. By the time it has attained two or more feet in height, it looks as if a child were under it and moving its arms about in all directions as if manipulating something underneath. It continues rising, oftentimes sinking somewhat to rise again higher than before, until it attains the height of about five feet, when its form can be seen as if arranging the folds of drapery about its figure. Presently the arms rise considerably above the head and open outwards through a mass of cloud-like spirit drapery, and Yolande stands before us unveiled, graceful and beautiful, nearly five feet in height, having a turban-like head-dress, from beneath which her long black hair hangs over her shoulders and down her back. . . . . The dematerialising of Yolande's body occupies from two to five minutes, while the disappearance of the drapery occupies from a half to two minutes."

In one of the illustrations published in her book she is photographed with her " spirit " Yolande. Later, she took hundreds of photographs, to test whether she could exert some mediumistic influence upon the

---

[1] *Shadow Land*, by E. d'Esperance. London. George Redway, 1898.

plate. On some plates, heads and nebulous human shapes were found beside the person photographed. Professors Butlerow and Aksakoff succeeded in obtaining materialisation photographs with Mrs d'Esperance. Oxley made the interesting experiment, unknown to the medium up to the time of the experiment, of mixing the seed of an Indian plant, *Ixora crocata*, with sand and water in a decanter, and requesting the medium to accelerate its growth. It is said that, under the eyes of twenty persons, the plant developed to a height of twenty-two inches, with a flower composed of some 150 four-star corollas and twenty-nine leaves.

Mrs d'Esperance lives in retirement in the country, or travels, and has quite ceased her mediumistic activity. (She died in 1919—*Tr.*)

The incompleteness and imperfection of the materialisations was already evident to the observers of the phantom " Yolande," which appeared with Mrs d'Esperance on 13th March 1896.[1] The heads sometimes gave the impression of masks, and this was also found by Comte Bullet during the photography of a phantom with another medium. According to his view, a flat surface is materialised first, and this is modelled subsequently. This view receives some support from the author's observations as recorded in this work.

As in Mrs d'Esperance's book Professor Mangin[2] describes materialisation as a fugitive structure suddenly generated, which assumes a human or animal shape. Its material is not permanent, but phantom-like. It contains *the minimum of substance necessary to produce in the witnesses the illusion that they have a living body before them*. Mostly it consists of outlines or sketches of hands or heads, and in order to save work in the formation of heads, the mysterious artist employs drapery. In a harmonious concatenation of all the best conditions a " Katie King " can be born and equipped up to the limit of illusion. She must vanish like the dream she is. The substance borrowed from the medium must return whence it came; the child disappears into the lap of its mother. In connection with the dress of the phantom Mangin asks whether it consists of "apports" or materialisations, and recalls the well-known scene in which Katie King cut off portions of her garment and distributed them among those present. She then filled up the gaps by simply covering them with the intact portion of her drapery. They were immediately filled up, and, in spite of the closest inspection, Crookes was unable to find a seam.

Similar to the above is the description given by the French physiologist, Professor Charles Richet,[3] of the process as observed in his Algiers sittings. " I see something like a white luminous ball of undetermined outline suspended above the floor. Then suddenly there appears, emerging from this white orb of light as from a trap-door, the phantom ' Bien Boa.' It is of moderate height. He is draped in a flowing garment with a belt round his waist. ' Bien Boa ' is halting and lame in his walk. One cannot say whether he walks or glides. . . . Without opening the curtain he suddenly collapses and vanishes on the floor. At the same time one hears the noise of a body falling on the floor. Three or four minutes afterwards the same white orb appears

---

[1] *Psychische Studien*, 1907, p. 119.   [2] *Annales des Sciences Psychiques*, Dec. 1907.
[3] *Psychische Studien*, 1906, p. 82.

in the opening of the curtain above the floor, then a body is seen quickly rising straight up and attaining the height of an adult, and then it again collapses on the floor."

Richet regards this as decisive, and says: " Before my eyes outside the curtain, a living body has been formed, which emerged from the floor and vanished into the floor." (There was no trap-door.) The photograph of the phantom taken by Richet on this occasion covers the upper body and the head of the medium. One might be justified in raising the objection that, viewed merely as a photograph, without regard to the conditions of the experiment, it does not prove the existence of any living being besides the medium, but that it gives the impression of a transfiguration, as already pointed out by Professor Gabriel Max.

Within the last forty years hardly any medium has stimulated the study of spiritistic phenomena to such an extent, nor earned as many convinced adherents among men of science, as Eusapia Paladino. The author followed her development for about sixteen years.

The first series of sittings took place in 1894, in the presence of Richet, Lombroso (Turin), Danilewski (Petrograd), and others.

In 1898 (May-June), 1903 (February-March), there were investigations in Munich in conjunction with German savants, and Professor Flournoy (Geneva). The author also took part in the tests of the medium arranged by Richet in August 1894 in the South of France, attended by the physicist Sir Oliver Lodge, Professor and Mrs Sidgwick, Frederick Myers and some French physicians. Lacking confidence in the accuracy of his own results, the author felt the need of repeated supplementary tests, and these took place at Rome (May 1896), Naples (May 1898), Rome and Naples (April 1902), Rome (March 1903), and lastly in Genoa and Nice (April 1909).

This lack of confidence was also the reason why no details have been hitherto published with regard to the results of these fifty-five sittings.

Meanwhile Eusapia submitted herself to further numerous and lengthy examinations by scientific commissions in Genoa, Turin, Naples, Paris, and other places. The careful experimental investigations of the General Psychological Institute[1] in Paris extended, with interruptions, over several years. As in the case of the author and others who have repeatedly and thoroughly examined the medium, the investigators reached, in general, positive conclusions in regard to the reality of certain mediumistic phenomena of a special kind. I cannot, however, deal with these in this Introduction. The phenomena observed were the motion of objects at a distance without

[1] "Rapport sur les séances d'Eusapia Paladino à l'Institut Général Psychologique en 1905, 1906, 1907, 1908," par Jules Courtier (*Bulletin de l'Institut Général Psychologique*, 1908, p. 415). *Présent.*—M. and Mme. Curie, Branly, Richet, d'Arsonval, Bergson, Langevin, Yourjewich, Miquel, etc. The Report confirms the motion, registered by automatic apparatus, of inanimate objects without contact with the medium, luminous phenomena, appearance of human shapes, contact and other telekinetic phenomena, and a certain proportion of fraud. For the majority of Eusapia's performances fraud could not be assumed. The conditions of control give a great probability against it; but the doubts occasioned by the frauds discovered, prevented the observers from speaking of a scientifically "impregnable" certainty of proof, and only admit of subjective judgments.

contact, table-tiltings, raps, the production of tactile sensations and similar performances.

Like Home, Slade, and Eglinton, Eusapia is chiefly a physical medium. The sittings mostly took place in a feeble red light, partly also in total darkness, but nearly all observers record some phenomena in a bright electric light.

By her long years of intercourse with sceptical savants she is accustomed to experimental conditions of the most varied kinds, and is herself anxious to maintain a good illumination and an accurate control.

Nevertheless, there is complete agreement among all these investigators, both those who have vouched for the genuineness of her phenomena, and those who are not convinced on this point, that Eusapia often deceives by well-known manipulations, that she knows how to free a hand or a foot, or even both hands, and thus brings about some of these phenomena mechanically with the aid of her own limbs.

Thus the author had already, in April 1894 in Rome, discovered the change of the hands and the use of a stretched hair for moving a letter balance. During a similar experiment in February 1903, in Munich, the author captured the hair which she used.

In the case of a sitting at Munich, in May 1898, Professor Lipps noticed that, instead of Eusapia's hand, he held the hand of the sitter controlling the left side of the medium. In this way she had freed both hands by a trick. Also the savants, Dr Eugen Albrecht, Dr Minde and Dr Loeb, who conducted the sittings in 1903, at Munich, found a regular freeing of arm or leg.

On the 22nd of February 1903 Professor Flournoy of Geneva controlled her left side during a sitting at Munich. The author stood behind the chair of the medium and saw, at the moment when Professor Flournoy felt himself touched on the right side, the sole of a foot and the heel quite clearly. It cannot, therefore, be doubted that the clever Neapolitan used her foot in order to touch the Professor while the latter believed he was controlling the foot.

On the 20th of February 1903 she produced a " direct writing " on my cuff. But I had remarked beforehand that she was playing with a pencil, and the point of this pencil was afterwards found to be broken off, and was probably used by her.

On the 11th of April 1894 she pretended to bring about a suspension of her body, a so-called levitation, in the dark, during a sitting at Rome, but I found that her foot was firmly planted on the table. She had therefore simply got on to the table. In fact, she utilised in a clever way, besides her usual and well-known tricks, the weakness of the observers. Thus she diverts the attention to the unoccupied side, and complains of too great pressure by those holding her hand. She is able to displace her chair by small and imperceptible jerks, so that she may, for instance, upset a small table standing behind her by a violent jerk of the back of her chair backwards (Munich, May 1898). Or she uses the train of her dress to pull objects towards her. Whole sittings were often filled with such manœuvres, which always aimed at outwitting the controlling sitters. And so it often happens that highly critical sitters see their expectations entirely realised, and believe they can explain all the phenomena by means of these frauds.

INTRODUCTION

During a sitting at Munich, which took place in a gathering of friends on the 4th of March 1903, there was a sudden appearance of a branch with red flowers. As we found afterwards, the branch fitted exactly on to the broken stem of an azalea bush which Eusapia had placed in her room. It is, therefore, quite probable that she brought the branch with her into the sitting room. If that was done intentionally, then this would, in my experience, be the only one during a long number of years in which she had prepared a phenomenon before the sitting. For, as a rule, she improvised her deceptions by a clever adaptation to the situation of the moment and by the simplest means, which were sometimes extremely naïve, barefaced and clumsy. For instance, when, during her farewell sitting at Munich in June 1898 the table would not tilt, she simply put her whole arm under the table and raised it up. Even in the case of those phenomena, which must be regarded as genuine, she often helps. Thus she uses the support of her shin to raise the table into the air, or employs curtains in order to manipulate more freely.

Although this mechanical production of mediumistic occurrences has often been observed by me, I have not been able to agree with the assertions of the English investigators (Sidgwick, Hodgson, and the conjuror, Maskelyne of London, 1895-6) that she worked with small apparatus brought into the sitting. I not only examined her dress with a ruler before every sitting, or had a special dress made for her, but I also had occasion to examine her whole luggage down to the last needle. Not the slightest suspicious objects, such as are required by every conjuror, could be discovered.

In Eusapia's case we may regard the following as the causes of her fraudulent performances: lack of productivity, incorrect control on the part of inexperienced and other sceptical observers, the suggestive influence of mental surroundings unfavourable to the proper psychic tone, the desire to fulfil the wishes of the participators, as well as bodily ailments or psychic discord. But, however frequent deceptions may have been in the case of Eusapia, they do not furnish any explanations of the genuine mediumistic phenomena observed under the most rigid control of the medium, as the author was able in numerous cases to verify.

Since she often fell into a deep trance, we must not judge her fraudulent practices without determining in every case how far she acted intentionally or unconsciously. The somnambulic activity of a medium must not be mistaken for deliberate fraud. Eusapia Paladino's performances have been examined several times by eminent conjurors (such as Rybka of Warsaw on the 13th of December 1893), and have been acknowledged in their written testimony. Thus the American conjuror, M. Howard, said the following on the occasion of Eusapia's sittings in America:—

" I have been a conjuror all my life, and have up to now exposed numerous mediums who produced physical phenomena, but I am convinced that this medium (Eusapia) actually produced elevations of the table, and I undertake to contribute a thousand dollars to a charity if any one can prove to me that Eusapia is unable to raise a table into the air without trick, without fraud and without help, excluding the use of fraudulent manipulations of knees or feet or any other part of her body or utensils."

Carrington, who, in conjunction with other conjurors, examined the Neapolitan, at the instance of the Society for Psychical Research, for several months at her home, and who also arrived at a result favourable to the mediumship of Eusapia, wrote in a letter addressed to *Light* :

" Several times I saw a third arm appearing, which closely resembled that of Eusapia. It proceeded from her shoulder and touched the experimenter sitting on the right. Both Eusapia's hands were visible on the table. During the sittings in the Columbia University a hole was made in the roof of the cabinet and one of the experimenters constantly observed the behaviour of the subject through this small opening while the phenomena took place. On three different occasions I saw strange projections emerging from Eusapia's body—once from the middle of her back—and then receding into her body. These pseudopods were wrapped in the material of the curtain, so that their consistency cannot be determined. The clearest observation was made of a pointed shape, about a foot long, which developed from her foot. It approached the small table, touched the top and threw objects standing upon it to the floor. All this was clearly observed."

With reference to Muensterberg's exposure of this medium, the well-known American psychologist, Professor Hyslop, says this :

" The report of Professor Muensterberg is not to be taken seriously, for it does not prove any actual fact, but only attempts an explanation."

Eusapia during the sittings fell into a deep hysterical somnambulism, and was often in a slightly dazed condition after the close. When the trance set in, she turned pale, her head swerved to and fro, and the eyes were turned upwards and inwards. She was hypersensitive, especially to the touch, and also to light ; she had hallucinations, delirium, fits of laughter, weeping, or deep sleep, and showed other typical hysterical convulsions. Digestive troubles also sometimes set in, especially when she had eaten before the sitting. In a sudden light or at a sudden rough touch, she cried out and shuddered, as she would under unexpected violent pain. Her comprehension was extremely rapid during her ecstasy ; she guessed the thoughts of those present very easily, especially if one of them suspected fraud.

As may be seen from the symptoms of the deep trance, great care and reserve are necessary during such experiments. Records made by authors familiar with the sources of error, and having great experience in the observation of people, should be accorded more weight. For this reason those materials seem to be the most valuable which are collected by experts, psychologists, physicians, nerve specialists, physicists, chemical anthropologists and official representatives of science. It is true that even such men may-be victims of refined fraud, but they employ scientific methods of investigation, and in the publication of their reports they risk their scientific reputations. Their

INTRODUCTION

responsibility, is therefore, considerably greater than that of any private reporter.

If, for instance, a savant like Morselli, Professor of Psychiatry in Genoa, who for many years conducted a literary war against spiritism, first took part as a novice and an unbeliever in the sittings with the medium, Eusapia Paladino, then convinced himself of the reality of mediumistic processes, and finally studied this subject with a scientific exactness and thoroughness, the judgment of such an eminent psychologist must be of great weight.

In reality he extended his investigation over several years, has studied the whole literature of the subject, and has finally published, in 1908, a work of 1000 pages in two volumes, which in exactness, scientific acumen, rigid self-control, and thorough information, can be compared to the best works of scientific literature.

He again and again emphasises that there cannot be the slightest doubt of the reality of the Eusapian phenomena, and in this the author entirely agrees with him, in spite of the fraudulent instances above specified. Besides, a large number of scientific authorities, both in Italy and elsewhere, have confirmed the authenticity of the phenomena with Eusapia under the most rigid control. According to Morselli, the explanation of Eusapia's performances by the fraudulent change of hands and feet is a thing of the past. " The time has come to break with this exaggerated negative attitude, this constant casting of the shadow of doubt with its smile of sarcasm."

Spiritism, according to Morselli's view, is a religion, and as such has its apostles, its priests, its dogmas, its ritual, and its sermons. He regards Eusapia's controlling spirit, " John King," as a suggestive creation from the medium's subconsciousness, as a fantastic dream image, as already shown by Professor Ochorowicz in Warsaw. Many phenomena are also in direct contradiction to the spiritistic teaching.

The physical phenomenonology of the mediums, whatever their names (Politi, Miller, d'Esperance, etc.), is to-day a matter of spiritistic tradition. Therefore, the savants are obliged to use the small table, magnetic chains, the control of hands and feet, the cabinet, darkness, the red light, plasticine and other limitations of the present investigation.

It is true that Morselli corrected this view by admitting that the phenomena themselves required certain conditions. Do not certain chemical combinations require to be formed in darkness in the laboratory? Do not photographic plates require a ruby light? And does not the night produce changes in the functions of animal and vegetable organisms?

It is, therefore, quite possible that the metapsychical or biodynamical performances of the medium are neutralised or impeded by light, which thus prevents him from producing the main phenomena of materialisation.

Control also paralyses the medium and influences him unfavourably; it often stops the occurrence of the phenomena. Morselli admits that mediumship is not a purely mechanical function like that of physical apparatus, but depends upon the psychic constitution of the person in question.

For this reason alone it is not right to demand objective results from the mediums in the sense of physics and chemistry, however desirable it may be to replace the record of the senses by registering apparatus.

Mediumship has its own essential conditions, which must be respected and studied by the observer. So long as spiritism develops outside scientific laboratories, the traditional usages of the sittings must be put up with. It is only when science has seriously tackled the subject that one can attempt to reduce the phenomena to a system. Modern spiritism has the same relation to the future science of mediumistic processes as astrology had to astronomy, and alchemy to chemistry. We must, therefore, endeavour to get beyond the state of raw empiricism in which we stand at present, to increase the confidence of the mediums in science and in its representatives, and use physical instruments and apparatus. Better even than dynamometers, balances and metronomes, in Morselli's opinion, is the photographic camera, since it gives positive proofs in the real sense of the word. In this connection, a large use has been made in the following investigations of photography, larger than has ever been done hitherto in the study of materialisation phenomena.

Although the nature of the various physical phenomena of mediumship is not yet entirely known, although in certain groups there is not yet any clear view of their subjective or objective character, various authors, like Aksakoff, Geley, Anastay and Morselli, have attempted the classification of mediumistic occurrences.

Thus Morselli describes as the parakinetic phenomena of mediumship the mechanical changes in or about inanimate objects touched by the medium, such as the oscillations, motions and liftings of a table, and the touching and motions of objects when touched by the hand of the medium. It is an open question whether the play of involuntary muscular action is able to give a sufficient explanation for all processes of this kind. One might have some hesitation in classifying such performances in any sense as physical mediumship.

Morselli has attempted to classify the Eusapian phenomena under the head of subjective and objective phenomena. Among the subjective phenomena he enumerates ten subdivisions; in the objective ones, eight classes with numerous subdivisions. To me this elaborate classification seems much too complicated, as well as unnecessary, in the presence of a subject in which the question of fact is not, as yet, sufficiently clear.

Since the present work only concerns itself with subjective occurrences and mental mediumship (modifications of consciousness, intellectual performances, dramatisation of personalities, automatism and psychography) in so far as they are necessary to understand the physical performances of Eva C., I refer those readers who wish to inform themselves in detail to the special literature, and particularly to the extremely careful investigations of Professor Flournoy in his work *Esprits et Mediums* (Geneva and Paris, 1911), as also to the observations of Mrs Piper by the British and American Societies for Psychical Research (communicated in their respective *Proceedings*).

INTRODUCTION

The most important objective performances of mediumship may be divided into two main groups :—

1. TELEKINETIC PHENOMENA.

This class comprises every sort of action upon inanimate objects without contact, such as oscillations, the moving of tables (attraction and repulsion), the levitation of objects (raising and suspension), inflations and motions of a curtain, the mechanics of motion connected with the so-called "apports," and finally the generation of musical notes and noises at a distance (including raps and other auditory impressions). Also effects upon musical instruments, direct writing—in a word, all forms of action at a distance, no matter whether in their case the manner of production by the mediumistic force was the same.

2. TELEPLASTIC PHENOMENA.

This group includes the so-called materialisation phenomena of the spiritists, *i.e.*, the production of forms and materials of organic or even inorganic matter, in accordance with definite conceptions and thought images of the medium, which may have their origin in the memory, or in the psychic under-currents of the medium, in the mentality of one of the witnesses, or (in the spiritistic sense) in forces and intelligences outside the medium.

On account of their psychogenic origin they may also be called "ideoplastic" occurrences. To these belong the alleged vital efflorescences observed in the case of Eusapia Paladino by Lodge, Richet and the author; the production of whitish threads (" Rigid Rays "); clouds and mists; materials resembling muslin used for the clothing of the apparitions or of the medium (during transfiguration); the appearance of forms of an undefined character; vague half-shadows; visible and tangible hands, fingers, and heads of structures resembling human limbs; impressions of these on lamp-blacked paper, or in clay; photographic reproductions of ideoplastic forms in various stages of development, including those invisible to the normal human eye; sketches of artistic reproductions of faces, or fragments of animal and human limbs; and finally, fully formed phantoms of distinct character and definite features and forms.

In the wider sense we may reckon among the teleplastic occurrences certain temporary changes in the state of aggregation of matter, as well as the dissolution and restoration of forms of distinct inanimate objects, *e.g.*, the celebrated "knot experiment," the interpenetration of matter, the introduction of objects not contained in the experimental room ("apports") and the production of luminous objects.

Beside the phenomena enumerated here, there are a number of phenomena the existence of which is doubted by an investigator as thorough and free from prejudice as Morselli, *e.g.*, change of weight of the medium, or of objects touched by the medium, and levitation of the medium (a telekinetic occurrence in the sense that the body of the medium itself is acted upon by the force in question).

During 1915 and 1916 Dr W. J. Crawford, Lecturer in Mechanical Engineering, Queen's University, Belfast, published some new and detailed investigations on levitation and raps. The medium is seated on a weighing-machine, and, when the table is levitated without any contact in a bright red light, her weight increases by approximately the weight of the table. Any vertical oscillation of the table is accompanied by an oscillation of the balance. The connection between medium and object is maintained by a " psychical structure," of unknown composition, derived from the body of the medium. This structure is of the " cantilever " kind, being fixed in the medium's body without other support, unless the objects levitated are heavy, when a support is found on the floor. The object is gripped by this structure in a manner resembling suction. Raps are produced by the impact of the hard end of such a " psychic rod " on a hard surface. See W. J. Crawford, D.Sc., *The Reality of Psychic Phenomena* and *Experiments in Psychical Science* (Watkins, London).

The sensations of cold, heat, and other radiations, which are often described, and which Morselli terms " thermoradiant " phenomena, are, when registered by sensitive apparatus, to be regarded merely as preparatory and concomitant phenomena of one of the real manifestations.

The physical phenomena—assuming them to be genuine—take the same course with all mediums. There are always the telekinetic and teleplastic processes classified above.

ON METHOD IN MEDIUMISTIC INVESTIGATIONS.

Even though the psychic and moral conditions of mediumship are not as yet sufficiently known, we may confidently say already that they lie apart from the normal course of psychic events. As in the case of mediums for mental manifestations, the hystero-hypnotic complex of symptoms plays a great part in the genesis of physical manifestations, for the stronger phenomena require, as a rule, the presence of a condition of deep trance.

Assuming that mediumship comprises genuine telekinetic and teleplastic performances, the possibility of such action is no doubt confined within definite limits. Its production corresponds to a certain degree of exhaustion of the medium's organism, and this conversion must be accompanied by a strong bodily reaction of the medium. The natural principle of conservation of energy is here also brought into action, and the forces seem to decrease with increasing distance. In an impartial examination of the subject we must, therefore, reckon with the possibility that the transformation process does not always follow a regular course, that it is accompanied by a strong reaction of the medium, and that it depends upon the momentary psychic constellation, and principally on the mood and bodily condition of the person under examination. In this sense we must regard the simultaneous sympathetic muscular contractions, which, especially in the case of Eusapia Paladino, were definitely established, as regular physiological accompaniments of telekinetic occurrences. To bring about the genesis of any desired effect, a strong psycho-physical effort, a vivid act of volition of the medium is required.[1] The person under test may, if the effort does not succeed at once, or if the forces available do not suffice, easily be led to assist, to some extent unconsciously, with the muscles, *e.g.*, to further the development of the phenomenon with a *coup de pouce*. Thus we get transition products of a mixed character, *e.g.*, help in table-tiltings, which the radical sceptic would inevitably attribute to fraud on account of the motor assistance observed.

During actions at a distance upon inanimate objects, many mediums move parts of their body in the desired direction in order to facilitate the transfer of force; for all experience points towards these medium-istic forces being limited in their effect, as already mentioned.

In the case of Eva C. also, the participation of the voluntary muscles could be regularly verified during the genesis of the materialisations. In both Eusapia Paladino and in Eva C. the violent muscular action, combined with pain, groans, and gasps, reminds one of the labour of childbirth. The expression " mediumistic labour " denotes, perhaps, quite definite and frequently observed physiological concomitants of telekinetic and teleplastic performances.

These motor concomitants of mediumship are a factor not to be neglected in observations. In combination with a vivid desire for success they easily lead to an unconscious mechanical execution of the task by the limbs.

Very frequently somnambulists play, or represent, the " spirit " themselves. As soon as a dream-like condition sets in, all consciousness of deception may be absent. In the case of the still more frequent representation of " spirits " by conjuring tricks, one always finds textile fabrics, clothes, beards, and other " properties " for the masquerade. Apart, therefore, from coarse prestidigitation, we have to consider three classes in the production of mediumistic occurrences :—

1. The unconsciously fraudulent representation of mediumistic performances in the waking and somnambulic states.
2. Mixed phenomena, combined with automatic reflex motions.
3. Pure unfalsified mediumistic phenomena.

Professor Ochorowicz[2] is probably right in distinguishing conscious deception, *i.e.*, the conjuror's dramatisation of mediumistic performances, from the frauds of mediumship. In the case of disguised, or open, somnambulism we should have unconscious deception without respon-sibility, since there is no consciousness of fraud. To the layman the medium may in that case appear to be awake, but the alteration in the eye, and in the whole psychic demeanour of the person under test, will not escape the trained medical observer.

The question of the substitution of illusory facts for genuine ones is not always easily answered. A reasonably reliable opinion on the character of the occurrence in question presupposes a rigid impartiality.

---

[1] The author has known cases in which the medium in a deep trance appeared quite passive, without participation or volition. But the psycho-physical exhaustion was always proportional to the performance.

[2] Ochorowicz. " La question de la fraude dans les expériences avec Eusapia Paladino " (*Ann. des sciences psychiques*, 2nd Sept. 1896).

There must be a combination of an extreme degree of scientific scepticism with a personal benevolence towards the medium. The accounts furnished by credible and reliable observers and found in the literature of the subject must be examined *sine ira et studio*. Many so-called exposures have exposed nothing but the ignorance of the exposers. But, on the other hand, we must bear in mind the important part played by subjective colouring, imagination, unavoidable errors of observation, lapse of memory, and strain effects, in such observations and reports.

We know that psychologists like Davey, Hodgson, and Lehmann could, after acquiring the necessary conjuring proficiency, deceive a number of calmly thinking persons, and impart to them a belief in their own mediumistic powers. And it cannot be denied that in the case of nearly all professional, and many private, mediums, the mechanical performance of some of their effects has been established. Thus in the case of Eusapia Paladino 10 per cent. of the phenomena are false, 15 per cent. doubtful, and 75 per cent. genuine, according to Morselli.

Conjuring tricks, which usually imply study and practice, must, therefore, not be put in the same category with mediumistic deceptions, at least, so far as mediums of the class of Eusapia Paladino and Eva C. are concerned. As a rule, mediums like these are placed at the mercy of their hosts or their investigators, who have every opportunity of examining their usually sparse luggage.

Besides, the conjuror is not dependent upon the malicious, hostile, or frivolous mentality of his audience. But the disturbing influences on the medium increase with the number of people present. The conjuror usually provides the necessary apparatus himself, changes the programme, and permits no interference with his experiments. In the case of the medium all this is reversed.

Now there are people who have the greatest respect for conjuring, and believe that art to be all-powerful. But this overestimate is solely due to ignorance.[1] If we consider it *a priori* impossible to protect ourselves against prestidigitation and other fraud practised by the mediums, we thereby declare the human senses to be incapable of scientific determinations of any kind. We should have to renounce all investigation, and particularly the psychological analysis of the insane, of criminals, and of simulators. Such an indefensible point of view clearly leads *ad absurdum*. A serious interest in this subject means, indeed, in the larger circle of savants and educated people, even now, a martyrdom for the investigator and the risk of being regarded as mentally inferior. Yet it is just the neglected subject of physical phenomena, constituting mediumship in the truest and narrowest sense, which deserves the attention and devotion of savants free from prejudice.

On the other hand, every serious investigator who undertakes this research must guard himself against the exploitation of his observations by visionaries to satisfy some need of religious belief. For the spiritistic hypothesis rests essentially on the metaphysical tendency implanted

---

[1] It is conceivable that a medium might combine genuine forces with conjuring tricks, just as professional soothsayers may have some real clairvoyance.

in mankind (experimental religion). As Richet very truly remarks[1] " We must make sure of the facts before we formulate general laws."

It appears to be extraordinarily difficult to place a fact upon so firm a basis as to be unshakable. This requires absolute accuracy. " It is a great drawback to scientific progress that spiritists, theosophists, mesmerists and mystics have erected such fanciful structures on such a tiny and insecure basis. Let us be satisfied with faultless experiments. Theory will follow in the natural course."

In another place Richet[2] writes similarly :—

" At the same time I do not consider myself justified in despising the 'metapsychic' facts, which must be methodically studied without prejudice. . . . We must not be appalled by what is strange . . . that which marks a discovery, the unforeseen, the unexpected, the new. It may clash with popular opinion, it may contradict the classic official teaching. Otherwise it would not be a discovery. And after it has come forward, it encounters a thousand denials. Even if it is as clear as the sun, it is not accepted. . . . It is only with difficulty that we form the conviction of having lived in error, of having made wrong assertions. . . . Only unusual phenomena astonish us. A thing appears true because we have often seen it, but not at all because we have understood it, for all natural phenomena are incomprehensible."

It is difficult, more especially for savants who have acquired a wide knowledge by hard work, to free themselves entirely from preconceived opinions and old habits of thought.

Many an investigator is not convinced by reason. Conviction only sets in when he has himself observed certain facts so often that their existence has become to him a mental habit, a familiar thing. Zollner[3] already found this psychic law of inertia, and added : " This is a curious phase of the human spirit, and is particularly strong in savants, indeed stronger, in them, I believe, than in others. For this reason we must not always regard a man as dishonest because for a long time he keeps beyond the reach of proof. The ancient wall of belief requires much siege artillery for its demolition."

Careful researches by English investigators have shown that human powers of observation are very imperfect. In his excellent work (already referred to) on *Superstition and Sorcery*, the well-known psychologist Lehmann of Copenhagen has fully dealt with the sources of errors of observation, especially in mediumistic investigations. These should be minutely studied by any one who approaches these experiments, so as to avoid self-deception as much as possible. Reports by persons lacking the necessary practice in observation should be received with caution. As a rule, there is hardly time during mediumistic tests, in presence of the often surprising and varying occurrences, to direct the attention to the most essential points. In this connection we must remember the conjuror's well-known stratagem of directing the attention to quite secondary matters. And, further, the employment of the

[1] Richet, *Experimental Studies in Thought Transference*, with a Preface by v. Schrenck-Notzing (Enke, Stuttgart, 1891).
[2] Richet, "The Future of Psychology" (*Ubersinnliche Welt*, Feb. 1907).
[3] Zöllner, *Abhandlungen*, Vol. II.

sense organs, especially in dark sittings, is not possible to the usual extent, the sense of sight being in abeyance. There are well-known errors in the mere estimation of distances, weights, etc., and therefore accurate measures in figures, etc., appear to be necessary. One is also easily deceived as to the direction and source of sound. Similar considerations apply to time. Sense impressions are often falsely interpreted ("illusion").

As a matter of fact we find cases in the experiments with Eva C., in which a materialised structure in the shape of a hand, which in the red light was not easily distinguished from a real hand, simulated the presence of the latter, while the real hand executed the expected mediumistic performance. Similar observations were made by Professor Ochorowicz with Eusapia Paladino. The author succeeded indeed, in photographically recording this interesting process. In the case of the Polish medium, St. P., also, it was sometimes difficult to decide whether the red patches visible in her lap were really her hands.

But the most frequent sources of error in the observation of mediumistic phenomena are gaps in the recollection. Unless a careful record is kept during each observation [1] a retroactive falsification of memory during the preparation of a subsequent record may reduce its value.

Facts and events are unintentionally mixed up, their order of succession is inaccurately recollected, apparently unessential points are omitted, and the report is unintentionally supplemented according to subjective interpretation. Thus the spiritist will, in accordance with his religious habit of thought, only retain that which he regards as essential, and his fancy will travel the old road in supplementing it. But, in the same way, the rooted associations of a determined opponent will render valueless an experiment which is successful in the wider sense, *i.e.*, which contradicts his negative conviction, so soon as the above-mentioned failure of memory sets in. Without hesitation he will unconsciously fill up the gaps of memory in his own way. He will see fraud where none exists, just as the believing spiritist will see manifestations of spirits where there are nothing but conjuring tricks. And since most people are already committed to some decided point of view, favourable or unfavourable, of these phenomena, it is exceedingly difficult to obtain quite unprejudiced and purely objective determinations.

In this way the author found, not only in the Munich sittings with Eusapia Paladino, but also in the experiments with Eva C., that the facts of the phenomena were afterwards distorted by learned witnesses under the compelling, though unconscious, influence of their anti-spiritistic habit of thought. Thus an eminent psychologist, who had observed Eusapia Paladino in the author's presence, asserts that during the well-known phenomenon of the inflation of her dress, he had seen a black rod manipulated by her feet, in order to pull forward some objects with the help of a hook attached to the rod. The author can guarantee the inaccuracy of this assertion, as he not only took part in observing

[1] For this purpose the Roneograph, brought out by Pathé Frères in Paris, is especially to be recommended. It is a sort of phonograph, whose wax plates receive the dictated record during the sitting and reproduce it afterwards.

the phenomenon, but minutely controlled the medium before and after the sitting.

Another observer is at present entirely convinced that Eusapia wears on her left shoe an iron sole, so that she can without detection withdraw the left foot and use it fraudulently, while the weight of the shoe standing on the foot of the controller on the left, is to produce the impression of a strong pressure with the foot. The numerous and detailed observations of the medium have not substantiated this hypothesis.

Another example : An observer of the sittings with Eva C. asserted in a supplementary record, written six months after the sitting, that the medium had only been examined over her dress, whereas the written record prepared by another savant immediately after the sitting gives an accurate account of the examination over the bare body, in conformity with the statements of the other witnesses.

These examples can easily be paralleled by similar experiences. Single determinations may often be of paramount importance for a decision as to the genuineness or falsity of a phenomenon.

We must add that in many mediumistic performances it is hardly possible for one person to execute the control and observation of the medium single-handed with sufficient accuracy. The help of a second observer must be secured. Now, however careful has been the control by these two trained and credible observers, however much both of them may asseverate that they had held the medium during the critical moment, yet it is natural that, in these extraordinary manifestations, most savants would rather assume an error of attention, or observation, in the case of the other controller, than acknowledge the genuineness of the phenomenon in question. That, at least, is the author's experience. And if, in spite of this, all objections can be met, the imagination will finally make some arbitrary addition or invention. The convenience of thought, the tough adherence to old preconceptions, is in most people too powerful to be put out of gear by any single observation.

If, therefore, we are to obtain reliable results, we must have a frequent repetition of the same occurrence, the same experiment, so that, after every experiment the objections and doubts suggested by mature reflection may be examined as to their justification during the repetition of the experiment. One should, therefore, always have a large number of sittings with the same medium—six at least—and arrange the whole method, so that the same experiment may be repeated as often as possible in the various sittings. The conditions may be changed, at discretion, at every sitting, so long as the externalisation of the mediumistic force is not thereby impeded.

How much emotional agitation, tension, expectation, fear, terror, and nervousness may hinder the power of observation and attention, inflame the imagination, and so produce errors of sense perception, amounting even to hallucination, is sufficiently known. Now, since as a rule—as Lehmann justly remarks—two people never commit the same errors of observation, their independent reports of the same event do not generally agree.

The same accuracy of proof as is demanded for the genuineness and objectivity of mediumistic phenomena must be furnished in an even higher degree for the negative proof, *i.e.*, for the presence of fraudulent manipulations when there is reason for suspicion. The latter problem is much the easier, but it requires a juridical accuracy in the establishment of guilt, *i.e.*, it is essential to the formation of a judgment that all positive and negative evidence be weighed before a final conclusion is drawn.

Any hasty generalisation, importing destructive criticism of the representatives of the opposite standpoint, must be regarded as unjust, illogical, and as the product of a very superficial acquaintance with the actual state of things. The fact that a medium has been detected in fraud under certain circumstances, cannot, as Eduard von Hartmann correctly observes, lead to the conclusion that the same medium has been nothing but fraudulent in every case and under the most varying conditions. " We must examine the conditions of each case, and one undoubtedly positive instance cannot be refuted even by a hundred negative ones.' Or will it be asserted, simply because simulation is often indistinguishable from hysteria, that all symptoms of hysteria are simulated ?

After all, the point is not whether errors and deceptions occur in this subject, as in many other fields of scientific activity, but simply whether, in this case, new and genuine facts of a special kind really exist. Even gold diggers must first separate the noble metal from its ore.

The author of this work, who has occupied himself more than twenty-five years with this subject, has had opportunities of observing mediums of all shades, both professional and private. In conjunction with other savants he has had occasion to reduce a whole spiritistic epidemic to its fraudulent causes (superstition and fanaticism) by means of careful and detailed investigations. He has become acquainted with the manipulations of the medium Eglinton, the sources of experimental error with the mediums Lucia Sordi and Linda Gazerra, which he has dealt with in special memoirs, and his own large experience has completely convinced him that conscious and unconscious fraud play an enormous part in this matter, and that nearly all mediums will, when the conditions are unfavourable, when their mediumistic powers are declining, or simply from greed and ambition, take to fraudulent or mechanical production of the phenomena.

According to my experience, I can only agree with Richet and Ochorowicz in regarding the psychic and moral conditions of mediumship, and of the trance condition as hitherto unknown, and in considering its aggregate of symptoms as different from the normal occurrences of psychic action. Indeed, it almost seems as if the tendency towards deception and to the mechanical production of mediumistic occurrences is a frequent quality of mediumship, just as simulation appears as a symptom of hysteria, or as *pseudologia phantastica* is inseparable from certain degenerative conditions of the brain.

We may be sure that absence of criticism, credulity, and the fanaticism of spiritists, have greatly hindered the education of mediums for scientifically useful objects. Fanatical eagerness to experience something *à tout prix*, to witness miracles, to receive signs from the " beyond,'' has rendered the crowd quite blind to the distinction between facts explicable according to the present conditions of psycho-pathology, and those which are not so explicable. The whole method of the spiritistic education of mediums, with their ballast of unnecessary conceptions, gives indeed an encouragement to fraud. When the believing congregation ends by seeing the work of a spirit hand in the falling of an umbrella, it is quite prepared to receive even the coarsest conjuring tricks of mediums as spirit greetings.

It is true that the violent excitement of the medium during the performance, especially in dark sittings, makes control very difficult, although on the other hand, it draws the attention of the observer beforehand to the occurrence of phenomena, and this guards him against surprise. We have already pointed out that the methods usual in science often here entirely fail the observer. It will, therefore, be a problem for future investigators to devise a special method for the examination of mediumistic processes.

We should, as Sir Oliver Lodge proposes, have a kind of psychic laboratory furnished for all kinds of experimental psychology and psycho-physics. Registration should, of course, be made independent of the sense organs, which are subject to deception, and should, as far as possible, be transferred to physical apparatus. A self-registering balance, the full use of photographic and electrical aids (such as photographs with ultra-violet light), the use of various degrees of brightness of light and of spectrum colours, thermometers, and other specially constructed instruments, may find their place in such an institute. Other apparatus of a more physiological kind would be necessary for investigations of the medium's organism (weight, temperature, respiration, etc.).

But of more importance than all these instrumental aids towards the study of this new force (assuming such to exist), would be the correct training of mediums for scientific investigations.

Such a dream of the future can, of course, not be realised in the narrow circle of a private residence, especially if the medium, as in the case of Eva C., is regarded as one of the family, and only resigns herself to these experiments voluntarily, and to a limited extent. Thus, in such a case, we have no complete independence in the arrangement of a laboratory, and the author found himself in the situation of an observer anxious to determine the existence of a new class of natural phenomena in the human organism.

In spite of this, it was possible, through the intelligent co-operation of the lady of the house, who conducted the mediumistic education of Eva C. with great ability, to make the conditions during the four years of experiment gradually more and more rigid and exact. The spiritistic group of ideas, which at first required the formation of chains, the singing and the addressing of the personifications appearing during the sittings, was afterwards put into the background, and during the last year played hardly any part. We had gradually discarded the spiritistic tradition by a slow education of the medium. Besides, all the sittings took place in a red light, so that during the four years there was not a single dark séance. We began with a single lamp and ended with a six-lamp chandelier of more than one hundred candle-power. The necessary dark room was furnished by the cabinet.

The experiments took place in two different Paris lodgings, in a villa at the seaside, and in the author's house in Munich, so that any preparation, of the walls or floor of the cabinet, for the hiding of objects, was practically eliminated.

The objective registration was based upon photography, which has been indicated by Lodge, Morselli, and other investigators as desirable. We began with a single camera, but at the end of the fourth year we sometimes had nine cameras, including several stereoscopic cameras, in action at the same time. From one to three cameras were then mounted in the cabinet itself. They were focused for short distances, and have been admirably serviceable. This method has not hitherto been mentioned in the literature of the subject, and was used for the first time with success. Unfortunately, a kinematograph, mounted by the author, for which a special electrical connection was arranged, gave no results in the case of Eva C.

That the control of the medium herself, both before and after every sitting, was executed with the necessary care is obvious.

The whole of the present work is really a monograph devoted to materialisation. For in the case of this medium, who is specially gifted for the production of teleplastic phenomena, it seemed advisable to develop this gift by suggestive education in every possible way, so as to form a firm empirical foundation for the study, by photographic means, of this teleplastic phenomenon so rarely found in mediums at present. It is possible that telekinetic phenomena, also, are founded upon a sort of materialisation, as indicated by the experiments of Professor Ochorowicz with Stanislawa Tomezyk. In this case also the process of materialisation might be regarded as the foundation of physical mediumship and as the point of departure of physical performances.

According to our observations, it is clear that the general direction and subject matter of the thoughts of the persons taking part in the experiments have an influence (either in a favourable or unfavourable sense), upon the psychic condition of the medium, and sometimes also upon the character of the phenomena produced. The mediumistic organism seems to be an exceedingly delicate reagent, very much open to the influence of suggestion. Strange as it may seem, active thoughts about exposures and trickery might, in the opinion of some investigators, suggestively influence the medium in this direction and lead to the employment of such manual aids. During any careful investigation one must also pay attention to this source of error, and one should exclude so-called professional exposers entirely from such observations, if they are such as scent corruption everywhere, without any appreciation of the psychological delicacy and difficulty of the problem, and prefer to assume collusion between the observer and the medium with a deceptive object, as the only reality in these occurrences.

Occasionally one finds savants with a compelling, but unconscious, idiosyncrasy as regards this field of investigation. They do indeed attempt to put themselves into a state of benevolence towards the medium, and to attune their mentality to the special conditions of the experiment. They even declare that they will be satisfied if an experiment succeeds under certain precautions, but, afterwards, they succumb to the strong influence of their unconscious mental resistance; they then bring forward quite senseless objections, and make every effort to avoid having to admit the possibility of these phenomena. Their view is that there is no other possibility than that of deception. Their whole effort, during the sittings, is not directed towards a determination free from objection, but simply towards detection of the fraudulent mechanism. That such a condition of mind may suggestively influence the instrument of research, and hinder its productivity, is shown by numerous experiences. Since this mediophobia belongs to the realm of pathological inhibitions, it is advisable to exclude persons subject to it from the sittings, as was done by Eusapia Paladino on account of the diminution of her powers, and so as not to be induced to practise fraud by such influence.

Nothing should be left undone to make the psychic conditions for the medium as favourable as possible. That is not always easy, especially if the medium, in consequence of his or her low state of education, has only a slight understanding of the precautions necessary for a scientific investigation. Nevertheless, we should never forget that the success of the experiment is bound up with the mood, the confidence, and the undisturbed comfort of the medium. By suspicion, even suppressed suspicion, by haughty or indifferent treatment, the instrument can easily be put out of tune. I again agree entirely with Eduard von Hartmann that it is not right that scientific men should refuse investigation of these manifestations, simply for the reason that they require conditions which are not always within the power of the observer.

Our lack of knowledge of the psychogenic factors, of the necessary physical and chemical concomitants inside and outside the medium's organism, as well as the absence of a tried experimental method for the investigation of the psycho-physical performances which really form a part of biology, distinguish these investigations from laboratory experiments or ordinary physiology. But even laboratory experiments are often dependent upon very complicated conditions, and, in any case, a physician does not allow his zeal for investigation to be influenced even by the most laboriously attempted deceptions of hysteria patients or insane persons.

This does not imply that any novice can, without further ado, without any experience or previous knowledge, without a study of the literature of the subject, prescribe to the medium his own conditions. The inevitable consequence of such procedure is a disturbing effect on the psychic condition of the medium and an interference with the mediumistic phenomena. If the mediumistic performances really represent a new kind of unknown force, every unprejudiced investigator must, in the first instance, make up his mind to be a passive spectator of what may be called a new class of natural phenomena. In the course of every observation of these occurrences, which depend upon such delicate conditions, he will learn to adapt himself to the peculiarities of this kind of investigation, as well as to the personality of the medium. As the confidence of the medium in the investigator increases, he will be allowed to exert an influence on the experiments, to choose the class of phenomena he wants to observe, and, finally, he will be allowed, even during the experiment, to exercise certain arbitrary interferences which will help him to arrive at a definite judgment.

The author used this method of investigation both in the case of Eusapia Paladino and Eva C. In both cases he was allowed, after a considerable number of sittings, and after the first suspicions had vanished, to make suitable interpositions and arrangements to facilitate objective determination. Still, one must not overlook certain difficulties inherent in the character of such persons. Fear and modesty may control young female mediums to such an extent that they resist investigation of the bare body, and indeed will refuse any experiment rather than allow such misinterpreted interference with their feminine feelings.

A medium of this kind is Linda Gazerra. The great gap in the conditions established in her case cancels the value of the whole work devoted to her by Imoda, as the author has shown in a special study, for any untrustworthiness in the experimental arrangements must necessarily shake the confidence of the critical reader, and must finally lead to a negative attitude even though the phenomena be genuine.

In all interferences with the phenomena themselves, we must also take into account the exaggerated sensitiveness, and condition of excitement, in which the medium's organism is placed during its particular performances.

The frequently observed vital efflorescences and the doubling of limbs apparently can give occasion for erroneous interpretations and mistaken interferences. Should the latter be coarse and brusque, they injure the bodily condition of the entranced medium in all cases. We must therefore establish the following fundamental rule:

All conditions, controls, interferences, and experiments must, as far as possible, be arranged in such a way that the play of these forces and the mediumistic performances as such, are not hindered or interrupted in their development or mode of action. This must be done, even at the risk of being accused of superficial and uncritical behaviour.

Fanaticism for exactitude may lead to the drying up of the fountain from which we wish to draw our material.

It is clear that the normal personality of the medium, as already shown by the whole somnambulistic objectivity of the type, is opposed to the psychic processes employed in the mediumistic performances as to something strange and compulsory. The mental contents of the mediumistic field and of the normal personality of the medium are usually self-contained, have no association with each other, and are brought alternately into nervous action. Thus we can understand the astonishment of the mediums about their own performances, their lack of remembrance of them, the feeling of strangeness in comparison with their own sphere of action, their frequent inability to determine beforehand the success or the kind of occurrences, and their sensation of innocence when found out in manipulations. Finally, we may understand their lack of appreciation of the importance of pure experiments as distinguished from occurrences exposed to objection.

Following up this train of thought further, we may suppose that soft substances, such as the flowing dress of the medium, curtains hanging near, etc., can be of some advantage, and may form conductors and reservoirs of power, from which the effects may take their origin, besides giving points of support for the materialised structures. Both for the materials for the furnishing of the cabinet, as well as for the dress of the medium (for which knitted fabrics are preferable), a black colour is to be recommended. For with a black background even the finest, hardly visible materialised fabrics can be seen. Besides, this colour increases the darkness in the cabinet, and thus contributes indirectly to the development of the phenomena. If care is taken that the medium has nothing white about her, the materialisation structures, appearing grey or white on a black background, are very convincing. Thus darkness behind these structures appears to be a necessity for the development of the teleplasm. Yet these thoughts, which are the product of uniform observation of various mediums, are not to be a rigid rule, but only a hint. All observations made by the author concerning mediums agree in this, that a white light has a hindering and disturbing effect on the phenomena, and an unfavourable action on the development of the teleplasm. It is possible that the education of the medium in this point also plays a part, for, on the other hand, I often succeeded in observing the course of the whole phenomenon from beginning to end in a red light or in the shade of the curtain in the case of Eva C. According to the spiritistic view, the closed cabinet opposes the dispersion of the fluid emanating from the medium. For the carping critic, the cabinet, the darkness of the reduced light, only exist in order to hide the manipulations by means of which the phenomena are fraudulently produced. That this easily understood view is generally applauded is not surprising.

The recent investigations by W. J. Crawford [1] have shown that white light acts destructively on the pseudopods or psychic projections from the medium's body necessary for the production of telekinetic phenomena. It appears to produce a molecular softening of the invisible " rods ; " while red light acts much more feebly. It is, therefore, necessary to consider the reflection, refraction and absorption of the light used in the séance room.

Professor Ochorowicz employed with success a faint blue light. So did Paul Gibier,[2] the Director of the Pasteur Institute in New York. But, in any case, the long-wave red rays are preferable, since they allow us to leave the shutter of the photographic apparatus open. On the whole it is better to renounce the show-pieces of the medium in the dark, and to use a faint illumination with a feebler manifestation. It is true that in a feebler light, and, therefore, also in the red light, we only see indirectly with the rods of the retina, which are more sensitive to light, and less to colour, whereas in fixation in a feeble red light,[3] we use the " cones," on account of their central position. But these, on account of their greater sensitiveness to colour than to light, in general give a feebler general effect. Objects on which the glance is fixed, or concentrated in a red light appear, therefore, feebler than they do subsequently on the photograph. The eye is very easily fatigued and subject to error. Hence it is advisable often to close the eye and to rest it, instead of fixing it with an effort for a length of time.

The exhaustion of the medium is, as a rule, in proportion to the strength of the phenomena. But the effort involved in the action of

[1] *See* p. 14. [2] Gibier, *Ann. des Sc. Ps.*, 1901.
[3] Graetz, " Physical Ray Phenomena," *Münch. Med. Wochenschrift*, No. 14, 1904.

the medium's organism is much greater when the composition of the audience is unfavourable. Occasionally the mood of the mediums may be adversely affected by unsympathetic personalities, or by contemptuous treatment; they are abashed, nervous, and incapable of any performance; for the latter necessarily involves a consciousness of capacity and the feeling of not being hindered. The somewhat suspicious refusal of very rigid conditions of control may be the result of a correct instinctive knowledge that they produce a psychic inhibition which places the whole result in jeopardy. Mediumistic activity may be compared with artistic creation. A good artist, be he musician, poet or painter, requires the necessary emotional state in order to develop his creative artistic power. He also is dependent on details of surroundings, trifling disturbances, bodily well-being, etc. This is also the reason why sittings in circles having a spiritualistic and religious colouring, in which the medium is almost venerated as a saint, are often attended by better success than the so-called scientific sittings. The wise experimenter will, therefore, take care to secure the necessary emotional state of the medium, and avoid any useless waste of power. He will be satisfied with one to three sittings, in order that the medium may recover, and from time to time he will allow longer rest intervals. Eusapia Paladino used to be very exhausted after every successful sitting, especially after she had been in a state of trance. She sometimes slept until the next midday, and was for the rest of the day apathetic, peevish, and monosyllabic. Her skin was usually cold after the sittings, her pulse rapid (110° per minute), and she had a strong feeling of fatigue. Her subsequent sleep was often restless and interrupted by vivid dreams. She had a sensitive feeling as to whether her performances had satisfied the audience or not, and put her ambition into the conviction of those present, meeting all their wishes so far as possible. After a failure, or perhaps a very strong effort, she might have a feeling of deep depression and increased sensitiveness. She then gave way to tears and lamented her sad fate. From a conjuring point of view all this would naturally be superfluous comedy, but from the psychological point of view it confirms the opinion of Richet, according to whom the psychic condition of the medium is different from the normal state, and requires further study. In the case of Eva C. also, where the number of negative sittings is very considerable, she feels much exhausted, according to the degree of her performances, and after exhaustive positive sittings she usually needs from twenty-eight to forty-four hours to recover the deficit in her strength. Also, she is often, on the following day, dazed, and complains of headache and lack of appetite.

Even in the case of the more or less spontaneous occurrence of her teleplastic activity, it may happen that, though for several days in succession she gives positive performances, she may remain entirely indifferent for weeks, and even months, afterwards.

No medium escapes the decreasing phase of efficiency, and in the case of professional mediums who make their living out of their sittings, it requires a great strength of character to withdraw, and to refrain from filling up the gaps by manual expedients, *i.e.*, by fraud.

Therefore the subsequent behaviour of such mediums, who in view of their usually feeble will-power are affected by momentary, including unfavourable, influences, is irrelevant to the experimental results obtained objectively by investigators when the former are in the fulness of their power.

Eva C. is not a professional medium, *i.e.*, she is not obliged to engage herself for sittings for money, but can return at any moment to her parents and sisters. But she prefers her independence and lends her remarkable power freely to Mme. Bisson and her collaborators for scientific purposes, from gratitude for the years of hospitality enjoyed in the house of the Bisson family. She has no binding obligation towards them; she is fully in possession of her liberty, and can discontinue the experiments whenever she likes. On the other hand, Mme. Bisson is undoubtedly under a moral obligation to the family of Eva C. to guard her against any injury to her health, or danger to her mind, and she also has to undertake a legal responsibility for the girl against such things as negligence resulting in bodily injury.

The method of education pursued in these four years has proved itself correct and appropriate, by the success of the experiments on the one hand, and on the other hand by the complete preservation of the bodily and mental equilibrium of Eva C. This indicates a delicate appreciation of the sensitive and abnormal nature of such persons.

FACTS AND HYPOTHESES

GRANTING the assumption that the mediumistic phenomena of telekinetics and teleplastics, including the intellectual manifestations, are not the product of fraud, we must at once frankly confess that, whether all phenomena have the same origin, or different origins, we cannot in any way explain them. This must not deter us from the attempt to put facts once acknowledged in proper order, to analyse them, to form auxiliary conceptions when terms are wanting, and to put forward hypotheses which only retain their temporary value so long as they serve the progress of knowledge.

A collection of facts is not yet a science any more than a heap of stones is an edifice. They must be collated, sifted and ordered, according to a definite point of view, in order that we may draw conclusions from them. It is therefore interesting to cast a glance at the present standpoint of these lines of investigation with a special reference to the theoretical interpretation of mediumistic phenomena. Most modern investigators are inclined to adopt the " subliminal " consciousness, proposed by Myers, as a basis for the explanation of the mental manifestations of mediums, including the phenomena of clairvoyance, psychometry, telæsthesia, etc. This subliminal consciousness comprises the transcendental faculties, and must not be mistaken for Dessoir's " subliminal consciousness," which only comprises normal faculties. Indeed, long before Myers, the philosopher Dr Carl du Prel, formulated a similar theory, with the sole difference that he denoted Myers's subliminal consciousness by the term " transcendental subject." The idea was therefore in existence, even before the time of Myers, and found considerable acceptance even at the time of du Prel.[1]

Since certain types of personification, which suggest an identity with deceased persons, cannot be explained fully by the theory of Myers (quite apart from physical occurrences), investigators like Sir Oliver Lodge, Hodgson, Lombroso, Flammarion and others, have been induced to return to the spirit hypothesis, and to the belief in personal survival.

---

[1] Reference may be made to the following: Myers, *Human Personality*. Carl du Prel, *Philosophie der Mystik*, 1885. Oliver Lodge, *The Survival of Man*. William James, *Psychology* and *Memories and Studies*, 1911. Maeterlinck, *La Mort*. Lombroso, *Hypnotische und Spiritistische Forschungen*. Delanne, *Apparitions Matérialisées*, Paris, 1911. Aksakoff, *Animismus und Spiritismus*, 1894. Flournoy, *Esprits et Médiums*. Von Hartmann, *Der Spiritismus* (1898).

Flammarion says on this subject: "At the same time it seems to me that the spiritistic hypothesis may be mentioned with the same right as the other, for all discussions on it have not proved that it is untenable."

Professor William James indicates a greater reserve in the following words: "If one sticks to the detail, one may draw an anti-spiritist conclusion; if one thinks more of what the whole mass may signify, one may well incline to spiritist interpretations;" and in another place: "Probably a strange will is also brought into account." In his *Psychology* William James does not hold back this conviction, and adds: "I communicate my view, not of course in order to convert any one to my opinion, but because I am convinced that a serious study of these phenomena is of the greatest importance to psychology, and because I think that my personal confession may lead a reader or two to approach the region of investigation which is usually treated with contempt by so-called men of science."[1]

In another place this great psychologist says:—

"Really powerful mediums are rare, but when one commences to work with them and descends into the dim regions of automatism, one is inclined to take many rare coincidences for rudimentary forms of truth. . . . The phenomena, infinitely complex in their elements, are as yet so little understood that concise judgments expressed by the words 'spirits,' or 'nonsense,' are equally unreasonable. As regards the question whether such types of phenomena which are ignored by official science exist, I am completely convinced that they do exist."[1]

A detailed discussion of the Anglo-American investigations centring round the experiments with Mrs Piper is contained in M. Maeterlinck's book *La Mort* (Paris—Charpentier, 1913). He says, among other things: "The survival of the spirit is not more improbable than the marvellous capacities which we must attribute to the medium if we deny them to the dead, and the existence of the medium is undeniable in contrast with that of the 'spirit.' The marvellous capacities astonish us because they are isolated. Fundamentally they are not more wonderful than our thought, our memory, our imagination. . . . On the whole the entire dispute is a question of fact which can only be solved by a series of careful experiments. The time for drawing conclusions has not yet come." For Lombroso, the totality of all observations of mediums forms so close a network of proofs that it resists all attacks of the most rigid scepticism.

His view approaches that of du Prel concerning the "astral body" and the solidarity of the phantom with the body of the medium, and he argues: "For, if the soul is reduced to a fluid material which only becomes visible and manifest under quite definite conditions, it surely belongs still to the world of matter" (when the word "matter" is not used in the sense in which it is used in the present doctrine of energy).

The two-volume book of Delanne represents, just like Aksakoff's *Animism and Spiritism*, the spiritistic point of view of the old school. These two works contain large collections of material.

On the other hand, Professor Flournoy (Geneva), without recognising, on the basis of sense observations, the reality of mediumistic

[1] Passage retranslated from the German (*Tr.*).

phenomena, still considers spiritism as an error, and believes it to be a serious mistake to ascribe the remarkable phenomena presented by mediums to the spirits of the dead.

He is convinced that the supernormal occurrences owe their genesis to hidden forces and laws which we do not yet know.

These materialisations do not offer a rigid demonstration of interferences from "Beyond," since the analysis of their psychological contents shows that they are merely creations of the medium's imagination, creations of his subliminal consciousness.

Among the best and most thorough works in German literature on this subject we may reckon the works of the philosopher, Eduard von Hartmann, who also assumes the reality of the mediumistic phenomena, but, apart from formal essential difficulties, he regards the spirit hypothesis as really superfluous, since in the case of both inspirational and physical processes, including materialisation, he depends upon the medium. Here we contravene an important principle of method: " The principles used in explanation must not be needlessly multiplied, and we must not suppose a second kind of causes so long as one kind suffices." The existence of these causes lying outside the medium is not proved, and the value of this hypothesis is only to be demonstrated by an explanation of the phenomena in question. Thus the assumption of such causes indicates a serious lack of critical caution.

De Vesme, the author of the three-volume *History of Spiritism* (Mutze, Leipzig, 1909), and Editor of the *Annales des Sciences Psychiques*, considers himself bound to maintain that a key will never be found which fits all the metapsychical phenomena, which he considers to be true as a whole. In the case of physical manifestations we may in his view discard the spiritistic hypothesis during experiments. But so soon as they are accompanied by manifestations of intelligence, or when we have to deal with purely mental phenomena, we need this hypothesis, but only as a *working* hypothesis. In other words, the experimenter must, in order to get results at all, adapt himself to the " dramatised personifications " under which all mediums in the somnambulic state carry out their performances during the sitting, but he must reserve himself complete liberty for a subsequent psychological analysis and explanation.

De Vesme also prefers, on the whole, the psycho-dynamic point of view, since it corresponds more closely with scientific minds than does the spirit hypothesis, though it may be difficult to bring all observations into harmony with it.

With Flournoy and De Vesme the author believes that the spirit hypothesis not only fails to explain the slightest detail of these occurrences, but that it impedes and hinders in every way serious scientific investigation. For the anthropomorphic need and the metaphysical tendency, slumbering deep within the human soul, have historically always taken charge of those objects and natural phenomena, which mankind could not explain with the help of the learning of his time.

That it is not impossible to bring about harmony between this problem lying on the borderland of human cognition and modern physical theory has already been pointed out by the well-known German chemist, Professor Ostwald, on the occasion of his review of Flammarion's work, *Unknown Forces of Nature*. Ostwald cannot escape the conclusion that, in the case of the scientifically useful materials collected by Flammarion, we have to deal with observed facts which we cannot, in general, justly deny. Special emphasis is attached to the point that nearly all mediums are fraudulent, because they cannot always produce the desired phenomena, and yet do not wish to lose their reputation for special gifts. They, therefore, employ artificial means if the phenomena will not come. But, even after deducting these deceptions, there remains, as Ostwald explains, such a large amount of well-authenticated fact that we must attempt to get into touch with it. Ostwald applies the energy theory in the following manner to the mediumistic phenomena. " Certain human beings are capable of transforming their physiological store of energy (which, as we know, is almost exclusively present in the form of chemical energy), of transmitting it through space, and of transforming it at prescribed points back into one of the known forms of energy. It results from this that the mediums themselves are usually much exhausted, *i.e.*, that they use up their bodily energy. A transformation into psychic energy seems also to be possible. The mediumistic form of energy can be compared, as regards velocity of propagation, with light, and it appears to have polarity, for there are persons whose actions neutralise each other. This view implies no fundamental contradiction of any laws of Nature. We have, therefore, the possibility of a science."

This science is regarded by Ostwald as in its infancy, since it is not yet possible to produce the phenomena at will. " But since apparently the mediumistic properties are not at all rare, but are found in nearly every other person, though only feebly developed, a rapid development, in the scientific sense, is quite possible, and will, perhaps, take place sooner than we think."

Though we may not share Ostwald's view as regards the frequency of mediumistic gifts, we must approve of his attempt to conceive and explain phenomena with the help of the energy theory of the Universe.

This theory also dominates the peculiar work written by Professor Staudenmaier, *Die Magic als Experimentelle Naturwissenschaft* ("Magic as an Experimental Science," Leipzig, 1912). This author thinks that the physical phenomena occurring with mediums must be produced arbitrarily and according to plan. Physiologically speaking, the specific energy, travelling over the various nerves, is driven in opposite directions from that which corresponds to normal working. In seeing, smelling, hearing and feeling, the specific excitation travels from the sense organs to the brain, and finally to the consciousness. In producing optical, auditory, and other hallucinations, we must learn to transmit the energy in a centrifugal direction. According to this view, which is opposed to the present doctrine of hallucination, we must suppose that virtual reality is at the base of the false perception. Staudenmaier seeks to explain the physical phenomena of mediumship by the expulsion of such forms of energy (*e.g.*, of motor energy from the fingers), as well as voluntary transformation of large quantities of energy in the nervous system. But as long as such experiments in " magic " cannot be produced in a manner free from objection, the hypothesis is not worth discussing. Perhaps the greatest advance in the knowledge of the elementary phenomena of materialisation is furnished by the experiments of Professor Ochorowicz [1] with the medium Stanislawa Tomczyk. In the first place, this experimenter observed the occurrence of "rigid organic rays," in 1893, in the case of Eusapia Paladino, and subsequently with the above-mentioned medium. These "rigid rays" are thread-like connections, which are formed between the fingers of the medium when she brings her hands together. These may remain invisible, and yet exert mechanical effects, as, for instance, by the motion and raising of small objects without contact. When condensed, they are visible and can be photographed. The author was present in Paris at such a sitting and can vouch for the accuracy of this observation. Besides, it was successfully tested by several Commissions, composed of photographic experts and savants. These rays can, however, not be compared with Reichenbach's "Odic Effluvia," nor with the "N" rays of Blondlot and Charpentier. We have here to deal with fluidic threads, which were also observed in the sitting with Eva C. by the author. Under a magnifying glass it appears that the thread is composed of points. Following up this study the author obtained radiographic drawings and impressions on black paper, and later, mediumistic radiographs of hands in total darkness, fluidic shadow-duplication of hands of the medium, with an imperfect impression on the negative, and finally impressions on the photographic negative corresponding to the thought images of the medium, *i.e.*, "thought photography." This thought image acquires a capability of externalisation, and thus produces an objective picture. Such an occurrence must be called "material ideoplastics." It furnishes a transition towards an understanding of materialisation phenomena, and is indeed of great importance for their explanation. Ochorowicz illustrated his systematic experiments by numerous photographs. Unfortunately, the other works are dispersed among periodicals, instead of being available to the reader in a continuous book. Not only the author's experiments with Eva C., but also those cited in what follows (which were obtained quite independently of Ochorowicz's observations), point in the same direction to an ideoplastic material expression of thought images of an optical character.

Dr Kotik,[2] of Moscow, put before a person acting as agent a clear sheet of notepaper, and a picture post-card, with a request to imagine vividly the picture transferred to the blank sheet, and to fix the attention upon the sheet for several minutes with that idea. Then the blank sheet, so treated, was shown to another person acting as the percipient and living in another place. This person's description regularly corresponded to what was represented on the picture post-card. Kotik assumes, in consequence of the success of a series of such experiments, that a psycho-physical radiant energy is secreted by the brain at the moment of thought, and can be transferred to a piece of paper; that it is there preserved, and subsequently may produce the same impression on the brains of persons having peculiar gifts. This energy, according to Kotik, possesses psychical and physical properties. It can, for instance, be collected on the surface of the body, and can be conducted or absorbed. He regards the subconscious self as the place of storage.

[1] *Ann. des Sc. Psychiques*, 1909, p. 41; 1911, p. 126.
[2] *Die Emanation der Psychophysischen Energie* (Bergmann, Wiesbaden, 1908).

According to his view, thinking is accompanied by the emission of brain-rays having a great penetrative power. These are accompanied by a psycho-physical element, which may have a small penetrative power, and another element, which is purely psychical. We have, therefore, in the experiments of Ochorowicz, a psycho-physical emanation analogous to the manifestations of radio-active substances and radio-active emanation. The small particles of the psycho-physical emanation he denotes by the term " psycho-physical atoms," or, in accordance with the newest views, as " psycho-physical electrons." Kotik believes that by means of this mysterious agency he is enabled to explain numerous actual phenomena of spiritism. However daring and unconvincing Kotik's arguments may appear at first sight, they indicate a path of research, and offer us a welcome auxiliary hypothesis for the comprehension of the occurrence of mediumistic ideoplastics in so far as their actuality cannot be denied.

In the work already mentioned by the author and discussed in detail, Imoda's *Phantasmal Photography*, numerous teleplastic portraits taken by flash-light are reproduced. Among these there is a photograph, taken at Professor Charles Richet's house, by De Fontenay on the 29th of April 1909, representing a rather distorted masculine face, with eyes directed upwards. Long after, on the 1st of March 1913, the newspaper, *Le Matin*, proved that this picture is strikingly similar to an angel head painted by Rubens. Comparing the two pictures, there can be no doubt that this picture was the model for the mediumistic reproductions. If, in consideration of the trustworthiness of both photographers, we may dismiss the possibility of fraud, we have here a typical ideoplastic reproduction by the medium, Linda G. This is supported by the following circumstances: The medium takes a great interest in painting, and has certainly seen the collection of pictures in the Louvre, where the original may be found. This Rubens angel head left a vivid remembrance in her subliminal consciousness. In the state of trance the dream memory of this head was translated into a reality. The image gives the impression more of an artistic recollection than that of a true copy, as we should expect, if there had been a virtual use of a photographic copy. Apart from the distorted expression in comparison with the original, the right eye is entirely covered with a black substance which may be regarded as a veil or hair which is not found in the original.

Besides, the picture as a whole departs considerably from Rubens's representation. According to the view of De Fontenay, the medium has materialised her dream impression. In any case, it is an interesting example of mediumistic ideoplastics, if we assume the genuineness of the phenomenon.[1]

Professor Morselli [2] has also adopted this view for the explanation of the Eusapian phenomena. He says: " In this case the idea of the phenomenon, as grasped by Eusapia in a waking or half-waking condition, rises into the medium's subconsciousness, where the still unknown bio-psychic power of mediumship elaborates it. It then

[1] See Schrenck-Notzing, *Die Phænomene des Mediums Linda Gazerra*, Mutze, Leipzig, 1912.
[2] *Psychische Studien*, 1907, p. 420.

externalises itself, and extends over a distance corresponding to her mechanical power as a luminous ' ideoplastic,' or ' materialised product.' During the more important phenomena the medium is always in a state of trance, and her own will is in abeyance. There is, so to speak, an automatic liberation of forces which we may term ' medianimic,' and which are stored in the nerve centres."

In another place [1] he admits that we know nothing, nothing, nothing as to how these things occur. Understanding must come later. He discusses no less than twenty-five explanations of mediumship. He regards the spiritistic hypothesis as superfluous, full of contradictions, uncultured, childish, too abstract and confused, and also as immoral, in the sense that it does not fit in with our religious and social ideals, and offends against human dignity. He also maintains that it is not proved by a single manifestation, at least so far as Eusapia Paladino is concerned. And the few communications which cannot be explained in this way, such as those of Mrs Piper and Mrs Thompson, do not offer a sufficient foundation for a magnificent edifice, such as has been attempted during the last few decades with such doubtful material.

The psycho-dynamical phenomena which Morselli classes under the provisional name of " medianimity," comprise indefinite, undefinable, and unintelligible capacities of the human organism, which perhaps every one possesses to a quite small and unrecognisable degree, but which some personalities possess to such an extraordinary extent that they succeed in expressing their vital and psychic activity beyond the limits of the body. These powers disappear with the mechanism which produces them, and have, therefore, no survival. The intimate dynamics of such capacities are unknown to us.

As one may gather from the above review, nearly all the investigators who have lately studied the phenomena of physical mediumship —which, in view of the psychogenic character of the occurrences must always retain some connection with psychical phenomena—incline towards a rejection of the spiritistic theory in favour of the psychodynamical conception, and towards a purely observational attitude, as represented by Morselli, Bottazzi, Foa, Richet, Ochorowicz, Kotik, Ostwald, Flournoy, de Vesme, de Rochas, Maxwell, etc. This is also the point of view adopted by the author in the following studies.

In this sense the observations with Eva C. were conducted as impartially and conscientiously as possible, the records written down after each sitting, and in the last six months even during the sittings themselves. Since Eva C.'s special gift is entirely confined to teleplastics or materialisation, the only possible objection that can be raised is that the materialisation products are somehow fraudulently smuggled into the sittings. The problem of control is, therefore, very simple. *It has only to guard against the introduction or handing in of objects and their subsequent removal.* Now, not one of the observers present in the course of four years was able to prove that prepared pictures or materials had been brought into the sittings or had been removed after use. Even the boldest hypotheses, based upon the mechanical production of the phenomena, have been refuted by a repetition of the experiments

[1] *Psychische Studien*, 1907, p. 545.

under modified conditions which paid special attention to the possibilities suggested. The result is, and remains, a negative one, that is to say, it remains favourable to the medium.

When, in view of the rigorous control of the medium before and after the sittings, it became impossible to cast suspicion upon her, the criticism directed itself upon her protectress, Mme. Bisson. But, quite apart from the unjustifiable and insulting insinuation against that lady, she has, in the spirit of a purely scientific research, repeatedly allowed herself to be examined by the author, both before and after the sittings, without any reason for suspicion ever being discovered. And, besides, if one really wished to continue this train of thought, with what motive could Mme. Bisson, living in Paris, try to deceive a foreign savant for four years, and with an even greater success in Munich, in the author's own workrooms, and under the suspicious eyes of German colleagues?

Financial motives are also put out of court by the favourable and well-regulated circumstances of the Bisson family. The lady's own expenses for these experiments (housing, clothing, and feeding of the medium for three and a half years, rent and furniture of the flat taken for the purpose of the experiments, extras for the sittings themselves) are many times those incurred by the author. Hysteria and a love of sensation do not play any part, since Mme. Bisson's bodily and mental equilibrium are intact. Besides, for spiritistic sensations more suitable objects could be found in Paris. There cannot, therefore, be the slightest doubt that Mme. Bisson, who also experimented with many other persons in the author's absence, has conducted this four years' investigation out of a pure interest in the subject, in the scientific exploration of the mediumistic problem. This is borne out by the French edition of her studies and observations with Eva C., written by herself, and published simultaneously with the present work. This step into publicity vouches for the authoress's *bona fides*. The imputation of fraudulent assistance is thus deprived of any reasonable basis.

In order to remain within the range of a rigid objectivity, the author has also published the subjective interpretations of the scientific witnesses, though, naturally, some of these opinions are negative, in view of the limited experience of the persons concerned. To the author, the most essential thing was the confirmation by independent witnesses of the effects they had observed. To form a judgment, the author had four years of observation to fall back upon. It is easily understood that a final judgment may be different from that of witnesses who have only attended a few sittings.

But the reader ought not to be swayed by the author's personal view. He should himself follow the development of the phenomena, with the aid of the records, and then form his own judgment.

In order, however, to offer the chance of a theoretical comprehension of the mysterious phenomena obtained with Eva C., the author thought well to give the above short review of the present condition of mediumistic research, with special regard to the present hypotheses and attempts at explanation.

Yet, in reality, it is more advisable to-day simply to verify, to observe, and to refrain from conclusions.

For, as Maeterlinck[1] truly remarks: "Let us not forget that we here have to deal with a science of to-day and yesterday, which is still groping for its utensils, ways, methods, and aims, and that in the midst of a night which is darker than the earthly night. Not in thirty years will be built the boldest bridge which has ever been audaciously thrown across the river of death. Most sciences have centuries of useless effort and barren uncertainty behind them, and among the youngest of them there are probably few which promise such a harvest, even in the first stages—a harvest which may not correspond to what we believe ourselves to have sown, but which already shows many buds of a strange and unknown fruit."

[1] Maeterlinck, "On Life after Death" (*Neue Rundschau*, Feb. 1913, Vol. II.).

MATERIALISATION PHENOMENA WITH EVA C.

Sittings of May and June 1909 (Paris).

Observers and Medium.

THE well-known author, Alexandre Bisson, whose dramas have also been performed in Germany, was induced by the phenomena observed in the case of Eusapia Paladino to collect further experiences on the subject of mediumship. He and his wife are neither prejudiced spiritists nor hypersceptical critics, but simply desire to serve truth without any preconceived opinion. The circle of friends, collected for this purpose by them, does not consist of credulous persons undertaking these researches on account of a metaphysical need, or with the object of establishing communication with the "Beyond." It consists of sober-minded observers, who wish to judge the facts in question on the basis of their own tests. For this purpose the arrangement of the experiments was directed towards the elimination of fraudulent manipulations and self-deception. Hence, at each sitting : complete undressing of the medium, strict examination of the cabinet, use of photography.

Through the kindness of M. Delanne, the author was introduced into this circle, which had already, for three months before his arrival, experimented several times per week. The medium was a young girl of the middle classes who had already shown materialisation phenomena in other circles, and had only come to Paris in 1908. Since the author is not justified in publishing details concerning her personal and family affairs, he need only mention here that although Eva C. has an unfavourable heredity, she has not passed through any serious illness. The relatives of the girl are all in respectable situations in industry, or the Civil Service.

Eva C.[1] is twenty-three years of age, of middle height, and slender build. She has fair hair and her body is well-nourished. She is said to have suffered in her second year from convulsions of nervous origin, but without any serious crises. Menstruation set in in the twelfth year, and is generally normal. Occasional tendency to bladder trouble after a cystitis six years ago. In 1907 she had an operation on her left eye for squinting (*Strabismus convergens*), and she is slightly feeble-sighted. At the age of seventeen to nineteen she had chlorotic symptoms, which have since ceased. Her internal organs are healthy, her pulse

[1] This report was written down by the author in June 1913, in the light of the four years' observations.

small and soft, 84 to 90 per minute. Her weight varies between 110 and 117 lbs. No signs of degeneration. Largest circumference of skull twenty-two inches. Fairly striking slant in the well-developed nose towards the left, but otherwise both sides of the face are equal. A few carious teeth. No disturbance of sensitiveness, or reaction to pressure, on tapping the skull. Eyelids equally wide on both sides. Pupils of normal aperture and prompt reaction to incident light. On the left a slight limitation of the field of vision. No disturbances of visual acuity or sense of colour. The scleral and corneal reflexes are present, but there is no reflex of the roof of the mouth or of the gullet. The deep-seated reflexes, such as those of the triceps muscle and the knee-cap, as well as the skin reflexes, take place without difficulty. The dynamometric force is fifty-two on the left, sixty-eight on the right. There are no disturbances of motion or equilibrium.

The ticking of a watch is perceived at eleven inches on the left and at twelve inches on the right.

Eva C. is very sensitive to olfactory impressions, while her sense of taste is normal.

The sensitiveness of the skin in the axillar region of both upper arms is exaggerated. There is a slight hyperæsthesia for pin-pricks, but the sensations of touch, heat and cold, of pain and of pointed and blunt objects, as well as suggestions of the muscular sense, are correctly perceived and localised.

Pronunciation, comprehension of words, and optical recollections are undisturbed. Hallucinations are denied. Sleep and appetite in general are good. Eva left school at seventeen and a half years. Her mediumistic gifts were discovered by accident when a relative operated in her presence with another test person. In her family circle spiritualistic sittings were held with Eva C. four or five years before the beginning of the Paris experiments. Another series of tests was made in the house of an English lady.

As regards her psychology there are no disturbances of attention. Eva easily follows conversations taking place in her presence, and sometimes shows a vivid interest. She is well-informed on general conditions of life, so far as they affect her personally, and readily answers questions about her life-history, and about events of the near and remote past. Her range of knowledge corresponds to her level of education. She can quote what she reads, hears, or sees, with facility, and can correctly render the details of a picture she has contemplated for a single second. She has a good memory for figures, and solves arithmetical problems without difficulty.

She has a vivid imagination, which is sometimes so exaggerated that truth and fiction can no longer be distinguished. She has a high suggestibility, especially for momentary impressions. She gives no coherent answers to abstract questions, such as : What is the difference between a storm and a hurricane ; why a stone falls to the ground and does not ascend towards the sky ; or how the political parties of her country are composed ? She obviously regards such questions as distasteful. There is very imperfect development of the logical faculty. Instead, there is a mechanical reproduction of opinions overheard, without the consciousness that these are taken from memory, and are not the result of her own thought. Her mood is unstable, and easily excitable. The momentary emotion dominates her mental life. She greatly depends upon her emotional state, and is quite inaccessible to any educational influences during her intermittent fits of temper. In such cases one must either await the subsidence of the crisis, which may last for days, or try to eliminate it by hypnotism and suggestion.

Her sympathy and antipathy towards people are very vivid. But her ethical feelings are purely egocentric. She has a lack of sincerity towards herself; but in social intercourse she usually gives a friendly, serene and amiable impression, though she knows how to hide her feelings in order afterwards to give way to them with an hysterical exaggeration. She is easily influenced and impulsive, and is readily led to make unfounded accusations, and to fall into fits of rage. The emotions are subject to sudden changes, so that depressions may follow a happy mood without any apparent reason. It is clear that in the crises above mentioned, in which Eva C. must not be regarded as responsible, nervous and other constitutional excitations play a part. Her sense of sex is feebly developed, but she has a vivid erotic imagination. No mania or compulsory ideas. Tendency towards bodily depression and self-pity. Exaggerated notions concerning her feminine charms and her influence over the male sex.

The great weakness of will in the character of the medium is explained by the prevalence of her emotional character, and by the lack of independence. She has a great faculty of adaptation to persons, and one might compare her relation to Mme. Bisson with that of a faithful dog to its master. But, in these circumstances, one can understand that Mme. Bisson cannot surrender her medium into other hands for the sake of experiments, since Eva would be equally accessible to the new influences as soon as she was accustomed to them.

This passivity is accompanied by great susceptibility to hypnotisation, as well as the faculty of accepting the ideas and intentions of the persons present at the sittings, and of realising these suggestively, or of allowing herself to be dominated by states of consciousness involving strong emotion.

At the same time, we can also understand the danger which the suggestive idea of fraud, in the minds of the persons present at the sittings, might imply for the medium.

Under such an influence she might be led to fraudulent manipulation, unconsciously suggested, because distinctly expected by such a person. The hysterical disposition, indicated by some of the abnormalities above specified, is placed beyond doubt by her general psychological condition. It is, however, not a case of an actual disease, which would imply hysterical fits and paralyses, but a constitutional peculiarity, which may facilitate the comprehension of the occurrences to be described in this book, in so far as they are affected by the personality of the medium.

After Eva C. had, during the first period of her mediumistic activity in the Bissons' house (from February 1909), lived outside, she was received into the family in the autumn of 1910, and lived at first in the studio flat of Mme. Bisson, who was occupied with sculpture. When the latter moved to a new place, after the death of her husband in the spring of 1912, Eva was given a room in the new flat. From the moment of her reception into the family she was always treated as one of the family, though she was constantly controlled.

As shown by records, some 40 per cent. of the sittings were without result in the first year, and 60 per cent. in the later years. In the aggregate, 54 per cent. In the successful sittings no phenomena, except materialisations, were observed; no other physical manifestations, such as those usually observed in the case of Eusapia and other mediums. Thus we find, in the case of Eva C., no raps, no table-tiltings, no " apports," no telekinetic phenomena, but her special faculty consists entirely in the production of materially formed bodies, beginning in barely visible and optically cloud-like or amorphous structures, and ending in the formation of solid materials, or organic shapes.

The records kept of the sittings preceding the 21st May 1909, by one of those present, relate to such phenomena. While at first only white patches of an irregular shape were observed, masses of material were gradually developed, and outlines of human forms. At first hands and arms of a sketchy outline, but without the rest of the body, became visible. The impressions were very fugitive and the red light was rather dim. It was found possible to increase the illumination gradually as the confidence of the medium increased, as well as the strength of the phenomena. These optical impressions only lasted a few seconds; apart from the rigorous control to which the medium was subjected before and after the sittings, both hands could in this period of experiment be observed to remain at rest in the same position while the occurrences took place. In the end some human faces were seen and flash-light photos could be taken. As a rule, the medium had no subsequent recollection of her trance condition.

SITTING OF THE 21st MAY 1909.

Present,—M. and Mme. Alexandre Bisson, M. and Mme. André Bisson, M. Chevreuil (Painter), Mr R. M., M. Delanne, and the author.

Scene of the Sittings.—Small room resembling a studio, situated on the fifth floor of the house, No. 199 Avenue Victor Hugo. This room was 17 feet long and 10 feet wide, and had a single door leading into an adjacent bedroom. This door led into a kind of recess, formed by a stove occupying 32 inches square, and having a chimney slanting towards the ceiling. The opening of this recess was closed up by means of a heavy curtain. The whole inner wall consisted of a black lining material; the piece hanging over the door had to be lifted if the door was to be opened. The lining was fastened by means of tacks.

In the same way the light wicker chair in which Eva sat was covered with black stuff. A careful examination of the cabinet and the chair gave a negative result. There were no secret doors or compartments. Wherever a hand could be introduced into the stuff this was done,

SITTINGS OF MAY AND JUNE 1909 (PARIS)

but with no result. The door itself was locked by me personally and sealed with my seal at all the sittings at which I was present, except at the sitting of the 21st May. The control after the sittings always showed the seals to be intact. At the sitting of the 21st May I kept the keys of the adjacent bedroom and of the experimental room in my pocket after having locked the doors myself. As soon as the medium had been hypnotised in the cabinet, which was originally done by the girl's relative, Mr R. M. (who, however, did not attend the later sittings), the curtains were closed. In order to divide the cabinet entirely from the room occupied by those present, a large brown meshed net had been nailed to the walls and ceiling of the cabinet. This could only be opened at one side to give access to the cabinet. At the beginning of each sitting it was also fastened to the floor, so that now the recess was entirely isolated. In these circumstances it would have been impossible to throw or smuggle any small parcel of material or any other utensil, from without into the cabinet. Afterwards, in November 1909, Mme. Bisson removed the cabinet into another room and omitted the net. Eva requires to be hypnotised from time to time during the sittings. This was done in the first series of sittings through the net, and in the second series by the hypnotiser entering the cabinet. The illumination of the experimental room was provided by a sixteen candle-power electric lamp, covered by several pieces of red paper or red cloth. By adding or removing some of these pieces one could make the room brighter or darker. As a rule, the illumination sufficed for reading the hands of a watch even near the curtain (Diagram 1).

Eva undressed before the sitting completely, and was requested to dress in the garments provided by those present, and carefully examined. This consisted of combined drawers and stockings of black knitted wool, without any opening, reaching to the hips and there sewn on to a simple black dress (bodice and skirt in one) belonging to Mme. Bisson, with half sleeves. She was then sewn up in this dress by Mme. Bisson. No other garment or undergarment was used. The opening at the neck, and those at the sleeves were also sewn up by Mme. Bisson, and Eva entered, as a rule, the experimental cabinet without shoes.[1] When Eva, after this examination entered the cabinet, it was safe to assume that no white or other materials or apparatus for the artificial production of phenomena could be hidden either behind the curtain or on her body. As soon as she had taken her seat (I stood beside her), Mr M. approached her, rolled up his sleeves to the elbows, and hypnotised Eva by mesmeric passes. In about half a minute she sank back and went into trance.

Mr R. M. retired, Mme. Bisson closed the curtain and fastened the net to the floor.

The duration of the sitting was from 9.20 to 10.50 P.M.

The first part of these sittings still took place under the spiritistic conditions and customs, which later were abandoned.

After a short time the medium desired the circle to sing. Then those present intoned all kinds of tunes in chorus, while the less musical ones hummed in time. After about half an hour the curtain was opened from 4 to 6 inches, but only for two or three seconds. I saw

---

[1] At several sittings gynæcological and anal examinations also took place.

the outline of a profile of a white-clad figure of the size of an adult, which was then seen about six times in succession, sometimes in profile, sometimes in front view. We could distinctly see a white-clad figure of middle size and strongly marked features, though we could not see whether it was male or female. On the head was a closely rolled turban of white stuff, covering the forehead and resembling a surgical bandage. The medium was not visible at the same time. Once the head was seen fairly close to the floor and rose rapidly, after which the whole form was seen in profile. The hands of the medium were partly seen as bright patches.

Under these conditions the phantom appeared once on the right side of the medium in the same costume. The curtain was drawn in from behind and opened again at once. The medium in her black dress stood before us. Hardly two seconds had been required to make the image disappear.

After the sitting Eva was again carefully examined, and so was the cabinet, but no suspicious circumstances were found.

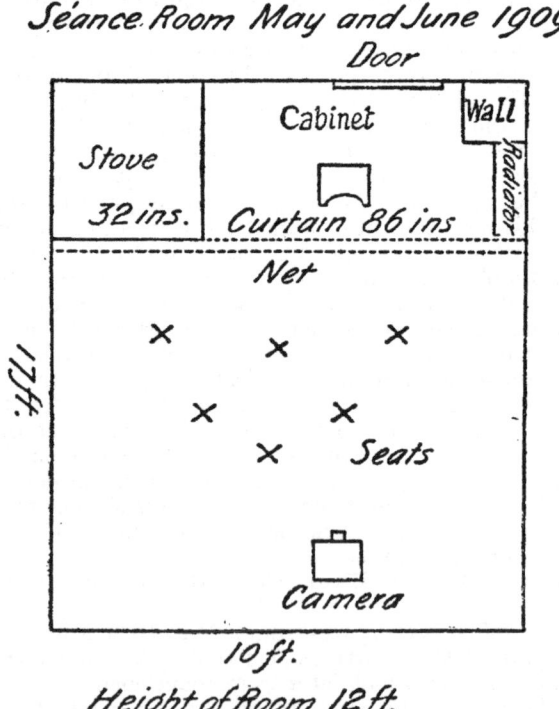

DIAGRAM I.

SITTING OF THE 25th MAY 1909.

Present.—M. and Mme. Alexandre Bisson, M. André Bisson (son of the last-named), M. Chevreuil, Mr R. M., Dr V. (Physician), and the author.

Preparations.—Control and dress of the medium, illumination, locking of the doors, etc., as on the 21st.

Time of Sitting.—9.35 to 10.20 P.M.

Before commencing the experiments the medium was undressed and Mme. Bisson performed a gynæcological examination.

Eva was to-day only hypnotised by her relative after the net had been lowered and fastened. Mr R. M. touched her fingers through the meshes and hypnotised the medium by Braid's method. I sat immediately in front of the curtains and saw, as a first phenomenon, a white and apparently soft mass, ascending on the side of the left ankle of the medium in the shape of a white column about 2 inches wide. It attained a length of about 20 inches and then disappeared. During this occurrence the left hand lay quietly visible on the left knee.

Shortly afterwards we saw during the next very short exposure a white-clad figure in front view, with its head surrounded by a turban-like bandage. The face was beardless, the dress of the upper body was light, of a bluish colour. The body was bent over in front, but no arms or legs were visible.

This figure showed itself three times, but only for a few seconds. It may have been the medium "transfigured."

When the curtain was opened for the third time the magnesium light was flashed. At this instant I clearly recognised a human face of female aspect.

Immediately after the exposure the medium opened the curtain and advanced towards the net from the cabinet. The difference of time between our perception of a white form and the appearance of the black-clad medium was only a few seconds. Even an expert conjuror would have found it difficult to make the white costume disappear in so short a period. I was the first to enter the cabinet. I examined the dress and body of the medium before the other persons had approached, also the cabinet, and the chair, and found that the seals were intact.

Mme. Bisson undressed the medium, and assisted her to dress, in my presence. Neither by me nor by any other observer was any white material or anything else found which gave rise to suspicion.

Eva's pulse was 90 before the sitting and 120 afterwards. A picture drawn by one of those present, but which is not here reproduced, showed the medium in white material. The front of the head is covered by this material down to the eyes and falls down as far as the hands.

[*Sittings of the* 28*th May and the* 1*st June unsuccessful.*]

Sittings of November 1909.

SITTING OF 13th NOVEMBER.

Place.—Avenue Victor Hugo, 199.
Present.—Baron Pigeard de W., Dr G. V., Mme. Bisson, and author.

The cabinet, transferred to a more suitable room, is lined entirely with black stuff; the floor is covered by a carpet which covers the whole room. The wickerwork easy chair is covered in black. Black curtains of a total width of 64 inches. The upper part of the cabinet is closed by a partition. The stuff is everywhere tacked on. Illumination by electric light on the mantelpiece covered with several sheets of red tissue paper which make the room rather dark. Near the lamp large print can be read, but not in front of the curtain, though the hands of the clock can be read there.

Before the sitting, detailed inspection of the experimental room. Solid floor, no depression. I pass my hand along the hem of the carpet to ascertain whether anything is hidden there, also under the stuff tacked on. The wardrobe and chair are similarly tested, but, in spite of every care, nothing suspicious is found which could have been used for the artificial production of the phenomena. Eva undressed completely and put on a knitted garment, which consisted of a combination of drawers and stockings. This reached to her waist, and was there sewn on to the black dress, and the sleeves and neck were sewn up as before.

The supposition that she might have secreted some white stuff in a leather case is negatived by the repeated examinations already mentioned, but, supposing she had succeeded in concealing a small packet and producing it at her neck, by pushing it upwards along the skin, the subsequent folding up of such an amount of stuff as would cover several square yards, packing it up, and taking it back to its hiding-place, would not have been possible in the time allowed (two to three seconds). (Diagram 2.)

Mr R. M., who had hypnotised the medium in the spring, was no longer present at these experiments. Before the sitting and after it, the author examined the medium: her arm-pits, mouth and feet. Eva entered the cabinet without slippers.

Baron Pigeard, who during the last summer had made the medium's acquaintance at Biarritz, hypnotised the medium from now onwards.

Eva took her place behind the curtain, P. sat down in front of her, touched her hands and fixed her eyes. The net was no longer used. For fraudulent assistance of the medium by one of those present could not be assumed, since the circle was often completely changed. Only the lady of the house was present at all sittings. Any suspicion against her is disposed of by the fact that the phenomena did not depend on her presence, for previously Eva C. had obtained the same results, in other circles, without Mme. Bisson.

The medium either held her hands on her knees or took hold of both sides of the curtain, to close the cabinet or half-open it for a short exposure of her creations. Sometimes she opened the curtain under the impression that the manifestations were already visible to us, but those present could see nothing.

Most frequently the optical impression was too fugitive, and so faint in the dim red light that no detail could be made out. This particularly applies to representations of whole figures, no matter whether these are to be regarded as genuine materialisations or only as transfigurations of the medium.

The first apparition, which occurred after about one hour, was on the right-hand side of the medium, and was preceded by a luminous haze on that side. I saw a figure, clad in light grey and partly white material, which was shown in half profile, and bent sideways over the medium's chair. The apparition lasted only one or two seconds.

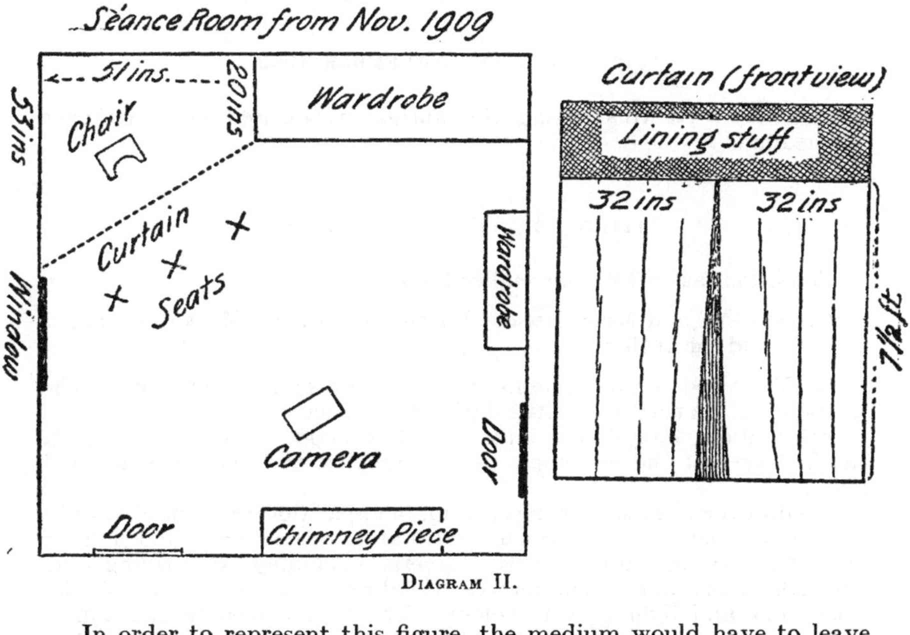

DIAGRAM II.

In order to represent this figure, the medium would have to leave her chair and stand on the right side of it. The garments of the figure appeared to be well fastened, but the impression was very fugitive and the medium was not simultaneously visible.

After a short time the phenomenon was seen again. This time it stood in front of the chair and showed itself in front view through the gap in the curtains. I thought I recognised the medium's face, and could distinctly see a turban covering the head.

Immediately the curtain was closed Eva groaned and wished to be soothed by the hypnotiser, Baron P. He opened the curtains, entered the cabinet and seized her hands. Neither he nor any of the others could see a trace of white material when the curtain was opened on the dark background.

Baron P. retired, closed the cabinet and sat down on his chair. He had hardly taken his place when the curtain was opened again, and this time a quite brightly clad apparition stood on the left side of the medium, a middle-sized figure. It showed no distinctly marked shape, but collapsed before our eyes, as though vanishing into the floor. This process was also very short, and allowed of no detailed observations.

In future, minor processes of imperfect materialisation will only be mentioned for purpose of completeness.

Eva was then awakened by the hypnotiser, and was examined by us again without our detecting anything suspicious. The subsequent examination which I made of the cabinet and the chair was also negative. The awakened medium had no recollection of what had happened during the sitting.

Sitting of 19th November 1909.

Negative. At this sitting the author hypnotised and awakened the medium.

Sitting of 21st November 1909.

Conditions as on 13th November 1909.

Present.—M. and Mme. Bisson, Baron Pigeard, Dr M., several ladies and the author.

Dr M. joined me in examining the cabinet and the medium. The red light was, on this day, a little darker than usual.

After about forty-five minutes a white strip, about a yard high, was first seen at the lower gap in the curtains, and then a white-clad figure.

Then, at the right side of the curtain, an apparition was seen, obviously taller than the medium, which put out a rather voluminous head seemingly wrapped up in veils. Several beginnings or attempts at materialisations were seen, masses of fabric of a cloudy or veil-like consistency and light grey in colour. These were seen several times, and once a long moving strip of white below, as if a hand had imparted a wavy motion to the veil.

We also saw the same white-clad female figure with turban as in the previous sittings.

Eva herself is not clear as regards the degree of development of visibility of these structures. Often she opened the curtains and said that the creation was complete, when those present could see no change either in the cabinet or in the medium. We may here have to deal with incomplete stages of development of the supposed process of materialisation which the medium passes through, and feels in her own body. But this process requires a certain increase or change, in order to become visible to the observer. Subsequent examination negative.

SITTING OF 25th NOVEMBER 1909.

Present.—M. and Mme. Alex. Bisson, M. and Mme. André Bisson, Frau von H., Messrs D., L., and Chevreuil, also Baron Pigeard, with his wife and the author.

The illumination was brighter than before, since two electric bulbs with red glass were attached to the ceiling chandelier (about twenty candle-power). The increased light enabled us to see details which could not be observed before.

A photographic camera was placed in front of the chimney, and beside it a paper cylinder about a yard high and half a yard wide to catch the magnesium vapour.

Hypnotisation by Baron Pigeard, who sat in front of the curtain. I sat immediately behind him at the best distance to enable me to observe what happened at the opening of the curtains. When the observer is too close it is impossible, if whole figures appear, to survey all the details in the short time of only a few seconds.

The medium before the sitting felt nervous and tired. Instructions about the behaviour of those present were given by the hypnotised medium in a whisper. These instructions were partly answers to the questions of Mme. Bisson and Baron Pigeard and partly independent statements.

Thus the question is always put, whether there is sufficient power to produce the desired manifestations, whether the circle is to sing or to form a chain, or whether the sitting is to be closed. Several times during the sitting the medium calls Baron Pigeard, and sometimes other persons, including the author, into the cabinet, and gives them her hands for a short time, as if she could, from this contact, derive power for the generation of the phenomena. As soon as Eva feels that the phenomena are about to take place, she asks the circle to sing. In quite a similar manner Eusapia usually asked those present to talk (*parlare*). The kind, character, and language of the songs are immaterial. Hymns or slow chants are as welcome as the Marseillaise, or tunes from *Carmen*. It is also immaterial whether or not the singing is in tune or in time.

We must here take into account that a strained expectation and an attention, too vividly concentrated upon the beginning of the phenomena may, according to the spiritistic view, interfere with the necessary psychic tuning of the medium. It is also possible that the fact of those present being occupied with an activity of the vocal organs perceptible to the medium, has a soothing effect upon the latter. A short-sighted scepticism, on the other hand, only sees in this a diversion of the attention necessary for conjuring tricks.

From the beginning of the sitting, about twenty minutes elapsed before the first phenomena were seen. The curtain was drawn open from within (by Eva's feet ?) and remained open for the whole duration of the ensuing phenomena, so as to form a triangular opening narrowing towards the top, through which the medium (in the trance condition), and the occurrences themselves could be fairly well observed in a good illumination.

The hands rested on the medium's knees and remained visible during the manifestations. Eva's head was bent towards one side and almost disappeared in the darkness. The hems of the curtains touched the knees of the medium from the outside.

Without any change in the position of the hands or the curtain, we saw first at the medium's left side, above her left hand, an illumination of the curtain at the height of about a foot and a half. This resembled a bright phosphorescent strip, which, however, was odourless. Then out of this there appeared, at about the level of Eva's head, a formless mass of a light grey colour, about a foot in vertical height, which disappeared and reappeared without a change in the position of the curtains or the hands. The shape appeared at first vague and indefinite, with a fluctuating motion, then it became visibly brighter and more solid, until it changed into a white luminous material, like a heap of the finest white chiffon veiling, apparently stretched out beyond the curtain by a hand and again withdrawn. Some of those present thought they saw a small female hand which held the stuff. In spite of the most accurate observation I could not perceive anything of this. The mass dissolved before our eyes, losing first its solid shape. Finally we only saw a light strip, which ascended from the quiescent hand and gave the impression as if a column of luminous smoke were ascending from it. The total duration of this remarkable process may have been thirty to sixty seconds. After a short pause some indefinite structures of various shapes were seen, which condensed to luminous strips and balls, moved about and changed their shapes, ascended and descended, disappeared and reappeared.

The strongest impression was obtained by the observers when the luminous smoke, proceeding from the region of the upper part of the body of the medium, changed into a long white band, about 2 inches thick and about 16 inches long, which, horizontally above the floor, at a height of $4\frac{1}{2}$ feet, joined the two hems of the open curtain, hanging parallel to the floor. If a comparison is allowable, which perhaps does not quite apply, we might compare the optical impression of this structure with the shape of a bleached human thighbone. In this apparently solid form, which ascended and descended in the air as a broad white strip, there hung a bright white veil-like material about 16 inches square, so that the whole apparition resembled a small flag held horizontally. Without changing the position, this form ascended to a height of about 6 feet, then descended, and remained twenty seconds before it disappeared. The optical phenomenon filled the whole opening of the curtains. The medium's hands lay as before motionless and visible on her knees.

It is impossible to describe this process as it was shown to our eyes. While the white column, condensed from amorphous material, sometimes gave the impression of a solid body, it usually appeared to stream through the cabinet in strips like a white creamy substance, sometimes proceeding in a straight line, sometimes breaking into zigzags

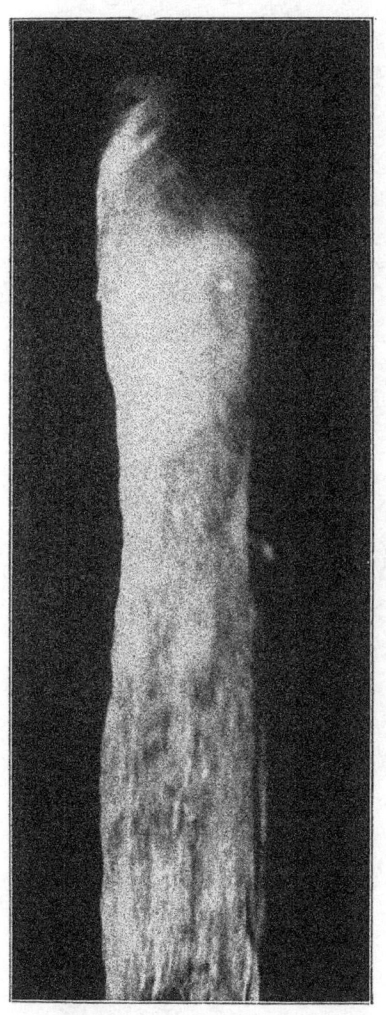

FIG. 1 PHOTOGRAPH BY MONS ANDRÉ BISSON ON 25 NOVEMBER, 1909

FIG. 3. DRAWING FROM REPORT OF SITTING OF 17 MAY 1910, MADE BY GAMPENRIEDER.

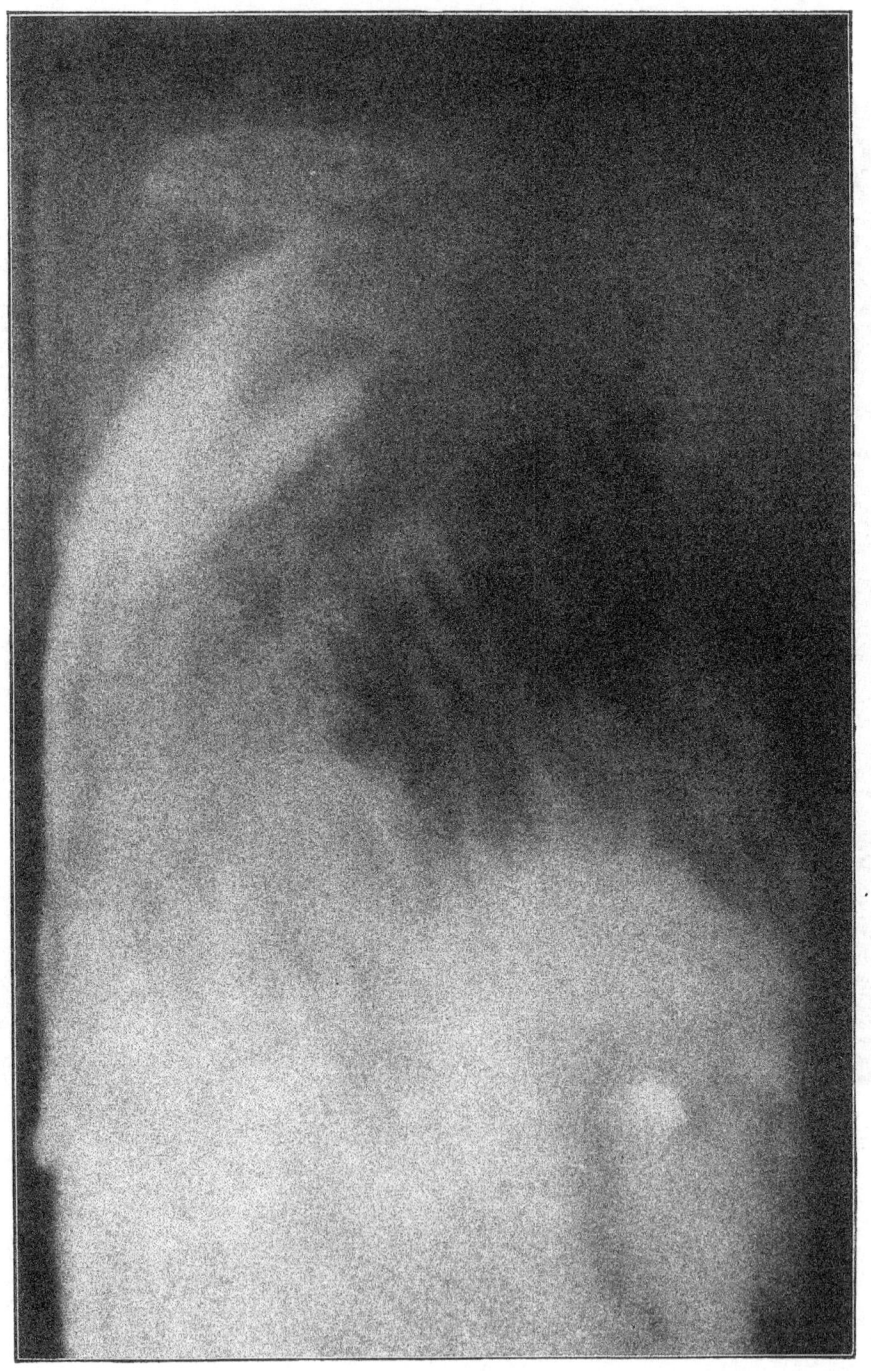

FIG 2. ENLARGEMENT OF THE HAND OF FIG. 1.

SITTINGS OF NOVEMBER 1909

or serpentine waves. Before its dissolution it became thinner, more colourless, resembling smoke, and then disappeared, usually in the direction of the body of the medium. The reddish light in the séance room increased the attractiveness of this interesting play of colours, bathing the nebulous and half-liquid or solid structures in a pale rose colour. The development of these creations took the form of an emanation of rays and streaks from the body of the medium as from a material radiation of energy, which however, probably influenced by unconscious volitional impulses, tended in its form towards definite representations, finally flowing back into the organism (like the rigid organic rays described by Professor Ochorowicz).

In the last successful sitting one could already recognise distinct attempts to produce human forms. Thus, in this sitting, the grey material repeatedly assumed a spherical shape, a more solid white nucleus formed within it, in size and shape like a human head, while the outer parts appeared to change themselves into veils and textile fabrics.

It was decided to attempt a photographic flash-light record with the consent of the medium. For this purpose a camera had already been set up before the sitting, opposite the curtain near the stove behind the observers. Behind it a paper cylinder more than a yard long had been suspended to receive the magnesium vapour.

The curtain was opened. We again saw before us a figure clothed in a long white flowing veil which covered the face (medium ?). The flash-light was ignited (Figs. 1 and 2), but, at the same moment, the paper cylinder caught fire, and it appeared as if the flames would spread. A panic took place among the audience, some of the ladies screamed with fright, and fled. But we succeeded in extinguishing the fire.

With a cry of pain the medium sank back into the chair gasping convulsively. Baron Pigeard at once entered the cabinet to soothe her, but the white clothing and veiling had disappeared. The medium had fainted, and lay in the chair bleeding from the nose, and the sitting had to be closed. I slowly wakened Eva by suggestion. A close examination of the medium and the cabinet showed nothing suspicious. No white or veil-like materials were found.

The whole fire episode was the work of a few seconds. A fraudulent medium would not have been able to hide the necessary masks and clothing during this unexpected interruption of her performance.

On awakening, Eva C. was obviously exhausted, and showed a trembling of the arms. Pulse 108. Subsequent control negative.

Hallucination of the witnesses, who all made the same observations, is excluded, since the photographic records confirm the optical impressions. A better illumination and a longer duration of the materialised structures rendered a more exact observation possible than on previous occasions.

No reasonable grounds for the supposition of fraud by the medium can be found, however strictly one may adhere to the view that these unusual occurrences require the greatest caution and scepticism.

The above record offers perhaps a contribution to the observation of a materialisation in the nascent state.

The picture taken on the 26th November shows the head of the

D

medium, who had obviously risen from the chair, in the opening of the curtains. A long veil, or an obviously very transparent soft white material, whose threads reminded one of cashmere wool, falls from her head to her knees. On Eva's hair on the right-hand side a soft vague and sketchy form of a miniature left hand (female), with a first finger pointing upwards, is to be seen. This starts from a sort of stalk or band quite continuous with the fabric, as shown by the magnification of the photograph, and which appears to be formed of the same stuff as the veil. With the help of an artificial hand-shape brought in for this purpose, consisting perhaps of cloth or paper, which then would have had to be placed on the hair under the veil, it would hardly have been possible to obtain this indefinite shadowy form with the soft fluid outline, though one has to consider a possible fault in the focusing of the apparatus.

Sittings of May and June 1910 in Paris.

SITTING OF THE 13th MAY 1910.

From the 9th December 1909 till 10th May 1910 Eva C. had gone to the Riviera, and had made no mediumistic experiments during this period. The resumption of the sittings coincided with the time of my stay in Paris. I was therefore able to be present at the first sitting after her arrival at the Bissons' house on the 13th May 1910. Though this six months' cessation was favourable to the recovery of the medium, we were prepared to have to commence from the beginning until Eva recovered the necessary practice in the production of the phenomena.

Present at the Sitting.—M. Paul D. (Bisson's nephew), M. and Mme. Bisson, Baron and Baroness Pigeard, and the author.

A stereoscopic apparatus for flash-light photographs, which I had brought with me, was put up before the sitting. The conditions, room and clothing of the medium were exactly the same as at previous sittings. But I may again emphasise that before and after every sitting I carefully examined the whole cabinet.

The complete undressing of Eva C. took place regularly in the presence of Mme. Bisson and the other female witnesses.

Costume: black knitted tights and black dress (no shoes). The dress in this and all subsequent sittings was sewn up to the tights, and also sewn up at the neck and at the sleeves, so that the body could not be touched without tearing the clothing.

Before each of the sittings now to be described, the author examined the medium's hair, nose, ears, mouth, teeth, arm-pits, feet, hands and finger-nails. During the whole following series of sittings I did not find anything suspicious either before or after the sittings, so that the objection that the medium might have concealed small packets of veiling, etc., appears unfounded.

SITTINGS OF MAY AND JUNE 1910 IN PARIS

The illumination consisted regularly of three ten candle-power electric lamps, under red glass. With this illumination large type could be easily read.

In these and the following sittings the hypnotising was performed by Mme. Bisson herself. On the 13th of May this was done in my presence at 9.40 P.M., after Eva had taken her seat in the cabinet. Only after the trance-like condition had set in did the others enter the room.

After about forty-five minutes we saw between the curtains a broad, bright, whitish wisp, proceeding from the mouth of the medium, like a broad band across her body and ending at the knees. Its length was 30 to 34 inches. During this phenomena her hands rested on her knees, and were distinctly visible, as was her head resting on the back of the chair. This apparition then disappeared. We then saw several times some grey or whitish flakes, clouds or wisps of an indefinite and varying shape. The nearest red electric lamp was then extinguished in order to increase the phenomena, but the brightness appeared to be nearly the same with the remaining two lamps.

For me, the only remarkable phenomenon in the second part of the sitting was the sudden appearance of a female form, wrapped in light grey veiling, whose head, as I noticed clearly, was swathed as in a turban in a cloth of the same colour. The figure stood there and opened the curtains for not more than one or two seconds. I had the impression of seeing the medium wrapped in veils. After the disappearance of this curious picture the medium made several attempts to produce similar phenomena, opened the curtain several times and asked if we did not see anything. But those present during these attempts only perceived Eva in her black dress. This and similar observations suggest the conclusion that the medium herself is not quite clear concerning the condensation process in her teleplastic action. She may feel that emanation is proceeding from her body, but in order to become visible to the human eye the process of condensation of all materialisations must have advanced to a certain point. It seems not always possible for the medium to recognise this point, unless the materialisation is rapidly and strongly developed.

The phenomena of this sitting were too inconstant and too feeble for photographic record. Besides, the colour of the veiling was of a greyish yellow, or whitish, and did not show a brilliant white, as in the previous sittings. The sitting was closed at 11.40 P.M.

SITTING OF THE 17th MAY 1910.

Present.—Dr V. (Physician), M. and Mme. Bisson, and the author.

Commencement at 9.30. Illumination, three lamps. Clothing and examination of the medium, and other conditions, as on the 13th May. Hypnotisation by Mme. Bisson. This time the phenomena commenced at once (Fig. 3).

The medium opens the curtain and lies on the chair in a passive trance. Her head turns sideways, so that the face is partly shadowed by the curtain. The hands rest on her knees before our eyes, and are held during some of the phenomena by my colleague, Dr V. (on the left), and myself. She bends the head back, so that it is fully illuminated. We see in front of the lower half of her face a cloudy mass, at first resembling a grey mist, which moves, grows and condenses, somewhat resembling a torn handkerchief of fine grey tulle. The lower hem was torn, and several small pieces and strips depended from it. The image dissolved. We attempted a flash-light photograph, but the ignition apparatus failed. The medium then asked me to enter the cabinet. Opening the curtain I knelt on the floor at her right-hand side, so that my head was exactly at the height of her own. Both my hands held her right hand, while her left held the curtain on that side. Then I saw immediately in front of my eyes a large striped, flocculent substance, which seemed to issue from her mouth, while she made deep respirations and convulsive muscular efforts. It grew and condensed. The structure may have been 2 or 3 inches broad, and 16 to 20 inches long. I approached my head to within about 6 or 8 inches, in order to observe more accurately, and saw this mass slowly sink with an inert motion, resembling a heap of the finest striped grey veiling. This followed every motion made by the medium's head, and yet appeared to detach itself from it. The structure disappeared behind the curtain. Her hands had not changed their position during the whole minute that this occurrence lasted.

The author left the cabinet and resumed his place outside it. The medium rested while the curtains were opened, moving her head deeper into the shadow, but her hands still lay upon her knees and were motionless.

After a short pause she exposed her head under the same conditions entirely to the light. To our astonishment we could no longer see her features, for her whole head was enveloped in a large veil-like cloud, from which bright fragments and strips hung down upon her breast and knees. Before our eyes this structure dissolved like a fog, and the face was again distinctly seen. During the last phenomenon her hands were held, Dr V. holding her right, and I her left. The curtain remained equally open from beginning to end. Immediately after the disappearance of the substance I examined her face, her scalp, her hair, etc., without finding anything by means of which this phenomenon might have been produced. The face was indeed quite moist as if with mucus. Her hands trembled (hysterical tremor). Her muscles showed a tendency to spasmodic contraction.

During the phenomena she groaned and trembled, and when she was awakened, after the sitting had lasted one hour and a half, she was very exhausted.

The conditions of experiment during the phenomena described constitute a great step in advance. The subsequent control was negative.

SITTING OF THE 20th MAY 1910.

Negative. Eva was indisposed. Hot and stormy weather.

SITTING OF THE 25th MAY 1910.

Present.—M. Chevreuil, Mme. Bisson, and the author.

Conditions as before, except that to-day four red electric lamps were lighted instead of three. But soon, at the request of the medium, one lamp had to be extinguished, so that the illumination consisted of three electric lamps.

As the corporeal examination before the sitting indicated, Eva had a piece of wadding in her right ear. She had just been treated by a dentist for toothache. The wadding was minutely inspected and put back in the ear. After the hypnotisation of the medium we took our places in front of the curtain, Mme. Bisson in the centre, Chevreuil on her left, and I on her right, and so we waited thirty-five or forty minutes for the occurrence of the first phenomenon.

Eva's head was visible through the open curtain. She took hold of the curtain on my side and moved it to and fro, as if she wanted carefully to expose a structure formed in the darkness tentatively to the red rays. But, in spite of the obvious efforts of the medium, we could not perceive anything. During the first phenomenon with open curtains, Chevreuil held her right hand and the author her left hand. Loud, convulsive coughing, muscular contractions in the arms, deep groaning and respiration. At first a nebulous, flocculent substance of irregular shape appeared, gradually condensing, and descending slowly from her chin to her breast, but retaining its connection with her mouth. On the left outer rim of this mass a thread-like projection of about 4 inches hung down. On my expressing a wish to see more clearly her head, which was bent towards the left, she brought it into the full light and shook it several times. We then saw that the grey structures already detached from her head had sunk into her lap. They resembled a grey, folded, filmy veil of a whitish colour. In attempting a photograph the magnesium ignition failed. As I went back to it the medium rose and came in front of the curtain. The mass of material adhered to her dress. She then sank back into the chair. As soon as I had resumed my seat she repeated the process above described once more. Again we saw the emanation of a smoky filmy substance produced as if by deep breathing. During this experiment she held the sides of the curtain with both hands, which were perfectly visible to us. Again the medium rose and left the cabinet and stood before me, her head inclined towards the left and holding the curtains as if for support.

Bringing my face to within 6 inches of her, I saw that a flocculent whitish grey mass floated from her mouth and hung down over her left shoulder, behind, down to her knees, in the form of a consistent substance. The structure might have been a yard long and some 6 inches wide, and resembled a large muslin veil of the finest texture. A draught would set it in motion. Eva remained about half a minute in this position. I expressed a wish to touch the fabric. But she said, perhaps out of nervousness: " Not yet, later."

While she returned behind the curtain and sat down, her hands remained tightly clenched on the hems of the curtain. The veil disappeared from my eyes in the darkness of the cabinet, as if dissolving into vapour. In this process, therefore, the hands did not play any part.

The conditions of observation of the whole process from beginning to end were rather favourable.

Before the last experiment of this sitting, and while the curtain was open, she took my hands in hers, and asked me to close the curtain as quickly as possible the moment she let go my hands.

After about half a minute she let me go, and I closed the curtain. Shortly afterwards she quickly opened the curtain with both hands, and we saw standing before us a female figure, covered from head to foot in fine white veils, the opening of the curtain being about 1 foot. After hardly one second the curtain was again closed, and then again quickly opened. We found Eva lying on her chair, and the mysterious veils had disappeared. Obviously the apparition was the medium herself wrapped in those veils whose production and disappearance we cannot explain.

Eva was then awakened and was again carefully examined. But neither on her body, nor in the black garment, nor in the cabinet, did we find a trace of that strange material which we had so well observed.

Sitting of the 27th May 1910.

Present.—M. and Mme. Bisson, M. Chevreuil, Drs V. and D., and the author.

Conditions as in the previous sittings. Eva was not well disposed to-day, and gave a sullen impression. The only phenomenon in this sitting was the appearance of a bright vertical wisp about a foot long and $2\frac{1}{2}$ inches wide on her left breast. Face and hands were visible before and during the phenomenon when the curtain was opened. The phenomenon disappeared after a short time, and the sitting had to be adjourned.

Sitting of the 31st May 1910.

No result.

Sitting of the 1st June 1910.

Examination as usual. Four combs were found in the hair, all other conditions as usual.

Present.—Mme. Bisson, M. Chevreuil, and the author.

Commencing at 9 o'clock. First phenomenon, 9.40.

Curtain opened—head and hands visible. Eva bends forward and opens her mouth. An amorphous material issues from it to a distance of about 1 inch beyond the lips. The medium first grasps the right hand of Mme. Bisson and guides the first finger to her mouth to touch the substance. Then she grasps my right hand and makes the same experiment with me. My finger touched a solid substance of dark or nearly black colour. The sensation of touch may be compared with the impression obtained by touching the dark skin of a mushroom. During the touch which she herself made with my finger, she gave a strong and painful shudder and trembled violently, and it seemed as if she made every effort to overcome her physical aversion to this touch. The mass then disappeared.

After a short pause Eva allowed her left hand to be held by Mme. Bisson, and her right hand by me. In this situation she rose from her chair, with her head bent towards the veil, so that the right-hand curtain covered her face. Again, as in a previous sitting, she tentatively brought her head into the red illumination until at last she exposed herself to the light completely. As before, a material issues from her mouth, which at first appears cloudy, then condenses and grows to a length of about 14 inches with a diameter of 3 or 4 inches. At first this cloud, resembling cigarette smoke, remained floating in the air without sinking. This time also she approached first Mme. Bisson's hand, and then my right hand to this structure, in order to touch it. The painful shudder was repeated at the touch. Great nervousness and self-abnegation were evident. In touching the cloud I had the sensation as if I destroyed a spider's web with my finger. She then drew her head behind the curtain and the phenomenon disappeared.

After a short pause for rest the bright light appeared on her left hip, the curtain being open and her hands resting visibly on her knees. Without any motion of the medium, this bright strip became broader and longer, assumed the shape of a veil bunched up and partly torn, and finally hung down over her feet. To obtain a photograph I returned to the apparatus standing 3 yards in front of the curtain, and at this distance I could still distinctly make out the structure, which hung down from her head over the whole of her left side. Eva now rose and stood in front of the curtain. In this case, also, the photograph was a failure. The phenomenon dissolved as if into invisible vapour.

During the next apparition the luminosity appeared first in her lap and over her right hip. It then fell like a wisp over her right knee, as if by its own motion, and hung down to her ankle. The lower end ended in a zigzag and resembled torn drapery. During this process I held the medium's right hand, and Mme. Bisson the left hand. The mouth had no connection with the fabric, as I proved by putting my finger into her mouth. In these circumstances the substance showed an independent power of motion. Having first hung down to the feet, it then crept like a snake slowly over the knee to the hip. The luminosity became ever smaller and the veil ever shorter, and disappeared between right hip and shoulder.

Towards the close of the sitting there was a repetition of the last phenomenon of the sitting of the 25th May.

I held both her hands in mine. She requested me this time to close the curtains as quickly as possible as soon as she released me.

I carefully executed her wish, and was about to sit down when the curtain, just closed, was quickly opened, closed again as quickly, and then opened for the second time.

At the first opening a female form wrapped from head to foot in light grey veils became visible. Although the optical appearance only lasted one second, I was able to notice that the veils were crossed over the head. Behind the veil there was a female face, whose features were, however, not recognisable, owing to the shortness of the exposure. At the second opening we found the medium reclining quietly on her chair. Not a trace of the veiled image remained. The double opening and closing of the curtain had hardly taken four or five seconds. In this space of time we saw, before and after the phenomenon, the medium dressed in black, and, in between, the brightly veiled image of an upright female figure.

The medium would hardly have had time to rise from the rather low chair, *i.e.*, from a half reclining position, to open the curtain twice and close it once. But that she should also have been able in this short time to wrap herself, with her own hands, in veils, to fasten them to her hair, and to make them disappear again, is quite out of the question. Even the ablest conjuror could not bring about a similar transformation in five seconds under the same conditions. Whether it was the medium which here appeared in veils, or whether we had here to deal with an ectoplastic projection of the female figure, is difficult to decide. After all his practice with Eva during numerous experiments the author is sure of having made no mistake in estimating the time.

The sitting closed at 11.10, with a final control of Eva C. and the cabinet, without anything suspicious being discovered.

SITTING OF THE 4th JUNE 1910.

Present.—Baron Pigeard, with his wife, Mme. Bisson, M. Chevreuil, and the author.

Commencement, 9.30 P.M.

At 10 o'clock I held the left hand of the medium and Mme. Bisson the right.

Head visible.

Suddenly the right wing of the curtain above her hand was illuminated from behind, as if a light were upon it. Then we saw, under the hem of the curtain, a white mass about 16 inches, which grew broader below and then vanished. Then the veiled figure already referred to was seen again. In order to take a flash-light photograph I struck a match, since the ignition apparatus did not work. The phenomenon disappeared immediately before the eyes of those present. Sitting closed.

SITTING OF THE 6th JUNE 1910.

Negative.

SITTING OF THE 10th JUNE 1910.

Present.—M. Chevreuil, Mme. Bisson, Mme. M. M., and the author.

This time Eva was indisposed (menses) and suffering from a cold, and only held the sitting to oblige the author, since he departed the next day. Otherwise the sitting probably would not have taken place. From 9.15 to 11.15 no phenomena. One of the three lamps was then extinguished, in order to make it easier for the medium. At last came the appearance of a light-coloured veil-like fabric, about 20 inches long, and issuing from the mouth. This developed with the curtain open, and while I held both her hands. The fabric lay like a large rag on her left shoulder and breast. This formation was preceded by violent efforts by the medium, who wished to produce something at any cost, and was accompanied by deep respirations, hysterical sobs and convulsive contractions of the arms.

The material only remained visible for a short time, and then disappeared.

The experiment was instructive, inasmuch as it showed that, even under very unfavourable conditions, a special effort of will on the part of the medium, combined with perseverance on the part of the sitters, may have some influence upon the result.

The medium lost a considerable quantity of blood during the evening; she also coughed a good deal, was feverish, fatigued, and hoarse. Final control negative.

OBSERVATIONS IN BIARRITZ.

THE sittings held after my departure in June 1910 did not yield any essentially new results. At the end of the month the Bisson family took up their residence in Biarritz for the whole summer, and Eva C. followed them in the middle of August.

During this new period of sitting the medium was hypnotised every day by Mme. Bisson in order to gain a suggestive influence upon the development of the powers of mediumship and the formation of the phenomena. The psychic condition during these hypnoses is identical with the trance of the sittings. Self-contained, it includes all memory images and conceptions relating to the sittings. The individual consciousness does not differ from the waking personality. It is always Eva C. who speaks, answers, and gives instructions and explanations. Never, during this period of her mediumistic development, does the change of personality, so usual in spiritistic circles, occur, in which imaginary individualities, regarded as foreign, speak or write through the medium.[1]

The mental contents of the second condition are not remembered

[1] This phase of mediumship was only observed several years later with Eva C.

after awakening, though the whole psychic character may appear clearer and less constrained. The kind of phenomena observed is the same as that found by me during the next Paris sittings to be described later.

According to Mme. Bisson the sojourn in a sunny climate had a favourable influence on Eva's mediumship, inasmuch as negative sittings hardly ever occurred. Her performances became stronger and prompter, and commenced to adapt themselves to the wishes of the circle.

The conditions as regards red illuminations and the clothing of the medium were the same as in Paris. The phenomena usually occurred with open curtain. The hands and head were visible, and the former were often held by those present.

In the sitting of the 30th August, at which the oculist, Dr T. B., was present, Mme. Bisson succeeded for the first time in drawing the teleplasm, or fundamental substance of materialisation, outside the region of the curtain and observing it carefully. Mme. Bisson writes on this subject in a letter of 2nd September 1910 :

" Eva's left hand rested in the hands of Dr B., who sat in front of her. Her right was held in both my hands. The curtain was fully opened. Suddenly I felt on my hands a cool sticky mass, which touched me. I took hold of it and brought it carefully outside the curtain, without letting go Eva's hand. The mass lengthened out in my fingers and hung down from my hand, and I could observe it for one or two minutes. But while I continued to unravel it carefully it dissolved and disappeared in my hands. It is very difficult to describe this substance. I had the impression of a flat, striped, thread-like, sticky, cool, and living substance. It was odourless, and had a light grey or whitish colour. My fingers remained moist from the touch. The phenomenon was repeated about eight times, and four times I was able to take hold of the mass and show it to Dr B."

In the sitting of the 2nd September this interesting experiment was continued. In this case the report is as follows :

" Curtains wide open. Dr B. held the left hand of the medium. A sort of veil or drapery proceeding from Eva's neck hung over her left arm down to the ground. She carefully led my hands, held by her left hand, towards the veil, and I took hold of it. She cried out : ' That hurts me, but I wish it all the same.' I drew the stuff towards me. It was quite similar to the mass which I had touched on the 30th August. Again the same sensation of cool, moist, living threads. My fingers became moist. Finally I drew the piece in front of the curtain and formed out of it a sort of veil, by spreading it out. This veil covered Eva's whole left side. Eva suffered severely. The whole fabric of stuff and threads was reabsorbed and disappeared."

Besides the phenomena obtained in previous sittings, the medium endeavoured, in this series of sittings, to form the teleplasm into human shapes. The members of the circle desired, for instance, a hand, a foot, or a head, and also sometimes wished for the form to appear in a given place near the medium. These experiments only partially succeeded, and the forms remained imperfect. Though the outlines of a hand or a head were recognised, they were not fully formed, and were extremely fugitive. Since the next report of my sittings deals exhaustively with this class of occurrences, any further details in this place are not called for.

But I might mention that Mme. Bisson had a sitting with Eva without any other witnesses, and during this sitting Eva wore nothing but a dressing-gown. After the beginning of the sitting Mme. Bisson persuaded the hypnotised medium to open the dressing-gown, and thus had, for the first time, an occasion to observe the emanation of the teleplasm from the bare body of the medium. It seemed to emerge primarily from the bodily orifices, mouth, teats, and genitals, and also from the hands and under the arm-pits. The emanation had a smoke-like or gaseous character, and formed clouds, from which structures, like veils and fabrics, and eventually all kinds of forms, resembling human limbs, developed.

After the return from Biarritz Mme. Bisson received Eva C. permanently into her house, where she was treated as a member of the family. This step eliminated the danger of the professional exploitation of her mediumistic power, for which favourable proposals had come from various quarters. It not only enabled her to exercise an absolute control of the young girl's mode of life, but also to conduct lengthy and uninterrupted observations of her powers, which developed more and more.

Sittings of October and November 1910 (Paris).

Preparations.

During the last series of sittings in Paris, the dark cabinet was arranged beside a window, which did not close perfectly. Since Eva C. was occasionally inconvenienced by the draught, Mme. Bisson arranged the cabinet on the opposite side of the room and, at the same time, enlarged it. All the walls, the floor and the roof consisted of black lining, sewn together by machine, in such a way that the inner space showed not the slightest opening, and appeared to be made of one piece. I may here mention specially that the cabinet was most minutely examined by me, before and after every sitting, with the help of an electric lamp. There was not the slightest opening through which one could put a finger. Even where the narrow side of the wardrobe touched the cabinet there was a wall of the black material. The area of the cabinet was larger than before. Length 7 feet inside, depth 4 feet. Above, it was entirely closed off at a height of 7 feet by a roof, so that it would have been impossible to introduce objects from above. The lining was tacked on to the floor and sewn up with the carpet. The curtain was made of the same black material and hung on rings running on a metal rod covered with a strip of lining. There was no connection with the wardrobe, the contents of which I examined. There was no double bottom or secret passage. There was no access to the interior of the cabinet except through the curtains. Door No. 2 led into the passage and was locked at the beginning of every sitting. Door No. 1 led into an adjoining room, resembling a studio, which had no other door.

The light straw armchair, which stood in the cabinet, had a rather high back, inclined backwards, and arm-rests. The seat sloped downwards behind, and was fairly long and comfortable, the lowest point being about a foot from the floor. This easy chair was also covered with black lining, and was thoroughly examined before and after every sitting, without, however, discovering anything suspicious.

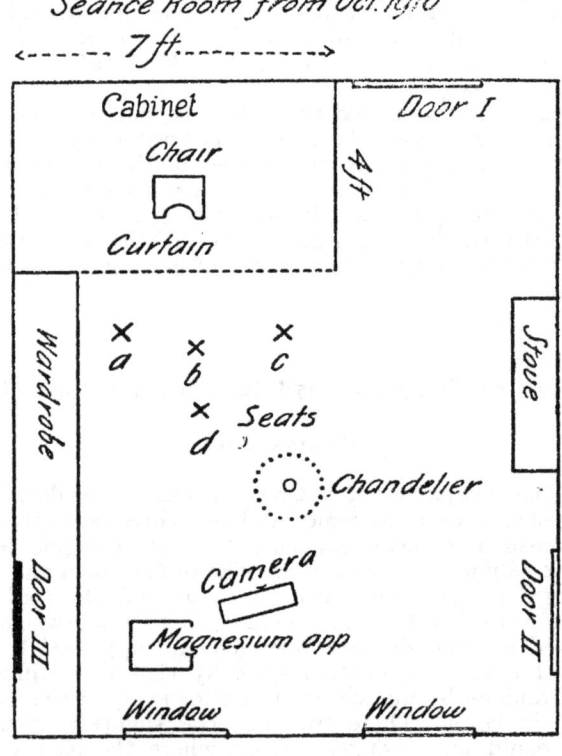

DIAGRAM III.

The illumination during the sittings was given by three or four twenty candle-power lamps in a pendant in the middle of the ceiling. Each of these lamps was contained in a ruby glass globe, as used in the development of photographic plates. This illumination continued during the whole of the sittings of this series, and sufficed for reading large print and for taking notes during the sittings.

Two cameras belonging to the author, one of which was a stereoscopic camera, were placed by him near the window (see plan of the

SITTINGS OF OCTOBER AND NOVEMBER 1910 (PARIS)

room), before every sitting. The red light permitted us to leave the camera open as long as necessary during the sittings.

The slides with the plates (manufactured by Hauff & Lumière) I put into the camera myself before each sitting, and I removed them myself afterwards.

For the flash-light several arrangements were tried successively (igniting rods, matches, fuses, caps). These worked quite irregularly, and were apt to fail at the critical moment. The electric ignition, on the other hand, turned out to be the most reliable when it was connected with the lighting supply by means of a plug adapter. A pressure switch held in the hand, with flexible cord attached, allowed of a quicker action of the apparatus than the previous arrangements. Afterwards the optical impression could be compared with the photographic result. As soon as a photograph was to be taken, those present withdrew from the opening of the curtain, in order not to obstruct the picture.

The clothing of the medium, before each of the sittings now to be described, was the same as in previous experiments. Eva undressed completely before Mme. Bisson (if requested, also in the presence of other lady witnesses), put on the knitted garment already described, which reached up to her hips, and over it, after very careful examination, the black dress, which only had an opening in the neck. On several occasions the medium allowed us to examine her in this half-dressed condition before the dress was sewn up in our presence at the neck and wrists, and sewn up with the tricot at her hips. But, even after this, she allowed us to make sure by touch that no materials or utensils were concealed between the dress and the skin. The tricot and dress were thin enough to show the whole superficial anatomy of the body through the light fabric. No contact with the skin was possible without either tearing or ripping the material.

In order to exclude the possibility of her having concealed rolled-up pieces of material in a hollow tooth, in her cheeks, in the external ear passages, or in her nose, I made her breathe before every sitting through the nose (each side separately), asked her to open her mouth widely, examined her cheeks, external ears and passages, her arm-pits and the felt slippers on her feet, as well as her hair and scalp. Often she removed the combs and black velvet ribbon from her coiffure, so that it was only held together by hairpins.

Immediately after every sitting the author examined all the seams of the dress, the hair, and dress, and body surface again, without ever discovering any suspicious change either in the medium or in her dress.

This examination and the sewing up took place regularly in the séance room. Immediately after the examination Eva entered the cabinet, sat down on the chair, and was put into the hypnotic trance by Mme. Bisson, by touching her hands and fixing her eyes. This lasted barely half a minute. The participators were always allowed to witness this process in the cabinet. Then Mme. Bisson closed the curtain and sat down on chair B or C. The chair A was regularly occupied by the author.

After the hypnotisation of the medium the white electric lamp was extinguished, the red illumination having been already switched on.

SITTING OF THE 19th OCTOBER 1910.

No result.

SITTING OF THE 22nd OCTOBER 1910.

Present.—Mme. Bisson, the author and his wife.

Examination and dress of the medium, and examination of the cabinet as usual. Illumination : three red lamps. Chair A occupied by the author, Chair B by Mme. Bisson, Chair C by the author's wife (see Diagram).

Commencement, 9 P.M.

The author sat barely 1 yard away from the medium, and could follow the phenomena even at a closer range. Very soon after the beginning of the sitting Eva opened the curtain with her hand, so that her whole figure became visible, but specially her knees and hands. We saw on the left some grey patches, hardly distinguishable from the black background, which gradually grew brighter and denser. Suddenly we saw about 16 inches above her left hand, which rested quietly by the open curtain, a shape having the outline of a human hand. This showed itself, disappeared and reappeared, remaining visible hardly more than a second, and reappeared again and again. I put forward my open right hand, and it was several times in succession touched, as by a blow from the hand-shaped body which was visible at the same time. Several times it passed over my face, from right to left, and I had the sensation of being touched by a strongly developed, and rather large, cool and moist male hand. My forehead after this occurrence was moistened as if by a sponge.

While the hand, apparently suspended in mid-air, and having the tips of its fingers directed rather towards the medium, was producing these effects, Eva's hands remained steadily visible and did not stir from her knees.

Just then we suddenly saw on the floor outside the curtain, opposite the chair C, the appearance of a bright patch where the curtain touched the floor, 15 or 20 inches away from the left foot of the medium (Fig. 4). On looking closer we had the impression that it was the limb of a living being (hand or foot) which emerged from the curtain. The shape was flat, about 3 inches long, and of a bright pink colour, and most closely resembled the four fingers of a left male hand, lying on the floor, with only the upper two joints of the finger showing. I knelt down, and made sure, at the same instant, with my hand, that both the medium's feet were in her slippers and had not changed their position. Her hands lay on her knees. In about half a minute this phenomenon disappeared.

Probably this was the same half-developed limb which had touched me. I could not perceive any finger-nails or any other details. The resemblance to a hand was only in bulk and outline. Its motions and the sensations of contact produced by it had an animal character.

In this sitting we again repeatedly saw, in various places and usually

SITTINGS OF OCTOBER AND NOVEMBER 1910 (PARIS)

joined in some way to the body of the medium, fabrics, resembling veils or clouds, in the form of delicate strips, threads, and fragments, and having a motion of their own. The medium's head was sometimes inclined towards the left, and in the shadow of the curtain, and, therefore, as a rule, invisible. But the manner of production was obviously the same as in previous sittings. During the preparation or development of the phenomena the medium groaned, gasped or whined softly, and one had the impression of a strong bodily exertion. Once Eva gave me both her hands during the development of these remarkable structures. At that moment a narrow luminous delicate ribbon, of some sort of veiling stuff, an inch or two wide, released itself from her lap, and appeared to connect both her hands from one thumb to the other. It only remained visible for a few seconds, and disappeared before my eyes, without her having released my hands from hers.

Eva wished to be hypnotised. Mme. Bisson entered the cabinet, placed her hand on her head, and encouraged the medium by suggestion. As she came out, some greyish fragments of the consistency of spider webs were found on the front of her dress and on her hair, but in a few seconds these disappeared, as if destroyed by the light. During the development of these apparently textile aggregates, I took the liberty of putting my head in between the open curtains to see what was happening there. Once I saw a greyish white cloudy column proceeding from her left upper arm, and, later, from her right upper arm. It was about 20 inches long and 2 or 3 inches thick, and at the upper end there was the form of a small female hand, endowed with a motion of its own, and with its broad side towards us. This hand executed graceful and beckoning motions, while the vapour column moved to and fro, as if keeping time with it.

Both the medium's hands lay quietly before us on her knees, fully illumined by the red light. Her head reclined on the back of the chair. The same phenomenon was repeated on the right-hand side. We could not see whether the palm or the back of the hand-shaped body was turned towards us, neither could we see any details in the design of the hand.

The same shape also appeared to execute beating and waving motions with something resembling a strip of muslin. This strip, in the course of its movement, became visible in front of the medium, and on one occasion touched my face (Fig. 5).

I also perceived a white patch in her lap resembling a strip of muslin bunched up. This disappeared rapidly without any perceptible aid from her hand. For the first time the author could, during this sitting, witness attempts at the formation of heads. But the optical impressions described in what follows were so swift, lasting barely a second, that the recognition of details appeared hardly possible, in spite of the closest attention. In this and the following sittings the forms resembling heads were shown mostly near the curtain on the medium's left, *i.e.*, in front of the medium, about 30 inches away from her head, and at the level of the head of a man of medium height standing upright. At first they were only fragments of heads, and partial formations, in which certain lines and forms, resembling faces, could be clearly recognised, while the rest appeared to be a dark undeveloped mass. Thus, I saw in this sitting a face looking upwards, in which I could recognise the bridge of the nose, the forehead, the hair and a rough outline of the head. A broad band surrounded the forehead. Owing to the fugitiveness of the impression, eyes and other details could not be recognised. The medium, of course, remained visibly seated on her chair during these phenomena.

Since the curtain appeared to be inflated on Eva's left side, I again inserted my head in the cabinet. To my greatest astonishment I then saw, on my right, behind the curtain, and as far as I could see suspended in mid-air, a completely developed female bust, with its head, neck and breast completely swathed in veils. This was at the height of a person standing upright, while on my left, tangible and fully illuminated, the medium's whole body lay stretched in the chair. The features of the apparition could not be recognised on account of the veiling. This appearance lasted about four seconds, and was clear, beyond all doubt, and most convincing.

The sitting lasted from 9.15 till 11.30.

The closest examination of the medium and cabinet after the mediun awoke, and before she left the room, yielded no result.

Sitting of the 25th October 1910.

Present—Mme. Bisson, her daughter-in-law, her two sons, and the author and his wife.

Time—9.15 till 11.30.

All conditions as on 22nd October.

Very soon after the beginning of the sitting Eva opened the curtain so that her hands and body could be seen. Her head appeared as a bright patch, which then grew gradually darker. I had the impression as if a grey misty veil was covering her face, and that it could, at last, be seen by the eye as a cloudy drapery falling over her chest and becoming more and more dense. This remarkable appearance seemed again to proceed from her organs of respiration, and ended in a sudden transformation of the fabric into a bright pink strip, resembling a veil, and extending from her mouth to the thumb of her right hand, with a thickness of about 2 inches. This appearance developed without any perceptible motion of the hands, which were resting on her knees before our eyes, while her head was inclined to the right. The bright band remained visible for about half a minute, and disappeared quickly, like an electric light when it is switched off.

The same process was repeated on the left side, the band joining her face with her left hand and appearing rather longer and more curved.

After this phenomenon had disappeared, we saw vague and indefinite forms, clouds and strips as they appear in nearly every sitting, which seem to furnish the elementary substance for the morphogenetic work. At least they represent a regular precursor for more distinctly marked outlines and plastic forms resembling human limbs (Fig. 6).

Fig. 5. Drawing after record of sitting of 22 October, 1910.

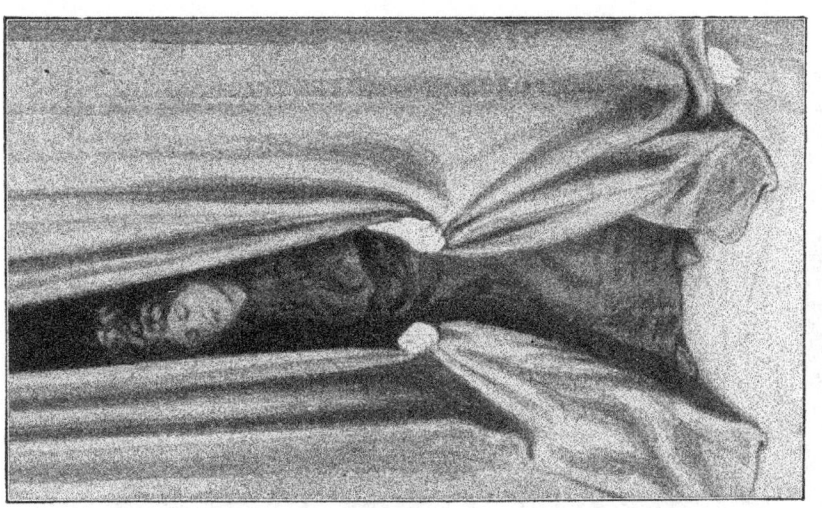

Fig. 4. Drawing after record of sitting of 22 October, 1910.

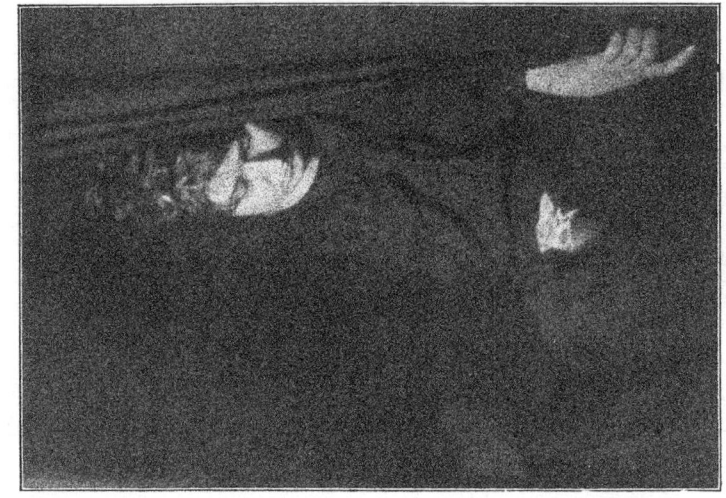

Fig. 7. Flashlight photograph by the author, 25 October, 1910.

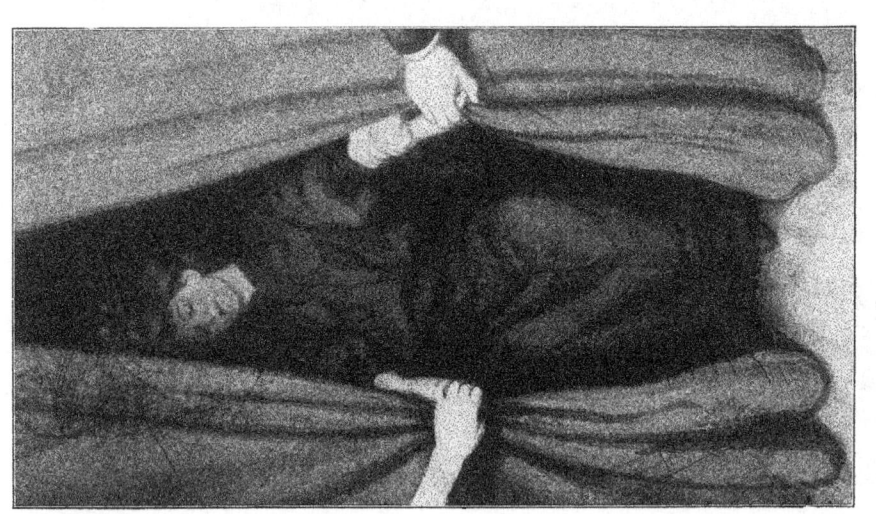

Fig. 6. Drawing after record of sitting of 25 October, 1910.

SITTINGS OF OCTOBER AND NOVEMBER 1910 (PARIS)

The next observation took place under even more stringent conditions. The medium placed, for purposes of control, her left hand in my right hand, and her right in my wife's right hand. Thus both hands were held and were visible in front of the curtain. She gripped the curtain with the fingers of the hand held by me, as if wishing to shield the impending creation from a too intense illumination. In these circumstances we saw on her left bare forearm between the wrist and the sleeve two completely formed hands lying on her forearm at right angles to it and resembling a woman's or child's fists. The knuckles, and the furrow between the fingers, were clearly recognisable, even at the first impression. The skin appeared a delicate pink in the red light of the room. Several times the medium exposed this plastic product to the light by the motion of her forearm, but never for more than a second, so that further observation of detail was not possible. This phenomenon also disappeared in the darkness of the curtain without any alteration in the control of the medium's hands. I now brought my left hand to the place where the fists had been visible, while my right hand still clasped Eva's left, and her right was held by my wife, and I requested to be touched. As quick as lightning a hand and forearm emerged from the curtain at the place indicated and touched the palm of my left hand. The touch was cool and moist and gave an impression as if I had been touched by the fist of a child, or the healed amputation stump of a child's arm. It lasted hardly half a second. This appearance seems very remarkable, especially as two senses were engaged in the control of the medium and the observation of the phenomenon. The opening of the curtain, at a height of about 50 inches from the floor, was about 28 inches.

We must add that it was repeatedly and very emphatically suggested to the medium by Mme. Bisson that she should form a hand. After the attempt at contact just described, Mme. Bisson, at my request, particularised the suggestion in the sense that a hand should become visible in the medium's lap between her two hands.

Meanwhile the lady of the house held the medium's hands, which had a soothing effect upon the latter. On one occasion we saw something resembling a small piece of a dark grey veil proceeding from the arm of the medium, covering the back of Mme. Bisson's hand and hanging down from it in the form of a strip 8 inches long. After a few seconds this structure disappeared before our eyes.

The curtain then closed further, so that we could no longer see the medium's left arm. Again I endeavoured to surprise her in her work of preparation by putting my head into the cabinet. To my greatest surprise I now saw, not two, but three forearms lying in her lap. The third arm, of a pink colour, had developed from the medium's left elbow outwards, was smaller than a child's arm, vague and transparent, and somewhat resembled a child's hand.

The suggestion that a hand should form between the medium's hands was repeated, although the appearance just described should perhaps have been interpreted in that sense.

What follows happened, however, under conditions less open to objection, inasmuch as her hands from beginning to end held the hems of the curtains, and were motionless and always visible. A bright, white patch, appearing red in the red illumination, and of considerable size, was formed in her lap, and appeared to consist of a moving and living material resembling an organic substance. From this material, elongations, resembling pseudopods, originated with a flowing motion, which soon assumed the form of the fingers of a skeleton hand. Finally the form, in its outline, completely resembled a white, transparent hand, in which, however, all finer details were lacking. One might perhaps produce a similar impression with a hand cut out of white paper.

I pressed the electric button in order to photograph the three hands, but the current only acted at the fourth pressure. By that time the form of the hand had already faded, and I only succeeded in photographing the white material in her lap (Fig. 7).

In any case the experiment is remarkable enough. The independent mobility of the aggregate, termed *teleplasm*, the clear endeavour to carry out our suggestion, and the production of a white form in the rough outline of a left hand, *i.e.*, without any recognisable aid of the medium's hands, which are always visible,—in a word, under careful control, are the elements constituting the value of this observation.

The stereoscopic photograph shows the medium with her head bent forward, sitting on her chair in the black dress. One sees distinctly the white stitches on the bodice of the dress. Both hands are visible holding the open curtain. The white mass is lying between her thighs, the distant part of it resembling a white cloth bunched up, with a projection in front showing the shape of a first finger. In front of this, *i.e.*, nearly between the knees, there is a hemispherical body flat at the top, the exterior of which seen in the stereoscope appears to be striped. On the enlargement of this picture the stripes appear to project parallel rays, which are visible over a portion of the black dress. The picture here reproduced does not show the same detail as the stereoscope.

The whole thing is very mysterious and unexplainable. How should Eva be able to introduce a spherical solid body, which, according to the picture, must be at least 6 inches across, into the sitting, in spite of our rigorous examination ?

The flash of the magnesium light gave a violent shock to Eva's nervous system, and, at the same time, brought about the total disappearance of the materialisation phenomena.

When Eva was to be awakened, about twenty minutes ensued before she regained consciousness. Pulse 100, small, and barely perceptible. Violent hysterical tremor in arms and legs, which only ceased after soothing suggestion. Traces of blood in mouth and nose. Tendency towards contraction of the voluntary muscles.

The structures and shapes produced by the medium were exposed to the light and to our observation, rather shyly and tentatively, and with evident reluctance. A fright, or a feeling of repugnance, even a fluctuation in the emotional state of the medium, seems to be able to destroy the teleplastic structures as if by magic, and to make them invisible. *This was also the inducement never to interfere, or to disturb her, but our endeavours, on the other hand, were directed towards strengthening the courage and confidence of the medium, so that a gradual training and adaptation to our wishes should enable her better to differentiate her products, to make them sharper and more plastic, and to expose them longer to the light.* On the other hand, a brusque procedure could entirely destroy any possibility of observation. That is why we had to resist the temptation to seize the white mass and to hold it in our hands. The following night Eva slept badly and felt out of sorts on the following day. As a rule, she requires two days to overcome the nervous exhaustion resulting from a sitting.

SITTING OF THE 28th OCTOBER 1910.

Present.—Mme. Bisson, the author and his wife.

Time of Sitting.—9.15 to 11.15.

Conditions as on 22nd October.

The curtains remained open from the beginning of the sitting. Since one of the flaps overshadowed the head, which was turned to the left, and reclined upon the back of the chair, the curtain was withdrawn further at the desire of the author. The medium's head was then entirely exposed to the illumination. I brought my head to within 16 inches of it, in order to be able to observe more closely. The features and the colour of the skin, which normally appears bright pink, were no longer recognisable. A veil lay on the face, and made it unrecognisable, as if the whole head were swathed in it.

Then there appeared the bright and nearly white outline of a hand lying on the shoulder, with the fingers towards the front, just as if a person standing behind the chair had placed a hand on the medium's shoulder. The shape, which from the formation of the fingers was evidently a left hand, appeared flat, and of a white colour. The optical impression was not at all that of real life (Fig. 8).

The medium's arms rested from the beginning of the sittings on her knees, so that, with the open curtain, they were always controlled and took no part in the occurrences. After several seconds the image disappeared, and the same process of development commenced on the left shoulder. This time I determined the period of visibility with a stop-watch. The structure remained visible to my eye exactly forty seconds. The fingers appeared as white strips of slightly vague outline and little plasticity, clearly marked off from each other, but without any detailed structure. Whether it was a right or a left hand could not be clearly distinguished on account of the imperfect development.

Without any change in the control, the long veil-like strip, apparently proceeding from the organs of respiration, reappeared. Since the head was turned towards the left, a part of this was seen on the left shoulder, whence it fell to the ground backwards, so that it was partly covered by the left arm, and only became visible again at the hip.

There followed some further attempts to form hands, but the structures disappeared at once, and appeared to have an insufficient consistency. My wish that the hand should grasp a small object (an ivory paper-knife) remained unfulfilled. During these morphogenetic endeavours I was able, on one occasion, to verify the existence of a second profile beside her head on the right, so that both profiles became visible side by side, and parallel to each other. I quickly put my head into the cabinet to see more clearly, and thought I observed the features of an old woman. The whole appearance lasted only a few seconds. An attempt to photograph the veil-like mass described above was a failure, because one of the ladies covered the medium's body at the moment of the flash.

Eva had, in the hypnotic trance, given Mme. Bisson on the previous day detailed instructions how to treat her after the flash-light photographs, which always produced a severe nervous shock. She demanded an instant closing of the curtain, the silence of the spectators and a period of rest. On carrying out these instructions the present sitting was continued with success.

This time there appeared between the curtains, opened to the extent of 15 to 20 inches, and high above the medium's hands, a white strip of fabric, which was pulled from one side to the other, as if by an invisible hand, with lightning rapidity, or waved with a beating or zigzag motion. This was repeated at an approximate height of 5 feet above the floor, six or eight times, and towards the front of the cabinet, while Eva's upper body lay back in the chair, and was approximately 3 feet from the apparition, and her hands were visible and motionless. I then requested to be hit in the face with the strip of material, and put my head into the cabinet. Suddenly I felt a pretty violent blow, as of a wet ball of stuff about the size of a walnut. It appeared to be attached to a cord, and hit my left eye so that it watered. The eye was even slightly painful after the sitting, and the conjunctiva was reddened.

This observation appeared to me as inexplicable as the others, since Eva's head and hands did not participate. That the curtain remained open during the first half of the sitting, and that I was able to look into the mysterious workshop as often as I wished, are the remarkable characteristics of this sitting. My wish to subject the materialised fabrics to the test of the sense of touch unfortunately remained unfulfilled. Those responsible for the experiments took the view that the further development of the medium must not be interrupted by such stipulations.

After the sitting the pulse was 90, and there was some fatigue. During the state of trance Eva is quite conscious of her activity. The extrusion of the material forming the teleplasm requires a great muscular and volitional effort, accompanied by groaning and whimpering. The same thing was noted in the case of Eusapia Paladino at the time of her performances.

In the semi-somnolent or somnambulic state, there is a close mental *rapport* with all those present, and particularly with Mme. Bisson, for whom Eva feels a close friendship. During the sitting she carries on a conversation with her protectress, tries to read her innermost soul, asks again and again whether her protectress is not tired, and whether she can see her creations, whether any ideas are preoccupying her; in short, she gauges with a correct instinct the psychological state of the sitters, often intervenes in their conversation, and corrects

Fig. 8. Drawing after record of sitting of 28 October, 1910.

Fig. 9. Drawing after record of sitting of 3 November, 1910.

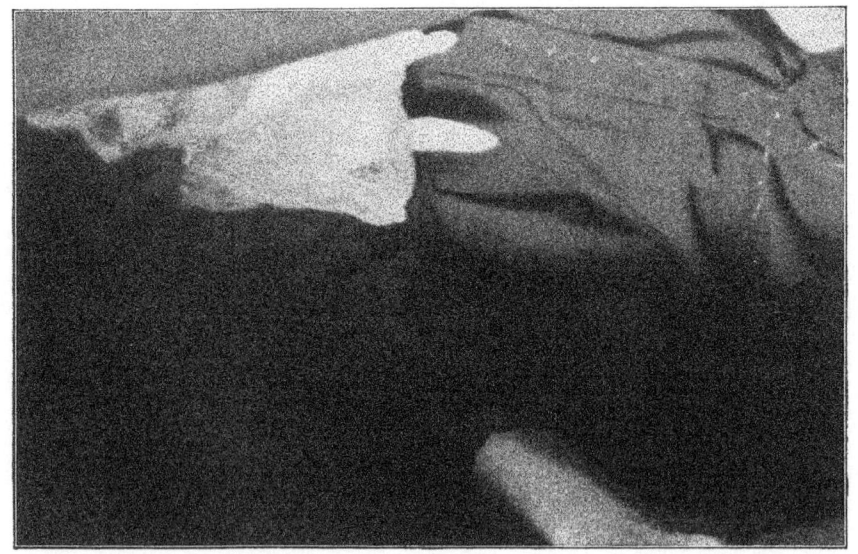

FIG. 10. FLASHLIGHT PHOTOGRAPH BY THE AUTHOR, 3 NOVEMBER, 1910.

FIG. 11. DRAWING AFTER RECORD OF SITTING OF 3 NOVEMBER, 1910.

SITTINGS OF OCTOBER AND NOVEMBER 1910 (PARIS)

erroneous interpretations, but shows great delicacy in avoiding saying anything which might be disagreeable to those present.

SITTING OF THE 2nd NOVEMBER 1910.

Present.—Mme. Bisson and the author. No result.

Eva had spent that day mostly in town shopping, and had been invited to lunch. She received a number of distracting and diverting impressions. Besides, the weather was bad, with wind and rain.

SITTING OF THE 3rd NOVEMBER 1910.

Present.—Mme. Bisson, Public Prosecutor M., and the author.

Time of Sitting.—9.15 to 11.30. All other conditions as before.

The flaps of the open curtain touched the medium's knees. The flap on the left-hand side moved gently to and fro, as if moved by her left foot, so that the left hand, seen on her knee in the red light, was sometimes seen and sometimes disappeared.

There was evidently great nervousness in exposing the ectoplastic product to the light, and to our gaze, for any length of time. During all the phenomena of this sitting her hands were visible, either resting on her knees or grasping the curtains. The first appearance was on Eva's right side, about the level of her head. It was a large, reddish, nebulous patch, 3 or 4 inches across, which gradually, before our eyes, and in the course of about half a minute, changed into a bright shape resembling a hand, larger than the hand of the medium, and resembling a rather large male hand. The dorsal surface, the formation of the fingers, and the division of the thumb, were clearly marked, but all finer detail, such as nails, wrinkles and knuckles were lacking. What we saw might be compared to a large white and rather flat seamless glove, which appeared pink in the red light. In a short time (twenty seconds at most) the form disappeared, and was replaced by teleplastic emanations of indefinite shape, such as patches and strips, which were mostly seen near the head and the right shoulder.

At Eva's request Mme. Bisson entered the cabinet several times, and put her hand on the medium's forehead. During one of these visits we suggested to the medium that she should materialise a hand with forearm. While the lady of the house held Eva's head in the cabinet, M. grasped her left hand and I her right. With this reliable control we saw before our eyes, and with open curtains, a bright patch lying in her lap, resembling a handkerchief. It appeared to be viscous and endowed with life, for it moved and altered its appearance, and assumed a shape about 2 by 8 inches. At the front of this shape, which was turned towards us, elongations appeared which resembled pseudopods. Finally, the outline of a whitish hand was formed. We saw before us the outline of a left forearm, about the size of a child's arm, but flat and without any detail. After about thirty seconds the form dissolved, returned into an amorphous mass of indefinite appearance, and then entirely disappeared.

In the course of the sitting I suddenly saw something resembling a bunched-up grey veil fall from her right shoulder into her lap. My wish to take this ball into my hands was not acceded to by the lady of the house. Mme. Bisson thought that any sudden intervention taking the medium by surprise would injure her health and jeopardise the development of the phenomena. I therefore abandoned the idea.

The material lying in her lap resembled a grey placenta-like pap, traversed by fairly thick round strips and cords. It was fairly immobile and remained visible at least two minutes. After a short closing of the curtains by the medium the material had disappeared, but the dress on her breast was lighted up. A white band about $2\frac{1}{2}$ inches thick, falling from her right shoulder into her lap, was partly covered at the shoulder by a fine bright transparent veil, and ended in her lap like a hand with three fingers. The whole structure most closely resembled a long white lady's glove, having only three fingers (thumb, first and third fingers), and perforated on the back by a hole nearly an inch long, which appeared as a black spot (Fig. 9).

The whole structure gave a flat and hollow impression. There was evidently an attempt to form a hand and forearm, but the necessary power was lacking for constancy, accurate delineation, detailed structure, and plastic form. The same shape altered its position, sank down, and remained lying in her lap. In any case this structure showed mobility of its own, and was visible without the co-operation of the hand in two places (right shoulder and lap). The shape remained fairly long, and showed itself for the third time during the flash-light exposure in front of Eva's face. The moment I saw the white mass with the fingers at about the height of the medium's throat, I ignited the flash-light (Fig. 10) with the electric button. I myself removed the plates in their slides and kept them until they were developed the following day. The plates entirely corroborate the visual impression, and prove that we had observed correctly. Magnification, and the stereoscopic transparency of these photographs on glass, permitted an accurate study of the structure.

The right side of the face is invisible and covered by a diffused apparently black and white mass, looking like a tangled mass of threads. From the right shoulder down to the breast a piece of veiling with a right-angled corner is hanging. Underneath this one sees two short white rounded strips, the outlines of which might correspond to the outermost joints of the first and third fingers of a rather large left hand. The stereoscopic pictures which we reproduced on glass distinctly show the transparent meshwork of a large net. Underneath, a white band bent outwards is seen, which would correspond to a thumb with its joint bent outwards. The shapes of the first and third fingers can be followed up under the net. In the place of the second finger there is a gap. The first finger projects and throws a distinct shadow on the dress of the medium. Eva's hands clutch the curtain. The strips resembling fingers show no detail. They appear flat, and have no seams, such as a kid glove would have. Besides, they are abnormally long, and larger than the medium's fingers.

SITTINGS OF OCTOBER AND NOVEMBER 1910 (PARIS)

One can hardly maintain that the photograph shows anything corresponding to a living form, but we seem to have before us the formation of the outlines of three fingers of a male left hand in a white material, the nature of which cannot be determined from the photograph.

The photograph is the final link in the chain of observations. It confirms the reality of the phenomena, as well as the correctness of our previous observations, in which we also saw an imperfect shape resembling an arm with three fingers. This remained constant, though appearing in three different places, and maintained its peculiar truncated character. I ought to mention that we had asked for the production of a hand, above or near her head, before we made the photographic exposure. She herself seemed to feel that the present stage of development was not ripe for the production of detailed forms, and asked us, repeatedly, to defer photography. On account of the extraordinary fugitiveness of the vitalised aggregates, a sudden and complete disappearance of the forms we saw was to be feared. For this reason I did not await her consent, but ignited the flash-light as soon as I could distinctly see the white shape at her head. Besides, these structures, even when imperfectly developed, are valuable for the study of such phenomena.

Immediately after the flash-light Eva, with a loud groan, closed the curtains she was clutching, but without altering the position of her convulsively closed fingers. Mme. Bisson closed the upper aperture, by sliding the rings together, and took hold of the right hand, while Monsieur M. took hold of the left. Her hands therefore remained after the photographic exposure in the position shown in the picture, not having been withdrawn behind the curtains, even for an instant.

This situation was still unchanged when, having removed the slides from the cameras, I took up a position behind the low chair of Mme. Bisson, which stood in front of the curtain, so that my head was about 2 feet higher than that of the seated lady, and about 18 inches in front of the curtain. Suddenly the latter was opened for about a second, in front of my eyes, to an extent of 8 inches at the most, and was immediately closed again, while nothing had been changed concerning the medium's clenched and closed hands (Fig. 11).

In spite of the shortness of the time I saw in front of me the face and upper body of a young and fully developed female swathed in grey veils down to the waist. The time of observation was too short to tell whether the face under the veil resembled Eva or not. In order to show herself to me, she would have had to stand up, and clothe herself with the veils. For this she required her hands as much as for the opening of the curtain. But her hands were visible outside the curtain. Their position corresponded with the sitting posture of the medium, and were held by two persons.

We must further ask: Could she rise from her chair without any noise and without the two persons sitting in front of her noticing anything? Her standing up would also have involved raising her hands to the level of the upright position. Neither of the controllers (who could not see the apparition visible above their heads) perceived the least change in the attitude of the medium. But the female body perceived corresponded in its height above the floor to the height of a female form standing upright. The apparition disappeared, with the same lightning rapidity and silence as it came. The question as to whether it was the medium, or whether it was a separate form, I cannot answer. In any case, the transformation of a shape resembling a hand, into long grey veils which enveloped a female figure down to the waist, without the aid of the medium's hands, is a riddle difficult to explain.

At 11.30 the sitting closed. Final and complete examination of the medium and the cabinet with no result.

Sitting of the 5th November 1910.

Present.—Professor Charles Richet, Mme. Bisson, and the author.

All conditions with regard to examination, dress of the medium, examination of the cabinet, and illumination, as in the previous sittings. Richet occupied the middle place in front of the curtain. I sat on his left, and Mme. Bisson on his right.

This time the phenomena began immediately after the commencement of the sitting and at the medium's left hand, as at the last sitting. We had a visual impression as if a slight black shadow passed, to and fro, along the back of the left hand. While the right hand remained quiet and visible in the opening of the curtain, the left was withdrawn from our gaze, now and then, by the curtain falling over it. Besides, the left flap of the curtain was stretched and inflated as if a living being were active behind it. The imperfectly visible head was bent towards the left and swathed in fine grey veils, which condensed more and more, and became visible on the breast and on the shoulder, so that, finally, we could make out a rough outline. When the condensation process of this grey material had made some progress, we saw a white or greyish luminosity, as if produced by white chiffon or veiling. These light grey patches of a vague shape showed themselves in turn on the right shoulder, on the left under the chin, on the lap, and then at the hem of the curtain, corresponding roughly with the height of Eva's head, which was about 3 feet behind. These patches, balls and bands occurred simultaneously in different places. They gave the impression of being independent of the body of the medium, showed a tendency towards the production of fingers and forms resembling hands, and were obviously directed by a psychic form of energy. The structures did not, however, suffer the light more than a few seconds. They emerged and disappeared, and had a tendency to avoid a lengthy exposure to light. Finally, we also saw on the medium's left side, on a level with her head, a white shape near the curtain, which resembled a female right hand and forearm, and disappeared after a few seconds. Some attempts to form heads were also observed, but these were more rapid and fugitive than the other teleplastic emanations. Among the suddenly appearing forms sometimes visible near the top of the curtain,' I once thought that I recognised the upturned face of an old man with a white beard, while at the same time the entranced medium, her head, body and hands, were completely visible. The two heads may have been 30 inches apart.

Fig. 13. Drawing after record of sitting of 5 November, 1910.

Fig. 12. Drawing after record of sitting of 5 November, 1910.

Fig. 15. Drawing after record of sitting of 11 November, 1910.

Fig. 14. Drawing after record of sitting of 11 November, 1910.

SITTINGS OF OCTOBER AND NOVEMBER 1910 (PARIS)

The play of whitish grey aggregations adjoining different parts of the medium's body then continued, her hands remaining at rest. One of these bands joined her head with her right hand. At the same time I saw emerging from the wrist or out of the sewn-up sleeve a white, apparently viscous mass which flowed down to the ground before my eyes (Fig. 12).

Suddenly, by an invisible impulse, this whole mass of elementary material was drawn across the right knee and then across the left knee of the medium, *i.e.*, right across the opening of the curtains into the region behind the left flap of the curtain, while the head and hands of the medium remained visible and immobile. Some attempts to form human shapes out of the teleplasm became evident on the right-hand side, behind the curtain, at the same level as before, and, apparently, due to an unknown volition. While Richet concentrated his whole attention on that process I looked into her lap to make sure that her hands were still there. But what was my astonishment when, instead of two arms, I perceived three! The third arm started from the right elbow. It resembled a long narrow strip of the size of a child's arm, and exhibited next the medium's right hand a small hand with five distinct fingers. Richet confirmed this observation when I drew his attention to it. We therefore saw at the same time four hands (Fig. 13), three in the *medium's lap, and a fourth in the process of development*, near the flap of the curtain on the medium's left, while the third hand, lying on the medium's lap, remained visible for about thirty seconds. Richet's right hand, which he held forward about a foot above the medium's visible hand, was touched by the hand coming out of the curtain. I ought to mention that we had wished to see hands, and had requested the medium accordingly.

After these phenomena had disappeared, we asked for the formation of a head. After a short rest-pause we saw a repetition of the phenomenon recorded in the last sitting, in which a packet of some kind of material was observed to fall. This time it fell into the lap of the medium, who sat in front of us with her hands visible. It fell as if projected from the roof of the cabinet by an unknown psychic force. This mass also disappeared from our gaze. Then began the development of forms resembling heads, which showed themselves with lightning speed behind the left flap of the curtain high above the medium and disappeared as quickly, so that there was hardly time to see the medium and the head simultaneously. In this case, Eva held the curtain flaps with hands always visible, and opened and closed them very rapidly. Since the effect was produced seven or eight times, I directed my attention exclusively to the medium, in some cases, while Richet observed the apparition of the heads. Occasionally, I could verify accurately that Eva lay in her chair, without any change in the position of her head and of her hands. In one case the phenomenon lasted two seconds, so that it was possible to see both heads simultaneously. The materialised head showed the features of a young woman whose hair was completely covered by a turban. In this I could distinctly see the slanting folds of the material. Unfortunately, the attempt at photography was a failure.

Towards midnight the sitting closed. Final examination negative.

Since the medium had a special veneration for Richet, she may have been satisfied with the good result of this sitting. In any case, she slept well the following night, and showed no after-effects to speak of.

Sitting of the 8th November 1910.

Present.—Mme. Bisson, M. Chevreuil, and the author.

No result.

The weather was rainy. Eva had, during the day, been shopping with her sisters, and had passed the whole day in town.

Contact with other people, and distractions, appeared to hinder the productions when immediately preceding a sitting. The medium herself attributed the lack of success to unfavourable atmospheric influences.

Sitting of the 11th November 1910.

Present.—Mme. Bisson and the author.

This day, as well as in all subsequent sittings, four twenty candle-power electric lamps were used.

Conditions as usual. The cabinet was again carefully examined with an electric torch. Eva's hair was held by a velvet ribbon (no combs).

Duration of sitting, 9.15 to 11.45.

Hypnotisation by Mme. Bisson.

Some twenty minutes elapsed before the phenomena set in. The curtain was half closed, and its left flap covered up Eva's left hand, which lay on her knee. Mme. Bisson, who sat opposite the left curtain, eventually pushed it back in order to see Eva's left hand. This unexpected interference provoked a violent reaction. The medium shuddered convulsively and complained strongly. For us, the whole occurrence had this interest—that on her left knee and underneath her left hand we saw a white mass, larger than a hand, resembling a white unformed aggregate endowed with life. This, under cover of the curtain, assumed the shape of a child's forearm, which seemed to attach itself from the outside to the medium's left elbow, and terminated in the outlines of a hand (Fig. 14).

We then suggested that Eva should produce a well-developed forearm with hand. The medium, whose hands were constantly controlled, evidently made strong efforts to carry out the suggestion. She made deep and audible respirations, and groaned and whimpered. At last we saw, on the inner side of her left arm, and starting from the elbow, the outlines of a left forearm, gradually becoming more distinct. A hand and fingers were formed in a rudimentary and imperfect way at first. But, before our eyes, this semi-liquid substance, endowed with some kind of animal life, changed its appearance, until it assumed the form of a correctly-drawn left hand, somewhat smaller than the medium's arm, and showing all the imperfections already mentioned as regards modelling, muscular development, detailed structure, and nails.

By closing the curtain, this structure was withdrawn from our gaze after barely fifteen seconds, and when the curtain was opened again, the apparition had crossed to the right side of the medium (Fig. 15).

This time the vitalised structure was detached from her body, and had the form of a double column of mist or smoke tapering towards the top. It ascended on her right side from the floor, and the two branches joined about the level of her shoulder, where they formed the dorsal aspect of a female right hand. The column may have been from 8 to 12 inches thick, and stood about 16 inches behind the right curtain on the floor beside the medium, whose whole body remained visible during the process. The hand then moved, beckoned to us, and appeared more distinctly formed, showing graceful lines like a living female hand. Although the teleplastic structure stood back in the cabinet, it was distinctly seen by all present, and for a sufficiently long time. I myself introduced my head for this purpose through the open curtain into the cabinet. The structure remained visible about twenty seconds.

When, after a rest-pause, the phenomena were continued, the same female hand lay on the right shoulder of the medium, with its dorsal surface and fingers towards the front.

Thereupon Mme. Bisson entered the cabinet in order to lay her hand on the medium's forehead. At the moment of her entry into the cabinet all the phenomena disappeared.

On continuing the sitting, I asked the medium whether some of the plastic material used for the materialisation process could be placed in a German-silver box I had brought for the purpose. The box had a well-closing lid, and contained a porcelain dish. It had not left my pocket. While the medium's hands clutched the curtains and remained distinctly visible, I brought the open box, held in my right hand, close to the curtain, at the level of about a foot above her right hand, while, at the same time, Mme. Bisson held my right wrist. At that moment the other two persons saw three well-developed fingers coming out of the curtain and touching the box. I myself could only see one finger, since I sat too far towards the left. This finger entered the open box on its narrow side and executed several shaking motions. I seized this moment to close the lid and hide the box in my pocket. On examining the dish afterwards in a white electric light I found on the inner narrow side of the porcelain dish, as if stuck to it, two pieces which, under the microscope, were recognised to be human skin [1] (Figs. 16 and 17).

Eva's hands, which held the curtains, remained during this experiment visibly under our control. During the final examination no defect of skin could be found either on the girl's hands or on her feet.

It appeared, from a microscopic examination, that the tissue was a piece of superficial epidermis, 16 mm. long, 11 mm. wide, and ¼ mm. thick. Even a simple magnification shows the

[1] Whether we have here to deal with tissue produced during the sitting, or introduced, in spite of the rigid control, or with an "*apport*," one cannot say with any certainty.

characteristic marbling of the skin, and a horny thickening of one half of it.

The second piece of skin, 12 mm. in diameter, is considerably thinner and finer. Under the microscope one distinctly sees the pigmented epithelium cells. The products do not in any point differ from the histological structure of human skin, but it is difficult to say from what part of the body they are derived.

After this experiment we asked for a hand above the medium's head for the purpose of photography. I went and stood beside the apparatus on my right, whence I could see through the open curtain everything happening on the left. Very soon a fairly large shape appeared above Eva's head, a shape which at a distance resembled a white male hand. The flash-light was ignited, and both photographs succeeded well (Fig. 18). Unfortunately, the plates only show half of what was perceived, because the left curtain half concealed the medium's face.

Owing to the various positions of the cameras, three fingers are seen on one negative, but on the stereoscopic negatives only two, and these are the backs of a thumb and forefinger of a left hand. On the picture with three fingers, half the hand is seen up to the wrist, the third joint of the first finger being bent, and lying in the inner corner of the medium's right eye. Hence the finger appears foreshortened. Whether the slanting shadow falling upon the upper part of the arm is due to that finger cannot be decided. Of the middle finger, only the first joint is seen, the second and third being bent in, or entirely lacking. On the stereoscopic plate the curtain covers this finger. The curvature produced by the metacarpal muscle of the thumb in a state of contraction is well developed at the root of the thumb, and the first and second joints of the thumb are distinctly outlined. No nail depression is seen on the thumb, although the tip has the natural shape.

Here, again, we cannot say what material the hand is made of. There is no question of a glove, because the outlines corresponding to the muscular modelling are too detailed. Besides, seams would be visible in some place or other. Nor does the material appear to consist of paper, for the sheen of white paper is easily recognisable on a photograph, and the fibres are seen in magnification. The freely-exposed thumb does, indeed, produce a flat impression, especially in the stereoscopic picture. But the photograph shows other and very remarkable things. We see a white and closely-twisted tissue, resembling veiling or lace, the end of which passed round the middle finger of her right hand.[1] This twisted strip is visible on Eva's lap, and is directed towards her left shoulder, which, unfortunately, is not visible. This tissue covers the wrist of the visible hand, and becomes visible again on her hair on the right side, falling upon her right shoulder. In the place where the thumb and forefinger join, a pointed white patch is seen on the hair, which is apparently due to the material lying on the head. We can recognise in the transparent unfolded tissue a folded margin and a net-like system of meshes.

[1] A comparison with numerous later photographs of the filmy teleplastic veiling shows a constant repetition of the same image, consisting of fibres, threads, bundles, and stripes, joined in meshes or nets, and sometimes in a parallel arrangement.

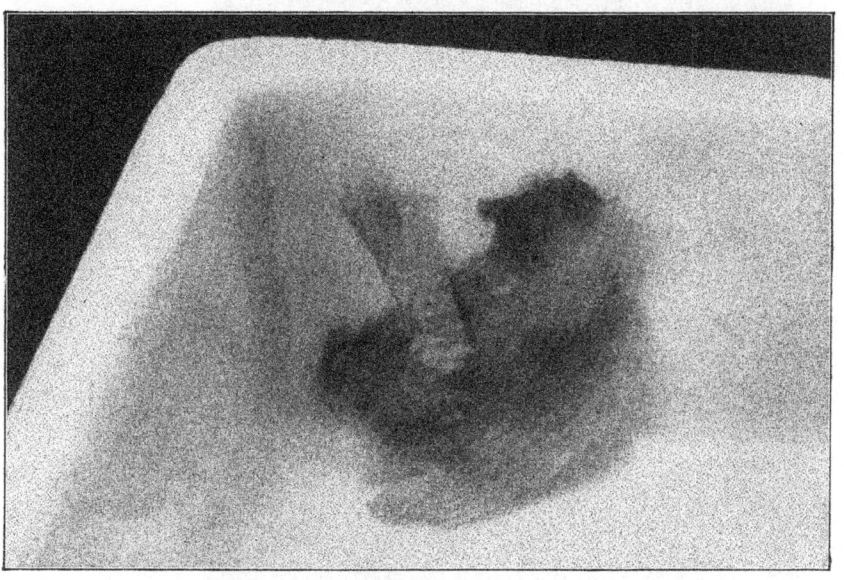

Fig. 16. Portion of the porcelain dish, with piece of skin.

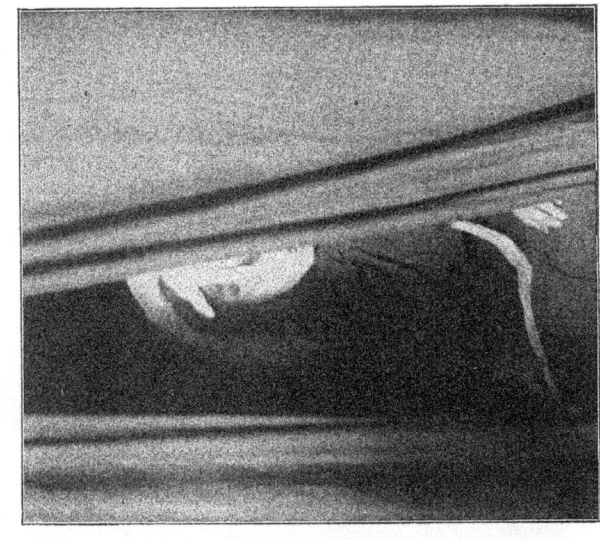

Fig. 18. Author's flashlight photograph of 11 November, 1910.

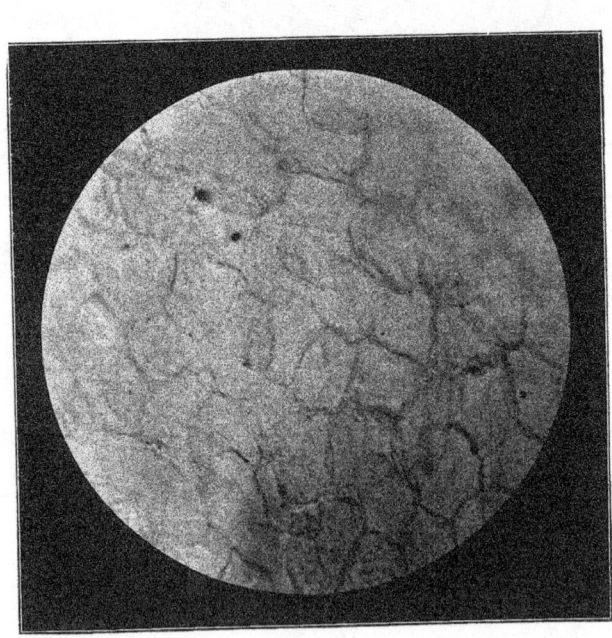

Fig. 17. Microphotograph of a portion of tissue from the piece of skin shown in Fig. 16.

On the magnification (Fig. 19) of the single picture, we can see, with the aid of magnifying glasses, that the second and third joints of Eva's left forefinger and middlefinger, as well as the second joint of the thumb, are enveloped in an extremely fine veil-like tissue, which also covers a portion of the finger-nails. This observation is confirmed by a detailed examination of the stereoscopic photograph.

If we assume fraud, what would have been the object of covering the left hand, which happened to be half covered by the curtain, and took no part in the principal phenomena, with veils of the finest material— a material which could only be discovered by the artificial means of magnification?

The sitting was continued after the photographs had been taken. The endeavours to show shapes of heads, in accordance with our wish, led to no distinct success. But, on one occasion, we saw in the curtain, rapidly opened and then again closed, a female figure draped from head to foot in veils, obviously the medium using the veils already formed and described above. The aperture of the curtain on that occasion was not more than 4 inches, and the appearance lasted only one second. The sitting ended at midnight. Final examination negative.

SITTING OF THE 15TH NOVEMBER 1910.

Present.—Professor Charles Richet, M. Chevreuil, Mme. Bisson, and the author.

During the day Eva had an emotional disturbance, and did not appear particularly disposed for a sitting. All conditions as before. During the examination the medium, dressed in the tights, allowed me to examine her bare upper body. It was also clear from an examination through the thin tights that no material was concealed about her lower body. The medium removed the three combs from her hair, so that the hair was only fastened by a velvet ribbon.

The development of the phenomena began again at her left hand, as in previous sittings, and took the form of bright shimmering strips, appearing at the shoulder and at the rim of the curtain. We repeated our previous request that Eva might allow the substratum of the materialisations to touch our hands. For this purpose M. Richet, Mme. Bisson, and the author, in turn approached their hands to that portion of the curtain where we had seen the white strip. All our hands were touched several times, the author having the impression as if several points of his right hand had been touched by a solid object with a slippery surface. It reminded him of moist, soft glove-leather. The material producing the touches did not remain motionless, and in spite of many attempts it could not be grasped. I also felt light blows on the palm of my hand, as if with whipcord, and I saw something resembling a ribbon crossing my hand. During this process Eva's hands were constantly controlled, and we could often see the outlines of her face. The blows were therefore undoubtedly not due to her hands, nor produced by her mouth.

After one such blow I closed my hand quickly and grasped something resembling a fine rubber cord, which, however, felt moist, and escaped from my fingers with a strong jerk and a serpentine motion, while the frightened medium gave a cry of pain.

We then asked to see a female head. For this purpose, as generally in this class of phenomena, the curtain was completely closed. It only opened at the moment of the phenomena, but we could always see both hands, and sometimes Eva's head during the exposure. The face we wished for showed itself six or seven times, always to the medium's left, and at a level corresponding to the head of a person standing upright. During the second appearance of the phenomenon, I could quite clearly make out Eva's head and hands.

During the third experiment I concentrated my whole attention upon the medium, and again verified that she lay in her chair without participating. The head images were visible hardly a second. The well-developed face corresponded to that of a good-looking young woman, and the forehead was covered by a broad band. As the head fell down I followed it with my eyes, and I saw it hasten towards the head of the medium, where it disappeared, as if reabsorbed by her body. On one occasion we had the impression that the medium had risen and sat down again. This observation led us to increase our watchfulness. In other cases the materialised head, and the medium, could be seen at the same time. Immediately after one exposure Eva opened the curtain, came towards me, and requested me to examine her. I found nothing suspicious. She then re-entered the cabinet in a somnambulic state, while Richet followed her into the cabinet, and placed his hand on her forehead.

On continuing the sitting another flash-light photograph (Fig. 20) was taken. It shows the medium holding both curtains, while Mme. Bisson's hand attempts to put back the left curtain flap. A twisted band, about 16 feet long and resembling lace, and having traces of a pattern, hangs from the medium's upper coiffure nearly down to her feet. A portion of it is undoubtedly attached above her forehead to her hair, while the rest of it disappears over her head towards the back. The meshed tissue of the material is very similar to that which at the last sitting lay on her head. On the magnification of the picture (Fig. 21), we distinctly see the last joint of a thumb and forefinger emerging from Eva's hair, which appear to hold the material.

After this experiment the sitting closed, and a very thorough examination of the medium and cabinet gave no result.

Sitting of the 18th November 1910.

Present.—Professor C. Richet, Mme. Bisson, M. Chevreuil, and the author.

Conditions as usual.

Eva was this day under the influence of menstruation, which had just set in. She felt fatigued, and complained of subjective difficulties. The sitting began at 9 o'clock. We waited an hour without any result.

For the comprehension of one of the phenomena about to be described, it should be mentioned that in discussing with Mme. Bisson

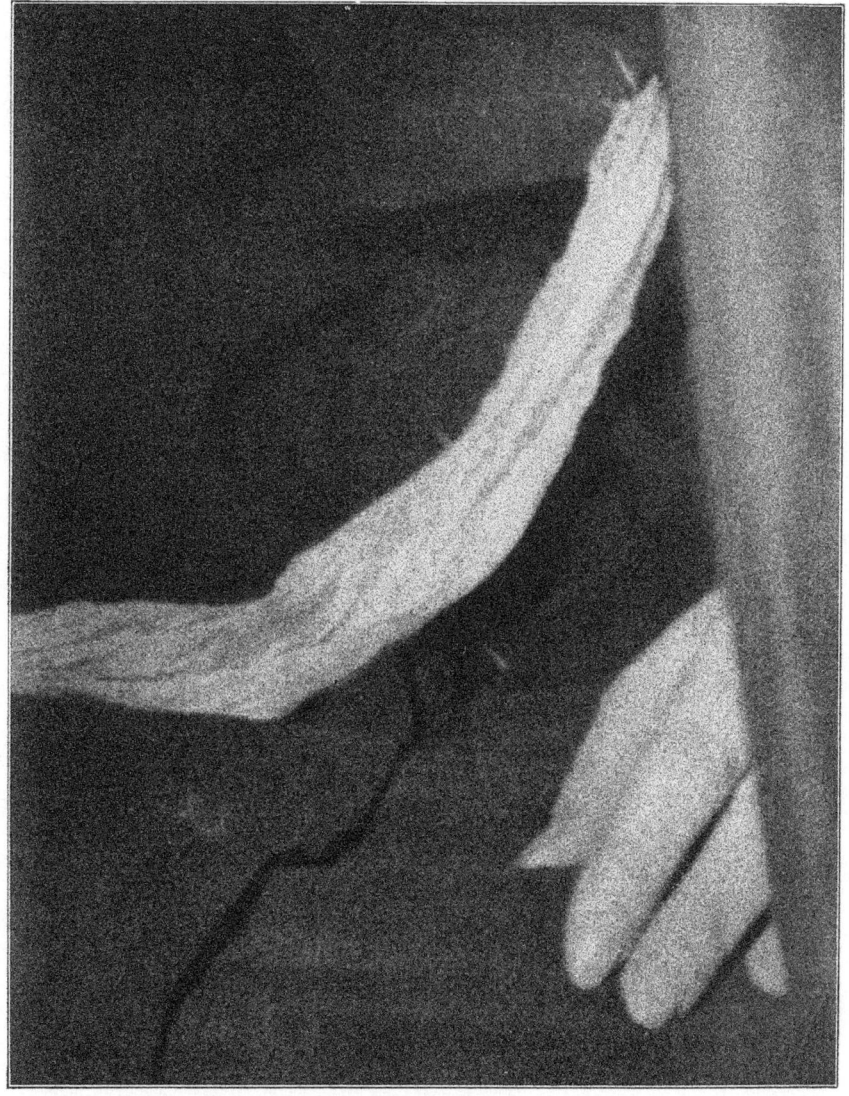

Fig. 19. Magnification of portion of Fig 18.

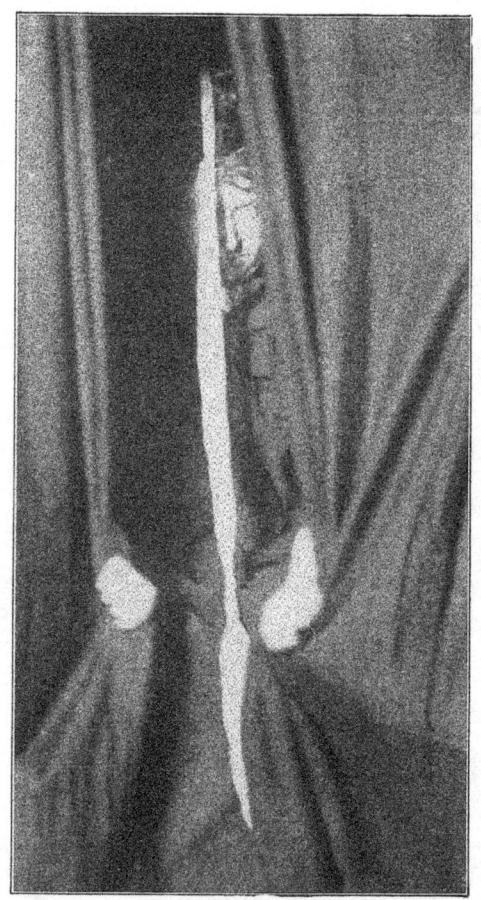

FIG. 20 FLASHLIGHT PHOTOGRAPH BY THE AUTHOR DURING SITTING OF 15 NOVEMBER, 1910.

the imperfect development of the photographic fingers, I had drawn attention to the absence of finger-nails.

After 10 o'clock the development of the teleplastic substance commenced. We saw in the opening of the curtain, while the medium's hands were visible and immobile, a broad luminous band, about 12 inches wide, in front of her chest, and then under her left arm, and also a white mass of material at the skirt of her dress, between her feet.

The simultaneous occurrence of teleplastic productions at the feet and under the arm is very remarkable, especially as its production occurred 2 feet from us, while the medium was quite visible and reclining tranquilly. Again we saw on her chest and in her lap some white ribbons and patches. The substance on her chest already gave an impression of solidity, and resembled a forearm, or a tibia, with hand and fingers, in skeleton form.

Exactly at the same place as before, *i.e.*, to the left of the left hand which lay on her knee, and about 12 or 15 inches above it, we saw a white shape emerging from the curtain, which disappeared again very rapidly.

During the next experiment (Fig. 22) Mme. Bisson held Eva's left, while I held her right in my left hand. All the hands were distinctly visible. At the same place as before a form became visible, which resembled a child's arm ending in a stump. It resembled an amputation stump. But this stump ended in three fingers (second and third joints only), whose total length was only about 1 or 1½ inch. This remarkable fragment was seen by all of us quite clearly. It was plastic, and otherwise resembled a living member. The shape approached my left hand, as it held Eva's right, and pressed two of the rudimentary finger stumps into the back of my left hand. The pressure lasted about two seconds, and was very firm, as if exerted by a cool, strong, moist male hand. The points of the nails were pressed firmly into my skin. This was probably in answer to the remarks I had made concerning the imperfection of the fingers photographed, and the intention may have been to prove to me, on my own body, that this intelligent creative power was also capable of producing finger-nails.

In order that there should not be the slightest doubt, the experiment was repeated three times. All those present saw the remarkable limb fragment during this phenomenon of contact. This performance was always accompanied by the groaning of the medium and an energetic display of will-power, just as was observed in the case of Eusapia Paladino. The manner in which the experiment was conducted, the control of the phenomenon through two senses, the simultaneous verification of the same appearance by all present, the absolute exclusion of any mechanical help by the medium, the threefold reproduction of the same experiment, and the rest of the conditions already stated, render this result free from any objection.

During the next experiment Richet held Eva's left hand while I held her right with my left. We wished to repeat the last experiment. I took the small metal box previously mentioned out of my pocket, opened it, and held it near the curtain, in the place where the shapes usually showed themselves, with the request that a portion of the teleplastic substance should be placed inside. Suddenly the box in my hand was seized by the stumpy fingers, one of them on the outside and the other inside, and was then forcibly pushed down, so that my hand, in spite of its resistance, was pressed down against my will. I saw the limb fragment, and heard how the porcelain dish rattled against the metallic case as the box was pushed down. This experiment also was twice repeated, rather slowly, taking three or four seconds. The medium's head was seen as a bright patch, and we held her hands. Again there was a great expenditure of energy and muscular contraction by the medium. This phenomenon was, therefore, perceived at the same time through the senses of sight, hearing, and touch.

The sitting then closed, and the subsequent examination was negative.

Sittings of December 1910 and January 1911.

AFTER the author's departure, in December 1910, the sittings were continued as usual twice a week. But no progress was recorded in the development of the phenomena, and at the beginning of December 1910 there was an unexpected interruption, as Mme. Bisson informed me by letter.

After the appearance of a number of teleplastic forms, at one of the sittings Eva requested Mme. Bisson to join hands with her through the gap in the curtain. This was done. Suddenly a strong, fully-developed, male forearm with hand became visible, seized the girl brutally against the breast and flung her violently back into the chair. The medium gave a cry of terror, and was so excited that the sitting had to be abandoned. It was several weeks before she recovered from the nervous shock, and it was Christmas before she was able to continue the experiments. This unwelcome interruption was probably the cause of the diminution of her mediumistic efficiency, which is clearly evident in the following series of sittings. The author considered it his duty, for the sake of an objective record, to mention this event, though it contradicts the experiences hitherto recorded ; but he refrains from drawing any conclusions.

SITTING OF THE 28TH DECEMBER 1910.

Conditions, illumination, and control as in the last sittings of November 1910.

Present.—M. M., Mme. Bisson, Professor B. (a German scientist), and the author.

Before the sitting three photographic cameras were set up by Professor B. and the author, a stereoscopic camera, and a camera taking pictures 9½ by 7 inches, about 10 feet in front of the curtain, and a camera 5½ by 3½ inches in the corner of the cabinet to the right of the medium. All three cameras had Zeiss lenses. The object of this

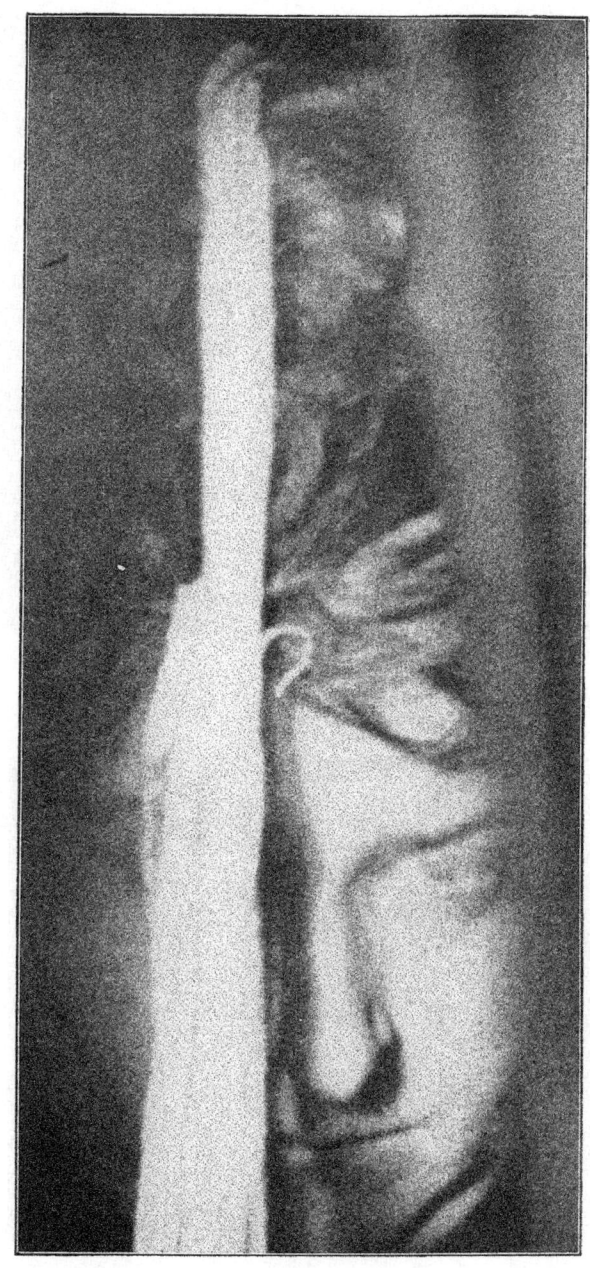

FIG. 21. MAGNIFICATION FROM FIG. 20.

Fig. 23. Photograph spoilt by wrong focussing. Flashlight at the sitting of 29 December, 1910.

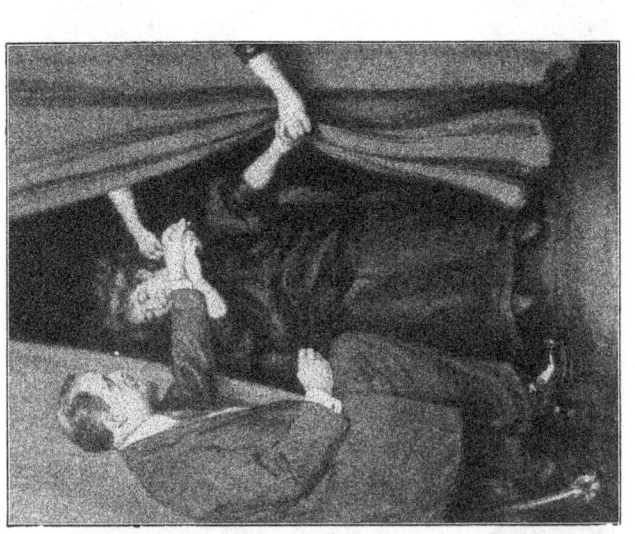

Fig. 22. Drawing after record of sitting of 18 November, 1910.

arrangement was to obtain side views of the various shapes, even if they were half covered by the curtain, as in some previous sittings. Unfortunately, the camera in the cabinet was, on account of the smallness of its field of view, not suitable for obtaining a picture of the occurrences at a distance of half a yard. Besides, everything not in the centre of the field would necessarily be out of focus. But the use of a photographic camera inside the cabinet means a considerable progress in the method of investigation, though the elaboration of this method requires the construction of special wide-angle lenses for photographing objects at close range.

Professor B., who only once before had attended a sitting (in a larger circle) conducted a specially careful and detailed investigation of the cabinet, of the chair on which Eva sat, and of the medium's dress. The bodily examination took place as usual before every sitting, while Mme. Bisson sewed the two garments together, but nothing suspicious was found. Professor B. took the place in front of the cabinet. The author sat at his left, Mme. Bisson at his right, and M. M. in the second row.

During the first half of the sitting Eva's hands remained visible on her knees and the curtains remained open. Immediately after the beginning of the sitting Mme. Bisson and the author perceived, on both the medium's shoulders, a barely visible luminosity which disappeared in the direction of her hips.

After about an hour, during which time the position of the hands was not changed, a pink luminous band, about 8 inches long, appeared to join the medium's two thumbs. It had rough, torn, and irregular edges, and changed its shape like india-rubber, some parts being bulkier than others. When the hands moved, this band contracted, and it became narrow on moving the hands apart. In some places the band was transparent, like a delicate veil. Its appearance might best be compared to an irregular, torn, and partly-twisted elastic and filmy band of tissue. It was observable for about a minute, and disappeared before our eyes, without our seeing any noticeable movement of the medium's hands. Shortly afterwards a thread-like band became visible, which ran down the middle of the dress from the knees to the feet, and corresponded, in length, to that of the medium's shins. This also disappeared very rapidly.

I then expressed the wish to see a freely suspended hand a little higher than her head, between the curtains. This point, as found by subsequent measurements, is about 3 feet away from the medium's head when she reclines as usual against the back of the chair, while the chair itself is always so placed that the curtains can be closed immediately in front of the medium's knees. When the hands rest on the knees this distance is exactly 27 inches. The cameras were focused on this point in this and in the following sittings. If the medium moves her head forward or takes hold of the curtain with her hands, it may alter this distance from 4 to 8 inches. But even then the distance from the body of the medium would be at least $1\frac{1}{2}$ feet.

A considerable time after the phenomena described had taken place, and after the curtain had been closed several times, thus hiding the hands, the distinct form of a hand appeared four times in succession, in the place indicated. Once it was a female left hand, with fingers longer than those of the medium.

F

The hands hardly remained visible for a second, so that it was not possible to concentrate the attention and the gaze upon Eva's body at the same time.

I succeeded, indeed, twice, and Professor B. once, in perceiving the medium's hands resting in her lap, while the third hand was visible. The author could distinctly see movements of the separate fingers of the hand shown (bending and stretching). Eva was unable to continue the sitting, and it had to be closed.

SITTING OF THE 29TH DECEMBER 1910.

Present.—M. .M., Professor B., Mme. Bisson, and the author.

When the medium put on the knitted hose garment, before the sitting, Mme Bisson, in my presence, introduced her finger into the medium's vagina. She was also explored by Professor B. and the author through the garment, but with negative result.

Assuming that a female medium wished to use the vagina as a hiding-place for closely rolled packets, *e.g.*, chiffon gauze, she would have to attach some kind of cord or ribbon to the packet beforehand, in order to be able to withdraw it. This cord would be detected during the exploration at the mouth of the vagina, and any finger introduced into the vagina would feel the foreign body. In the case of persons with a very wide vaginal entrance, it might be possible to withdraw the packet by means of the fingers, deeply inserted. But such a manipulation supposes that the genitals are not separated from the hand by any partition, even a knitted one, and that the person is in a standing or reclining position. She might have touched the external genitals through the garment, but could not have penetrated to any depth.

The hiding of objects in the anal aperture, and their withdrawal from it, is even less possible, on account of its closure by a firm ring muscle, which hinders the introduction of a finger. Hidden packets can only be withdrawn by means of a cord of suitable strength, the external end of which would have been immediately discovered during the corporeal examination ; but never with the sole help of the person's own finger.

The restoration of the material to its hiding-place would be even more difficult. It presupposes a careful folding-up and packing in the darkness of the cabinet. An introduction of the packet into the anal opening would be almost unthinkable without the use of vaseline. But all such manipulations are doubly difficult in the dark.

The bodily, and especially the gynæcological, examination, the sewing-up of the tights to the dress, of the dress at the neck and wrists, dispose of these objections, since the medium cannot touch her own skin except at the head. Besides, the manner of appearance and disappearance, and the automatism of the materials and forms produced, tell against the possibility of fraud.

As soon as Professor B. had convinced himself that Eva had no material or apparatus concealed about her person, the sitting commenced in the usual way. The examination of the cabinet, illumination, hypnotisation, as usual.

After about half an hour's waiting a bright patch appeared under

SITTINGS OF DECEMBER 1910 AND JANUARY 1911

the medium's left hand. Eva opened and closed the curtain several times, thus alternately exposing the patch to illumination and shading it. Eventually it grew towards the upper arm and the right hand, so that it had a rectangular appearance. Length, 12 to 14 inches; width, about 4 inches. She then took both my hands and brought the first finger of my left hand towards the material lying in her lap. I was surprised when my finger touched a firm, hard, rounded object, with a rough surface. The sensation was like touching a rough bone. The object I touched appeared of a pink colour, and lay on the medium's left thigh.

We then asked to see a hand. After a pause of ten minutes, during which the curtain remained closed, she opened the curtain again. A broad white band fell like a veil from the left upper side into the lap, like a flowing mass. The portion on her lap seemed mobile and changed its shape. We could distinctly see stripes, and the slowly developing design of a limb. Eva's hands clutched the curtains, and at that moment I ignited the flash-light (Fig. 23).

The curtain had immediately to be closed, since Eva whimpered and groaned in great fright.

Finally we saw, during a quick opening and shutting of the curtain, a veiled female face, probably the face of the medium. Eva's hands then became hot, always a sign that she could not produce anything more. A renewed and minute examination of the medium, as well as the chair and cabinet, after the sitting, had no result. As soon as she had changed her dress Professor B. examined the séance dress, to see if any moisture adhered to it, but nothing suspicious was found. The sitting closed at 11.30.

Unfortunately, the photographic record is not clear. The camera (7 by $9\frac{1}{2}$ inches) obviously stood too near the curtain, so that the medium's left hand, holding the curtain, cannot be distinctly recognised. We see the white material falling from a point on a level with Eva's head, out of the curtain over her left shoulder into her lap, but without any detail. The shape of the mass resembles, in its rough outlines, a lower leg with ankle and foot in the course of formation.

On the basis of this photograph we can only assert that it confirms and amplifies our optical impression, and therefore offers a strong argument for the actuality of this mediumistic process, under the precautions described. It should be noticed that the material emerges from the left curtain at a point higher than Eva's head, although her left hand was visible to us holding the curtain.

SITTING OF THE 3RD JANUARY 1911.

No result. Eva had been on the 1st and 2nd January staying with friends, and was still probably under the diverting influence of their hospitality.

SITTING OF THE 4TH JANUARY 1911.

Present.—Mme. Bisson, her sister, and the author.

Conditions as before. Complete, including gynæcological, examination. Commencement, 10.30. The first phenomena appeared at 11.30.

Eva meanwhile breathed deeply and audibly, showing light tremors, and had cold and moist hands. She gave an impression of suffering.

Several times Mme. Bisson, who sat on a low wicker chair in front of the curtain, had to hold her hands. Under these conditions we saw at a level of 17 inches above Eva's visible hands, which were held by those present, some well-developed structures, resembling limbs emerging from the curtain on the left, at a distance of 20 to 23 inches from her head. These objects appeared eight times in succession. The medium requested me to bring my head near the aperture of the curtain. In order to entice the apparition further outside, I brought my forehead closer, but not sufficiently so. Twice this hand-shaped structure attempted by very rapid motion to reach my forehead, but without success. When I further reduced the distance, I twice felt a strong and distinct touch on my forehead, while the medium appeared to make a great muscular effort. The touch resembled that of a broad, strongly-developed finger of a large male hand (or a big toe?). I distinctly felt the pressure as from a soft finger-tip, together with the feeling of cool and moist human skin. Just as a gymnast contracts the muscles of his body with an extreme effort of will in order to bring about a single extraordinary muscular feat, so Eva, with many gasps and groans, endeavoured to bring about a contact by means of this structure, which was obviously amenable to psychic direction. The course of this phenomenon was characteristic, and was observed by me in the same manner in the case of Eusapia Paladino, although the two mediums had never seen each other in their lives.

The duration of contact might have been one or two seconds, but the structures stretched forward remained visible hardly one second, so that one can only state the fact without saying anything about the detailed building-up of the limbs. And, generally, the appearances are the more fugitive the less close the connection with the body of the medium, while the phenomena taking place at the body itself show a greater durability under light and observation.

Again, we saw at the same part of the left curtain a white form about 8 inches long and 4 inches wide. The medium called out " prenez-le." I pressed the electric button. The light flared up, and convinced that I had this time obtained a specially interesting photograph, I took charge of the closed slides.

It should be mentioned that during the last phenomena Eva's hands held both sides of the curtain, and were, therefore, distinctly visible. This time, also, the sudden interruption of the phenomena by the light meant the end of the sitting. But before I had asked for Eva's awakening she requested Mme. Bisson to unpick the seam between tights and dress. When this was done, she asked me to examine her. In the course of the gynæcological examination I introduced the middle finger of my right hand pretty deep into the vagina, without, however, finding anything beyond a softening of the epithelium. It is, therefore, certain that the genital passage was not used as a hiding-place. Eva was awakened, and passed a restless, sleepless night. The sitting closed at midnight

To our great surprise the development of the plate gave a negative result. The photographs as such are successful, especially the stereoscopic ones. Eva lies on the chair with her body stretched out, and her head rests on the back of the chair, which is quite visible. The mouth and eyes are tightly compressed, and the face screwed up as if blinded by the light. Her arms are stretched out, and both hands clutch the sides of the curtain, so that they are visible with the fingers outward.

The camera mounted inside the cabinet (Fig. 24) showed a portion of the left curtain from the inside. Embedded in its folds one sees a white, round sphere with a shadowy patch above it. Above the shadow is a faintly illuminated broad cross-streak of a cloudy character. The first impression made by the photograph upon photographic experts is that the white sphere is a flare spot produced by the diaphragm of the camera in consequence of a reflection. In this sense the second cloudy circle, which becomes visible upon magnification, and partly covers the first circle, is also interpreted. On the other hand, no reflecting objects were contained in the cabinet, and the white patch gives the impression of a real solid ball rather than of a circle. The view is confirmed by the manner in which the feebler cloudy structure forms a slanting cover towards the back. But assuming the circle were the result of reflection, how shall we explain the misty luminosity extending downwards and getting brighter below on which the sphere is lying? Also, the broad, cloudy cross-band above the sphere. These two things are not due to errors or accidents during exposure, but correspond to structures really present.

We must also remember that white luminous balls have been seen by numerous observers of materialisation phenomena, and have been described by them as preliminary stages.

Finally, it is also remarkable that the sphere and the luminous streaks were photographed at the very spot on the hem of the curtain where I saw the white substance emerge beyond the curtain at the moment of photography. We must, therefore, reckon with the possibility that the white-formed substance observed by us changed into the shape of a sphere. But the retrogressive process, and the displacement towards the origin, occurred more quickly than the ignition of the flash-light by the button. Now it is quite possible that the camera in the cabinet may have photographed a fragment of the mass, in retrogressive development, as it retired behind the curtain.

Taken by themselves, the feeble photographic results of this sitting prove little or nothing. In connection with previous results they tell against any suspicion of a possible fraudulent arrangement of the occurrences. But for the investigator who sees here the working of unknown forces, any detail, however small, may become significant. The discussion of these side issues, therefore, appeared desirable.

SITTING OF THE 6TH JANUARY 1911.

Present.— Mme. Bisson, M. M., and the author.

Conditions as before. An external examination of genitals through the tights gave a negative result.

After nearly an hour's waiting, a bright luminosity appeared under the medium's left arm. While the medium, as usual, clutched the sides of the curtain, her hands being visible during the whole phenomena of this sitting, a small arm with hand appeared on the left, but hardly remained visible a second. In the short time no details could be observed.

After this we saw an equally fugitive, but recognisable, male hand (Fig. 25) in side view, with its thumb in front, and its finger stretched upwards. As already stated, the distance between the hand and the medium's head was from 20 to 27 inches, and the distance from her hands 16 to 24 inches.

While Eva held both curtains and moved them to and fro, a narrow bright band developed between her hands, and increased to a width of 3 inches and a length of 12 to 14 inches. The material appeared to be elastic, viscous, and endowed with a mobility of its own. Before our eyes it transformed itself into the shape of a human forearm, which was rather long and provided with a hand. The latter lay across the right hand of the medium, while the elbow portion lay on the base of the thumb of the medium's left hand and vanished behind the curtain. The strip then became thinner again. Eva closed the curtain for a moment, and when she opened it again the same play of a more or less liquid, variable form recommenced. This time it corresponded to a human lower leg, the sole of the foot touching the medium's right, and the toes being directed upwards. The knee portion disappeared above her left hand behind the curtain.

This whole metamorphosis resisted the influence of the light and of our gaze unusually long, perhaps sixty seconds, but never showed a permanent firm shape. The constantly changing momentary creations only resembled human limbs in their outline.

Before awakening, Eva again asked for the tights to be detached from the dress and submitted to a gynæcological examination. The introduction of my right middle finger into the vagina gave a negative result, as did the remaining examination of medium, dress, cabinet, and chair.

Sittings of March and April 1911 (Paris).

SITTING OF THE 13TH MARCH 1911.

Present.—Mme. Bisson, her sister, Professor Richet, M. de Fontenay and the author.

Time of Sitting.—10 to 11.30.

Illumination and control as in previous sittings. Arrangement.— Mme. Bisson in the centre, in front of the curtain; the author on her left; Richet on her right; De Fontenay in the second row.

The cameras were set up by me before the sitting at a distance of 10 feet, one camera for plates 7 by 9½ inches, and a stereoscopic camera. In addition, De Fontenay set up a "veroscope," at a distance of 10 feet and a height of 6 feet, on the wardrobe.

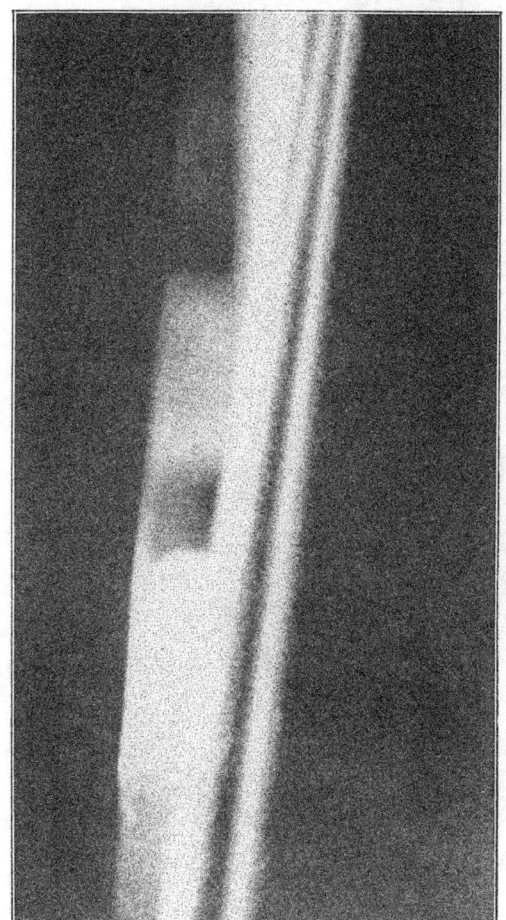

FIG 24. PHOTOGRAPH TAKEN BY FLASHLIGHT WITH CAMERA INSIDE THE CABINET. (SITTING OF 4 JANUARY, 1911).

Fig. 25. Drawing after the record of sitting of 6 January, 1911.

SITTINGS OF MARCH AND APRIL 1911 (PARIS)

The phenomena began about twenty to twenty-five minutes after the commencement of the sitting. When the curtain opened for the first time the medium's hands rested on her knees. The skirt had subsided between her knees, and in this depression we saw a whitish, jelly-like material, 8 or 10 inches long and about 6 inches wide, and endowed with its own mobility. On approaching my head I could distinctly make out the form of the hand of a child of one or two years. The half-flexed first finger and thumb were directed towards us. The other three fingers disappeared downwards. The whole structure exhibited a rather inert motion, and remained visible for one or two minutes. During this time, Eva opened and closed the curtain several times. In the ensuing part of the sitting hands, of various shapes and sizes, appeared from the right and left of the curtain. Several times they appeared in the medium's lap, where they remained longer than the others (several seconds), and could, therefore, be more carefully observed. The visual impressions interpreted by us as hands were manifested about thirty times, while the medium's hands were visible on her lap all the time, or were holding the curtains. In some cases the curtain before us fell so far over the medium's right knee that the left hand disappeared from my view. In such cases I asked Professor Richet, who sat on the right, whether he could see the medium's right hand from his side, and he always answered in the affirmative.

It is impossible to describe at all adequately the impressions we obtained. Out of a rich store a few are worthy of special mention. Thus, I saw a small closed female hand, which appeared to be wrapped in a veil, the end of which hung down. From this I distinctly saw two finely modelled female fingers emerge. On the first finger I could see the shape of a nail. The phenomenon lasted about three seconds and was repeated several times, being withdrawn behind the curtain and then again emerging into the light. Another, and rather better developed hand was exposed at the same place, *i.e.*, to the right of the medium, and appeared to be a large male hand, with partially flexed fingers. I observed one of these fingers carefully, and compared it with those of the medium's visible hand. It was twice as large as Eva's fingers.

During another phenomenon, which took place to the left of the medium, the hand of an adult appeared as a white compact mass, in which the formation of a hand and fingers could be distinguished in low relief. The whole thing recalled a white block of marble, from which only the profiles of fingers and hand emerged, while the interstices between the fingers were filled with the mass.

During one such materialisation Richet held the left and the author the right hand of the medium. The curtain was pretty widely open. Suddenly, out of the dark on the left of the medium's head, a hand and forearm, visible up to the elbow, appeared with a downward motion towards the medium's lap. At the same time a hand became visible at the level of her shoulder. I could not distinctly see this hand on account of my sitting on the left, whereas the other persons could see the phenomenon better. No details could be made out beside the unmistakable outlines.

In contrast with this, and while the medium grasped both curtains with her hands, a white patch formed between her feet in front of us, and from this a white column of smoke curled upward (Fig. 26). At its upper end a distinctly visible hand formed, ascending to Eva's knees, and then disappearing.

When another hand was observed on my left, *i.e.*, to the right of the medium, I quickly inserted my head behind the curtain and saw that this hand, thrust into the illuminated portion of the gap, was attached to a white column which had the approximate length of an adult's forearm. It emerged from the elbow-joint of the medium in an upward and forward direction half to the left, while her own forearm rested on her right thigh, so that two forearms appeared to issue from her elbow. Although shaded by the curtain, the appearance, owing to its light grey or almost white colour, was bright enough to be distinctly seen against the faintly illuminated background. The hand itself moved, the fingers bending and stretching. The whole emanation did not last long enough to perceive any details.

After this we saw a white mass developing on her breast, starting from her neck. During its development Eva gave Richet her left and the author her right hand, and expressed a wish to be photographed in that situation. Though closely observing this self-moving and evervarying substance, I did not succeed in recognising a perfectly clearly materialised hand. Fearing lest the mass might disappear again, I gave, after about thirty seconds, the sign to switch on the electric current.

The three photographs (Fig. 27) are quite successful, and will be described at the end of this record. The curtain was at once closed, in order to allow Eva to recover from the shock.

Although in other sittings the flash-light exposure generally meant the end of the phenomena, this time the medium was able to continue her performances. We saw several veiled heads on Eva's left, and at about the height of a person standing upright, but these hardly remained visible a second.

The medium several times requested Mme. Bisson to hypnotise her by laying her hand on her forehead. The lady of the house entered the cabinet and closed the curtain behind her. As she was emerging, and closing the curtain behind her, a veiled female head became momentarily visible. The whole occurrence took place with such rapidity that the head had already disappeared at the second opening of the curtain, even before Mme. Bisson had sat down. The medium repeated this experiment three or four times, calling her protectress into the cabinet each time. The bodily contact with her seemed to strengthen and soothe Eva. The impression made was as if Mme. Bisson were about to draw the picture of the head, by an invisible thread, out of the curtain behind her.

The mixed series of heads, amounting to about a dozen, shows some variations. In one case a rather long bright fragment hung down from the nose or chin of the materialisation. On another occasion the figure recalled the head of an incompletely sculptured marble bust, as in the case of the hand previously described.

Although I was unable, from my seat, to see Eva's head at the same time, I did not have the impression that she could have produced these

FIG 26   DRAWING AFTER RECORD OF SITTING OF
13 MARCH 1911.

FIG. 27. FLASHLIGHT PHOTOGRAPH BY THE AUTHOR, 13 MARCH, 1911.

SITTINGS OF MARCH AND APRIL 1911 (PARIS)

faces, which appeared instantaneously, as if projected by a magic lantern, by means of her head alone. The time available for putting on, or removing, a mask, and setting up and dismantling the phantom, only amounted to one or two seconds in most cases. Another head, emerging from the curtain on the left, distinctly showed female features, eyes, and veil. The nose resembled Eva's nose, and the phenomenon recalled the photograph of the 13th May 1910. Whether, in this last case, the medium had risen, and had shown herself to us veiled ("transfigured"), cannot be decided. This is possible, although the picture itself appeared finer, more ethereal and delicate than Eva's face.

This day's experiments were remarkable for the sculptural character of the teleplastic projections. Some of the head and hand shapes resembled unfinished plastic works of marble, plaster, or clay, on a white background. Perhaps this extraordinary circumstance is explained by the fact that Eva inhabits a room connected with Mme. Bisson's studio. She is surrounded by sculptures of all sorts, and has, through the artistic activity of her protectress, daily opportunities of observing the various phases of the development of such products. Memory images of this kind may have influenced her mediumistic productions.

The last remarkable phenomenon of this sitting was the emergence of an extraordinarily voluminous mass of white fabric from the roof of the cabinet, and mainly from the strip hiding the suspension of the curtains at a height of 7 feet. It resembled a large bundle of muslin, entering the gap of the curtains from above, and falling down and disappearing in the dark. The quantity would have sufficed to clothe an adult person completely. In this, and the previous occurrences, Eva's hands held the curtains, and opened them at each new phenomenon. Half an hour after the flash-light exposure the sitting was closed. Still in the hypnotic condition, Eva took off the tights and asked to be gynæcologically examined. This and the rest of the examination was negative.

The photograph of the 13th March 1911 shows the medium in the cabinet on her chair, with her face turned to the right and painfully drawn. Her left hand is held by Professor Richet and her right by the author.

From the opening of her dress at the neck a white, flocculent mass of material, about 6 inches wide in the middle, extends over her chest to her right thigh, forming a voluminous package of material in her lap, and then falling down outside over her left thigh, and ending in a point.

The stereoscopic image, taken from the wardrobe, distinctly shows the round hem of the neck opening. The substance is not, therefore, as one might conclude from the photographs, taken at the same level, tucked in like a napkin, but is freely fixed to the material of the dress.

The mass itself is not a uniform structure like, *e.g.*, a large piece of muslin, but shows a loose consistency with quite a rough exterior, like fur or wadding, composed of a bundle of stripes and cords, resembling lint or wool, intermixed with transparent veiling. The stereoscopic transparency shows the structure more clearly than the simple photograph. Just in the middle, on Eva's breast, there lies a solid piece of a flat white substance, larger than a hand, and resembling a white paper glove. One also distinctly sees four finger-tips, two of which are flattened and bent upwards, also an excrescence pointed upwards, and above it a solid, round, plastic structure recalling a thumb-joint with a nail. The flat white and sharply bordered piece also emerges in a point from under the substance on the right side, and can be recognised through the substance lying over it.

On her left shoulder is a flat form resembling a hand, with an extra long thumb; the finger-tips bent upwards, and the little finger twisted about its own axis. This shape resembles not so much a glove as a very fine, soft, white paper shape. Any one who is not familiar with the observation of mediumistic processes will jump to the conclusion that this is gross fraud, and will see an intention of producing the optical impression of hands, by means of rough models made of some fibrous material. Here, again, the examination of the photograph alone is not sufficient to form a judgment. One must take into account the record of the sitting in conjunction with further data.

Sittings of the 8th and 18th April.

An unusually interesting photograph (Fig. 28) was taken by M. de Fontenay at the sitting of the 8th April 1911, in the author's absence. Eva sits on the chair, both her hands being held by two gentlemen present. A broad scarf-shaped band, with a distinctly parallel striping, runs across her head, entirely covering it nearly down to the forehead. The left portion falls over the breast in the shape of two long fibrous fragments, while the other end of the shawl, lying more in the shade on the right, or darker in colour, also consists of parallel stripes, and allows two white rounded ends, of a plastic appearance, to emerge below, producing the distinct impression of plastically modelled fingers. The photograph (Fig. 29) taken by De Fontenay on the 18th April is also instructive when the stereoscopic transparency is examined. While Eva's hands are being held and the curtain is wide open, the medium is seen on her chair with her head bent forward. Over the back of it there is something like a broad cloth, adhering to the hair like soft and yielding material, and extended like a shawl. The two ends hang down on both sides to the middle of Eva's chest, the left portion ending in a leaf-shaped branch, turning and widening upwards. The whole appears to consist of one piece, as shown in the photograph. This photograph is remarkable by the fact of the fabric being thick, soft, and yielding at the top, like a woollen material, while the two extremities, hanging down, give the appearance of a thin, sharply bordered, flat structure, resembling paper. This clearly marked contrast in the consistency of the same piece of material is remarkable.

If the teleplasma can undergo such changes, this picture may be regarded as an instructive preparation for the flat, sharply bordered materials, resembling paper, occuring so often at later sittings, as, for instance, in the portraits of heads.

Fig. 28. Flashlight photograph taken by Mons de Fontenay at sitting of 8 April, 1911.

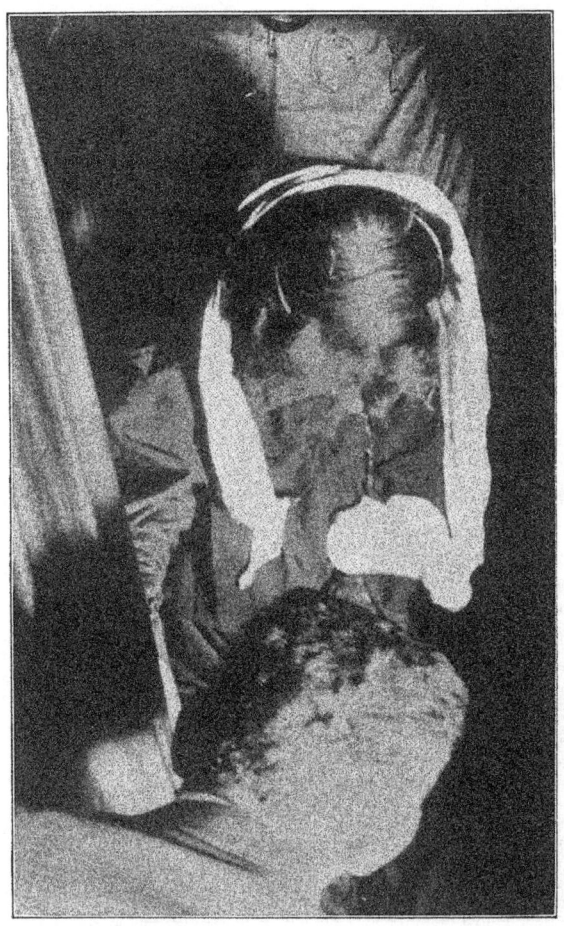

FIG 29 FLASHLIGHT PHOTOGRAPH BY MONS. DE FONTENAY AT SITTING OF 18 APRIL, 1911.

Sittings of May and June 1911 (Paris).

THE experiments undertaken between 13th March and 8th May 1911 neither showed any progress, nor any deviations, from the previous phenomena. More than two-thirds of these sittings were negative, and the positive phenomena fell short of previous performances. My arrival in Paris on 8th May 1911 occurred during this unfavourable period.

The first four sittings at which I was present, 8th to 23rd May, were without result, and one sitting had to be abandoned on account of the sickness of the medium. The first change in Eva's condition took place at 8 P.M. on the 18th May, when Mme. Bisson had, as usual, hypnotised the medium. While the latter was alone with the medium in the cabinet, a smoke-like substance suddenly began to emanate from Eva's mouth, while her hands were being held. In order not to weaken the medium, in view of the sitting arranged for the next evening, the hypnotisation was stopped. Still, the sitting on the 19th May remained negative.

SITTING OF THE 23RD MAY 1911.

Present.—M. de Fontenay, Mme. Bisson, and the author.

The conditions were the same as regards inspection and control of the medium and cabinet, as well as dress and illumination. On this day only three electric lamps were lighted, since the electric circuit had become defective.

This, however, did not make any perceptible difference to the lighting of the room.

Although no less than seven photographic cameras had been set up, no flash-light photographs were taken, on account of the short visibility of the very unstable phenomena.

After waiting three-quarters of an hour, a grey and gradually growing mass was seen on the medium's lap, about the size of a large cocoa-nut. Eva's hands were visibly clutching the curtains. The mass of material appeared to weigh down Eva's thin dress, sank in the depression of the dress, and changed its shape with an independent motion. Looking closer, I recognised the form of a very small child's hand, which, however, did not remain there long. Eva drew the curtains together. After this some forms in the shape of hands appeared, on the left-hand side, at the part of the curtain before referred to, but these were too fugitive to make out any detail.

At Eva's wish the participators, one after the other, approached their foreheads to the curtain and were touched several times. The pressure perceived by the author at such a contact was always that of a fairly large member, having a cool, hard skin. For a finger the mass producing the contact seemed to be fairly broad, and reminded me rather of a large toe, or the thumb of an unusually large hand. To eliminate any doubt, I repeatedly made sure during the experiment that Eva's left knee had not left its place.

PHENOMENA OF MATERIALISATION

The author therefore reasoned as follows :—

If the hand, or whatever member it may be, is as clearly developed as the touch suggests, it should be able to grasp and hold an object.

With this idea he took a piece of cardboard, the size of a post-card, out of his pocket, and held it in the place where the member appeared, requesting it to take hold of the cardboard. Immediately there were attempts to grasp the cardboard, but without success. The cardboard was clearly touched, moved to and fro, and pressed against my hand, but without being really grasped. Perhaps the object was unsuitable. I therefore put it away and held out my handkerchief. It was immediately seized, and was pulled out of my hand and thrown behind the curtain with a violent jerk. Afterwards it was found to the left of the medium on the floor. I then held up a golden brooch belonging to Mme. Bisson, provided with four short golden chains with breloques (4 inches long and weighing one and a third ounces). The brooch was also grasped by the ends of the chain, pulled to and fro as if in play, and then thrown with a strong jerk behind the curtain, where it fell to the ground.

During this phenomenon Eva's hands were held by M. de Fontenay and myself. Her head lay in the shade of the curtain, on the back of the chair. Eva talked during these occurrences, so that the mechanical participation of her mouth is excluded. The last performance had fatigued the medium to such an extent that the sitting had to be closed.

For the critical discussion of these observations it should be pointed out that although the three experiments were extemporised, they still succeeded. They could, therefore, not have been prepared for in any way.

Final control negative.

SITTING OF THE 24TH MAY 1911.

Conditions, participators, and cameras as on 23rd May.

The medium passed the night of the 23rd-24th without sleep. Yet she wished for a further sitting on the 24th.

During the first hour Eva lay obviously in a deep sleep, and did not attempt to produce phenomena. She appeared unconscious and unconcerned. Her regular breathing was the only audible sign of life. According to our experience no phenomena occur during this stage of deep somnolence. As soon as a partial awakening from the deep sleep occurs, and a stage of active somnambulism sets in, in which the second personality dominates Eva's reduced consciousness, mediumistic performances may be expected.[1]

During the phenomena there is always a spiritual connection of the medium with those present, even when the medium appears sunk in a passive lethargy and quite taken up with the act of production. But, as a rule, she takes part in the conversation of those present, puts in remarks or instructions, and sometimes asks questions, *e.g.*, whether

[1] This is an individual peculiarity, and not common to all mediums.

the developing creation is already visible to us. As before mentioned, Eva's personality reappears in the somnambulic state, but combined with an increase in her mental functions.

During the deep sleep the connection with the external world is almost broken off. The deep sleep may often be converted into the half-awakened state of consciousness by verbal suggestion, unless it occurs spontaneously after some time. On this occasion Eva began to enter the state of active somnambulism after about an hour. She gave signs of life, entered into the conversation, and showed, by blowing actions of the mouth and deep audible respirations, the endeavour to materialise.

The somnambulist appeared anxious to continue where she had left off the day before. Just as was described in the last sitting, we saw plastically developed hand shapes emerge several times in succession from the left curtain, in the same place as before. On my stretching forward my left hand it was touched several times on its palm, and again I had the impression of being touched by a big toe. An attempt at photography failed, the phenomenon having disappeared at the moment of the flash. After the photograph, a forearm and hand became visible, and a fist appeared at right angles to her right hand. Those present were several times touched on the forehead and hand. Final examination negative. Close of the sitting, 11.15 P.M., after a duration of an hour and a half.

SITTING OF THE 27TH MAY 1911.

Present.—M. S., Mme. Bisson, and the author.

Three cameras; conditions and illumination as on the 23rd.

The whole sitting lasted twenty minutes, and showed nothing new.

A nebulous mass was seen in the medium's lap, and fugitive shapes, of very short duration, between the curtains.

SITTING OF THE 29TH MAY 1911.

Present.—M. de Fontenay, Mme. Bisson, and the author.

Conditions as on 23rd May. Six cameras. A camera, specially prepared for close-range photographs, was attached to the wall in the cabinet on the medium's right. Three cameras faced the medium, and two were on the wardrobe.

The kind of phenomena seen did not differ from those of the last sittings. Some forms, resembling human members, became visible at the curtain to the left of the medium, about 2 feet above her hands, and about 32 inches from her head. Touches on the forehead and hand, as in previous sittings. The skin was hard and cool, and the touching surface was wider than a finger.

The failure of the last photographic exposure suggested to the author the idea of providing for the rapidly disappearing structure a point of attachment (Fig. 29).

PHENOMENA OF MATERIALISATION

I took a cigarette from my case and requested the medium to grasp the cigarette when held against the curtain gap by means of the materialised structure. Since I had no success, Mme. Bisson held the cigarette towards the spot described. At the moment when the structure approached the cigarette, touched it and became visible, the flash-light was ignited.

Eva's hands at that moment grasped the curtain. In spite of the nervous shock consequent on the photograph, the phenomena continued. Among these should be mentioned the appearance of a small child's hands between Eva's hands, as they rested on her knees. This hand lay across the medium's lap, opened and closed into a fist. It also several times beat with its palm upon the back of Eva's right hand, and we could distinctly hear the clapping sound. In this case, therefore, the visual impression was confirmed by the sense of hearing.

At Eva's request, Mme. Bisson then took both the medium's hands in hers. Even under those conditions the small mobile hand remained visible.

Final control negative. Sitting closed at 11.30.

The negative (Fig. 30) produced by the camera facing the cabinet (7 by 9½ inches) shows in the background the medium's face with the mouth half open, both hands in the foreground grasping the curtain. Above the left hand, about the level of the medium's head, we see a portion of a plastically-formed member in a curious foreshortening. It is undoubtedly a left foot. One sees the big toe as if seen from below, with a distinct fold of skin on the ball of the foot, and the tips of the second and third toes. The lower surface of the big toe projects beyond the horizontally-held cigarette, so that the latter nearly touches the tip of the second toe. It looks like an attempt to hold the cigarette between the first and second toe. The stereoscopic apparatus confirms the picture, and particularly the plastic formation of the member.

The cameras standing on the wardrobe, and being pointed down from above, give a different picture, in this sense—that one sees the cigarette lower, and the first and second toe projecting beyond it. A careful examination of the magnified photographs eliminated any doubts that this member could be anything but the point of a foot. The author's first impression was that it belonged to the medium's left foot.

In order to examine this question in greater detail, I went as soon as the plate had been developed, i.e., before either Mme. Bisson or the medium knew the result, to the séance room, and made them give me the black knitted tights used by Eva for the sittings.

The material covering the sole of the left foot did indeed show some holes nearly an inch wide, apparently due to ordinary wear, but not large enough to allow the three toes and the ball of the foot to pass through—these amounting to about one-third of the foot, according to the photograph.

Further investigations with the medium in the cabinet show that it is impossible for Eva to raise her left foot so high, and to put it in the place where the toes were photographed, while maintaining the upright position shown in the photograph.

Fig 30. Flashlight photograph by the author,
29 May, 1911.

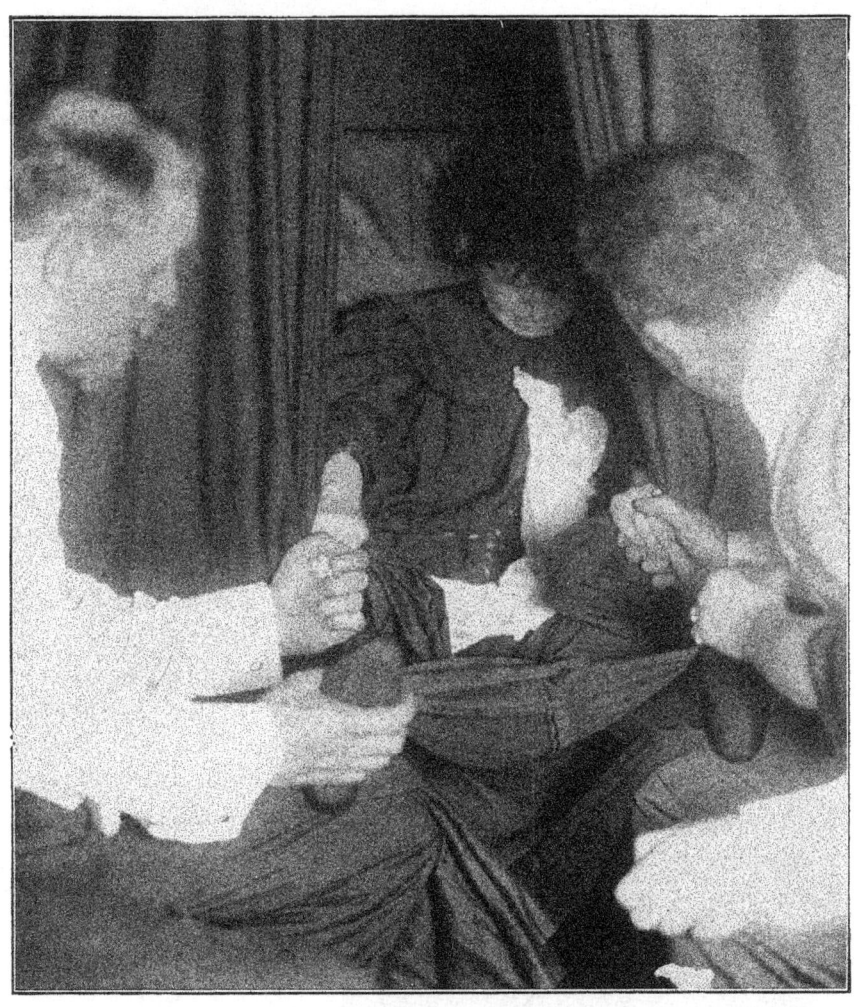

FIG. 31. FLASHLIGHT PHOTOGRAPH BY THE AUTHOR, 7 JUNE, 1911.

SITTINGS OF MAY AND JUNE 1911 (PARIS)

The left leg would have had to be raised outside the left arm. Finally, the size and the build of Eva's left foot do not accord with the structure photographed. Measured by comparison with the length of the cigarette, the medium's big toe is relatively larger than the toe photographed. Although, on our part, all possible objections were investigated, the evidential force of this photograph does suffer by the presence of the holes in the sole of the stocking. In order to guard against such a source of error in the future, the author bought a new pair of black woollen tights, made in one piece, which extended from the feet to above the hips. These were regularly used in the following sittings.

SITTINGS OF THE 3RD AND 6TH JUNE 1911.

Without result.

SITTING OF THE 7TH JUNE 1911.

Present.—M. de Fontenay, Mme. Bisson, and the author.

Sitting commenced at 9.30 P.M. The defective electric lamp having been repaired, four electric lamps lighted up the room during the whole sitting. Conditions and control as usual. Eva this day wore the new tights. She undressed in the séance room and put on the séance costume in our presence, after we had carefully examined it.

Five cameras were ready, two on the wardrobe, two facing the curtain at a distance of 10 feet, and one in the cabinet, which, as usual, had been carefully searched.

Obviously, in consequence of the discussion of the toes photographed, the medium demanded a special control of her feet. She stretched herself on her chair, and laid them on our knees, so that M. de Fontenay had charge of her left foot and I of her right foot, outside the curtain. She also gave me her right hand and M. de Fontenay her left hand. Her head was visible as soon as she had opened the curtain with the hands held by us. The control demanded by the medium herself, which, in addition to an illumination by four electric lamps, placed her hands and feet entirely in our power, and excluded all co-operation of these members during the production of the phenomena, may surely be taken as meeting every objection. In these circumstances there appeared on her left side, at about the level of her head, but more than 20 inches away from it, the distinct form of a left hand, with a portion of an arm corresponding approximately in size to a female hand.

This strongly luminous, strongly outlined, and freely suspended structure, apparently made up of a paplike mass, quickly moved down to about the middle of her breast, and disappeared behind the curtain. The whole process took two or three seconds—rather a long time—and was repeated five times, so that we had sufficient time for exact observation. The fingers were separated and directed downwards, but showed no skin colour, nor any other detail. In fact, they accurately corresponded in their appearance with those hand shapes which we had photographed on several occasions.

Special interest attaches to the undoubted perception that the hand shape appeared to be quite flat, as seen in previous photographs. We had, therefore, under these rigid conditions, the freely suspended flat sketch of a female hand endowed with independent motion. In spite of its imperfect development, it was mobile, and independent of the medium's body. The whole observation is of importance in connection with the criticism of the glove-like forms seen in several photographs. It tells against the hypothesis of fraud, and in favour of the genuine character of this peculiar formative process.

Releasing the foot, I extended my right hand into the curtain and asked to be touched on the palm by the materialised hand. Four times it approached to within about 4 inches, but it regularly disappeared again, as if repelled by the radiation from the human skin.

Again, at a critical moment, unfortunately the electric circuit for the ignition of the magnesium failed. On this occasion it would have been easy to photograph the freely suspended hand, since it remained exposed, for several seconds, to the influence of our gaze and to the light. The fault in the circuit was found and remedied, so that, at least in the second half of the sitting, a photograph was possible. After we had taken our places again, and had re-established the previous control, we soon saw on Eva's breast, and in her lap, that veil-like mass which had once before been photographed. I approached my hand in order to grasp it, but it regularly receded before me and disappeared. While the medium's hands and feet were held by the observers as described, we saw a veil-like strip, about 4 inches broad and 20 inches long, descending from the left-hand upper region. It was more feebly developed, and was less distinctly seen, than the previous phenomena (Fig. 30).

On again perceiving the apparently woven fabric, in the medium's lap, the flash-light was ignited, and the phenomenon disappeared at the same moment.

The sitting closed at 11.30. Examination of the medium and cabinet negative.

Taking into account the wearing of the new tights and the strict supervision of her extremities, the results of this evening form a justification for the medium, as they prove that Eva does not require either her hands or feet for the production of the phenomena.

The photographs (Figs. 31 and 32), both simple and stereoscopic, show the following aspect : the author holds the medium's right hand and right foot, while her right foot rests on his left knee. On the other side, De Fontenay holds her left hand with his right, her left foot rests on De Fontenay's left knee, and is held by Mme. Bisson's hand. In his left hand De Fontenay holds the press-button for igniting the magnesium light, and his thumb is just exerting the pressure.

The medium herself has her head bent forward. The features indicate a certain energetic concentration of the will. On her chest is seen, at the height of her shoulders, a broad white fabric resembling muslin, which falls down into her lap and is shaded just where it bends

Fig. 33. Flashlight photograph by de Fontenay, 10 June, 1911

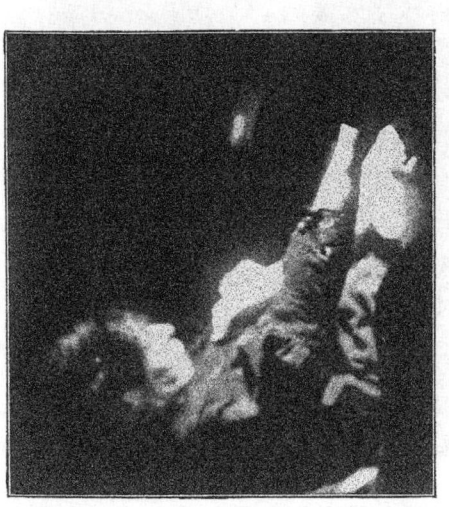

Fig. 32. Lateral view (photographed in the cabinet) of the phenomenon shown in Fig. 31.

Fig. 34 Flashlight photograph by de Fontenay, 24 June, 1911.

to the left, while it vanishes on her right side into the material of the dress. On the left side, the fabric is transparent, and underneath it are seen two sharply-defined forms, resembling finger-tips cut out of white paper.

The photograph taken by the camera set up in the cabinet (Fig. 32) shows the medium in profile. In that photograph the fabric gives the impression of a material strongly bulging forward, and having a sharp edge below, recalling, to some extent, a mass of plaster of Paris. One also recognises the form of a finger-tip. The upper part of the fabric is surrounded by a radiating aura. But whether this is simply the effect of the luminous white colour on the photographic plate, or is produced by the composition of the fabric, is difficult to decide.

Further Observations during June and July 1911 (Paris).

SITTINGS OF THE 10TH AND 24TH JUNE 1911.

ON the 10th June 1911, M. de Fontenay succeeded in photographing the material radiating from the top of the medium's head (Fig. 33). Although the picture is somewhat blurred, the stereoscopic transparency shows the situation best. Eva sits with head bent forward in the cabinet. A broad strip of white material runs from the back of her head, on the left, over the top, and ends in a fork with a projection. Two broad strips branch out from the main portion, backwards and downwards, while a portion resembling a leaf, and attached to the main body by a narrow stalk, lies over the hair in front. The photograph (Fig. 34), taken on the 24th June 1911 by De Fontenay, in the author's absence, is interesting as throwing a light on the genesis of the so-called transfiguration, *i.e.*, in the spiritistic sense, the medium takes upon herself the part of the " spirit," endeavouring to dramatise the character of the person in question, by clothing herself in the materialised fabrics. This transition stage is found in nearly all materialisation mediums. The literature of the subject records a large number of attempts at exposure of mediums thus impersonating " spirits," *e.g.*, that of the medium Bastian by the Crown Prince Rudolph; that of Crookes's medium, Miss Cook; that of Mrs d'Esperance, etc. In all these cases the medium was seized, but the fabrics used for masking immediately disappeared, and were not afterwards found.

In our case, Mme. Bisson held the medium's right hand. The medium had risen from her chair, bent forward, and stretched her head out of the curtains, while her left opened the curtain. Of Eva's face we only see the nose, a portion of the cheeks, and the mouth. The whole upper head, and the upper half of the nose, is bound up in a striped dark material in several layers and in the form of a helmet, so that the eyes are completely covered. Over this is a fabric recalling, in its transparency and in its uniform parallel pattern, the previous creations. A second and larger packet of material, of the same composition, is held in her mouth. This material hangs down upon her hands, and seems connected with the head-covering. For this interesting masquerade a considerable quantity of some bright transparent material, also of some dark material, would have been necessary.

Communication by Letter.

The following description is contained in a letter of Mme. Bisson to the author, of the 3rd July 1911 :—

" At nine o'clock last night (2nd July 1911) I hypnotised Eva, as usual, in the cabinet. I had hardly approached her when she threw herself on one side, with her mouth open, and with that stertorous breathing that you are familiar with. Much astonished, I closed the curtains behind me and remained with Eva in the cabinet, holding her two hands and waiting, as I foresaw the occurrence of phenomena. Eva's hands had grown cold, and the stertorous breathing continued. Then I saw, descending from her left shoulder, masses of material, which fell over her chest down on the right side.

" I then asked that the mass should come to me. Almost immediately after I had uttered this wish, a large packet was thrown on my head from behind. It glided over my face and eyes, moving independently like an animal with a moist skin. I had the sensation as of touching a snail, and the material had a peculiar smell, difficult to define.

" During these occurrences I continued to hold both the medium's hands. The living material glided along down my back, hanging over from one shoulder to the other, and entirely enveloping me, something like what is seen in the case of the medium in the last photograph.

" The whole mass dissolved quite suddenly and disappeared, while I still held the medium's hand. After a pause of several minutes, Eva said to me, ' It will now come into your hand. Stretch out your hand as flat as possible, and bring it near my left side.'

" She then took, my right arm in both her hands, and in this position I stretched forward my right hand. Immediately afterwards I felt, in the hollow of my hand, something resembling a pigeon's egg, which, however, was connected with Eva's left shoulder by a broad band of the substance. I then withdrew quite slowly, still holding this egg-like substance in my hand, and my arm still held by both Eva's hands. Thus I gradually got into the light at the opening of the curtain.

" The material has an ash-grey aspect, and is traversed by threads like a delicate skin. It is cool, moist and living. I slowly approached my left hand to the material, touched it and followed it with my hand up to its origin. A large knot of dense and tough substance was found emerging from Eva's left shoulder.

" Suddenly the material was withdrawn from my right hand, and I felt that it receded towards Eva's left shoulder, escaping from under my hand.

" Another pause, after which the phenomena recommenced. Laying my right hand on Eva's left shoulder, and holding with my left her two joined hands, I felt myself pulled and touched on the hair with the fingers.

"Thereupon Eva took my right arm in both her hands. This time the material was thrown on my right hand and on her hands, completely enclosing our hands. I then commenced to pull again and to draw the material outwards, proceeding as tenderly as possible, in order not to hurt the medium. When I began to examine the material, it had curled right round my hand. Suddenly Eva made a movement with her hands, lying on my arm, and involuntarily pulled at the material held by me. It obviously frightened and hurt her, for she screamed, and gave me great anxiety. I tried to soothe her, but she complained of a strong nausea. The material, this time, quickly disappeared on her left breast. The nausea continued for about ten minutes. Immediately after the scream she fled, in her hypnotic condition, out of the cabinet into the room, and would not return. I soothed her gradually, and awakened her outside the cabinet."

In a letter of the 9th July, the above communications were supplemented as follows, in answer to some questions of mine :—

"As I stood in the cabinet, and Eva's stertorous breathing commenced, I carefully opened the left flap of the curtain behind me, and the light thus entering, allowed me to see the phenomena. In holding the material in my hand, I had the impression of some dense but soft matter, neither quite hard nor quite soft. The material penetrated Eva's dress, and, the moment I touched the shoulder with my left hand, it quickly disappeared. Eva felt all my movements, including that by which I touched the material. The touch itself does not make her suffer, but it hurts her when I begin to draw the material away. A pin inserted in the material would cause Eva pain.

"One might succeed in removing the material as soon as the materialisation is sufficiently separated from her. But one must not try to cut off a piece, or to pull it away brusquely, while the material is still in connection with her. In any case, one must avoid hurting her by an incorrect procedure.

"In her somnambulistic condition, Eva says : ' It is not I who produce or create. It is an entity independent of me, which borrows material from me, and can go out beyond my body. That cannot take place in the light and in the daytime.' This is also corroborated by the circumstance that she has produced phenomena at moments unexpected by herself or by me. She claims to submit to an unknown power, which directs her. She, therefore, never knows whether she can produce or not. She looks upon herself simply as a machine."

Sittings of July and August 1911 at St Jean de Luz.

THE Bisson family had taken for the summer of 1911 a villa at St Jean de Luz, a picturesquely situated watering-place 10 miles from Biarritz. The medium, Eva C., accompanied them thither.

In order to continue his observations, the author went to Biarritz in July, and between the 21st July and the 26th August 1911 he took part in eighteen sittings.

Experimental Room.—A room on the ground floor, with a single entrance, was reserved exclusively for the sittings. An inspection of the external walls showed no opening, or access, except the window. The window itself had wooden shutters, which were closed before every sitting. Also, the only door was locked, before every sitting, with a key, which the author, or one of the other sitters, kept in his pocket.

The cabinet arranged for our purposes had walls lined with thin black material, and had a roof at a height of $7\frac{1}{2}$ feet. The separate portions of the material were joined by a sewing-machine, and had no folds or pockets into which one could have inserted a finger, much less a hand. The curtains were mounted on rings running along a metal rod. They consisted of the same black stuff, sewn on to the lining of the cabinet wall at the sides. A light wicker chair, enamelled black, and partly covered with the same material, was used by the medium as a seat. Everything else can be seen from the Diagram.

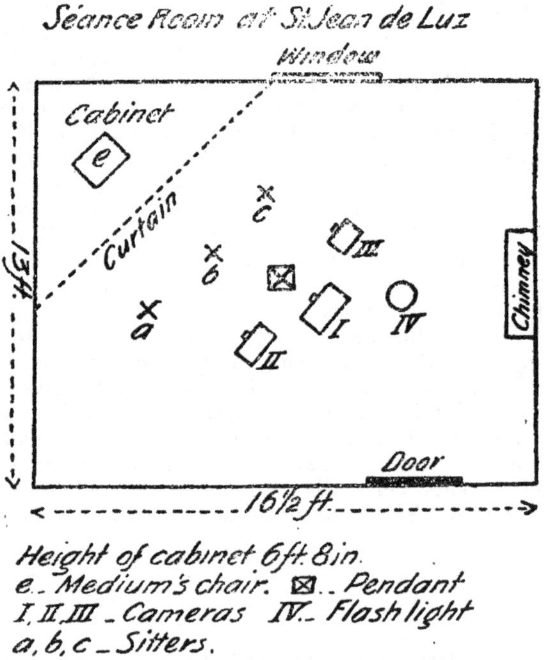

Height of cabinet 6 ft. 8 in.
e. Medium's chair. ⊠..Pendant
I, II, III — Cameras IV.— Flashlight
a, b, c — Sitters.

DIAGRAM IV.

Illumination.—The pendant hanging from the centre of the ceiling had four electric lamps, the middle one of thirty-two candle-power and the three others of sixteen candle-power each. The thirty-two candle-power lamp was surrounded by a red globe. The other three only had a simple shade of red glass; but, since the carpet and ceiling appeared nearly white, they gave such an intense light that at first we also reduced these lamps, by encasing them in red globes, so that the electric light then had to traverse a double layer of red glass.

Since the room then appeared too dark, we removed the ruby globe from one of the lamps before the sitting of the 2nd August, while the other two lamps retained their double red-glass envelope. This illumination made the room appear considerably lighter than it did in Paris.

If we desired to reduce the light we could switch off the sixteen candle-power lamps, so that only the thirty-two candle-power lamp shone through a white and a ruby glass.

The dress of the medium consisted of the tights supplied by the author in Paris, which enveloped her up to the hips, and a black dress made at St Jean de Luz, without any trimmings or collar, which closed tight round the neck, and was, before each sitting, sewn up behind, from the neck down to the waist. Furthermore, Mme. Bisson, before every sitting, joined the tights to the dress by a close-stitched seam passing round the waist, and sewed up both sleeves at the wrist, in such a way that the sleeves fitted closely to the wrist. For this purpose eight or nine white threads were necessary, which were always joined by knots.

The searching of the medium took place before and after each sitting, in the same way as in Paris. The medium entered the room with the séance costume, and put on the tights in our presence. Before every sitting we were allowed to insert the hand between the dress and the skin, to make sure that no white veils or similar things were concealed about the body. Besides this, the hair, nose, and mouth were examined, but always without result.

The inspection of the cabinet, before and after the experiments, by the various sitters, never showed anything remarkable, in spite of the greatest care.

The hypnotisation of the medium was done regularly by Mme. Bisson, who took a seat in front of the cabinet, and always under the eyes of those present. Fixation of the eyes and touching of the medium's hands sufficed to put her into a state of trance in barely half a minute. Only after this was the white light extinguished, so that the red lamps alone were burning.

The photographic exposures during the sittings were prepared by the author, and were all carried out with his three cameras, placed some 10 feet in front of the cabinet.

The magnesium itself (about a tenth of an ounce) was ignited by the electric current derived from the mains, with the help of a pear-push held in the author's hand and connected by a flexible cord. All the slides were inserted by the author himself. The cameras were opened in the red light only, and remained open during the whole sitting. It only required a pressure on the contact to photograph any situation which appeared suitable to the author. The first three sittings of 21st, 22nd, and 25th July were without result.

SITTING OF THE 28TH JULY 1911.

Present.—Mme. Bisson ; a German physician, Dr A., and the author.

Commencement of the experiment at 8.45. Conditions of control as above. Dr A. himself searched the cabinet, the séance costume, and the medium before and after the sitting, and took charge of the key of the room. Illumination as above described.

Very soon after the commencement of the sitting some large patches were seen on the medium's upper arm, and some strips about a foot long.

We formed a chain. Mme. Bisson sitting in the centre gave her right hand to Dr A. and her left to me. Eva gave her left hand into Dr A.'s right, and her right hand into my left, so that the circle was closed, with the curtains open. The latter, however, the medium held with her thumbs, so as to be able to bring the phenomena from the shade into the light, by moving the curtains.

Her feet were stretched out and lay in Mme. Bisson's lap. Under these conditions two large faint patches appeared on her upper body, changing from place to place ; then some sketchy, white, imperfectly developed structures, which were not visible to us longer than from one to three seconds, but which already showed a tendency to the formation of hands.

The shapes were flat, emerged from a mass showing automatic motion, and showed finger-shaped excrescences, which seemed to move of their own accord. Finally, we saw emerging from the curtain on the left, a clearly drawn female right hand (of the size of Eva's hand), with a forearm swathed in a wide sleeve, resembling veiling or lace.

This shape was not apparently in direct connection with Eva's body. It remained visible for two or three seconds, but was flat, as if cut out of paper.

During further formations of this sort, which all showed a tendency to take the shapes of hands or arms, the flat character became less noticeable. More or less plastically developed forearms, with hands, showed themselves about six times.

In one case, a hand came from the medium's left side and disappeared on the right, behind the curtain. This appearance was at about the level of the medium's head. I may add that, during the whole of these occurrences, the head was always under the scrutiny of our eyes, and often exposed to the light. Out of the series of visual perceptions, which only represent repetitions and variations of the same theme, a few characteristic ones may be mentioned.

While the conditions of the experiment remained unchanged, so that Eva's whole body was under control, she closed the curtains with the hands held by A. and by me. Suddenly, a third hand appeared about a foot above Eva's hands, in the shape of a fist, emerging from the curtain. It was plastically well developed, but appeared to possess only three fingers.

In a few cases we saw hands above her head, with fingers pointing forward. On the whole, the phenomena appeared less distinct and less materialised than during the last observations in Paris. This may have been due to the brighter illumination and change of climate.

Among other appearances, I may mention a broad veil-like mass, which came from the left shoulder, descended into Eva's lap, showed automatic motion, and disappeared before our eyes.

Only once after the majority of the phenomena mentioned occurred did Mme. Bisson enter the cabinet, in order to soothe the tired medium by placing her hand on her forehead.

Then, when Eva's hands became warm—a sign that she could not produce anything more—the sitting had to be closed.

Still in the state of somnambulism, Eva rose, approached Dr A., and asked to be searched. Dr A. verified that all the seams and the whole dress were in order, and was the first to enter the cabinet for the final search, which was also negative.

SITTING OF THE 31ST JULY.

Negative.

M. Bisson, on the 30th July, had a paralytic stroke, with left-sided hemiplegia. This sad occurrence, the excitements and anxieties in the family, brought about by it, and the sleepless night spent in nursing him, from the 30th to 31st July, disturbed the psychic equilibrium of the sitters required for a successful sitting.

SITTING OF THE 2ND AUGUST 1911.

Present.—Mme. Bisson, Dr A., and the author.

Conditions as on the 28th July. Time, 9 to 11 P.M. Illumination as above.

The medium's body, including mouth, nose, hair, and arm-pits, her dress and the cabinet, were thoroughly examined by Dr A. and the author. Without the knowledge of the ladies concerned, Dr A. had made a red mark on Eva's dress, in order to make sure that there was no substitution of clothing.

Dr A. also watched most minutely the process of hypnotisation-from beginning to end. Mechanical aids towards the production of phenomena were not found hidden anywhere.

A quarter of an hour after the hypnotisation, what we may call the "transformation of energy" in Eva's organism began. This time the large white mass seemed to issue from the mouth, which was bent to the left. The substance extended from the left shoulder, in the shape of large patches, 8 to 12 inches wide, on to her breast, and changed their character several times. Eva's hands, meanwhile, held the curtain, and were constantly visible. The substance appeared several times lying on her hair, and flat forms of hands were seen.

At the commencement of this stage, Eva gave her two hands to Dr A. and myself, as in the sitting of 28th July. These hands we held during the ensuing phenomena without interruption. But the medium's thumbs held the curtains, in order to be able to close them more or less, and so regulate the light falling on the materialised products. She also laid her feet on our knees, her left foot on Dr A.'s, and her right on mine. The head, as in the sitting of 28th July, was always under scrutiny, and was seen by me during nearly all the phenomena. By this procedure Eva had excluded all her limbs from co-operation in the phenomena. Our first optical perceptions during this period were at about the level of Eva's head. At first we saw large indistinct patches which, with a gradual and automatic flowing motion, formed themselves into flat hands without any detail. Their colour was white, but appeared reddish under the illumination. Their size was variable. Sometimes the forms resembled female hands, and sometimes male hands. On one occasion a male forearm and hand, clothed in a sleeve and extending up to the elbow, proceeded from a point at the level of her head. This arm made a rapid movement downward towards a position in front of her face and disappeared.

A further group of optical images developed at her right hip under the elbow, *i.e.*, on my side, in such a manner that they were covered by the curtain and invisible to me, but were clearly observed by Dr A., who sat directly opposite. Dr A. found that this substance developed into a hand. Then followed a rest-pause. The curtain was closed and the limbs liberated.

The same conditions were then restored as regards the control of hands and feet. On reopening the curtains the mass, invisible to me, lay on her right shoulder. Dr A. observed that a hand emerged from this viscous and apparently luminous substance. He also thought he observed the lifting of this hand from the body of the medium, and some motions of the fingers.

On his giving the sign for the ignition of the magnesium light, I pressed the button. The photographs were successful, and confirmed the accuracy of the visual impressions, especially the stereoscopic plate.

The photograph (Figs. 35 and 36) shows the control of the hands and feet. Mme. Bisson holds the medium's right foot, lying on my left knee, the tip of her left foot projects beyond A.'s left knee. Both her hands, which hold the curtain, are held[1] by A. and me. The medium's head is bent and clearly visible. The seam in her dress is clearly seen, and behind the head a portion of the back of the chair.

On her right shoulder is a broad mass resembling a thick white cloth, and hanging down to the middle of her chest. Over her shoulder, at the sleeve, a flat white hand, with four clearly-drawn fingers, is seen, the joints of which follow the rounding of the shoulder and appear bent in front. The whole of the back of the hand is distinctly seen, and the relative sizes are correct. The thumb is not there, but the first finger and the part of the hand which would join the thumb is seen to merge into a white substance without any demarcation, as if the hand were only part of the whole substance. Besides the fingers, there is a narrow stalk which emerges from the base of the hand backwards and points over the shoulders. The form of the hand is flat, and its surface lacks

---

[1] Visible on the original plates. This part was omitted in the above picture, so that the other foot is not seen.

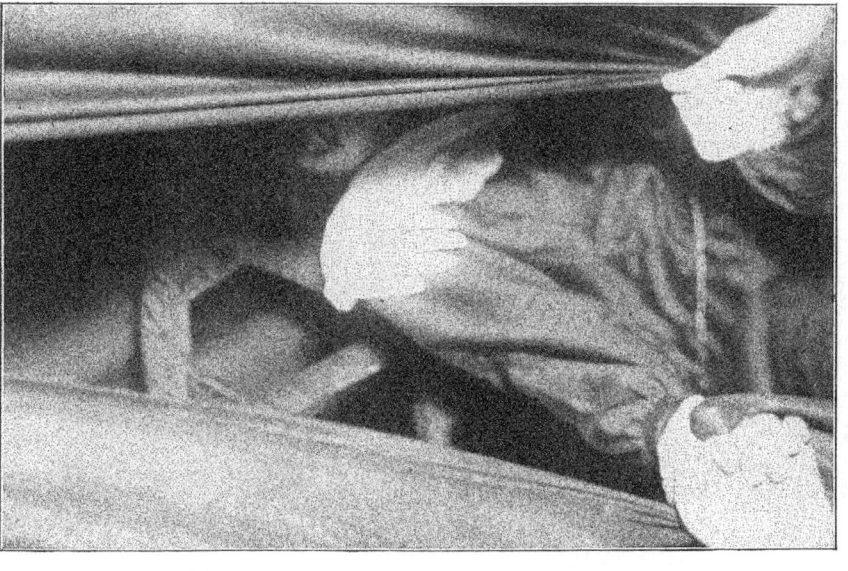

Fig. 36. Situation of Fig. 35 taken simultaneously by the author with a second camera.

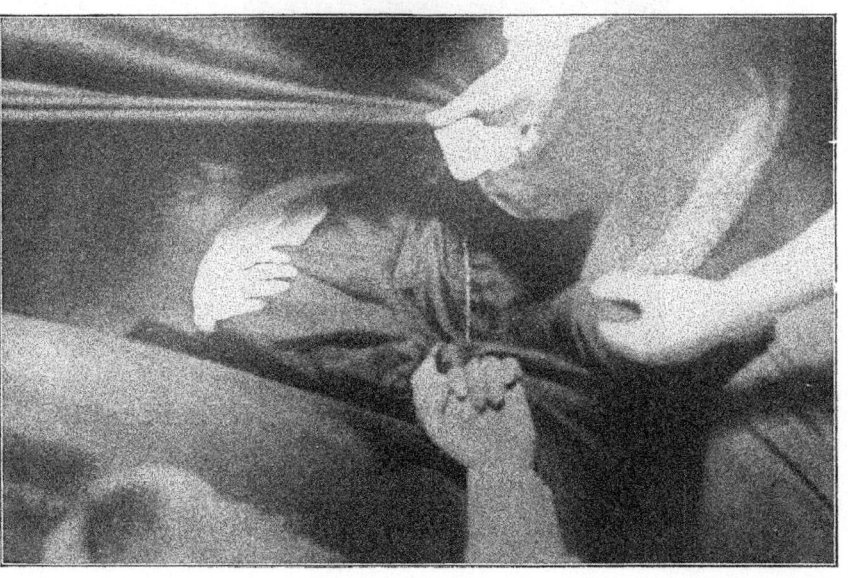

Fig. 35. Flashlight photograph by the author, 2 August, 1911.

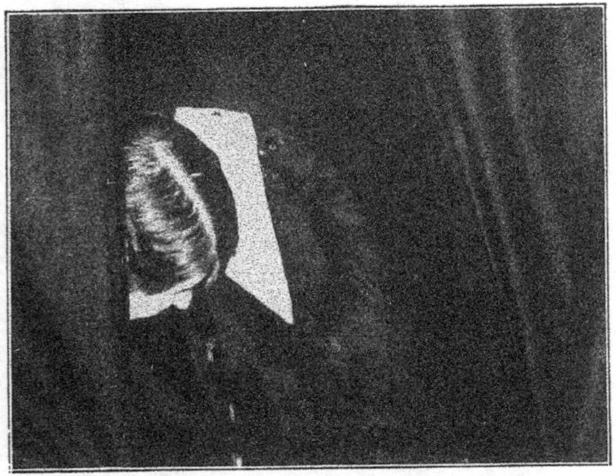

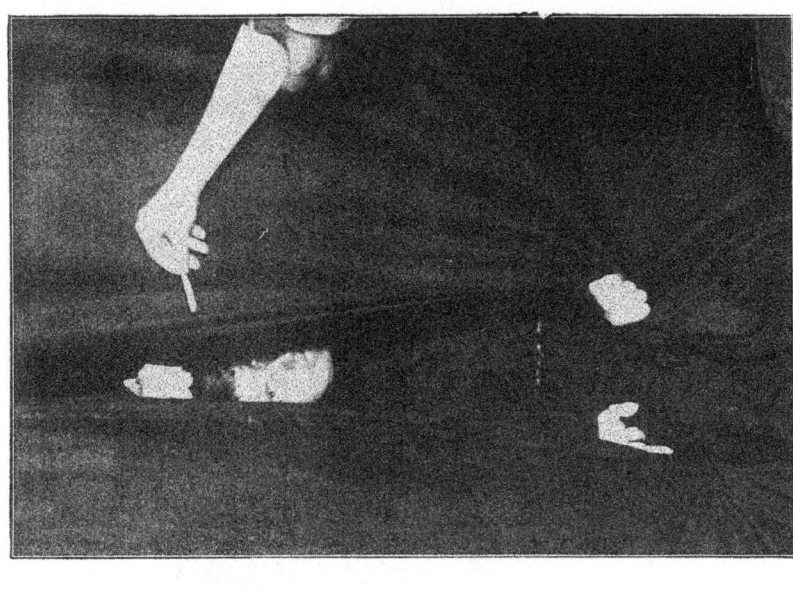

Fig. 37. First flashlight photograph by the author, 11 August, 1911.

Fig. 38. Second flashlight photograph by the author, 11 August, 1911.

all detail. This whole experiment is of interest, inasmuch as Dr A., while controlling all the medium's limbs, observed the growth of a hand-shaped body out of an automatically-moving substance, from beginning to end, and gave the signal for the photographic record when he considered the process terminated. The photograph confirms the correctness of the appearance. In this case the time of observation was about one minute.

When the flash-light flared up Eva screamed. Mme. Bisson took her handkerchief and entered the cabinet to wipe Eva's face and mouth. When she came out and showed us the handkerchief it was quite wet, and showed traces of blood.

After a short pause the sitting continued. The hands and feet were left free, but the hands could be regularly seen during the occurrences about to be described, either lying on her knees or holding the curtain. The appearance of hands and arms at a level of the medium's head was repeated several times.

On one occasion Eva closed the curtain, though her hands remained visible at the curtain from without. Suddenly, I saw at a height of 16 inches above her hands, a fist, which fell like a meteorite in front of our eyes and disappeared on the floor.

While Eva's hands rested visibly on her knees, and the curtain was half open, suddenly a third hand grasped the left-hand flap of the curtain from within and closed it. This third hand, at Dr A.'s wish, gave a tap on the back of his right hand.

Subsequently some misty or cloudy spherical forms, about the size of a head, became visible above Eva's head. On one occasion the profile of a human face appeared instantaneously on the left. Then a piece of veil came on the left, out of the curtain, and fell on Eva's hand. It was large and transparent, so that the hand could be seen through it, and was withdrawn by a turning motion, while Eva's hands were quite motionless.

After the conclusion of the sitting a detailed examination of the medium and cabinet was undertaken. Eva had emerged from the curtain in the somnambulic state, and requested to be searched, but the final examination was without result.

SITTINGS OF THE 5TH AND 7TH AUGUST.

Negative.

On the 5th August Eva was out of sorts before the sitting, and strongly resisted all attempts to awaken her from the somnambulic state. In order to produce a slight shock in her nervous system, the author took a needle and made a prick in her neck. The medium reacted to this harmless intervention with a violent fit of rage, followed by an hysterical crisis, with nausea and convulsive weeping. Not quite completely awakened, she went to bed, and turned up the next morning with her head wrapped up. Even shortly after the sitting a red patch, the size of a florin, was observed on her neck, probably the result of an auto-suggestive local hyperæmia.

It was only on the 6th August, in the evening, after very serious representations by Mme. Bisson, that Eva's excitement subsided.

Sitting of the 8th August 1911.

Sitters.—Mme. Bisson and the author.

This day Eva took part in a motor excursion, and was apparently well disposed.

Conditions as on the 2nd August.

Eva showed the strongest desire to produce some phenomena, but for a long time her efforts remained unavailing. In order to facilitate the process of development, the author reduced the light, extinguishing the three sixteen candle-power lamps, so that only the thirty-two candle-power lamp remained.

Then followed feeble attempts at materialisation. First, at Eva's left shoulder, some grey and indefinite cloudy patches were seen; then, while her hands were visible, a three-cornered mass, the size of a 5s. piece, appeared in her lap, which sometimes was bright and sometimes was darker, then disappeared and reappeared. It finally receded, leaving only a bright point, which slowly vanished.

This evening's experiences are instructive, inasmuch as they show that the phenomena do not solely depend on the medium's will, but that other entirely unknown factors play a part in their genesis.

Sitting of the 9th August 1911.

Sitters.—Dr A., Mme. Bisson, and the author.

Conditions as on 2nd August. Minute inspection of medium and cabinet.

Immediately after the beginning of the sitting the well-known large strips and veils were perceived at her left shoulder. These were in constant motion, while the visible hands were at rest. They fell down, changed their shape, and swathed Eva's left lower arm as with a bandage. On one occasion they sank down to the floor, and remained lying in the cabinet on the medium's left, without her making any movement.

Dr A. then took Eva's left hand, and the author her right, as described in the sitting of the 2nd August. She placed her feet in the lap of the lady of the house, who sat between us.

Under these conditions the same play of formations began, already repeatedly described, sometimes to the right of her head, sometimes to the left of it, sometimes above her head, which remained constantly under our supervision. Some of these formations took the form of hands.

We then expressed a wish that a hand might be formed, independently of her body, *i.e.*, without any visible support, and that this hand should grasp a cigarette, held by Mme. Bisson against the left curtain. We then saw a bright, freely suspended white patch, which condensed and seemed to form a hand. This hand made several attempts to approach the cigarette. There were five or six such attempts without the desired result. This cloudy structure invariably recoiled from the cigarette, at a distance of from 4 to 6 inches. But Mme. Bisson's hand, holding the cigarette, was several times touched through the curtain.

The formative tendencies were at work for about twenty minutes. Sometimes we distinctly saw hands, which, however, did not remain visible for more than a second. Again, as in the sitting of the 2nd August, a hand emerged out of the curtain from the left, disappearing behind the curtain on the right, at the level of the medium's head. On the whole, the formations had a less developed and more fugitive character than in previous sittings.

We thereupon released the hands (held up to then), though we could control them during the ensuing phenomena, when they usually held the curtain.

At this stage of the sitting there was a remarkable appearance of a hand above Eva's head. It appeared a faint grey, was finely drawn, with fingers directed downwards, and wrists. I had the impression of its being a right hand. This optical appearance was also fugitive, and limited to about one second.

Dr A. was able to recognise, above Eva's head, a spherical structure. Then there emerged from the left curtain, always at the level of Eva's head, some white veils and patches, which receded extremely rapidly, and gave the impression as if a third person behind the curtain brought about these phenomena.

Just as a white ball of this description, about the size of a child's head, was exposed again, I pressed the electric button for the magnesium light. Of the photographs taken, only the stereoscopic plate shows a positive result. Both the medium's hands, and especially the whole left forearm, are distinctly visible on it. The whole upper body is behind the right curtain, while at the left curtain, at the level of the medium's head, the remainder of the white mass is distinctly seen. There is no connection between this structure and the medium's right arm, which is about 14 inches below.

The experiment must therefore be regarded as a successful one, for a portion of the receding structure was caught by the camera. The optical impression made upon the sitters could not be reproduced, since the withdrawal of this substance took a shorter time than the ignition of the flash-light. This experiment proves the extraordinary mobility of structures clearly separated from the medium's body. After the photograph the phenomena tailed off to such an extent that the sitting was closed. Final examination negative.

SITTING OF THE 11TH AUGUST 1911.

Sitters.—Mme. Bisson and the author.

Conditions as on the 8th August. Illumination by all the four lamps.

Hardly was the white light switched off when a groaning from Eva indicated the beginning of the phenomena. She herself opened the curtain from time to time, and exposed the products of her remarkable power to the red light. The same misty and veil-like substances were produced, mostly connected with her body, on the right and the left, on her chest and in her lap, on the shoulder or at her head. The high back of the chair served as a support. We saw on Eva's left a white mass, which was photographed by me. All three cameras gave the situation in successful photographs (Fig. 37), each camera in a different way, according to its position. On the stereoscopic picture the medium's body covers the material, which lies like a napkin over the high chair back. The camera for the 7 by $9\frac{1}{2}$ inches photographs gave a negative on which part of the mass is covered by the head and left upper arm, while the third photograph ($3\frac{1}{2}$ by $4\frac{1}{2}$ inches) shows a long strip, hanging down the back of the chair as far as the seat, and crossed by the left arm. A corner of the material is bent forward on the inside, and where it is folded over the back it shows a hole.

The observation as described is given by the author according to the actual facts, without any comment, and will probably create the impression among persons not familiar with this subject that we have here to deal with simple fraudulent manipulation of a white piece of material resembling a handkerchief.

After the photograph was taken the sitting was continued. Out of the mobile fundamental substance a distinctly visible third hand of flat appearance formed in Eva's lap. On this occasion I also saw, at 12 inches above her head, a fairly well-formed hand. When the phenomenon repeated itself several times, and again appeared above her head, I again took a photograph, which is highly remarkable (Fig. 38). In the place of her right hand we see the flat hand observed several times, of which three fingers and the larger part of the back are visible. The three finger-shaped flat projections are unequal, and, as in the case of a hand photographed on the shoulder during a former sitting, they show depressions which apparently adapt themselves to the folds of the dress. The substance, therefore, seems in this case to be soft, yielding, and pulpy, and seems to adapt itself to its support by gravity, as showed by a magnification not here reproduced. The inaccuracy of the design is also characteristic, the second finger being obviously too long. The first and second fingers show the same foldings, probably due to a fold of the dress crossing them. If we wish to adopt the view that it was an artificial production, it could not have been a paper hand, since, on account of its lightness and consistency, it would not adapt itself to its support. The magnification neither shows the structure of textile fabrics nor that of leather, such as a glove. Textile fabrics of the same diameter would probably be too light and too little flexible to fit thus into the fold of the dress. We see, in the same photograph, above Eva's head, a remarkable four-cornered

Fig 39 First flashlight photograph by the author, 16 August, 1911.

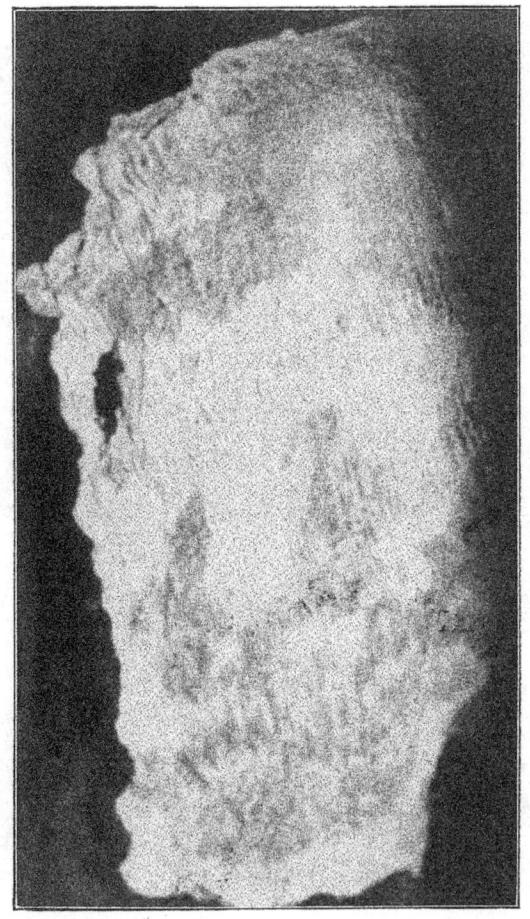

FIG 40   MAGNIFICATION OF PORTION OF FIG. 39.

structure, with a shape of which the lower part is irregular. One may assume that the medium's right hand held above her head supports this substance.

Whether the hand shape on the lap is to produce a deceptive appearance of Eva's right hand, in order to maintain the usual scheme of optical control, we can only guess. In this case we should have a genuine phenomenon with a fraudulent tendency—the image of the right hand of the medium being deceptively represented, in order that Eva's living hand should produce phenomena, and give us the impression as if it were the product of materialisation.[1]

After the second photograph the phenomena were continued. A strip of material, about 12 inches wide and 20 inches long, was thrown over to us out of the curtain, but withdrawn immediately. We also saw, coming from the left, a hand well developed in all detail, with a forearm and five fingers spread out (medium's hand?), while both Eva's hands (one a pseudo-hand?) lay visibly on her lap. This structure made a turning motion, remained visible for four or five seconds, and was then withdrawn. From the forearm depended a rather large piece of a veil-like substance. This same hand touched the back of my left hand, and pressed the tips of its fingers into my skin, so that I clearly felt the finger-nails (obviously Eva's hand). After this a very large hand, wrapped in a white cloth, became visible, its outline being visible through the cloth. This outline also produced strong touches on our heads when brought near to the curtain, ruffling the hair.

The sitting then closed. The photograph leaves the question open whether one of the hands lying on her knee did not, in this phenomenon also, simply present the deceptive image of a hand, in which case the very material character of the final phenomena is explained as being due to the action of one of the medium's hands.

Sittings of the 13th and 14th August.

Negative.

Sitting of the 16th August 1911.

Present.—Mme. Bisson and the author.

Conditions as on the 11th August.

Immediately the red lights had been switched on—I had not even taken my seat—the veil-like strips and patches began to appear at various parts of the medium's body, on the right or left, on her breast, or in her lap. There were also sketchy hands on her lap, and on her head, and a white drapery over her face, of which I took a photograph (Fig. 39). On this we see a fairly large piece of material, rather too densely woven for a veil, which falls from the head to the middle of the chest, and entirely covers Eva's face. Narrowing towards the bottom, this oblong substance ends in a rectangular piece. The frag-

---

[1] This possibility of deception is already known from the sittings of Eusapia Paladino.

ment on the right has a hole in it, and gives the impression of a piece of linen dipped in viscous white paint. It seems to vary in density, and to be transparent in some places; also to have a greater consistency at the irregular wavy rims than in the centre. The magnification (Fig. 40) shows a broad regular strip running down in parallel lines.

During one of these experiments, while Mme. Bisson held both the medium's hands, I observed that a flat hand appeared on Eva's hair, and made distinct motions with all the five fingers. It seemed to lie on her head with the fingers pointing forwards, and became immediately visible when Eva bent forward. She did not accede to my wish to touch the product.

On the appearance of a veiled female face, which could not be immediately recognised as Eva's face, in the opening of the curtains, the author took a second photograph (Figs. 41 and 42), in order to clear up the matter. The sitting was then closed, and the final examination was negative.

The second photograph reproduces the medium holding the curtain at the instant when she rises from her chair, and bends forward her head, which is covered with a white cloth. The cloth has ? distinct longitudinal stripe, and is laid across Eva's head from the left to the right shoulder. We still see a small portion of the chin and a bit of the nose. The cloth covers the whole head and leaves a triangular opening. There is a small hole about the region of the nose. A critic would at once have the impression that Eva had put a handkerchief over her head, and, indeed, the picture gives this superficial impression, but, as we see on further inspection, especially of the stereoscopic plate, there is below the three-cornered aperture, and low down on the neck, an irregular ring-shaped piece of substance, from which a broad, voluminous round stalk, with a longitudinal stripe emerges, like the stalk of a mushroom. This is continued under the cloth in an upward and right-hand direction (Eva's hair?). Where the stalk touches it the cloth shows a clear impression outward. This dark grey structure cannot be explained by the photograph.

In this sitting also the medium was obviously anxious to mask herself with her teleplastic productions.

Sitting of the 20th August 1911.

No result. Eva, on the first day of her indisposition, was in a very unfavourable mood. In the somnambulic state she became violent, and did not want to give any more sittings, but to go home. Her nervous irritability rendered her treatment difficult.

Sitting of the 21st August.

Sitters.—Mme. Bisson and the author

Conditions as usual. Second day of menses.

A patch about the size of a fist appeared immediately at the beginning of the sitting, in the medium's lap, and changed into a broad band

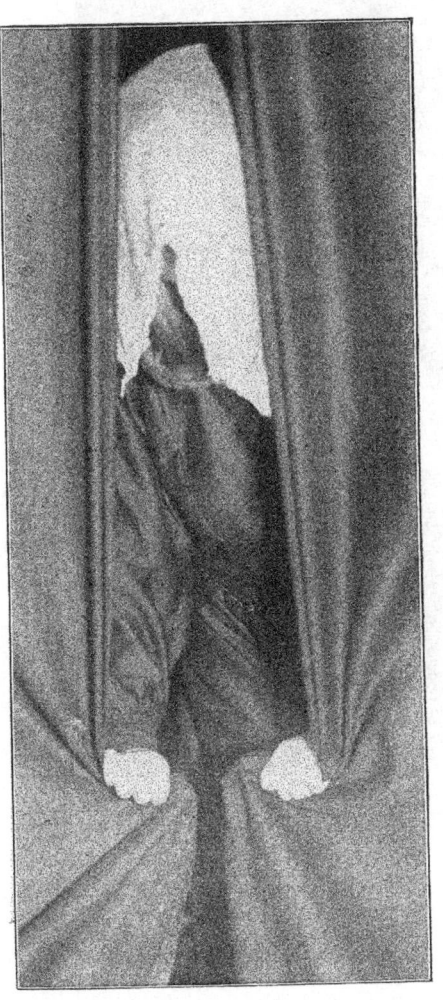

FIG 41 AUTHOR'S SECOND FLASHLIGHT
PHOTOGRAPH, 16 AUGUST, 1911

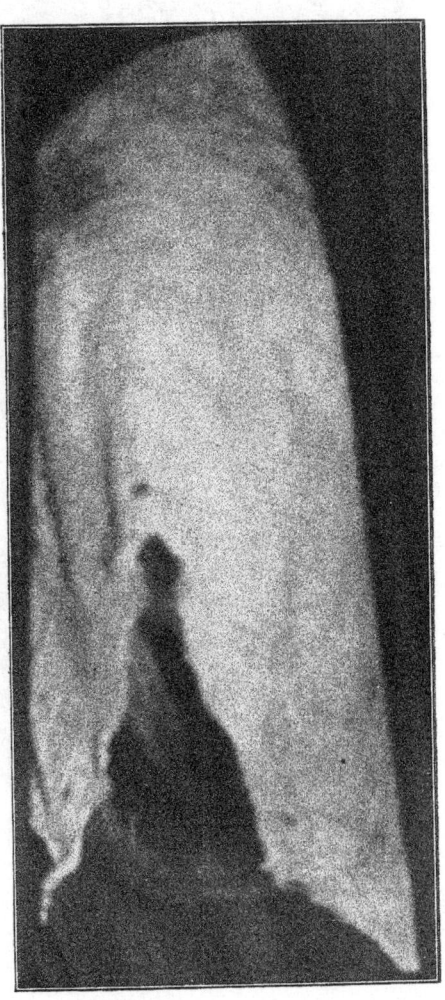

FIG 42 ENLARGEMENT FROM FIG. 41.

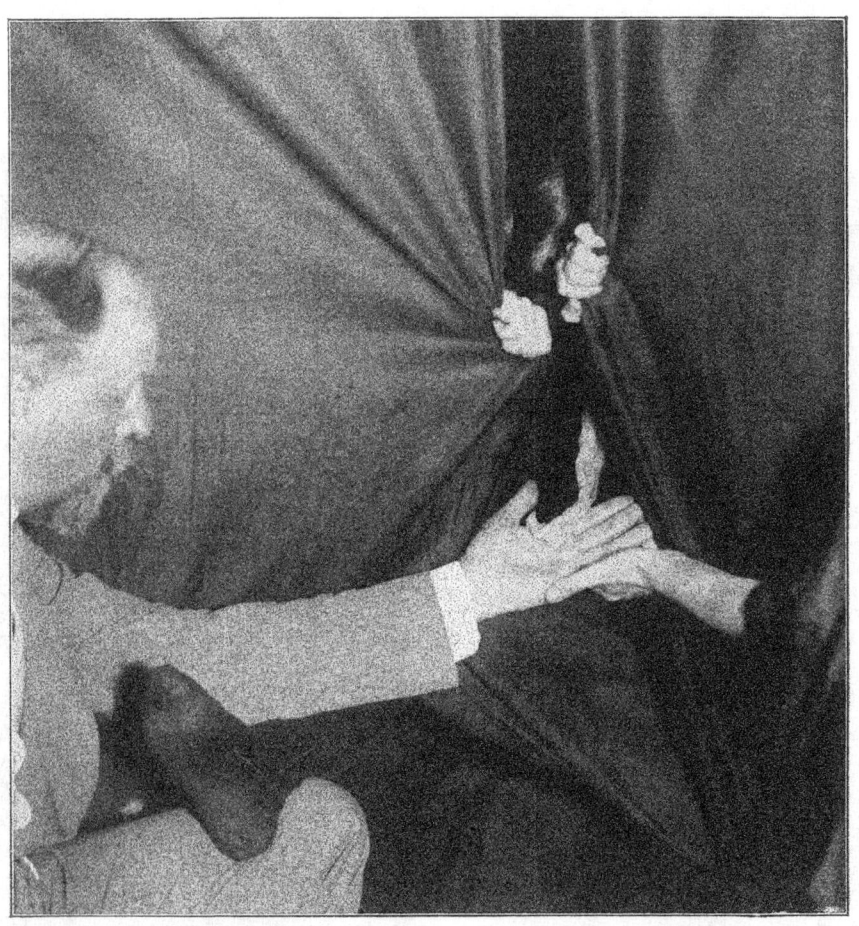

FIG. 43. FIRST FLASHLIGHT PHOTOGRAPH BY THE AUTHOR, 21 AUGUST, 1911.

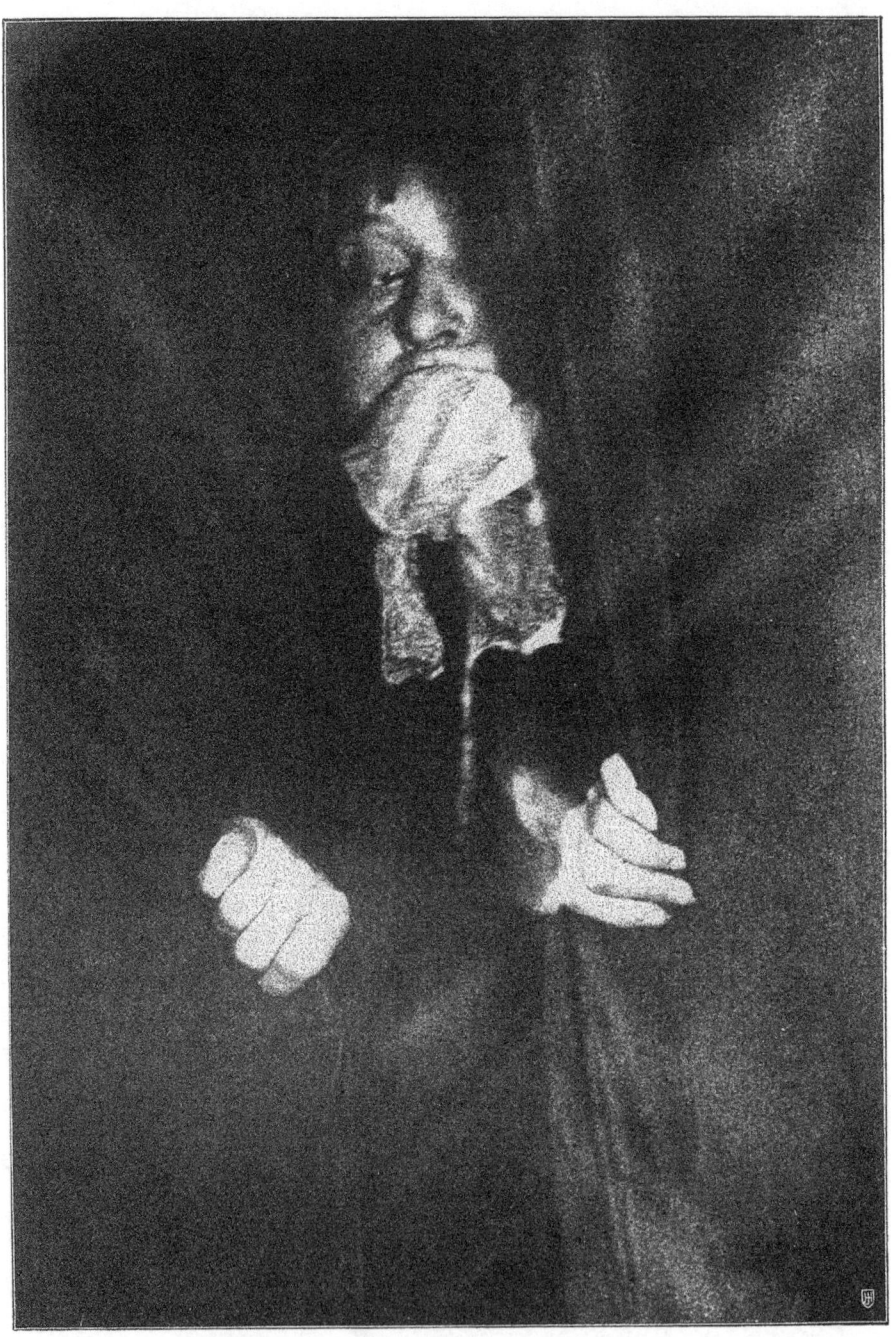

Fig. 45 Author's second flashlight photograph, 21 August, 1911.

joining one hand to the other. Then followed the usual changes of position of the substance from one part of the body to the other, and the automatic changes of shape, while the medium's hands were controlled. Eva's hands were held by Mme. Bisson and by me, and her right foot was placed against mine, or laid on my knee, while Mme. Bisson controlled her left foot. Her hands grasped the curtains, and the head was visible from time to time. Under these conditions she attempted to fulfil my oft-repeated wish that the material should be placed in my hand. Again and again there appeared in the light a long fragment of the fabric, apparently in direct connection with her body, and directed by the motion of the body. Evidently somewhat nervous during this experiment, the medium asked that Mme. Bisson should join her left hand to my left hand. Mme. Bisson accomplished this by touching my hand from below with her open fingers. The two hands thus joined we first held higher than the hands of the medium, and then about 10 inches lower. In this situation the end of a long piece of fabric was repeatedly placed in the palm of my left hand, though at first it was always withdrawn again very quickly. At last, after six or eight attempts, the fragment remained so long that I had ample time for a photograph. This photograph (Figs. 43 and 44) gives an accurate view of the situation, and it succeeded with all the three cameras. The strip, which finally remained in position for six seconds, started from Eva's mouth, as shown by the stereoscopic transparency, and ended in my hand.

It was partly transparent and flexible, like rubber. The substance lying in my hand seemed to me heavy in comparison to its size, and comparable to a heavy organic substance (mesentery ?). It was moist, cool, and viscous, and gave the impression of a long, irregular, fibrous strip of skin, of definite design and consistency.

I may mention that during this occurrence my extended hand was touched both from below (on its back) and from above. The mechanical co-operation of the medium in this must be excluded, on account of the conditions.

This experiment realises a long-desired result. I was intentionally passive, for any grasping or pulling or closing of the hand might have resulted in a fit, and ended the experiment.

After this, hands in various shapes appeared, some of them with sleeves, veils, and forearms. On one occasion I could observe a flat hand with long pointed fingers, which descended in front of her face.

Although the room was filled with magnesium vapour, a second photograph (Fig. 45) was taken, which is perhaps the most interesting of all those taken at St Jean de Luz. On the cleaned and enlarged plate we see both the medium's hands holding the curtains, and her head stretched through the opening. The curtains touched the face, so that the projecting part of the latter, and the piece of material issuing from the mouth and held by it, are *outside* the curtain. The larger and more compact piece has two rectangular terminals of different breadth. From the inner edge of the left-hand piece a thin thread falls down to the back of Eva's left hand. The third joint of the middle finger of the left hand is covered by a patchy amorphous material, which seems to coalesce with it.

The piece of material held in the mouth shows a pattern of parallel stripes. Three broad flat stripes and two quite short ones run from Eva's left cheek to the lower edge of her chin on the external surface of the fabric, suggesting the initial process of the formation of fingers. These lie partly in the fabric itself, since the cross-hatched pattern is visible at the same time.

Perhaps even more remarkable than the structure itself is the radiation phenomenon visible in the picture. The materialised products, as well as the parts of the medium's skin lying in front of the curtain, emit rays in three directions, which cross the folds of the curtain. The origins of these rays correspond exactly with the parts named. Neither photographers nor physicists could explain this remarkable phenomenon satisfactorily, although it was natural to bring the magnesium smoke filling the room into question. The author simply mentions the fact as shown by the plate, though it is possible that a simple physical solution may be subsequently found.

Towards the close of the sitting veiled heads appeared in the gap of the curtain, though it was impossible to decide whether they were Eva's head or independent formations. No accurate observation was possible.

Sitting closed after a duration of two hours. Final examination without result.

Sitting of the 23rd August 1911.

Sitters.—Mme. Bisson and the author.

Conditions as in previous sittings.

This day Eva showed a cheerful disposition. Hardly had the trance condition set in—I hardly had time to open the cameras—when the phenomena began, with the appearance of a long strip passing from the chin, over the knees, to the floor.

After the well-known movement of the substance, a veiled head appeared again, which we immediately recognised as Eva's head.

Our efforts on this occasion were directed towards prevailing upon Eva to place a piece of material in the porcelain dish used on previous occasions. Mme. Bisson made several suggestions in this direction, and held the dish before my eyes, against the gap in the curtains. Eva's hands grasped the curtain. While the hands and arms were motionless I observed that, after several attempts, a long filmy strip slid forward with a creeping motion over the medium's left forearm (coming from her mouth ?), and inserted a tentacle resembling a living member into the porcelain dish. This substance was withdrawn with a sharp jerk. This was repeated three or four times. At the third attempt the material completely filled the dish, flowing together in spirals as if by its own weight.

After the tentacle had been withdrawn, we were requested to see what was in the box. On close examination we found on the bottom of the porcelain dish, 3 or 4 cubic cm. of a transparent viscid liquid (without air bubbles). I preserved this secretion in order to have it examined on the following day in a pharmaceutical laboratory at Bayonne.

During the experiment itself Eva's head was bent to the left, and did not come near the dish.

A loud noise in the water supply waked the medium, and the sitting came to an end.

Final examination negative.

The analysis of the liquid gave the following result :—Colour, none ; appearance, slightly turbid ; consistency, liquid, not viscous ; smell, none ; precipitate, whitish ; reaction, slightly alkaline.

Microscopic examination :—Numerous plate epithelia, some saliva granules, some fat grains, numerous epithelium granulations, and a large number of meat particles. The liquid also contained traces of potassium sulpho-cyanide. The dried residue was 8·6 grammes per litre. Ashes, 3 grammes.

Conclusion.—The microscopical and chemical character of the liquid shows that we have to deal with cell detritus and saliva. The remnants of food also indicate the mouth as the origin. One cannot decide from the examination whether the organic remains are derived from the material, or simply from the epithelium of the mouth and the salivary glands.

Sittings of the 24th and 25th August.

In presence of Professor B., a German scientist. Negative.

Sitting of the 26th August 1911.

Sitters.—Mme. Bisson, Professor B., and the author.

Duration, 9 to 11.15. Conditions as in the other sittings.

Professor B. examined Eva's dress, the body surface, including mouth, hair, and arm-pits, as well as the cabinet, and declared, before the sitting commenced, that he had found nothing which could be used for the artificial production of the phenomena.

The hypnotisation of the medium was watched by Professor B. from beginning to end.

Very soon, hardly a minute after the beginning of the sitting, a large reddish patch became visible on Eva's breast. While her hands held the curtain, the substance appeared in her lap, the size of a hand. It grew and assumed a triangular shape, and then diminished and disappeared before our eyes. This patch was joined to the head by a band which moved with the motion of her head. Mme. Bisson then entered the cabinet in order to sew up a seam which had given way in the medium's tights. From this moment till the end of the sitting Professor B. and the author held the medium's hands, while her feet rested on the knees of these two observers.

Under these conditions we first saw a broad strip coming from her mouth and reaching down to her knees. This irregular strip, grey and partly transparent, emerged from the left side of the curtain under the hand held by Professor B. (length about 6 inches and width about ½ inch) and disappeared from our view, after Professor B. had been several times touched on his right hand from below.

The material reappeared from the left over Eva's arm, and its end was laid on the open right hand of Professor B. as he brought it near the curtains, while Eva held his wrist. It gave him the impression of a mass of soft dough tapering towards the top. The whole occurrence lasted three to five seconds. As Professor B. was slowly withdrawing his arm from the gap of the curtain, the substance was suddenly withdrawn and disappeared.

Professor B. had the impression that the object touched by him was moist, cool, and comparatively heavy, as if a reptile had sat on his hand. After this experiment, Professor B. was asked to feel behind the curtain with his right hand, held by the medium at the level of Eva's visible head. He then, at a distance of 10 to 12 inches from her head, touched something which felt like a broad vertical band, independent of the medium's body. This contact also reminded him of a reptile with a cold moist skin.

In repeating the same experiment, the author had the impression of touching a moist, cool, firm, and fibrous fabric. After this, the same ribbon gave a blow on his face from the closed curtain, and a third hand emerged for an instant from the curtain.

When Eva then opened the curtains, her head was covered with a white cloth hanging down over her neck, which quite corresponded with the photograph taken on the previous occasion.

She then turned her head to the left. As I sat on her right, I could observe that this cloth was slowly drawn away from her head on one side, so that her face became gradually visible. As already mentioned, the hands were held by Professor B. and myself during these phenomena.

The sitting closed. Final control negative. Professor B. was the first to enter the cabinet. The medium, still in a somnambulic state, allowed herself to be examined by the author (including a gynæcological examination).

COMMUNICATION OF PROFESSOR B.
CONCERNING HIS OBSERVATIONS.

THE author engaged in a correspondence with his friend, Professor B., who had been present at some sittings, but who, as a non-medical man, is unfamiliar with the medical and psychological aspects of the investigation. The following points are culled from his impressions thus communicated :—

" 1. There was certainly no other person in Eva's cabinet, nor could any one have entered it without detection. This excludes all attempts at explanation based on the assumption of a confederate.

" 2. I satisfied myself, by searching the cabinet and chair before the sitting, that nothing was hidden there which could have been used afterwards.

" 3. My search of the medium convinced me that she had no fabrics, veils, etc., or anything that one could feel about the exterior of her body. Even if she had, I do not see how she could have produced them, so long as she was sewn up (but I emphasise the fact that the seam once parted and was renewed during the sitting).

" 4. As regards the nature of the materials which I have seen, I repeat that, to the touch, it gives the impression of a moist organic substance. But that is only my personal impression.

" In these circumstances, which dispose of quite a number of explanations suggested, I must, in accordance with my way of thinking, ask myself the question : How can these phenomena be artificially produced under the given conditions ? "

Professor B. then suggests the possibility that the medium secretes a particularly consistent mucus, uses it in some way to form the shapes seen, and finally swallows it.

This suggestion need not be discussed in this place, more especially as it is ruled out by subsequent observations.

Further Observations in St Jean de Luz, September 1911.

Sitting of the 11th September 1911.

The photograph (Fig. 46), taken on the 11th September in the author's absence by M. Bourdet, shows the medium with her hands held by Mme. Bisson and M. Bourdet. Eva's head is completely covered by a white disk-shaped structure which, after intensifying the negative, shows the drawing of a male head, with its front portion cut off by the curtain. In its design, the picture corresponds completely to the male face subsequently photographed by the author on the 5th November 1911, in Paris. In the photograph of the 11th September, it looks rather flat, like a drawing, whereas in the picture of the 5th November it looks plastic and mask-like. Since the design of the hairy portions, of the eyes and the whole face, shows no difference from the picture of the 5th November, the reader may refer to the detailed description given in the discussion of the sitting of the 5th November.

Sittings of the 10th and 11th September 1911.

The following report is taken from a letter of Mme. Bisson, of 12th September 1911, from St Jean de Luz :—

" On the 10th September Eva proposed that we should try to produce phenomena alone, as she felt so strange. Although we had arranged for a sitting on the 11th, I hypnotised her at 8.45 P.M. Immediately after hypnosis the characteristic breathing began, and a curious materialised form appeared on the medium's left shoulder, even before I had closed the curtains. I sat down in front of the cabinet.

"The material then detached itself from Eva's shoulder, and a white patch moved over the dark background of the cabinet. I held Eva's hands all the time.

"Eva then opened the curtains very wide, and I beheld at the back of the cabinet, about 20 inches from Eva's head, a sort of face which seemed to look at me, although it was not possible to recognise any detail. I counted altogether seventy seconds without the apparition making any movement. Eva's hands were always in mine.

"Obviously attracted by the phenomenon, Eva extended her arm (still holding my hand) towards the disappearing apparition, screamed, and fainted away. Afterwards she told me that the materialisation, injured by the strong incident light, had suddenly retired to her body, making her so ill that she lost consciousness. I then closed the curtain, still holding Eva's hands, and allowed her to recover a little.

"Quite gradually she opened the curtains again, and again I saw a head at the back of the cabinet beside that of Eva. For nineteen seconds this apparition remained motionless. Then it decreased and gradually disappeared.

"Suddenly Eva requested me to undo the seams. She removed the clothes and sat naked in front of me. Then followed a series of remarkable phenomena.

"A large, flat, dark-grey patch appeared on her breast, white at the rims. It remained for some time, and then disappeared in the region of the navel. I clearly saw it being reabsorbed there.

"The curtains were then kept closed for several seconds, without my releasing her hands. A round patch again appeared on her skin at the opening of the curtains. It had the same kind of shape as the first, but was larger. To this was joined, in the left ovarial region, a large, black, ball-shaped structure, white in the middle and dark grey at the rims. With the curtain open, I counted twenty-two seconds. Suddenly the material folded itself together at right angles to the axis of her body, and formed a broad band extending from hip to hip under the navel. This apparition then folded up and disappeared in the vagina.

"On my expressing a wish, the medium parted her thighs and I saw that the material assumed a curious shape, resembling an orchid, decreased slowly, and entered the vagina. During the whole process I held her hands. Eva then said, 'Wait, we will try to facilitate the passage.' She rose, mounted on the chair, and sat down on one of the arm-rests, her feet touching the seat. Before my eyes, and with the curtain open, a large spherical mass, about 8 inches in diameter, emerged from the vagina and quickly placed itself on her left thigh while she crossed her legs. I distinctly recognised in the mass a still unfinished face, whose eyes looked at me. As I bent forward in order to see better, this head-like structure rose before my eyes, and suddenly vanished into the dark of the cabinet away from the medium, disappearing from my view. Again the medium fainted.

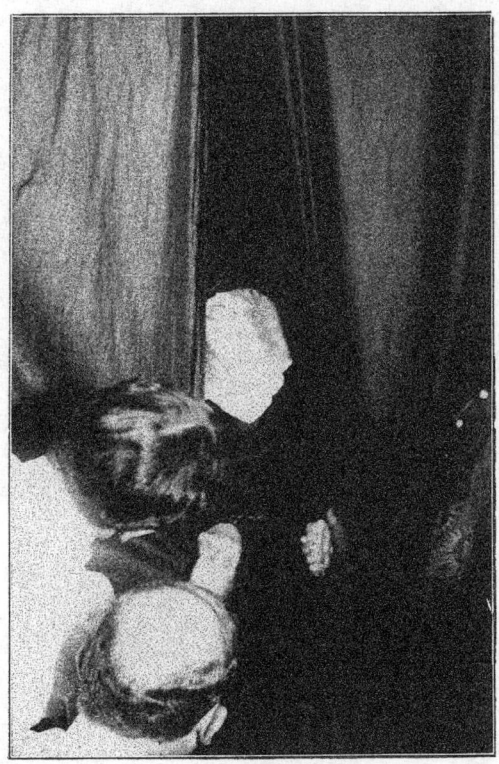

FIG. 46. FLASHLIGHT PHOTOGRAPH BY THE AUTHOR, 11 SEPTEMBER, 1911.

FIG. 47. FLASHLIGHT PHOTOGRAPH BY THE AUTHOR, 1 NOVEMBER, 1911.

"When Eva, in her armchair, had recovered her somnambulic consciousness, I saw, eight times in succession, a head covered with veils, which was quite detached from the medium. The phenomena then ceased, and I closed the sitting at 10 P.M.

"In spite of these exhausting results, Eva, at a sitting on 11th September, at which the physician, Dr B., and the author, Bourdet, and his wife were present, again produced, some twenty times in succession, a materialised head, with a distinct forehead and grey and white veilings; then a wonderfully-shaped profile drawn upon the material as a base. Beard and hair were also represented in the material. I had the impression that this profile resembled a deceased near relative of mine, but I do not wish to assert anything—I only believe that I saw it. The sitting closed at 11 P.M."

Sitting of the 26th September 1911.

In a letter from St Jean de Luz (September 1911), Mme. Bisson communicates the following result :—

"The day before yesterday (26th September 1911) I hypnotised Eva while she sat naked in the cabinet. As she had said she felt numbed, I had decided to have a sitting alone with her. She had hardly entered the trance when the phenomena appeared in great number. This time they began in her neck and at the top of her head. A face was quickly formed, and supported on Eva's head. When I noticed the strength of the phenomena, I asked the medium to concentrate her whole power upon my being able to obtain a piece of the material. This was refused, on the ground that the connection of the material with Eva's body was too close, so that it would injure her. But I could try and take some hair from the materialised head. I then grasped the end of a piece, which hung down, with my left hand. During the first three attempts to detach a piece, Eva screamed. Only at the fourth attempt did I succeed in doing so. I immediately switched on the white light, and was considerably astonished to hold in my hand a lock of fair hair, which did not in any way resemble Eva's darker hair. My hand was covered with mucus and moisture. Understand clearly—I thought I tore off a piece of material, and I had a bundle of hair in my hand. During this whole process Eva held my hands by the wrists, in order to be able to withdraw them if I hurt her too much. If this remarkable occurrence had not happened to myself under extraordinary conditions, in a red light, with a naked medium, in my own house, and in a cabinet constructed by myself, I should never have credited the reality of such an unheard-of phenomenon. I sit for hours and think over it, without finding the least explanation."

Sittings of October and November 1911 (Paris).

On 25th, 27th, 29th and 30th October negative sittings.
Eva was indisposed, suffered from bladder troubles, and the menses

were retarded by nine days. After the negative sitting of 30th October she went to bed while still in the hypnotic condition. Mme. Bisson followed her. Suddenly the medium, already in bed, began to breathe stertorously, and requested Mme. Bisson to remove the bedclothes and control her abdomen. Favoured by the light still coming through the window, Mme. Bisson was able to verify the recurrence of the materialisation process, the phenomena this time emerging from the genital passage. She carefully lighted up in order to observe better, and saw a digital excrescence between the *labia majora*, parallel to the thighs at first, and afterwards crosswise. Every time the light fell upon this product, Eva reacted violently and painfully against it.

On the morning of the 31st the menses had set in, the retardation of which appeared to have been the cause of the stoppage of the phenomena.

On 31st October Eva remained the whole day dazed and uninterested. In the evening, Mme. Bisson dressed her in the séance costume in order to hypnotise her in the cabinet. The author was not present. Hardly had the somnambulic condition set in, when Eva requested Mme. Bisson to loosen the seam joining the tights to the dress. In the red electric light, Mme. Bisson observed a material emerging from the navel, whose shape and movement resembled vaseline pressed out from a tube. The viscous substance emerged in a columnar form, and fell by its own weight, spreading out and widening, and forming on the skin a hand without any detail. The colour of the material was grey, but gradually became brighter and whiter. Mme. Bisson closed the sitting, as she wished to preserve Eva's power for the next evening.

Sitting of the 1st November 1911.

Sitters.—Mme. Bisson and the author.

Séance room and cabinet as during the last series of sittings held in this room. The large Gothic wardrobe, standing against the long windowless wall opposite the chimney-piece, had been removed from the room, so that now the room contained no objects or furniture not required for the sittings. (See Diagram 5.)

With the space thus gained, the pendant, with four twenty-five candle-power electric lamps in ruby globes, was hung immediately in front of the cabinet. Two of the globes were contained in additional red glass cases, so that their light had to pass through a double red screen, while the others had only a single red-glass screen. This arrangement greatly increased the illumination of the room. As soon as the eye had got accustomed to the reduced light, every detail of the room was clearly visible, and large print and the face of a watch could be distinctly read. Since the light was above our heads, it fell from the right into the cabinet, on opening the curtains, so that the foreground of the cabinet was better illuminated than the background.

The easy chair in the cabinet had been replaced by the chair used in St Jean de Luz, as the latter had a low back and a perforated seat. But in this chair also the various rods were either lacquered black or covered with black stuff.

SITTINGS OF OCTOBER AND NOVEMBER 1911 (PARIS)

The two tables in the room served for keeping the articles required for photography and the magnesium light. The flash-light apparatus (A) was ignited by means of the electric supply. The contact push and its cord, 14 feet long, was placed beside the author at the seat (a).

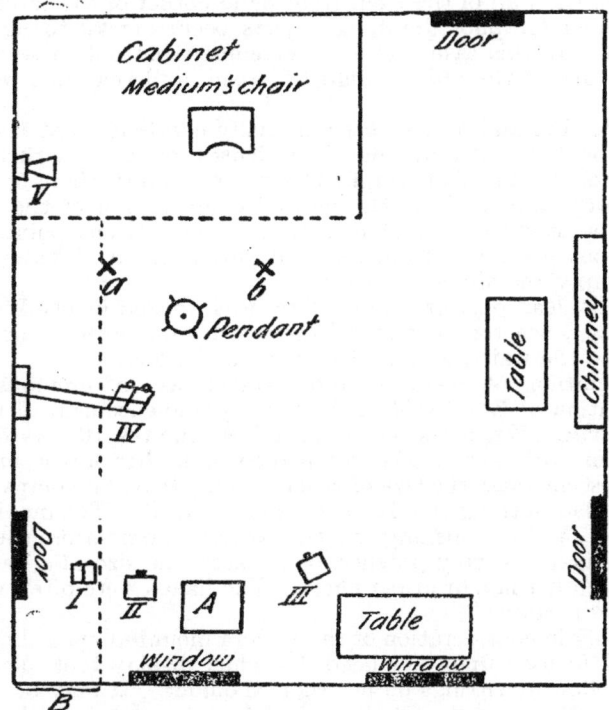

I, II, III, IV, V.—Cameras (I & IV stereoscopic)
a.—Seat of the Author
b.—Seat of Mme Bisson
A.—Flashlight apparatus
B.—Wardrobe leading to the cabinet,
(removed Nov. 1911)

DIAGRAM V.

Arrangement of the Cameras.—Among the author's five photographic cameras there were two stereoscopic cameras, one of which (II.) was mounted at a height of 45 inches, and at a distance of 10 feet from the cabinet, while the other was placed on a shelf fixed against the wall, 6½ feet above the floor and 7 feet in front of the cabinet. The two stereoscopic cameras took pictures $3\frac{1}{2}$ by $5\frac{1}{2}$ inches. The largest camera (II.) took 7 by $9\frac{1}{2}$ inches pictures, and stood fairly in the middle, in front of the cabinet, 10 feet away from the medium's chair, while a smaller camera (III.), taking $3\frac{1}{2}$ by $4\frac{1}{2}$ inches, was focused on the gap in the curtain, and was intended to reproduce the phenomena in the foreground at the curtain itself. Finally, the author had set up a fifth apparatus (V.), $3\frac{1}{2}$ by $5\frac{1}{2}$ inches, on a square wooden support, fastened to the wall of the front right-hand corner of the cabinet. This was intended for photographing objects occurring 20 to 80 inches in front of it. In this case, we must remember that only a small portion of the surface of the object could be taken, and that this would be in side view.

Cameras IV. and V. had been specially constructed at the author's request for the sittings, since the lenses on the market are not designed for taking photographs in close proximity thereto. The five cameras were intended for the mutual confirmation of the negatives, and for the study of the objects taken from various points of view, from various distances, from different sides, and in different sizes, as well as simply and stereoscopically.

As at St Jean de Luz, the medium was dressed in black tights and black dress, sewn together round the waist, and sewn up behind from the neck to the waist, and at the wrists, as before.

Examination of medium and cabinet as in previous sittings. Hypnotisation of Eva by Mme. Bisson. Commencement of the sitting about 10 P.M. When the medium, a few minutes afterwards, opened the curtain with her hands, we perceived in her lap a bright pink phosphorescent mass the size of a hen's egg. It had a compact appearance, and had nothing cloudy or veil-like about it. The medium closed the curtain, and on opening it again shortly afterwards, the material appeared again as grey patches, or packets, the size of a hand, at her shoulders, in her lap, or at her chest. The hands were often withdrawn behind the curtains.

Probably in consideration of the camera mounted upon the medium's right, and focused upon her head, the chief display took place in this and the following sittings on her right shoulder. It may be mentioned that the author had repeatedly asked for phenomena to be produced at this point, upon which the cameras were focused, and this was actually done, for a materialisation on Eva's left shoulder would have been hidden by her head from the camera inside the cabinet. An object appearing further away from her body would have been beyond the field of the apparatus, and, even with different focusing, could probably not have been photographed at the same time as the medium. Our whole endeavour was concentrated upon regularly taking the medium and the materialisation together on the same plates.

The product appearing on her right shoulder was not sufficiently clearly visible when the curtain was opened, since the pendant, hanging rather towards the right, illuminated chiefly the foreground of the cabinet, as already mentioned, and the background only on the medium's left. On account of this indistinctness, Eva allowed me to illuminate the structure by means of a red electric torch specially reduced by

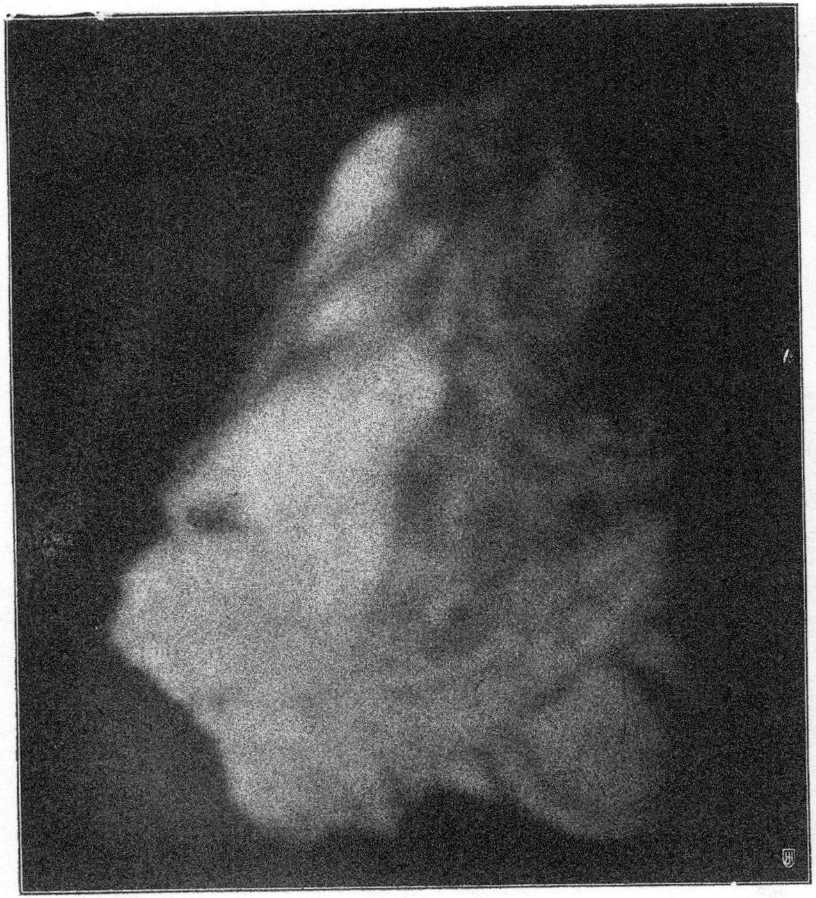

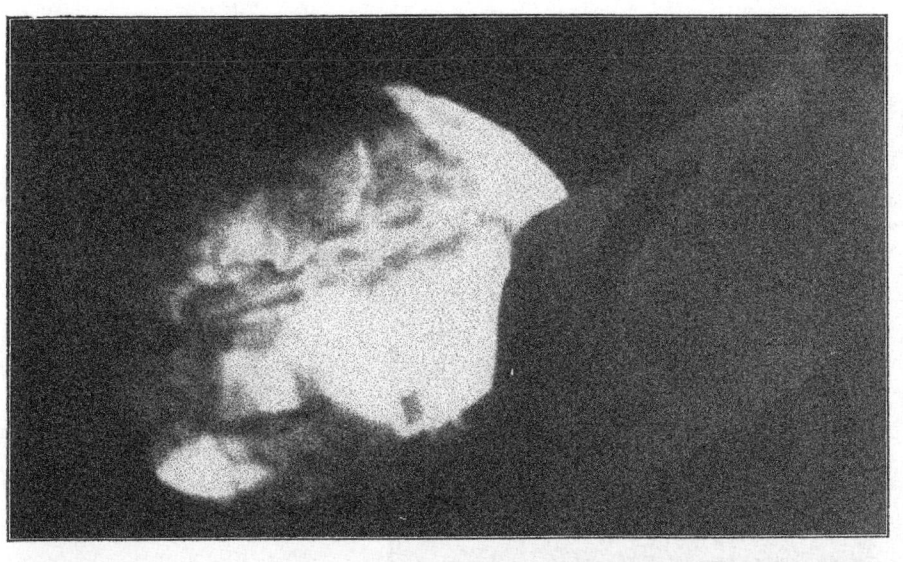

Fig. 48. Magnified portion of Fig. 47.

The same object taken from within the cabinet. Lateral view, magnified.

FIG. 49. AUTHOR'S FLASHLIGHT PHOTOGRAPH, 5 NOVEMBER, 1911.

FIG 51. OBJECT SHOVN IN LAST FI SIMULTANEOUSLY TAKEN FROM WITHI THE CABINET

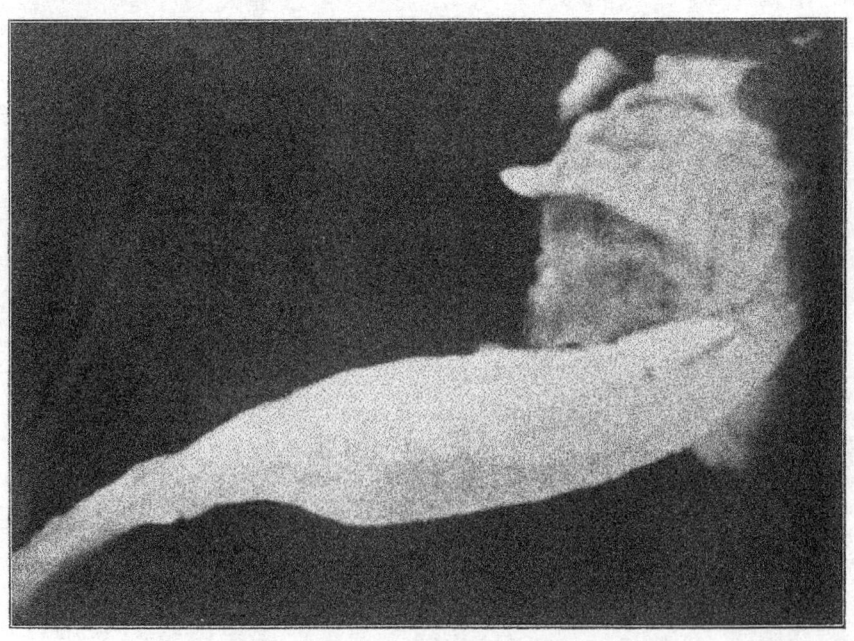

FIG. 50. PORTION OF FIG 49, MAGNIFIED.

SITTINGS OF OCTOBER AND NOVEMBER 1911 (PARIS)

means of transparent black stuff as soon as she opened the curtain, so that I could observe more distinctly what occurred on the right side of her head. This was done very quickly, but about eight times in succession. I thus saw on Eva's right shoulder a white mass partly covering her head, and showing the indistinct profile of a face. The hair of the head-like structure seemed to be of a lighter colour than the medium's hair. The medium's face and the materialisation were turned away from each other, and gave the impression of a Janus head.

At the next opening of the curtains I ignited the flash-light and obtained admirable photographs with three of the cameras. The shock produced by the flash had broken Eva's power. The structure had disappeared without leaving a trace. The sitting was closed, having lasted one hour. Strict examination followed. Dress was intact, but moistened by menstrual discharge, which tells against the possibility of concealing objects. Search of cabinet also negative. Eva went to bed in the somnambulic state.

The photograph (Figs. 47 and 48) shows for the first time in three years' observation a clearly-marked, but imperfectly-modelled, male profile, in which the nose is wanting. The whole gives the impression of an unfinished sketch of a death-mask made with the help of a soft, white, pulpy substance. The small photograph, taken by the camera in the cabinet (Fig. 48, second picture), gives the complete outline drawing of a head. The line of the chin is covered by Eva's sleeve. That which, in the small photograph taken with the cabinet apparatus, looks like the neck of the head, is nothing but Eva's chin, as shown by comparison with the other photographs. In all the photographs the nose is wanting. In the photograph with the cabinet camera, and in the stereoscopic transparency, we see a black veil-like fabric falling over the forehead, left eye, and the region of the nose, so that two-thirds of the forehead and the whole nasal region are covered. The mouth is represented in rough modelling as a square hole, while the design of the lips is clearly perceptible.

The left corner of the mouth is serrated. Where the hair would begin on the forehead there is a white piece of material forming a transition to the mass, which must be interpreted as hair, and which extends from the left ear down to the neck. It must be remarked that this curious grey, roughly-fibred material, covered with numerous small white shadows, gives on the photograph the impression of hair. Whether we have to deal with real hair cannot be decided from the photographs, neither by the positives, nor by the magnifications. It is doubtful whether any right half of the face is there to match the left profile. This whole structure, which has a distinct relief, may be compared with an extremely rough sculptor's model in a white, soft-yielding material, the first attempt at a death-mask of a male face.

As shown by this sitting, there is an imperfect attempt at forming the shape of a face out of the white fundamental substance.

The production gives an immediate and convincing impression of an elementary natural product, as distinct from the impression which would be produced by the shape of a face mechanically prepared for fraudulent purposes.

Sitting of the 4th November.

Negative. On this day Eva made an excursion to see some relatives. Her attention was possibly thereby deflected too strongly from her mediumistic activity.

Sitting of the 5th November 1911.

Sitters.—Mme. Bisson and the author.

Conditions as before. All the cameras had been opened since the red light was established. A change in the suspension of the red lamps allowed of a better illumination of the cabinet.

As soon as Eva had entered the hypnotic state, she asked, " Juliette, do you see anything ? "

I had feared another negative sitting, since the more vivid accompanying conditions (groaning and stertorous breathing) were absent this time. But hardly had Mme. Bisson directed her attention to the interior of the cabinet when a pink luminous mass of material fell from the roof of the cabinet, like a shooting star, into Eva's lap. It might have been the size of a child's hand. It immediately disappeared from the medium's dress.

When the light again fell into the cabinet, its rays illuminated a long vertical strip, resembling veiling or muslin, standing about 4 feet away from the medium, and having a length of from 4-6 feet. The medium then worked the curtain in such a way that she again and again opened and closed it, obviously in order to avoid the destruction of the formation by a lengthy exposure to light. In this case we could observe the changes in the strip, standing by itself behind her on the left, at least ten to fifteen times, although not distinctly, on account of the distance and the half-shadow. The top of the strip seemed to be surmounted by a half-round shape resembling a head. This ghostly phenomenon showed no connection with the medium, who was sitting quietly in her chair, and whose hands, at the same time, were constantly visible at the curtain. Every time it exposed itself, hardly for longer than a second, to the light, and always returned into the dark. It looked as though the repetition of the process had for its object a gradual adaptation to the light. Sometimes it seemed as if the head portion were growing more distinct, and the strip growing longer. Gradually a freely-suspended form, with a long white train, approached the gap in the curtains, traversing a path of about 6 feet. Here I had the impression of seeing a masculine face, with its upper half finished, while the lower was covered with a fragmentary mass, and was not all developed.

In spite of a repeated approach towards the curtains, the appearance of the face seemed to change. Once I thought I recognised a profile consisting of a mosaic of small white pieces, and of a stratified modelling,

SITTINGS OF OCTOBER AND NOVEMBER 1911 (PARIS) 123

resembling a sculptural form in the rough. The forehead and the hollows of the eyes were always easiest to recognise.

Eva asked for the red electric torch already mentioned, and made some attempts at illumination behind the curtains, in the first instance talking in a low voice to the form standing beside her. I heard expressions like the following :—" Pourquoi ne veux-tu pas ? " " Il faut s'habituer à la lumière." Again opening the curtains (probably with her feet), Eva illuminated the structure with a torch. This time I could not, indeed, recognise a head, or anything resembling it; but in its place a white bunched-up cloth about the size of a man's handkerchief, and the long strip hanging down. She then returned the torch.

Mme. Bisson, who wished to get a clear impression of the features, waited until the phenomenon was visible again, and approached the cabinet quite closely, put her head through the curtains, and claimed distinctly to recognise a masculine face with a full beard. The apparition then became visible in front of Eva's chest, whence it seemed to advance into the gap of the curtains. In one of these attempts I succeeded in observing quite closely a masculine face, with a pointed beard and closed eyes, between her hands, which held the curtains. The perception was so distinct that an optical illusion is out of the question. In consideration of the position of the camera, we expressed a wish to see the phenomenon to the right of the medium.

At first we saw, still on the medium's left, just at the hem of the curtain, a white strip about 20 inches long, which became visible several times behind the hem and parallel to it, near the middle. Then a separate white mass, not quite the size of a hand, showed itself round the hem of the curtain outside, remaining visible for about twenty seconds, and then disappeared.

At the next exposure, I just saw that her right shoulder was covered with the white luminous mass, and I quickly ignited the flash-light.

The phenomenon disappeared at once. When Eva had been carefully examined by me, with a negative result, she was taken to bed in a dazed condition. A final examination of the cabinet gave no result.

During the whole sitting Mme. Bisson only entered the cabinet twice, the first time being after the phenomenon in the corner had become visible several times.

As the successful negatives show (Figs. 49, 50, 51), Eva has her head bent forward to the left at the moment of exposure. Her whole profile and her hair are seen as far as the right temple. The hands keep the curtain open. A mask-like form is tilted over her hair. A white and partly-transparent fabric hangs from the hairy portion of the mask over her right upper arm, and disappears behind the curtain. Tapering towards the hair of the medium, the upper half of the veil is covered by a broad crosswise portion, but the object of this is not clear from the picture. The whole fabric is some 4-6 inches away from the chin and neck of the medium, and only touches Eva's body again on her upper arm. The medium's head, with the apparition, appears to be some 4-6 inches away from the back of the chair, against which she only appears to lean her left shoulder. One also sees behind the face profile a white flat mass, about the size of a hand, with an irregular-pointed margin hanging over the back of the chair.

We now come to the mask itself. We see, at the first glance, that it is intended to represent a male head, although in an extremely rough and imperfect form. The line of the profile is so clearly marked on the stereoscopic transparency that it gives the impression as if the mask-like form were cut off, and had no right half to its face. The left visible portion is clearly modelled in relief. The portion representing the nose is much too long, and too much curved and distorted, and reminds one of the nose of Cyrano de Bergerac. The hairy portions—beard and hair of the head—are distinctly seen in the right proportion as dark patches adjoining the face. Instead of the lines of the mouth there is a lip depression in the profile covered by a moustache, with hair which appears to be very short and rough, as well as curly, like fur. While the beard, on all the plates taken from in front of the cabinet, is obscured by the veil in its lower portion, it is seen in the photograph taken from within the cabinet to continue into a broad "imperial" beard, and the straight line of the lower chin becomes visible. On this plate the point of the nose appears to be cut off, which is explained by the lateral mounting of the camera. The modelling of the strongly-flattened and receding forehead is not completed on the picture. One cannot escape the impression that the unknown sculptor had left his work unfinished, or had been interrupted in his work by the flash-light. In this case the rest of the material available would naturally remain lying on the back of the chair. The position of the closed eye is indicated in an approximately correct place by a broad black shadow, which is slightly too long. The line of the eyebrows looks like a similarly sketched second eye, and is much too high, though the beginning of the hair is in its right place.

The hair itself is distinctly shown as a dark grey rough mass at the corner of the forehead. In the middle of the head there lies a small irregularly-shaped piece of white material. The ear is absent. In its place we see a few broad rough strips and irregular projections in relief, as well as parallel clefts, which had already occurred in the earliest representations of heads, and which recur, together with folds, in nearly all head forms.

Perhaps the reader will not prevail upon himself to recognise a masculine face-mask in this very clumsy, irregular, and imperfect form. That its left side is evolved in relief, *i.e.*, plastically, is placed beyond all doubt by an inspection of the transparency, but the mask appears to be hollow, and nothing in it bears the marks of life.

Sittings of the 7th, 9th and 11th November.

Negative.

A friend of the medium's family had come to Paris during these days, and daily claimed Eva's company. Such invitations appeared to absorb the medium's attention so completely that one could count upon negative results.

SITTING OF THE 12TH NOVEMBER 1911.

Sitters.—Mme. Bisson and the author.

Time, 9 P.M. Control and illumination as before.

A few minutes after the beginning of the sitting a semicircular flat mass, the size of a man's hand, appeared on the medium's lap, between her hands, which rested with fingers spread out on her knees. The fingers themselves appeared to be joined by a fine web-like membrane of a grey and veil-like appearance, which filled up the intervals between the fingers of both hands. Where this web touched the skin there was a shadow. It is, therefore, also possible that this fabric was only covered by her fingers, and only gave the optical impression of such a junction.

While Eva was thus passively allowing the materialisation process to take place, an electric bell suddenly rang in the next room, the signal for the sick nurse of the master of the house. Eva took fright, and the material observed immediately disappeared.

The creative process, which requires the undisturbed passivity of the somnambulist, was interrupted. Only after a pause for rest did the mass become visible again, in the form of more or less large irregular patches, at the shoulder and in the medium's lap.

Next, a compact mass formed on the right beside her head, which again resembled an imperfect human profile. Then a long white veil appeared above her head, while she opened the curtains with her hands, and this veil disappeared behind her head. The uppermost point of the veil was about 20 inches above her head. Then the white veil rested on her head, covering it like a nun's head-dress.

White patches and fragments were seen disseminated over her body, but the mediumistic force did not seem to suffice for real formations, or further transformations. Even these feeble phenomena disappeared after about half an hour. Eva declared herself unable to continue the sitting. She appeared to have been waked from the trance condition and disturbed in her work by the ringing of the bell. Perhaps she was still under the influence of the visit above mentioned. These feeble and diffused phenomena can only be regarded as the result of an unfavourable psychic tuning.

The final examination gave a negative result.

SITTING OF THE 14TH NOVEMBER 1911.

Negative.

SITTING OF THE 16TH NOVEMBER 1911.

Sitters.—Mme. Bisson and the author.

Control and illumination as before.

The phenomena of the sitting about to be described were obtained without the participation of the medium's hands. For the latter were either steadily visible on her knees, or they grasped the two curtains in order to close them or open them, and only seldom were they withdrawn from observation. Often the hands were seen resting in the shadow of the curtain when we unexpectedly looked behind the curtain. I repeatedly assured myself, by a turn of the head and a withdrawal of the curtain, as to the inactivity of the hands during the sitting. The medium's head was visible as soon as the curtain was sufficiently opened. Sometimes she did this with her feet, which was easy, since, as a rule, she does not wear slippers during the sittings. In some cases one even had the impression that while the feet were at rest the curtains were opened or closed by an invisible power.

The medium's head, lying on the back of the chair, only became visible when the curtain was sufficiently widely opened to enable the light to shine upon it, or when the medium herself changed her position in order to bring the head into the light.

A few minutes after the commencement of the sitting (9 P.M.) a vertical white strip about a yard long appeared on the left, beside the medium in the corner of the cabinet, *i.e.*, about 30 inches from her left shoulder. It again looked veil-like, and appeared to be held and moved at a higher level than her head. The light falling slantingly into the cabinet enabled us to verify that this structure had no visible connection with her body, but appeared to be independent and quite separated from Eva. Its profile entered the illuminated portion of the cabinet again and again. At the upper end a mass was bunched together. The hidden power seemed to be at work, for we heard noises as if textile fabrics were being rubbed together, and we also saw lively motions in the veil-like matter. Eva left the curtain open for a fairly long time, so that the appearance stood the light longer than usual. As it approached the curtains we recognised the outlines of a large hand. Quite clearly we saw three middle fingers holding a veil, and retiring with a turning motion behind the curtain.

The white shape did not disappear, but became visible again and again at the back of the left curtain beside Eva's left knee. Since my place on the opposite side permitted me to see behind the curtain, I saw in that place a broad, white, columnar mass, 16-20 inches long, and forked at the top and bottom.

The curtain was closed and again opened. Now the right curtain covered both hands, which, however, could still be seen in the shadow. Starting from her body and crossing her left lower arm, in the illuminated portion of the cabinet, two strongly luminous strips about 2 inches wide and 8 inches long, and somewhat resembling the bones of a lower arm, became visible. These ended in prolongations, resembling indistinct fingers, or skeleton hands, which appeared to unravel an extremely fine and strongly luminous mass of threads, resembling a spider's web, on the medium's dress, this mass becoming apparently broader by the withdrawal of the left curtain. The optical impression of this play belongs to the most curious observations of this mediumistic period. On one side the inactivity of Eva's arms and hands, which at any moment could be verified by a glance into the half-opened cabinet; on the other side—that is to say, to the left of the medium—these arm-like projections proceeding from Eva's body, which appeared to unravel a tangle of innumerable luminous threads and transparent veils. This picture showed a constant motion, a visible working of the mysterious power. It is not conceivable that, with the help of any known technical appliances, such a performance could be brought about.

The whole phenomena lasted from a minute to a minute and a half, a comparatively long time, until the interesting play was withdrawn from our gaze by the closing of the curtain.

Eva then requested Mme. Bisson to enter the cabinet and hold her head. She reports that the white material was now again on Eva's left side, but separated from her body. Mme. Bisson touched it. While she was still in the cabinet, her left lower arm was completely enveloped in the delicate veiling. During this time I was able to observe that Eva's two arms did not stir from their place. Mme. Bisson then endeavoured to bring her arm slowly into the light, and she eventually succeeded. On her left arm hung a fragment of material about 8 inches long, which gave an impression similar to that photographed in St Jean de Luz, as it lay in my hand.

The bringing forward of the material on the arm was evidently painful to Eva. She screamed, and at the same instant the whole mass disappeared into her mouth with a lapping and chewing motion, as Mme. Bisson in the cabinet could verify.

After a short pause the plastic process appeared to recommence. Eva said she felt the development of the material about her abdomen. She quickly seized my hand and guided it to the region of the navel. To my great astonishment I felt through the thin stuff a small knot, the size of a cherry, on the left of the navel. Under my touch I felt the knob getting smaller until it disappeared, as if it had been flattened out or absorbed into the medium's body.

The same process repeated itself under Mme. Bisson's hand at the medium's left breast. In order to show me the process, and without informing Eva, Mme. Bisson took my hand and led it to the place indicated. The medium, who obviously regarded this interference as a disturbance, screamed with fright, so that the experiment had to be discontinued without result. This nervous shock stopped the generating force immediately, so that, in spite of verbal suggestion and lengthy waiting, no more phenomena occurred. This unexpected interference also deprived us of the photograph we had hoped for.

The sitting was closed with the ordinary examination of the medium and cabinet, without result.

This experience teaches us again that it is advisable to let such experiments be preceded by an understanding with the medium, and that any method which, without consideration of the medium's nervous condition, takes her by surprise, or proceeds by violence (*e.g.*, the grasping of the structures, which has often been proposed by savants inexperienced in this subject), totally misses its object in the case of the " genuine " medium, since the fountain of observations is dried up by the psychic shock which always results from such interferences.[1] The

---

[1] If it is a case of mediums who only operate in the dark, who refuse bodily examination and other methods of control, and give serious grounds for suspicion of fraudulent manipulation, it is the duty of the experimenter to interfere without compunction.

same negative result also occurs often enough when Eva agrees with the interference, or even undertakes it herself. In this connection I may mention an occurrence from a later sitting. Eva attempted to illuminate the materialised structures with a red lantern which we handed her, but they disappeared, and did not reappear that evening. The flaring-up of the magnesium light also produces a sort of injury which, although expected and desired by her, always shortens the sitting, and often brings it to an end.

On 17th November Eva was out of sorts, and we expected that the sitting arranged for the 18th would be negative. For this reason Mme. Bisson, who had had no opportunity of hypnotising Eva on the 17th, went to the bedside of the sleeping medium at one o'clock at night, at the author's suggestion. By verbal suggestion she easily transformed the normal deep sleep into a state of hypnosis with *rapport*, as was clear from Eva's answers. Mme. Bisson made some verbal suggestions with regard to the sitting of the 18th, and as to her psychic attitude towards it.

On the 18th itself Eva was constantly in the society of her protectress, who, during the afternoon hours, was busy with sculptural work in her studio. By her conversation also, Mme. Bisson sought to stimulate Eva's interest for the sitting of that evening. This kind of psychic preparation was of astonishing success, as will be seen by the report of the evening sitting.

Sitting of the 18th November 1911.

Present.—Mme. Bisson and the author.

Conditions as usual.

The appearance of a white patch, very soon after the beginning of the sitting (9 P.M.) to the left of the medium, which appeared to change into a long, narrow, veil-like strip, implied the commencement of a positive sitting. Finally, the veil lengthened out to 7 or 8 feet, and approached the gap in the curtains, while the medium's hands were controlled, so that it was in the full light.

As the phenomenon was repeated and more closely examined we saw a hand, which appeared to grasp the veil above and pull it along; the lower end seemed to trail along the floor. Then Eva's body was covered with the material, particularly her face and shoulder. On one occasion I thought I recognised beside Eva a face in profile, which did not resemble the medium, and quickly disappeared. When, subsequently, something white again appeared, clinging to Eva's hair, as the curtain was opened, I ignited the flash-light. The successful photograph (Fig. 52) does not show a head, but material, in the shape of two superimposed leaves, attached to the back of Eva's head, and corresponding in size to her face. The lower leaf is quite white, and resembles a handkerchief. Over this there lies a rather larger piece of grey stuff of a patchy and veil-like structure, with two deep parallel folds and several smaller folds. The ribbons appear torn, and in two places have small thread-like projections resembling the fur of a rat or rabbit.

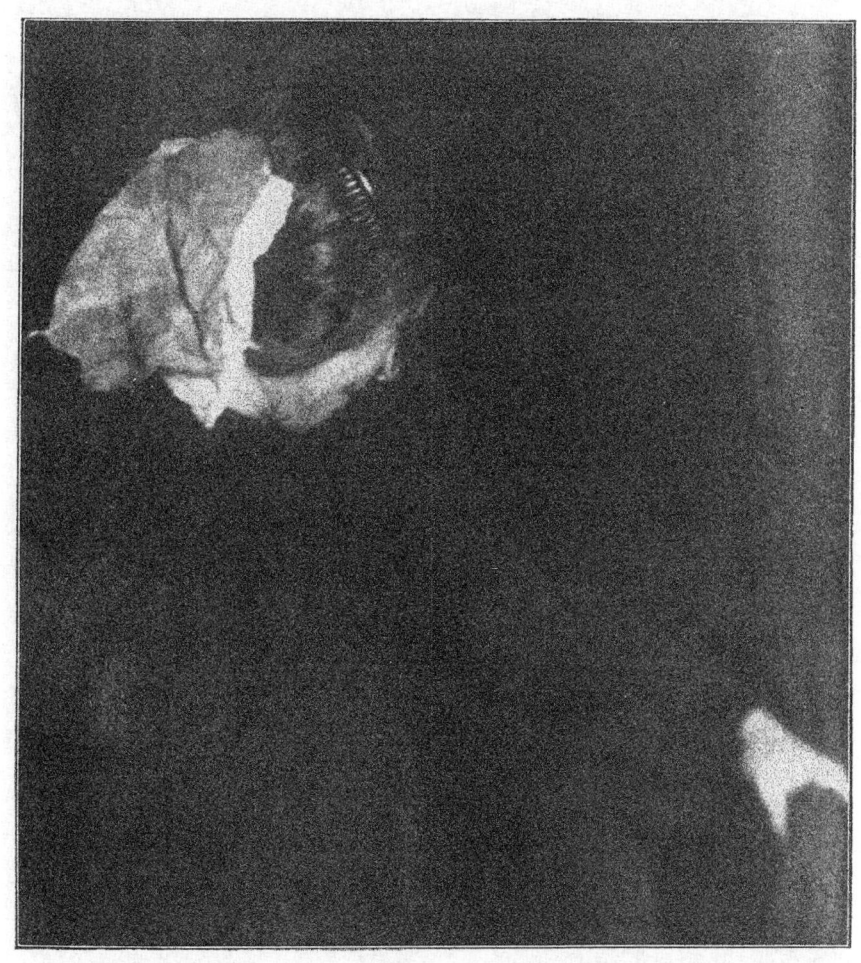

FIG. 52. AUTHOR'S FIRST FLASHLIGHT PHOTOGRAPH, 18 NOVEMBER, 1911.

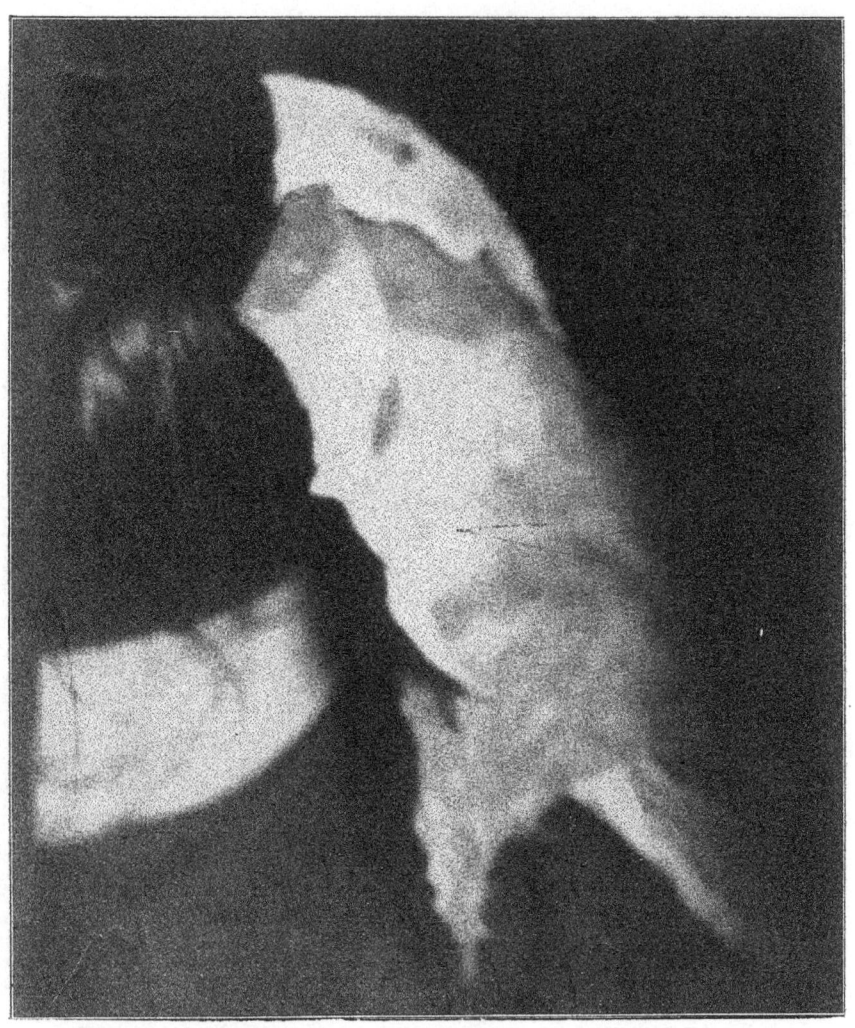

Fig 53. Author's second flashlight photograph, 18 November, 1911.

A third of the substance appears light grey, and the rest dark grey, with a rough surface.

With reference to later sittings, it may be mentioned here that these dark felt-like or fur-like substances play a great part in later photographs, especially of modelled structures, and are mostly used for the representation of the hairy portions of faces and heads. It is only by the close examination and comparison of the stereoscopic transparencies with the simple photographs that this material is recognised, which now appears for the first time on the negative.

As the sitting progressed, the author obtained a clearer and clearer impression that this material would form itself into a face. As the head-like structure approached the gap of the curtains, it gave quite a flat impression, not like a picture, but like a mask of a face, on which the features of a face were to be modelled by the sketchy insertion of small grey and white patches of some soft material. Thus, a black pointed beard was most clearly marked, while the features were only very roughly sketched. This remarkable thing moved freely, and drew a long white veil after it, which suddenly detached itself and fell to the ground, while the mask-like object disappeared backwards. When, on the medium's left side, an oblong white mass was again exposed, the author took another photograph (Fig. 53), after which the sitting had to be closed on account of Eva's fatigue.

The final examination was negative.

The second photograph shows an oblong, white, and rather thick piece of material issuing from the back of Eva's head, as if attached to her hair, falling over her left shoulder and upper sleeve, and disappearing in the dark of the cabinet. The material is closely folded. On its upper portion, at the level of Eva's head, it gives the impression of stiff crumpled paper with sharply-cut edges.

On this there lies a piece of the grey, flat, rough-haired substance above described, which resembles below a masculine beard and moustache. At the place of the nose is a great dark patch. The part corresponding to the face is a dark grey colour. Where the hair joins the forehead the dark grey substance commences again. Over that again is a white cross-piece. The eyes are absent. The part corresponding to the right half of the face is bent outward. The whole consists of a flat sharp-rimmed structure, formed of two pieces of material, lying one over the other, the upper one having a dark colour. The shape recalls the process of formation of an incomplete mask.

The comparison of the first picture of this sitting with the second suggests that the two kinds of material photographed and described are used for the reproduction of flat mask-like shapes of faces, the dark fur-like material being used for the hairy portions.

Sitting of the 21st November 1911.

The medium told us that she had waked in the night, or rather half-waked, and had seen a large white heap of material on her chest, which greatly frightened her, but she soon went to sleep again.

SITTING OF THE 22ND NOVEMBER 1911.

Present.—Mme. Bisson and the author.

This time Eva had a veiled look and did not feel well. Her hands were cold and her pulse accelerated. There was no preparatory hypnotism, as she seemed well disposed. Careful searching of her body and dress, and of the cabinet, gave no result. The cameras were fixed at a distance of 12 to 14 feet. The magnesium charge was $3\frac{1}{4}$ grammes.

Immediately after the beginning of the sitting a white mass, the size of her two hands, appeared in her lap. In order to get a good result, and not to disturb the development by the light admitted by the repeated opening of the curtains, the author asked Eva only to open the curtain as soon as a shape was sufficiently developed. Thus, at the author's special wish, the curtains remained longer closed this time, in order to allow the materialisation process to ripen.

The question of the artificial production, or the fraudulent manipulation, of the manifestations may be now regarded as settled, at least for Mme. Bisson and the author, especially in view of the remaining conditions governing the sittings. In any case, there is no occasion to refer to this question of control by a special verification as each new phenomenon arises. The interest of the highest possible advancement of the phenomenon is greater than the constant diversion of the medium's attention towards the control, as such control hinders the natural development of the phenomena and reduces the efficiency. The general course was the same as in previous sittings. To the left of the medium in the corner, at the first exposure, a white form was visible, resembling a pile of white stuff. This mass was about 5 or 6 feet from the curtain and 28 inches from Eva's face, and appeared about to assume a head-like form, but the curtain closed again. Eva whimpered and groaned, with deep and loud expirations, and appeared to suffer, and be profoundly troubled. Then we heard a rustling as if some silk material was being crumpled. When the curtain was again withdrawn, the incident light seemed to illuminate a female face, which shyly and slightly exposed itself to the light and approached us. The apparition was on the medium's left. At our request, Eva, who herself wished for a good photograph, caused the phenomenon to take up her position on the right side of her head, so that it could be taken simultaneously by the various cameras, and fall within their fields of vision. (Possibly she arranged it with her hands.)

I then requested her to decide the moment for exposure herself, according to her own feeling, by opening the curtain widely. This was done. The author pressed the electric button, but the action failed. To discover the fault, I unscrewed the push, but Eva called out " C'est le contact." This meant the plug in the wall. I should not have had this idea, but should have looked for the fault in the attachment of the flexible cord of the ignition apparatus, in one of its screws, or in the hygroscopic character of the magnesium powder. But it was found that the plug had actually been put in the wrong way.

Fig. 54. Author's flashlight photograph of 22 November, 1911.
(*Front view*)

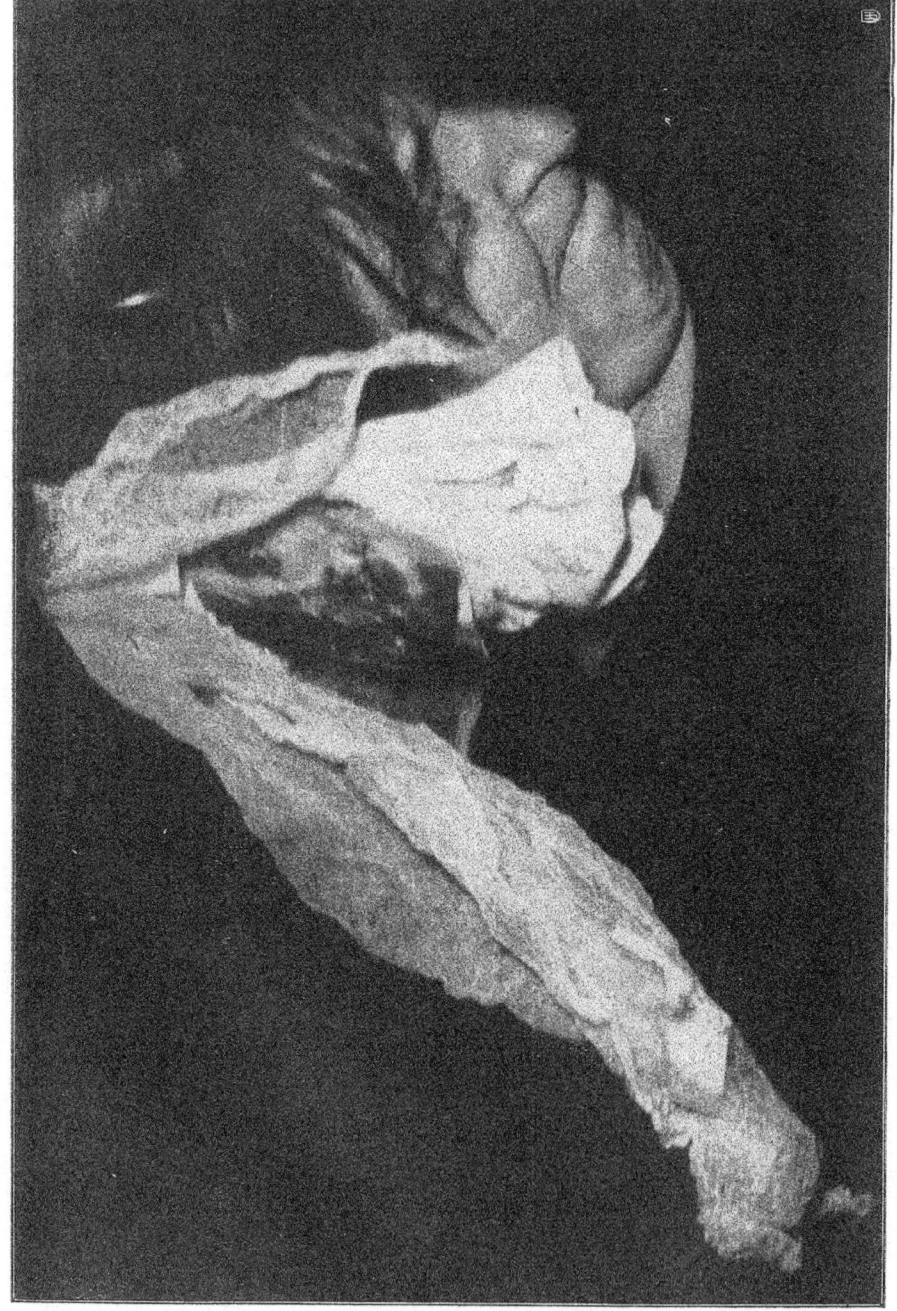

Fig. 2. Magnified portion of Fig. 1.

When, after this interruption, the medium opened the curtains again, the flash-light was ignited. After a short pause the sitting was continued. Then a head, apparently freely suspended, approached the opening of the curtains, and was, clearly recognised by Mme. Bisson and myself. In size it resembled a child's head, which was clothed like that of a nun with a white veil. During these creations Mme. Bisson, as if moved by an unconscious impulse, suddenly seized Eva's left hand. At the same moment I saw the head, which was on the medium's left, sink to the ground with lightning speed and disappear, just as an object maintained in suspension by some electric attraction would fall immediately on breaking the circuit. The face itself gave me a sketchy and unfinished impression.

When the little head showed itself again the author heard Eva speak at the same time. She wished that Mme. Bisson should cut a lock of hair off the head. As the apparition approached, Mme. Bisson took, with her right hand, a pair of scissors which I held out to her. Her left hand was guided by Eva's right hand towards the head situated at the rim of the curtain. Mme. Bisson then, under my eyes and while I could observe everything quite closely, took a lock of hair and cut off a length of about 4 inches. She at once gave half the hair to me, and I took charge of it.

The materialised structure suddenly disappeared in the direction of the medium, accompanied by a scream from Eva. It seemed as if the substance dissolved and was reabsorbed by the medium's organism. A detailed examination showed that the tights had traces of moisture near the left calf to the extent of the size of a hand. The patch had no odour, and resembled the serous moistening of bandages over wounds. Otherwise the subsequent examination was negative.

As the successful photographs show (Figs. 54, 55 and 56), Eva has widely opened the curtains with her right hand, so that her whole body is visible. Her face, bent towards the left and front, is painfully contracted. The centre of the materialised structure corresponds to the position of her right ear. In an artistic frame of white veils we see two-thirds of a pretty female face, appearing to be about half the size of Eva's. The forehead, left temple, and ear are covered by the veil, and the right eye and the right temple by hair hanging down.

The stereoscopic picture leaves it doubtful whether the left upper half of the face is developed at all. The left eye, directed towards me and inwards, is as natural and vivacious in expression as it would appear in a good photograph from life, and seems designed accordingly. With the help of masks, reproduced photographs, or hairdressers' models of heads, a similar result cannot, in the opinion of artists and other experts, be obtained.

The excellent drawing of the face, the softness of the finely-modelled form of the small head, lightly inclining to the right, the shadows everywhere strictly corresponding to the direction of the incident light, increase the impression of natural truth. In spite of the smallness of the face, it corresponds more to the type of a young woman's than a child's face. The pretty mouth, with the dimples in its corners, the slender and regularly-built nose, the rounded and rather broadly developed chin, the well-nourished curve of the cheek, together with the vivacious expression of the eye, express a certain brightness and contentment which might correspond to an age of twenty to twenty-four years.

The manner in which this small face presents itself in its frame of veiling makes an artistic impression, and even suggests a trace of coquetry and vanity. In any case, it argues a careful preparation of the toilet. The materials falling in natural lines are partly transparent, with flat solid pieces devoid of structure. The edges visible on the photograph run, as in almost all the other photographs, in very wavy or pointed lines, with irregular corners and hanging fragments and threads, but never in straight lines. A regular pattern, which might give an indication of the mode of weaving, cannot be seen either in the transparencies or in the magnifications. The side version of the picture by the camera inside the cabinet is also excellent. Here we see the small head more from in front, and the portion of the coiffure covering the left ear becomes visible. The rounded form of the face is more clearly marked. The shadows, again exactly corresponding to the incident light, especially to the left, on the chin, mouth, and nose, have here become a little brighter and softer.

Yet the face, in spite of the completed details, does not give a finished impression. In the magnifications we see several fissures and patches (*e.g.*, on the left cheek, in the corner of the mouth, and on the bridge of the nose) which resemble either pimples or a fine veil, folded and torn in some places. But these might also be due to fissures in the ground substance out of which these forms are made. Under the veil covering the forehead we see the regularly folded white material used as a base for covering the right side of the forehead.

The whole picture, in its expression, in the position of the head, in its drapery, and in the manner in which the veils are arranged and fall, makes such a natural, elemental, and harmonious impression, in spite of its incompleteness and sketchiness, as would be astonishing in an instantaneous creation of nature.

The back of the head is wanting. We have before us only a flat, one-sided development of facial relief, which lies flat against Eva's right ear, and even appears fixed above against the hair by a small projection.

Owing to the fact that the longer piece of material on the right lies with its outer edge on Eva's right shoulder, and so is prevented from covering the right half of the face, a hole is created between the right half of the face and the veil arrangement—a sort of cave, which is clearly seen in the stereoscopic transparency. The unfinished surface, which would correspond to the other half of the face, is covered by something black, which looks like hair hanging down, and cannot, in any case, be regarded as developed. There are important arguments against a possible doubt that this remarkable face is in reality plastic, *i.e.*, developed in low relief, rather than in one flat piece, with a face drawn or photographed upon it. The fall of the shadows corresponds exactly with the direction of the incident magnesium light. A difference between these shadows in the front view picture produced by the

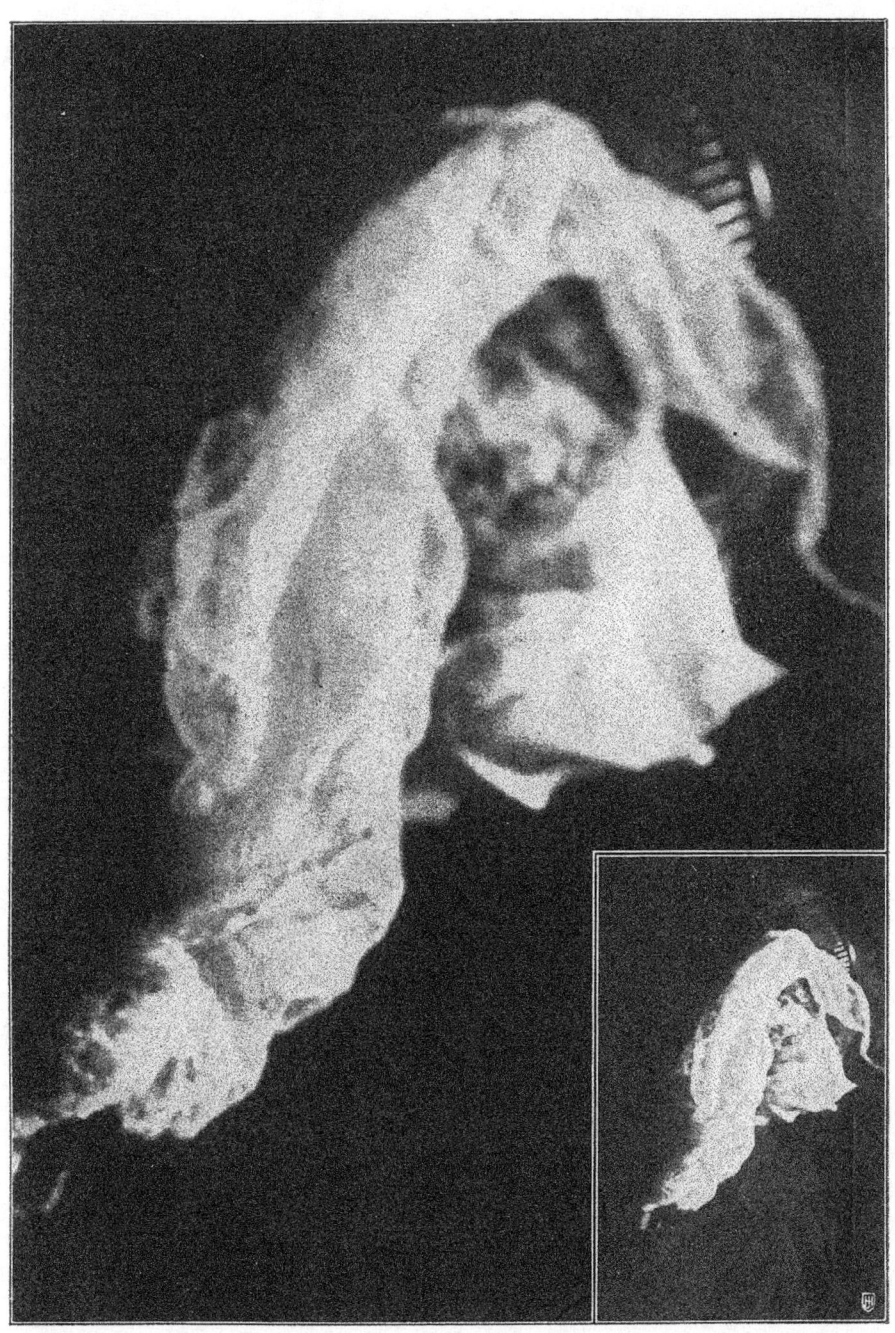

FIG. 56. LATERAL VIEW, WITH MAGNIFICATION, OF FIG 54, TAKEN FROM THE CABINET

I A

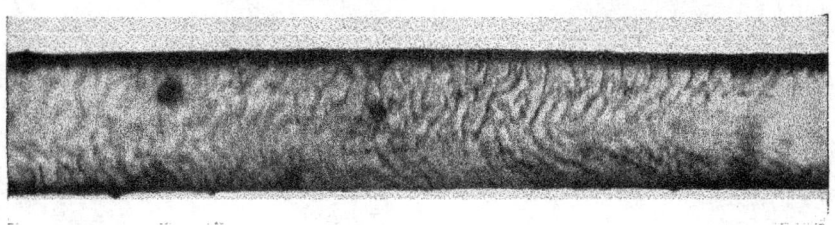

II A

I B

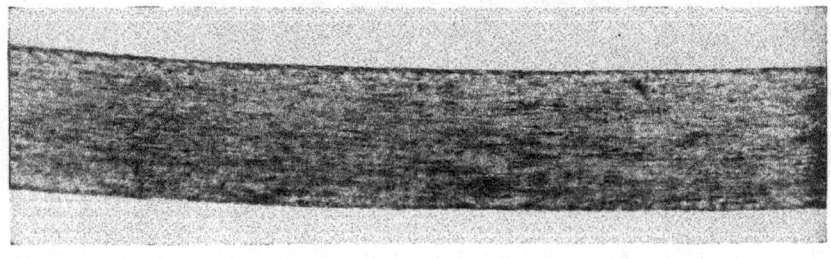

II B

FIG. 57. MICROPHOTOGRAPHS OF EVA'S HAIR (II) AND "ESTELLE'S" HAIR (I).

SITTINGS OF OCTOBER AND NOVEMBER 1911 (PARIS)

camera in the cabinet and the profile picture of the external camera would be impossible in the case of a photograph previously illuminated, or in the case of a product of lithography or graphic art, also provided with shadows before exposure. Although this would suffice to decide the question, I arranged for the careful measurement of the different stereoscopic pictures magnified to 6 feet. The distance between the two cameras brings about certain changes in size and in the design of the chief features on the negatives, and these sizes were correctly measured, with special reference to the nose projection. The difference amounts to $1\frac{1}{2}$ mm., which is easily understood, considering the smallness of the objects measured, and this again gives a further proof of the plastic relief of the face. Also, the high light on the eye corresponds with the incident light, and argues a convex form of the eyeball, which increases the living impression.

The hair obtained at the same sitting is evidently derived from the strands of hair seen hanging on the right half of the face down to the neck. After the sitting I cut a lock of hair from the medium, with her permission, so as to get material for comparison. While Eva's hair showed altogether a brunette character, the hair taken from the small head was light blonde. This impression is completely corroborated by the chemical examination and microphotography of the samples of hair of Eva and "Estelle" (the name by which the medium denotes the face photographed), which was made by Dr Steiner in Munich.

In the samples of hair, the expert says that the marrow cylinder is absent, so that it must be regarded as hair of the head. That we have to deal with human hair is shown by the microphotograph of the hair in air (magnified 440 times). The epidermis (Fig. 57) is furrowed crossways over the whole width in a manner characteristic of human hair only. The microphotographs of the two hair samples, in glycerined gelatine, bring out the difference between the two samples as much as the microphotograph in air. While Estelle's hair only shows slight pigmentation, Eva's hair is distinctly provided with granular pigment. Seen in polarised light, both samples show double refraction, with the optical axis in the direction of growth.

Treated with sulphuric acid, potash, and chromic acid, both samples split up into elementary fibrils without showing any peculiar characteristic features.

The differences in the two hair samples as regards pigmentation, structure of the fibres, and of the epidermis, does not yet make it certain that the hair is drawn from different individuals, since different colours of hair grow in one and the same person. The difference in the epidermal structure may be due to different ages of the hair. But the expert noticed, when treating the samples with warm sulphuric acid (80 per cent., temperature 50° C.), that the sample taken from Eva dissolved into its fibrils much more cleanly than Estelle's hair when treated in the same manner. Eva's hair dissolved very naturally into its elements, while Estelle's hair not only showed this dissolution, but a partial solution of the fibrils themselves. This difference indicates a difference in the chemical constitution of the substance, which is not seen in one and the same individual. It is therefore probable that both samples of hair belong to different individuals.

SITTING OF THE 25TH NOVEMBER 1911.

Present.—Mme. Bisson and the author.

Conditions as in previous sittings.

After several exposures of a white material on Eva's left shoulder, I saw, to the left of her head, a white disk-like structure. At the next opening of the curtain I turned on the current, and took a photograph. The sitting was then closed, and the final examination was negative.

The pictures (Figs. 58 and 59) are very successful, and show Eva with compressed mouth and closed eyes in her chair. The face is turned half to the left. A fairly long fragment of material, about 2 inches wide, and folded several times, joins the back of her hair with the left curtain from within, and appears to be fastened at both ends (by Eva's hands?). From this hangs a second piece of fur-like substance, the size and shape of a lady's handkerchief, forming a rectangular flat surface with irregular margins. This is attached to the strip by its narrow edge. An examination of the piece of material in the stereoscopic transparency shows that the surface is covered with numerous irregular folds, both small and large. The light grey centre is well marked off in the middle, from the darker and broader margin. The whole makes an impression more of rough fur or skin than of a woven fabric or a product of wood fibre. In its whole composition it recalls the piece photographed on the 18th November 1911. As we shall see later, the same substance is used as a base for the head structures.

Observations in December 1911 (Paris).

THE physical need towards materialisation often occurred spontaneously with Eva at odd times, and appears to depend upon her physical condition.

As already mentioned, Mme. Bisson was in the habit of hypnotising Eva every evening in the cabinet (but in her day dress), in order to maintain the suggestive *rapport* and to influence her psychic condition favourably towards the sittings.

In a letter of 9th December 1911, she reports as follows :—

" Yesterday I hypnotised Eva as usual, and she unexpectedly began to produce phenomena. As soon as they began, Eva allowed me to undress her completely. I then saw a thick thread emerge from the vagina. It changed its place, left the genitals, and disappeared in the navel depression.

" More material emerged from the vagina, and with a sinuous serpentine motion of its own it crept up the girl's body, giving the impression as if it were about to rise into the air. Finally it ascended to her head, entered Eva's mouth, and disappeared.

" Eva then stood up, and again a mass of material appeared at the genitals, spread out, and hung suspended between her legs. A strip of it rose, took a direction towards me, receded, and disappeared. All this happened while Eva stood up. She then sat down on the floor, supported her head on her joined hands, and her elbows on my knees. At that moment another broad strip of material appeared, lying across her knees. At one end of it the shape of an imperfectly materialised, but quite recognisable, hand became visible. A further mass of material appeared on Eva's left shoulder. Then the whole mass disappeared and did not reappear."

The above report is supplemented by a letter of 13th December, which contains answers to questions put by the author. It appears that the material vanished after its first appearance as if it had been dissolved, also at the end of the sitting. During the whole process the curtains were open, and the red lights were burning as during the sittings. Mme. Bisson was in front of the cabinet and Eva inside. During the upward motion of the strip, from the genital passage to the mouth, the material showed slowly undulating movements.

At one moment the material rose in the air, and seemed to try and detach itself from the medium's body, while Eva was motionless. It gave the impression of being directed by some unseen force, while she herself was passive. Slowly, as if of very light weight, the material sank back.

Mme. Bisson was able to observe these phenomena from beginning to end without interruption. The colour of the material was grey, without transparency. She adds: " I know that these facts, having been observed by me alone, are therefore of less value in the eyes of many savants. Discoveries increase in importance in proportion to the amount of the observational material. Even if you, and other sitters, do not succeed in obtaining the same results as I, my collected experiences, committed to writing, may yet serve the truth. It is quite natural that I, who live with the medium, and observe her the whole day, hypnotising her regularly, should get to see more than savants, who only participate from time to time."

In a letter of 11th December, Mme. Bisson touches the question raised by the author as to detaching a piece of the material produced by Eva. She refers to the fact that the well-known medium, Mrs d'Esperance, was seriously injured in her health by one of those present grasping the transfiguration : " To an invitation to Paris, this lady, who was not a professional medium, but gave sittings solely in the interests of science, replied that she would never again offer herself for any kind of experiments, not because she lacked confidence in her own powers, but because she mistrusted the savants, who, in her somnambulic condition, had grasped the material. In consequence she was seriously ill for several months, and had never regained her full health. Yet I know that it would be of the highest scientific interest to obtain a piece of this material. In my opinion, its analysis would only yield organic substances derived from Eva's body. At the present moment, when the phenomena originate in the vagina, they would probably only contain cells, and cell products, corresponding to the anatomical structure of the vagina. I therefore do not wish to employ any force or compulsion which might injure the medium, quite apart from the unpleasantness I might thereby incur with her relatives. Believe me, she prefers her health to any sort of phenomena. She lends herself to these experiments to please me. She has no conception of the importance of the phenomena, not being sufficiently well informed. Nor does she want to read anything about them, and keep herself up to date. Every day she tells me that she is bored, and wants to marry. Still, I have the desire and the intention to possess a piece of the material. But I wish to get it from her, *i.e.*, with her consent. I expect to succeed by great patience and perseverance, but not by violence. Do not say that Eva runs no risk. You cannot be sure of that, since you do not know yourself what the material consists of, nor how it is connected with her body. In yesterday's sitting I saw, about ten times running, a completely materialised hand of an extraordinarily firm consistence, which several times touched my hand, and each time laid a piece of veil on the palm of my hand. The little finger and thumb were joined by a fine ribbon. I never saw a hand as clear as this."

Answering some questions concerning the phenomenon, the lady supplemented her report in a letter of 16th December as follows :—

" While the materialised hand touched me, both Eva's hands visibly held the curtain, and in order to be quite certain I touched both Eva's hands with my left hand."

She continues her report (letter of 11th December) as follows :—

"Suddenly Eva declared she felt nothing more. She hiccoughed as if about to vomit, complained of sickness, and said : ' I wish to go to bed without being wakened.' I therefore took her to bed. She appeared to suffer, and cried out. I hesitated to waken her, but suddenly she said I was wrong to close the sitting, as ' they ' (meaning the entities in the mediumistic sense) were annoyed, since they were still there and wanted to show themselves.

"Thereupon the phenomena commenced again in the bed, the material again emerging from the vagina, as some days before. Eva lay stretched on her back, and I knelt in front of the bed. The mass emerging from the genitals had the shape of a thick and solid strip, passing along the thigh, and appearing to recede into her body. Suddenly she exclaimed, ' Look, look, it comes again ; I feel a head.' Then a round and fairly solid sphere, of the shape and size of a billiard ball, fell into my hand as it lay with the palm upwards between her legs. Also another, quite small, one. The sphere was attached to her body by a ribbon. I thus held in my hand this mysterious living mass, which moved on the palm of my hand. I rose with the intention of closing my hand in order to achieve the long-desired success, when suddenly the whole thing disappeared from my hand as if it had been vaporised. I searched in the bed and under the medium, but found no trace. All had disappeared, and remained so.

"Eva felt free and at rest, and I could go to bed. Can you give me the key to these mysterious occurrences, which I report to you just as I have experienced them ?"

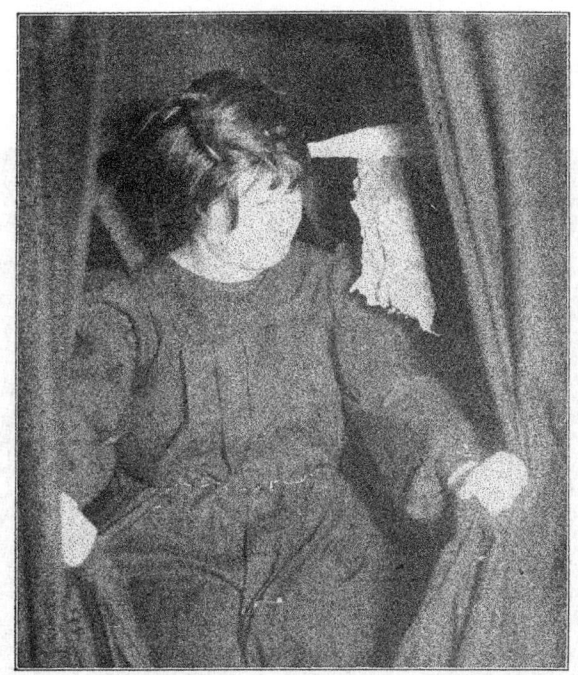

FIG 58. AUTHOR'S FLASHLIGHT PHOTOGRAPH OF 25 NOVEMBER, 1911. (*Front view*)

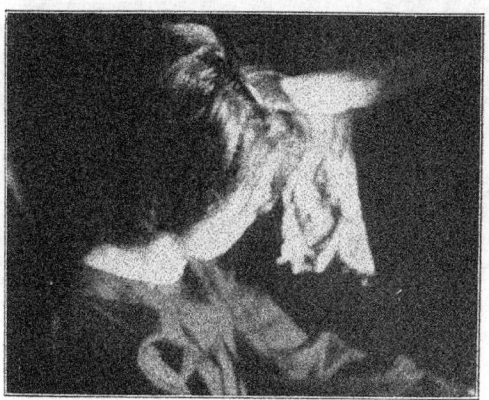

FIG. 59. THE SAME TAKEN IN SIDE VIEW FROM THE CABINET

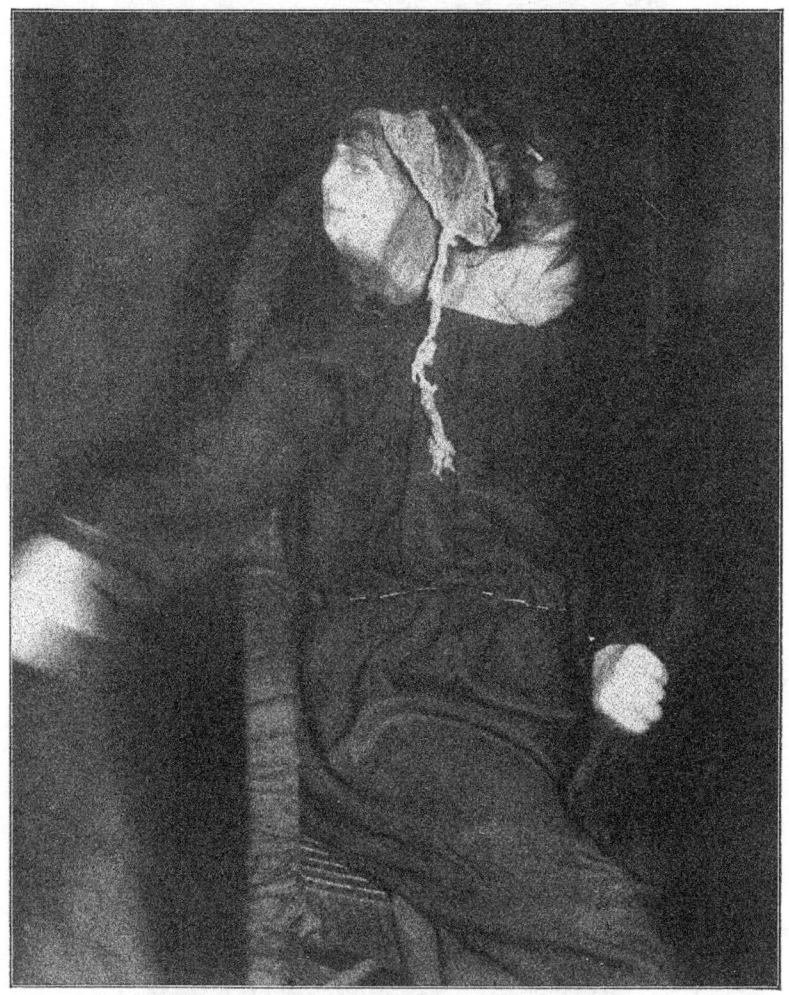

Fig. 60. Flashlight photograph by the author, 30 December, 1911.

Further, Mme. Bisson reports in a letter of 18th December 1911 :—
" Last night I held a sitting, in which a lady took part. After the entity ' la petite Estelle ' had shown itself several times, a male face appeared, and three times I clearly recognised my deceased nephew. The apparition disappeared slowly, being wafted upwards. Then the medium said, ' I see nothing more, nothing at all.' I then wanted to awaken Eva, but found her still so dazed that I took her to bed in that condition. I did not leave her, but waited to see if anything further would happen. Ten minutes after she had lain down, the stertorous breathing began again, and she fell into catalepsy. Then phenomena appeared in the region of the vagina. A flat ribbon of material emerged from the genitals, remaining joined to them by a small junction. I touched it and pulled at it (which made Eva scream), and hoped to withdraw a small piece hanging loose. But, unfortunately, I did not succeed, as Eva resisted too much, and the whole product was reabsorbed into the vagina. The material was white, and showed in the centre a black patch like a hole. After it had disappeared, Eva exclaimed, ' Oh, I suffer no more ; I feel very well.' I let her lie, and·suggested to her to sleep well till the morning. She awoke refreshed the next morning, and was cheerful the whole morning. But already by 2 o'clock on that day she became numbed, and her eyes assumed a peculiar expression. The afternoon passed without anything special happening. But hardly had I hypnotised her at 9 P.M. when the entity ' la petite Estelle ' showed itself seven times in succession, but too far behind the curtain to be photographed."

Sittings of December 1911 and January 1912 (Paris).

SITTINGS OF THE 27TH AND 29TH DECEMBER 1911.

Sittings negative.

Eva's attention had been distracted by the presence of a friend of the family in Paris. She appeared nervously excited, and passed through one of those crises which take several days to subside.

SITTING OF THE 30TH DECEMBER 1911.

Sitters.—Mme. Bisson and the author.

Conditions, control, and illumination as in previous sittings.

Immediately after the extinction of the white light and the setting-in of the somnambulic state, Eva made the well-known noises of long-drawn expirations and stertorous groaning and gasping. Hardly had I taken my place to the medium's right, when a white mass, double the size of a hand, became visible in her lap. During the following twenty minutes the psychophysical efforts continued. The substance changed its place, and at the next exposure we saw it on Eva's head. I requested her to show the female face previously photographed, which, according to the medium, belongs to an entity " Estelle," and this was promised. Also, the head was to be visible in a larger size than before.

After another ten minutes the curtain opened again, and I saw attached to Eva's head, on the right side, a female face in profile, swathed like a nun. The bandage went over the forehead and covered the ears, but the image was only visible for a moment in the light. When next the curtains were opened the head stood a little lower, about the level of her chest, 20 inches above her right hand. I then saw the same pretty female face quite distinctly, and I was so surprised by the natural colour and the life-like expression, that my first impression was that it might be the (not simultaneously visible) head of the medium swathed in material (" transfiguration ").

I communicated this idea to Mme. Bisson, and did not attach to the phenomenon the importance which it assumed afterwards.

Again I addressed a request to the medium—or, rather, to the intelligence here at work—that " la petite Estelle " might expose herself for photography at the right place, *i.e.*, to Eva's right, since the camera inside the cabinet was focused on that point. As soon as the female profile showed itself again, I switched on the current.

The nervous shock produced by the light resulted in a tetanic contraction of the medium's voluntary muscles. Respiration ceased, and was only slowly restored. After the exposure Mme. Bisson entered the cabinet, in order to soothe Eva and enable her to recover.

After she had recovered and the plates had been changed, the female face was seen again. This time, however, the curtain covered Eva's head, so that the profile of the materialised female head could only be seen through the magnesium smoke in the room. In bearing and position the two heads, taken within seven minutes of each other, are equal. After this the sitting had to be closed, on account of the exhaustion of the medium. The subsequent examination showed that the tights were stained with blood in the genital region (menses). Eva had removed the usual bandages before the sitting.

On developing the photographs (Figs. 60, 61, and 62) it was found at once that the female face seen and photographed by the author did not belong to the medium. The photographic results of the five cameras count among the best of the collection. The two stereoscopic pictures differ only in the size of the objects shown, while the two profile photographs, *i.e.*, that of the interior lateral camera, and that of the 7 by $9\frac{1}{2}$ inches camera, show the same head, but from different points of view.

The female face—one-third smaller than the medium's head, but, according to my wish, larger than the last photograph of Estelle— covers with its back portion the whole of Eva's head (turned to the left and forward) from the right ear down to the neck of the dress. It appears as if growing out of the medium's neck. The neck of the apparition, visible along its whole length, is attached like a stalk to Eva's neck, as if growing from it, and this gives the picture the character of a Janus-like double head. Unfortunately, a fragmentary hanging strip of the much-folded grey and white head-covering covers with its shadow the very point where the two heads appear to join.

The face, completely developed in its design, is regular. The particular characteristics of this type are: the lines of the small

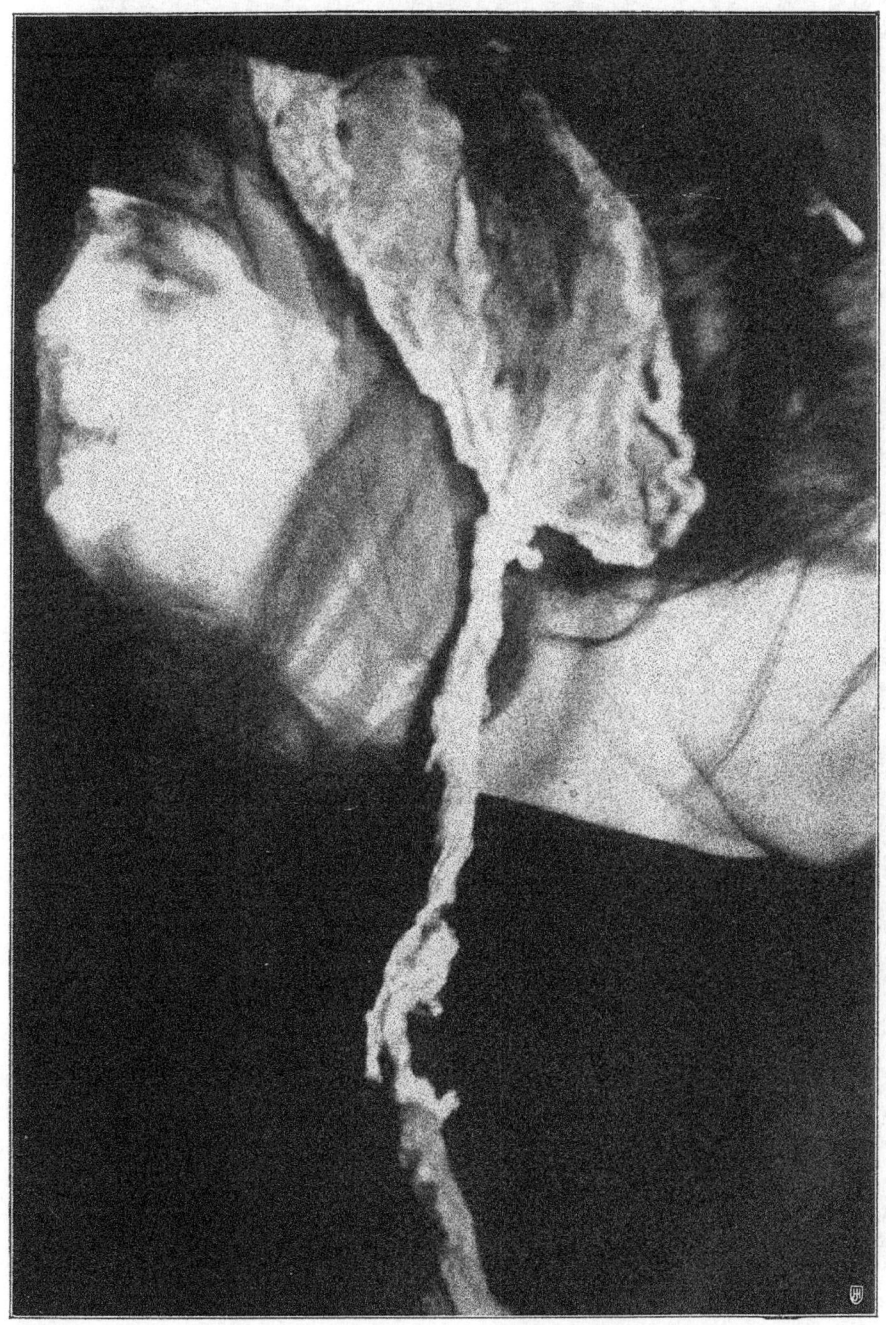

Fig. 61. Magnification from Fig. 60.

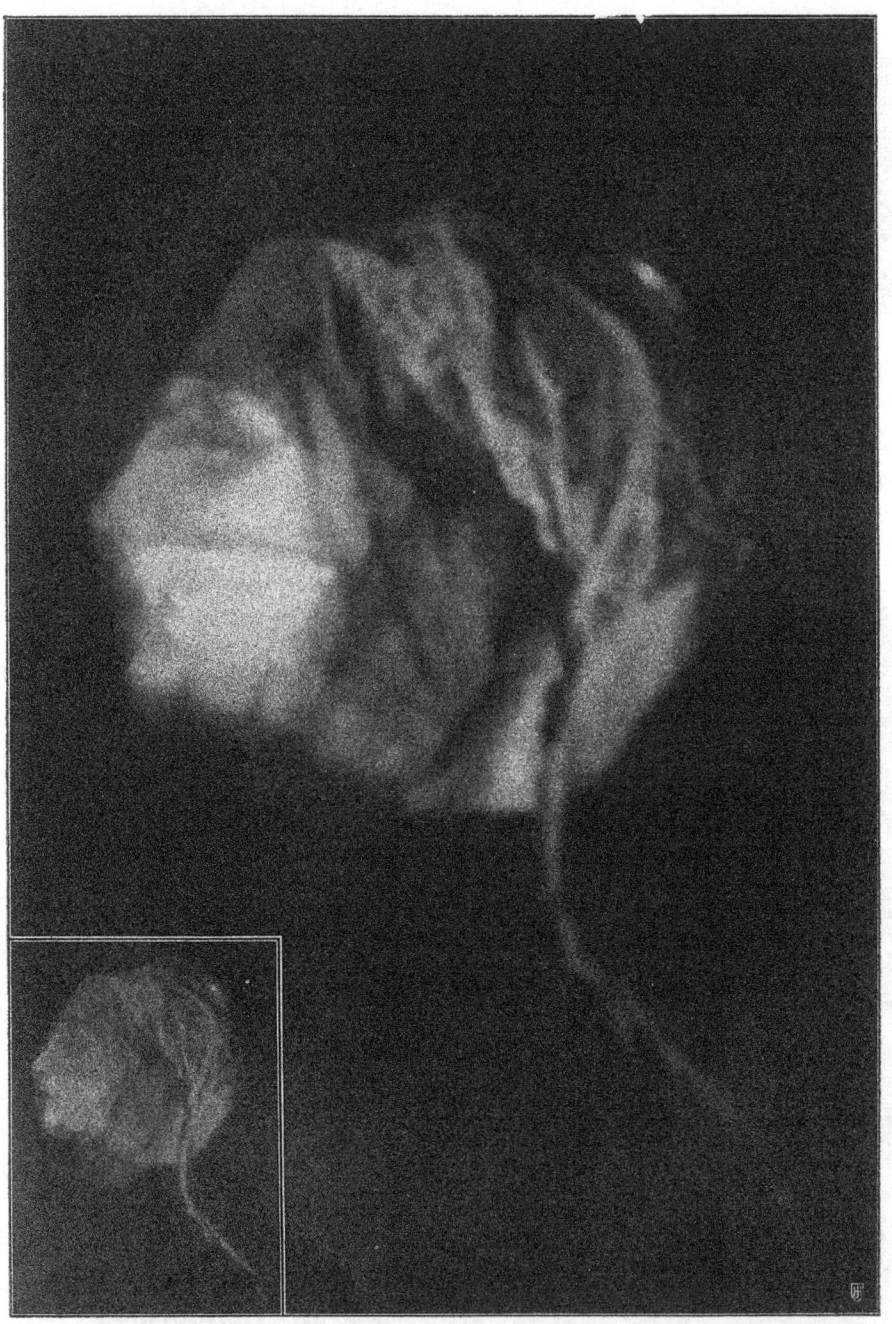

FIG. 62 SIDE VIEW OF FIG. 60 TAKEN INSIDE THE CABINET, WITH ENLARGEMENT.

SITTINGS OF DECEMBER 1911 AND JANUARY 1912

bridge of the nose, which, without an indentation, passes into the forehead in almost a straight line; the fine drawing of the side of the nose; the comparatively great distance between the nose and the upper lip; the small closed mouth, with straight thin lips; and the rather short rounded chin, tapering forward and appearing almost angular in this photograph, with its lower line almost as if cut straight where it passes towards the throat.

The rather large, well-shaped, and deep-set eye has a dreamy expression, and is almost half covered by the upper eyelid. The left cheek, on the other hand, gives the impression of a dull surface without high lights or half shadows, without folds or modelling, and this does not contribute to the vivacity of the expression. The forehead down to the eyebrows is capped with a thick, dark grey, felt-like stuff, which, however, seems to dissolve into transparent veils, and completely envelopes the face and head. This veil, carefully arranged in folds, is joined in a loose knot under the chin. Over the junction of the hair of the two women there lies the cap-like fabric already mentioned, from which a strip hangs down to the middle of Eva's breast.

The observer's curiosity as to how these two heads are joined is left unsatisfied. The magnified picture taken by the inner camera corresponds, by virtue of its finer drawing, to the classical profile, and recalls heads on Etruscan and Greek vases—as a work of art it is an excellent production. From the study of these photographs alone, one cannot decide how far these face forms are developed plastically. To me, personally, the profile view of the face appears flat, while the whole drapery of the head, including the veils, consists of real materials. The stereoscopic photographs leave no doubt of this.

Neither can the question be decided as to whether there is a right half of the face, nor whether it is plastically developed. In beauty of form and purity of drawing, this face stands in the foremost rank.

The second negative (Fig. 63), obtained at the same sitting, is somewhat veiled by the magnesium smoke in the room. It only gives the head of "Estelle," which, when magnified, appears softer, more vivid, and more plastic than in the last photograph.

It shows some essential differences from the first picture. We see nothing of the lace cover of the head, while the turban-like head ornament remains, and is more closely bound. In addition, the shape of the chin is more rounded, and the expression brighter, and, generally, the second photograph looks more complete than the first. There is a remarkable difference in the way the head is held in the two photographs. In the first one the face is stretched forward, so that the throat and the lower chin form nearly a straight line, whereas, in the second picture, they are distinctly curved by the head being withdrawn. This is clear on comparing the stereoscopic pictures with the others.

In a careful examination of the first two photographs, as compared with the three-quarter profile taken from the side, the differences in the lenses used, and the different positions of the cameras, must be taken into account. Nevertheless, the slightly different shadows in the three pictures show that it was not a rigid form on an immovable foundation, as, for instance, a drawing on paper.

Sittings of the 2nd, 3rd and 4th January 1912.

Negative.
This failure is possibly explained by the various diversions and entertainments connected with the New Year. My disappointment was not lost on Eva. On the 4th January she made great efforts to bring about phenomena, and, in the somnambulic state towards the close of the sitting, she said, " Je voudras lui donner ma tête si je pourrais." So she was ready to make every sacrifice in order to satisfy the sitters. This little observation shows how easily a professional medium might, under less rigid conditions, be influenced by the strong suggestion of her own ambition, and the keen desire of the sitters, and led to indulge in fraudulent manipulations.

The despair of the medium also shows that the production of phenomena does not depend only upon her own will, though she may, indeed, be able to furnish psychic conditions favourable or unfavourable to the occurrence of phenomena. Even a strong deflection of her attention, a vivid mental preoccupation, and other things (*e.g.*, a letter from a friend, a question of dress, visits, stimulating conversation before the sitting, impatient waiting for late sitters), suffice to destroy the necessary passive and receptive condition of the mediumistic mind, which is so essential to the phenomena. In such cases a sort of psychic impotence brings about an inhibition of the necessary emotional state, and a resistance to the physiological process of teleplastic emanations; hence the unsatisfying condition of trial, and failure sets in.

Sitting of the 5th January 1912.

Sitters.—Mme. Bisson and the author.

Conditions as usual.
Even before the sitting, while in the waking state, Eva gave a peculiar dream-like and dazed impression (condition of slight hysterical absence). Mme. Bisson said, " Elle est déjà prise." Hypnotisation required barely fifteen seconds. The author opened the camera in the cabinet while Mme. Bisson held Eva's hands. Immediately after hypnotisation, while the curtain was being drawn, we heard loud, long, and deep expirations, lasting from three to twenty seconds. These expirations gave the subjective impression as if with this intense breathing she exhaled some kind of material.

Mme. Bisson steadily held her hands. After about five seconds, Eva disengaged her left hand, and used it for opening the curtain, so that both hands still remained visible. We then saw attached to her head, which was turned to the left, a white mass, 20 inches long, with torn and ragged edges. She opened and closed the curtains several times without changing the position of her hands, as described. The material had then disappeared from the head, shoulder, and upper arm, and could not be discovered anywhere in the cabinet.

Obviously the substance had separated from her body in order to

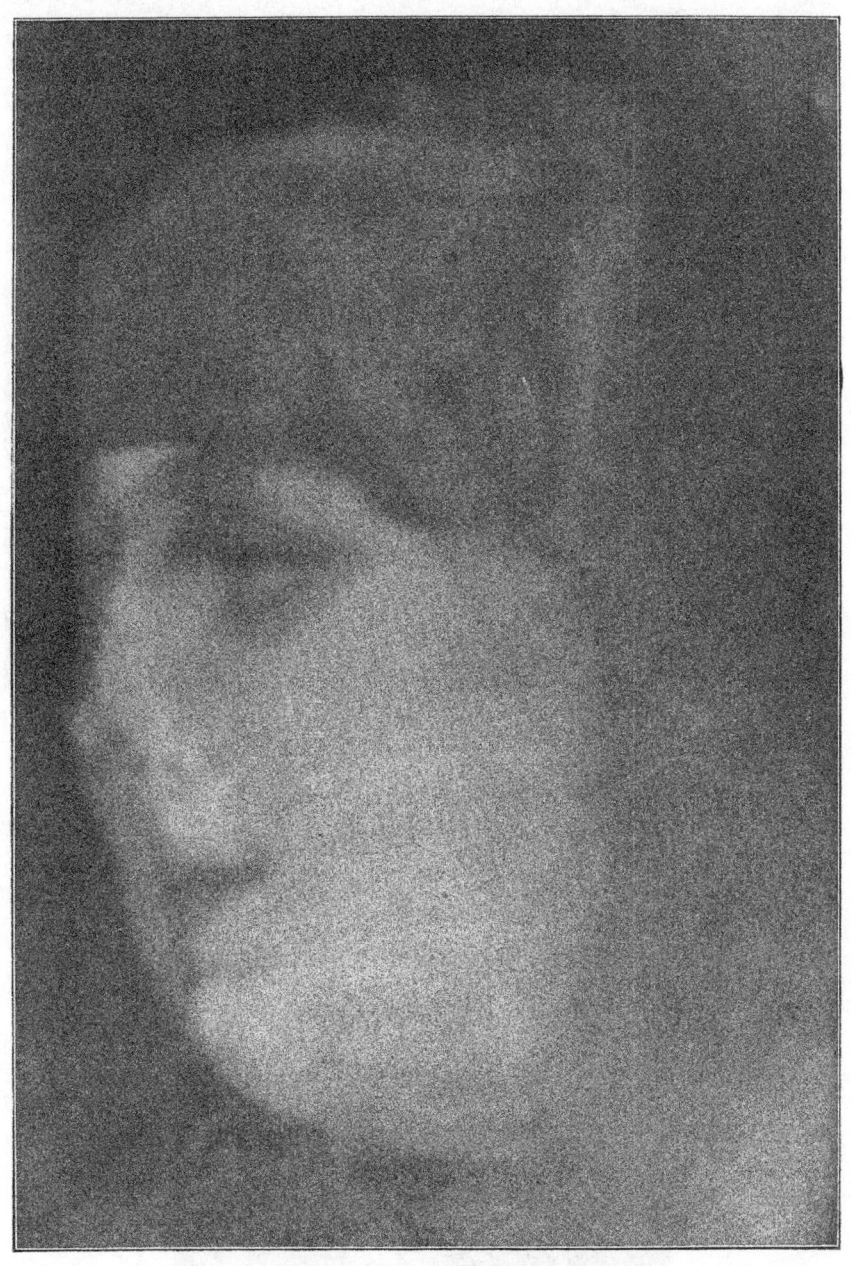

Fig. 63. Magnification of part of author's second flashlight photograph of 30 December, 1911.

Fig. 64. Author's first flashlight photograph, 7 January, 1912.

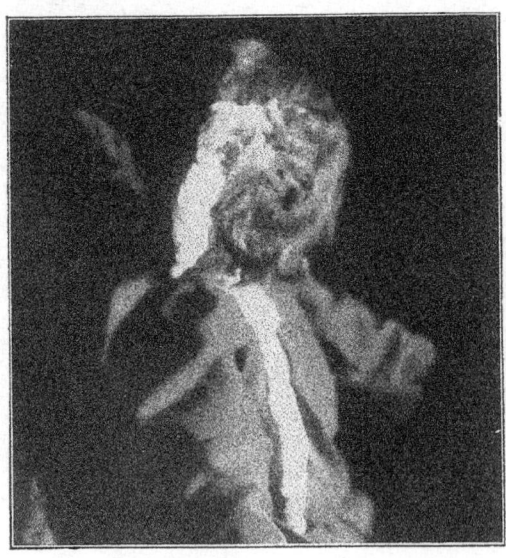

Fig 65. Side view of last picture, taken inside the cabinet

SITTINGS OF DECEMBER 1911 AND JANUARY 1912

serve as material for the coming phenomena. We expressed a wish to see again the female face, described by the medium as " Estelle," which had been photographed at the last sitting, and this time we wished to see it in front view, and with a smiling expression.

Eva then withdrew her hands. The curtain remained closed entirely for about a quarter of an hour, while her gasping and whimpering indicated that something was happening. During the next exposure the curtain usually remained open for about three seconds, so that we had sufficient time to make a general survey of the picture, with its chief characteristics.

First, we saw, in front of her face, the upper part of a male face, which appeared plastically developed, with forehead, eyes, and temples, but resembling a mask half cut off. The place of the nose was taken by a long, narrow, white fragment which was freely mobile. The mouth and lower jaw were absent. The eyes could not be recognised. I could not make up my mind to take a photograph, since I wanted to secure a finished, and more distinctly developed, face.

After this rough shape had shown itself several times we saw, to the right of Eva's head, the lower half of a male face, again resembling a portion of a mask. The mouth was half open and seemed to smile, as we had wished. There was no beard.

Next we saw, in the left corner of the cabinet, a white head-like patch, separated from the medium, and standing about 6 feet high. It gave the impression of a beardless male face in profile. This imperfect formation did not approach us, in spite of several invitations. As we could distinctly see through the rather narrow gap in the curtains (3 or 4 inches wide), the object had separated from the medium's body. Eva herself expressed a wish that it should come forward and become more distinct. As this wish still remained without response, she borrowed my little red electric torch in order to illuminate the product herself. But when the light fell on it the apparition immediately disappeared, and did not come again that evening.

Again we saw on Eva's right shoulder a white veil-like mass, and noticed a female face in miniature, the size of a small child's head, seen from the front.

Eva asked us to wait for the photograph, as the head would grow larger. She again borrowed the little red torch and illuminated the apparition, so that I could observe it more closely.

My first impression was that of a flat picture framed in a cleverly-arranged veil. Without a knowledge of the conditions, one might be tempted to consider the apparition as fraudulent, and as brought about by well-known means. When the curtain again opened, I had the distinct impression that this female face was plastic and modelled in low relief, and had therefore changed its appearance. The colour of the face was grey, and the size of the head corresponded to that of a child about two years of age.

After that a white mass developed in the same place without a distinct form or features. This disappeared completely, and the sitting ended. Final examination of cabinet and medium negative.

We must deny any life-like character to the forms seen to-day. They were simply fragments of a mask-like or picture-like character.

SITTING OF THE 6TH JANUARY 1912.

Negative.

SITTING OF THE 7TH JANUARY 1912.

Present.—Mme. Bisson and the author.

Conditions as usual. Commenced at 8.30 P.M.

Eva had very cold hands before the sitting. The curtain remained closed for half an hour, while Eva's behaviour indicated positive results. After half an hour I saw through the barely-open curtain a white mass pretty high over the medium's head. The whole behaviour of the medium gave an impression of deep trance and great effort.

Only towards 9.45 did she give glimpses into the cabinet by opening the curtain, saying that "la petite Estelle" wanted to show herself to us. Eva had turned her head to the left, and I could see perched on her hair a female face in profile, not quite normal size, the two faces being turned away from each other. The forehead and head were draped with white cloths and veils.

Curiously enough, Eva exclaimed beforehand, "I see hair—much hair." (The photograph taken subsequently furnishes the explanation of these words.)

Nevertheless, the profile, which resembled the female face photographed at the previous sitting, gave a less clear impression. After several efforts by the medium the face appeared to grow more distinct. A long fragmentary strip hung down from her right shoulder.

As soon as she opened the curtain again, I closed the electric contact, and changed the plates at once. Meanwhile, Mme. Bisson entered the cabinet, in order to soothe the Eva, who had been violently affected by the light, and was trembling. She says that as she entered the cabinet the apparition disappeared, though Eva had not changed her position. But in the left corner of the cabinet she saw a long white structure, resembling a strip of muslin. When Eva had recovered, some minutes later, Mme. Bisson resumed her place. Immediately the same female face appeared, in the same place.

After changing the plates and adjusting the flash-light powder (about seven minutes) I resumed my seat, and, during the next opening, I took a second photograph. The structure disappeared, like the others, without leaving a trace, and the sitting had to be closed.

Eva showed an accelerated pulse of 104 per minute, and, after being carefully searched, she was taken to bed in a shaken condition. Some mucus and a little blood issued from her mouth and genital passage. Final examination negative.

The observations of the sitting were confirmed, on all essential points, on the development of the plates.

In the first series (Figs. 64, 65 and 66) we see a pretty female profile perched on the right-hand portion of Eva's head and neck, and resting

FIG. 66. ENLARGEMENT OF PORTION OF FIG. 64.

Fig. 67. Author's second flashlight photograph, 7 January, 1912.

SITTINGS OF DECEMBER 1911 AND JANUARY 1912

on her right shoulder. This seems to consist of a white mass, and shows little indication of plastic modelling, as far as the face alone is concerned. The lower part of the profile (the line from the corner of the mouth to the nose) is surprisingly long as compared with the upper part.

The face is covered by a fine transparent veil, which appears to be torn in the region of the left eye. The forehead, which is slightly too low, is encased in black shiny material, which covers the head like a cap, and then covers the hair in curious loops and knots, folded something like black taffetas.

Besides this bandage there are three layers of a veil-like substance, appearing partly light grey and partly dark grey. The particularly fine turban-like arrangement, which could only be unravelled by careful study of the stereoscopic transparencies, forms the principal origin of a rich variety of broad, well-dressed locks of hair, covering the whole hinder portion of the face, from the eye and the corner of the mouth backwards, so completely that only in one place does the white base shine through. The colour of the hair was dark (black in the photograph). It ends on Eva's shoulder in curls, turned upward and appearing as if singed with curling-irons. Underneath these a long transparent veil hangs down to Eva's hips.

The stereotyped expression of the first photograph, and the disproportionately small eye, do not allow this picture to seem true to life. The side-view, taken from the interior of the cabinet during the same flash, shows a vague profile, and is too indistinct to justify any conclusions.

While in this case the face is directed rather upwards, the second photograph shows the same formation with a slight inclination downwards. The downward flowing curls have disappeared, the head is covered in the same way in front, but the cheek portion of the face is freer. Instead of the hair there is a conglomeration of grey, black, and white veils. The hanging white veil appearing in the first picture is now collected into a narrow strip, fastened to the back of Eva's head with a knot, and, hanging down to Eva's neck, it forms the termination between the hair of the medium and the attachment of the formation.

In the second profile photograph (Figs. 67 and 68) the expression of the face is more clearly brought out. It seems pleasanter, and the lines of the profile are strikingly soft. The cheek is traversed by a crease, or crack, which is also indicated in the first picture. The composition and arrangement of this head appear to be a remarkably artistic performance, quite apart from the question as to how it was done.

The question now arises as to the origin of this hair. We see real black-looking hair in long shiny strands, well dressed and arranged in curls. Does this hair belong to Eva's head, or is it a sort of materialised wig? My personal impression favours the simpler assumption, viz., that Eva's coiffure was opened out broadly, and used for decorating the picture, especially as the lowermost curl can be followed direct from the medium's hair. It is dressed in the same way, and is as long as the rest of her hair, and similarly arranged. The cap-like structure is therefore only apparently the division between the two heads. It is partly attached to Éva's head, and gives the impression of an independent coiffure. In the second series of pictures the curls have disappeared, having been restored to Eva's head, and their place is taken by the veil conglomeration already referred to. That this extraordinarily artistic arrangement could be produced in the dark, without a mirror, by some power as yet unknown, is in any case remarkable.

The following point appears much more remarkable than any hitherto enumerated. In photograph (1) we have an upward position of the head with a downward gaze, whereas in photograph (2) we have a downward position of the head with an upward gaze. On the first picture the upper eyelid covers half the pupil, and is therefore half closed ; while on the second picture the upper eyelid is wide open and the pupil, with the high light, is completely visible.

All the negatives, including the stereoscopic ones, show the same state of things, which is therefore not due to some accidental indistinctness. This change, in conjunction with the better modelling of the corner of the mouth, which is drawn slightly upwards, produces a pleasant impression in the second picture, which also appears more finished.

If we take into account that all the rest of the characteristics of both profiles, including imperfections and faults, are identical in the two pictures, and that both photographs were taken in succession with an interval of about seven minutes, and with the same experimental conditions, we may consider the fact established that in both cases we have to deal with the same picture, which, in consequence of its non-rigid, variable, and half-soft condition, was modified and perfected, before the second photograph, by the anonymous artistic intelligence.

SITTINGS OF THE 9TH, 10TH AND 12TH JANUARY 1912.

Negative.

SITTING OF THE 27TH JANUARY 1912.

Alex. Bisson, the author, whose wife had devoted herself in the most generous manner to the exploration of mediumistic phenomena, succumbed, after six months' illness, to the effects of a paralytic stroke.

Eva, who lived in the house and was treated as a member of the family, was affected by the occurrence as much as any of the family. Although a few positive sittings took place in the author's absence, the productive power of the medium entirely ceased between 20th February and 22nd March, although several times a week experiments were regularly tried.

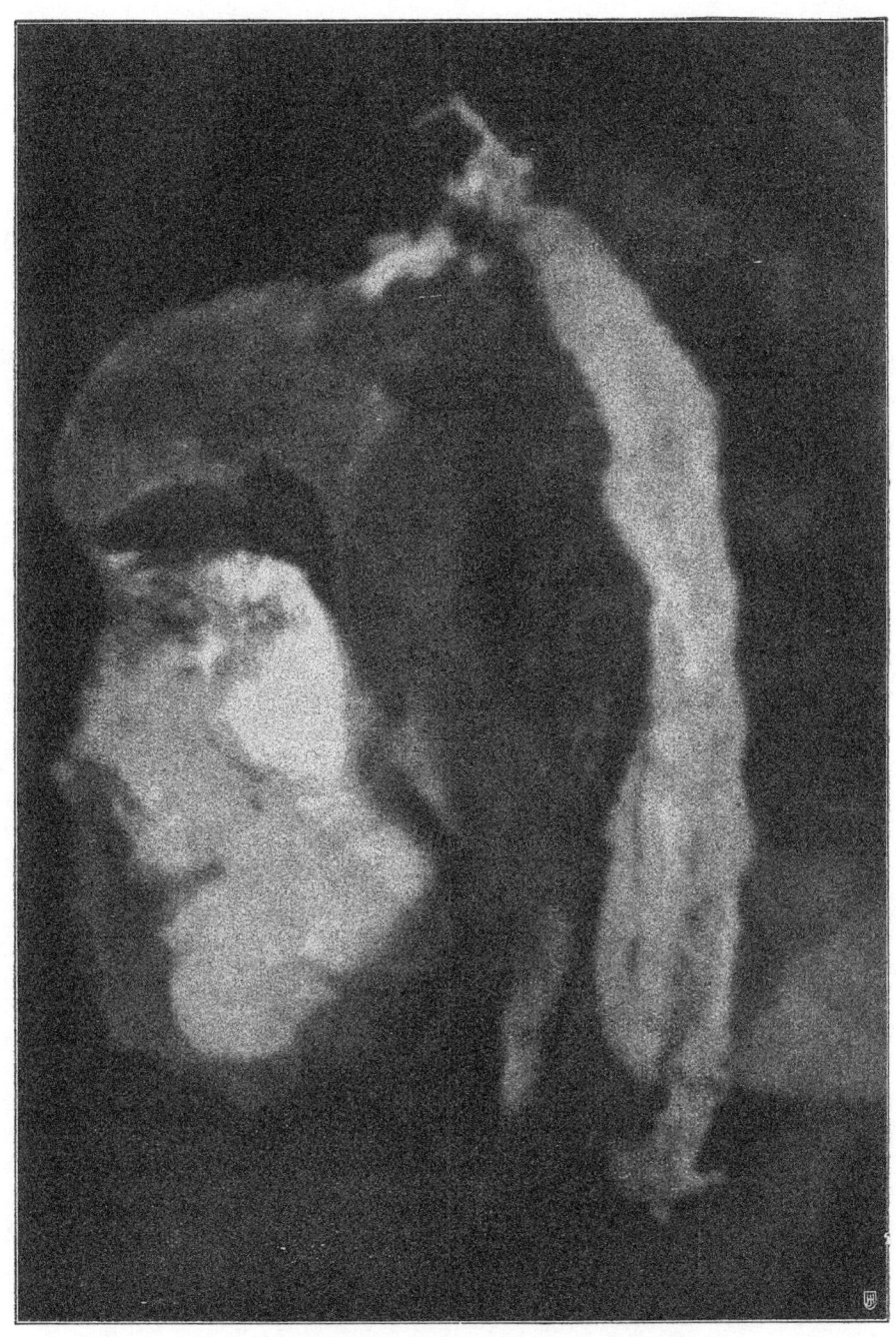

FIG 68   ENLARGEMENT OF PORTION OF FIG. 67.

FIG 69   MME. BISSON'S FIRST FLASHLIGHT PHOTOGRAPH, 14 FEBRUARY, 1912.

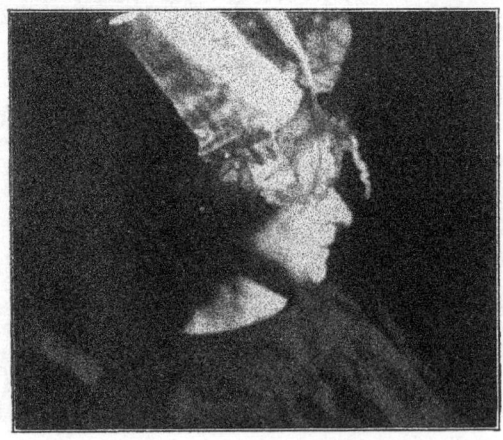

FIG. 70.   SIDE VIEW OF PREVIOUS PICTURE.

Observations in March and April 1912 (Paris).

SITTINGS OF THE 5TH AND 14TH FEBRUARY 1912.

MME. BISSON writes in a letter, dated 8th February 1912 :—" On 5th February 1912, shortly after the death of my husband, Eva was occupied in a psychographic exercise, when she suddenly stopped and produced what was for me an extraordinary phenomenon of incarnation (dramatic representation of a personality in the trance condition). M. Bisson appeared, represented by Eva, and spoke to me with his own voice and his own gestures. He repeated the last words addressed to me before his death, with his own intonation and characteristics. I ought to say that, since my return from St Jean de Luz in October 1911, *i.e.*, during the last three months, Eva had not entered the sick room. During this performance the medium breathed very audibly. Without desiring to convince you or to make any reflections on this event, I must confess that the impression made upon me was a very deep one. The girl then fell into catalepsy, and recovered very slowly." On 15th February, also, Mme. Bisson observed the same procedure, and she reports : " This time I put a question which M. Bisson alone was able to answer. The reply was appropriate."

During a sitting on the 14th February 1912, in my absence, Mme. Bisson took two photographs. When Eva had been hypnotised, a portrait appeared which was not apparently drawn from life, but reproduced from memory of a picture. It appeared first between Eva and the curtain, then on her head (Figs. 69 and 70), and finally on her shoulder (Fig. 71).

It recalls the painting by Leonardo da Vinci of Monna Lisa, which had disappeared from the Louvre. It is quite possible that the numerous reproductions of this picture in the public press left a permanent impression on the memory of the medium, and that the portrait of the 14th February was the result.

The head, seen from the front, is quite flat, and is attached to Eva's hair by a round neck piece, being bent slightly backwards. The drawing is somewhat stiff and conventional, like the portraits of old Italian and German masters, but otherwise very purely and carefully executed The identity of the Monna Lisa is vouched for by the prominent cheek bones, the short double chin, the broad bridge to the nose, the deep-set dark eye (without high lights), and the long loose hair. The drawing of the left eye, and of the eye-sockets, is not only out of proportion, but also wooden and amateurish. Two white spots (of teleplasm ?) lie on the hair and the left eye, covering the latter, and these recur in all the pictures of the series. It is interesting to note how the artist has given the impression of wavy and curly hair-dressing by the distribution of light and shade. The basis for the hair silhouette, with its sharp outer margin, is the dark material product already previously referred to, which has no resemblance to cardboard, but which has a soft and more felt-like character. Both on the face and on the hair are numerous folds running across the portrait. On the head, towards the left, there is a real veil hanging down over Eva's face, and in the second photo-

K

graph this covers a portion of the hair on the right, and otherwise shows differences of arrangement.

After several weeks' cessation, during my absence, the phenomena were resumed on the 22nd March, and the new series of experiments was attended by M. de Vesme, Editor of the *Annales des Sciences Psychiques*, and also, in turn, by the sons of Mme. Bisson.

The photographs from this period are mostly head fragments or preliminary stages in the development of faces, but are more valuable on account of their originality, and their curious form. The endeavour towards fuller formation is perceptible throughout.

SITTINGS OF THE 2ND, 8TH, 14TH, 15TH, 20TH AND 23RD APRIL 1912.

In the sitting of 2nd April M. de Vesme photographed too early. The curtains were not sufficiently widely open. Only the photograph with the apparatus in the cabinet succeeded.

We see, in the side view, on the back of Eva's head a white mass resembling a small tower, which has not yet acquired a distinct shape, and which reaches nearly down to her neck below (Fig. 72). It seems to be composed of ribbon-shaped pieces twisted together. The observation of the sitters (André Bisson, M. de Vesme, and Mme. Bisson) that the exposure was made during the beginning of the materialisation and therefore too early, is confirmed by the photograph. We have here apparently amorphous teleplasm in a stage preliminary to the development of a face. This is indicated by the structure and composition of the substance.

The photograph (Fig. 73) taken on 8th April was again due to M. de Vesme. The head, only developed as far as the nose, is placed on Eva's hair like a helmet. The mouth portion is not yet developed, and forms an open, narrow, rectilinear base for the upper half of the face, the latter being framed in a white fibrous mass as in a wig. The remnants of this half-formed substance hang down in one mass on the right side of the face down to the medium's shoulder. The picture forms a valuable contribution to the study of heads in course of development.

The front view of the medium, taken by De Vesme on 14th April, shows on the hair a portion of material in which three finger-points are developed in low relief, while two ribbons joined in a loop hang down towards the forehead (Fig. 74).

The side view of the same picture, taken inside the cabinet, and with the same flash, give another view quite independent of the front view. The substance is built up on the top of Eva's head, and points upwards, while broad bands of matter pass down the parting of the hair, and also towards the back. A face can only be recognised as a shortened profile turned towards the ceiling. The forehead is somewhat compressed and drawn out in length. The hair is well marked from the forehead to the ears. The eyelid, nose, and upper lip are unmistakable, although imperfect. The lower part of the whole head disappears in the white fabric lying round chin, ears, and neck, like a bandage, and this fabric also joins the face with the base and materials

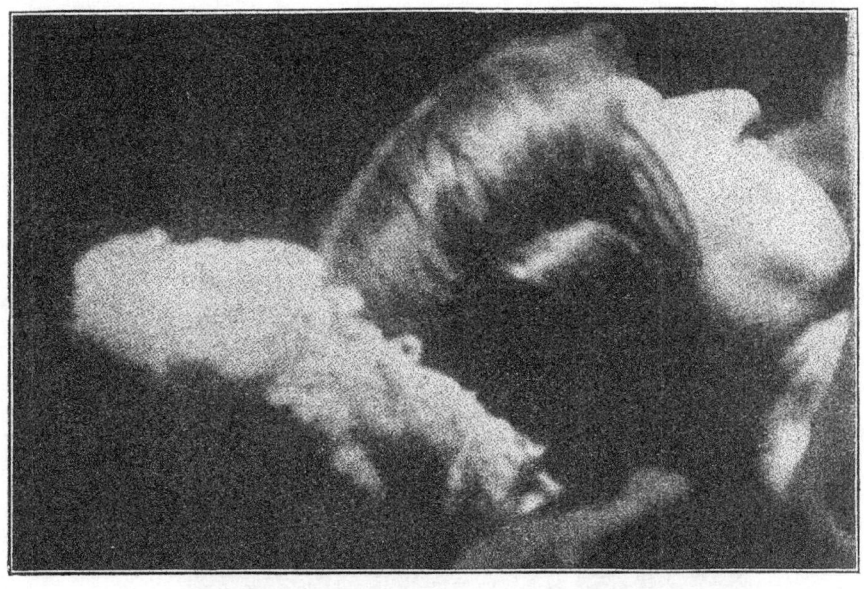

FIG. 72. DE VESME'S FLASHLIGHT PHOTOGRAPH OF 2 APRIL, 1912.

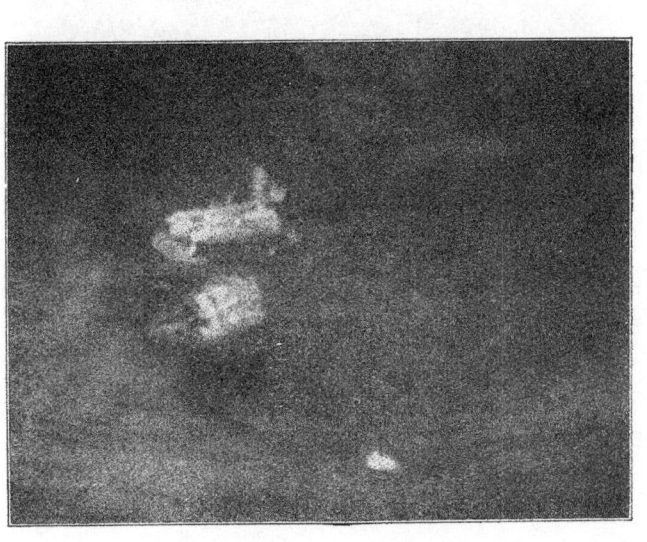

FIG. 71. MME. BISSON'S FLASHLIGHT PHOTOGRAPH OF 14 FEBRUARY, 1912.

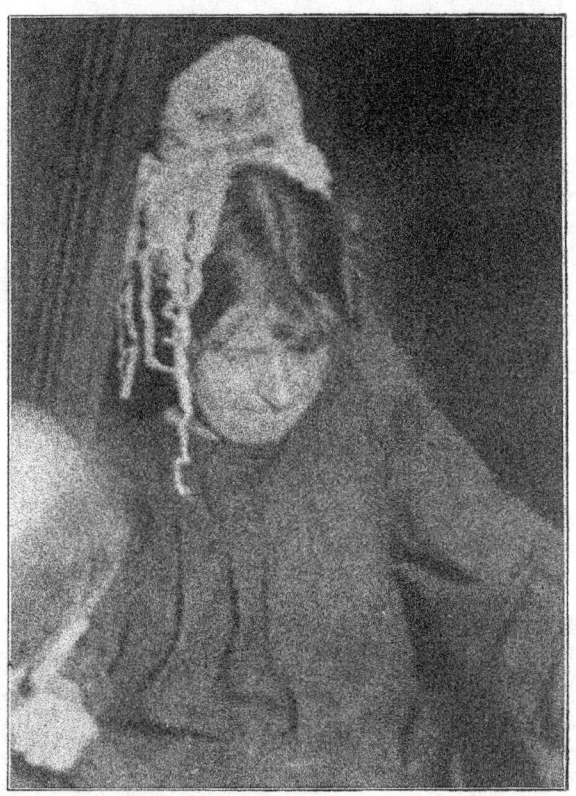

Fig. 73. De Vesme's flashlight photograph of 8 April, 1912.

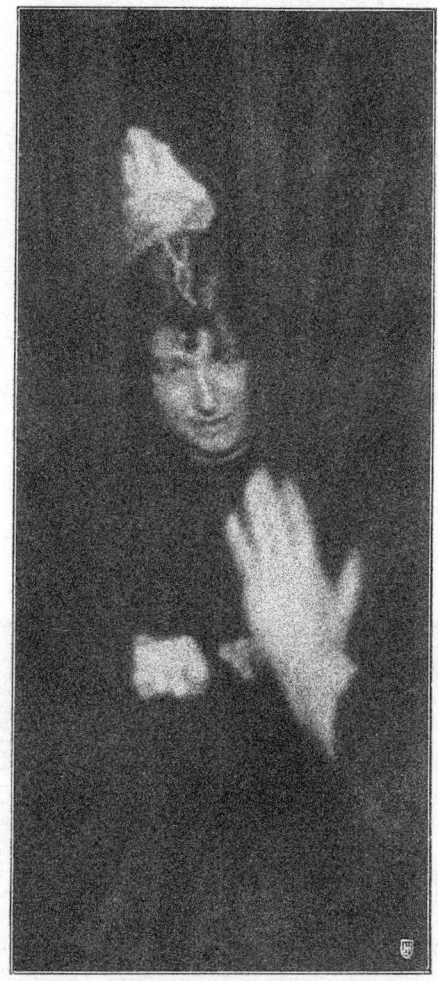

Fig. 74. De Vesme's flashlight photograph of 14 April, 1912.

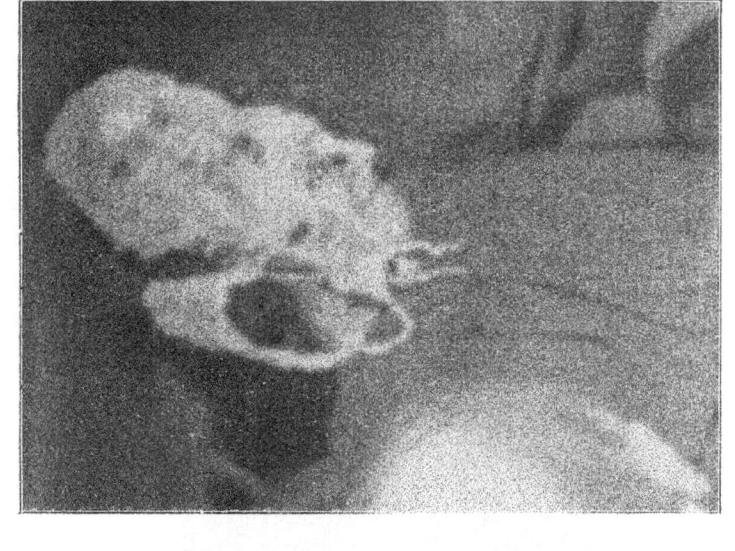

Fig. 76. Mme. Bisson's flashlight photograph of 15 April, 1912.

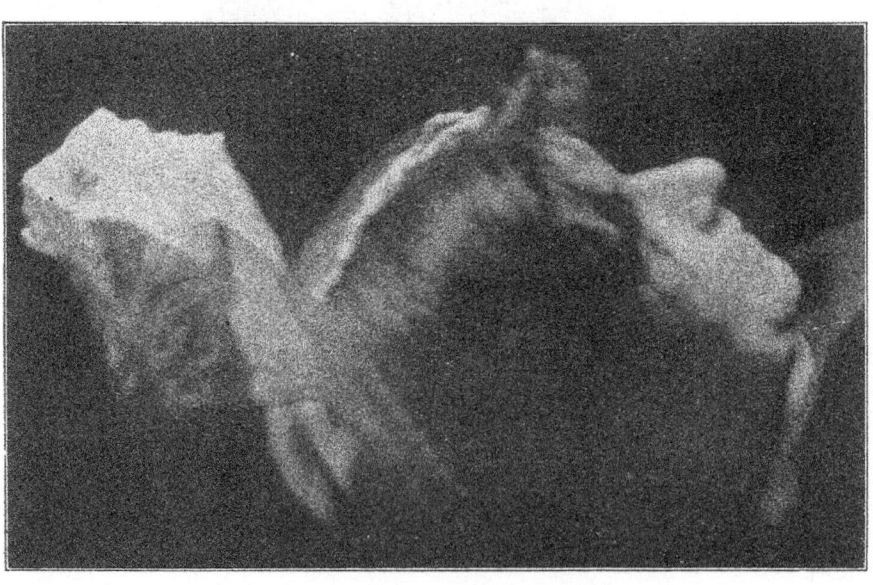

Fig. 75. Side view of the previous picture (from within the cabinet).

on the head. Again a fragment, a further link in the genesis of teleplastic head forms (Fig. 75). Here, for the first time, we see two different and independent structures represented by the same materialised substance. From the front it appears as three fingerpoints, while the negative in the cabinet shows a female face turned towards the ceiling. A rare phenomenon! Another imperfect formation is shown by the photograph, taken on 15th April 1912, also in De Vesme's presence, and consisting of a female face on Eva's head (Fig. 76).

The left side, as compared with the right, seems to be displaced a little upwards, as indicated by the higher and slanting position of the right supra-orbital region. The chin portion is obviously unfinished. Again the hair is arranged like a white wig, and there is a streak (a rent, or the lower veil margin) across the face, over the bridge of the nose. As in the case of the former head arrangement, this face, in the stereoscope, gives the impression of a plastic form in low relief. In the tangle of fragments of material hanging down, two parallel strips of a finer, muslin-like material proceeding from the mouth, are conspicuous. The whole structure is remarkable for its imperfections and its grotesque appearance.

A few days later (20th April 1912) M. André Bisson,[1] son of Mme. Bisson, took a further photograph, in which Eva holds the curtain with her hands. The head is turned towards the left. In front of her face, and, therefore, certainly 20 inches behind the left curtain, we see a broad rectangular formation with irregular margins, which is either separated by the back of the chair or hangs free (Figs. 77 and 78).

This packet of material is joined to Eva's mouth by a broad band, appearing dark grey or black in the photograph, which passes from the open mouth slantingly upwards. From the neck of her dress, in two places, we see small quantities of material projecting over the hem, and corresponding in shape to three flat glove-fingers. On the magnification of the picture these projections seem to coalesce with the epidermis of Eva's throat, and one cannot say definitely whether they are tucked in and bent round, as one might conclude from the first impression. The magnification gives no hint of a textile product, since the structure gives more the impression of a ribbon without any characteristic markings. A further interesting study is furnished by a picture taken by Mme. Bisson on 23rd April, especially in the side view. In a mass of amorphous substance the size of a head, and consisting of heaps or packets of miscellaneous hanging strips and fragments, we see the beginnings of a face formation, including two eyes and a broad thick nose, and beneath it some beginnings of a mouth. Everything else is imperfect, but yet gives an impression of an elementary creation *sui generis*. Unfortunately, both views are ill-defined (Figs. 79 and 80).

Sittings in April 1912 (Paris).

BETWEEN 1st and 10th March the author was present at six sittings, all of which were negative.

[1] M. André Bisson holds an office in the Ministry of Finance.

Sitting of the 29th April 1912.

Present.—M. de Vesme, Mme. Bisson, her son Pierre (aged 13), and the author.

Conditions as during previous experiments.

Eva fell into a deep, quiet sleep which resembled normal sleep. No bodily symptoms (stertorous breathing or whimpering) indicated that the psychic condition necessary for the occurrence of phenomena was present. She remained dumb, and did not seem to stand *en rapport* with those present.

After a fruitless waiting of three-quarters of an hour, Mme. Bisson tried to convert the passive state of sleep into a light active somnambulism by laying on her hand, and making urgent verbal suggestions. Eva began to show greater activity. She spoke and moaned, and her respiration became loud and vigorous. After 10 o'clock a white wisp appeared over her left shoulder while her head was bent to the right. The hands, which were always visible, opened and closed the curtain, and then remained motionless on her knees, while she opened and closed the curtain with her feet.

We then saw some small white hand shapes enter the circle of light near her head, and disappear again with lightning rapidity. On one occasion a shape resembling a child's hand appeared to grow with a revolving motion, and then to disappear suddenly. On several occasions Eva's head and hands were simultaneously visible during the phenomena. Some of the images gave the impression of a well-developed female hand, but they hardly remained visible for a second.

In order to observe more accurately, I rose and stood behind Mme. Bisson, who sat in the middle in front of the curtain. I then clearly recognised a hand shape, coming out of the dark of the cabinet and disappearing, while De Vesme simultaneously controlled both the medium's hands. After the last apparition Eva declared that "Berthe," who had latterly assumed control of the medium in the spiritistic sense, had gone away and would not return. She rose, came out of the cabinet, and allowed herself to be completely examined, the result being negative.

The sitting closed towards 11 o'clock. Eva had had a bad day, and was in a bad humour, though we could not discover the cause of it.

Sitting of the 30th April 1912.

Present.—Mme. Bisson, M. de Vesme, M. Pierre Bisson, the author and his wife.

Conditions and control as in the previous sittings.

My place was to the right of the medium, as usual.

Since a large number of the phenomena happened to occur on this side, the author could not observe them, while those sitting on the medium's left had the advantage.

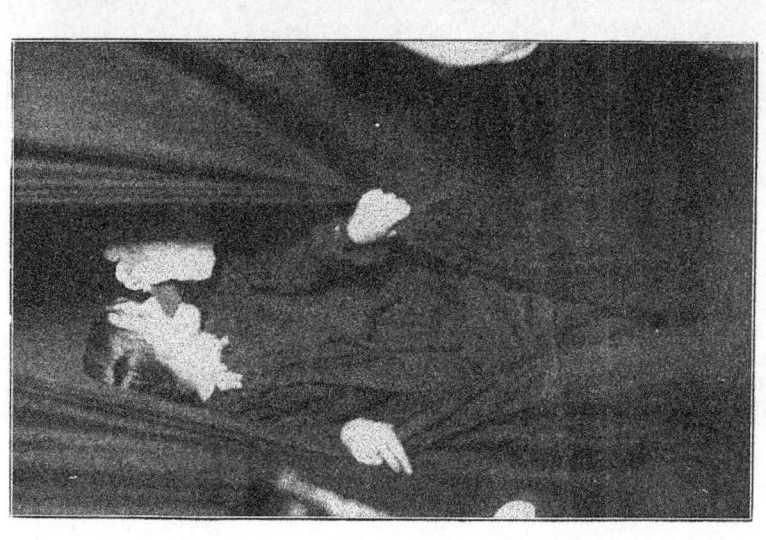

Fig. 77. M. André Bisson's flashlight photograph of 20 April, 1912.

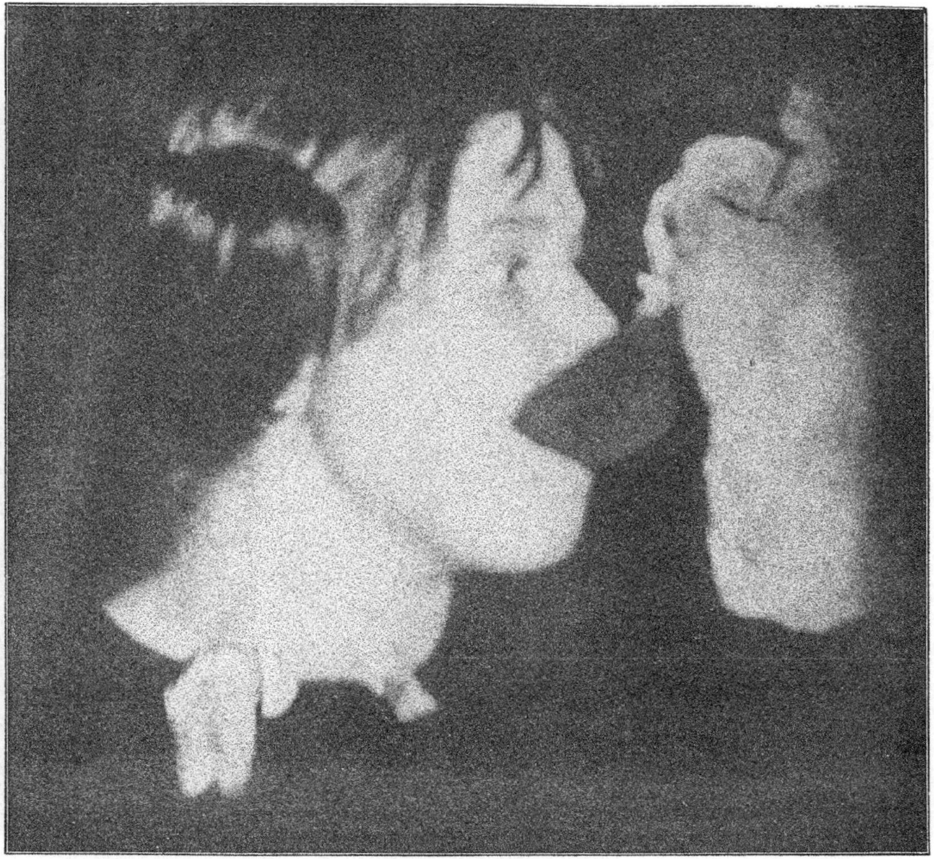

Fig. 78. Enlargement of portion of previous photograph.

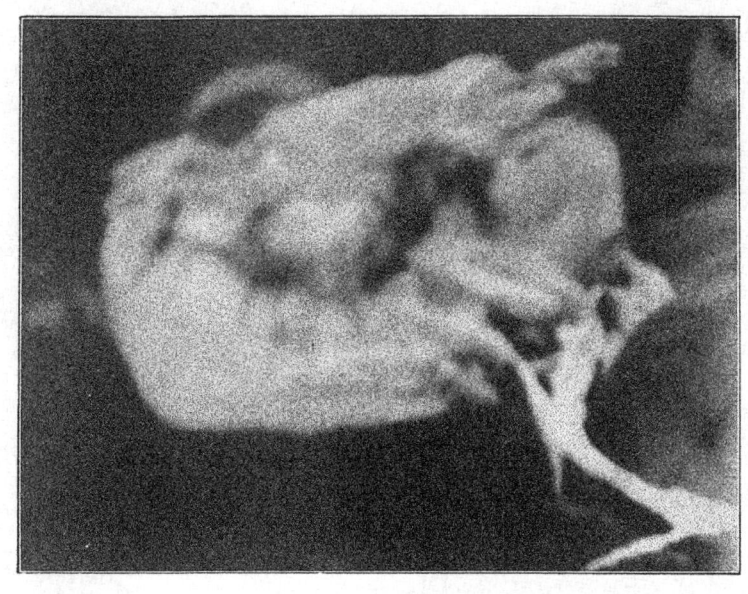

Fig. 80. Side view of previous picture.

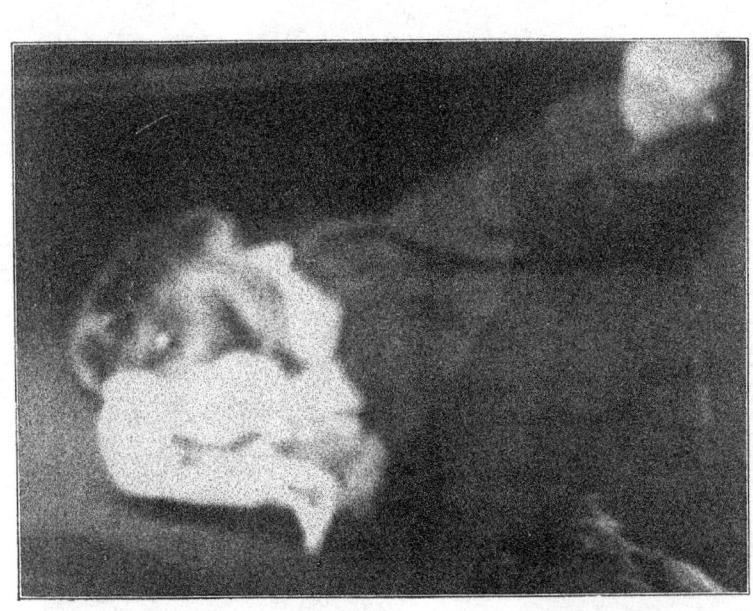

Fig. 79. Mme. Bisson's flashlight photograph of 23 April 1912.

Immediately after the extinction of the white light, a white hand shape appeared on the left, at the level of the medium's shoulders, while Eva's hands during this and the following observations always remained quietly on her knees, and often enough were simultaneously visible with the phenomena on the opening of the curtain (with the feet).

Some ten or fourteen times the same form of a hand appeared, usually on the right side of the head, but it was too fugitive to be photographed.

After Mme. Bisson had been touched on her right hand, which she stretched into the cabinet at the level of the medium's head, my wife's extended hand was grasped by a hand with broad, cool and round fingers (Eva's fingers are small, narrow, and pointed). Then something white appeared on Eva's left shoulder, but nothing could be recognised.

The phenomena then disappeared, and the sitting seemed at an end, but on the urgent suggestion and request of Mme. Bisson the hand became visible once or twice, though very fugitive. Final examination negative.

Thus ended the last sitting in the Bissons' flat, Avenue Victor Hugo, in Paris.

On 2nd May the author was present at the dismantling of the mediumistic cabinet, consisting of curtains, walls, and roof. He examined the whole construction, the material, the walls, etc., again, without finding anything remarkable. The lining had no holes anywhere and the walls were intact.

PSYCHICAL PHENOMENA.

FOR the understanding of what follows, it seems important to insert here some remarks on the class of psychical phenomena already mentioned, which Mme. Bisson usually observed alone with Eva in the hypnotic preparatory sittings. In a few cases the author was present at these. The original object of these experiments was to tune the psychical condition of the medium, in a manner favourable for materialisations, by means of a suggestive *rapport*, to counteract her mental inhibitions, to concentrate her attention and her interest on the phenomena—in short, to attain by a systematic psychical training a gradually increasing arbitrary influence over the development of her abnormal psycho-physical performances.

Although Eva's peculiar character, combined with a certain indifference regarding her peculiar faculties, was very inaccessible to educational influences in the waking state and offered great resistance in the somnambulic state, the subsequent results have justified the correctness of the procedure.

As already mentioned, the psychical personality of the somnambulist differs from that of the medium in the waking condition. The latter is rather indifferent to the results of the sittings, but gladly occupies herself with feminine problems—the cut of a new dress, a new hat, some amusement, a harmless flirtation, a compliment on her looks, can engage her whole interest, change her emotional state, and influence her course of action. To these were added, at irregular intervals, fitful lapses of temper, not warranted by external conditions, spells of anger, under the influence of which she sometimes lost her self-control and plied those about her with unfounded accusations. The appreciation of the scientific importance of her faculty was lacking. Any acknowledgment of her mediumistic performances she used to regard as a compliment to her female nature. Her interest in the photographs taken during the sittings was slight. She rarely inquired of her own accord how they had succeeded, and hardly noticed it when the photographs were not shown to her at all. On the other hand, Eva possesses a passive and fundamentally good-natured disposition, and gives the unprejudiced observer the impression of a harmless and modest young girl. When she is in emotional equilibrium she is bright, childlike, and amiable, and is much pleased by any small attentions shown to her.

Her hysterical temperament explains, perhaps, this psychological diagnosis. That Mme. Bisson faced the great difficulties necessarily attending the daily intercourse with a girl of a lower educational level for several years, for the sake of mediumistic investigations, must be specially acknowledged, besides her other services to the cause.

From time to time Eva had the same succession of emotional crises. First, a latent state of tension, bad humour, and embitterment, which might last for days, and was always followed by negative sittings. Often Eva declared that the sittings were nothing to her, that she wanted to go back to her people.

In such cases Mme. Bisson acquiesced in her wish, and made her pack her boxes. This action, in conjunction with an authoritative bearing, or a suggestion in the somnambulic state, often led to a termination of the mood, in a flood of tears, and an entire reversal of the emotional state. After the reaction Eva was always willing, tractable, amiable, and sociable. She was easily influenced, and the sittings were successful.

It is possible that the state of control, on the basis of a hysterical disposition, produces a state of embitterment and tension—a sort of *ressentiment*.

The character of the somnambulic Eva is not fundamentally different from that of the medium in the waking condition. But her whole nature appears spiritualised, elevated, better balanced, and more sensitive. Obstinacy and fits of temper are not often observed; only in rare cases is the irritable mood carried over from the waking into the somnambulic state. Displays of anger, as a rule, occur only in consequence of interference, possibly necessary, by the sitters, which hurts her feminine sense of honour or modesty. Any abrupt and unexpected procedure, *e.g.*, awakening her (pin-pricks), touching the materialisations (attempted exposure), making a thorough gynæcological examination, or expressing doubt as to her honesty, may produce anger, violent disturbances of pulse and respiration, hysterical crises, and fainting fits.

The psychic adjustment of the medium is of the greatest importance for the success of the experiments. As already mentioned, she feels the phenomena to be something foreign to her, and a sort of compulsion, in spite of the efforts she herself has to make in producing them. According to Eva's conception, the phenomena are brought about by intelligent powers, independent of herself, by means of her own vitality and psychical energy.

If, in this sense, we wish to judge the psychological relation of the medium towards the phenomena, for the practical purposes of the sittings, we may distinguish three periods or emotional stages.

Phase I.—In this phase Eva's state is unfavourable. Bodily indisposition, ill-humour, lack of will-power, preoccupation of the attention by extraneous subjects, reluctance, and indifference to the required psycho-physical effort, and its resulting fatigue, hinder every kind of production, even when the intelligent power outside her is active and wishes to manifest itself. In such cases there are always negative sittings.

Phase II.—The medium's general condition is favourable. She wishes to fulfil her task. But the will-power is too weak for the mediumistic act. In this stage the medium requires strong suggestive encouragement by her protectress, or by those present, in order to overcome the resistance of the inertia. She herself has a feeling of requiring some help, and even expresses it by the words " Aide moi, Juliette ! " But one of the conditions for the occurrence of positive effects is that the intelligent personified factor, felt by her to be an independent entity, wishes to manifest itself. She usually expresses this by the words, " Je le (or les) sens," or " Je ne le (or les) sens pas."

It is only when these two factors co-operate that results can be expected, but, in spite of the favourable psychical adjustment of the medium, her efforts remain fruitless if the presence of the factor referred to is not felt during the sitting.

Finally, there is the possibility of a negative sitting if, in spite of every effort, the inertia cannot be overcome. The phenomena brought about in Phase II. are mostly feeble, or of medium strength, and are always accompanied by strong bodily reactions of the medium (pressing and gasping, violent muscular contractions, a quick pulse, and expressions of pain).

Although the author has taken into consideration the medium's subjective view, it does not follow that that view is correct. On the contrary, the observer even gets an impression that the medium produces the phenomena on her own initiative alone, especially when they consist in the production of simple aggregations and forms. This also is suggested by the frequent adaptation of the phenomena to the wishes of the sitters, as when they urgently suggest the occurrence of some definite phenomena (*e.g.*, a hand, a female or a male face).

Phase III.—The medium is under the influence of a sort of fit of compulsory organic necessity towards psycho-physical emanations. This shows itself in a certain confusion of consciousness and a tendency towards spontaneous production. In such cases one must carefully postpone the productions until the time of the sitting, or the sittings must be arranged as quickly as possible, in order to produce the necessary relief. The preparatory symptoms consist of a dazed and dreamy state, a feeling of sickness, a veiled gaze and quickened pulse (100 to 110 beats per minute), a feeling of uneasiness, loss of appetite, and sensory symptoms (such as a swelling of the mammary glands). In this case the hands are always remarkably cool.

As soon as the communication is made to the sitters " Elle est prise," one can reckon on the certainty of a positive sitting. The phenomena in this phase occur immediately after the extinction of the white light, and are often perfectly developed—as, for instance, in the form of head shapes. In some sittings the author had not even enough time to open the cameras, which requires only a few seconds.

The phenomena thus produced are, as a rule, durable in the light, and resist certain interferences, so that one can sometimes take three flash-light photographs in succession.

The production of the phenomena is usually accompanied by a great relief for Eva, " Elle est dégagée." The sitting therefore acts as a liberation, although great exhaustion may follow for twenty-four hours.

But if any complete relief takes place, this may occur after she has retired to bed, and take the form of unusual materialisation phenomena, sometimes associated with the genital organs.

In this fitful occurrence of the materialisation impulse, the medium is blindly subject to a stronger power, and does not seem to be able to resist it by her own will. The subjective factors, mentioned in Phases I. and II., are quite placed in the background.

Instead of this period of active production, we may have a variation of the same condition in the shape of a latent tension, lasting for several days, and relieved by several minor eruptions of phenomena. If no relief is obtained at the sittings, these phenomena may take place irregularly during the day (mostly in twilight), or during the sleep at night, which then passes into a state of active somnambulism.

In general, the observer is forced to the assumption that, in the production of positive results, an intelligent factor, independent of the medium, comes into play, although it seems immaterial whether that factor is to be looked for in the medium's subliminal consciousness or not. For the purpose of experiment we must take into account this apparently independent will-power, and must come to an understanding with it concerning the method of procedure.

There is some justification for speaking of a duplex personality in the case of Eva, although it may only be a case of a freer development of her *psyche* in the trance condition. Her manner of expression in somnambulism is better, she appreciates the importance of her mediumistic performances, and makes an effort (though not always) to produce a favourable emotional state by a passive behaviour. She usually shows a certain emotional softness, and instinctively reads the desires and thoughts of the sitters. There is also a greater suggestibility and a more vivid play of imagination. During the phenomena themselves her whole effort is directed towards making them as convincing as possible to the sitters, and towards being strictly controlled. Several times she rose from her chair immediately after a production of phenomena, stood in front of the curtain, and demanded an examination of her body and her dress; or she took a red or white electric torch in order to illuminate the phenomena, if they were not sufficiently clearly visible for us. Often enough she destroyed the phenomena by this procedure. Or, after the end of the sitting, she may demand tests which do not even appear necessary to those present. Thus she sometimes would undo the tights and ask for a gynæcological examination.

Her relation to Mme. Bisson in somnambulism is that of love, attachment, and gratitude. While the waking Eva always addresses her protectress respectfully and in the plural, the somnambulist uses the singular, and usually calls her " ma petite Juliette." She is anxious about Mme. Bisson like a mother about her child. When Mme. Bisson is fatigued, or out of humour, she always inquires the cause, gives amiable consolation, and wishes to hear her voice. Her attention and her detective sense are exaggerated; nothing escapes her in the conversation of the sitters, as her frequent apposite remarks testify. The exception from this rule occurs in the states of deep trance during production, in which she gives an impression of great suffering, resembling the pains of parturition, and is quite occupied with herself. On a few occasions I have observed a trace of hysterical supersensitiveness and affectation. When her nerves are shaken by the shock of the sudden flash-light, or when she tries in vain to produce phenomena, she is soothed by Mme. Bisson touching her hands, and head, and the region of her heart. She asks Mme. Bisson to comfort her and to help her own efforts, by an exertion of her will-power. This whole behaviour is foreign to Eva's character in the waking condition, and indicates a difference in the two states of consciousness.

The presence of her protectress, who has her fullest confidence, probably became a psychological necessity for her production in the course of the several years of training and habituation. Owing to her great lack of will-power in the waking and somnambulistic states (often found in mediums), she requires psychic guidance, and constant incentive, from without. The importance of the spiritual link joining the two women, for the production of phenomena, is easily underrated. Mme. Bisson has, so to speak, become an indispensable active psychic supplement to her, since she just possesses the qualities lacking in her, knows Eva's mentality intimately, and during the frequent incidents of the sittings, which would leave any other experimenter helpless, she always finds the right means to restore the disturbed psychical and physical equilibrium of the medium.

If, therefore, some savants assert that Mme. Bisson's mere presence at the sittings constitutes a source of error, this shows a deplorable lack of understanding of the complicated mechanism of the mediumistic occurrences, quite apart from the unworthy attempt to cast suspicion upon an experimenter, and exclude her from her own work, because she is not of the male sex, or has not passed through a regular University course. No doubt some other person could undertake the part of the hypnotiser, with all its consequences, in the case of this medium, if Eva gradually got accustomed to the other person. I may recall that in the first period of the experiments in the Bissons' flat, one of Eva's relatives and Baron Pigeard hypnotised the medium, and that before the Bisson period a series of sittings took place in the residence of an English lady in Paris.

The hypnotic education which Mme. Bisson has given to her medium has been directed systematically towards progress and the higher development of the mediumistic faculties, and towards the preservation of the suggestive and authoritative state of dependence. Thus she has adhered to the rule of hypnotising Eva on the days on which materialisation sittings did not take place. If, on the day of the sitting, the medium was not favourably disposed, or for other reasons, she also hypnotised the medium on the days of the sittings themselves. The hypnotic sleep, often prolonged for several hours without experiments, was also an excellent means of disposing of the symptoms of exhaustion, which often followed positive sittings on the next day, and also of eliminating slight disturbances of humour and nervous affections. That this whole procedure was successful is shown by the gradual increase and higher development of the mediumistic performances, while the bodily and mental equilibrium of the medium remained intact during four years of experiments, which were sometimes very fatiguing.

The mental manifestations of the somnambulist usually took the form of automatic writing, or speaking in simple or dramatised form. Ostensibly such entities, or personifications, manifested through the medium, were regarded by the medium during the materialisation sittings as the originators of the phenomena, and as giving rise to the objects photographed. During the last month the chief guidance of the medium was undertaken by an " entity," calling herself " Berthe." This entity was supposed to guide the pointer held in Eva's hand with lightning rapidity over the table of letters, while Eva, with closed eyes, and without any apparent participation, leant her head against Mme. Bisson's shoulder, and appeared quite unable to control the composition of letters by her right hand, or to read what she had automatically written. Mme. Bisson, even, could hardly keep pace in noting down the letters, and, in any case, during this operation she did not appreciate the sense of what was being written. The subsequent study showed messages giving a connected sense, usually referring to a sitting, and giving explanations and instructions as to how to treat the medium.

" Berthe " presents a self-contained psychological existence elaborated in detail. Whether she manifests through Eva psychically or physically, in both cases her action is relatively less trying for the medium than the manifestations of other personifications, especially male ones. She also expresses herself, though more rarely, directly through the mouth of the somnambulist, and addresses her as a third person, so that Eva repeats verbatim what " Berthe " communicates to her. " Berthe " is even dissatisfied with Eva's behaviour in a waking condition, criticises it intelligently, gives advice how to treat Eva, and how to cross her ideas and plans, and promises, on her own part, a psychic influence upon her. (Thus, in one case, in compliance with such a promise, she manifested herself unexpectedly in Eva's waking state by a sudden semi-somnambulic trance with a complete change of disposition.) On several occasions, during the observation of Eva's somnambulic inspiration, Mme. Bisson observed a "lucid" moment, in which apposite remarks were made concerning occurrences beyond the range of the knowledge of the medium. In some cases these also referred to future events. I ought to remark that the whole material of observation was entered, after every sitting, by Mme. Bisson in a note-book, which allowed of an accurate verification afterwards. Such utterances always came spontaneously in the form of communications from the somnambulist, or from "Berthe," as a product of an inspiration originating in the Unconscious. In almost all cases, messages of this kind were correct, while answers to questions were usually incorrect and unreliable.

The course of our whole four years of investigation was directed towards the impartial record of facts, uninfluenced by any theory. We succeeded in gradually liberating the materialisation sittings from the influence of the spiritistic tradition (formation of a chain, singing, etc.), and we only made such concessions as were indispensable conditions for success (*e.g.*, dark cabinet, red light, etc.).

If the results of our objective researches, in spite of ourselves, may yet be explained better by a spiritistic theory than in any other way, we must put this down to our lack of influence upon the quality of the phenomena, not to any bias in the experimenters. Without wishing to prejudice this question, the author is of the opinion that, even though most of the spiritistic phenomena should turn out to be true, an animistic explanation is to be preferred, and that it does, on the whole, suffice.

This remark appears necessary in view of the case now to be related. Shortly after the death of M. Bisson a new psychical entity manifested itself through Eva in the trance state. It came into play in a very sudden manner, and in apparent conflict with the medium, with violent defensive motions and convulsive muscular contractions. This personification called itself "Alexandre Bisson." It spoke through the mouth of the medium, with a deep voice. It only remained for a short time, and caused profound bodily exhaustion to the medium. I myself have never seen this "incarnation," and only know of it through the reports of my collaborator, who, after thirty years of happy marriage, would know her husband better and more exactly than any other person. Indeed, according to her report, the personification "Bisson" commanded the memory, the language, the mode of expression, and the character of her dead husband. Mme. Bisson was convinced that she was in the presence of the psychic existence of her husband. She repeatedly asked him questions which he alone could answer, and his answers were always correct. M. Bisson, when alive, stammered, especially when in a state of excitement, and this stammering occurred in the conversation.

The communications of the type "Bisson" referred to his family life, to the completion of a drama left unfinished, and to our sittings. "Bisson" said we were on the right way, and should not allow ourselves to be discouraged by anything from continuing with the investigations.

It also appears remarkable that the personification "Bisson" usually occurs at "critical" moments. Occasionally there were moments in which Mme. Bisson had lost courage, in consequence of the difficulties caused by Eva's character, and the opposition offered to her suggestions. When inclined to discontinue these investigations, or depressed by family troubles, the type "Bisson" regularly appeared, in order to console his wife with words known to her in his life.

We must ask ourselves: "Is it possible for a girl, with Eva's lack of education and gifts, to create a true psychic copy of the personality of the deceased, and even subconsciously to make his mentality and knowledge her own?" Even assuming an unusually highly-developed somnambulic detective sense, such a psychological reconstruction would remain a remarkable and puzzling performance.

Sittings of May and June 1912 (Paris).

THE new flat, Rue Georges Sand 33, contained two completely separated rooms, one of which was used entirely for the sittings, and could be locked, so that, besides the sitters, nobody had access to it in the absence of the observers, not even the servants.

The dark cabinet was now in the corner opposite the window. The photographic cameras were mounted in the usual way. One camera was placed in the cabinet to the right of the medium's chair, and the rest outside.

The author intended to use here, for the first time, a kinematograph (Pathé Frères), and in order to provide for the necessary illumination by a projection apparatus, he had caused a special cable to be laid. But the experiment was attended by such extraordinary and unexpected difficulties that the plan was not carried out in the first instance.

The author was present at the construction of the cabinet. It consisted of two side walls joining in a corner and a roof, all provided with a black lining. The floor of the cabinet was also covered with black. In front of the curtains a carpet was nailed to the parquet floor, in order to avoid unnecessary noise by walking during the sittings. The accompanying Diagram gives the necessary details (Diagram VI.)

SITTING OF THE 5TH MAY 1912.

Present.—Mme. Bisson and the author.

Negative.
Illumination by five red lamps, eighty to one hundred candle-power. The dress of the medium and control, as in the Rue Victor Hugo. Hypnotisation by Mme. Bisson. During somnambulism Eva was extremely timid. The whole surroundings appeared strange to her.

SITTINGS OF MAY AND JUNE 1912 (PARIS) 157

SITTING OF THE 6TH MAY 1912.

Present.—Mme. Bisson, the author and his wife.

The dress and control of the medium and the cabinet were as in previous sittings.

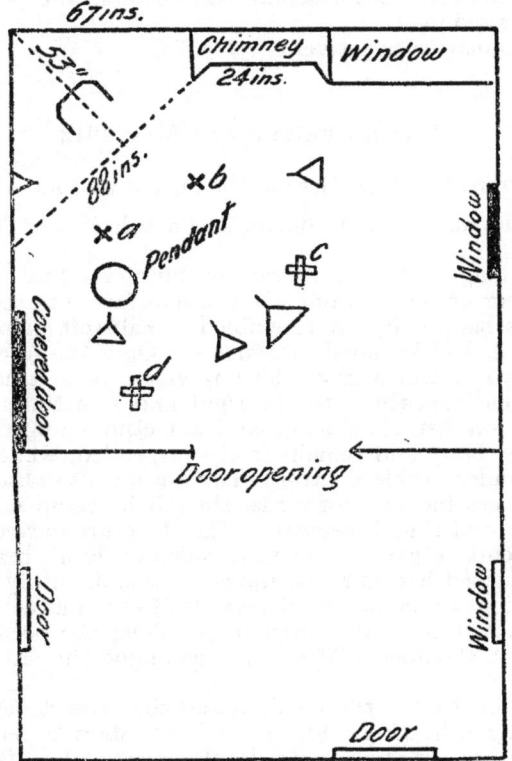

DIAGRAM VI.

Strong and loud expirations and gasps were heard. After about forty-five minutes there appeared above Eva's head a white shape the size of a fist, then a light-coloured smoke-like wisp issuing from her mouth. Then we saw, in the gap of the curtains, sometimes from the left, sometimes from the right, a white shape resembling a hand, sometimes looking like a clenched fist, and sometimes like several bent fingers. The phenomena were obviously independent of her body, and followed each other so rapidly that the time was too short for a photograph. For the half-hour during which the phenomena lasted the medium's hands remained clasping the curtain, and were continually exposed to the red light.

Final examination negative.

Sitting of the 8th May 1912.

Present.—Mme. Bisson, the author and his wife.

Dress, illumination, and control as on 6th May. Commencement, 9.30 P.M.

Loud and long-continued expirations during the first twenty minutes. At the opening of the curtains a mask-like face was seen attached to the medium's back hair. It resembled a half-soft pulp, traversed by softer material, and kneaded into shape. Only the forehead and eyes were recognisable, which gave the impression of a female face. This shape was seen, sometimes to the right and sometimes to the left of the medium (on her shoulders), and sometimes appeared to detach itself from her body and remain freely suspended, while her head and hands were under visible control. The author also observed that this form three times inclined forwards, though he could not tell whether Eva's head moved simultaneously. The structure moved forward once as far as the curtain gap. Once it subsided on Eva's head. While the lower part touched her hair, the upper part sank slowly backwards, as if the formation was about to flatten itself out and cover Eva's head as with a veil. I succeeded in photographing the peculiar formation on Eva's right shoulder. After the flash-light the sitting had to be closed.

Final examination of the medium and the cabinet negative.

The photographs (Figs. 81, 82 and 83) show a remarkable half-finished structure arrested in its development. It is fastened to the hair of the back of Eva's head on the right, and does not appear to exceed in size the face of a new-born baby or a fairly large doll.

If we wished to make a comparison, we might say as follows :—
The whole thing looks like a half-finished sketch of a female face-mask from nature, composed of pulp and softened cardboard and fragments of veil-like material, or perhaps made of a special mass resembling plasticine. The forehead, cheeks, nose, and eyes, and the upper face generally, are sufficiently finished to recognise the intention of the modeller to compose a female face. Where the point of the nose should be, a break goes right across the face, dividing it into two storeys, the lower storey being pushed backwards in comparison with the upper,

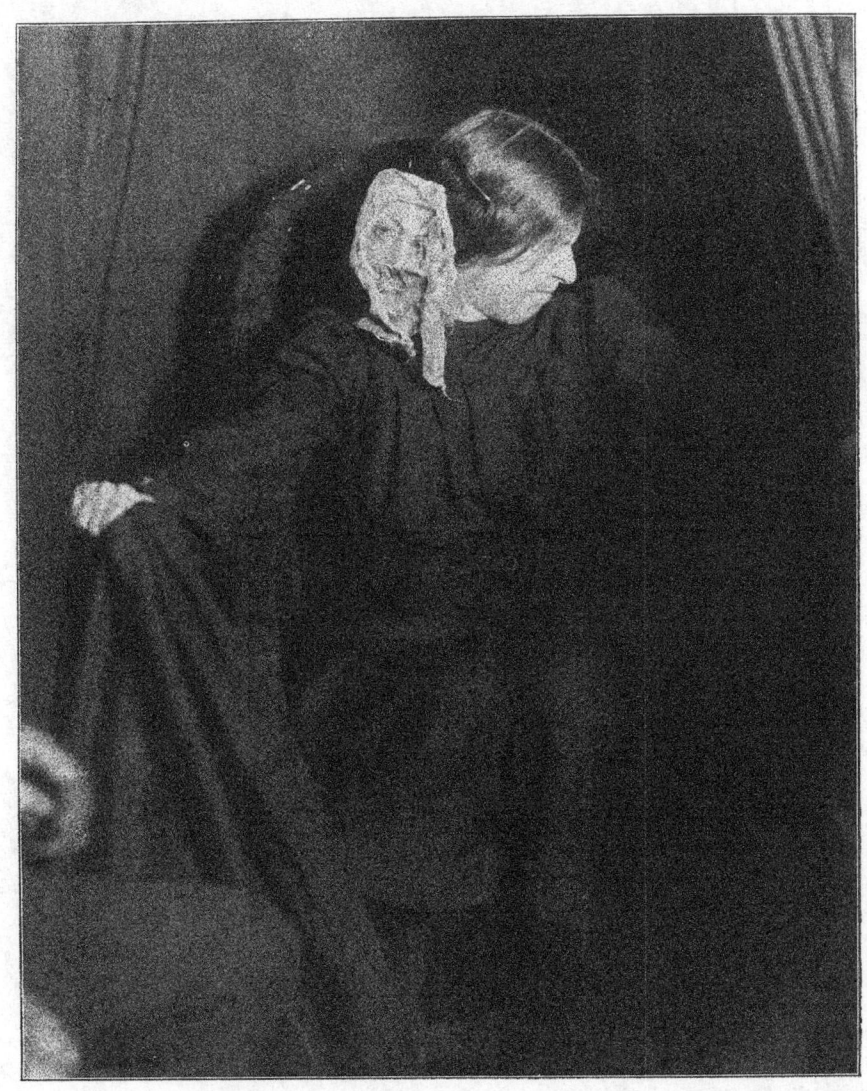

FIG. 81. AUTHOR'S FLASHLIGHT PHOTOGRAPH OF 8 MAY, 1912

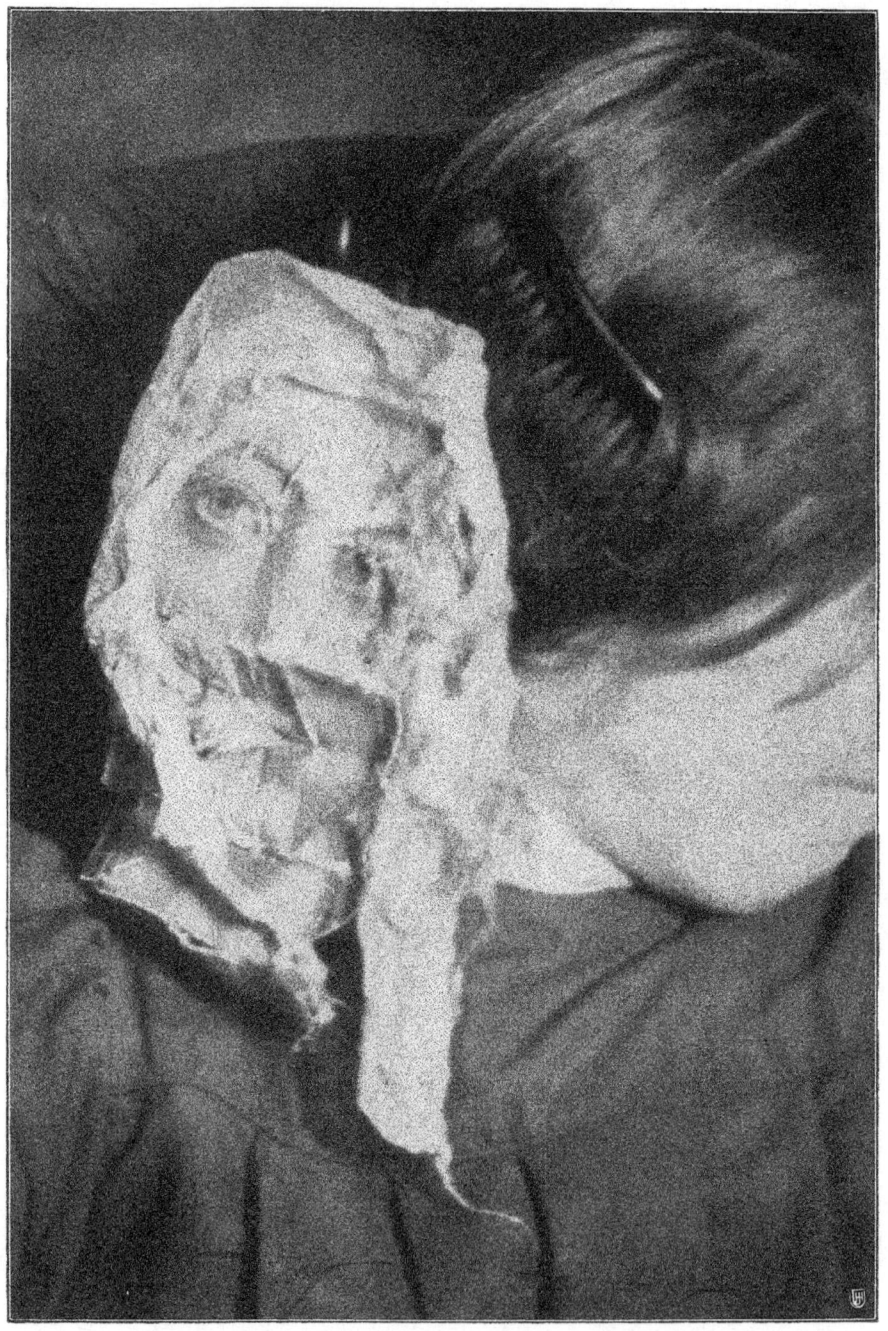

FIG. 82. ENLARGEMENT OF PORTION OF FIG 81

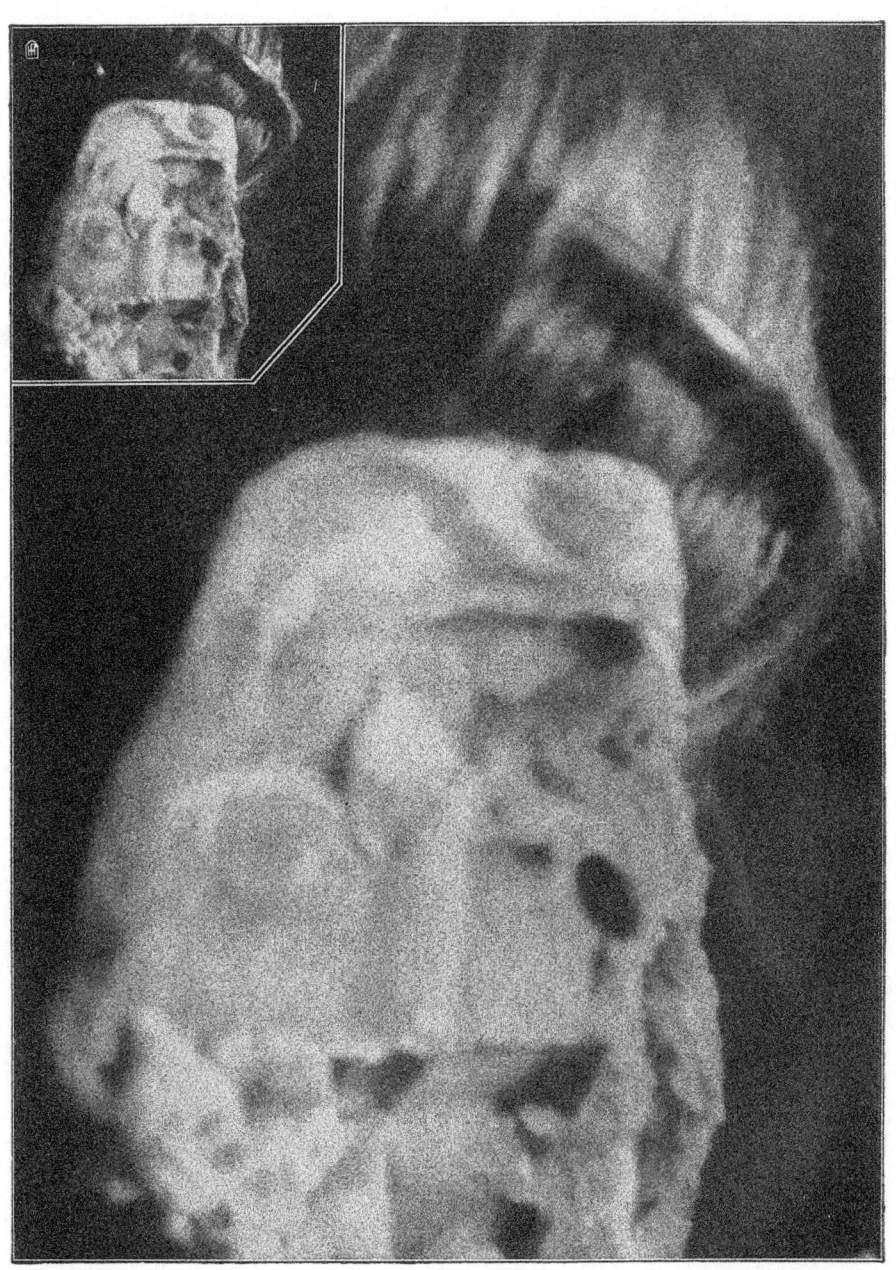

FIG. 83. LATERAL VIEW OF FIG. 81 TAKEN INSIDE CABINET, WITH ENLARGEMENT.

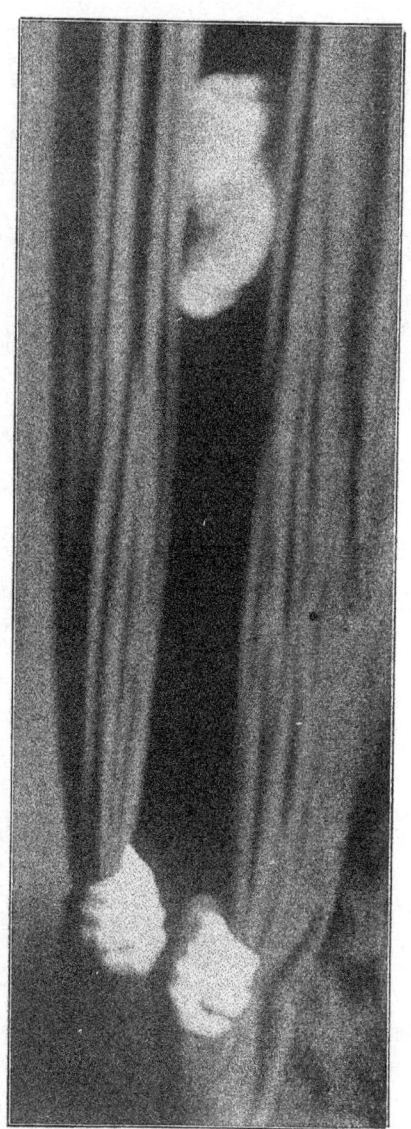 

FIGS. 84 AND 85. AUTHOR'S FLASHLIGHT PHOTOGRAPHS OF 14 MAY, 1912.

FIG. 84. FRONT VIEW.   FIG 85. VIEW FROM THE LEFT.

but under the rents and creases and fragments we can distinctly see a mouth, with broad lips and the left part of the chin (magnified front photograph of the 18 by 24 inches camera). The left side is out of drawing, and the left eye squints.

The face is surrounded by fabric in the stereoscopic photograph, and shows a distinct low relief, like a sculptural sketch for the mask of a female head. The surface of the formation is covered by numerous folds, holes, and creases, while the lower half appears to consist of several broadcloth or paper bands unfolded, placed one upon the other, and organically joined and felted up with a veiling material. A crumpled mask, such as can be bought, would have a more complete appearance, and would hardly be organically connected with cloth fragments and veils, as is the case with the present structure.

Sittings of the 10th and 11th May 1912.

Negative.

Sitting of the 14th May 1912.

Present.—Mme. Bisson and the author.

Conditions as in previous sittings.

During the hypnosis, on the 13th May, Mme. Bisson had suggestively prepared Eva for to-day's sitting, so that she was more favourably disposed.

About a quarter of an hour after hypnotisation a long veil-like strip of matter appeared, covering first the medium's breast and then the left upper arm, with a large part hanging down over her dress on the left. This strip, about a yard long and about half a yard wide, and resembling fine muslin, was fixed on the back of the curtain at Eva's left, while her hands remained fixed to the curtain, and it was repeatedly seen in the light, quite separated from her body.

Although a round globular mass showed itself several times, we could not recognise any features. Yet Eva pointed with a finger to the structure opposite her, and said, "Don't you see? Here's the nose, here's the mouth, etc."

When the white round form appeared clearly in the curtain gap I ignited the flash-light.

Sitting closed. Final examination negative.

Before the sitting Eva weighed not quite 120 lbs. After the sitting she weighed 119 lbs., though there were slight oscillations of the balance, owing to her restlessness.

An examination of the photographs (Figs. 84 and 85) taken at this sitting shows that Eva's hands grasped the curtain at about the level of her knees, and that 3 or 4 feet above, rather higher than the level of her head, there is a white elongated shape, which looks like a cloud. On the stereoscopic picture, which is rather more successful, is seen a white compact mass emerging from the left curtain, to the back of which the invisible portion of this shape might be fixed, although in the front view the left margin of the material does not seem to touch the curtain on the same side. Whether this structure, 8 inches long and 4 inches wide, consists entirely of the primitive elementary substance of materialisations, or veil-like or other stuff, cannot be judged from the photographs alone. The medium's head was over 3 feet behind the form, and for the first time in the series of experiments we have succeeded in photographing this material, apparently used for forming heads and faces, quite separated from the medium, and apparently freely suspended in the curtain gap.

SITTING OF THE 15TH MAY 1912.

Present.—Mme. Bisson and the author.

Conditions as before.

In order to make the conditions of control still more rigid, Mme. Bisson allowed me to search her from head to foot before the sitting, so as to dispose of the allegation that she could have supplied any objects to the medium in the cabinet for producing the phenomena. Eva was not favourably disposed on this day. When the first half-hour had passed, without result, there were no indications of a positive action by the medium, so Mme. Bisson began to talk to Eva, urging her to put an end to this condition of indifference by an energetic concentration of the will, and the direction of the attention to the occurrence of phenomena. Eva then asked her: " Venez, Juliette, me tenir la tête," and Mme. Bisson entered the cabinet and touched the forehead and neck of the medium about one minute with her hands.

After we had again made urgent requests for positive efforts, we saw at last (about one hour after the sitting commenced), in her lap, a packet of white material, which moved and finally assumed a rough outline of a white female arm, lying across her lap, while the medium's hands held the curtain.

The author then expressed a wish to be allowed to touch this substance. Eva then brought my right hand towards the mass, but with obvious reluctance and instinctive fear. The author touched a firm, cool, moist mass, which, however, disappeared at his touch as if by magic.

Some white amorphous material appeared several times in her lap, but Eva's power did not seem to suffice for any further development of the phenomena, so that the sitting had to be closed.

Final control negative. The medium weighed, before the sitting, 119 lbs.; afterwards, 120 lbs.

SITTING OF THE 17TH MAY 1912.

Present.—Mme. Bisson and the author.

Eva's weight before and after the sitting was 118 lbs. Conditions as usual.

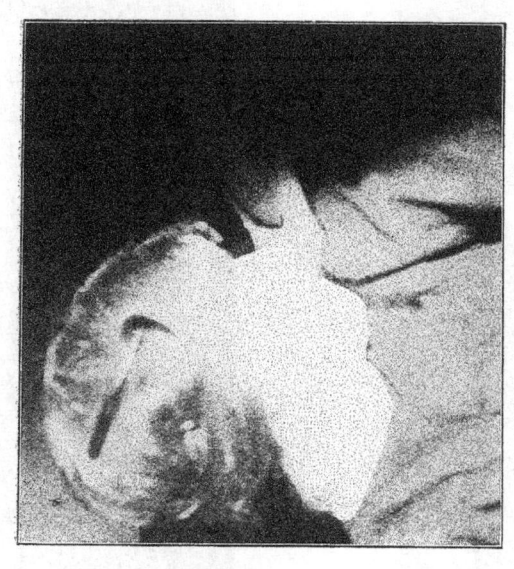

Fig. 87. Author's flashlight photograph of 20 May, 1912.

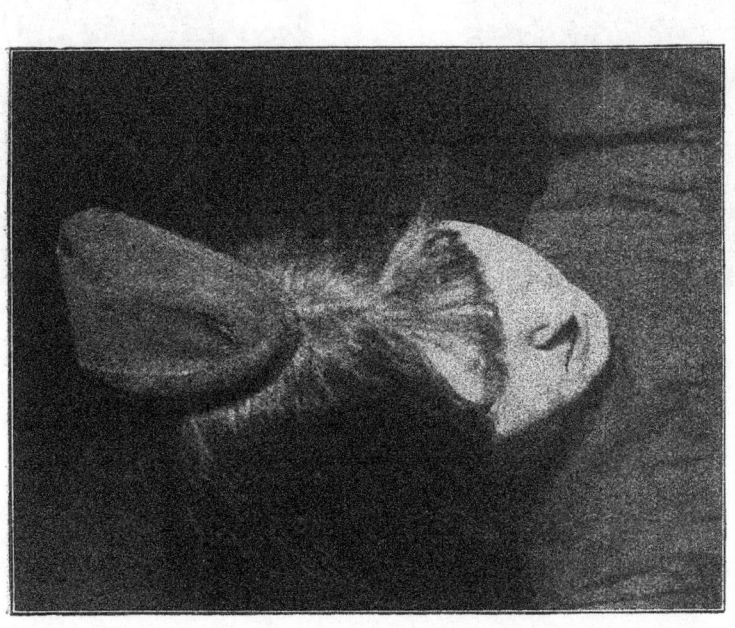

Fig. 86. Author's flashlight photograph of 17 May, 1912.

 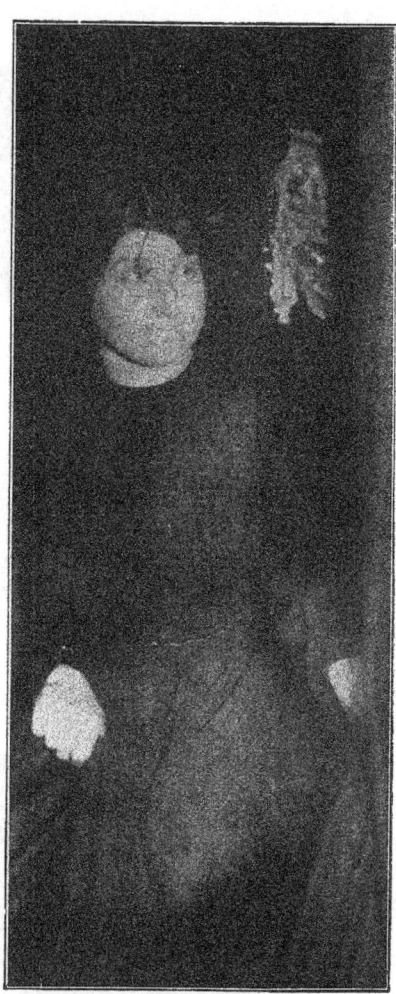

FIGS. 88 AND 89. FLASHLIGHT PHOTOGRAPHS OF 21 MAY, 1912.
LEFT: FIRST PHOTOGRAPH. RIGHT: SECOND PHOTOGRAPH.

While the medium's hands held the curtains half open, a grey smoke-like wisp, some 8 or 10 inches long, appeared to emerge from the medium's mouth, accompanied by convulsive groans and long-drawn expirations. Towards the end it gradually became denser and whiter, and from this end there emerged the unmistakable outlines of four obviously flat white fingers of middle size, which were kept in constant motion, as if by a draught, and changed their shape every moment. When the curtain was opened wide the material was separated off, and became visible first on the shoulder and then, in a very remarkable shape, on the head, giving an impression of white.

The electric contact was pressed and a photograph taken. The medium was exhausted, and the sitting came to an end. Final examination negative.

The grey shape visible on the photographs (Fig. 86) lies on the middle of the medium's head, and resembles an old felt slipper bent backwards, but of miniature size. The stereoscopic picture shows Eva's feet, also in felt slippers. By its appearance and quality this picture is quite out of the run of the series of observations, which show a more or less uniform tendency of development.

Sitting of the 20th May 1912.

Present.—Mme. Bisson and the author.

Conditions as usual. Examination, also, of Mme. Bisson, as on the 15th May.

In this sitting the phenomena took approximately the same course as in the last. White wisps and balls on the lap and shoulder, and the mouth phenomenon as described on 17th May. The material attached itself again to the back of the left curtain, and sometimes passed beyond the hem of the curtain into the circle of light. The request to take hold of a proffered cigarette was not fulfilled. In her efforts to carry out the request, Eva moved the curtains pretty rapidly to and fro. I saw distinctly, from my place near the right curtain, that the white mass was drawn to and fro with the left curtain, as if it was attached to it. When the mass reappeared on the left shoulder I took a photograph, and the sitting came to an end.

The photograph (Fig. 87) taken in this sitting is very similar to the last. Again an object resembling a slipper, which appeared to me white, comes out grey in the photograph. It lies on the left shoulder, and is apparently held with the mouth. The long bag-shaped object broadens out backwards.

The similarity of the object to that photographed in the last sitting is too striking to be overlooked. Both shapes belong to the same kind, and show on the whole the same composition and design, without being absolutely identical. In the course of the sittings we observed repeatedly that the tendency towards identical forms continued over several sittings. This experience was repeated later in the case of face formations, whose type and chief characteristics were sometimes preserved for several successive sittings.

Sitting of the 21st May 1912.

Present.—Mme. Bisson, her younger son, and the author.

Conditions as usual.

On this day Mme. Bisson did not enter the cabinet during the whole sitting. After somnambulism had set in we heard loud expirations and stertorous breathing.

The white material first seen on the medium's lap is again supported behind the left curtain, exposing itself to the light from time to time. The impression given was as if Eva rolled up the curtain with the fingers of her left hand and drew it back slightly at the same time. On opening her hand, the curtain fell back over the image. This process indicates a fixation of the object or image on the inside of the curtain. We saw the features of an imperfectly-formed face, which, on account of its favourable position, I photographed (Figs. 88 and 89) three times, changing the plates after each exposure. I then saw a long white fragment, and had the impression as if the face were suspended in mid-air, subsequently moving back towards Eva's head, in order to lie on her hair. Eva asked us to give her the red electric torch, and illuminated the rather flat image, from which a number of flakes and fibres hung down, resembling white curls made up of thick cotton thread.

After this occurrence the author sat inside the cabinet on the floor, with Eva's consent, in order to observe any further phenomena from the back. Unfortunately, the medium was too exhausted to continue the sitting. I then entered the cabinet before anybody else and examined Eva over the whole skin. Nowhere could I find anything suspicious, neither on her body nor in the cabinet. Sitting closed.

All three series of photographic records show pictures of the same object.

This day's type of face corresponds in its structure and its composition to that of 14th May. While the latter was attached to Eva's hair, to-day's structure is quite detached from the medium's body, and is obviously attached to the curtain inside, or supported by it.

In the second series the face appears in the same place, and in the stereoscopic photographs gives the impression of free suspension, but that may be an optical illusion, as a fold of the curtain, pushed back by the medium's left hand, furnishes a support for the image. The hem of the curtain projecting forward throws a shadow on the image.

The whole form of the object recalls a first sketch of a face in wet plaster or *papier mâché*. We find the same building up of the face in storeys as on 14th May. The face terminates in the upper lip, the lower part being displaced backwards and showing a gaping hole—at least, in Series I. The eyes are just recognisable, the bridge of the nose is twice broken, or at least traversed, by two great rents. The whole consists of a conglomeration of fragments of an unknown mass, like the sketch of a face-mask in low relief. The structure is flat, like that of 14th May.

The photographs of the second and third series closely resemble those of the first, differing only in details. Thus, in the second series, a deep rent appears on the right cheek, which is absent in Series I.

To-day's experience is interesting, inasmuch as in the sittings from 14th to 21st May the same type recurs with extremely characteristic faults and imperfections.

SITTING OF THE 24TH MAY 1912.

Negative.

SITTING OF THE 25TH MAY 1912.

Present.—Mme. Bisson and the author.

Strict examination of both women and the cabinet before the sitting, as on 15th May 1912. Illumination and other conditions as in previous sittings.

Since the weight of the medium, both before and after the sittings, showed no material change, these weighings were not continued.

Commencement, 9.15 P.M. Bodily reactions indicate positive performances. Half an hour after hypnotisation a white patch was seen at the level of the medium's head on the back of the left curtain, and after Eva's left hand had several times carefully rolled up the curtain. The patch turned out to be a flat white hand, with wrist and part of an arm, attached to the curtain in such a way that the fingers hung down. The author had the personal impression of a lifeless form without motion of its own. By pulling in or rolling up the curtain three fingers were made clearly visible. The phenomenon was observed more easily from my place than from that of Mme. Bisson. Since I perceived no motion, I saw no chance of a proffered cigarette being grasped. The shape of the hand was elongated. It appeared mummified and shrivelled, and was provided with extraordinarily long and pointed fingers. In thickness it appeared flat, but thicker than a hand shape made of leather or paper. Its thickness might have been about one-fifth of an inch. Shortly afterwards some fingers appeared at the same level, but this time they were alive, and grasped the curtain inside and out. My whole attention was turned towards Eva's left hand, and when the curtain was withdrawn again I saw the flat hand-formation on her left knee instead of the real hand. There is hardly a doubt that the living fingers grasping the curtain were those of Eva. This situation, already photographed at St Jean de Luz, is psychologically explained by the endeavour to fulfil our wish for the grasping of a cigarette. Since the flat lifeless shape did not suffice for this, the somnambulist exchanged the parts of the living and the lifeless hand.

Doubts of this kind were just passing through my head when a new phenomenon attracted my attention. Both Eva's hands were clearly visible on her knees, when suddenly a third hand, coming from the left, crossed Eva's left hand, touched it on the back with the finger-tips, and then quickly withdrew. This phenomenon occurred several times in succession, but so quickly that I did not succeed in taking a photograph of it.

These two contradictory events happened in close succession, and were observed with equal exactness and impartiality. In the course of the sitting the curtain-rod suddenly came loose, so that it hung down. Yet I tried to photograph the hand. The photographs failed on account of the disturbance mentioned. Only the stereoscopic transparency shows how Eva's left hand opens the curtain widely, and how she looks back towards the back of the cabinet. One sees a white elongated shape with fingers recalling a long female glove attached to the back wall, but no such thing was found during a strict search of the medium and the cabinet. The object had disappeared without a trace.

Close of the sitting, 11 P.M. Final examination negative.

Sittings of the 27th, 28th and 30th May 1912.

Negative.

Sitting of the 1st June 1912.

Present.—Mme. Bisson and the author.

Commencement, 8.45 ; end, 10.30 P.M.

On this day Mme. Bisson hypnotised the medium at 5 P.M. in preparation for the evening's sitting. The personification calling herself " Berthe "—the controlling spirit in the spiritistic sense—announced through the somnambulist's mouth extraordinary phenomena for to-day's sitting. " Berthe " would endeavour to show us the head of a person closely related to us, and would, if possible, appear simultaneously. She would see if we would recognise her.

Before the sitting Eva had a dreamy and dazed expression, and already showed a quickened pulse two hours beforehand. The definite announcement of a positive result induced us to make the examination of the medium and the cabinet as thorough and as strict as possible. As in all previous sittings, the medium undressed completely and put on the black séance costume, consisting of tights and dress.

Illumination with red light, aggregating about one hundred candle-power.

Eva had hardly been hypnotised on her chair by Mme. Bisson when she breathed loudly and stertorously, with every sign of deep trance. The teleplastic creative process commenced at once. At the place in the curtain which had been made familiar by practice, and in which the phenomena had shown themselves at the last sittings, *i.e.*, on the inside of the left curtain, at about the level of the medium's head, a white luminosity, as of a strip of muslin 20 inches long, became visible. Eva then tried gradually to expose the image to the light by rolling up the left curtain flap with her left hand, and thus gradually allowing the red light to fall upon the object, obviously fixed inside.

To my greatest astonishment I seemed to recognise in the masculine face, shown with the well-known drapery of veiling, but sketched as with black chalk on a flat surface, the features of Alexandre Bisson, the husband of my collaborator, who had died in January 1912.

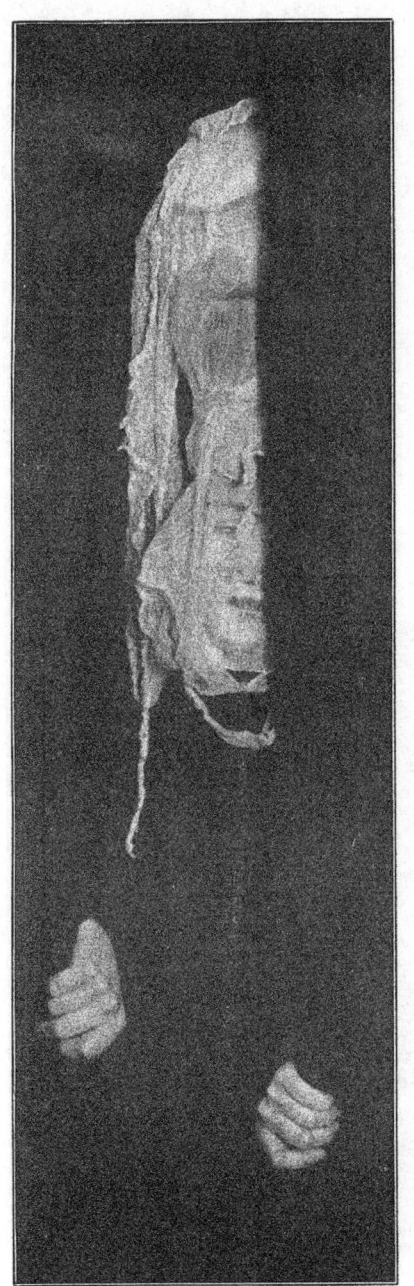

Fig 90 and 91. Author's flashlight photograph of 1 June, 1912 (second series), on the right: enlargement.

FIG. 92. AUTHOR'S THIRD FLASHLIGHT PHOTOGRAPH OF 1 JUNE, 1912.
PORTRAIT OF M. BISSON.

SITTINGS OF MAY AND JUNE 1912 (PARIS)

Although I saw that she had immediately recognised her husband and showed deep emotion, I was not certain of my impression, and considered the possibility of a self-deception. As soon as the face showed itself again, I ignited the flash-light by means of the electric contact in my hand. After changing the plates, I succeeded in taking two further photographs, so that out of the three series of photographs, taken with five cameras, nine successful photographs are available for study, the remaining photographs having been unsuccessful. Before the third flash-light the object appeared smaller than before the first. Mme. Bisson claimed to have recognised two heads during the first exposure—a male head and underneath a female head (the portrait of the entity " Berthe ")—and this was corroborated on developing the plates. The pictures of the third series only contained one face.

The pictures (Figs. 90, 91, 92 and 93) recall face-masks artistically composed with clever veil drapery, but without any signs of real life, in spite of the greatest portrait resemblance. Besides, no plastic development of the features could be established with any certainty either in the sittings or from the photographs, while the base of the pictures appears to me to resemble paper. The transition towards the pictorial representation of the face proceeded in stages, since in the beginning, as in previous sittings, the only thing to be seen was material in rather large veils and fragments, with which Eva would sometimes cover her own face.

In spite of the three flash-light exposures, the phenomena continued. The structure now appeared on the left shoulder. Eva illuminated it first with the red and then with the white electric torch, but the image, in which I distinctly perceived a male bearded face, with a high forehead, would not suffer the light, and disappeared behind the back of Eva's chair towards the back of the cabinet, without Eva having changed the position of her hands. Since I had closely followed the image from the shoulder, I did not let it go out of sight, but rose and put my head deep into the cabinet, bending over Eva as she sat quietly, and keeping the curtain closed under my chin. In this way a ray of light passed over my head, through the top of the curtain, on to the back of the cabinet, without disturbing the medium. The male face then stood facing me like a male portrait in life-size, fixed on the back wall, remained for about six seconds, and then revolved about its own axis flat on the wall, the upper part of the face falling down, and finally disappeared towards the floor behind the medium's back. During this whole observation Eva's body was motionless, and under my observation. The image was entirely separated from her. Its motion and disappearance appeared to be under the control of an unseen power.

Thus ended this extremely remarkable sitting, during which Mme. Bisson had not entered the cabinet at all. Eva rose from her chair and stood in front of the curtain. She tore open the seam joining the black tights to the dress, so that I could make a complete bodily examination. Again I searched her with the greatest care, made her open her mouth, examined her hair and ears, and performed a gynæcological examination, without finding anything either on her body or on the séance costume. The subsequent examination of the cabinet was also negative. The image I had seen falling had totally disappeared.

Eva was much indisposed after the sitting, and several times vomited blood—about a wine-glass full, mixed with food remnants. She also complained of headache. The condition of exhaustion lasted several days.

The author was, as usual, present at the development of the plates. The first and second series showed two faces, one above the other—a male face above and a female face below—while the third series only showed a male face. The remarkable similarity of the male face to that of the late author, Alex. Bisson, is immediately obvious. Proofs of the photographs sent to members of the family were recognised by all the relatives (wife, four children, etc.) and friends of M. Bisson, as his portrait at the age of about thirty-eight. When Eva saw the pictures she fainted. The author made some tests himself, and showed the pictures to persons who had known Bisson in his life. These persons also recognised the deceased at first sight.

The third exposure shows the complete life-sized face of a bearded man, with his head bent towards the left, and directing a look full of expression upon us from behind the curtain. The curtain covers half the left eye. Eye-glasses are distinctly seen on the eyes. Several veil-like fragments hang down from the right side of the head. From the point of the nose, part of the mouth, and nearly the whole beard, are covered by partly transparent material hanging down for a length of from 8 to 12 inches.

Among the remarkable characteristics we may mention the high broad forehead, the straight line of the hair, the deep-set eye-sockets, the vivacity and cleverness of the eyes, and the short sight (glasses), all being peculiarities of the late M. Bisson, as may also be seen by comparison with extant photographs. A closer examination of the stereoscopic picture also shows that the corner of the mouth, visible on it, is directed downwards as in photographs from life.

The beard is comparatively long. In portraits from life, M. Bisson's beard is rather shorter. But at various times in his life M. Bisson wore his beard in various shapes and lengths, so that this point is not important.

The first and second series of photographs, which show, below Bisson's portrait, the pretty features of a young woman, reproduce the same sketch of a face corresponding in every detail to the photograph just discussed (Figs. 90 and 91). Only the draping of the veiling is different. The veil in this case covers the greatest part of the hair of the head, and hangs down in streamers quite a yard long, which form, in the middle, a fairly compact mass, part of which was photographed by the camera inside the cabinet, *i.e.*, from behind (Fig. 93).

The partly transparent veils are themselves thickened at the hems, and show a pattern of parallel fibres.

The female face, the deeper shading of which suggests the beginning of a plastic modelling, has regular and good features, though its expression may be described as rigid. Both these faces, placed one above the other, are lacking in the finer half-shadows, which are, for instance, expressed so clearly in the medium's face beside them.

We have, therefore, here to deal with flat images draped with veil material, with artistic sketches, soft charcoal, or other black and white

SITTINGS OF MAY AND JUNE 1912 (PARIS)

drawings, but not with photographs from nature or reproductions of photographs, though the portraits themselves have a natural expression. Quite apart from the fact that no photograph of Bisson exists in half-profile with the expression and position of our pictures (as shown by inquiries within the family), the sketchiness of the drawings, and the lack of fine modelling of the face, speak against the possible use of a photograph. Thus, even the worst photographic reproduction would never give the outlines of the eye-glasses in such an irregular, half-finished and distorted way as is shown in our pictures. The same remarks apply to other details when closely examined, *e.g.*, the artistic treatment of the beard, the eye-sockets, the forehead, etc. While in the photographs from life both eyebrows make a straight line, in our pictures they proceed in obtuse angles upward and outward. In spite of the obvious defects of drawing, the liveliness of the expression, especially of the eyes, is not surpassed in any extant photograph. And it was just the intelligent vivacious eye which distinguished Bisson's physiognomy. Very characteristic of the deceased was the breadth and shortness of his nose. If one of his photographs had been used, how was it that this particularly characteristic part was covered? There would be no sense in it, but we find the same principle in other materialisation photographs. Perhaps the rendering of this part offers special difficulties for the teleplastic projections. Or the artistic intelligence made a special point of showing in the face sufficient characteristic traits to ensure recognition, and of saving any further unnecessary and superfluous additions for the sake of economy of power. Thus the contrasts between the vivacious expression of the face on the one hand, and the imperfection and lack of details on the other, would be explained by this impressionistic tendency.

As regards the position of the medium's head in the photographs taken from the interior of the cabinet, Bisson's portrait and the stereoscopic pictures show that the upper part of her body is about 3 feet behind the images, and completely separated from them, while the hands are visible at the curtain in all the pictures. The lateral view from within the cabinet is of special interest as giving a section of a portion of the teleplastic creation from behind, with an estimated diameter of 6 inches.

The result of the sitting of 1st June 1912 is probably one of the most interesting results of our four years of observation, always supposing that fraudulent manipulations were excluded by the experimental arrangements. We are face to face with the fact that the features of a deceased person are reconstructed in a portrait by mediumistic power. The injurious effect which a fact of this kind, with its apparent fulfilment of the far-reaching hopes of spiritualism may exercise on superstitious minds, must not be underestimated. For this and other reasons we refrain from any theoretical interpretation of the fact, and confine ourselves to a simple record of the observations.

Sitting of the 4th June 1912.

Negative.

SITTING OF THE 5TH JUNE 1912.

Before the beginning of this day's experiment, Bisson's three sons appeared in the séance room (the eldest is employed in the Ministry of Finance, the second is an airman, and the third is a thirteen-year-old schoolboy) to express their thanks for copies of the photographs, and their deep emotion on beholding the features of their late father, obtained in so remarkable a manner. Another visitor was a painter, R. M., a friend of Bisson's of twenty years' standing, who presented his congratulations on the success of the sitting of 1st June. He also, at the first glance, had recognised his friend from the picture.

Present.—Mme. Bisson, her son Pierre, and the author.

Conditions as in previous sittings.

About fifteen minutes after hypnotisation I saw a long white wisp or veil, which appeared to come from the back wall of the cabinet, and hung down over Eva's left shoulder. This gradually advanced, as could be seen on the repeated opening of the curtains, until finally the features of a female face were seen in the upper portion. While the medium's hands were quiet and visible, the head, with its tail of long veiling, moved up along the left hem of the curtain, as if the head were creeping up, until it nearly reached the curtain-pole (9 feet up), and then rapidly descended. A photographic record was made with a flash-light.

A white hand also appeared at the curtain, and when Mme. Bisson approached her head, she was pulled by the hair, while Eva's hands remained visible. On closer inspection I recognised the same glove-like form which we had observed and photographed on 25th May 1912. This ended the sitting. Final examination without result.

The negatives of to-day's sitting (Fig. 94) show the same female type of face as that photographed on 1st June with M. Bisson, and they appear in the same favourite place on the back of the left curtain. By mounting a stereoscopic apparatus just opposite at the right curtain, I had succeeded in getting a front view of the face only half-illuminated behind the curtain, whereas the other cameras, owing to the slanting position of the head, only show a distorted picture.

The position of the head is vertical, and at right angles to the curtain, which is touched by the left ear. The nice-looking female face, with its natural expression, is now undoubtedly in low relief, and is surrounded by fabrics, wisps, and fragments, which fall over the face down to the mouth. A rich bundle of the finest veil-like fabric hangs down on to Eva's left shoulder, and four white finger-tips project from it, obviously belonging to the hand which we observed during the sitting.

The side view taken from within the cabinet corroborates this picture, and shows that the fingers look flat, as if cut out of paper, and are quite irregularly formed.

As regards the modelling of the face, the nose appears to be distinctly developed, and to project in the right proportion. In the same way the eye-sockets, mouth and chin appear to be plastic impressions, like the work of a competent artist. The shadows of the face are strong, deep, and correctly arranged.

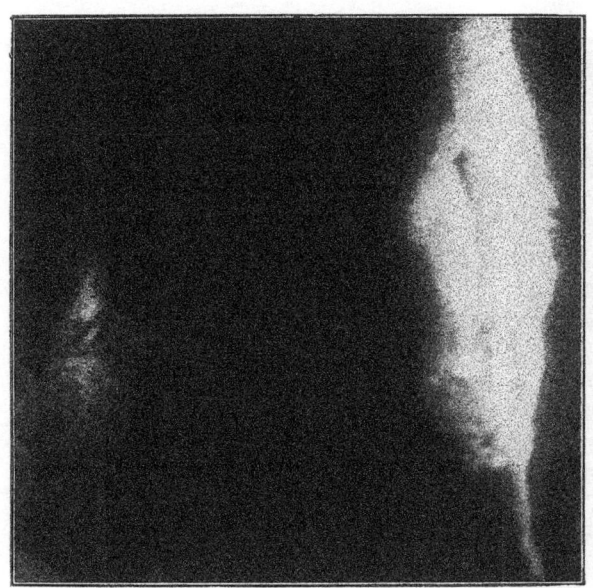

Fig. 93. Photograph of a cross section of Fig. 90, taken inside the cabinet.

FIG 96. SIDE VIEW OF FIG 95, TAKEN WITHIN THE CABINET.

The extremely fine veiling stuff resembles a spider's web, and bears a remarkable likeness to the productions of the medium Stanislava P.

Observations in June and July 1912 (Paris).

FROM 12th to 24th June there were chiefly negative sittings, or positive ones with slight results. Only on 24th June Mme. Bisson succeeded in taking a new photograph. This sitting was attended by Dr Bourdet (an author), his wife, and young Pierre Bisson. In the face shown, Mme. Bisson recognised the features of her deceased nephew, Georges Thurner, a literary man. She succeeded in taking the photograph with three cameras, which confirmed the observation. In a letter of 1st July, she communicates the following: "Yesterday I showed the photograph of 24th June to my sister (the mother of Georges), without telling her anything or making any remark. The impression made upon her was an unexpectedly violent one. She exclaimed, ' Georges, my dear son, it is you! My God, my God, how wonderful, and yet how terrible!' Then she broke into sobs and tears."

Similar emotions were produced by the appearance of the portrait in the case of a grandmother and an aunt of the deceased.

At my request, Mme. Bisson asked her sister to give her a statement in writing, and this is as follows :—

" MY DEAR JULIETTE,

"Immediately on seeing the photograph I recognised my deceased son Georges. I am grateful to have a proof that he thinks of me, and am looking forward to seeing him again some day.

" Yours, with all my heart,
" EUGÉNIE."

After these statements, one is justified in assuming that the picture obtained on 24th June bears a close resemblance to the deceased Georges Thurner.

The technical composition of this image (Fig. 95) is extremely curious. A comparison of the stereoscopic transparency with the side view and the front view shows very clearly two layers in the structure. The upper and outer layer exposed to the light shows a clean-cut surface, consisting of a thin layer resembling paper, and in its size and its outline corresponds to a life-sized male face with a long beard, beyond which it projects below. On this surface are two projections, one in the place of the right moustache, and the other in the place of the lower beard on the right. The lower one is bent upwards. The lower termination of the surface is straight, as if cut off with a knife. On this groundwork, which appears to be fixed to the left curtain, there is the drawing of a man's face, from twenty-five to thirty-five years of age, in half profile, with eyes turned towards the left, and generally resembling a brown charcoal drawing. A striking, and, at first sight, rather strange peculiarity, is a deep indentation running parallel to the mouth across the whole beard, from which two other indentations descend, in parallel lines, to the lower edge. The one on the left crosses the horizontal indentation, makes a deep cut, and disappears in the white of the left cheek. The rectangular and parallel character of the crease is even visible on the back of the lower portion (Fig. 96), so that the whole structure resembles a rectangular balloon.

The lower layer of this whole head-composition projects beyond the leaf-shaped upper layer in an irregular shape below, covers the whole back of the picture, as shown by the side view, and appears at the right forehead with a fold as of a transparent veil. The visible hair of the right side and the point of the nose are plastically added to the drawing to increase the vivacity of the expression.

On the forehead the veil is twisted up into a thick cord, which replaces the bridge of the nose, and passes into the tip of the nose. Whether the dark broad full beard is drawn or composed of the dark substance previously mentioned cannot be decided from the photographs. The principles of formation are the same as in the other pictures. The author of this head is less concerned with anatomical accuracy and technical completion than with the psychical expression. In spite of the simple realism in the use of the means of presentation (drawing supported by sculptural presentation and decorative veil ornaments), the desired impression is produced, and the essential character is maintained.

The short, straight, tight-closed mouth, with comparatively large nostrils, strong bushy eyebrows, the earnest eyes turned towards the left (which, however, are very badly drawn), in connection with the long square beard, give to the portrait the expression of manly dignity, severity, and decision. It is just this production which, more than many other pictures of our collection, combines the negative and positive qualities of the unknown artist, as regards technical construction, use of material, and artistic treatment.

In the sitting of 21st June (also held in the author's absence) Mme. Bisson perceived three types; first, the type of her deceased nephew, Georges; second, the type " Berthe "; third, the type of her deceased husband, Alex. Bisson. Of the latter, she succeeded in making a new portrait, which is quite different from that made by the author on 1st June. While the author's photograph is three-quarter face, we find on 21st June a full-faced portrait. Although both negatives represent the same object, they have hardly any common characteristic, and on the negative on 21st June the eye-glasses are wanting.

Mme. Bisson is of the opinion that the photograph of 21st June represents her husband, as he was in the last years of his life, while the pictures of 1st June represent an earlier period of his life.

Now we might ask: Is this a portrait of the deceased at all? The author can answer this question in the affirmative by what he remembers of Bisson, and after the study of photographs. The picture (Fig. 97) shows the following :—

Eva's distorted face is turned to the right, while the portrait appears to lie on the left side of her head, or to be attached to it. The sharply contoured head is drawn in broad lines under the thick transparent veil, covering the whole flat surface. It is drawn as if by a heavy awkward hand of a sculptor making a charcoal drawing. The hair is wanting, or is entirely covered by the veil. The line of the

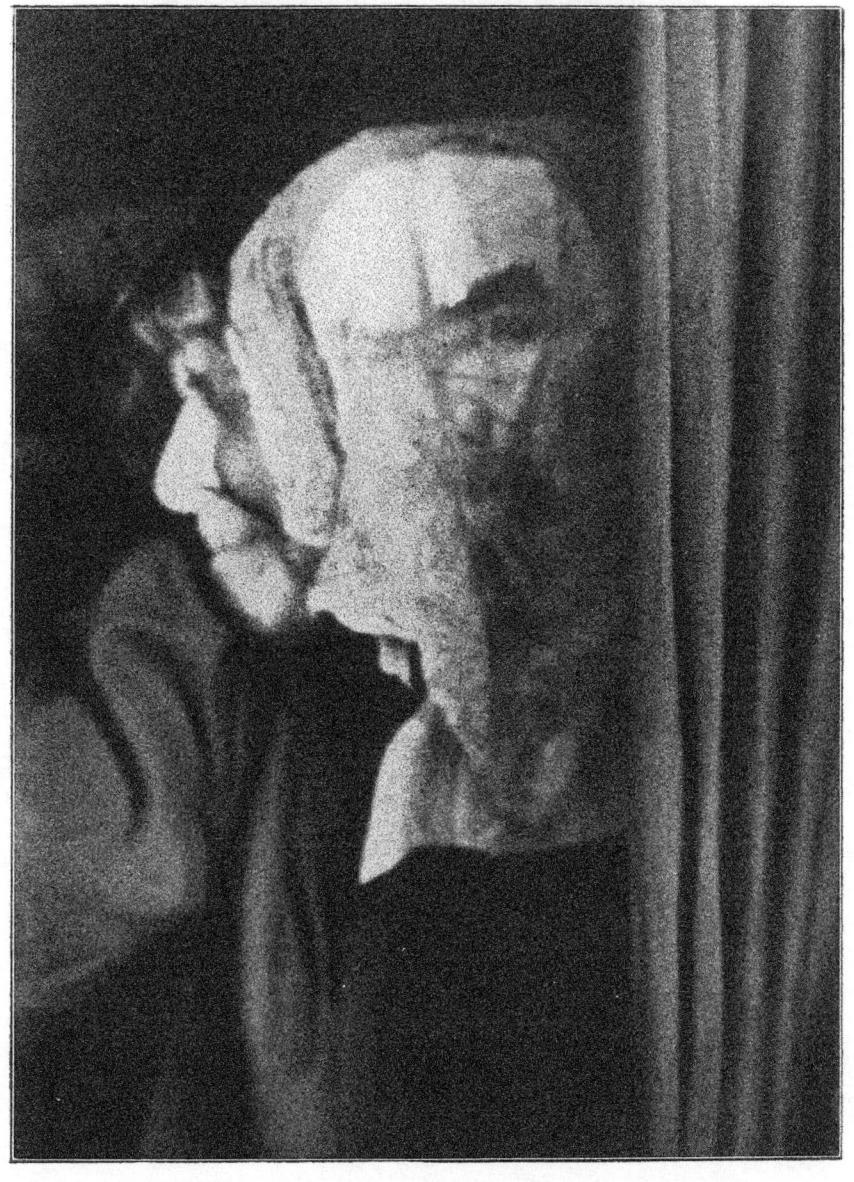

FIG. 97. MME. BISSON'S FLASHLIGHT PHOTOGRAPH OF 21 JUNE, 1912.

Fig. 99. Sid
Fig. 98 ta
within the

Fig. 98. Mme. Bisson's flashlight photograph of
6 July, 1912.

eyebrows here also makes an obtuse angle, instead of being straight, as in the photographs from life. The eye-sockets, especially the left one, are so strongly marked by deep dark shadows that one might describe them as plastic. The expression of the eyes is extremely vivacious, especially in the left eye, which is less covered by veils. The nose appears to be rudimentary, and only a stump is seen. On the other hand, the falling line of the bushy moustache corresponds exactly to the photographs from life, and the building of the forehead, the eye-sockets, and especially the eyes, removes all doubt as regards the resemblance to Bisson. A piece of material resembling paper projects from the veil below. The arched forehead appears as if split by a broad vertical fissure in the middle. There are also three parallel creases crossing it downwards at equal intervals. The lower portion of the face vanishes under the veils.

In this production, also, an artistic will has attempted to materialise its interpretation, and has strongly emphasised the main points, in order to produce the desired resemblance, with the least expenditure of power. The present portrait is no doubt designed from nature, and not after photographs. In spite of its coarse imperfections it produces a much more living impression than the reproductions from life. The technical treatment is exactly the same as in previous pictures.

The production of two entirely different types of images of the same deceased person, without any help from existing photographs, must, in any case, be recognised as a very remarkable mediumistic performance.

In the sitting of 6th July another fragment of a face was photographed (Figs. 98 and 99), consisting of a right eye with a piece of cheek and forehead, framed with fabric and veil draperies. The whole object appears to be fixed to the curtain, which is rolled up by Eva's hand. The life-sized eye might correspond to that of a female person. This fragment of a face is the last flash-light photograph produced at Paris in July 1912.

In the second half of July Mme. Bisson and Eva were alone in the family villa at La Baule at the mouth of the Loire, in order to make preparations for the move from Paris. On 19th July Mme. Bisson hypnotised her medium in the photographic dark-room of the house while the door was open, *i.e.*, in semi-darkness. Eva wore her day costume. Suddenly the female image known as " Berthe " showed itself several times on Eva's clothed body. This observation is interesting as a spontaneous materialisation, without cabinet and without séance costume, occurring in half daylight.

SITTINGS IN JULY, AUGUST AND SEPTEMBER 1912 (MUNICH).

ARRANGEMENT OF THE EXPERIMENTAL ROOM.

In response to the author's invitation, Mme. Bisson and Eva C. stayed in Munich from the 25th July till 13th September 1912, and sittings were held in a room adjoining the author's working-rooms, and arranged for the purpose (*see* Diagram).

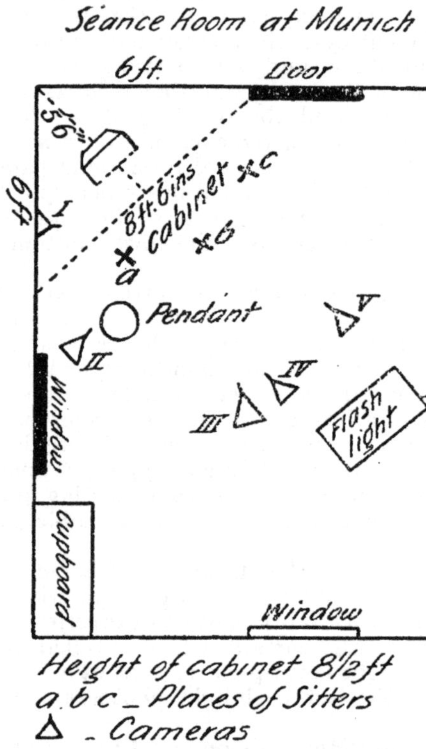

Diagram VII.

Séance Room at Munich

(Height of cabinet 8½ ft. *a, b, c* — Places of Sitters. △ — Cameras.)

For the construction of the cabinet a large three-cornered wooden framework had been prepared, having two sides, 6 feet wide at right angles to each other, the extreme ends of which were nearly 9 feet apart, and were joined by the curtain-rod. This gave a cabinet 4¼ feet in depth and 8½ feet high. The cross-bar in front was 8 inches wide, and to its inner surface was attached a stereoscopic camera (Zeiss Protar, $F = 1.6$ inches, f/18, 3½ by 5 inches), enabling me to photograph the occurrences inside the cabinet from above at a distance of 30 to 60 inches.

The whole framework was movable and collapsible, and was covered with a thin black cotton lining, as was the ceiling and the floor of the cabinet. A second photographic camera ("Special Wiphot," 3½ by 5 inches, Rietschel Linear Anastigmat, f/4·8, $F = 4\frac{3}{4}$ inches) was placed in the corner of the cabinet on the medium's right, at a height of 57 inches, in order to photograph the occurrences near Eva's head and shoulders, at a distance of 40 inches (as in the Paris séance room). The camera could be worked on the medium's right by drawing back the curtain, which was only fixed to the framework for the upper half of its height, while the left curtain was nailed to the framework all the way down, so that no connection could be established with the medium on that side. The easy-chair intended for the cabinet was partly painted black and partly covered with black material. It consisted of basketwork, with a simple smooth seat and back.

The electric pendant held five lamps with red glass bulbs, two of sixteen candle-power and three of twenty-five candle-power, thus yielding an illumination of one hundred candle-power, which sufficed for reading the hands of a watch and large print, especially on the seats in front of the curtain.

The electrically-ignited flash-light was contained in a large metal box, 10 feet away from the cabinet, with its door opening towards the cabinet, the frame of the door being covered with a transparent incombustible fabric. A tube joining the box to the stove-pipe immediately removed the smoke of the burnt magnesium powder. This arrangement enabled us to take several photographs in succession without being inconvenienced by the magnesium smoke.

Besides the two cameras already mentioned as placed in the cabinet, four other cameras were used, mounted in places which remained the same in all the Munich sittings. These cameras were furnished with Zeiss lenses. There were two stereoscopic cameras with Tessar lenses, $f/6·3$, $F = 4\frac{1}{2}$ inches; one camera 7 by $9\frac{1}{2}$ inches, $f/6·3$, $F = 14$ inches; and one $3\frac{1}{2}$ by 5 inches, $f/4·5$, $F = 6$ inches.

A kinematograph by Pathé Frères, for which an electric projection lamp with an instantaneous shutter provided the illumination, was also in readiness, but it could only be brought into action once, and that without success. For this reason the position of the kinematograph is not shown on the Diagram.

The electric contact for igniting the flash-light was provided with sufficient flexible wire to enable the author to work it from his seat. All the electric arrangements of the séance room derived their current from the house installation.

SITTING OF THE 25TH JULY 1912.

Present.—Mme. Bisson, Dr Specht, and the author.

Negative.

During this and all the following sittings Eva wore the well-known Paris séance costume, consisting of black tights, with stockings in one piece, and the black apron dress. As in Paris, Mme. Bisson, in our presence, sewed up the medium before each sitting in the room adjoining the séance room, after a bodily examination. The seam passed round her waist in order to join the tights to the dress, and then up from the waist to the neck, as well as round the wrists. The costume remained in my house, and was closely examined before and after each sitting by the sitters, with the help of an electric torch shining through it. Only after completing the preparation of the costume, and after searching the medium, did the two ladies enter the séance room together with the other sitters, the room then being illuminated with white electric light.

Eva took her seat in the cabinet and extended her hands, Mme. Bisson taking hold of her thumbs. Hypnotisation was carried out, by fixation of gaze and suggestion, in thirty to sixty seconds. Mme. Bisson then sat back. One of those present closed the curtain and extinguished the white light, while the red light was burning all the time. The hypnotisation process described was the same in all the sittings.

Besides the above precautions, the sitters also examined the cabinet before and after each sitting. The windows were closed by wooden shutters and curtains and the doors locked with keys, which, in some sittings, were put in charge of the observers. Dr Specht had on the 25th spent an hour and a half, in the afternoon, in the séance room, in order to examine it, and especially the cabinet, thoroughly in every part.

Sitting of the 26th July 1912.

Present.—Mme. Bisson, Dr Specht, and the author.

Time, 8.30 p.m. Examination and illumination as on 25th July. I passed my hand over the medium's skin under the dress and found that there were no veils or other objects concealed. Dr Specht followed my hand from the outside. Eva undid her hair, opened her mouth, and pronounced vowels. The examination of her teeth, ears, arm-pits, and feet had negative results.

Specht carefully followed the process of hypnotisation. The white light was extinguished by the author at the moment when Eva was hypnotised and subsided into her chair. Mme. Bisson sat in the middle in front of the curtain, I on her left, and Specht to the right. Eva held the curtain closed for about twenty minutes, while breathing stertorously, as in the Paris sittings. When she opened the curtain I saw beside her left elbow a white mass, which was fugitive but clear enough to be recognised.

A few minutes later, Mme. Bisson and the author saw a male face, with a dark beard, on the left behind Eva, resembling the photographs of the type Bisson. I exchanged places with Specht. When the curtain was opened again, the latter thought he saw an object resembling a skull. During the next phenomenon Eva's head, resting on the back of the chair, and her hands, opening the curtain by about 8 inches, were all visible. Above her left hand a bright wisp about 5 inches long appeared, which seemed to be self-luminous. After this the image of the type " Bisson " was seen to advance slowly into the circle of light and expose itself to view. It was above the medium's hand behind the left curtain, and appeared flat without any relief. Specht had the impression that the image had become clearer after the medium's forced expirations and blowing. The image disappeared. Eva declared, after a short time, she did not feel any more. The sitting was at an end. She rose, walked up to Dr Specht, tore open the seams, and allowed him to examine her thoroughly. Result, negative, as was also the searching of the cabinet.

SITTINGS IN JULY, AUGUST AND SEPTEMBER 1912

Dr Specht considers the phenomena unexplained, and that the proof is complete as far as the facts are concerned. Only he wished that the white light should be switched off after the curtain had been completely closed. The sudden change of illumination produces a blinding of the eye for a short period, and this only disappears when the eyes have got accustomed to the red light. This involves a source of error, for if fraud was intended, one could at that moment pass objects to the medium in the cabinet without detection.

SITTING OF THE 28TH JULY 1912.

Present.—Mme. Bisson, Dr Specht, and the author.

In order to eliminate all sources of error and possible objections regarding Mme. Bisson's part in the phenomena, the latter asked to be examined before the sitting. She entered another room and undressed completely in the author's presence. She wore a chemise, knickers, stockings, and shoes, all coloured black, and over them a long black dress in one piece, which was carefully examined. Neither in the shoes, nor under the stockings, was anything suspicious found. A strict search of the hair and the surface of the body gave negative results.

I then conducted the lady into the room adjoining the séance room, where she sewed up Eva, in our presence, into the séance costume, after the medium had been examined as on the 25th July. That the costume and cabinet had been previously searched by Dr Specht goes without saying.

We then entered the séance room together. Eva was hypnotised as on 25th July. Mme. Bisson closed the curtain, and took her place in front of it on the left. Only then, at a sign from Dr Specht, did the author extinguish the white light.

During the first twenty minutes the medium breathed and blew heavily. Then, as the curtain was opened, there appeared on the left, behind the medium, against the wall, at the level of her head, the same male image as we had observed on 25th July. It was shown four times. Dr Specht regarded it as remarkable that during the first exposure the picture was visible in a place from which it had disappeared at the second exposure, reappearing in the same place at the third opening, although Eva's hands had been visible all the time, and had not left the curtain for an instant. At the urgent request of Mme. Bisson, that the phenomenon might come forward, the portrait changed its place, placed itself on Eva's head, then on her right side, then partly disappeared from our view, finally fixing itself on the back of the curtain, on the left. Eva tried carefully to expose the structure gradually to the light by manipulating the curtain. During the next opening, I worked the electric contact for the flash-light.

Until then Mme. Bisson had not entered the cabinet, but now she extended her hands, which were held by Dr Specht, into the cabinet, in order to soothe the frightened medium, by placing her hand on her head and her heart.

The image corresponding to the type " Bisson " showed itself a few more times, while I looked after the plates, but Eva declared herself to be exhausted, and could not continue the sitting.

The sitters having been requested not to leave their places, the white electric light was switched on. The first to enter the cabinet was Dr Specht, who examined the cabinet and the medium without finding anything which could have served for the artificial production of what had been seen.

Mme. Bisson, still sitting in her place, was then searched from head to foot with a negative result. Dr Specht then declared that the experimental conditions were perfect, and that the impression made upon him by the occurrences was favourable and positive.

The photographs (Figs. 100 and 101) taken at the sitting of 28th July show through the gap of the curtain, which is only 10 or 12 inches wide, the medium on her chair, with her head bent to the right. The left curtain is partly rolled up by her left hand. At the level of Eva's head we see an elongated, flat, sharply-cut picture, of a substance resembling paper or cardboard, with a bearded male face. The image appears to be fixed with its left side against the back of the left curtain, and to extend at right angles to it in a direction towards the wall, so that, with the exception of the lowest portion, the whole image was invisible from in front, and only visible from the medium's right, where the stereoscopic camera was mounted.

The image looks quite distorted, the nose being wanting except for a stump under the eyes. Two broad creases pass over the forehead parallel to each other. One of these ends at the root of the nose, while the other passes over the left eye down to the corner of the mouth. A short distinct crease passes horizontally over the left temple. The rectangular surface at the bottom, especially the lighter-coloured continuation under the beard, shows numerous creases, projections, and folds. The whole form is produced on such a dark, black, partly grey, and spotted ground that the features can only be made out after prolonged study.

In spite of its flat construction, this production resembles an unfinished sculptural sketch in grey clay. On account of the depth of the shadows we get the impression of a low relief about the mouth and eye-sockets. Any one unacquainted with the conditions of the experiments would consider the appearance of this mediumistic product very suspicious. He would take it for a crumpled, spoilt, mask-like portrait, with eyes too small in comparison with the other features, which are themselves out of proportion. But a closer examination will not be satisfied with that. For the whole thing looks bizarre. In spite of its flatness, it looks kneaded, with an unusual distribution of darker and lighter portions, of real forms, and formless pieces of material.

Whether paper or cardboard creases have the character of the creases in the picture must be left in doubt. The vertical rent over the left eye gives the impression as if the face consisted of two portions. The treatment of the whole portrait, in its design and execution, appears rough and clumsy. The margin, shown in the picture taken by the opposite camera, projecting beyond the right curtain, does not show the creases characteristic of crumpled paper, nor the hard substratum peculiar to paper, but looks rather like a soft yielding material (Fig. 102).

FIG 100 AUTHOR'S FLASHLIGHT PHOTO-
GRAPH OF 28 JULY, 1912

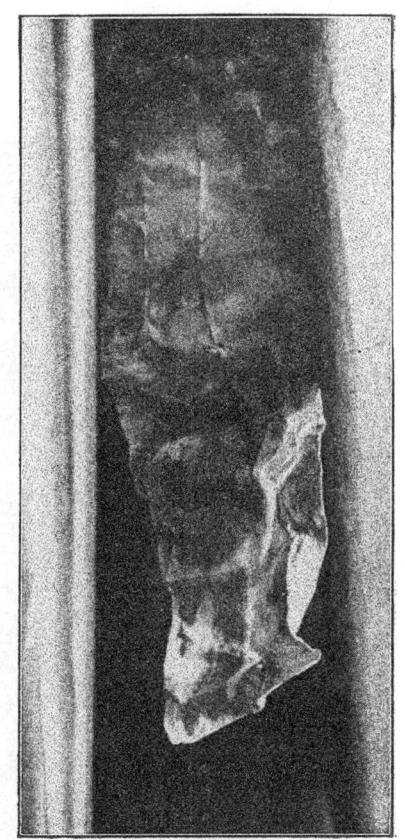

FIG 101. ENLARGEMENT OF FIG. 100.

FIG. 102. AUTHOR'S FLASHLIGHT PHOTOGRAPH OF 28 JULY, 1912.

SITTINGS OF JULY, AUGUST AND SEPTEMBER 1912

The very defects of this strange product characterise it in a manner such as could hardly be paralleled by the crumpling of ordinary pictures or masks.

Although the author could hardly expect from Dr Specht, after only two positive sittings and poor phenomena, a final judgment, either *pro* or *con*, he received from him a letter dated 6th August 1912, from Sweden, whither he had meanwhile departed, and I may as well quote some passages from it, as they show in a typical manner how a man's fresh recollections of his own observations cannot hold their own against his habitual thoughts and rooted prejudices. He writes :—

" Even at the end of the second sitting I was firmly convinced that the phenomena were impostures, but the source of error pointed out by me (premature extinction of the white light) was eliminated in the third sitting. I observed all that happened during and after hypnosis ; I also considered it impossible that there was a corporeal contact between the medium and Mme. Bisson after the disappearance of the phenomena. I was, therefore, speechless after what I had seen. I was face to face with a riddle. Indeed, in the third sitting, what I saw appeared monstrous to me. For I had the impression that, while the phenomena appeared, disappeared, and reappeared, the medium had her hands continuously at the curtain at the level of her knees. It seemed to me quite impossible to produce the phenomena as they appeared in the third sitting by trickery. Thus my impression after the third sitting was quite different from what it was after the first and second. It was a favourable one, as I said at the time.

" To-day, after over a week has passed, I am convinced that everything was trickery. The black background, the injunction against touching the products, may be specially noted, because the deception is not possible without. Nor do I consider myself competent to discover tricks by which the snake-charmers of Ceylon perform their feats. In spite of the closest search of the two ladies, something may have escaped you, and why should you not have been deceived for three years ? My impression, on the whole, is that we are shown materialisations which do not exist."

On account of this negative attitude, Dr Specht was not invited to further sittings.

SITTINGS OF THE 30TH AND 31ST JULY.

Present.—Mme. Bisson, Dr Kafka (Privatdozent in Psychology), and the author.

Negative.

In order to meet the requirements of scientific sitters still further, Mme. Bisson resolved to change her dress like the medium before the sittings, and the author selected for this purpose from her wardrobe a light grey thin dressing-gown, which, like Eva's séance costume, was kept in the séance room.

Eva C. seemed little satisfied with her stay at Munich. She did not feel happy in the strange surroundings, wished to depart, and showed no interest in the sights of the strange city. It was notable that before the sitting of 31st July she had a decided squint.

Sitting of the 3rd August 1912.

Present.—Mme. Bisson and the author.

Conditions, hypnotisation, etc., as in previous sittings.

Prolonged blowing expirations. After about twenty-five minutes we saw, against the dark background, the distinct shape of a white half-mask of a face, near the medium's head, with two black eye-holes. When the curtain opened again the male face, as in the last sitting, appeared, and in this case its pictorial character was clearly preserved, on the left, behind the medium, against the wall. Both rents across the forehead were clearly visible.

The medium seemed to make great efforts. She whimpered and moaned as if in pain, and there followed some unusually deep tones, with a convulsive tetanic stretching of the whole body. Suddenly she screamed as if in violent pain (such as might be produced by a surgical operation), and made lively defensive movements, as if repelling a strange power intruding upon her. This incident obliged Mme. Bisson to enter the cabinet and look after Eva. Slowly she grew calmer, but the sitting could not be continued. Final control negative. Eva squinted strongly, complained of indisposition, and vomited some blood.

Sitting of the 5th August 1912.

Present.—Mme. Bisson, Professor Albert von Keller (painter), and the author.

Conditions.—Examination of the medium and Mme. Bisson as on 28th July.

Before the sitting Eva was restless and complained of palpitation, a sign that we could expect a favourable sitting. Already in the afternoon, during the preparatory hypnotisation in their lodgings, Mme. Bisson had to waken the medium and cut short the procedure, because even at that early hour the medium's whole behaviour indicated the immediate occurrence of phenomena. Otherwise, the success of the evening sitting might have been interfered with.

It was only after Professor von Keller had made a preliminary examination and declared that there was nothing suspicious, either about the two women or about the cabinet, that the hypnotisation commenced, in the same manner as on 28th July.

The curtain was not yet closed, and the white light was still shining,

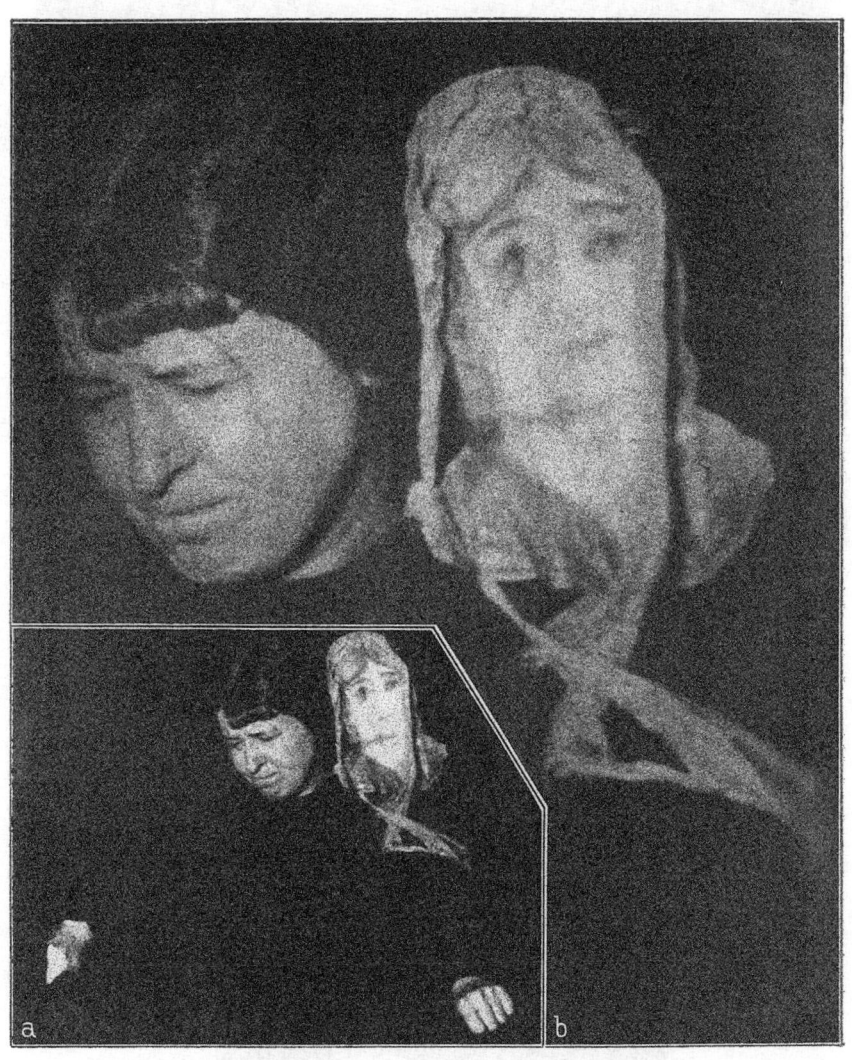

FIG. 103. AUTHOR'S FIRST PHOTOGRAPH OF 5 AUGUST, 1912.
(a) ORIGINAL.   (b) ENLARGEMENT.

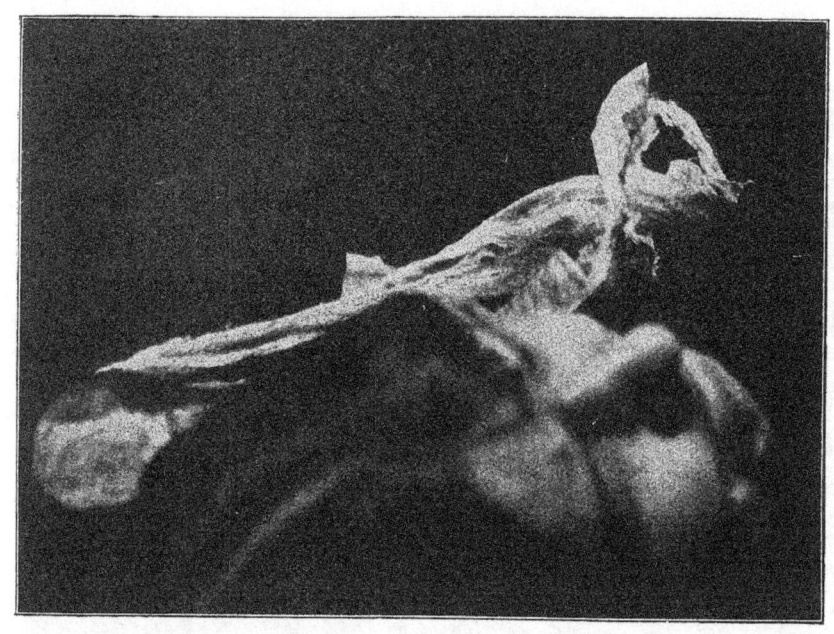

Fig. 105. Enlargement of Fig. 104.

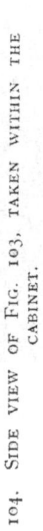

Fig. 104. Side view of Fig. 103, taken within the cabinet.

when the well-known loud sound of expiration set in in great strength. The author had hardly time to switch off the light and sit down when the first phenomenon appeared through the slightly open curtain, in the shape of a long wisp of material on the medium's left upper arm. This peculiar shape appeared on the left, behind the medium, and we recognised a female face, which repeatedly changed its position, appearing sometimes on the medium's breast, and sometimes on her right or left shoulder, while the hands, as she opened and closed the curtain, were continuously visible.

As soon as the image was again seen on the medium's left shoulder, the first photograph was taken, which, on this day, produced less shock than usual upon the medium. While the plates were being quickly changed, the image took up a position against the wall on the left. This situation was quickly photographed again, and then a third photograph was taken, at the moment when the female face emerged between the curtains at the level of Eva's chest. The female face withstood even the third magnesium flash, and showed itself several times afterwards. It was only when the author switched on the electric arc-lamp for the purpose of a fourth photograph that the mediumistic activity was impaired, so that the phenomenon disappeared without a trace. The white electric light was then switched on, while all the sitters remained in their places. The final examination, undertaken by Professor von Keller and the author, was negative, both as regards Mme. Bisson and the medium, as also was the examination of the cabinet.

In spite of the comparatively fatiguing performances of this sitting, Eva was not over-tired, and slept well.

On the first of the eleven successful photographs (Fig. 103) the facial muscles of the medium are convulsively contracted, as if by strong concentration of the will. The female face on her left shoulder is somewhat vague in its details, and in its softness resembles a Japanese picture, painted or drawn on the finest silk. It is half suspended, and half leaning, with its right side against Eva's apparently black hair, while there seems to be a lower point of support in the two ribbons of material hanging down on each side of the head-dress, and crossing on Eva's upper arm. The remaining parts of the head, especially the neck covered with a creased collar, are freely suspended, and are separated from Eva's shoulder, as shown in the stereoscopic photographs.

Again we have to do with the product of an artistic activity, a sort of sketchy drawing of a portrait, but certainly not a photographic reproduction from life, quite apart from the question whether the performance is valuable or not, whether it is made by an amateur or a professional, or what is the base on which it is drawn, whether paper, fine gauzy fabric, or some plastic substance. It is obvious that the cap-like head covering is treated technically in the same way as the face and collar. This is clearly shown on the stereoscopic photographs. On the supposition that the whole was a drawing, the cap also would have been drawn. But then the cap ends in long distinct folded ribbons, flowing down over Eva's upper arm, and continuing in broad bands of material. Here, then, the drawing would suddenly be converted into a plastic reality. On the other hand, the cap might be of plastic material, with a drawing on the surface. But this is not at all the impression conveyed by the picture. However this may be, the transition from the pictorial to the plastic is a pleasing characteristic of the image. The uniform treatment of the whole image is also shown by the numerous folds of the collar, which appears to consist of the same material as the cap.

The enlargements show that the whole portrait is covered by numerous parallel rents and creases, the most conspicuous of which cuts vertically across the right eye.

Some irregular transverse creases are also seen on close inspection. An impartial observer, who did not know the origin of the head, might assume that thin paper had served as a basis for the portrait, and had then been unfolded and smoothed out, showing traces of such folding. This supposition can hardly be brought into harmony with the woolly character of the cap, ribbons, and collar. But if the image is an artistic sketch on a woven basis, the peculiar character of the creases, which could be easily smoothed out in a fabric, would be difficult to explain.

This question is answered with some certainty by the photograph taken from within the cabinet (Figs. 104 and 105), which shows the product taken in profile from behind.

On this photograph we see that the product consists of a single fabric, in the shape of a soft, clinging, fibrous mass. Paper would look in profile like a clear rigid surface. But here, on the other hand, the head ends in a wide rounded parcel of material.

On the stereoscopic transparency Eva's dress, over her right thigh, shows a number of white patches, and another such patch appears in front on the right, under the seam of the hip. As was observed at later sittings, such patches are due to the emanated teleplasm, and are residues of the organised material.

In the second flash-light photograph of the same sitting (Fig. 106), the medium inclines her head towards the left, and holds the curtain wide open, so that we can now distinctly see the image fixed to the background on the left. Very probably it is the same female portrait. But a thick and broad parcel of material, with a straight lower rim, hangs over the left half of the face down to the chin. Starting from the image, a cord, over 3 feet long and irregularly twisted, joins Eva's head with the image. Its lower end passes up to Eva's right ear, ending in a loop. There are two knots in the cord. A second such cord branches off downward on the left and falls over the medium's left upper arm.

The termination of the face on the right is different, in this picture, from the last. While in the first photograph the face ends in a straight line on the right, so that the ear is not visible and the cap on the head appears flat, in the second picture the lower half of the left ear comes out clearly, and the line of the throat down to the collar curves down in a natural way. The line of the hair and its covering rises plastically from the foundation. The portion between ear and throat appears to be filled with a veil-like material. On the left side of the face we only see portions of the nose and mouth, the remainder being covered by the curtain, while the whole lower portion of the image is the same as

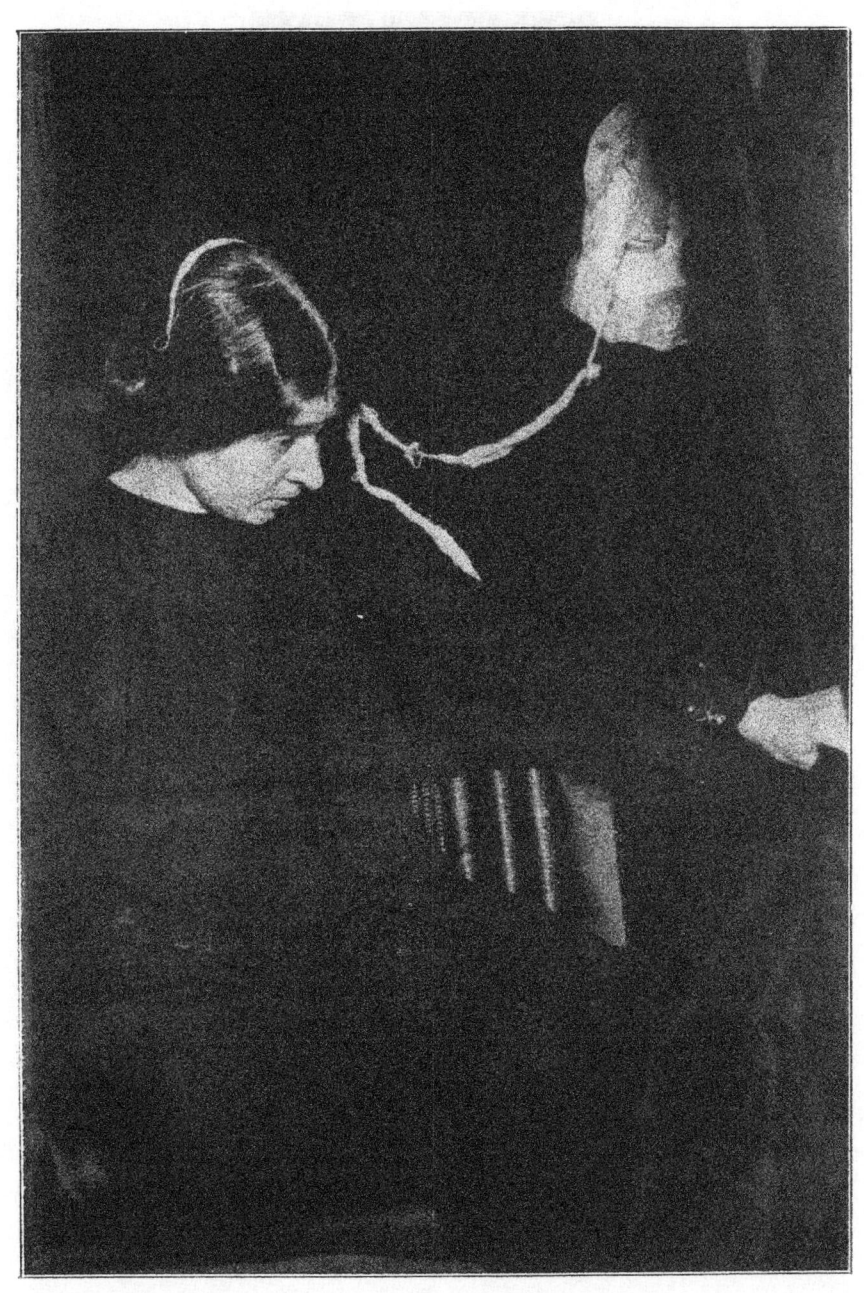

FIG. 106. AUTHOR'S SECOND FLASHLIGHT PHOTOGRAPH, 5 AUGUST, 1912.

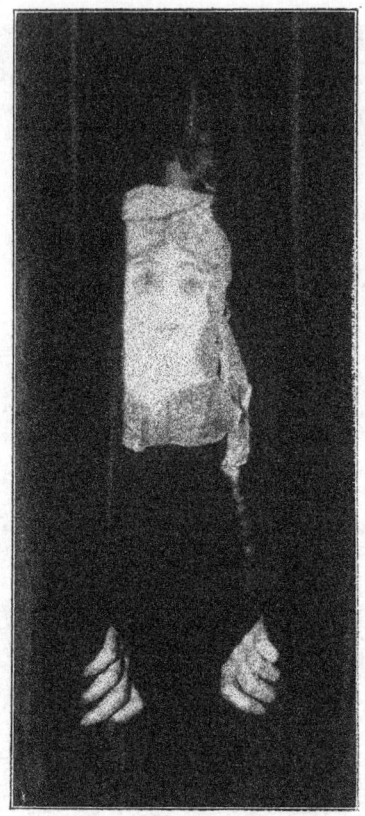

Fig. 107 Author's third flashlight photograph, 5 August, 1912.

SITTINGS OF JULY, AUGUST AND SEPTEMBER 1912

in the first negative. On the breast of Eva's dress, about the region of her heart, a new long white patch has appeared, which was absent in the first picture.

The third series of photographs of this sitting (Figs. 107 and 108) shows a much more distinct picture, quite in front in the curtain gap, and from 8 to 12 inches higher than Eva's knees.

On the first photograph the image does not appear to be quite developed. It resembles the face of a young woman of about twenty-five years. The face gives a slender and juvenile impression, owing to the way in which it terminates at the side. The right cheek is a little distorted down to the chin. The whole sketchy, and somewhat vague, drawing shows a remarkable softness and delicacy which may be intentional.

Quite different is the third photograph. Here we see a pleasant, round, female face, which might correspond to an age of about forty years. The features come out clear and distinct, especially the correct curves of the left cheek (Fig. 108). The double chin is clearly marked, and the mouth, nose, and eyes are more distinct than in the first photograph (Fig. 103). The collar also is broader in the middle. The ribbons of the cap have disappeared, and the head covering is converted into a piece of fabric (lace ?) lying on the parted hair. From the head covering a broad ribbon falls down on the left side over the collar, ending in twisted fibres, which exactly resemble the threads of an unravelled woollen cord.

Those portions of the picture which represent the hair, the fabric, and the collar give the impression of being formed of the same material, as they do not differ in structure or colour. Here, again, we have a combination of plastic, fabric, and pictorial drawing forming a harmonious whole. The technical process employed in these phenomena, and the artistic development, seem to be the same in all the pictures.

The sceptic will direct the severest criticism against the last picture, as it is crossed with parallel folds and rents, just like the first. One involuntarily recalls the cracks in old portraits painted on wood, which would appear just like this.

The most interesting conclusion yielded by a comparative study of the three photographs of 5th August seems to me to consist in the perfection of the third photograph, as compared with the first. In both cases we have the same type of face, and, indeed, the same person, as shown by a comparison of the expression of the eyes and the design of the nose, forehead, and eye-sockets. In the first portrait we might have before us a woman of twenty-eight years, and in the third portrait the picture of the same lady at the age of forty. The ethereal, delicate, and undeveloped young woman has become a fully developed, portly woman of mature age. The manner of dressing the hair with the head covering, and the collar, also correspond to the spirit and taste of the two different ages. Either that, or the second picture is a much more perfect portrait than the first, though only separated by a short interval of time. In any case, we have not to deal with rigid drawings or an unchanging surface, but with a mobile and varying product, showing changes in numerous details.

Sitting of the 7th August 1912.

Present.—Mme. Bisson, Professor von Keller, Dr A., and the author.

Negative.

Sitting of the 9th August 1912.

Present.—Mme. Bisson, Dr A., and the author.

Examination.—Mme. Bisson was examined by the author in a separate room, as on 28th July. She put on the light grey dressing-gown, which had been examined carefully by Dr A. with the help of an electric torch. After she had taken off her shoes, we made sure that nothing was concealed in her stockings, nor in her hair. We also examined her mouth, arm-pits, and ears.

We then entered the room adjoining the séance room, where we found Eva, who had put on the séance costume, after examination by Dr A. Close examination of the medium's body, hair, mouth, and ears gave no result. The cabinet had already been examined by Dr A. We then entered the séance room. Hypnotisation as on 28th July, while the white electric light, standing on the table, brightly illuminated the hands of the two ladies. Hypnotisation was complete in thirty seconds. Mme. Bisson retired, so that she was from 3 to 5 feet from the curtain. Dr A. closed the curtain and took the lady's hands. I switched off the white light. As soon as our eyes had got accustomed to the red light, Dr A. released Mme. Bisson's hands. During the sitting he sat, or lay, in front of the cabinet, while Mme. Bisson took her place behind him.

As soon as the behaviour of Eva indicated a positive sitting, by the loud blowing expirations after hypnotisation, the author quickly opened the cameras.

I had hardly sat down in my chair when the medium opened the curtain and showed on her left upper arm a long white wisp, which afterwards covered her head. The left hand often disappeared behind the curtain, while the right hand usually remained visible.

During the next opening we perceived a pictorial female face on her left shoulder. Eva said she had not sufficient power, and would have to take hold of the materialisation with her hand in order to pull it away from herself towards the curtain. She asked us to wait for the photograph, "Celà suit ma main." The manipulations with the right hand were observed by us. As soon as I again saw the image, I ignited the magnesium powder. Mme. Bisson then laid her hands, which were held by Dr A., on the medium's neck and heart. On this occasion he again saw something white on Eva's left shoulder. Then the curtain was closed.

Continuation of the Sitting.—The white mass on the medium's shoulder appeared again. This time the author, without warning, illuminated the object with the white light of a pocket-lamp. We saw

Fig. 103. Enlargement of Fig 107

Fig. 109. Author's first flashlight photograph, 9 August, 1912.

a flat triangular structure about the size of a hand, with dark rims and a white centre. It stood the exposure of the white light for about three seconds, and then, turning about a vertical axis, it disappeared backward and vanished from our sight. When the female face appeared again I made a second exposure. The medium was exhausted, and the sitting closed.

The cameras were closed while all kept their places. The white electric light was switched on. Dr A. found all the seams in Eva's dress intact. The medium was subjected to a strict search, with a negative result, and after it was finished Mme. Bisson, who had not left her seat, was also examined, with the same result. After the two ladies had withdrawn the cabinet was examined. As in the previous sittings, Eva was wakened from hypnosis after the final examination.

Of the first series of photographs (Figs. 109 and 110), taken on 9th August, the stereoscopic transparency, which was most successful, shows that Eva had opened the curtain with her right foot, and was holding, with her right arm stretched over her head towards the left, a sort of mask, while the original place of her right hand on her knee was occupied by a white mass. The junction of the thumb and forefinger of the left hand is also marked by a narrow, flat strip of matter which passes over the back of the hand. This was the first occasion on which the stereoscopic apparatus attached to the roof of the cabinet was brought into action. For the study of the shape, dimensions, and proportions of the object photographed in the sitting of 9th August, we have at our disposal two stereoscopic photographs, one from above and one from in front, as well as a side view taken from inside the cabinet.

A comparison of these three photographs makes it quite certain that the mask held by Eva was a profile of a female face modelled in low relief. It is cut off sharp and flat at the back, and the whole face rises on this flat base in a hemispherical form to an approximate height of 2 inches. That the shape is modelled, and does not consist of a sheet of paper bent by the hand, is clearly proved by the photographs taken from within the cabinet. The broad covering of hair over the forehead clearly projects down to the right ear, and the right temple is also clearly arched. The ear appears to be covered by hair. The portion of the face exposed to the light is traversed by rents like the " craquelures " of an old picture. From the inner corner of the right eye, which is just visible, a thick black line, probably a rent, passes to the right eyebrow, but without continuing downwards.

Such a rent is also seen in the photographs of the 5th August (Fig. 108), but in this case it commences in the eye and passes downward, while the upper eyelid remains free. The negatives of the 9th August show the reverse case, the rent beginning in the same place, but passing upward. This peculiar coincidence does not, therefore, prove the identity or similarity of the two objects. Unfortunately, all the other portions of the face are covered by the shadow of the curtain, so that this mask-like face cannot be compared with the other pictures. But, on account of their well-marked plastic development, these photographs form an important supplement to the numerous flat pictures.

Eva exhibited the structure to the sitters apparently by holding it by the part corresponding to the hair. A severe critic would object not only to the mask-like appearance, but also to the manner of demonstration. He would contend that the white mass on the lap is intended to represent a hand indistinctly visible in the shadow. But if in this case something is represented which does not exist, Eva, in her waking condition, could not be made responsible for such an action while hypnotised. In any case, this view does not affect the central point of the mediumistic phenomena. This consists in the creation of these objects and their disappearance. All the experimental conditions employed up to now, which exclude the concealment of objects, have not brought us any nearer to the solution of this question.

A free suspension of the materialised objects was, in all the sittings, only observed when combined with rapid motion. But in order to become visible when at rest, the object seems to require a point of support, such as the dress of the medium, the curtain, or the back wall. It is therefore easily understood psychologically that when Eva endeavours to show the materialised product to the sitters, she touches it, places it, or even fastens it somewhere, and that these manipulations require the use of her hands. This applies especially to such sittings in which her mediumistic power does not suffice. It is less objectionable as regards the sitting of 9th August, as Eva announced, in her own words, the co-operation of her hands. The appearance of the picture by itself, without a knowledge of the records and experimental conditions, must necessarily produce an incorrect and unfavourable impression.

The second photograph (Fig. 111), of 9th August, shows at once the same type of female face as was photographed three times on 5th August. Essentially we have again a flat pictorial production with sharply-cut margins, which is apparently fastened to Eva's hair above and touches her left shoulder below. The triangular head covering, with rounded points, projects in a straight line over the forehead, and casts a shadow upon it like a superimposed piece of fabric. The patchy grey, narrow, twisted strips hanging down to the collar on both sides of the face are obviously intended to represent hair. The right-hand position of the collar, which in its shape resembles that of 25th July, seems to be a superimposed piece, as does the head covering. The left cheek, which in the third photograph of 5th August is so typically rounded, here gives a twisted impression, and the anatomy resembles that of an old woman. In the drawing of the mouth and nose also we miss the firm lines of the forty-year-old woman of the previous sitting. The double chin is no longer clear, but the chin appears to have grown more pointed and less firm. The face looks thin, wrinkled, and shrivelled, although, on the whole, it preserves the roundish type of the age of forty.

The somewhat ill-defined sketchy drawing of nose, eyes, and forehead, as well as the whole structure of the face, suggest that we may have here a greater age (sixty-five to seventy years) than on 5th August. The treatment of hair and clothing also supports this. While the twenty-eight-year-old "Berthe" wears a coquettish cap with long streamers joined in a loop below, the head covering of the forty-year-old person has been simplified. It is still placed on the hair in a picturesque

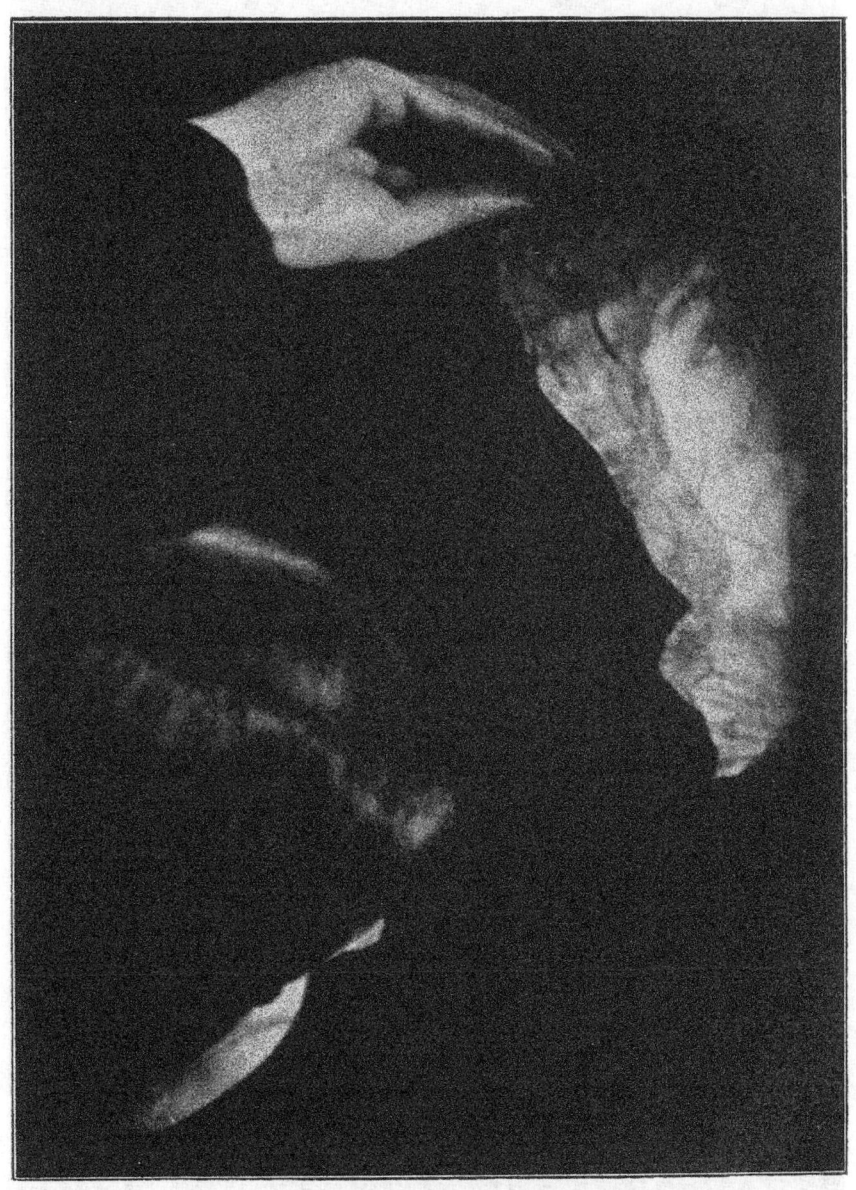

FIG. 110   ENLARGEMENT OF FIG. 109.

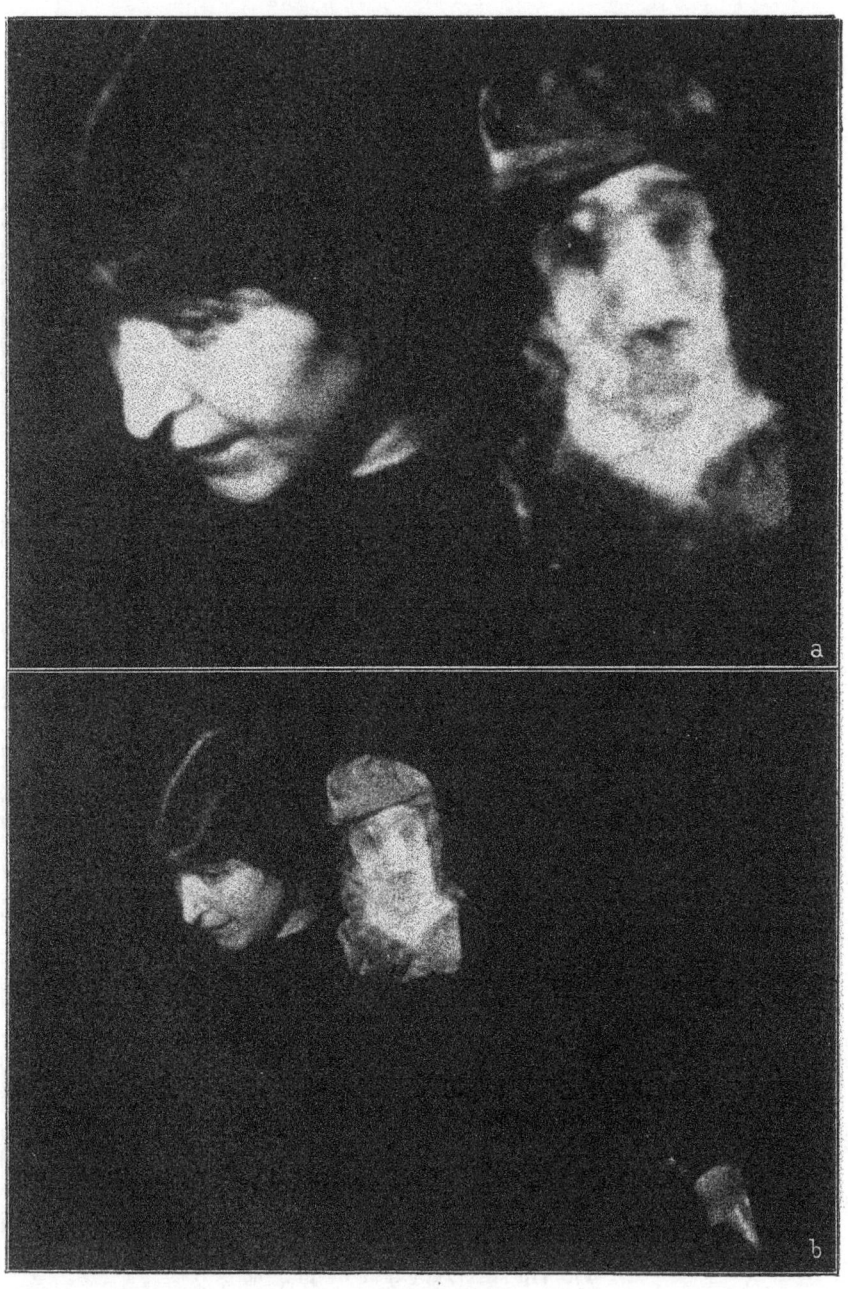

Fig. 111. Author's second flashlight photograph, 9 August, 1912.
(a) Enlargement   (b) Full picture.

manner, and ends in a shorter streamer, but it suits the dignity of that age. The person of, say, sixty-eight, shows less interest in her appearance, as shown by the unadorned and unbecoming piece of material laid over the head. The hair, still nicely parted at forty, hangs down over the temples in a haphazard way in the last picture.

This view of the pictures only occurred to the author four months afterwards, during a minute comparison of the photographs, and neither the medium nor Mme. Bisson knew about it. The reader should form his own judgment on the basis of the three pictures.

Finally, we ought to notice that in the picture a small packet of white material lies on the shoulder beside the chin. The stereoscopic pictures also show that the material observed on Eva's left thigh, in the first photograph, has left behind at two places some traces in the form of white patches.

Assuming that the manifestations of 9th August were fraudulently produced by Eva, this implies the smuggling in (against all the precautions taken) of—

(1) A plastic mask of natural size, apparently made of some solid material;
(2) a head shape of paper or textile fabric; and
(3) a quantity of substance, the size of a hand, which leaves traces on the dress.

These products would have to be well packed in a small compass, concealed on the bare body, in spite of all precautions, brought into the cabinet, opened out, used, then folded up into equally small packets, and again concealed about the bare body, so that the most thorough search could discover nothing! A conjuring performance of this kind would be novel, and would reveal a world of deception hitherto unknown. But, *so long as no such trick is actually performed under the same conditions, and cannot be performed, the discussion of the hypothesis seems superfluous.*

Sitting of the 14th August 1912.

Negative.

Sitting of the 15th August 1912.

Present.—Mme. Bisson, Dr A., and the author.

Control.—Mme. Bisson changed her dress in the author's presence, in his study, and was strictly examined by him. She wore a black chemise, knickers, and over them she put on the grey dressing-gown, after it had been examined by Dr A., and fastened it with a grey belt, which had also been examined. An examination of her hair, ears, etc., was also negative.

Eva entered the room adjoining the séance room in the séance costume. The author undid her hair and examined the whole surface of her body, including her arm-pits, mouth, nose, ears, hands, and feet, all with a negative result.

Eva was then sewn into the séance costume by Mme. Bisson, as already described. The seams were so close that one could not pass a finger through them. Dr A. conducted Eva into the séance room, after it had been very strictly examined by him. After his examination, nobody had meanwhile entered it. Eva took her seat in the cabinet. After Dr A. had made sure that Mme. Bisson's hands were empty, the hypnotisation took place in such a way that Mme. Bisson grasped Eva's thumbs, which were stretched forward out of the cabinet, and fixed her gaze until, in half a minute, a state of trance had set in. Mme. Bisson then withdrew her hands, and Dr A. closed the curtains. Mme. Bisson sat from 5 to 7 feet from the curtain, on the floor, and gave her hands to Dr A. Only then was the white light switched off, and the red light left burning. As soon as the eyes had got accustomed to the illumination, Dr A. released Mme. Bisson's hands, and also sat down on the carpet between her and the curtains.

The phenomena commenced immediately. With the well-known physical accompaniments, Eva's hands grasped the curtain and showed a long white wisp on her breast about 16 inches long and 3 or 4 inches broad. The curtains were then closed. In about ten minutes they were opened again, and a white disk, about the size of a head, with no motion of its own, was shown by rolling up the curtain into the medium's left hand. It looked flat, white, and rectangular. The curtain was released and fell back. During the next opening Dr A. found on the same structure a crumpled corner projecting into the séance room, and finally the sitters recognised the features of the image. It was then suggested to the medium to bring about distinct, and, if possible, freely suspended materialisations, and not again to withdraw the hands which held the curtain.

Under these conditions, while the hands were visible and quiet, the next opening showed a mass of the size of a head, some 20 inches above Eva's hair, between the curtains, and this mass glided downwards and backwards and disappeared with a turn towards the back. During the next opening of the curtain the left curtain was rolled up, and, at the same place as before, a white, flat face profile became visible, with its hinder part (neck, etc.) covered by the curtain. A flash-light photograph was taken, and the sitting closed. Mme. Bisson did not enter the cabinet during the sitting, and while the photograph was being taken she was held by Dr A.

The white electric light was switched on. Mme. Bisson did not leave her place. The medium was undressed by Dr A. and the author, with the exception of the tunic, which opened down the back. They examined her mouth, nose, ears, toes, hands, arm-pits, and the whole skin, with a negative result. The author also conducted a thorough gynæcological examination, in the course of which Eva was much affected, and broke into tears. Nothing suspicious was found. After the medium had been examined, Mme. Bisson removed her outer dress, and was searched by the author in the presence of Dr A. without the slightest thing being found which gave rise to suspicion. The subsequent examination of the cabinet and the séance room was also negative.

FIG 112. AUTHOR'S FLASHLIGHT PHOTOGRAPH OF 15 AUGUST, 1912.
(a) FRONT VIEW. (b) ENLARGEMENT OF (a) (c) VIEW FROM THE LEFT.

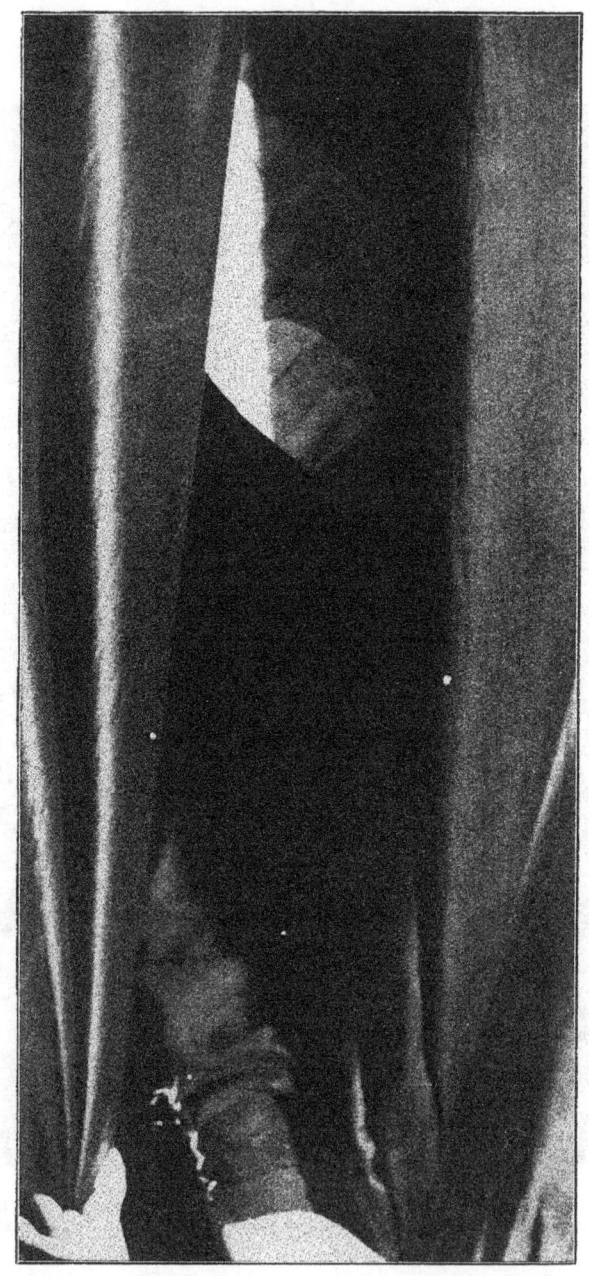

FIG. 113   ENLARGEMENT OF A STEREOSCOPIC SIDE VIEW, TAKEN OUTSIDE THE CABINET, 15 AUGUST, 1912

The picture (Fig. 112) obtained on 15th August is interesting in many ways. An artistically complete female face and profile looks out of the left curtain, which is held up by Eva's left hand. Its gaze is directed upwards, and the curtain cuts off the whole back of the head, from a line in front of the left ear. Again we have not to deal with an object reproduced from nature, but with an artistic impression. The features are extremely sharp in all their details, and finely drawn. There is something Madonna-like about the facial expression, and the whole conventional interpretation and treatment of the subject recalls the Directoire period. In consideration of the softness of the outer margins of the face, the clearness of the modelling, and the clever distribution of light and shade, we might consider the face as plastically formed, and the stereoscopic negative taken from the roof also supports the idea of a mask in low relief; but this might be due to the slanting position of the image. This point cannot be decided with absolute certainty from the photographs. The impression of hair is only produced by the dark colour and shading, on the same ground substance.

The profile is continued in a white wisp, which is very clearly reproduced by the third stereoscopic camera (Fig. 113) placed at the side. At the first glance, this white strip looks like an unfolded piece of white or grey paper, or like a width of a close textile fabric. The visible portion is some 10 to 12 inches wide and some 25 inches long, and is crossed by numerous parallel creases, which are about an inch apart. The lower half appears to be repaired by sticking on a semicircular patch. At right angles to these creases, which also come out in the face as delicate rents or lines, there are two strongly-developed furrows along the whole length of the strip, the first of which ends on the temple of the face. The broad, flat, paper-like strip ends above in the female profile, and then forms the stalk or continuation of the image, which touches the inside of the left curtain at its lower end, where it may possibly be attached. However favourable may be the impression conveyed by this portrait study, the analysis of its material composition has a sobering effect. Anyone who does not realise the rigorous precautions taken, must necessarily assume that a packet, folded together in numerous rectangular folds, was fraudulently introduced into the séance room, and subsequently unfolded. This stiff broad sheet, partly repaired by a supplementary piece, might then be supposed to have been fixed on the inside of the left curtain, in such a manner that the face profile, cut out on the upper end, would just enter the light to show the profile. In that case, the second stereoscopic apparatus mounted near the right-hand curtain must be taken to have revealed the mechanism used in mounting the picture.

We have here one of those cases where the appearances are against the medium, but only because this piece of material forming the support bears an extraordinary *resemblance* to a paper unfolded and fixed. But this single argument does not suffice for establishing a serious hypothesis of fraud. The technical process yielding a product which happens to produce the optical impression of a folded and crumpled paper, might very well be due to the character of the mediumistic production. For we see the same process in nearly all the images. Everywhere we see rents and creases, and, in the majority of them, a flat structure, and a predominance of the purely pictorial character, though occasionally there is low relief. We must bow before the facts, however strange, so long as we have not found the explanation.

Sittings of the 18th and 20th August.

Negative.

On the 21st August, Dr A. drew my attention to a number of fresh holes which he had observed in the left-hand curtain. These holes, in his opinion, were made by pins used for fixing the images. In fact, we found, at a height of 40 to 50 inches, and at a distance of 12 to 16 inches from the hem of the curtain, a group of pin-holes in pairs. I had, indeed, on several occasions pinned the curtain flaps together. But this group of pin-holes was at a height of 67 inches, and near the hem of the curtain, and, therefore, had no connection with the supposed suspensions. The corroboration of Dr A.'s observation led us to shift the whole cabinet structure and to search the back wall with a thirty candle-power lamp, as several images had been observed apparently fixed to it. Here, also, we found about sixteen pin-holes in pairs, which roughly corresponded to the position of the images. The place in which these were found was at a height of 43 inches, and 3 feet from the corner of the cabinet. It should be mentioned that in that neighbourhood (about 8 inches away) a light-coloured spot was found resembling the spots sometimes left behind on Eva's dress as a residue of the materialised mass. On one occasion, on 5th August, an image had appeared on the right (the third photograph of that sitting), and this was fairly low, at the level of the back of the chair. A strict search revealed in this position three very small holes, 40 inches above the floor and 5 inches away from the hem of the curtain, which might be due to pins.

It goes without saying that the use of pins for fixing the images would be a negative factor of considerable importance. For, in this case, a pin would have escaped our strict examination, which is quite possible, since the combs and hair-pins were not taken out of the medium's hair, and since a pin might very well have been hidden in the cabinet, in spite of the most painstaking precautions.

On the basis of this fact many readers will certainly come to the conclusion that the images were fixed with pins. If we adopt this view, we encounter the question of where the pin came from. If these images, in spite of our precautions, were introduced by fraudulent manipulations, the pin is quite a natural addition, and we might assume that Eva had secured and hidden the pin in the waking state with a fraudulent intention.

There is no trace of any evidence for such fraudulent preparations. The observations, extending over three and a half years, speak to the contrary. The conditions under which the sittings took place exclude the introduction of pictures and other objects. Besides, as we had occasion to observe later, other methods of fixation were used, such as adhesion by means of the material itself. The spot on the back wall is possibly a residue of this kind of fixation. That there is a fixation of the materialised products on the curtains, is amply proved by the series of experiments already described.

In any case, we are obliged to distinguish between the question of suspension or location, and the mediumistic creation itself. I observed, in a later sitting, that the medium was capable of producing a picture, but could not place it in a position favourable to the observer. During the whole sitting the hands were outside the curtain, and, therefore, not in operation. In these circumstances manual help would be intelligible, and would not argue against the genuineness of the phenomena. In view of the careful control and the convincing positive results, too much importance should not be attached to this matter, even though we may not completely understand the negative indications, whose existence cannot be denied. Besides, in spite of the very suspicious coincidence of the position of the images with that of the pin-holes, we have no complete proof, but only circumstantial evidence, that pins were used at all, and that the pin-holes were connected with the suspension of the images. For, when the cameras were being focused upon the places at which phenomena had previously appeared, sheets of newspapers had been pinned on in order to get the focus. This applies particularly to the kinematograph. We have the proofs in the test photographs, and in the testimony of the photographer concerned in the adjustment of the cameras. Thus my photographer writes as follows :—

" DEAR SIR,

" In answer to your inquiry, I beg to say that I perfectly remember in one case, when I had no assistant, pinning a piece of newspaper to the black curtain of the cabinet in order to focus the cameras. It is quite probable that I fixed the same sheet, with the same pin, also on the back wall or on the chair, but this I cannot remember after all this time.

" Yours, etc.,
" DR GEORG HAUBERRISSER."

Much later, after the Munich sittings had been ended, a pin was found in the covering of the left arm-rest of the chair used by the medium. It was stuck in from below, so that only the head could be felt in the seam. Possibly the upholsterer who covered the chair had left the pin in the seam, so that there was a possibility of using it during the sittings.

We may regard this point as unsettled. We may ignore it, or we may see in it some negative evidence, but whatever our view of the matter, it cannot alter the positive results already obtained.

Finally, we must not forget that the phenomena continued just as before without any new pin-holes in the curtain, and without pins, in spite of more rigorous precautions for controlling the hands, and that the images were again fixed to the curtain without leaving pin-holes behind. We must conclude that in exploring the unknown country of mediumism we must count upon numerous surprises and contradictions, and that we have no right to admit one apparently inexplicable fact, and then to reject another fact, simply because it does not fit in with our suppositions.

Sitting of the 23rd August 1912.

Negative.

Sitting of the 24th August 1912.

Present.—Mme. Bisson, Dr Kafka (Privatdozent of Psychology), M. S., and the author.

I quote the following from M. S.'s report of this sitting :—

" There were three cameras in front of the cabinet and two in the cabinet. There was a red light of medium intensity. Mme. Bisson put the medium into a trance, while Dr Kafka and I strictly controlled her hands. After a short time the medium's breathing became stertorous, and after half an hour changed into strong gasping. The curtain was opened. The medium was greatly disturbed, moaned, and shook convulsively. Some grey mass appeared near her head. But I attributed this appearance to my fixed gaze in the red light, which came from the left. After a short time I saw near the medium's left ear a sharply-defined strip, about 6 inches long and $\frac{1}{2}$ inch wide, which was brought into the light and somehow disappeared suddenly from my view. The curtain was then closed, and the medium's stertorous breathing increased. The curtain then opened again, and the hands did not leave the curtains. Suddenly a large white mass appeared in front of the medium's head, as if emerging from behind the curtain. It was not quite so brightly illuminated as the strip had been, but had the distinct shape of a head in front view, somewhat like a roughly modelled and softened mask of white plaster, but of a softer consistency. It was observed for two or three seconds. The medium closed the curtain with a strong convulsive movement. The clenched hands did not apparently leave the curtains. After some time the breathing became quiet. Mme. Bisson went up to the medium and awakened her, while we carefully controlled her hands. The medium was then searched, in the bright light of the adjoining room, by Dr von Schrenck and Dr Kafka, but nothing was found."

The author must add the following comments :—The phenomena only set in after an hour's waiting. The final searching did not take place in the adjoining room, but in the séance room itself. The medium was greatly frightened by the falling of an object into the flash-light box, and the phenomena ceased. Mme. Bisson had to enter the cabinet in order to calm Eva. The latter suffered from cough and general indisposition, and coughed some blood. The final examination was negative.

Sittings of the 26th, 27th, 28th and 29th August 1912.

Negative.

SITTING OF THE 30TH AUGUST 1912.

Present.—Mme. Bisson, Dr Kafka, the author and his wife.

Although Eva did not feel well this day, she had eaten heartily at 7 o'clock, and was constantly under the supervision of Mme. Bisson, who would have noticed if she had concealed any object about her person. At the author's request, Mme. Bisson searched Eva's luggage down to the last thread, without finding anything in the least suspicious. The medium was examined as detailed by Dr Kafka in his report, appended to the record of the sitting of 11th September (*see below*).

The sitting commenced at 9.15 P.M. The medium went into a deep trance after hypnosis. She made loud gasping expirations, and whimpered as if in pain, so that positive results were to be expected.

The hands lay in the first instance on her knees, and the author, who sat on the right, could see her left hand through the gap in the curtain, and made sure that it remained immovable.

Then followed about fifteen minutes, during which the curtain remained quite closed, and after this we saw on the medium's left shoulder a grey or brown strip resembling a veil, and falling over her upper arm into her lap. "The exposure was very short and the impression indistinct" (Dr Kafka's report). The curtain was then closed.

Then we saw, while the medium's hands held the curtain, a white mass on her lap, which Dr Kafka describes as "a whitish indefinite mass about the size of a hand."

From my place I could see an obviously flat finger, while Mme. Bisson saw the shape of a hand, and Kafka only saw an indefinite mass. While before this the curtain had been repeatedly opened and closed, "the medium's hands now remained constantly visible at the curtain" (Dr Kafka's report).

Dr Kafka proceeds: "A change in the mass could not at first be seen during the exposures, which lasted only one or two seconds. But, later, two finger-shaped projections seem to have formed. After a considerable pause, during which the hands always remained at the curtains, the flat white mass in the medium's lap changed into a brownish structure resembling the shape of a scorpion." The author perceived irregular projections, which gave the impression of being soft and semi-liquid. The medium again closed the curtains without withdrawing her hands. After this the ladies and the author saw a white mass extending from the medium's head to her shoulder, but this was not seen by Dr Kafka.

At a signal the author seized Eva's hands, while first Mme. Bisson and then the author's wife illuminated the cabinet with a white electric torch. Much terrified, Eva screamed, struggled, and gave cries of pain.

The white mass disappeared instantly. But I saw on her right shoulder, where the throat joined the dress, a transparent fabric of mouse-grey colour, about $2\frac{1}{2}$ inches long and a little over an inch wide. I asked Dr Kafka to seize the piece. The medium screamed, struggled in my grasp, and made violent movements. Although Dr Kafka snatched at the piece as quickly as he could, he only succeeded in touching Eva's dress and the skin of her throat. The piece of fabric had disappeared. It was only after we had made sure that what we had seen had disappeared that we withdrew the torch. According to Dr Kafka's report, the strip had a brownish colour, but the effect of the red light on the apparent colour has to be taken into account.

Dr Kafka writes as follows concerning this attempted exposure :—

" At Dr von Schrenck's request I snatched at the substance, but the medium, moaning pitifully, made strong motions with her whole body, and especially with her neck, so that I could not seize anything. I felt no moisture on my hand. The lamp was extinguished and the medium retired behind the closed curtain, trembling, breathing heavily, moaning, and complaining of pains. Mme. Bisson also was greatly excited and incensed at this interference. Since the medium's condition did not improve, Mme. Bisson entered the cabinet and embraced her." Gradually the two ladies regained their composure. The forcible procedure had naturally produced a profound emotional disturbance in the medium.

Yet she wished to continue the sitting and produce new phenomena for the flash-light photograph. She rose several times from her seat, stood in front of the curtain, and requested to be searched, but we declined and asked her to resume her seat.

The author was convinced that nothing more would be seen, when suddenly the curtain was opened and the image of the type " Bisson " appeared in front of her face on a disk-like surface. It was immediately recognisable, and also showed the broad black strip over the forehead, as shown in Mme. Bisson's third series of photographs (Fig. 97).

It must be said that, from this moment until the complete cessation of the phenomena, the medium's hands did not leave the curtain, and remained visible to all of us.

The two ladies claimed to have seen that the image fell from above downwards and forwards over the medium's face. At the next opening the disk appeared on her right shoulder (without help of her hands). These occurrences followed very rapidly in one or two seconds, or just as much time as was required for the successive opening and closing of the curtains. After the last exposure she barely closed the curtain and opened it during the same second. She rose, stood in front of the cabinet, bent her head forward so that we could see the neck, and shook her head. The object we had seen had disappeared with lightning rapidity, like the switching off of an electric light.

On this incident, Dr Kafka reports as follows :—

" During a new exposure, a disk was seen more clearly on the right, just by the head of the medium. She then quickly closed the curtain, jumped up, took a step outside the cabinet, requested to be searched, but was pushed back into her chair by Mme. Bisson. The medium had bent her head and trunk forward right out of the cabinet, so that we could see her neck, but we could see no trace of the phenomenon. After a pause the medium was seized with a violent cough and vomiting, and something was caught in her handkerchief. This turned out to be a grey crumb."

We have above the report of two occurrences—first, an unsuccessful attempt at an exposure ; second, the subsequent appearance and dis-

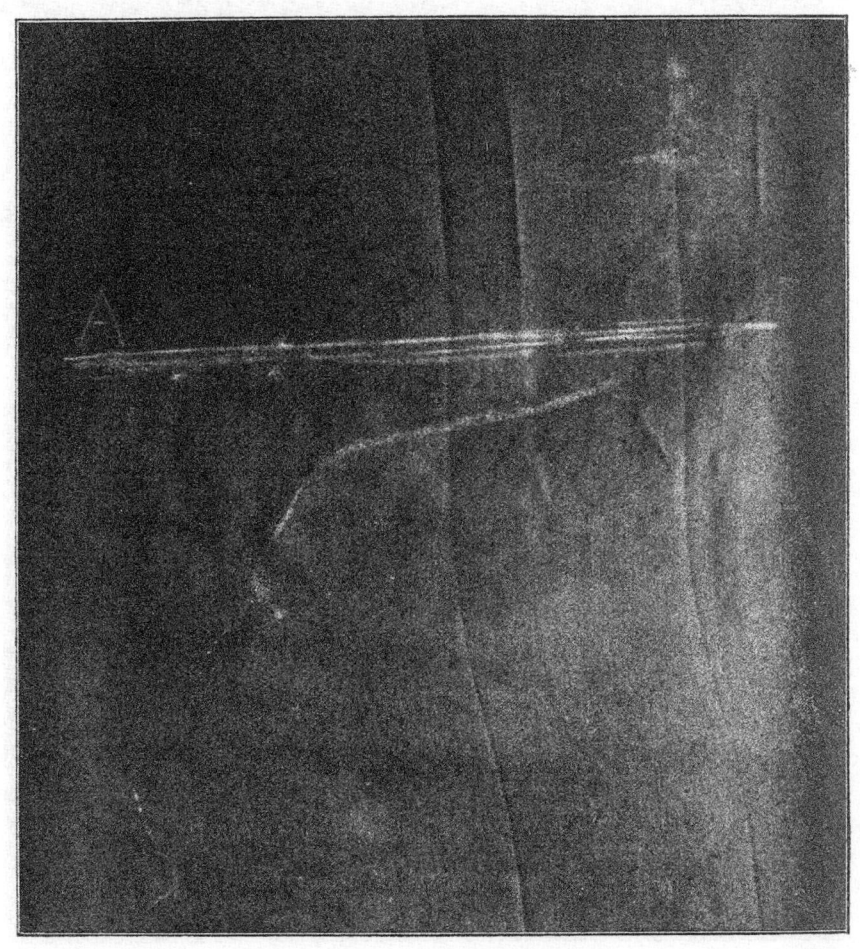

FIG. 114. PHOTOGRAPH OF A LONG PATCH ON ·EVA'S DRESS THE PARALLEL LINES MARKED A SHOW THE LINE OF THE WAIST.

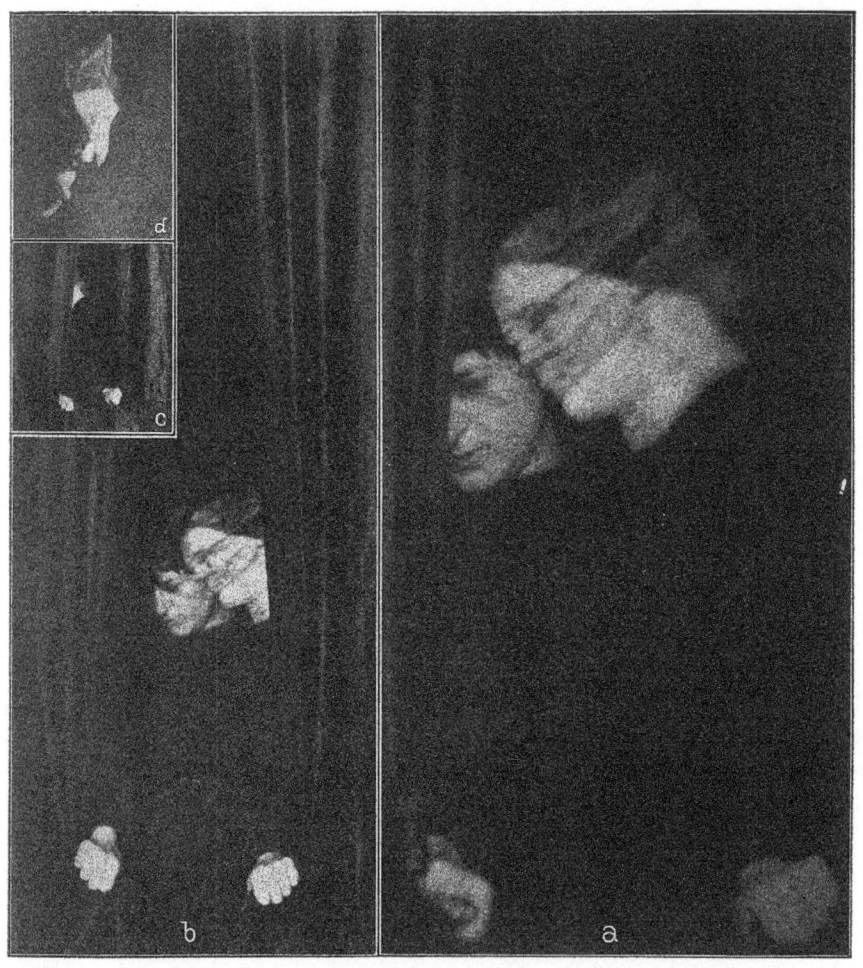

FIG 115 AUTHOR'S FLASHLIGHT PHOTOGRAPH OF 10 SEPTEMBER, 1912.
ON THE LEFT: FULL PICTURE. ON THE RIGHT: ENLARGEMENT. AT TOP: LATERAL
VIEWS FROM WITHIN THE CABINET (*c*) AND FROM WITHOUT (*d*).

appearance of a disk-like image, with a male portrait within a few seconds, while the co-operation of the hands was excluded.

The sitting was closed at 11 o'clock, owing to Eva's exhaustion. The subsequent search in a white light, although conducted with the greatest care, remained without any result. During this process the medium fainted away. She had to be taken in the hypnotic condition to a couch in another room. She then recovered, but fell into another deep fainting fit, from which she was restored with the help of alcoholic stimulants.

The medium was still in a state of trance when we conveyed her in a motor-car to her lodgings, where she was at once put to bed. The fainting fits were repeated three times in the night, and Mme. Bisson, who watched by her bed till 4 o'clock in the morning, took half an hour to bring her to, out of one of the fainting fits.

When I visited Eva at 11 o'clock next morning, she was still in a dreamy state, complained of pains in her breasts, coughed and vomited about a wine-glass full of blood.

The disturbance in the medium's condition lasted four days. We arranged a several days' excursion into the mountains. The fresh air and the excitement of the change of landscape gradually obliterated the traces of Eva's indisposition, so that we could resume the sittings on 6th September.

During the subsequent examination of the cabinet, on 30th August, we found on the floor some small white particles, the largest of which was the size of a pea, and was flattened. They gave the impression of small balls of paper crushed with a shoe. The séance costume, especially the inside of the tights, showed a large number of particles resembling a fine dust.

A microscopic examination of the white particles showed wood fibre, such as is used for the manufacture of paper and cardboard. We therefore probably have to deal with paper or a product resembling paper. The fine dust also consisted of wood fibre. This discovery might be explained by some paper adhering to the shoes of the person entering the cabinet, which was then detached in the cabinet, and that the tights had been thrown on the parquet floor and gathered some dust. The circumstances do not seem to have any connection with the phenomena.

The small crumb, the size of a pin-head, which had been ejected from the mouth during the sitting, when microscopically examined, turned out to be a small piece of wood. Eva had visited a Somali village at the Munich Exhibition, and had there bought from a nigger one of the wooden rods they use for cleaning their teeth, such as they offer to every visitor, and had used it for the same purpose. A small piece of wood had stuck between her teeth, and had then been found, so that this circumstance also is explained in a natural manner.

SITTINGS OF THE 6TH AND 7TH SEPTEMBER 1912.

Negative.

SITTING OF THE 8TH SEPTEMBER 1912.

Present.—Mme. Bisson and the author.

Control.—As in previous sittings. Time, 9 to 11 P.M. The medium's hands were visible during the whole sitting.

After about three-quarters of an hour the first phenomenon appeared in the shape of a fragment of fabric hanging from Eva's mouth. At the next opening of the curtain we saw wisps of material on the breast of the dress and in Eva's lap. Suddenly there appeared a grey cord, resembling twine, which appeared to consist of very fine twisted skin. It started between forefinger and thumb of the left hand, which was in front of the curtain, and continued in a straight line towards the medium's head, disappearing in the darkness of the cabinet. The curtains were opened only 1 or 2 inches, so that only the 6-inch piece outside the curtain was clearly visible. This stretched string then suddenly disappeared behind the curtain, reappearing immediately in the medium's lap. At least, I saw there a long line, faintly luminous, as if phosphorescent, which disappeared under my gaze.

During this whole experiment Eva's hands had not left the curtain. Her body was quite steady, so that the phenomenon could be observed quietly for ten to fifteen seconds.

On touching the medium's dress several times, it was noticed that the places where the material had appeared were moistened as with a sticky substance. Sitting closed. Final examination negative.

An inspection of the dress showed on the breast, and in the lap, a number of irregular whitish-grey spots. The most conspicuous of these was a strip 9 inches long and 2 or 3 inches broad below the waist, which was placed just where I had seen the luminous cord disappear. We may therefore conclude that this strip remained on the dress as the residue of the cord-like substance.

The author considered this connected observation so important that he caused the patch to be photographed (Fig. 114) and some microscopic preparations to be made of the residue and of the other spots. The analysis will be given in a special chapter in connection with similar later discoveries.

SITTING OF THE 9TH SEPTEMBER 1912.

Present.—Mme. Bisson, Dr Kafka, M. S., and the author.

Duration, 9 to 11.15 P.M. Control as on 30th August 1912.

It was only at 10.30 P.M. that a bright wisp became visible on the dress, which moved over to the left at the level of Eva's upper arm, while her hands and body were motionless. It was about half an inch wide, and over 2 inches long.

Sitting closed. Final examination negative.

When Eva, on the evening of the 9th September, had returned to her lodgings, she suddenly cried in her room, " Quelquechose sort de moi! " and could hardly be pacified. Mme. Bisson put her to bed at once, and on examining her, she found a mass, 4 inches long and 1½ inches thick, projecting from Eva's vagina. But when she tried to seize it, it was drawn in with a sudden jerk (Mme. Bisson's report).

Sitting of 10th September 1912.

Present.—Mme. Bisson, Dr Kafka, M. S., the author and his wife.

Control and hypnotism as on 30th August 1912.

In spite of the medium's strong exertions (deep expirations), it was only after three-quarters of an hour that the curtain was opened (the medium's hands were partly invisible), and a white mass appeared on her left at the level of her shoulder. This process is described by Dr Kafka as follows :—

" It was only at a later exposure that I could observe that a white head-shaped disk moved past the medium's head from the left. During this phenomenon the medium's hands were visible at the curtain. The medium then completely closed the curtain, in order, as she said, to gather force, and during this pause she on one occasion closed the curtain particularly tightly from within. During the next exposure two white structures, resembling arms, appeared twice, which both appeared to proceed from the medium's mouth."

M. S. perceived a fairly large grey mass coming from the left at the level of the medium's shoulder, and compared it in appearance to extremely fine muslin, having the colour of smoke, which, however, did not give the impression of lightness, but fell by gravitation, and might have been a moist textile fabric. The phenomenon disappeared while the curtain remained open, and Eva's hands remained at the curtain.

The author had the impression as if another personality, standing behind the curtain, had suddenly moved a white disk towards the medium's head and withdrawn it, while the curtains were steadily open, and were held by both the medium's visible hands. The successive exposures occurred at such a rate that the visual impression was too fugitive to perceive any detail concerning the shape and appearance. On my questioning them, the two men both said that the structure resembled an arm. Although the author feared to be too late with the ignition of the flash-light, he still decided to switch it on as quickly as possible during the next exposure. This was done, the plates were changed, and I was quite in the dark as to what had been photographed. But of one thing I was certain, and that was that this white object had been photographed at the moment of its quickest motion, and its greatest independence of the medium's body.

Mme. Bisson declared that she had seen the shape of a head in the flash-light. The ignition of the flash-light produced a crisis in Eva, which was dealt with by Mme. Bisson.

The sitting was closed, and the final examination gave a negative result.

The development of the plates (Fig. 115) showed as a result the profile of a female head nearly normal in size, but slightly smaller than Eva's head. We have here to deal with a flat, sharply defined portrait, with a neck-piece which appears comparatively broad. It is freely suspended in a direction at right angles to the medium's temple. The face, with its regular features, just covers Eva's left ear, and it looks as if the nose and forehead touched the medium, but that is only a guess, since the photographs do not decide this point. All the rest of the silhouette of the head hangs free, the back of it standing higher than the front.

The structure gives the impression of an unfolded paper, as is suggested by the many parallel creases. The hinder portion of the head appears entirely enveloped in a dark grey cloth, or perhaps the dark covering is intended to produce the impression of hair. The forehead is strongly arched and low. The nose is short, the lips small and curved, with a projecting upper lip and dimples, the chin is strong and middle-sized. The deep-set eyes are directed upwards. The ear is indicated, but by a fault of drawing it is placed too far backwards. The neck is broad. The two last points tell against a portrait from nature. A transparent veil, with its hem coming from chin to ear, covers the face.

We certainly have not to do with the same picture as was produced on the 15th August. For on the latter we find a higher and less projecting forehead, and much longer nose of different shape, as well as other small deviations.

The stereoscopic view from the top of the cabinet corroborates this description, and shows, apart from the flat and pictorial character, two strong-marked vertical folds, like those of a concertina, as if the paper had been unfolded towards the right and left. From the standpoint of a purely objective judgment of the photograph, without any consideration of the experimental conditions, we should have to conclude that we have to deal with a profile of a head, drawn on a foundation of textile fabric or paper, and afterwards cut out, folded up, and then again unfolded, retaining traces of the folds.

As regards the artistic treatment, we miss the naturalistic character. Like many of the previous ones, it appears conventional and stereotyped in expression. Yet the features themselves are well modelled. Again we see the great contrast: on the one hand, the mediumistic phenomenon photographed under the best conditions while in rapid motion; and, on the other hand, the disappointing negatives: the shape of a head, apparently cut out of paper or some textile fabric, and provided with pictorial detail.

A one-sided scepticism will surely arrive at an unfavourable conclusion. But, even after taking into account all the actual circumstances, the question remains unsolved: How can such a picture be produced, and disappear, and move freely without the co-operation of the medium's hands?

SITTING OF THE 11TH SEPTEMBER 1912.

Present.—Mme. Bisson, Dr Kafka, M. S., the author and his wife.

Control, illumination, and hypnotisation as on 30th August 1912. Time, 9 to 11.30 P.M.

SITTINGS OF JULY, AUGUST AND SEPTEMBER 1912

Hardly had the curtain been closed when long stertorous expirations were heard, accompanied by deep tones, recalling the " belling " of stags. A single expiration lasted for from five to twenty seconds. Eva's whole behaviour indicated a deep degree of trance (in the mediumistic language. " Elle était prise "). The moaning and pressing was interrupted by whimpering cries of pain.

The phenomena commenced at once after hypnosis. I may remark here that the whole sitting was devoted to the root phenomenon of materialisation, *i.e.*, the generation, motion, and disappearance of the plastic substance, and that during the several hours of the sitting the curtains remained uninterruptedly open. The process of materialisation began on the medium's left breast, about the level of her shoulder. Later. the phenomenon was seen at various places—on the front of her dress and in her lap. The visible material took the shape of wisps, cords, shreds, and projections, and especially of a very fine mouse-coloured skin, of a transparent texture, resembling spider's web. The colour often appeared a reddish-violet, or resembled dull red rubber on a base of black velvet. On one occasion a long strip developed before the eyes of those present out of an apparently phosphorescent, reddish, and seemingly liquid patch, but it grew pale and disappeared as quickly as it had come.

With Eva's consent, the fairly wide strips on her breast, three or four in number, were illuminated by white electric light and touched with the fingers. Under the influence of the light they lost their red colour and their visibility. The touch showed a sticky colourless substance. In the author's opinion, this very fine fabric is liquefied by the influence of light.

Dr Kafka believes that the wisp reflects the light, and thus acquires the appearance of a solid substance of definite shape.

Dr Kafka says about this :—" During the next opening a wisp appeared near the medium's shoulder and left breast, which, though partly reflecting the light, actually consisted of drops of liquid, as could be proved by illumination and touch. The liquid moistened the hand, and when rubbed off with a handkerchief, left distinct traces. Then suddenly, while the medium held the curtain open, a ragged strip of a brownish colour appeared on the medium's left hand. The medium's hands and chest were clearly visible during these phenomena, since the curtain was always held open. The lower arm and elbows were, however, in the dark. After some time the strip disappeared, as if suddenly jerked upwards."

On this the author remarks as follows :—" The impression of this phenomenon was as if, from the sleeve, a rather voluminous brown earthworm, about 3 or 4 inches long, had crept on to the back of the left hand, nearly down to the knuckles. The front portion of this self-moving shape turned in the form of a hook. as if it wanted to return. But suddenly the whole structure was jerked back, and disappeared as it had come."

M. S. describes his impressions as follows :—" Suddenly there appeared in front of the curtain, on the medium's left hand as it lay on her left knee, a dark strip, or ribbon, ending in a strongly indented, leaf-shaped, terminal about the size of half-a-crown, which moved in the direction of the knuckles, and jerked several times backwards and forwards."

All the three observers agree in having seen on the medium's left hand a rather long ribbon-shaped substance, having a motion of its own. To the same class of phenomena belongs the following, described by Dr Kafka :—" The medium requested me to give her my hand, so that the material might be laid upon it. Three times in succession a strip of material appeared, which seemed to emerge from the darkness above, and was drawn over the palm of my hand, giving me the impression as if somebody had drawn the end of a rope lightly across it."

M. S. gives the following graphic description of his impressions of these phenomena :—" Suddenly we saw, proceeding from the left shoulder towards the medium's heart and lap, some clouds of thick, greyish-red masses, which laid themselves over the hands of Dr Kafka and the Baroness von Schrenck, filled the latter's hand, and flowed over it, in the shape of a twisted band, having the thickness of the cord of a dressing-gown, into the medium's lap, where they deposited themselves like heavy cigarette smoke in the folds of the dress, and subsequently withdrew themselves. Dr Kafka and Baroness von Schrenck emptied their hands into a porcelain dish, and a small residue of a dark liquid remained behind in the white dish. During this process I did not observe the medium. Mme. Bisson requested the medium to place some material in the dish herself. The small dish was held in the medium's lap. The mass advanced and retired, laid itself like a smoke ring into the small dish, withdrew again from it, entered it again, and finally about 1 c. cm. of the dark liquid remained in the dish, which was then covered and put away. At about the same time the head of the medium—who was greatly excited, and who shook convulsively and groaned deeply at each touching of the mass—was bent forward, and appeared covered with large curved masses resembling curls."

The same phenomenon is described by Dr Kafka in the following words :—" During the pause the curtains this time remained open. The medium's hands were distinctly visible, and I held her right hand with my left. The medium's hands lay on her knees, and I suddenly felt my hands moistened with liquid. Mme. Bisson took the porcelain dish, in order to catch the material. Then we saw several times pieces of brownish material, which at first remained suspended over the dish. at a certain distance, then lightly touched it, until finally a distinctly visible brown strip of a textile appearance, seeming to come from the medium's head, entered the dish and remained in it about four seconds, then disappeared at once, appearing to leave behind a liquid precipitate. Immediately after this the medium put my hand into her mouth, so that I might examine it, but I could only feel the teeth and the tip of the tongue, and nothing else. The medium then expressed a wish to take off the tights, and did this, against the advice of Mme. Bisson, who, however, finally helped her to do so. The medium took my hand several times and guided it to her breast or her lap, so that I could always make sure that the outside of the dress was moistened with liquid. Once she put my hand on her breast, and I suddenly noticed that a smooth and quite soft piece of material moved upwards under my hand, then returned and placed itself on the back of my hand, whence it finally disappeared upwards. At the level of her navel a piece of the same material, a few inches long, seemed to emerge from the dress and then to withdraw itself. At the level of her breast some liquid matter, in the form of drops, emerged twice from the dress, and, on one occasion, spurted with considerable pressure into my hand. The material, on its emergence, appeared warm, darker than my hand, and had no recognisable taste or smell, although the medium's hands are strongly perfumed, and this perfume was transferred to my hand. I wiped off the liquid with my handkerchief, but Mme. Bisson had already got some of the liquid in her hand, and let it drop into the porcelain dish, even before a strip of the material had entered it.

"After a pause for rest, during which the curtains were entirely closed, the medium tried, at Mme. Bisson's request, to produce a phenomenon in her lap. After some exposures giving no result, some brownish material appeared in her lap, and some white substance on her head, and after a further pause a white substance, the size of her hand, appeared in her lap. During an attempt to make a kinematograph record of this substance, the medium, screaming loudly, fell into a fit, and was pacified by Mme. Bisson in the usual way in the cabinet. After this the liquid phenomenon showed itself a few more times, and during the subsequent examination Dr von Schrenck found the medium's skin to be dry."

In the above reports the author quotes from the observers present, because they sat in front of him, and therefore stood in direct relation with the medium. As a supplement to Kafka's report, I may say that the colour of the material can vary. Sometimes it looks quite white, then reddish, by reflection of the red light, resembling red rubber, which Kafka probably expresses by the word "brownish." The bits and strips are sometimes dark mouse-grey, and grow brighter the thinner and more transparent the structure. The liquid in the porcelain dish gave a viscous impression, but a fine grey film seemed to cover its surface, and the chemist who examined the liquid could give no information about this film.

That it is not a case of dust, but of a special substance, is clear from similar later observations, with the same medium, in Paris, where a grey film was also observed to lie over the liquid. This observation corresponds with that of the colour of the veil-like fabric. It was only after two hours of observation through the continually opened curtains that we regarded the sitting as practically closed for that day, and gave our consent to the complete closing of the curtains, so that Eva might rest undisturbed and collect power for the kinematograph experiment.

M. S. and the author went up to the kinematograph, which stood 10 feet from the curtain. Even at that distance we observed the materialisation process between the medium's knees, where, at Mme. Bisson's request, the mass was to appear. M. S. and the author saw a ribbon-shaped white mass about the size of a hand. The electric arc was turned on and M. S. worked the apparatus. The medium fell into a screaming fit and immediately closed the curtains. This ended the sitting.

Final control negative, but the dress was full of whitish spots which remained moist after the sitting, just in the places where the structures had been observed. The tights showed nothing unusual. The kinematograph experiment was a total failure. It appears that the film was spoilt by a mistake in the subsequent treatment.

REPORT OF PRIVATDOZENT DR KAFKA

CONCERNING THE

SITTINGS OF 30TH AUGUST AND 10TH AND 11TH SEPTEMBER 1912.

THE initial examination is the same for all the sittings. I examined the cabinet with the electric torch, felt the walls, floor and curtains, to make sure that nothing was hidden behind them. A similar examination was made of the wickerwork chair covered with black cloth and placed in the cabinet. I also examined the medium's black dress, outside and inside, by incident and transmitted light. This costume was handed to the medium, who put it on in a neighbouring room. When she returned, she was examined by Dr von Schrenck, who passed his hand over the bare trunk and legs, as well as outside over the feet and toes. After this examination, the medium was sewn into the costume by Mme. Bisson in the presence of the sitters, the tights being sewn to the waist of the dress, the sleeves being sewn round the wrist. After this, Dr von Schrenck made the medium open her mouth and blow, and examined her nose, hair and ears. The medium was allowed to retain her hairpins. She then entered the brightly lighted séance room and sat on the chair inside the cabinet, the curtains of which were open. While I stood by and observed the motions of the medium and Mme. Bisson, Mme. Bisson took the medium's hands, and put her into a trance, by fixing her gaze. The medium lay back in her chair. Mme. Bisson withdrew in the full light, and I closed the curtains. Then the white light was switched off, and the illumination consisted of five electric lamps (total candle-power 100, according to von Schrenck), enclosed in ruby glass globes. After the eye had got adapted to the light, one could read large print, at a distance of 2 or 3 yards from the lamps.

SITTING OF THE 30TH AUGUST 1912.

Present.—Mme. Bisson, Dr von Schrenck, his wife, and myself.

Initial control and hypnotisation as described.
After some time the medium opened the curtain, and a strip of greyish-brown matter seemed to lie on her left shoulder. The exposure was, however, very short and the impression was indistinct. The medium then closed the curtains completely, so that the hands were not visible, but soon the curtain opened slightly, so that one could observe the medium's hands through the gap, and see that they were describing grinding motions on her knees. The medium then opened the curtain completely, and we saw, in her lap, a whitish, indistinct mass about the size of a hand. Several times the curtain was opened and closed, but from this moment the hands always remained visible at the curtain. During the various exposures, which lasted one or two seconds, no change in the mass could at first be discerned, but afterwards two finger-shaped projections seemed to have formed. After a lengthy pause, during which the hands remained visible, the white flat mass in the medium's lap was replaced by a brownish structure, approximately of the shape of a scorpion. After a short exposure of the phenomenon the medium again closed the curtain. At the next opening of the curtain Dr von Schrenck and Mme. Bisson declared they saw a white mass on the left shoulder which, however, I could not confirm. This mass was then illuminated by Mme. Bisson with a torch, while Dr von Schrenck held the medium's hands. The medium made convulsive movements, and the white mass on the left shoulder disappeared, according to the other observers. On the right side of the neck there now appeared a thin brownish strip, emerging from the dress by a few inches,

which in structure resembled a coarse, porous, textile fabric. This strip did not alter its appearance during the three or four seconds that it remained visible. At Dr von Schrenck's request, I snatched at the substance, but the medium, whining pitifully, made violent motions with the whole body, and especially the neck, so that I got nothing, nor did I feel any moisture on my hand. The lamp was switched off and the medium retired behind completely closed curtains, trembling and breathing deeply, moaning and complaining of pains. Mme. Bisson also appeared very excited and incensed at this interference. As the medium's state did not improve, Mme. Bisson entered the cabinet and embraced her. She was then pacified, and Mme. Bisson's excitement subsided.

The medium then opened the curtains several times, though nothing was to be seen. After several such unsuccessful exposures, a disk, resembling a head, appeared in front of the medium's face. The medium closed the curtain again, but in such a way that, during the whole phenomenon, the hands remained visible. During the next exposure the disk was seen more distinctly on the right, quite near the head of the medium, who then quickly closed the curtain, jumped up, took a step outside the cabinet, and expressed a wish to be searched, but was pushed back into her chair by Mme. Bisson. The medium had bent her head and shoulders forward quite outside the cabinet, so that we could see her neck, but we could not see a trace of the phenomenon. After a pause, the medium had a violent cough and vomited. The vomit was caught in a handkerchief, and the sitting was closed. The medium emerged from the cabinet, and was examined by Dr von Schrenck in the same way as at the beginning. The result of the search was negative. During the examination the medium fainted, and had to be taken away in a state of hypnosis. During the subsequent examination of the cabinet, a pellet, the size of a finger-nail, resembling paper, was found on the floor of the cabinet. A further test proved it to be paper of unknown origin. In the vomit, we found a grey crumb, about the size of a pin-head, which, on analysis, was found to be chewed wood. According to Mme. Bisson, the medium had, on that afternoon, chewed some wood. Nothing else was found in the handkerchief or in the cabinet.

SITTING OF THE 10TH SEPTEMBER 1912.

Present.—Mme. Bisson, Dr von Schrenck and his wife, M. S., and myself.

Initial control and hypnotisation as usual.

The curtain was completely closed so that the hands of the medium were also invisible. After waiting three-quarters of an hour, the curtain opened several times without result, and, after that, the other observers claimed to see a white strip over the left shoulder. I could only observe during the later exposure, that a white disk, resembling a head, moved across the medium's head from the left, while the medium's hands were visible at the curtain. The medium then closed the curtain completely in order, as she said, to collect power, and during this pause she once closed the curtain from within particularly tightly.

During the next exposures, two white structures resembling arms appeared twice. I had the impression that they proceeded from the medium's mouth. The phenomenon looked as if a rolled-up rubber tube (like that used in a well-known toy) was unrolled by blowing into it. The phenomena disappeared while the curtain remained open, and the manner of disappearance could not be accurately observed. For the third time an elongated structure appeared, which, to M. S. and myself, resembled an arm reaching down from the medium's left shoulder. This phenomenon was photographed while the medium's hands grasped the curtain. The ignition of the flash-light produced a crisis in the medium, and to pacify her, Mme. Bisson bent over her and embraced her. The curtain was again closed, but, in spite of all the medium's efforts, no further phenomena were seen.

The medium again has a violent fit of sickness, vomiting mucus and blood, and in the mucus there are again small crumbs, which, however, this time, according to a microscopic examination made at Dr von Schrenck's request, consisted of food fragments. During the final control Mme. Bisson objected to Dr von Schrenck opening the seam by which the tights are fastened to the medium's dress, and performed that service herself. The searching of the medium and the cabinet was carried out as before, and gave a negative result.

SITTING OF THE 11TH SEPTEMBER 1912.

Present.—Mme. Bisson, Dr von Schrenck and his wife, M. S. and myself.

Initial examination and hypnotisation as usual.

The medium's hands were not at first visible. The phenomena commenced very soon, and, in the first instance, some white beckoning forms appeared above the medium's head, rather resembling those tube-like structures which, in the last sitting, appeared to proceed from her mouth. Mme. Bisson then asked the medium whether she would permit any illumination of the phenomena, and received an answer in the affirmative. During the next exposure, a strip appeared on the left breast which, in part, reflected the light, and actually consisted of drops of liquid, as could be proved by illumination and touch. The liquid moistened the hand, and when wiped off with a handkerchief left distinct traces. Suddenly there appeared, on the medium's left hand which held the curtain open, a ragged strip of brownish colour. The medium's hands and chest were steadily visible during these phenomena, as the curtain was open, but the lower arms and elbows were in the dark. After some time the strip disappeared, as if it were suddenly jerked upwards. Then Mme. Bisson laid her hand, which I held in my own, on that of the medium, and requested that the material should appear on her head in front of the curtain. That did not happen, but the medium requested me to give her my hand so that the material might be laid upon it. Then, three times in succession, a strip of material appeared, as if emerging out of the darkness above, and it crossed the palm of my hand, giving the impression as if somebody lightly drew the end of a rope across my hand. During the pause, the curtains remained opened all the time. The medium's hands were distinctly visible, and I held her right hand with my left. The medium's hands lay on her knees, and I suddenly felt my hands moistened with liquid. Mme. Bisson took the porcelain dish, in order to catch the material. Then we saw, several times, pieces of the brownish material, which, at first, remained suspended over the porcelain dish at a certain distance, then lightly touched it, until, finally, a distinctly visible brown strip of a textile appearance, seeming to come from the medium's head, entered the dish, and remained in it about four seconds. It then disappeared upwards, appearing to leave behind a liquid precipitate. Immediately after this, the medium put my hand into her mouth, so that I might examine it, but I could only feel the teeth and the tip of the tongue, and nothing else. The medium then expressed a wish to take off the tights, and did this against the advice of Mme. Bisson who, however, finally helped her to do so. The medium took my hand several times and guided it to her breast or her lap, so that I could make sure that the outside of the dress was moistened with liquid. Once she put my hand on her breast, and I suddenly noticed that a smooth, and quite soft piece of material moved upwards under my hand, then returned and placed itself on the back of my hand, whence it finally disappeared upwards. At the level of her navel a piece of the same material, a few inches long, seemed to emerge from the dress, and then to withdraw itself. At the level of her breast some liquid matter, in the form of drops, emerged twice through the dress, and on one occasion spurted with considerable pressure into my hand. The material on its emergence appeared warm, darker than my hand, and had no recognisable taste or smell, although the medium's hands are strongly perfumed, and this perfume was transferred to my hand. I wiped off the liquid with my handkerchief, but Mme. Bisson had already got some of the liquid in her hand, and let it drop into the porcelain dish, even before a strip of the material had entered.

After a pause for rest, during which the curtains were entirely closed, the medium tried, at Mme. Bisson's request, to produce a phenomenon in her lap.

After some exposures giving no result, some brownish material appeared in her lap, and some white substance on her head, and, after a further pause, a white substance, the size of her hand, appeared in her lap. During an attempt to make a kinematograph record of this substance, the medium, screaming loudly, fell into a fit, and was pacified by Mme. Bisson in the usual way, in the cabinet. After this, the liquid phenomenon showed a few more times. During the subsequent examination, Dr von Schrenck found the medium's skin to be dry. An examination of her genitals was resisted by Mme. Bisson. Various white spots remained on the dress where the teleplasm had appeared. Nothing remarkable in the cabinet.

The result of the observations I should summarise as follows :

The sittings did not appear absolutely convincing, either in the negative or in the positive sense. One cannot maintain that in the first sitting the substance emerging from the neck had disappeared in my hands, since the possibility is not excluded that a substance of slight consistency might have been rubbed into the skin by the medium's movements. Mme. Bisson's entrance into the cabinet during the crises of the medium supplies, of course, a source of error which cannot be neglected, although the sitters did not protest against it, in order to avoid any possible injury to the medium's health by the long-continued crisis, and also in order not to produce an unfavourable impression on the disposition of the two ladies, who are in close "rapport," and thus interfere with the success of the sittings. The initial and final examinations only prove that no bulky object is concealed anywhere, but are hardly sufficient absolutely to exclude the possibility that an artificial product, packed into an infinitesimal volume, was smuggled in, and afterwards disposed of by some trick, such as swallowing or rubbing out. The folds visible in the photographs of heads are suspicious in any case. Any experience gained at these sittings only seems to prove that the medium's hands take no part in the modifications and disappearances of the substance before the crisis, nor in the change of place of the head-like disk after the crisis. But I must remark that in two photographs, which Dr von Schrenck kindly showed me, the medium's right hand is obviously concerned in the motion of the phenomenon, while on the right knee there is, in one case, an amorphous mass, and in another case a mass resembling a hand, which might be intended to simulate the presence of a real hand. I cannot indeed confirm this hypothesis by my own experience, but the repeated request, made by the medium to the sitters, to fill up the pauses between the phenomena with conversation, might indicate an attempt to divert attention. The photograph of the phenomenon occurring in the second sitting furnishes a very remarkable proof of the unreliable character of visual perceptions, showing, as it does, that a phenomenon described by two observers as resembling an arm was, in reality, a well developed head. On the other hand, it is remarkable that the stereoscopic photograph gives the impression that the medium's head, the phenomenon, and the curtain were only a short distance apart from each other, while in reality the phenomenon was about 20 inches from the curtain, and its distance from the medium's head cannot be accurately determined. The great uncertainty of the sense organs seems also indicated by the fact that the other observers sometimes claimed to see cloud-like phenomena, dotted with luminous points, while these appearances were obviously really produced by subjective excitation of the retina.

In the third sitting we find that the liquid which appeared to come from the dress moistened it in several places. The responsibility as to whether Eva had concealed under the dress some bladder filled with liquid must be laid upon the initial examination. Dr von Schrenck and M. S. also maintain that the liquid did not come out of the medium's mouth, a point to which I paid no attention. I could not observe that the brownish ragged material was converted into liquid, for I saw either a material liquid from the beginning in the form of drops, or I saw ragged fragments of it executing gliding motions and disappearing into the dark. On the other hand, the amount of liquid collected in the sitters' hands, and dropped into the porcelain dish, seems to have increased after the material had laid itself into the dish, and had again disappeared from it. But I should not care to assert definitely that the ragged material had converted itself into liquid, or *vice versa*. I cannot also say whether the medium's head was always motionless during the jerking motions of the ragged material, as Dr von Schrenck and M. S. maintain, but these motions did indeed appear to take place without the co-operation of the medium's hands, trunk, or feet.

The microscopic investigation gives the typical structure of an albuminous liquid filled with cells, with or without nuclei (epithelium). In my own preparation there are also fat globules. Although Dr von Schrenck did not detect the presence of fat in his preparations, the question as to whether the liquid is to be described as colostrum should be more closely investigated, and the medium should be examined for accessory milk glands. Also the possibility of a profuse perspiration, or the secretion of lymph, is not to be discarded *a priori*. As regards the time distribution of the phenomena, it should be said that the sitting of 30th August was the first positive sitting after five negative ones at which I had been present, also that, after the crisis of the 30th August, on account of the medium's exhaustion, no sittings took place for a week, and that the sitting of 9th September (the fourth after the crisis, but the first at which I again assisted) was also without result.

Final Remarks on the Munich Sittings.

THE exposure scene at the sitting of 30th August had really a negative result, yet Dr Kafka does not perhaps consider this evidential, since he had not seen the manifestation on the left, which disappeared before our eyes. On the other hand, he admits that the veil-like piece observed by him on the right shoulder was withdrawn from his gaze. It is not clear whether it disappeared from our observation by an unknown process, or whether the veil-like fragment was removed by movements of the neck and shoulders. The process is still mysterious if, as Dr Kafka assumes, the piece had been rubbed away, for it would surely have left traces on the dress or on the body, whereas no such traces were found.

That Mme. Bisson's presence could not explain a single one of the phenomena was already proved finally in previous sittings. The experimenter cannot be expected to go through this unpleasant part of the proof from the beginning at the entry of every new savant into the sittings. Besides, there is no reasonable justification for throwing suspicion on Mme. Bisson, simply because the phenomena cannot be explained through the medium alone, and because it so happens that, in this case, an experimenter of the female sex trained the medium with indefatigable patience and self-sacrifice, and demonstrates the result. Even with all the precautions taken on the 15th August, which have almost the effect of vivisection in the case of a sensitive person, every unprejudiced observer of good will, open eyes, and clear intellect can easily recognise that the occurrence of phenomena is not, in any case, bound up with Mme. Bisson's personality, but Mme. Bisson does know how to foster the phenomena by her great educative and suggestive influence. Furthermore, her entrance into the cabinet, during the two sittings described by Dr Kafka, was necessitated by the strong nervous crises produced on the medium in the first sitting by our attempted exposure; and in the second, by the author's unexpected switching-on of the electric light, *i.e.*, solely by our own conduct. And when all is said, there is surely a legal and moral responsibility resting on those immediately concerned as to the medium's health. Our own procedure alone (and the author does not exclude himself) produced on 30th August several profound and *genuine* fainting fits of the medium.

In these investigations we are face to face with unknown quantities which must be respected; with a subject which has its own conditions, and cannot be treated like a mathematical formula, or like a piece of mechanical clockwork.

Occurrences which depend to such a great extent upon the psychical adjustment, not only of the medium but of all those present, cannot, in spite of their real existence, as yet aspire to the objective force of demonstration that is insisted upon in a physical, or even a physiological, experiment.

The possibility of an adjustment of these phenomena to conditions prescribed by us, and by our habitual mode of thought, has distinct limits. When these are reached, it is the business of the investigator to accept the laws peculiar to the new region in the light of previous experience, and to alter the experimental conditions accordingly.

If a small artificial product could be smuggled in, in a small compass, as Dr Kafka believes, in spite of the control, the initial control would have entirely failed in its object. If the possibility of an exact initial examination is denied in principle, and conjuring thus declared to be almighty, that means the abandonment of all evidential determinations.

So long as no details are given as to how and where such artificial products are hidden, a general assertion of this kind can only be taken as a confession that the critic is baffled, or that he is dissatisfied as to the accuracy of the control. But these two assumptions must be rejected, since the initial control was carried out with every care, and we can say, quite definitely, that such packets are not hidden either on the body of the medium or in her dress. So long as the control is not proved inaccurate, the assumption lacks all justification; or, to put it legally, it is not the accused who has to prove his innocence, but his accusers alone who are bound to produce proof of his guilt. The right to an assertion of guilt does not exist in law so long as the proof is not brought.

A special discussion is required of the question of hysterical rumination, brought forward by Dr Kafka. The fact that hysterical patients can sometimes bring up into their mouths objects they have swallowed, by an antiperistaltic motion, after the fashion of ruminating animals, cannot be doubted, although the cases are rare, and require special pathological conditions. By numerous observations, and even by photography, the part played by the mouth in the phenomena is well defined. This objection, already considered by the author on a previous occasion, is in any case worthy of discussion. A number of circumstances could be adduced in favour of this hypothesis: the emergence of the substance from the mouth, the repeated appearance of shreds hanging out of it, the frequent vomiting of blood after the sittings (where the gullet was proved to be the origin by microscopic examination), the repeated disappearance of the substance into the mouth, and the mixture of saliva with the material, as proved in Biarritz, all these are weighty arguments for the theory.

It cannot, and must not, be denied that the organs of respiration and nutrition appear to be concerned in many cases in the production of the substance, even if we assume a special possibility of mediumistic production of this transitory matter. But, in the first place, a proof is required that hysterical rumination occurs at all in Eva's case, for after two years of observation no indication of this has been noted by her daily companions.

Hysterical rumination is a pathological act of vomiting which is voluntary on the part of the person concerned. But such a person cannot make any selection among the contents of his stomach. He must vomit whatever is there at the time, *i.e.*, food diluted with liquids and gastric juice. In bringing up a swallowed object, traces of the contents of the stomach and of gastric juice would certainly be brought up as well, which would leave spots on the dress, and thus betray their origin.

In the case of the present investigations, we have only to consider products consisting of paper, or of some textile fabric (wool, cotton, thread, silk), *i.e.*, soft materials capable of being folded up. But such soft, fibrous preparations, in the form of small packets, would in any case be attacked, decomposed, softened, and impregnated by the gastric juice and the liquid contents of the stomach. They would show distinct traces of where they had been. They could hardly have that clearness, firmness, and diversity of form found in the materialisation products, but would show a defective and softened condition.

The process would be still more difficult if these products were packed in a solid case, which would at least have to be the size of a walnut, and were then swallowed and brought up again. The voluntary bringing-up of solid objects is much more difficult, and very painful, and does not always succeed at the first attempt. Since the contents of the stomach are three or four pints in bulk, and very variable, the further question arises as to how many antiperistaltic motions are necessary to bring the object into the mouth. What then becomes of the matter brought up during the first motions? And how could a flat drawing, the size of a head, be disengaged from its case, unfolded, smoothed out, placed in position, folded up, and pressed into the same volume so as to fit into the case and be swallowed again—all this in the dark and without the help of the hands? And, finally, what about the packing up of the plastic forms, the mask-like products? Could these also be concealed in the stomach?

As soon as we follow this process in detail and try to translate it into practice, the answer is obvious.

In any case, Eva, as a rule, took her dinner two hours before the sitting, and was sometimes observed during the five, or even seven, preceding hours, so that the swallowing of artificial products would have been noticed.

Since food-remnants or gastric juice were never found, since such manipulations could not have been concealed for four years, and since at the sittings themselves, even with an open curtain, nothing was ever found which could be interpreted in this sense, there is no justification for such a theory. And, finally, in many cases the phenomena were observed to commence in the medium's lap or some other place, quite unconnected with the mouth or the digestive organs.

During his experiments with Eva C., in December 1912, the Paris physician, Dr R., a specialist for digestive troubles, made Eva eat bilberry jam half an hour before the sittings. Yet the material emerging from the mouth during the subsequent sittings was white. If it had come out of the stomach it would have been red, since bilberries colour the whole contents of the stomach. The medium did not know the object of the experiment.

Yet the fact remains that the mouth plays an important part during the generation and disappearance of the products.

Dr Kafka is right in calling attention to the uncertainty of sense perceptions, and the occurrence of optical illusions. Here the author agrees with him entirely, and it was for the very reason that he has made the freest possible use of photography. As regards his experience of the 10th September—in which he thought he saw an arm-like appearance, while the photograph showed a head—the main point seems to have escaped attention. If the object seen had remained at rest, we should all, no doubt, have gained a distinct impression. But the object moved at a distance of 20 to 30 inches behind the curtain, from the dark region of the cabinet on the left several times, towards Eva's head with a great speed (her hands being visible). Also, it remained in the circle of light for barely a fraction of a second, and disappeared suddenly into the darkness. The optical impression was therefore too fugitive, too rapid to be discerned clearly. In this sitting the curtain remained open both before and after the phenomenon, since the same process of appearance and disappearance was repeated several times. The photographic record confirms this, and shows a freely floating head. The situation is particularly clear in the stereoscopic transparency, which, contrary to Dr Kafka's opinion, shows the distances practically right.

On the other hand, there is justification for Dr Kafka's remarks concerning the appearance of face and head-forms, so very contrary to our expectations. As a matter of fact, we have to deal in some of these phenomena with objects of an artistic character, such as drawings on a white base, sharply cut out and showing creases, as the author has already explained in connection with previous sittings. But the improbability of the appearance is not in itself a sufficient argument against the genuineness, or the metaphysical origin, of the products. The objections raised on this point are the more easily understood, since a head-form was only once photographed in Dr Kafka's presence. Surely a final judgment on this matter requires more numerous experiments than could be carried out in Munich.

Sittings in October and November 1912 (Paris).

THE experimental room for the sittings now to be described was the same as in June 1912. But the observations at Munich had led Mme. Bisson to construct an entirely new cabinet. The skeleton of this cabinet was a wooden framework covered with new black lining material. The size was determined by the position of the stove, and was the same as before, except that the roof was higher, being 9 feet. The broad wooden cross-beam, to which the curtain-rod was attached, allowed of the attachment of the stereoscopic camera used in Munich.

As regards all the remaining details, the position of cameras, etc., nothing was changed from the arrangements at the sittings in June, so that no new description need be given.

The author examined the curtains and walls carefully, but nowhere did he find pin-holes or any other defects in the lining material.

The pendant was strengthened by a twenty-five candle-power lamp, and there was also a red electric lamp suspended in the cabinet in such a manner that it could be switched on and raised or lowered from the outside.

SITTINGS OF THE 25TH, 26TH, AND 28TH OCTOBER 1912.

Negative.

SITTING OF THE 30TH OCTOBER 1912.

Present.—Mme. Bisson and the author.

Control.—Dress of the medium as in the Munich sittings.

Eva's disposition during the whole week was unfavourable, and was probably the cause of the negative sittings. On this evening Mme. Bisson asked the medium to hurry a little with her change of dress, whereupon Eva refused to have a sitting, and locked herself into her room. The next day she wrote a letter of apology to the author.

SITTING OF THE 2ND NOVEMBER 1912.

Present.—Mme. Bisson and the author.

Control and illumination as on 30th October 1912.

Eva held the curtain open with her hands, and endeavoured to adapt herself psychically to the occurrence of phenomena. We heard long and short expirations. Without a change in the disposition of the hands, a patch of a dark grey colour, changing into white, became visible on her left shoulder. Then, while the curtain remained open, a white strip, like a chalk mark, appeared in the same place. Suddenly a disk-like structure emerged out of the dark, with a motion forward over Eva's left shoulder. I recognised a female face, obviously on a flat surface. The hands had not left the curtain during the whole development of the picture, and the curtain had remained open. I took a flash-light photograph.

After the image had shown itself several times, while the plates were being changed, the sitting was closed. Final examination negative.

The photographs of this sitting (Figs. 116 and 117) are not among the best, owing to faulty focusing of the cameras. On the left side of Eva's head we see an oval female face in front view and natural size, but it is narrower than the medium's face, and turns round towards her, with a strong bending of the head towards the right. The right temple touches Eva's hair. Otherwise, it seems to float freely, and touches neither Eva's shoulder nor the back of the chair. The gaze is directed upwards in accordance with the position of the head. Both eyes look slightly distorted. Mouth, nose, and chin are regular and nicely drawn. The whole structure is probably flat rather than plastic, although this cannot be decided from the photographs. From the point of view of criticism, it is interesting to note that the picture occurred with open curtains and hands always visible.

NINE SITTINGS FROM THE 4TH TO 17TH NOVEMBER 1912.

Negative.

Unpleasant family news had an unfavourable influence upon Eva's disposition. She was ill for several days and vomited blood. According to the microscopic analysis made in the Antoine Hospital, the blood is drawn from the gullet, a symptom which is frequently combined with hysterical rumination.

SITTING OF THE 18TH NOVEMBER 1912.

Present.—Mme. Bisson and the author.

Control.—Although it had been often proved that the medium's hands took no part in the development and disappearance of the pheno-

FIG. 116. AUTHOR'S FLASHLIGHT PHOTOGRAPH OF 2 NOVEMBER, 1912

FIG. 118. AUTHOR'S FLASHLIGHT PHOTOGRAPH OF 27 NOVEMBER, 1912. FRONT VIEW.

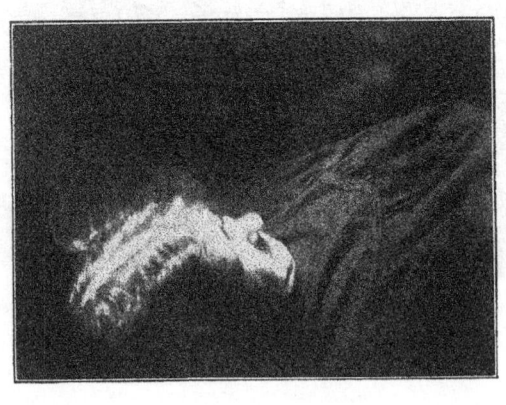

FIG. 117. SIDE VIEW OF FIG. 116.

SITTINGS IN OCTOBER AND NOVEMBER 1912

mena and remained visible, yet we had noticed in most of the sittings, and especially during the total closing of the curtains, a temporary drawing back of the hands which, with new observers, always gave rise to the suspicion that Eva's hands participated in the production of the phenomena. For this reason Mme. Bisson accepted the author's proposal to change the control in such a manner that Eva's hands should not leave the curtain during the whole sitting, or, at least, until the complete development of the head forms. They should be constantly illuminated and visible to us.

In order to increase the accuracy of the record, the author wrote his report, from the 18th November onward, during the sitting itself.

The remaining conditions were as on 2nd November. When I extinguished the light, Mme. Bisson held Eva's hands, which grasped the curtain, and were placed outside the curtain on her knees. From this moment the five fingers of both hands were illuminated before our eyes. The author also touched these from time to time, to make sure that they were really Eva's hands.

9.1 P.M. Commencement of sitting. Hypnotisation complete in thirty seconds.

10.40 P.M. In spite of nearly two hours of waiting, no phenomena. New control seems to present a difficulty. Strong suggestion to encourage the medium.

10.45 P.M. Whimpering and stertorous breathing. Eva says she feels the impending occurrence of phenomena. Her trance seems to deepen. Her hands are motionless in the same place.

10.55 P.M. Curtain opens. On the medium's left thigh there appears a mass, nearly an inch wide and 6 inches long, so that, in spite of the long waiting, the proof of the occurrence, and a positive result under the more rigid conditions, is obtained.

11.4 P.M. The material has altered its place, passing on to the left shoulder, and looks like a white cloth. Hands visible all the time on the knees, holding the curtains.

11.9 P.M. A veil-like fabric on Eva's face. The gasping becomes harder, she says: " Oh, Juliette, c'est dur, aide-moi ! "

11.22 P.M. Control unchanged. I observed a flat white disk, the size of a head, lying horizontally on the left shoulder like a sheet of paper.

11.25 P.M. I distinctly recognise the female face photographed on 2nd November, but reversed, the forehead being directed forward. The whole gives the impression of a chalk drawing on the white ground. The narrow oval face is very noticeable. Hands constantly visible in their place.

11.28 P.M. On the shoulder there is now nothing but a white mass. resembling a folded handkerchief.

The former form has disappeared. I took up a white electric torch.

11.50 P.M. Hands still visible. Suddenly I illuminate her lap with the lamp. In the black folds of the dress there are several white fragments or white pieces resembling lint. These do not seem to withstand the light, and disappear.

11.55 P.M. Mme. Bisson illuminates the medium's lap. Instead of the white mass, some apparently viscous, light grey drops and some liquid material are seen. With a glass rod I took up some of these drops and placed them on a microscopic slide, for a subsequent microscopic examination.

12.4 A.M. With my permission, Eva released the curtain, which, however, remained open, and sat beside the chair on the floor. Again a sudden illumination with a red electric torch. White patches and fragments lie on the seat of the chair beside the medium. She screams and clutches with her left hand at the chair, whereupon everything disappears, as if by magic. Medium's hands empty. No further phenomena.

12.30 A.M. End of the sitting. Final examination negative.

We may say with certainty that the picture on the left shoulder was produced without participation of the hands. That it remained there, and could not be put upright nor fixed, may be due to the exclusion of manual help.

Sittings of the 20th and 22nd November 1912.

Negative.

Sitting of the 23rd November 1912.

Present.—Mme. Bisson and the author.

Control.—As in previous sittings.

This day Eva, as a preparation for the sitting, remained in a state of hypnotisation from 3.30 to 6.30, under Mme. Bisson's supervision, in her study.

Immediately after hypnotisation, and before the white light was switched off, both Eva's hands, holding the curtains, were laid on her knees in front of the curtain, and during the three hours' sitting they remained illuminated by the red light, and clearly visible. On the extinction of the white light, Mme. Bisson held Eva's hands. The record was kept during the sitting.

8.45 P.M. Hypnotisation and beginning of the sitting. Hands visible.

9 P.M. Groaning and whimpering. Mme. Bisson is requested to help in the production of phenomena by an effort of will: " Demande bien, ma petite Juliette."

9.5 P.M. Groaning and gasping, accompanied by an effort of the ventral muscles.

9.6 P.M. Eva crosses her hands at the curtain, holding the right curtain with her left hand and *vice versa*.

9.10 P.M. Increase of the painful efforts. Eva feels the coming of mediumistic phenomena. She says, " Cela va venir."

9.11 P.M. Stertorous breathing and long expirations. " Cela vient, je le sens."

9.16 P.M. She brought her hands again into the original position, and they remained visible, holding the curtain. Without altering this position, Eva stretches her head out of the cabinet and asks Mme. Bisson to place her hands on her forehead and neck, which was done, but under the strict supervision of the author.

SITTINGS IN OCTOBER AND NOVEMBER 1912

9.25 P.M. Crossing of the hands in the light as at 9.6 P.M.

9.31 P.M. Eva puts her head out of the cabinet and asks, " Juliette, tu vois ? "

9.36 P.M. Restoration of the original position of the hands as at 9.16. Eva talks a lot and is very restless. " Cela vient, je le sens. Oh, c'est dur ! "

9.45 P.M. Renewed painful gasping and moaning. In consequence of the manipulations of the curtain, the curtain rings are separated so far on the curtain-rod that light falls into the cabinet from above. At Eva's request, Mme. Bisson mounts on a chair and closes the curtain. No change in the position of the hands.

9.50 P.M. Eva again puts her head out of the cabinet, and Mme. Bisson pacifies her by laying her hand on it.

9.59 P.M. More pains. " Cela vient."

10.3 P.M. Mme. Bisson holds Eva's hands in hers in front of the curtain, so that they remain always visible.

10.21 P.M. Stronger efforts and motions.

10.22 P.M. Curtain opened. " Tu vois, Juliette," she says. Deep long-drawn respiration.

10.28 P.M. In spite of several changes of position, made during the hour and a half of the sitting, the hands had not been withdrawn within the curtain for one moment, but were always visible in the red light, only now I had the impression of a vague vaporous form above her head, though this might have been an optical illusion.

10.29 P.M. Hands still visible in the same place.

10.30 P.M. Curtain opened. An illuminated patch about the size of half a crown, and apparently of the consistency of skin, becomes visible about midway between the medium's thighs, but only for an instant, for it is withdrawn with a rapid motion towards her body, and disappears. The curtain is closed while the hands remain visible.

10.32 P.M. The muscular efforts are accompanied by a chewing action, as if Eva had something in her mouth. She shows some feeling of animal satisfaction, interwoven with states of tension and painful sensations.

10.45 P.M. The hands hold the curtains closed, thumbs touching, and all ten fingers being visible. She draws the thumbs about an inch apart, and, between them, a piece of material is seen, exactly the colour of Eva's skin. This lies in front of the curtain, and becomes larger, thicker, and longer under my gaze. It is prolonged backward, while in front it takes the form of a small clenched doll's hand of ivory. This miniature structure, of about the size of a small plum, ends in a ribbon about an inch wide, running back towards the body of the medium, and, while the body remains steady, it is suddenly withdrawn, and apparently reabsorbed.

10.48 P.M. Deep groaning noises and slight cramp in the arms.

10.50 P.M. A larger piece of veil-like material is seen on the breast and left upper arm, like torn, ragged, and transparent material. Length about 12 to 15 inches.

10.59 P.M. Hands still visible at the curtain. Eva is quieter, having passed the climax.

11.10 P.M. A white mass of material on her left shoulder.

11.14 P.M. The curtain being opened again, the author bends his head forward behind the curtain, so that he can observe the white stuff on the shoulder. Again I see a flat, white disk, larger than a head, of oval, irregular form, lying horizontally on the left shoulder. On the light background there is a male face resembling a charcoal drawing, with chin towards the back wall. It is remarkable that on the upper lip a moustache emerges plastically, as if at the position of the upper lip, on a larger drawing on cardboard, a real moustache had been stuck on. During the closing of the curtain a rustling is heard, as if soft paper were being rubbed.

11.18 P.M. Hands unchanged. Curtain opens. The disk is still in the same place, and makes a motion upwards and forwards, the back portion raising itself. This motion was apparently aided by a simultaneous motion of Eva's head.

11.25 P.M. During the next opening I saw the picture rolled up like a paper-bag, with its point touching Eva's mouth, while the broad opening pointed upward.

11.27 P.M. Everything has disappeared without a trace. Eva opens the curtains very wide and stretches forth her head. I looked at the back of the chair, and the sides of the cabinet, and illuminated everything with a white torch. From the beginning to the end of the sitting the hands had not left their place for an instant, and so could have had no connection with the genesis, motion, and disappearance of the phenomena. The sitting was continued, but without any further result, and was closed at 12.10 A.M. Final examination negative.

Sittings of the 25th and 26th November 1912.

Negative.

Sitting of the 27th November 1912.

Present.—Mme. Bisson and the author.

Control.—As at the sitting on 23rd November.

Several hours of hypnotisation during the afternoon as a preparation.

9.1 P.M. Hypnotisation in thirty seconds. The hands to-day also remained visible in the light, in front of the curtain, until the phenomenon was well developed.

9.15 P.M. Great restlessness and groaning, as well as the usual respiratory symptoms.

9.22 P.M. An irregular wisp appears on the medium's breast, reaching down to the belt.

9.30 P.M. A long grey fragment hangs out of the mouth. No details can be given, as the exposure was too short. Mme. Bisson holds my porcelain dish under the fragment, and also catches in her hand some drops of a liquid material, which she also puts into the dish. The latter finally contained 1 c. cm. of liquid.

9.35 P.M. Strong muscular efforts. Eva lays her feet in Mme. Bisson's lap.

9.40 P.M. Painful whimpering and moaning.

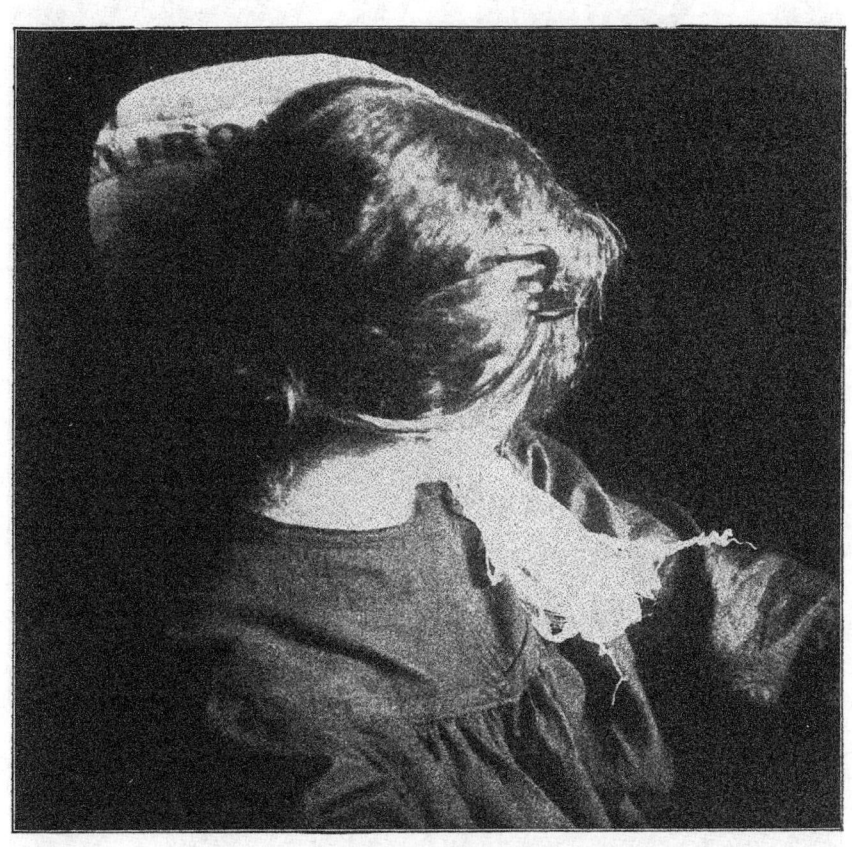

Fig 119 Side view (enlarged) of Fig 118
taken within the cabinet

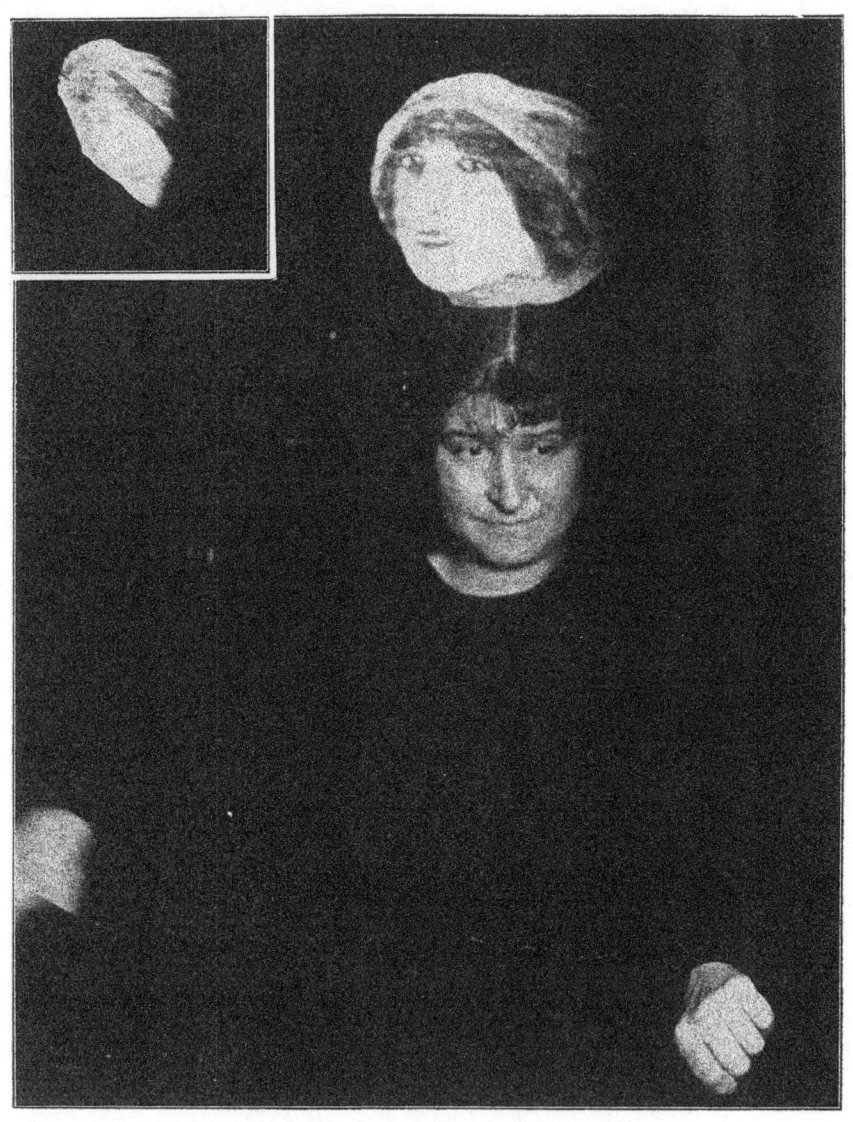

FIG 120   AUTHOR'S FLASHLIGHT PHOTOGRAPH OF 30 NOVEMBER, 1912.
FIG 121 (INSET)   SIDE VIEW OF FIG. 120

9.45 P.M. Opening of the cameras, while keeping an eye on the position of the hands at the curtain.
9.55 P.M. " C'est dur ! je vois une tête."
10.15 P.M. Pause, without change in the position of the hands.
10.20 P.M. The whimpering grows stronger, and more laborious. No change in the position of the hands.
10.30 P.M. Exposure of a head image, first on Eva's breast and then on her shoulder. Possibly a small portrait, but it cannot be distinctly recognised. Up to now the hands have not been withdrawn behind the curtain for an instant.
10.42 P.M. Flash-light. As the curtain opened I seem to see a white disk with a fragment depending from it. The phenomenon disappears totally.
10.50 P.M. End of the sitting. Final examination negative.

The liquid caught in the porcelain dish looks viscous and colourless. It has no smell, and a grey film seems to lie over it. Microscopical preparations were made.

Development of the negatives produced a surprise, inasmuch as they showed only a veil-like disk, without the drawing of a head. At the moment of the flash-light Eva had turned her head to the left, so that she covered the structure attached to her hair on the left. We therefore see the outer semicircular edge of a wisp falling down on her left shoulder, with a form resembling that of previous pictures (Fig. 118). The camera, in the roof of the cabinet, shows that a flat white disk, about the size of a head, lies on the medium's hair.

Of much greater interest is the result of the photograph taken with the camera inside the cabinet (Fig. 119), giving pictures $3\frac{1}{2}$ by $5\frac{1}{2}$ inches. Here the flat object, which projects behind the medium's head towards the back, appears with four distinct parallel vertical creases, which are also shown in the stereoscopic photograph. There is a narrow horizontal strip, also interrupted by creases, on which we can recognise the words " Le " (small type) " Miro " (large type). That is evidently meant to be " Le Miroir." We can just recognise the top of an " I " following the " O," but the next " R " is covered. I cannot form any opinion on this curious result.

Sitting of the 29th November 1912

Present.—Mme. Bisson and the author.

Conditions as on 27th November.

Mme. Bisson only saw the proofs of the photograph of the 27th November immediately before this sitting, and was as much puzzled by the result as was the author. Eva did not notice anything, but thought that the photographs had been failures, through an unfortunate turning of the head towards the left. She did not see the proofs before the sitting, nor were they discussed with her. Eva did, indeed, say to Mme. Bisson at midday on the 29th, during the preparatory hypnotisation, " Berthe wanted to show you something special." Mme. Bisson hypnotised her at 9.30 P.M. Hardly had she gone into hypnosis when she said the word " Miroir." She then continued,

" Elle (Berthe) voulait vous écrire autrefois, elle voulait vous envoyer sa pensée ecrite. Vous êtes pour elle son miroir. Elle se revoit ici. Vous avez une photographie d'une pensée de Berthe. Elle a la joie de se créer un autre image." ("She (Berthe) wanted to write to you the other day. She wanted to send you her written thought. You are her mirror. She sees herself here. You have a photograph of the thought of Berthe. She has the joy of creating another image for herself.")

On questioning her further, Eva said that the matter attached to her head had not been a picture, but had only been intended to materialise that word for us.

To-day's sitting was negative. It ended at 11 P.M.

Sitting of the 30th November 1912.

Present.—Mme. Bisson and the author.

Eva was hypnotised in the afternoon as a preparation for the evening sitting.

Control.—As on 23rd November 1912. Eva's hands were brought in front of the curtain, in the white electric light, immediately after hypnotisation, and remained visible till after the appearance of the materialised picture.

9.10 P.M. Moaning and bleating noises. She says, "Juliette, demande bien," which means that Mme. Bisson is to support the medium's efforts by an effort of will.

9.20 to 9.25 P.M. Mme. Bisson sees, on the medium's breast and shoulder, initial materialisations in the form of fine misty structures.

9.28 P.M. Eva is restless, puts in remarks, but takes care that her hands are always visible at the curtain. Her feet are stretched forwards, and lie between those of Mme. Bisson, who sits facing her.

9.30 P.M. She draws the curtain to and fro, possibly to allow light to fall upon some product.

9.35 P.M. The well-known respiration becomes more active, there are plenty of sounds and indistinct words, giving the impression that Eva had something in her mouth which hindered speech. We hear whining, gasping, and pressing, and the hands grip the curtain convulsively.

9.37 P.M. For the first time to-day the author sees a long strip of white material falling from the left shoulder down to the breast. The hands are constantly controlled. During repeated exposures, the material appears to become more compact, and to assume the shape of a white disk the size of a head.

9.55 P.M. On the disk lying on her breast, I notice features as if drawn with charcoal, but cannot say whether the face is male or female.

10 P.M. Moaning and whining.

10.6 P.M. We hear a rustling as if paper were being rubbed together, while Eva's hands are steadily visible.

10.11 P.M. Eva asked us to postpone the photograph, as the face was not yet sufficiently clearly developed. With my permission, she then drew back her hands. I assumed that she would use them to fix up the picture, but had no objection to that, as I had already seen the picture partly developed.

Fig. 122. Enlargement of Fig. 120.

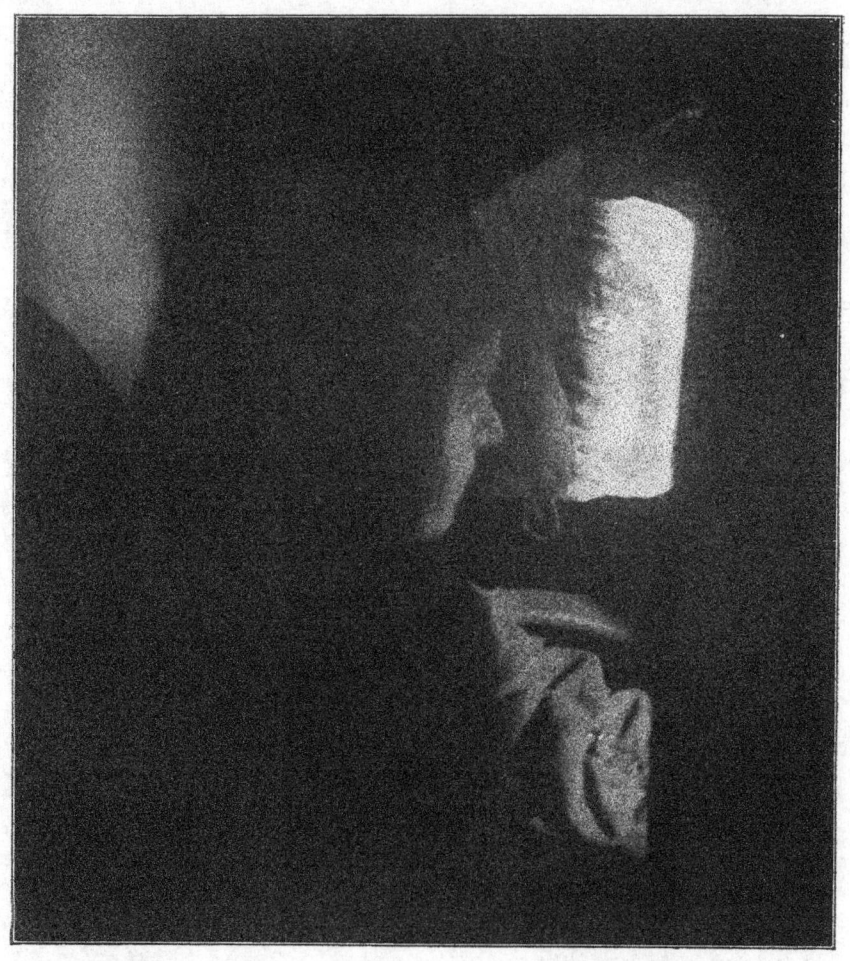

FIG. 123. AUTHOR'S SECOND PHOTOGRAPH OF 30 NOVEMBER, 1912.

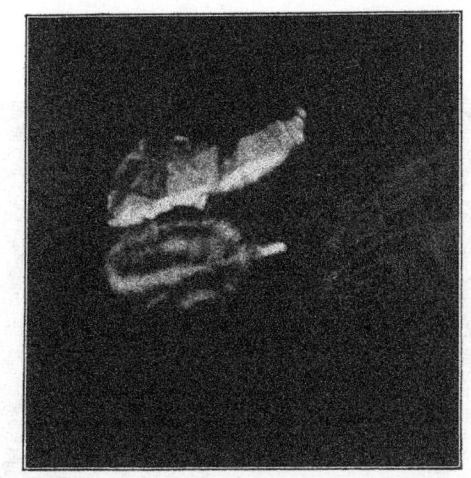

Fig. 126. Side view of Fig. 125, from within the cabinet.

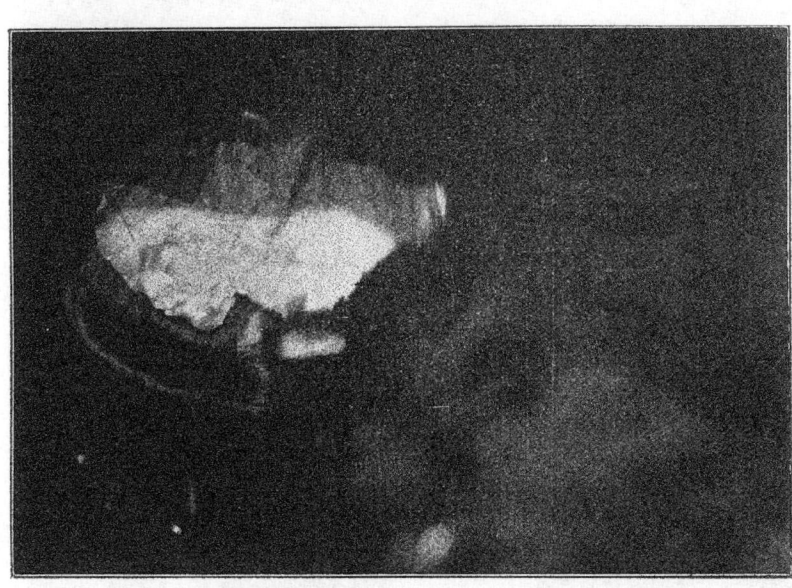

Fig. 125. Mme. Bisson's flashlight photograph of 30 December, 1912.

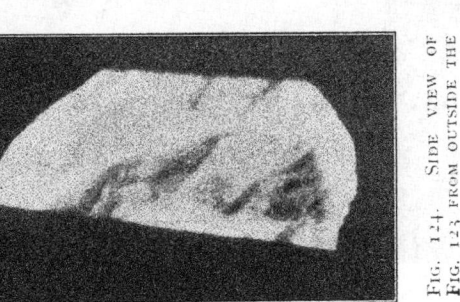

Fig. 124. Side view of Fig. 123 from outside the cabinet.

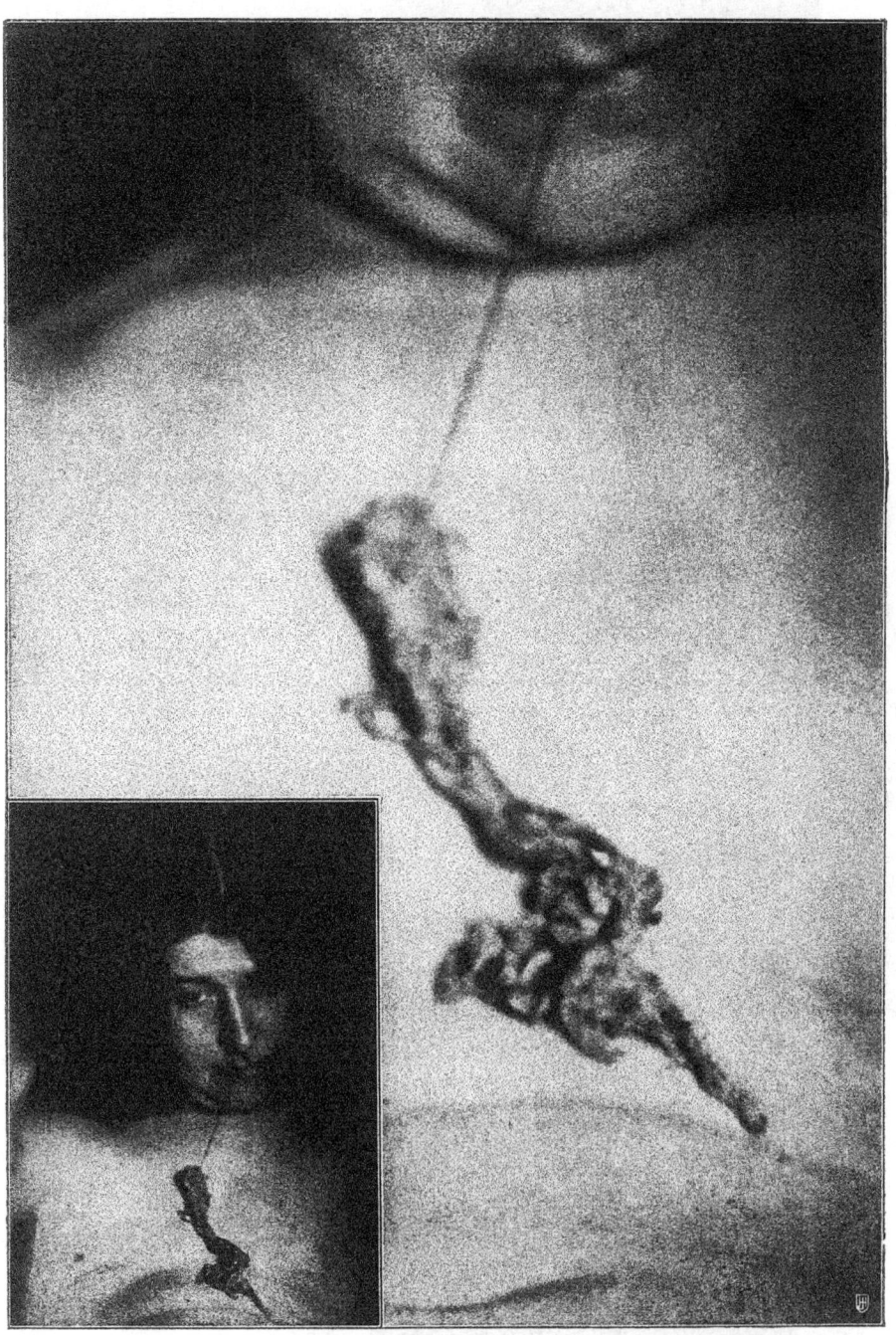

FIG. 127   MME. BISSON'S FLASHLIGHT PHOTOGRAPH OF 5 JANUARY, 1913, WITH ENLARGEMENT.
(RETOUCHED.)

SITTINGS IN OCTOBER AND NOVEMBER 1912

10.46 P.M. After several exposures, I see a structure on her head, and ignite the flash-light. I change the plates at once. Then I stand behind Mme. Bisson, and see on Eva's head, in a half-inclined position, a female face on a sort of disk. It resembles a coloured drawing on Japanese paper.

10.55 P.M. The image is now seen on her left arm, and seems to stand at right angles to the curtain at the level of Eva's head.

10.59 P.M. Second photograph.

11.5 to 8 P.M. She shows the product in several exposures to Mme. Bisson, who sits opposite, holding both flaps of the curtain at the bottom with her left hand, and obviously manipulating the picture with her right, moving it up and down, or trying to detach it from its position (Fig. 123).

11.11 P.M. Mme. Bisson claims to have seen the image on the back wall.

11.13 P.M. The author illuminated the cabinet unexpectedly with a white electric torch. Everything had disappeared without a trace. The sitting was closed. Final examination of the medium and cabinet negative.

The successful photographs (Figs. 120, 121, and 122) of this sitting show us, on Eva's head, a life-sized female head, in the form of a drawing on a disk cut out. The eyes are very far apart, and the forehead and the left ear are invisible, being entirely covered by hair. The nose is broad and curved, and the open mouth shows the teeth. The hair surrounds the face like a wreath, and over the back of the head and part of the neck a white cloth is draped.

From the artistic point of view the portrait may be considered as extremely finely drawn and interesting. The vivid expression, especially that of the eyes, has something animal and bloodthirsty about it, full of spirit. The half-open mouth and the lips, which appear to be reddened, indicate sensuality.

The outer circle of cloth gives a remarkable yielding and rough impression, as if the mass were some soft material product, and it shows no resemblance to the sharp margins of cardboard. In general, the whole veil-drapery of the hair, especially as seen in the stereoscopic photograph, looks extraordinarily delicate and realistic, like a real veil. We cannot escape the impression that in this case a sketch, commenced by drawing, had been finished by modelling.

In the second picture (Figs. 123 and 124) of 30th November the same image hangs by a black wiry cord, with some branches attached, which joins the left curtain with Eva's hair. A small piece of whitish substance is attached to it. A veil-like fabric, of extraordinarily loose composition, is also suspended by it, and covers the whole face, so that only the left side can be seen. Here, as well as in the side view of the image (Fig. 124), we distinctly see a slanting parallel fold, which cannot be seen in the first picture. The portions of the face lying under the veil in the shadow, especially nose and mouth, are distorted and no longer recognisable as such. The decomposition process seems to have already begun, and is perhaps the cause of the fold. Since Eva had been allowed to withdraw her hands before the first photograph, there is nothing against the assumption of a manual arrangement of this remarkable picture. An inspection of the curtain did not, as one might expect, show a pin-hole at the point where the cord had been fastened, but a whitish spot, resembling the spots which sometimes remain as a residue of the substance on the dress. The fastening, therefore, might have been accomplished by sticking on the chain.

The whole circumstances here described are very peculiar, especially since there were no aids towards the production of such a complicated collection of things, either on Eva's body or in the cabinet. If, therefore, we admit, in principle, the materialisation process, we may make up our minds to assume that the means of fastening the artistic products are generated and disappear in the same way as the products themselves.

Observations in December 1912 and January and February 1913 (Paris).

AFTER the author's departure, Dr R., the specialist for digestive troubles already referred to, in connection with Dr Bourbon, continued the observations under the same conditions as the author.

In the first positive sitting of 9th December, phenomena of moving material began similar to those of the last Munich sitting of 11th September 1912. During the final control of the cabinet, Dr R. found on the floor a piece of soft, grey, half-liquid material, which was preserved for chemical and microscopic examination.

As shown by Mme. Bisson's communications, the further sittings up to 20th December 1912 were negative, but for some minor phenomena.

It was only on 23rd December that phenomena began again to appear, and in the first instance in presence of Mme. Bisson only, who on that evening operated with the medium in a naked condition. About this she writes as follows in a letter, dated 24th December 1912 :—

"At first the material emerged from the vagina in the shape of a ribbon split at its lower end. Then it jumped on to Eva's shoulder. Finally the female image ' Berthe ' appeared under Eva's chin, as if stuck to her breast, with its face turned sideways. The medium's mouth remained inactive in this case. Then the head appeared on Eva's shoulder, following the motions she made with her chin. I insisted that Eva's hands should never leave the curtain, in order to get her accustomed to that requirement, although I was operating with her alone. The phenomenon could be followed without interruption. During the process of the formation of the face I heard, without seeing anything, the curious noise resembling the rustling of paper rubbed together, the curtain being open. Eva's hands either grasped the curtain or lay in mine. During the noise I held her hands. The sitting lasted one hour."

SITTING OF THE 30TH DECEMBER 1912.

Present.—Mme. Bisson.

A further photographic record (Figs. 125 and 126) of a perfectly flat face-fragment, closely resembling in design and composition the head

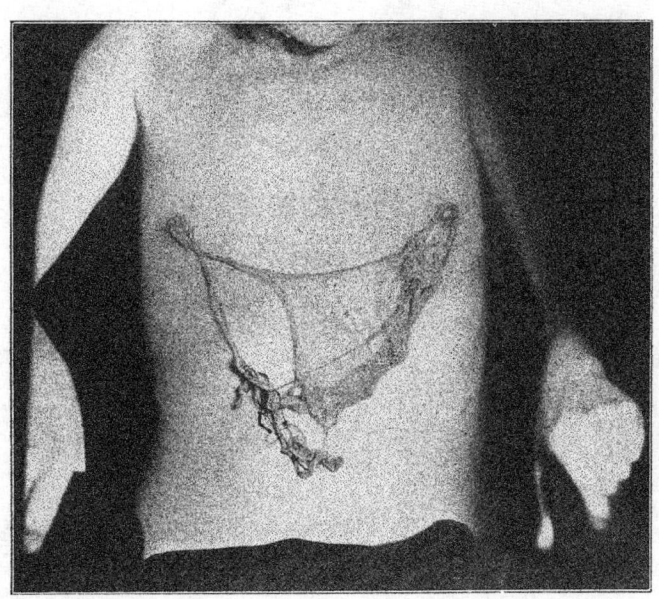

Fig 128. Mme Bisson's flashlight photograph of 5 January, 1913 (Retouched.)

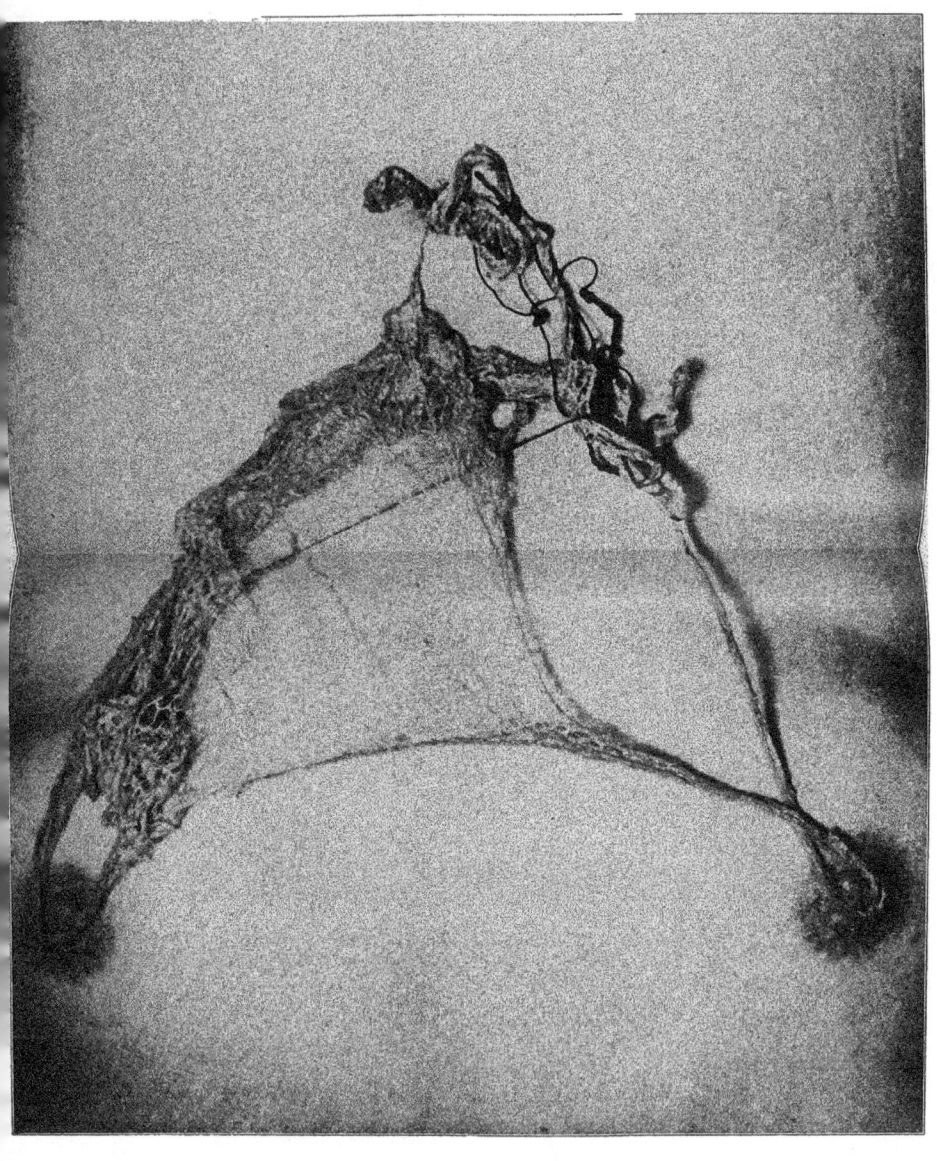

FIG 129 ENLARGEMENT FROM FIG 128

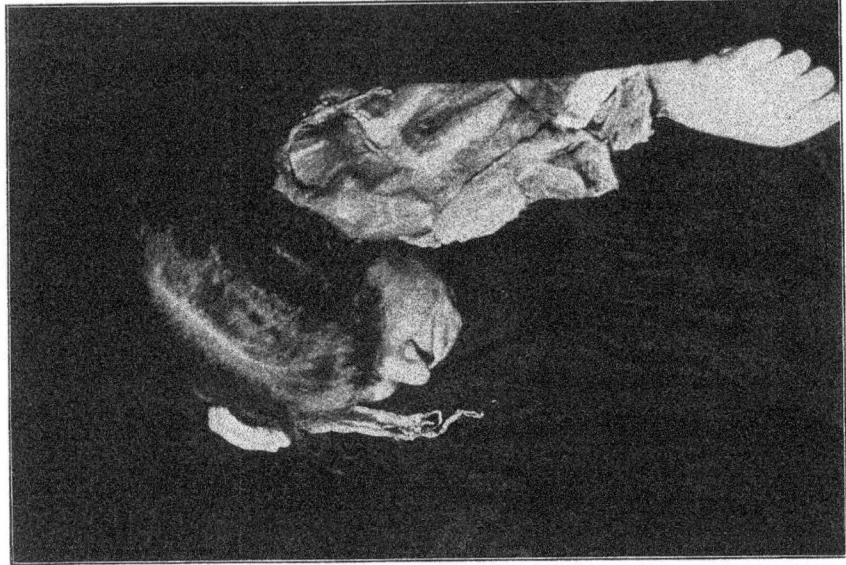

Fig. 131. Mme. Bisson's second flashlight photograph of 6 January, 1913.

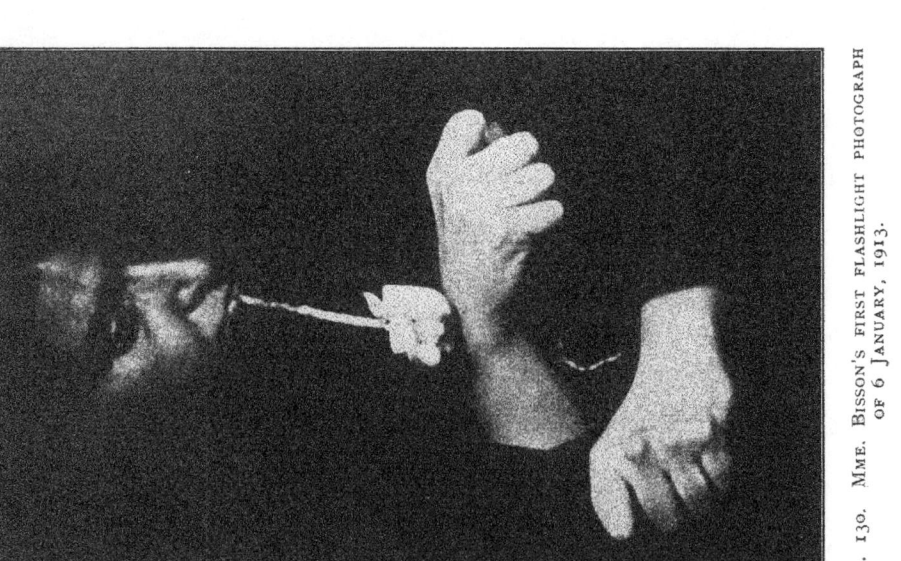

Fig. 130. Mme. Bisson's first flashlight photograph of 6 January, 1913.

photographed at Munich on 10th September 1912, was made on 30th December. The image, resembling a crumpled and then smoothed-out sheet of paper, is fastened to the medium's hair at her left temple, and casts a shadow on her face, which is turned to the right. Under the mouth a piece seems to be torn out at right angles. The dark-shaded portion corresponding to the hair is prolonged downward disproportionately, and shows a number of deep creases and rectangular superpositions of the same thin, paper-like substance, giving the impression as if they were laid or stuck on. The design of the face leaves no doubt that this portrait is intended to represent the woman photographed at Munich on 10th September. The outer margins of the profile are torn, especially at the nose, and in other ways the outside of this object is too defective and crumpled to permit a detailed comparison. As regards the experimental conditions, the medium's hands were not once withdrawn during the sitting, being at the curtain under Mme. Bisson's eyes, so that the medium could not use them.

The appearance of the same image, or type, of face or artistic production during sittings, separated by considerable intervals, has been observed on several occasions.

Sitting of the 5th January 1913.

Present.—Mme. Bisson.

The sitting of 5th January 1913, in which Mme. Bisson operated with the naked medium alone, shows a great step in advance, inasmuch as she succeeded for the first time in photographing the teleplasm on the medium's naked body. The illumination was the same as in all the sittings. During this sitting also the hands did not leave the curtain, and were therefore controlled from beginning to end in such a way that the medium could not use them.

The first photograph of 5th January (Fig. 127) shows the hypnotised medium with open eyes holding the curtains open.

According to Mme. Bisson's report, the photographed material came from the region of the navel (as if emerging from it), and moved like a living reptile in serpentine windings or jumps, upwards over the skin. Suddenly a thread-like connection was formed between the medium's mouth and the material. At that moment the flash-light was ignited. The material resembles a collection of skinny substance of intestinal origin, and is obviously composed of numerous loops, shreds, and strips. In spite of the disturbance by the flash-light, this packet of teleplastic matter did not disappear, but fastened itself with two loops formed out of the substance to the medium's teats, joining them to the navel in the shape of a three-cornered net, as shown in the second flash-light photograph (Figs. 128 and 129) of this sitting. The very remarkable product shows on the left a broad coherent strip, consisting of an irregular tangle of meshes of different sizes. The middle piece is stretched and transparent, so that the net-like character of the structure, and the medium's skin under it, are distinctly seen. The whole is traversed by irregular branches of varying thickness, which in turn are joined by a fine threadwork, in parallel lines, or in numerous small polygons, like a delicate stretched animal membrane. The lengths joining on to the teats and the navel consist of quite irregular thick cords of the same ground substance. Some black knotted threads, one of which cuts across the net, and is even woven into the meshes, do not differ in any way in appearance from textile fabrics (black yarn ?), and offer a striking contrast to the irregular structure closely resembling a natural product (mesentery), which forms the dominant characteristic of the phenomenon and shows itself in the projections, cords, and attachments.

Immediately after the second photograph, Mme. Bisson stood back in order to close the cameras. At that moment Eva arose, frightened by this disturbance, and still covered by the material, emerged from the cabinet, and sank fainting into Mme. Bisson's arms. At the same moment the mass disappeared. The medium recovered slowly under the care of her protectress.

Sitting of the 6th January 1913.

Present.—Mme. Bisson.

The first photograph (Fig. 130) of this day's sitting shows the hypnotised medium, whose hands remained under observation from beginning to end, with open eyes, head bent forward, and crossed hands, which hold the curtains. On her left wrist there lies a compact piece of white substance, with two finger-shaped attachments pointing forwards, while behind the left curtain a shred hangs down. The piece of material is joined to the mouth by an irregular cord.

Second photograph (Figs. 131, 132, and 133). Eva's left shoulder, from the left forearm to the ear, is covered by an obviously flat, deformed, and distorted face portrait, prepared on a soft base. The left curtain passes over the nose slantingly downwards. The right eye and the upper bridge of the nose are clearly drawn. There are several deep clefts at right angles to each other, as if the picture had been made by combining and superimposing several pieces. The substance itself has the same irregular character as before, and does not resemble the structure of textile fabrics or paper.

Of greater interest than this image are perhaps the two fragments of fingers lying on the hair over Eva's right temple, and consisting of three joints in a flexed position. Only about half of the third phalanx is visible. The position of the nail is clearly marked, especially in the front finger, and the whole drawing is finely executed. Not much can be said about its plastic development, since there are no stereoscopic photographs. The foundation substance does not show the histological structure of epidermis, but that of our teleplasm. The soft flowing lines of the drawing, and the covering of part of the lower line by the hair, are notable. A shred-like piece of material also hangs down on the right from Eva's hair on to her shoulder.

Sitting of the 9th January 1913.

Present.—Mme. Bisson.

Medium half naked, dressed only in the tights. The hands were

Fig. 132. First enlargement from Fig. 131.

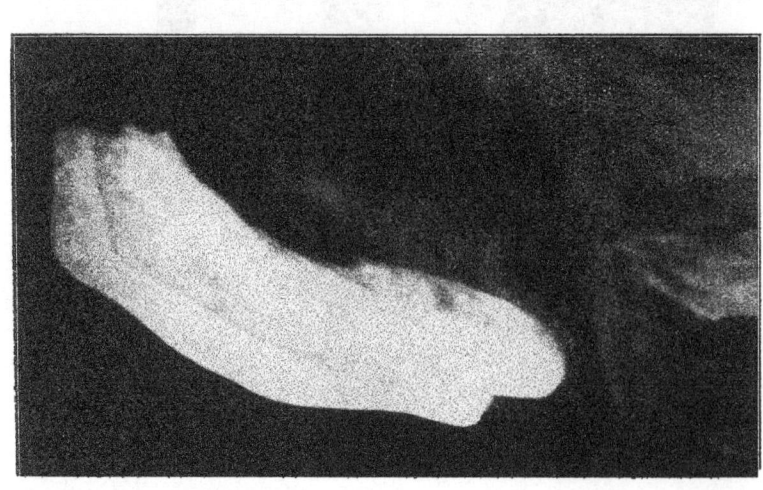

133. Second enlargement from Fig. 131.

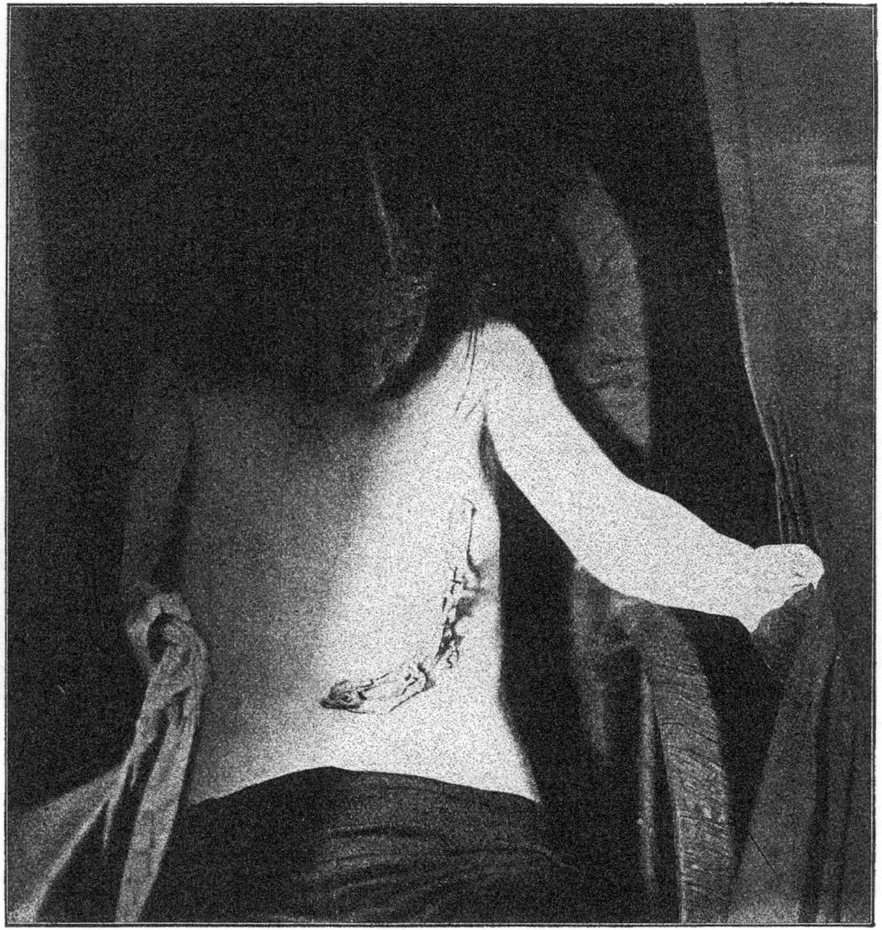

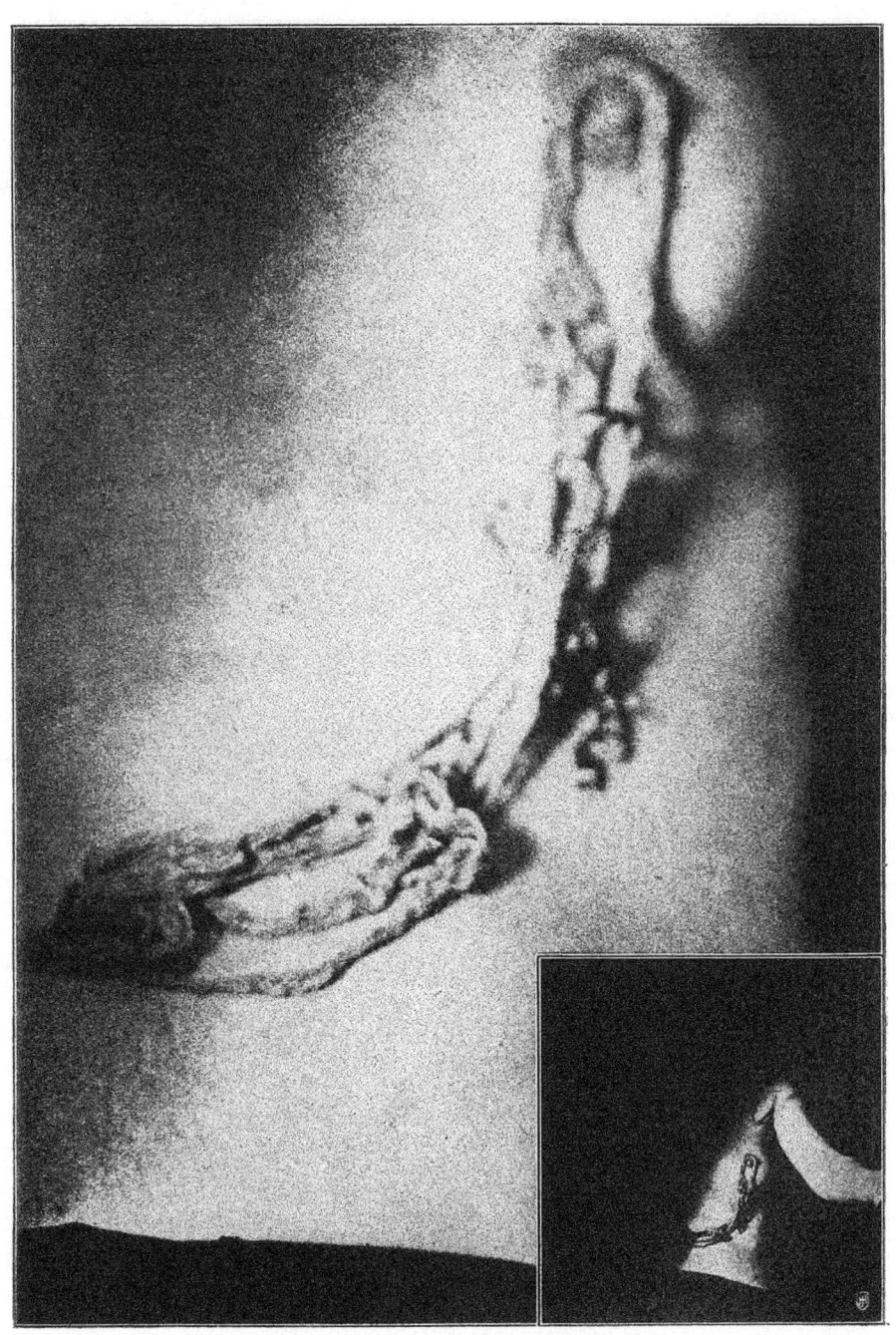

FIG 135. MME. BISSON'S FLASHLIGHT PHOTOGRAPH OF 9 JANUARY, 1913, WITH ENLARGEMENT FROM FIG. 134

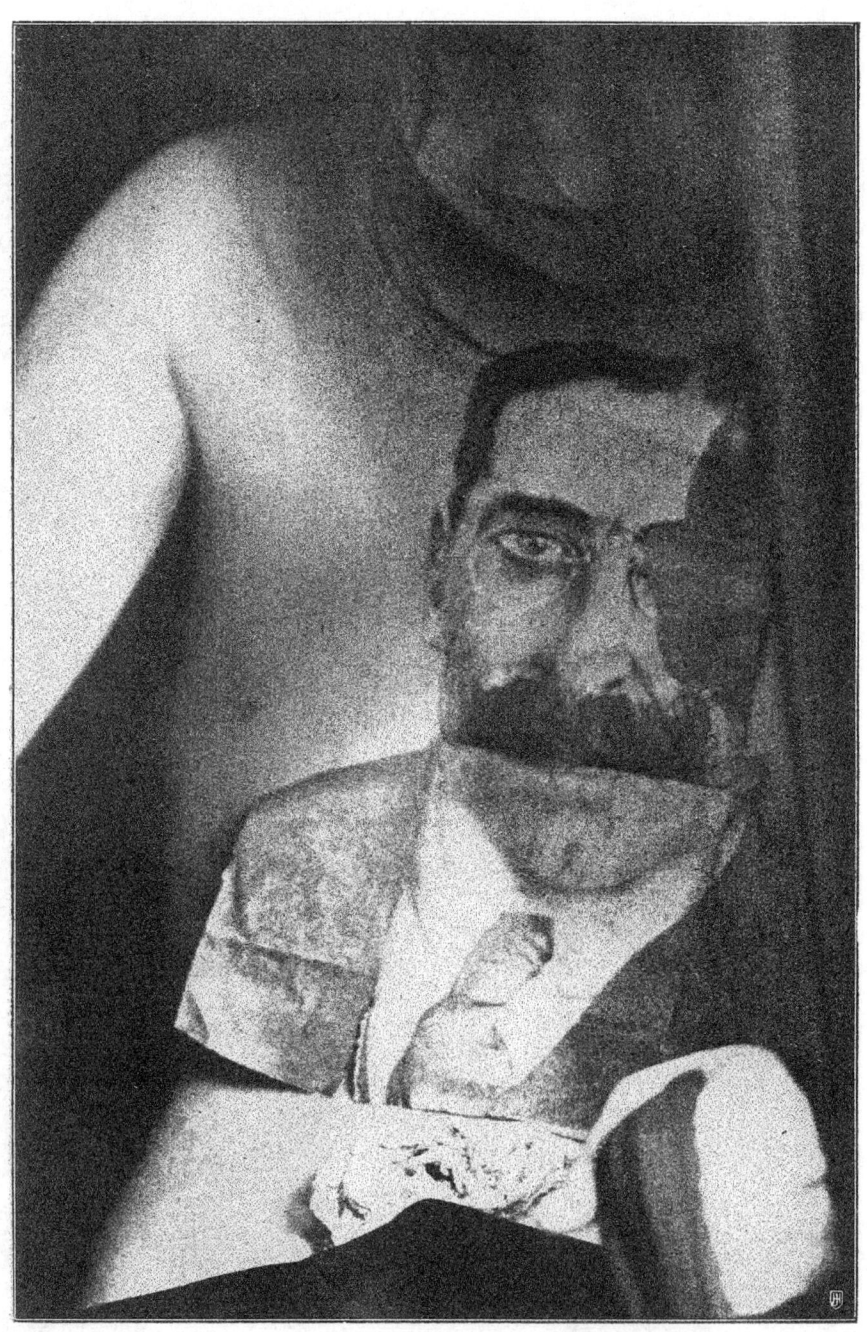

FIG. 136. MME. BISSON'S FLASHLIGHT PHOTOGRAPH OF 19 JANUARY, 1913.

visible at the curtain during the whole sitting, and took no part in the production of the phenomena.

This day the material formed itself at the teats and the navel, fastened itself with a cord on the left teat by an automatic motion, and joined itself below with the navel, which forms the centre of the end piece, and is clearly seen on the photograph (Figs. 134 and 135). As in the picture of the 5th January, the teleplastic substance is composed of cords, shreds, and strips in a free arrangement. In the sitting of 6th March Eva demonstrated the same phenomenon to the author on her bare skin in such a manner that he could, by his own eyes, confirm the accuracy of the photograph of 9th January. After the ignition of the magnesium powder on 9th January, Mme. Bisson endeavoured to withdraw carefully and slowly from the cabinet, in order to close the cameras. At that moment the teleplasm crept like a living thing with a rapid independent motion down the black tights on to the carpet, and, detached from the body of the medium, it crept outside the cabinet towards Mme. Bisson. When it had advanced about a yard in front of the curtain, Eva suddenly rose and fell forward on to the floor, covering the material with her body, and lay there in a faint. When she was lifted up nothing was to be seen, the substance having been apparently reabsorbed by her body.

Sitting of the 19th January 1913.

Present.—Mme. Bisson.

Conditions.—Medium nude, except for a black cloth over abdomen and feet. Hands visible at the curtain during the whole sitting. The photograph taken at this day's sitting (Fig. 136) marks an advance, inasmuch as the investigator succeeded in photographing, besides some teleplastic material, a male portrait on Eva's naked body.

We see the medium with head bent forward, holding the right curtain wide open, while the left curtain is tightly stretched, and cuts off the left side of the image.

Over the medium's navel there lies a packet of material of the same description as in the last sittings. The broad life-sized portrait, joined to it by a short ribbon, covers nearly the whole body, from the navel to the neck, and from one hip to the other, and is obviously a pictorial product on a thin or paper-like base, which seems to be cut out. It has several square folds, which clearly indicate a sheet regularly folded at right angles, and subsequently opened out.

We have here an artistically successful male face with a lively expression. The whole plan, the drawing and shading of the head, and especially the way in which the moustache is placed over the straight fold, are remarkable. The opening of the waistcoat, the tie, and the shape of the collar correspond to the modern fashion, and impart an up-to-date character to the picture.

The left forehead, the cheek, and the left eye are covered by a black sheet. A detailed observation shows that the middle of one eye is seen near the left temple displaced towards the outside, as if this displacement were due to a fault in the act of artistic creation.

The contemplation of this mediumistic product will no doubt give rise to the greatest misgivings on account of its paper-like, sharply cut, flat appearance, and the regular square creasing in the drawing itself. An unfolded picture smuggled in could hardly look different, unless we consider that the combination of fine detail, as in the drawing of eyes and forehead with coarse angular sketchiness (moustache) speaks for the originality of the design, and therefore against a stereotyped picture executed according to a definite artistic principle. Yet the creases and furrows of the picture fit together so accurately that the author was led to cut out the outlines of the head in paper after an enlargement and to fold it up according to the creases shown in the photograph, with the result that the various creases fitted accurately.

Sitting of the 13th February 1913.

Present.—Mme. Bisson.

Conditions.—Medium nude. The feet, resting on Mme. Bisson's knees, are covered with a black cloth reaching up towards the hips. Eva's hands do not leave the curtain during the whole sitting.

This day's flash-light photograph (Fig. 137), which only succeeded in the stereoscopic camera, shows again a face portrait on the bare skin.

Eva sits on the chair in the cabinet with her head bent forward, and opens the curtain with her right hand, while with the left she tries to draw it as a protection in front of the head, which covers the whole abdomen up to the breast. The flat male face shown in low relief gives a front view with the gaze directed towards the right. The nose is distorted and a failure. The right eye is distinctly recognisable, while the left eye is covered by Eva's left hand. The ground substance on which the form is developed seems to be soft, for it adapts itself to the contour of the body. The lower part of the face stands out in accordance with the convexity of the abdomen, while the region of the eye has sunk into Eva's waist. The forehead again bends upwards, corresponding to the position of the thorax while sitting.

Perhaps the most striking point about the face is the fully developed pointed beard, which emerges plastically from the basis, and seems to consist of a curly-haired or felt-like mass, unless we have to do with real hair, a point which cannot be decided from the photographs (*see* the stereoscopic photograph). The face is framed, very curiously, on the right side by a strip of white material, having the thickness of a finger, while the left side is hidden from observation by the medium's hand. On the second photograph of the 13th February Eva's right hand covers the forehead.

We may certainly conclude from the above details that the object is not a portrait drawn on paper, but is a flat mask in low relief, with a soft and fairly cohesive basis, but with quite a realistic development of the hairy portions. The shortened view of the half-concealed structure in the enlargement does not allow us to form an opinion as to the facial expression. But on the second (smaller) photograph the left eye is remarkably lively, whereas only a straight line of the thickness of a finger is there to indicate the moustache. Here also a rough,

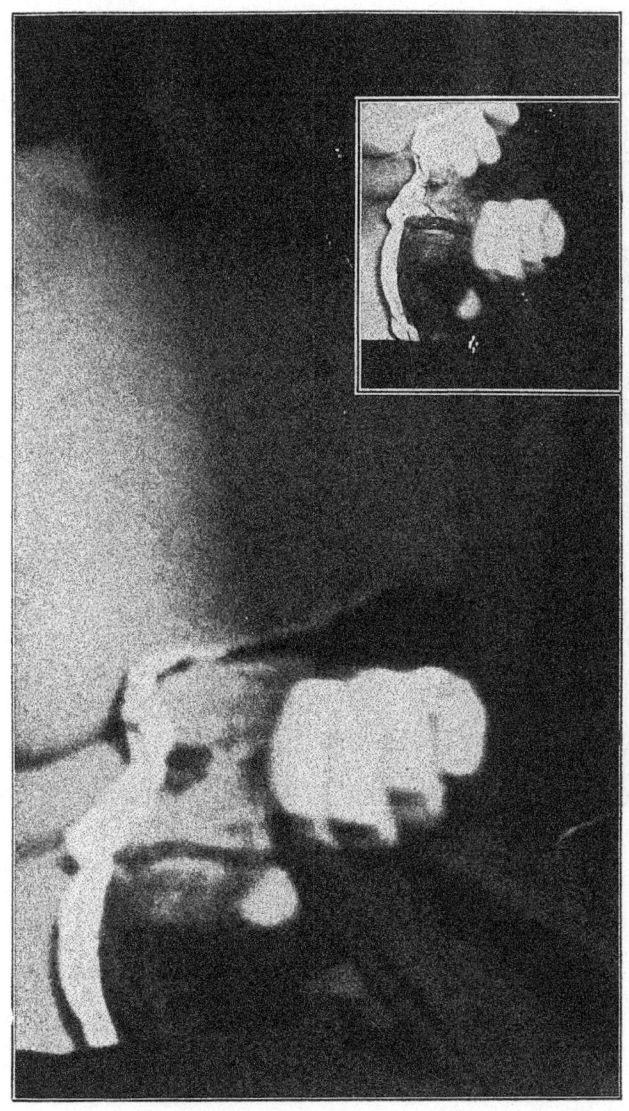

Fig 137   Two flashlight photographs taken by Mme. Bisson, 13 February, 1913.

FIG 138 MME. BISSON'S FLASHLIGHT PHOTOGRAPH OF 23 FEBRUARY, 1913 FIRST PHOTOGRAPH OF AN ENTIRE PHANTOM, TOGETHER WITH NUDE MEDIUM (RETOUCHED).

FIG. 139 SIMULTANEOUS VIEW OF FIG 138 FROM ABOVE (ROOF STEREOSCOPE).

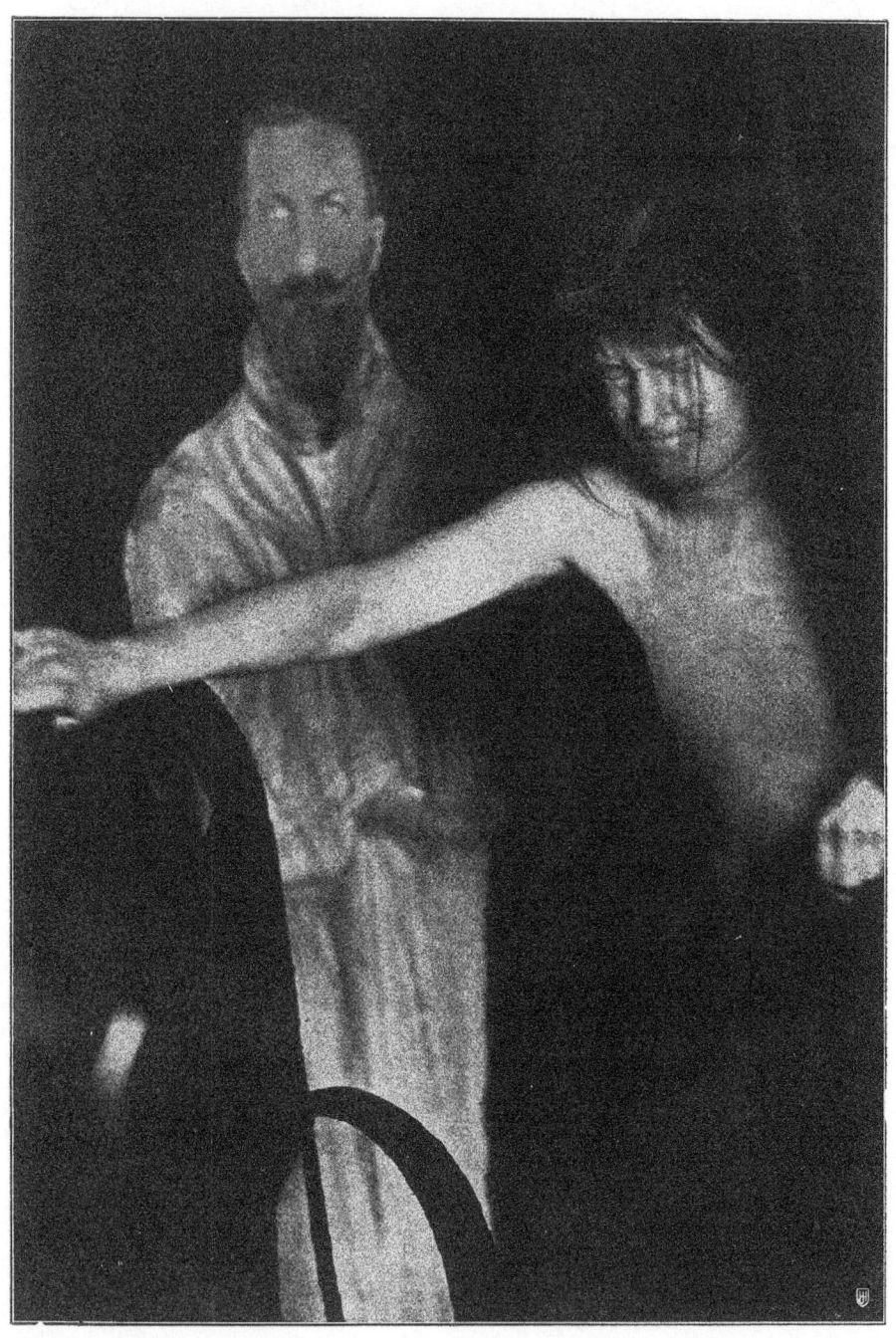

FIG. 140. MME BISSON'S FLASHLIGHT PHOTOGRAPH, SIMULTANEOUS WITH FIG 138. WHOLE PHANTOM, WITH NUDE MEDIUM. (RETOUCHED.)

wooden, sketchy scheme is combined with a lifelike expression as on the negative of 19th January.

SITTING OF THE 23RD FEBRUARY 1913.

Present.—Mme. Bisson.

Since 4 P.M. Eva complained of pains and swelling of the breasts. After dinner she suffered from palpitation. A sitting had not been planned for this Sunday evening. Still, Mme. Bisson was led by the medium's curious behaviour to hypnotise her in her day dress in the cabinet after supper. Hardly had Eva entered the trance condition when she asked to be undressed, threw off all her clothes, and discarded even the black cloth with which she had been covered during previous sittings.

A deep trance followed, but of a character different from that of previous sittings. Curiously enough, no material appeared on her body to-day. Suddenly, after about thirty minutes, on opening the curtain, a life-sized phantom with male features appeared behind Eva's chair in the corner of the cabinet, fully developed already at the first exposure. Eva rose, stepped aside, and opened the curtain with her right hand, in order not to cover the phantom with her body. Flashlight photograph. In spite of the shock the figure, which moved freely without feet, ending at the lower hem of its cloak, remained where it was, and allowed itself to be illuminated by Eva's electric torch six times in succession. In addition, Mme. Bisson switched on the red lamp in the background of the cabinet. A second photograph failed, because the phantom had withdrawn sideways out of the field of the camera. It disappeared without a trace in the direction of the back wall.

In the successful photographs (Figs. 138, 139 and 140) the nude medium stands at the left curtain, holding it with her left hand, while with her right hand she has opened the other curtain far enough to allow the phantom to be plainly seen. Her features express a strong, painful effort of will. On the photographs intended for publication, Eva's naked body was, for obvious reasons, retouched in such a way that the sex characteristics (breasts, etc.) are not seen.

The phantom, clad in a long white mantle, stands at the right-hand back wall of the cabinet, with crossed arms, and upward gaze, and, by its height and attitude, gives an impression of solemnity. The face is complete, without fragments, shreds, etc., as seen so often on former heads. The face is long and oval, the forehead high and narrow, the nose long, broad, and well developed, there is a long pointed beard and a well-arranged moustache, and the left ear is clearly outlined. A broad coat collar covers the throat, which is wrapped up. In the triangular opening two buttons are visible, as of a waistcoat. The left hand disappears in the white mantle, resembling a bathing wrap. We only see a triangular black patch, while, on the right hand, fingers are indicated. The regular features express earnestness and dignity, as in a conventional Christ-head.

While the face of the phantom appears entirely pictorial and flat, like a drawing (this is corroborated by the foreshortened stereoscopic picture taken from the roof of the cabinet), the cloak, on comparing the various photographs, seems to show a certain reality in its material composition. Yet the figure as a whole gives a unified and harmonious impression. A detailed study of the stereoscopic transparency, with its strongly foreshortened image taken from the roof of the cabinet, leaves no doubt that two parallel folds or rents traverse the whole mantle vertically, as if it had three divisions, and opened to both sides.

On the negative of Fig. 138, and in the stereoscopic photographs (from the front and from above), a sickle-shaped, cloud-like structure is seen above the medium's right hand. This is not due to a fault in the plate, but had a real existence, though it cannot be explained. Perhaps we have here a physical accompaniment of the materialisation process.

By the success of the sitting of 23rd February, the four years of Mme. Bisson's self-sacrificing activity were deservedly rewarded. For her, and for every impartial observer in her position, the actuality of the production of phantoms by mediumistic power must be considered as proved, especially as more rigorous experimental conditions could hardly be imagined. Indeed, in the whole literature of occultism, in so far as it is to be taken seriously, there is no proof of observations of teleplastic projections simultaneously visible with a nude medium. Photographs of phantom and medium on the same plate are a great rarity. But a naked medium, deprived of every chance of concealing materials for the artificial production of the phenomena, photographed on the same plate with the phantom, is unprecedented.

Sittings during February and March 1913.

SITTING OF THE 26TH FEBRUARY 1913.

Present.—Mme. Bisson and the author.

CONDITIONS as in November 1912, but the medium, at the request of the two physicians, Dr Bourbon and Dr R., who attended several sittings, undresses in her room and enters the séance room dressed only in a blue dressing-gown. Here she receives the séance costume from the physicians (in this sitting from me), puts it on behind the screen, and is then sewn into it in the presence of the sitters, after an examination of her body surface. She had therefore neither time, nor opportunity, to hide any object on her person. Then the sitting commences as usual after the hypnotisation of the medium.

The illumination is still brighter, as now six red lamps are used. No result.

SITTING OF THE 27TH FEBRUARY 1913.

Present.—Mme. Bisson and the author.

Conditions as on the 26th. Nose, mouth, arm-pits, hair, and body surface examined by the author as before.

SITTINGS DURING FEBRUARY AND MARCH 1913

Mme. Bisson hypnotises the medium more deeply, with urgent suggestions to show a phantom.

The hands were laid on the medium's knees in front of the curtain before the white light was switched off, and were held by Mme. Bisson, and remained in that position, or in a crosswise position, or visibly held by Mme. Bisson's hands, until the end of the sitting, without ever withdrawing themselves from control by a withdrawal into the cabinet.

The curtain was also open during the whole sitting, in the sense that there was always a narrow gap through which one could see Eva's head. Her feet were stretched out in front of the curtain, and were held by those of Mme. Bisson. The record was kept by the author during the sitting.

9.5 P.M. Beginning of the sitting. Immediate deep stertorous breathing and expirations. Hands continually visible at the curtain.

9.10 P.M. A white shred-like, rather broad, flat mass emerges from her mouth and falls over her left shoulder and left breast.

9.15 P.M. Continual whimpering. A flat mask-like structure is seen on the left shoulder.

9.20 P.M. Suggestion by Mme. Bisson. " Détache-toi bien." Hands still visible.

9.21 P.M. During the next exposure I distinctly saw the male face already photographed by Mme. Bisson on the naked body of the medium. It gives the impression of a flat, somewhat diagrammatic, bearded mask. The face is framed in a kind of ring-shaped wall, and the face photographed on the 13th February is distinctly recognised.

9.22 P.M. Eva takes Mme. Bisson's hands, as if she wanted to strengthen herself by the touch. The structure is now visible in Eva's lap, and disappears from my eyes while the curtain is open.

9.23 P.M. No trace left.

9.25 P.M. Neither on her breast, nor in her lap, nor on her head, is there a trace of the structure. She sometimes puts her head into the curtain gap, when she wishes to touch it with her finger, to push her hair from her face.

9.26 P.M. She now holds the curtain with crossed hands, moans, and appears to make great muscular efforts in order that the form may be seen again.

9.30 P.M. She puts out her head, without altering the position of the hands, to ask if we see anything, to which we say " No."

9.36 P.M. She asks Mme. Bisson to hold her hands, in order to gain power.

9.40 P.M. Strong whimpering, with a distinct sensation that the face will be seen again.

9.44 P.M. At her request, Mme. Bisson enters the cabinet, opening the left curtain widely so that she can be seen. She holds Eva's head in her hands, encourages her, and emerges again.

9.46 P.M. The structure is again seen on the left breast, but appears less developed and less solid than in the first impression. It looks like a transparent white mask. We abstain from photographing it, hoping that the form will become more distinct.

9.48 P.M. Eva lays her head on the hands which still visibly hold the curtain. The gap becomes very narrow, since the hands touch each other.

9.50 p.m. Nothing more is seen, and everything seems to have disappeared. Hands still at the curtain.
9.56 p.m. New efforts by Eva.
10.1 p.m. Mme. Bisson again takes Eva's hands.
10.10 to 10.15 p.m. The medium rests, and no further sounds are heard.
10.16 p.m. Eva has the impression that she cannot produce anything more. Close of the sitting. Final examination of the medium and the cabinet negative.

Result of the Sitting.—Appearance, disappearance, and change of position of a mask-like male face, without the co-operation of the medium's hands.

Sitting of the 4th March 1913.

Present.—Mme. Bisson, Dr R., Dr Bourbon, and the author.

The medium, completely undressed and clad only in a blue dressing-gown, enters the room and puts on the carefully examined séance costume in our presence. While Dr R. examines the arm-pits and the mouth, with the help of a silver spoon, Dr Bourbon undoes the medium's hair and puts it up again, having found nothing remarkable, and also examines her ears. Blowing through each nostril shows that the nose is free.

9.14 p.m. After examination of the cabinet, Mme. Bisson hypnotises the medium in the white electric light. The medium's hands are on her knees, and are held by Mme. Bisson.
9.15 p.m. Extinction of the white light. Illumination by six red lamps.
9.17 p.m. Hands still held by Mme. Bisson.
9.18 p.m. Hands released, but rest on medium's knees, visible to us.
9.35 p.m. Some efforts to produce phenomena.
9.43 p.m. Mme. Bisson again takes Eva's hands and makes energetic suggestions towards production.
9.50 p.m. Eva crosses her hands.
9.57 p.m. The trance seems to have deepened, and we hear plaintive whispering and long forced expirations. Apparently the process of materialisation is commencing, although it encounters great resistance.
10.1 p.m. An object appears on the medium's breast.
10.5 p.m. Dr R. holds Eva's left hand, Dr Bourbon the right. The curtain is half opened.
10.10 p.m. On the left shoulder there is a shred, clearly produced from the mouth.
10.15 p.m. Emanation process from the mouth continues. Since the head is exposed to the light, we clearly see a ribbon-shaped piece hanging from the mouth. As Dr R. finds by touch, the dress has become moist and sticky in some places on the chest.
10.21 p.m. Mme. Bisson opens the seams and takes off Eva's tunic, so that she sat dressed only in the tights.
10.22 p.m. The medium's hands are held by the physicians as before. Eva is embarrassed, crosses her arms, and tries to conceal her breast from the two men.

10.25 P.M. Some dark grey patches, the size of a florin, appear on the skin, especially on the left breast, but the appearances are too fugitive to form a definite opinion.

10.40 P.M. The emotion of the medium at being unclothed in the presence of men is obviously very strong, and produces inhibitions which do not allow of the development of the phenomena, which on this day are weak in any case.

11.10 P.M. Closing of the sitting. Final control negative. While, on the one hand, the method of this day presents a step in advance, inasmuch as the medium was made to produce her remarkable power in a nude condition, we see, on the other hand, that the process of emanation is exceedingly easily hindered, and brought to a stop, by psychological conditions, since the medium feels herself hemmed in by the too rigorous procedure of the experimenters, or by the premature exposure to the light of the phenomenon in a nascent state, followed by critical analysis from every side. This possibly explains the fact that the intensity of the phenomena diminishes, as the methods of observation become more exact.

Sitting of the 6th March 1913.

Present.—Mme. Bisson and the author.

Eva enters the séance room at 8.30 P.M. dressed only in the dressing-gown. In my presence, she takes it off and puts on the carefully examined séance costume. She opens her mouth, sounds vowels, and blows through her nostrils. Arm-pits, hair, and ears are examined.

When it is proved that she has nothing concealed anywhere by which she could produce the phenomena, she takes her seat in the cabinet, which has also been previously examined, and is hypnotised by Mme. Bisson in my presence. During the whole sitting the hands are visible, either lying on her knees or holding the curtain.

8.45 P.M. Mme. Bisson holds Eva's hands. The white light is switched off.

8.49 P.M. Mme. Bisson releases the hands which now hold the curtain. The curtain itself remains more or less open during the whole sitting.

8.50 P.M. The medium is obviously resisting. Her whole expression shows the absence of the deeper trance.

8.55 P.M. " Demande bien, ma petite Juliette." Groans and exertions of the ventral muscles.

9 P.M. More violent efforts. Condition of "mediumistic labour," deep long-drawn expirations.

9.3 P.M. " Cela me prend, Juliette."

9.5 P.M. Hands still visible, lying on her knees, and holding the curtain. As soon as she opens her knees, I see between them, in a fold of the dress, a strip about 3 or 4 inches long and about the thickness of a pencil, of a pink colour, the first sign of a positive sitting.

9.8 P.M. At various parts of her dress, and in her lap, small pink lines and points become visible, obviously material emanating from her body through the dress, and now forming a sort of precipitate. This substance seems to be partly liquid, and partly solid, its density comparable with that of a very delicate web. On touching the luminous portions, they feel moist and sticky.

9.11 P.M. Hands still visible.
9.15 P.M. Greater exertions.
9.16 P.M. " Je le sens, Juliette."
9.20 P.M. Hands crossed at the curtain.
9.22 P.M. Plaintive whimpering. Mme. Bisson holds her hands to encourage her, and then releases them again.
9.30 P.M. Pause for rest. Hands visible.
9.35 P.M. " Cela vient, je le sens."
9.38 P.M. We now see the distinctly formed bearded face, in front of her head, like a mask. As her head moves, the lower part of this picture swings to and fro, and gives the impression that it consists of a soft, skinny substance.

9.40 P.M. During the next exposure a ribbon nearly an inch wide, with ragged, irregular edges, becomes visible between her hands. On opening her knees and then separating her hands, this band stretches to a length of 8 to 10 inches. Suddenly, while her hands are at rest, this band is jerked upwards towards her head, as if drawn from above, the middle of the band going first, and then disappearing in the region of her mouth. One cannot say whether this material was reabsorbed by Eva's organism, or simply served to build up the materialised face. In any case, the appearance was remarkable.

9.41 P.M. I took a photograph at the next exposure. Unfortunately, Eva just then closed the curtain, so that the first series was not successful.

9.47 P.M. After the plates were changed, the second exposure was made, Mme. Bisson, sitting in front of the curtain, pressing the electric button.

9.50 to 9.55 P.M. The image was seen a few more times and disappeared, although the hands, from the beginning of the sitting until now, had never been withdrawn from our gaze. Eva, being anxious to show the automatic mobility of the substance, herself proposes to take off the tunic.

10 P.M. Mme. Bisson opens the seams, takes off the tunic, and Eva is only dressed in the tights, her upper body being nude.

10.3 P.M. She opens and closes the curtains alternately, to allow of the development of the material on her body in the dark, and then to expose the products for a short time to the red light.

10.5 P.M. During several exposures I saw distinctly a self-moving, net-like, skinny mass, about the size of a plate, and in the form of a shred with a long strip attached, depending from her left breast. Before my eyes, this mass detached itself and disappeared in the region of the navel. The optical impression corresponds approximately to the pictures taken by Mme. Bisson on 9th January 1913. My subsequent observation, therefore, confirmed the correctness of the photograph. Since such a photograph is already in our possession, no new photograph was attempted to-day.

10.10 P.M. Eva demonstrates a few times more, with portions of substance in the form of knots the size of walnuts, as well as packets and veils, on her neck and upper body. These structures did not

FIG. 141. AUTHOR'S FIRST FLASHLIGHT PHOTOGRAPH OF 6 MARCH, 1913.
(FROM ABOVE, INSIDE CABINET.)

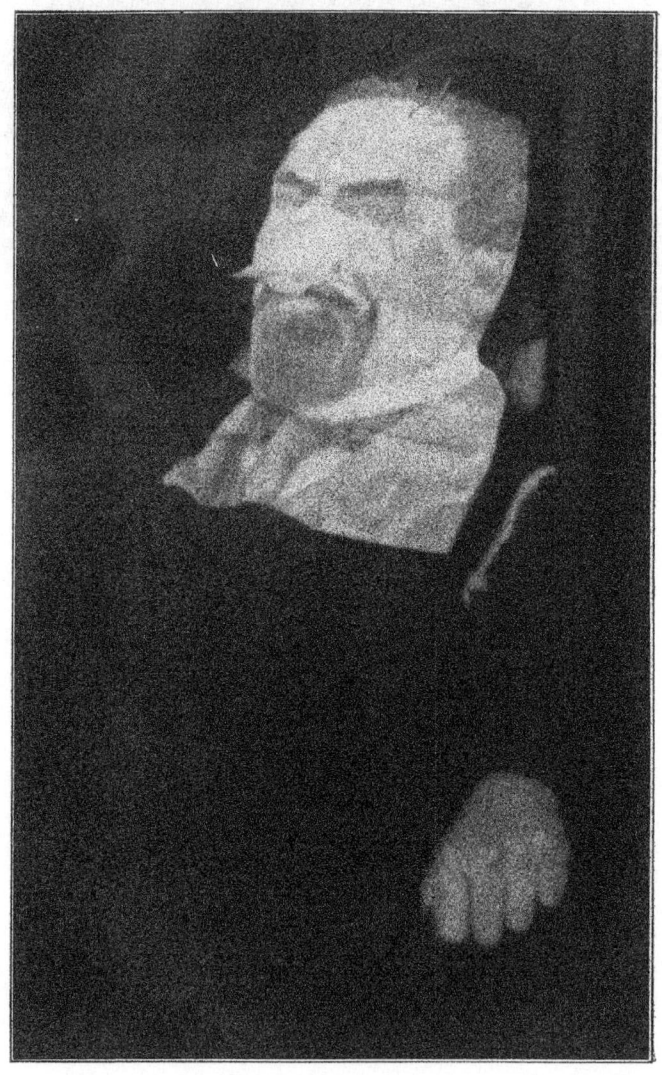

FIG. 142. AUTHOR'S SECOND PHOTOGRAPH. 6 MARCH, 1913.

withstand the light, they always disappeared, even after a few seconds of exposure to light.

10.20 P.M. Close of the sitting. Eva's skin is covered by a viscous moisture, on her left breast and in the places where we saw the material. The tunic itself is quite permeated with moisture near the left breast, and shows several moist patches on the inside and outside.

Final control of medium and cabinet negative.

While the first flash-light photograph, taken by the cameras in front of the cabinet, was a failure, the negative of the stereoscope mounted inside the cabinet above the medium's head shows a curious result, which is the same in both pictures (Fig. 141).

We look down from above on to the seat of the chair, which stands outside the curtain, and both the medium's hands holding the curtain are visible. With a magnifying glass we can even recognise the sleeve of the left forearm. To the right of it, in a corner of the cabinet, *i.e.*, at an approximate distance of 43 inches from Eva's body, we see a white structure consisting of a compact, irregularly shaped head-piece, the size of an adult female fist, to which is attached a curved tail-piece, about half an inch thick and about 12 inches long. The shape resembles that of a spermatozoon or neuroblast. The material of which it is composed must be strongly self-luminous, and shows a feeble aura, otherwise the camera would not have made so clear an image of it. Since the dark cabinet contains no self-luminous objects, and since white textile products or white paper possess no luminosity in the dark, it can only be a case of a materialisation product which corresponds to observations in other sittings. Repeatedly we saw white luminous strips, with the head-like attachment, apparently of a textile nature, and more or less long, which altered in shape and size, and were detached from the medium's body. We have, therefore, here probably a primitive materialisation in an embryonic state, the appearance of which corresponds to organic structures known in nature. It appears to float freely. This phenomenon also belongs to those which can hardly be imitated artificially.

As regards technique, flatness, and artistic design, the author's second flash-light photograph (Figs. 142, 143, and 144) of 6th March closely resembles the photograph taken by Mme. Bisson on 19th January. As in previous observations, the male portrait drawn on paper or thin fabric, and cut out sharply, is fastened to the right side of Eva's head, covering it almost completely. The folds of the foundation material cut across the image in sharp parallel lines, and even, to some extent, interfere with the artistic impression, as at the point of the beard. The whole nose is covered by shreds of material folded several times. The manner in which the hair of the beard is treated (by short strokes), as well as the collar and eyeglasses, allows of no doubt that we have here a pictorial sketch. The treatment of the eyebrows and eyeglasses resembles the picture of M. Bisson obtained on 1st June 1912.

As the portrait of 19th January, so also the present one shows the shirt front and tie. The expression of the eyes is peculiarly life-like, and the image appears to be fastened to Eva's hair by threads or a pin. The conception, composition, artistic execution, and technical treatment of the material, as well as the impressionistic rendering of the theme, indicate the same artistic individual as that indicated by the authorship of numerous previous portraits. Born of the same artistic intuition, they prove themselves to be different works of the same hand.

Observations in March, April and May 1913 (Paris).

SITTING OF THE 24TH MARCH 1913.

Present.—Mme. Bisson.

IN a letter, dated 26th March 1913, Mme. Bisson writes:—" On Monday evening I hypnotised Eva in the cabinet in the red light as usual. She wore her day dress, since, owing to her unfavourable psychic disposition, I did not expect any phenomena this day.

" I took her hands and suggested to her ' Go to sleep quickly.' She at once fell back into her chair, and immediately afterwards arose, already in the trance condition, and said, ' He is there, he is there! Undress me quickly!' She almost tore her dress off, and I helped her until she was quite undressed. Then she seized my hands and pressed them violently, with the words, ' Look, look! He forms himself! He is there!' I thought I saw something large on the back wall of the cabinet, to my left. Eva remained standing, leaning against me, then pressed my hands, stood back a pace and screamed with pain, while her whole body was shaken with convulsions. She cried out, ' Touch the cord on my back.' I stretched out my hand and felt under her waist a moist cord-like structure which joined Eva with the phantom. The cord detached itself while Eva leant against me. I saw the phantom illuminated. It consisted of a long, broad strip standing vertically on the floor, at the top of which I recognised a face. Eva stretched back her arm, and the broad strip wound itself once round it, while the head-piece pointed vertically upward.

" After the structure had detached itself again, Eva called out, ' See how he forms himself! Press my hand hard to give me power.' I now saw with my own eyes how the phantom broadened out, how the shoulders took shape, and I used this moment to take a flash-light photograph, fearing that the vision might disappear. It is probably the same form as that of 23rd February. Unfortunately, I had no time to prepare all the cameras, and only the two large ones were in action.

" With the ignition of the magnesium powder, everything disappeared. The whole occurrence happened in a few minutes, and already at 9.30 I could put the girl to bed. The subsequent examination of the cabinet was also negative to-day. On the following day Eva had no recollection of what had happened, and did not know that the phantom had returned.

" For me the proof is complete. The recollection of the sitting of Monday can never be effaced."

At the first sight one recognises the apparition of 23rd February. There is the same head, the same broad, long white cloak, and the arms crossed over the breast, but the head is less distinct this time. The whole appearance resembles an old portrait, painted on wood, and

FIG. 143 SIDE VIEW, ENLARGED, OF FIG 142.

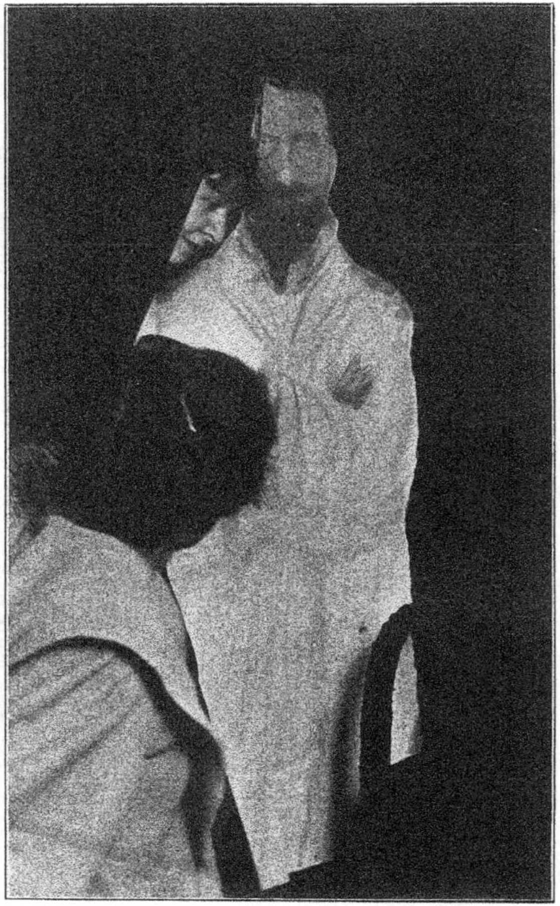

FIG. 145. MME. BISSON'S FLASHLIGHT PHOTOGRAPH OF

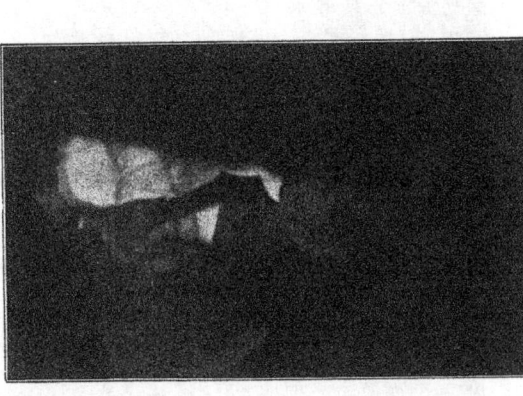

FIG. 144. SIDE VIEW OF FIG. 142, TAKEN FROM INSIDE THE CABINET.

rather badly preserved. While the apparition of the 23rd February showed eyes turned upwards and towards the right, so that the whites were distinctly visible, the look of the phantom of 24th March is straightforward, without the sideways position of the eyes. The lids are smaller and less open. The left ear of the 23rd February gives the impression of a completely modelled shape. Over the outer temple, on the right, there is a vertical, straight, and deep cleft, with irregular margins. A narrow piece ending it hangs outside on the head, as if torn off, or perhaps the process of composition is not quite complete. On the left part of the forehead there is a long, black patch. The outlines of the rather vague, full beard are on the whole the same as before. The buttons closing the cloak at the top are also the same in both pictures; while the coat collar in the picture of 23rd February ends in a rectangular cut crossing the larynx on the right, that same ending is now on the left side. The opposite side, on both negatives, is lower and more open. The upper edge of the cloak on 24th March, which looks as if drawn by hand, shows a torn hem, in contrast with the soft regular lines shown in the negative of 23rd February.

Four fingers of the left hand, in two of which the nails are indicated by white patches, are clearly seen in the photograph of 24th March. The outer lines are very rough and sketchy, like a painter's sketch of a hand for a picture, and seem to lose themselves in the background. The cloak itself occupies a much wider space in this new photograph than it did on 23rd February, with the left sleeve passing at right angles across the cloak, thus enlarging the upper outline of the figure, in contrast with the lower part. In consequence of the folds which broaden out downwards, the left marginal line of to-day's phantom is straight, without allowing the sleeve to project, as on 23rd February. The phantom appears to end at the lower hem of the mantle.

The photograph of 24th March (Figs. 145 and 146), as a whole, gives the impression of a flat drawing, on a foundation having a pattern like linen. While on both pictures the heads appear flat (which is confirmed by the cleft in the second picture), the mantle in the first picture shows soft, deep creases, and, looking stereoscopically from above, the observer does not get the impression of a flat drawing. Unfortunately, there are no plates available for 24th March other than the picture here reproduced. The arrangement of the folds is different from that of 23rd February, being less developed, flatter, and more like an outline drawn with a pencil. Yet the outer margin, when magnified, shows fibres and threads which suggest a fibrous material.

Of the medium herself, the only thing visible this time is the head, half cut off by the curtain. From a comparison of the two pictures, it is therefore quite clear that on 23rd February and on 24th March we have two different representations of the same object, of the same personification. The differences between the pictures taken of the same type, but on different evenings, may be compared with the different poses of a person at a photographer's, and are mainly due to different positions of the body, owing to displacement and changes in the external lines and the folds of the dress thus produced. If we had to deal with an object smuggled in for the sake of a ghost apparition, i.e., with a finished product on a rigid foundation, there would have to be at least two representations of the same head, with different positions of the eyes, for in this case the medium would certainly have had to exhibit a different face on 24th March from that shown on 23rd February. Although this assumption appears very improbable on comparing the two pictures of the same type, the smuggling in of a whole phantom is already excluded by the experimental conditions of the two sittings.

From the point of view of teleplastic projection, the differences of the two representations of the same phantom are very interesting. The same optical conception of a portrait endeavours to realise itself on two evenings by means of the psycho-physical energy at the medium's disposal, with the result that the identity of the type twice represented is proved, while the numerous changes and differences of the two pictures indicate mobility and variability of the artistic will behind the scenes in the details and shades of the conception, as well as the incompleteness in the material process of creation.

As in nearly all the teleplastic formations observed by us, the elementary formative principle never produces rigid and unchangeable products, but the photographed emanations always indicate a mobile, soft material basis, which is highly changeable and rapidly perishable.

Sitting of the 1st April 1913.

On 1st April 1913, in the author's absence, but under the usual experimental conditions (strict initial examination, searching of the mouth and hair, etc., and hands visible at the curtain during the whole sitting), in the presence of Dr Bourbon and M. Bourdet (an author), a long cord-like structure was photographed (Figs. 147 and 148), consisting of two ribbons, one of which hung down in the form of a long torn shred as far as the waist, while the other was looped round an anatomically well-developed finger, consisting of three joints, so that the flexed finger appeared to be held by a loop passing round the second joint. The nail position was distinctly developed, and under the first joint a crease is visible, produced by the bending of the first and second joints. Although we have here quite a plastically developed finger in the natural size of an adult female hand, one cannot make out, in the enlargement of the picture, whether the surface of the fragment has the characteristic appearance of human skin. The material of the strip by which the finger is suspended is fixed at its upper end to the breast of the tunic, and resembles in form and composition the other teleplastic products.

Sitting of the 2nd May 1913.

Before the sitting of 2nd May (also in the author's absence), Dr Bourbon arranged experimental conditions of increased rigidity, by proposing that Eva's entire head, after she had been sewn into the séance costume, should be surrounded by a veil, fastened to the neck all round by sewing. In addition, Eva's hands at this sitting also remained constantly at the curtain. Under the conditions named, a male head picture developed in Eva's lap, its lower part separated by a neck-piece, while the upper pointed freely upwards, and was not

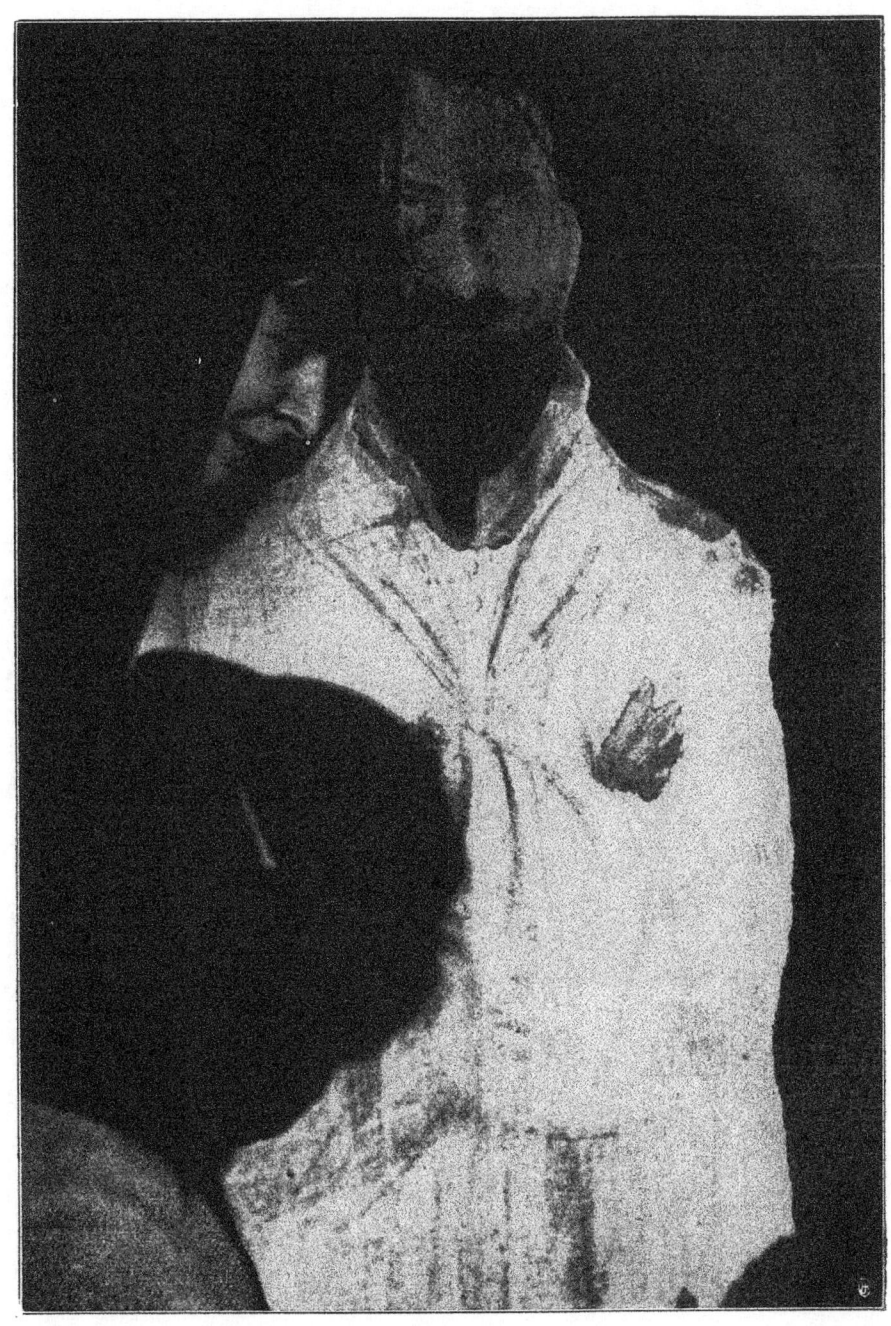

FIG 146 ENLARGEMENT OF FIG. 145.

FIG. 147. MME. BISSON'S FLASHLIGHT PHOTOGRAPH OF 1 APRIL, 1913

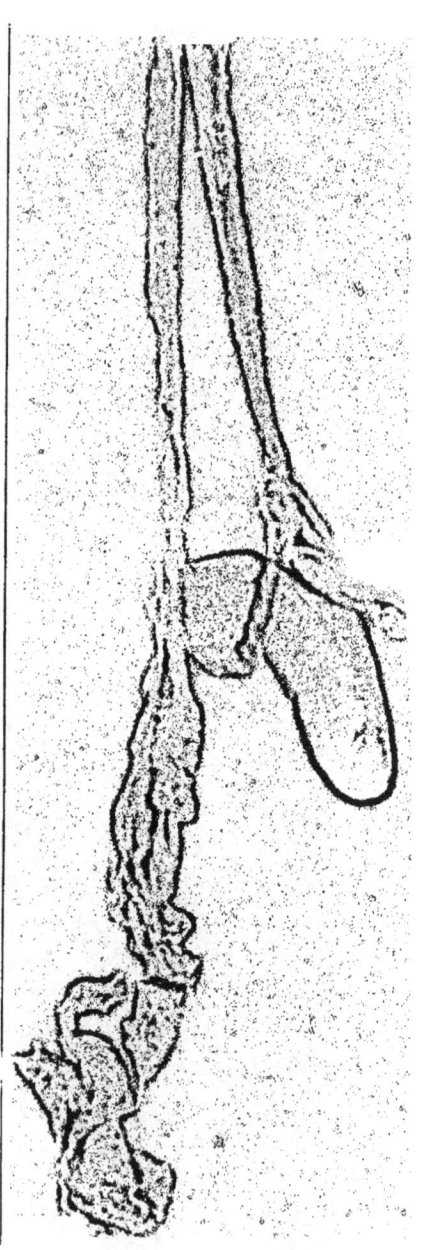

FIG. 148 ENLARGEMENT OF FIG 147.

leaning against the dress. This product (Fig. 149) shows all the characteristics already seen in previous creations.

Upon the forehead of the portrait (which looks as if cut out of paper, with a sharp margin and rents at the top), we clearly see a square piece of the same structure as the rest of the picture, stuck on. Numerous creases, some of which are parallel, traverse the face—one of the most noticeable of these being a crease passing in a straight line from the mouth to the ear, this rent being in turn traversed at right angles by another passing over the upper jaw. Numerous smaller bunches of creases suggest a folded paper subsequently smoothed out. The right eye, which is somewhat deformed, appears pressed slantingly inwards, in contrast to the correctly placed left eye. The lower jaw is remarkably short. The broad correctly shaped nose, the compressed mouth, the lively expression of the eyes, and the look towards the left, give the impression of a great liveliness in the whole artistic treatment, which is shown by the eyeglasses and the beard, as obviously that of a charcoal or pencil drawing. The whole design, the technical treatment and composition, admit of no doubt that this creation is from the hand of the same unknown author as the rest of the male pictures of the last series.

Sittings in May and June 1913 (Paris).

SITTINGS OF THE 6TH AND 7TH MAY 1913.

Negative.

SITTING OF THE 9TH MAY 1913.

Present.—Mme. Bisson, Dr Bourbon, and the author.

Control.—This day, for the first time, a black woollen knitted garment was used for the medium's whole figure, only leaving the hands and head free. This garment, prepared at the suggestion of the Paris physicians, consisted of one piece, and had only one opening at the back, from the waist to the neck. The medium entered the séance room dressed only in the blue dressing-gown, which had been previously searched, and, in our presence, she changed into the woollen garment after it had been carefully examined, whereupon Mme. Bisson closed it along the back with close stitches. She also sewed up the sleeves so that they fitted tightly round the wrists.

During these operations Dr Bourbon examined her mouth with a spoon, asked Eva to blow her nose into a handkerchief, undid her hair, and examined hair and ears. Finally, the medium's head was enveloped in a black veil of strong tulle, which was sewn all round to the neck of the dress as on 2nd May. A final examination of the seam round the neck showed that the stitches were too close to allow a finger to pass. Only Eva's hands remained free, and she was allowed to retain the ring on her right hand. The examination of the cabinet gave a negative result.

Illumination as in March 1913.

Eva took her place in the cabinet. Mme. Bisson took her hands and hypnotised her by fixation as usual.

9.23 P.M. Hypnotisation. The white light is switched off by the author, while the medium's hands lie still in those of Mme. Bisson.

9.25 P.M. Mme. Bisson releases Eva's hands. These grasp the curtain and remain visible at the curtains during the whole sitting, though now and then the arms are crossed. They are sometimes touched by the author.

9.40 P.M. In spite of long-continued expirations, and obvious efforts by the medium, no results. Her hands are warm.

10.10 P.M. Suddenly Eva commences to whimper, makes muscular efforts, and gives cries of pain.

10.12 P.M. The hands become cool. Efforts continue. Mediumistic labour.

10.14 P.M. A white wisp, about half a yard long, penetrates the veil, before our eyes, and places itself upon her left upper arm. Those present claim to have seen a finger in it. The author only sees the wisp, and opens the cameras.

10.17 P.M. The wisp lies over the left arm and the medium's thighs. The author ignites the flash-light and changes the plates at once.

10.25 P.M. The wisp is again visible.

10.28 P.M. Eva feels the disappearance of the phenomenon. Her hands have not left the curtain for a moment.

10.30 P.M. Close of sitting. The medium steps in front of the cabinet, gets the seams undone, and takes off the whole séance costume in our presence, opens her mouth, and is again searched, with no result. She retires to rest while in the somnambulic condition.

Nothing is found in the dress. Neither veil nor tricot are moistened. The cabinet is also examined without result.

The photograph (Figs. 150 and 151) taken shows the medium sitting on the chair clothed in the tricot and veil, with a white, broad strip hanging from the left wrist down to the right thigh. As shown by the enlargement of this strip, its structure, like that of the material previously described, shows meshes, thick parallel threads being held together by short cross filaments, so that the whole gives a net-like impression and a polygonal pattern. The material is soft and fibrous, like the finest cashmere wool.

SITTINGS OF THE 13TH AND 14TH MAY 1913.

Negative.

SITTING OF THE 16TH MAY 1913.

Present.—Mme. Bisson, Dr Bourbon, M. de Vesme, and the author.

Conditions as on 9th May. Woollen garment, head sewn into the veil, which was sewn on to the tunic round the neck. Hair, mouth, and nose examined by the author.

Three cameras were in the cabinet and four outside, also a stereoscopic apparatus furnished by Dr Bourbon and a camera of Mme. Bisson's

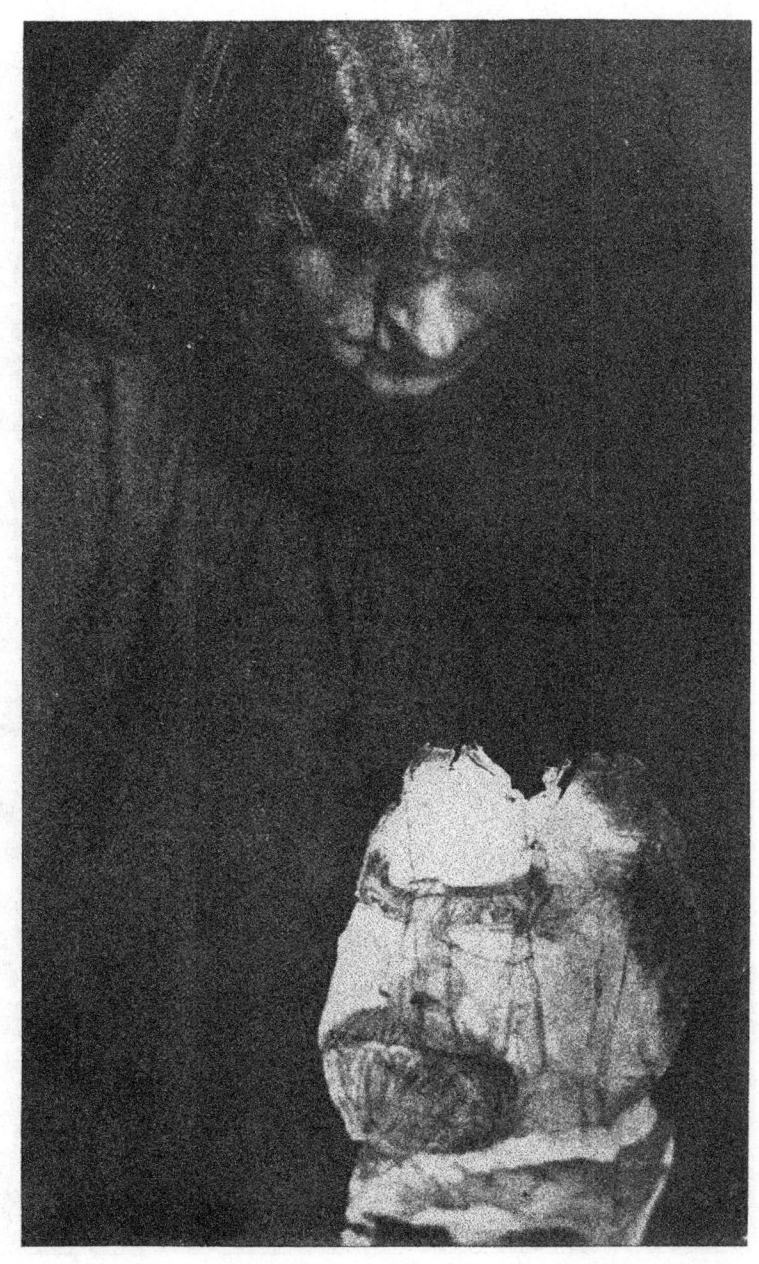

FIG 149. MME BISSON'S FLASHLIGHT PHOTOGRAPH OF 2 MAY, 1913.

Fig 150. Author's flashlight photograph of 9 May, 1913.

SITTINGS IN MAY AND JUNE 1913

($4\frac{3}{4}$ by 7 inches)—nine cameras altogether. The record was taken during the sitting, as usual.

9.5 P.M. Commencement of sitting. Hypnotisation and extinction of white light as on 9th May. The hands remain visible at the curtain during the whole sitting, and never disappear behind it. They move during the convulsive efforts accompanying the productions. The curtain is grasped with the *vola manus*, the smaller fingers being uppermost. Then the fists grasping the curtain are turned so that the thumbs are uppermost. During mediumistic labour there are strong stretchings of the arms, the curtain being gripped, and used as a support for the hands.

9.9 P.M. Strong moaning, expiration, and pressing. The forearms are crossed, the right hand holding the left curtain and the left the right. Then the normal position is resumed.

9.11 P.M. "Demande bien, ma Juliette!" which means that Mme. Bisson is to support the medium by effort of will and words. Since at present, after the farewell of the controlling "Berthe," no other "personification" has taken her place, the suggestions of the sitters only had reference to the medium, in order to induce her to make greater efforts.

9.15 P.M. Stertorous gasping.
9.17 P.M. Complaints of pain. "On me fait mal, Juliette."
9.25 P.M. A white substance becomes visible hanging out of her mouth like a large tongue, and appears to penetrate the meshes of the veil. The author opens the cameras.

9.32 P.M. After those present had seen not only a veil-like substance, but at its end a finger, the author ignites the flash-light during the next exposure, and immediately changes the plates.

9.33 to 9.38 P.M. Dr Bourbon and M. de Vesme observe the white material on the breast, and a fragment of a finger, which in size and shape might belong to an adult female. Dr Bourbon and Mme. Bisson ascertain that this finger is quite plastically developed, can move its joints, and that it bends and stretches. Then the strip lengthens, changing into a sort of cord, and jumps on to the right arm, finally remaining in the lap. Here the author saw the finger lying between the medium's knees quite closely. The bed of the nail is distinctly visible. While I changed the plates, this jointed fragment of a finger was laid in the right hand of Dr Bourbon, and there performed a rotating motion about its axis, so that there can be no doubt as to its plastic development. The sensation caused by the contact was that of a solid, cool, moist object. Lying in the medium's lap, the stretched finger rose freely with its tip upwards, and fell back. Then the whole thing was withdrawn and disappeared as if reabsorbed by the medium.

9.40 P.M. Still the characteristic efforts of the medium continued, so that further phenomena might be expected.

9.44 P.M. She takes Mme. Bisson's hands. Continued psychophysical efforts.

9.46 P.M. In spite of convulsive movements in the arms, no further phenomenon occurs. With the words "Cela me quitte, le fantôme viendra demain," the sitting closes.

9.47 P.M. Eva rises and emerges from the curtain. In the white electric light a careful final examination is made. The veil shows no holes, and the seam connecting it with the dress is nowhere defective. The single stitches are so close together that a finger cannot penetrate. Inside the net there is one large tortoiseshell hair-pin, which had fallen out of the hair. The front lower portion of the veil is thoroughly moistened. The seam along the back is also intact. This is now undone. Eva handed the whole tricot to Dr Bourbon, put on the blue dressing-gown, and went to bed while in the somnambulic state. Final examination of the séance costume and the cabinet negative.

Dr Bourbon (physician) put his impressions of the sitting of 16th May into the following words, addressed to the author :—

" DEAR COLLEAGUE,
"In accordance with your wishes, I am quite prepared to communicate to you briefly my impressions of the sitting which we attended, together with Mme. Bisson and M. de Vesme, on 16th May.

" The medium's head was completely enclosed in a black tulle veil, firmly sewn to the neck-piece of the tricot, as has been the practice lately.

" Very soon the medium commenced to breathe stertorously. In this sitting the hands remained always visible on her knees, unless they were holding the curtain. During the whole sitting the curtains were not completely closed for an instant. All the phenomena observed by us were, therefore, always under our eyes, and at a distance of not more than half a yard.

" At 9.20 P.M. Eva bends forward towards us, and we see the substance emerging from her mouth while within the veil.

" Very soon afterwards I perceive that something is hanging out of her mouth and moving up and down over her breast. It was a finger suspended by a cord of the well-known substance. The finger touches me, and in answer to an observer I say that it feels dry. Again the medium takes my hands and places them under the structure. I then felt, and saw distinctly and clearly, a finger which was moist and cool, and which fell into the hollow of my hand, where it turned to and fro for some moments. Its weight appeared to be the weight of a full-sized finger. The phenomenon then disappeared. Eva then let me feel the veil which, near the mouth, was soaked with mucus. Soon afterwards, without much change in the position of the curtains, the phenomenon was repeated while the hands remained always in the full illumination. I could now clearly recognise the finger, which was suspended by a grey substance consisting of two or three portions, and which moved up and down across the medium's breast. This finger executed distinct bendings two or three times, and then disappeared from view, as if it had ceased to be illuminated.

" This manner of disappearance is often observed.

" Eva then rested with her hands in her lap, which held the curtain open in the same way as before. Suddenly I see something white between her hands, which are about 4 inches apart. I draw the attention of the sitters to this, and we ascertain that it is again a small finger parallel to the medium's fingers. This finger then stretches out slowly, and we find that it lies on a mass of the same substance joined by a

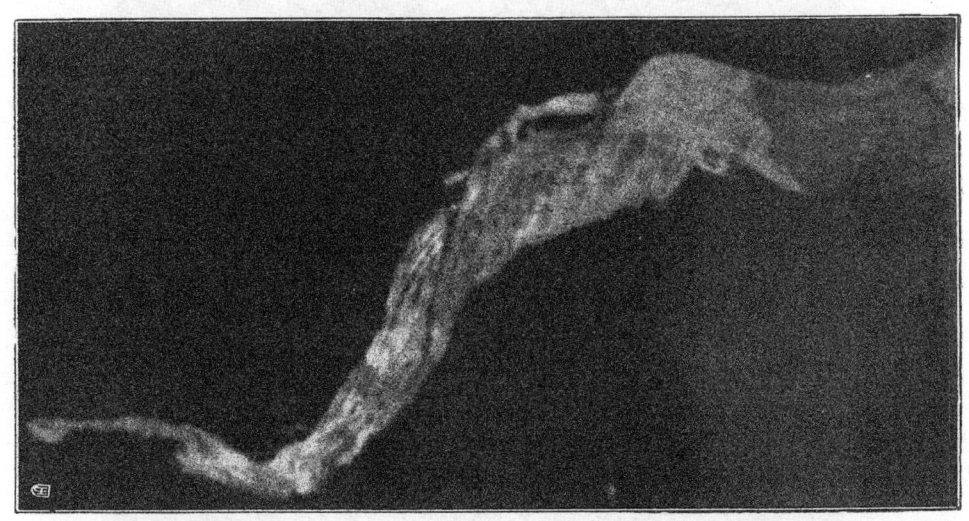

FIG. 151. ENLARGEMENT OF FIG. 150.

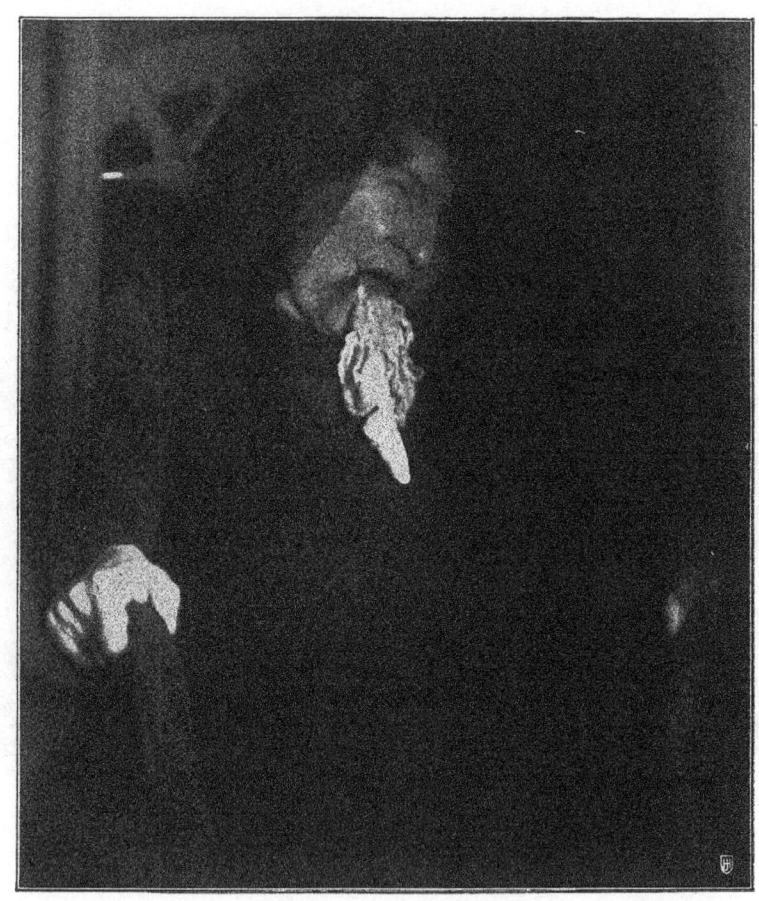

FIG. 152. AUTHOR'S FLASHLIGHT PHOTOGRAPH OF 16 MAY, 1913.

cord to the medium's body. Some moments afterwards the whole phenomenon disappeared in the gap of the curtain, whereupon, in spite of our wishes, nothing more was shown.

" In the course of the sitting a flash-light photograph was taken of one of the most important phenomena which we have yet observed—that is to say, the penetration of the substance emerging from the medium's mouth through the veil. With an expression of happiness at being able to place my testimony at your disposal,

" I remain, dear Colleague,
" Yours sincerely,
" Dr HENRI BOURBON."

In a letter of 19th May, addressed to the author, M. de Vesme gives his impressions of this sitting as follows :—

" . . . Although I did not myself examine the medium, thinking that an examination by two physicians would suffice, I can say this, that I saw that hair, nose, and mouth of the medium were examined, that Dr Bourbon's examination of the mouth took a long time, and that the seams were also carefully examined.

" During the sitting I was interested to see whether the attention of the experimenters would be constantly concentrated on the control of Eva's hands, so that we could say, with a clear conscience, that the hands never disappeared from the eyes of the observers. My place was to the right, and a little further from the curtains than the other chairs. It is true that under these conditions I several times saw the left hand disappear from view, but as soon as I altered my position and approached the curtain, I always found that the observers sitting in front of me, and therefore better placed, could see the hands all the time.

" As regards the phenomena, I first saw a white mass in the form of a long tongue hanging out of the mouth of the medium outside the veil. After an interval of some minutes, while the curtain hid the medium's body from me, I again saw the tongue-like white structure, to which a thread was now attached, which hung down to Eva's knees. This thread, which gave an impression of a navicular cord, held a finger suspended. When I saw it, it was in a flexed position, but I could not, like the other observers, myself ascertain any motion in it. But I can bear witness that this finger raised itself upwards from the medium's dress. My position rendered observation difficult. Thus I could not see the nail-bed on the finger. Also, I did not touch it, as did Mme. Bisson and Dr Bourbon. On the other hand, I see no possibility that this whole phenomenon could have been brought about in a fraudulent manner.

" Yours sincerely,
" DE VESME."

A close examination of the veil after the sitting gave the following result :—A tulle veil is attached to the neck of the tricot by a double or treble row of close stitching, in the form of a thick ruche, about an inch across and having a length of 11 inches. An attempt to penetrate the fastening at any point with a pencil, without injuring the seam, was unsuccessful. The mesh of the veil itself is one-twelfth of an inch wide. On putting on the tricot, the veil has only to be sewn on to the back of the neck in order to isolate Eva's head completely. In reality, Eva's body is under these conditions as if it were enclosed in a cage, which only leaves the hands free.

The photograph (Figs. 152, 153, and 154) of 16th May completely corroborates the observations as stated. Eva's mouth is wide open. A part of the veil is slightly drawn into the mouth. We see distinctly that, over the whole under lip, a broad, striped, and fibrous mass, recalling a leafy vegetable structure or tangled felt, hangs out of the medium's mouth, emerging, apparently, between the tip of the tongue and the lip. At the end of this tangle of fibres there hangs a plastically developed finger of natural size, cut off at the middle of the first joint. The second joint is grasped by the fibrous cord, and is only connected with the rest of the mass by this cord.

These details are corroborated by the side view from the right, and by the negative taken from above on the left, inside the cabinet, especially as regards the distinct plastic development of the finger. The excellent photograph obtained with Mme. Bisson's camera shows, in its enlargement, the nail-bed as observed by the author in the further course of the sitting. A second photograph (Fig. 155) shows that the veil after the sitting was quite intact. A piece of white paper was placed inside the veil in order to let the pattern appear more clearly.

The photographic documents from the sitting of 16th May, in conjunction with the agreement of the observations made by the sitters, and the fact that Eva was completely enclosed in the tricot and veil, as in a cage, while her hands throughout the sitting were observed by four people, and never escaped visible control, bring us a proof of the penetration of the teleplastic substance through a closely meshed tulle veil, which was found intact both before and after the sitting. From this we may conclude that the material has a loose, half soft, variable structure, which only forms, as shown in the negatives, after it has emerged from the mouth and veil. It is also probable that the finger fragment only developed to its natural size after penetrating the tulle, finally assuming the sharply marked and anatomically correct form of an adult finger, with nail-bed, as observed by Dr Bourbon, Mme. Bisson, and myself. The subjective and objective determinations were made on 16th May 1913, under the most careful conditions, so that it will not be easy to raise well-founded objections against the completeness and accuracy of the demonstration.

SITTING OF THE 17TH MAY 1913.

Present.—Mme. Bisson and the author.

Conditions.—To facilitate the production of a whole phantom, Eva this time put on the former séance costume (tights and tunic). It was sewn up only at the sleeves and neck. The back remained open by leaving the back seam unsewn, as this phenomenon is usually joined to the medium on her back. No veil was put over the head.

On the afternoon of the 17th May the male personification "Dors-

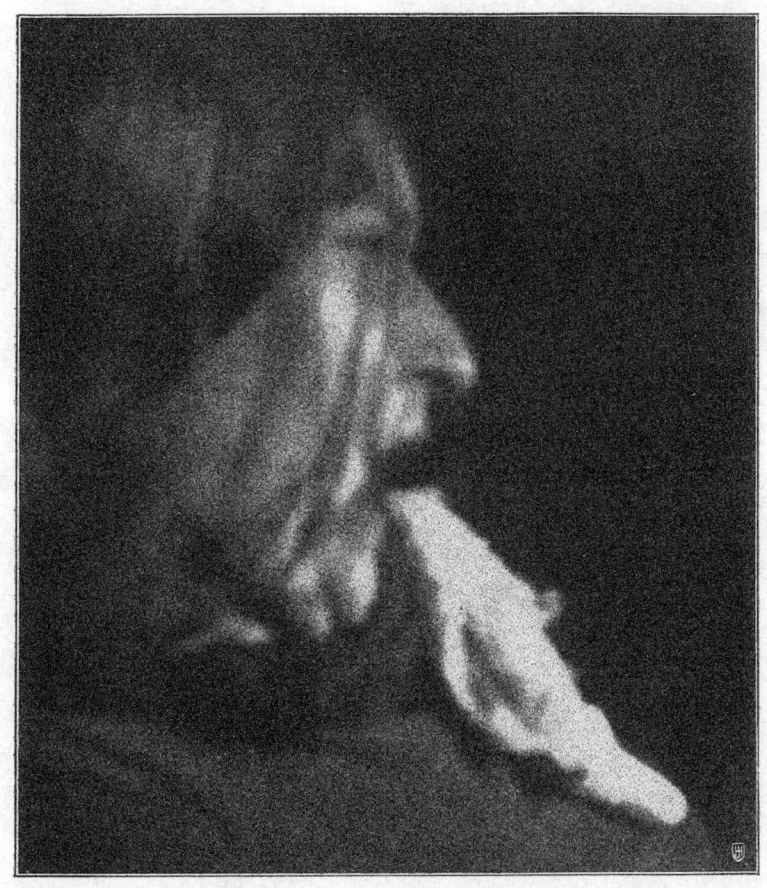

FIG. 153. SIDE VIEW OF FIG. 152.

Fig. 154. Enlargement of Fig. 152.

FIG. 155   PHOTOGRAPH SHOWING THE VEIL INTACT AFTER THE PHENOMENON SHOWN IN FIGS. 150 AND 151.

SITTINGS IN MAY AND JUNE 1913

mica" had announced, by automatic writing through the medium, its appearance for 8.30 P.M. Before the sitting Eva's pulse was accelerated. Other conditions and illumination as in previous sittings.

8.15 P.M. Hypnosis. Hands always visible. Distinct signs of trance.

8.17 P.M. Medium asks leave to remove the tights, and is only clad in the tunic, open behind.

8.20 P.M. Sounds of painful exertion and groans. Exclamations like " Oh, ma Juliette! Ah!"

8.21 P.M. Strips of white material on the left arm.

8.24 P.M. Great excitement and restlessness. Hands always at the curtain, but move to and fro with the curtain, sometimes crossed, and subsequently restored to the normal position.

8.28 P.M. Eva rises and steps into the left corner of the cabinet, her head bent forward, but keeping hold of the curtains. A white mass about the size of a head emerges from her mouth and is visible on the inner side of the curtain. Since to-day we wanted to see a phantom, we agreed not to take any notice of other phenomena, so as not to interfere with the process of development. Eva sat down and rested.

8.31 P.M. She says " Cela travaille."

8.35 P.M. Hands always visible. Pause continues.

8.40 P.M. A renewed whimpering and loud deep sounds.

8.45 P.M. The medium rises, steps back to the right, and cries out, " Oh! mon Dieu, Juliette, il me tire." This may be taken to mean that the point of attachment for the expected phantom was on Eva's back, as observed previously by Mme. Bisson. The medium therefore feels drawn backwards, and yields to the sensation.

8.47 P.M. The medium sits down and rests.

8.50 P.M. Renewed long expirations. Eva expresses a wish that we should not take any notice of the phenomenon now occurring, so as not to interrupt the process of development. I therefore turned my head sideways towards Mme. Bisson, but still kept my eye on the happenings behind the left curtain, facing me as I sat in front of the opened curtains. Then I saw, while both Eva's hands held the curtains open, over her left forearm the distinct appearance of a male face, on which the contrast between the black hair and the white ground was distinctly marked.

9.1 P.M. Whimpering and pressing. Eva rises, holds one curtain with both hands, and—

9.5 P.M. Passes into the right corner of the cabinet, sits down, and asks Mme. Bisson to hold her hands.

9.10 P.M. Louder cries of pain, mediumistic labour, accelerated respiration, hands cool.

9.15 P.M. We rise and look behind the curtain. Mme. Bisson maintains that she recognises in the dark corner the head of the phantom, photographed by her behind the medium's head. The author can only vouch for seeing a broad white band, with its upper end higher than Eva's head, on the back wall in the corner of the cabinet. We take our seats again in order to induce the phantom to advance more into the middle of the cabinet

9.18 P.M. Eva sits down.

9.20 P.M. Further great efforts. We close the curtain above her hands, so that they are no longer visible.

9.30 P.M. The medium suddenly feels her power vanishing, or the connection can no longer be made. In short, the sitting had to be closed without our being able to perceive the structure generated in the darkness. Final examination negative. Eva was very much exhausted, went to bed in the somnambulic state, slept restlessly, rose at one o'clock to cool her head with cold water, then went to sleep properly.

SITTING OF THE 18TH MAY 1913.

Negative.

SITTING OF THE 19TH MAY 1913.

Present.—Mme. Bisson and the author.

Initial examination, séance costume, and programme as on 17th May 1913.

Eva, dressed only in the blue dressing-gown, enters the séance room, and takes from the author's hands the tunic and tights, which she puts on, but she is only sewn up at the wrists and neck. The dress covers her like a wide full shirt slit down the back.

After her hair, mouth, ears, and hands had been examined, as in previous sittings, while she sat on the chair in the cabinet (which had also been carefully searched) she is hypnotised by Mme. Bisson. Illumination as on 17th May.

8.21 P.M. Extinction of the white light. Eva's hands are well in front of the curtain, and remain uninterruptedly visible during the whole sitting, even when she stands up.

8.25 P.M. Long-drawn expirations and mediumistic efforts.

8.35 P.M. Mme. Bisson holds her hands, while the moans and muscular efforts increase.

8.37 P.M. Mme. Bisson releases her hands, which, however, remain visible. Whimpering and cries of pain, trembling voice, and great excitement. Hands and feet are cold. She takes off the tights and sits on the chair, only clad in the tunic.

8.40 P.M. The whimpering and groaning become more vehement, and continue as in the case of a person undergoing a lengthy and painful operation.

8.41 P.M. Gasping and accelerated respiration, with open mouth.

8.50 P.M. The pains seem to diminish and Eva appears to rest.

8.51 P.M. Renewal of strong mediumistic pains. " Cela me prend au cou."

8.55 P.M. On the right, beside the medium's head, the author sees a white mass. The curtain is intentionally kept closed above the medium's visible hands, so that the materialisation process can develop completely and is not interrupted by premature illumination.

8.59 P.M. Mme. Bisson continues to encourage the medium. With urgent suggestions that a whole phantom may show itself, she takes Eva's hands and supports her effort of will.

FIG. 156. AUTHOR'S FLASHLIGHT PHOTOGRAPH OF 19 MAY, 1913.

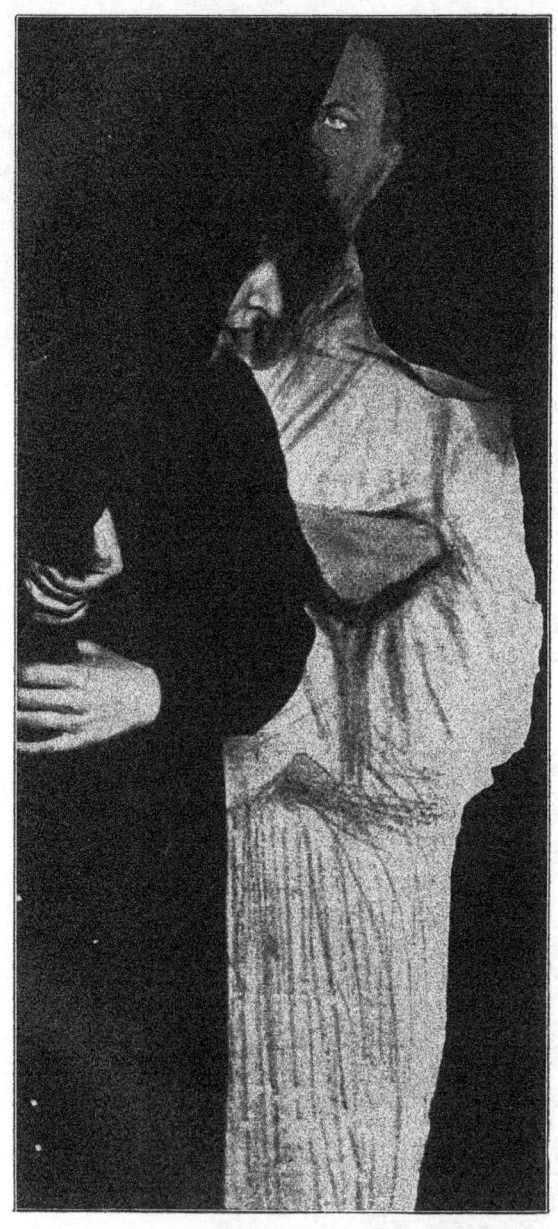

Fig. 157 Simultaneous photograph by Mme Bisson, 19 May, 1913.

SITTINGS IN MAY AND JUNE 1913

9 P.M. Eva rises, still holding the curtain so that her hands remain visible, but so that the materialisation process can take place in the dark.

9.3 P.M. Convulsions shake the medium's body. Whining with pain she throws herself into the chair. While her hands are being held, a broad white mass becomes visible on her left forearm, and is drawn upwards.

9.15 P.M. Stertorous and accelerated breathing. Long-drawn muscular efforts. She cries out, " Oh ! ma Juliette, il me fait mal, il me tire."

9.20 P.M. Eva again rises, quickly steps towards the right, and remains standing in the corner of the cabinet.

9.25 P.M. The medium takes Mme. Bisson's hands and follows the motions of her arms, and moves them up and down several times at the back wall of the cabinet, as if one were to pull a bell-rope.

9.30 P.M. She releases Mme. Bisson's hands, grasps the right curtain, and says, " Juliette, appelle-le, je le vois."

9.35 P.M. She starts opening the right curtain while standing. Mme. Bisson recognises the male personification " Dorsmica," already twice photographed.

9.38 P.M. As Eva opened the curtain wide I saw behind her, as if protected by her body, what appeared to be a white male figure taller than the medium. In order not to miss the opportunity, I immediately ignited the flash-light, although the apparition stood too far sideways beyond the field of view of the lenses to be photographed by all the cameras.

Immediately after changing the plates I entered the cabinet, the curtains having remained open. The apparition had disappeared like lightning at the ignition of the flash-light. Eva sank exhausted into Mme. Bisson's arms, who placed her carefully in her chair. Immediately afterwards the author searched the cabinet and the medium, but nowhere could a trace of the apparition be found. The medium changed from the séance costume into the dressing-gown, and was immediately put to bed. The space of time between the changing of the plates and the final examination of the medium and the cabinet was only a few seconds. Close of the sitting, 9.40 P.M.

On the tightly stretched black cloth lining of the cabinet, under the wooden cross beams, there were two white spots about the size of a five-shilling piece, corresponding approximately to the middle of the back of the phantom, as it showed itself at first. But, as proved later, these patches were on the left of the photographed phantom. If there is any relation between the patches and the phantom, we must assume that the apparition made a lateral movement towards the corner of the cabinet, as, indeed, Mme. Bisson claims to have noticed. In any case, it is remarkable that other whitish patches are found on the back wall, corresponding to the position of the phantom previously photographed. These have the same appearance as the patches on the dress when subjected to microscopic analysis, and probably also contain cell detritus.

The stereoscopic camera, mounted on one side, gave a front view of the medium and phantom, which is unfortunately not very well defined (Fig. 156).

A second stereoscopic apparatus, placed in front of the cabinet, only shows the left side of the phantom, while Mme. Bisson's camera, being slightly turned to the left, gives a better result, which, however, only shows half the phantom (Fig. 157).

At first sight, one recognises the male figure with white mantle photographed on 23rd February and 24th March, and this time it closely resembles the first photograph. Again the apparition is half a head taller than the medium, and the lower edge of the mantle, as shown by the photograph taken from above, is from 4 to 8 inches above the floor. Again the whole structure is flat, like a picture on linen, or something resembling leather; in any case, some coherent material.

On the author's negative the head is bent slightly to the left, in contrast to the upright position of the two previous pictures. The eyes are open, the gaze is directed half upwards as in the photograph of 23rd February 1913. But the eyelids are less open, so that, especially on the right side, the eyeball is not so prominent as in the first photograph. The pupils are also somewhat further to the right. In a word, the opening of the eyelids is flatter in our picture than in the first photograph. The high light, corresponding to the incident illumination, is remarkable, and so is the distinct marking of the unusually black pupil of the left eye in Mme. Bisson's photograph. Over the forehead, upwards from the nose and in prolongation of the latter, there is a fold resembling a ridge, which is pointed where it joins the hair.

As we see from a comparative study of the two stereoscopic transparencies, the nose and supra-orbital region are clearly marked out in low relief, as in a mask, and the beard gives the impression of rough hair, and therefore of reality. The prominent bridge of the nose continues, as already mentioned, in a ridge up to the hair. Another cross fold runs from the end of this ridge to the right, across the hair of the forehead. A part of the ridge is crossed by a crease in the forehead on the right. The whole head portrait lies flat on the broad beam of the cabinet frame as if fastened to it. Towards the right of it we also see two nails, which were hammered in by the author for suspending the photographic apparatus.

The further development of the features appears to have been done by drawing or painting materials, and does not show any essential changes in comparison with the first picture.

The distance between the medium and the materialised image is indicated by the broad shadow thrown by her body on the phantom standing behind her. The shoulder of the phantom is less sloping in the last photograph than in the two previous ones, so that the shoulders appear broader and squarer. With the aid of the roof stereoscope we recognise at the left shoulder, which is bent forward at the top and sharply cut off, that the whole character of the structure consists of a white plate, of fair consistency, finished by pictorial means. Besides some remarkable parallel creases at the level of the knees, which on Mme. Bisson's photograph are hardly visible, the photograph shows distinctly projecting folds, which are plastically developed on the obviously soft ground substance, especially in the lower portion of the mantle. The outer line of the mantle also runs more irregularly than in the first pictures, and shows certain separate pieces, as well as fibres or threads. On the enlargement the drawing of the mantle is clearly seen to consist of strokes.

Various lines are thick and soft, and as if running into the foundation. They are of varying depth, and are again and again broken by gaps, and contain thick points of a deeper colour. Generally speaking, we cannot escape the impression that the strokes consist of more or less closely united points, grains, or particles of different sizes and colourings, like the " organic rays " observed by Ochorowicz. On the larger scale the strokes, consisting of separate pieces or joints, recall the anatomical structure of certain kinds of reeds built up of regular joints or layers. As in the previous pictures, the arms are folded and the hands are invisible. But, in place of the left hand, we see a fairly large triangular piece of substance, with a broad dark rim, the character and significance of which cannot be explained. The covering of the throat is the same as in the first picture.

We have here, for the third time, a representation of the same male type, but the differences in the three separate pictures of 23rd February, 24th March, and 19th May, and in various photographic poses of this individuality, are so great that they could not be produced by any fraudulent use of one and the same image. It would at least have been necessary to smuggle in three life-size pictures of different appearance. Besides, on the last negative, we find an advance from the flat to the plastic in the design of the head. It must be remembered that the pictures of 24th March had the precise character of painted canvas, which is partly seen in the negatives of the last series also. Unless we doubt the reality of this remarkable materialisation process, we might expect that, in the course of time, a further plastic development of the phantom would take place. In this case the flat pictorial development of the psychic composition, or individuality, which is to be realised, would only be a necessary transition stage in the materialisation process towards those creations and figures which, in appearance and in motion, resemble real life, so that finally, as in Crookes's phantom " Katie King," we cannot distinguish them from real living organisms.

The author's result of 19th May 1913 confirms the observations and photographic records of Mme. Bisson on 23rd February and 24th March, and for this reason alone it is of definite value in deciding the question of phantoms.

Sittings of the 20th and 27th May 1913.

Negative.

Sitting of the 31st May 1913.

Present.—Mme. Bisson.

The medium this day wore the tunic with tights. Immediately after the beginning of the sitting the phenomena began, with the usual physiological accompaniments, in the form of materials streaming out of the mouth. Mme. Bisson observed that a small complete finger, tied up with this material, emerged from the mouth. This shows that the attachment is not made outside the mouth. The finger then grew to the normal adult size of a female finger. During the next exposure two further fingers were formed, which were joined by cords to the mouth and the rest of the material. The medium, in this case, had the sensation of having produced a whole hand, and she asked her protectress if she did not perceive it. Finally, Mme. Bisson carefully caught the finger stump in her own hand, touched it on both sides, and pressed it so that the medium cried with pain. In this case she observed that the finger felt like a real finger, like a consistent firm body, with a cool and skin-like exterior.

In the further course of the sitting a piece of material emerged from Eva's mouth and laid itself across the medium's hands, which were held by Mme. Bisson, and of this a photographic record was made. It was all drawn into the medium's mouth as the light flashed up. During the sitting Eva's hands were continually visible and under control.

The enlarged photograph (Fig. 158) shows the medium's hands separated from below by Mme. Bisson's hands. A cord-like piece of material hangs from Eva's mouth over her right hand and down to the end of her first finger. To this band a round white structure is attached which, however, can hardly be called a finger fragment. A broad triangular attachment is seen on the upper part of this white fragment, and appears to coalesce with its surface. The manner of attachment on this day is quite different from that in the case of the finger of 16th May.

SITTING OF THE 2ND JUNE 1913.

Negative.

SITTING OF THE 3RD JUNE 1913.

Present.—Dr Bourbon, M. Bourdet, Mme. Bisson, and the author.

Conditions.—Eva puts on tights and tunic, and is sewn up from the neck to the waist and at the wrists. The tights were not sewn on to the tunic, because the medium often wishes to take them off during the sittings. Control as in previous sittings.

8.50 P.M. Hypnotisation in thirty seconds. The hands remained in visible control during the whole sitting. The trance condition on this day was much quieter.

9.30 P.M. A rather bulky material streams out of the mouth in the form of thick strips and threads, corresponding approximately to those photographed in the case of the veil phenomenon.

9.35 P.M. Material becomes visible on her lap in the shape of a long strip, to which a small structure, resembling a finger, appears to be attached.

9.45 P.M. New exposure. The miniature finger attached to the substance becomes visible—below the medium's hands, and as if protected by them while they grasp the curtain— and touches Mme. Bisson's hand. The impression is conveyed as if a long elastic rubber band emerged from the mouth and connected it with the finger. As soon as this is touched it is drawn back into the mouth with an elastic jerk, and disappears.

10.15 P.M. At the next opening of the curtain the substance hangs in broad strips out of the mouth, and at the lower end a finger seems to be attached to it. Mme. Bisson illuminates the phenomenon with a

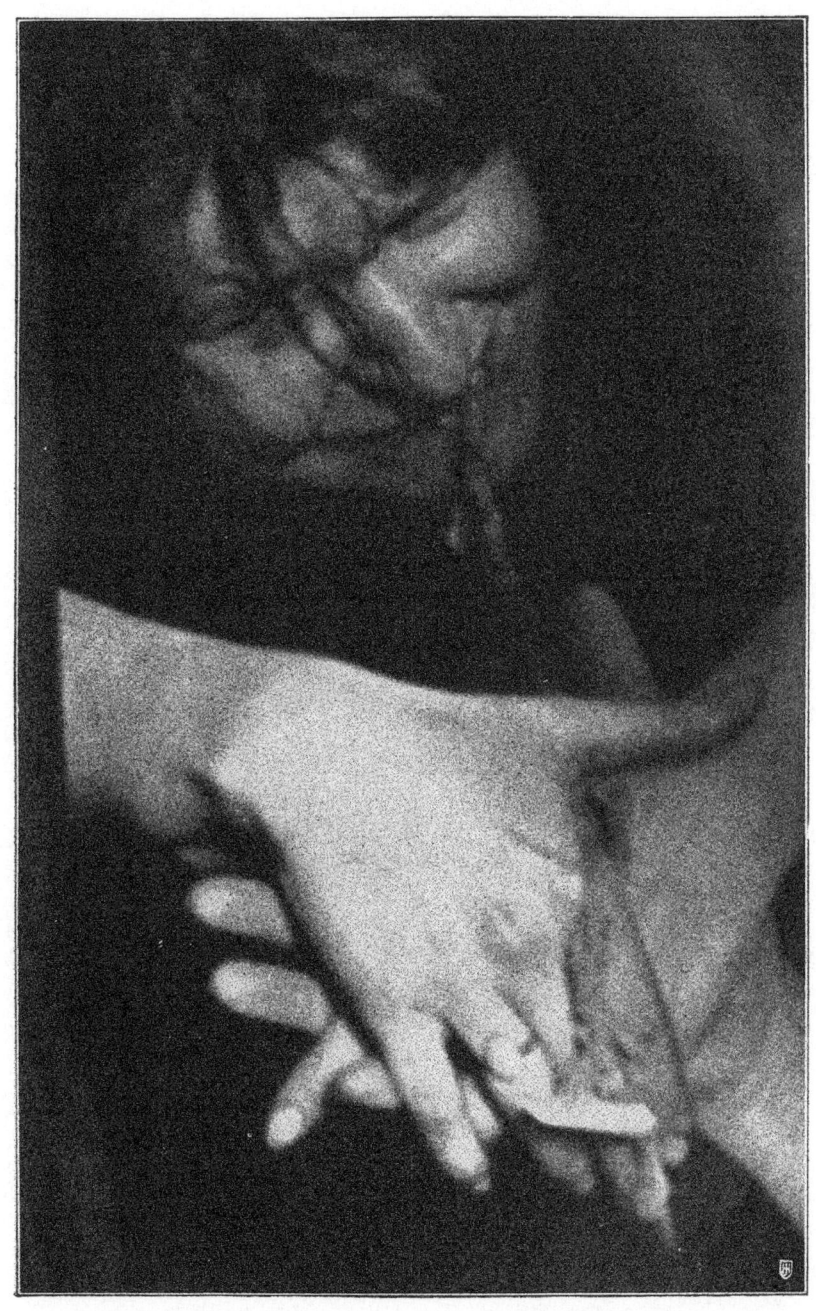

FIG. 158. MME. BISSON'S FLASHLIGHT PHOTOGRAPH, 31 MAY, 1913.

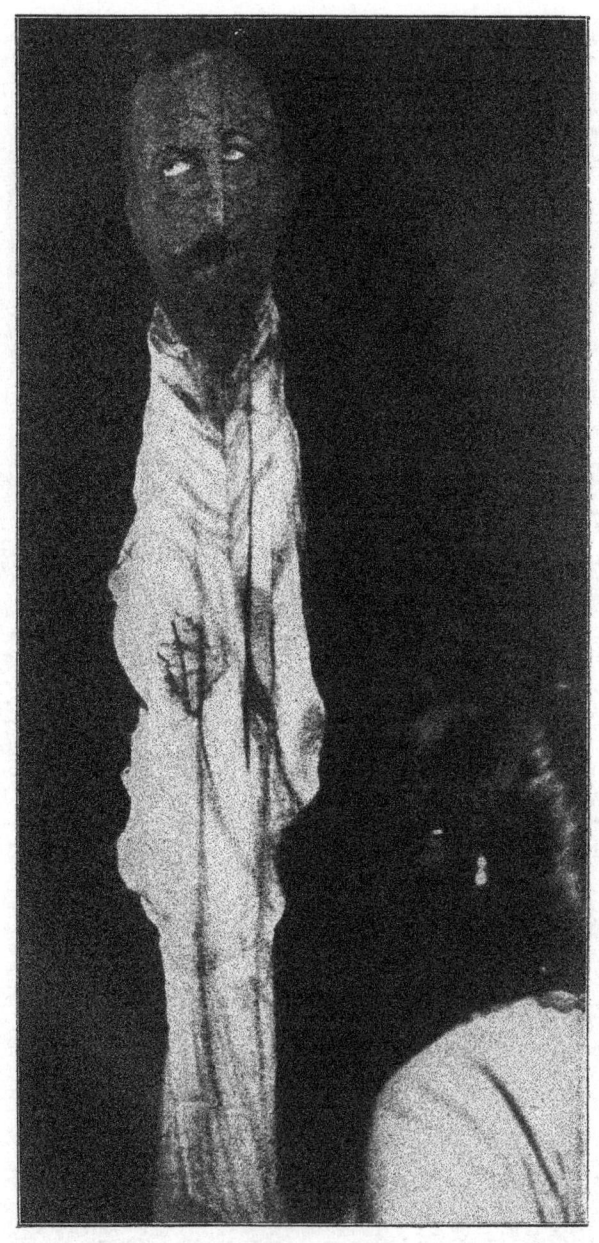

Fig. 159. Mme. Bisson's flashlight photograph of 8 June, 1913

red torch. It is about 3 or 4 inches thick. Beside it, the dress of the medium is moistened in strips on her breast, and shines pink in the light. While the material itself looks grey, the more compact portions, like this finger, appear white.

10.20 P.M. The form changes its shape. Sometimes it looks like a long narrow band, sometimes like a bulky packet. The phenomenon shows at various parts of the medium's upper body, once on her hair, and then on her right, or left, shoulder, but only remains visible for about a second. Eva is extremely timid, and protects the structure from the light and the sitters' gaze, like an anxious mother protecting her child. On the whole, the mediumistic efforts on this day are less violent and painful, but, on the other hand, the phenomena are feebler and more fugitive.

The phenomena only occur after energetic suggestive words by Mme. Bisson, as if the medium's own will power was not able to overcome the impediments.

10.28 P.M. Close of sitting. Negative result of the final examination.

Observations in June and July 1913
(Paris and La Baule).

ON 8th June Mme. Bisson hypnotised the medium at 8 P.M. without the intention of producing phenomena, but hardly had Eva entered the trance condition when, with whining expressions, she appeared to be defending herself against some intrusion. Then she undressed, and remained in a suffering condition for about thirty minutes. She rose, became restless, and moved to and fro in the cabinet. Mme. Bisson herself then entered the cabinet, sat down on Eva's chair, while Eva stood beside her, and left the curtain sufficiently widely open to observe the materialisation process. She held Eva's hands, but released them from time to time, in order to allow her to put her arms right up. Then Eva bent down and complained of pains in the back. Mme. Bisson saw a packet of material emerging from Eva's body at her waist, in the form of smoke taking the aspect of rays, and surrounded by a clearly visible " aura," or ring of light. This whole appearance then vanished, but now she saw, at the back of the cabinet, behind the medium, the outlines of the phantom against the back wall. Eva then clasped her back with both hands and complained of pains in the lumbar region. The phantom formed a head with a white strip hanging down from it. It followed Eva's movements, and became longer and broader, as if Eva were going to duplicate herself. As soon as the undeveloped phantom was sufficiently clearly seen, Mme. Bisson pressed the electric button. With the flash of the light everything vanished without a trace. At 9.15 P.M. Eva was able to retire to her bedroom. (Letter of Mme. Bisson, dated 9th June.)

The plan to photograph the phantom in the nascent state had succeeded, for instead of a figure the negative (Fig. 159) gives only a white strip with a finished head. The length of the whole thing corresponds to the size of the phantom, as seen in previous pictures, while its width amounts to about one-third of the former distance between the shoulders. The whole phantom is traversed vertically by five long parallel rents or depressions, the most noticeable of which cuts the face quite sharply into two portions at the corner of the left eye. These two portions are not even correctly joined, so that the left eye is too high in proportion, and the left nostril appears to be cut off. The observer gets the impression as if the drawing of the face consisted of two pieces, and was to have been developed by separating these two pieces and filling up the gaps. This unfinished process taking place on a flat surface without plastic development is also indicated in the clothing by the long parallel rents, which are lost below in the folds of the mantle. The position of the hands is quite different from that in the previous phantoms. The expression of the face and the position of the eyes are similar to the previous photographs, except that the left side of the face, being undeveloped, appears too narrow. Both eyes show high lights corresponding to the incident light, and exhibit an essential difference in the drawing from the previous phantoms, especially as regards the opening of the eyelids and the direction of the gaze. This is particularly remarkable in the eyeball and the inner corner of the right eye. A close comparison between the four phantom pictures proves that, if we assume fraud, it is impossible that the same image could have been shown all the four times. On this assumption four different models must have been used. The presence of real high lights also is not explained, nor the tendency shown in the pictures to widen out in the same plane. The textile character of the mantle is shown by small threads, which project from the margin of the picture, which otherwise is flat and disk-like. Although this photograph looks suspicious at the first glance, and was also produced after the close of our experiments, the author still considers it desirable to publish it in the collection, since it may be of interest for the study of folds and rents, such as were characteristic of the former photographic records.

In describing the first phantom photograph, attention was drawn to some rents observed by means of the roof stereoscope, which traversed the figure from top to bottom. They are most likely the residues of the same process of development, which is now seen in its incomplete stage. In describing the negatives of a female head (30th November 1912), it has already been pointed out that folds occurred in the materialised forms undergoing observation. Now we observe the same process of folding during the development of the phantom. Whatever may be our point of view on this matter, the negatives mentioned seem to show that the process of folding occurs not only during the origin of the structures, *i.e.*, before the complete materialisation, but also during their recession, *i.e.*, their de-materialisation. The criticism, which takes no account of the experimental conditions, will hardly forgo this opportunity for an unfavourable decision, and will use these folds as an argument to show that these structures are unfolded from a packet previously folded up. But this assumption is hardly supported by the peculiar character of these folds, which resemble parallel rents, and one cannot understand how the whole phantom can be fraudulently produced in this manner. Besides, the whole controversy becomes meaningless if we consider the experimental conditions, since we must not forget that these experiments took place with a nude medium, and that

Mme. Bisson would have been the person to be deceived, although she sat on the medium's chair and followed the whole process on Eva's naked body. The problem is therefore a deeper one, and cannot be disposed of by such superficial criticism.

For the last time before the close of this work the same phantom was observed by Mme. Bisson on 4th August 1913, in their country house on the Loire (La Baule). This time it occurred outside the curtain, while the medium lay behind it in a deep trance, in the easy-chair, without any sign of life. The face of the phantom was perfectly modelled, and resembled that of a living person, while the lower part of the mantle, formed of soft material, lay on the knees of the observer sitting in front of the curtain. And yet the surface of the mantle gave the impression of a drawing.

A further letter of Mme. Bisson's relates that in the sitting of 13th June, which was attended by Dr Bourbon, she observed the tip of a small finger with a nail, which penetrated Eva's dress, grew in size, and also changed its shape. It remained visible for several minutes between the medium's knees, was quite independent of the substance hanging out of the mouth, and finally appeared within the veil which enclosed Eva's head. One of the observers also succeeded in touching it inside the veil, and subsequently outside. This material had a grey colour, and felt like a mass having a fair consistency and thickness.

On 17th June Mme. Bisson was able to touch a completely formed finger which emerged from Eva's mouth, again in Dr Bourbon's presence. She followed up this finger while it penetrated through the veil, without tearing it, and without altering its own consistency.

On 21st June the experiments were continued. Eva guided one of Mme. Bisson's fingers into her mouth. On this occasion she felt a materialised finger, wrapped in material, on the tip of Eva's tongue. It appeared to adhere to the skin of the tongue and the gums, and to emerge from them. On feeling the back part of the tongue and the mouth, these turned out to be quite free and intact, thus indicating that only the front half of the tongue was concerned in the materialisation process. She felt a nail on the same finger, and raised it with the nail of her own finger, whereupon the medium gave a cry of pain. This interference stopped the materialisation process. Everything was reabsorbed, and did not appear again that evening.

On 29th June Mme. Bisson and Dr Bourbon again observed two fingers attached to the material. These fingers advanced in front of the curtain and laid themselves in the hands of the two observers. In this case the fingers and the substance were black instead of the usual grey or white colour.

On 23rd July 1913 (in La Baule), at 3 P.M., several completely formed fingers wrapped in material, three of which showed nails, emerged from the vagina of the hypnotised medium, moved upwards over her skin, and disappeared without a trace at the moment when Eva awoke spontaneously with a cry of terror.

The above communications, received by letter, are not without value as a supplement to the previous observations already related.[1]

[1] Cp. Juliette Alexandre-Bisson, "*Les Phénomènes dits de Matérialisation.*" Felix Alcan, Paris, 1914.

RESULT OF THE MICROSCOPIC EXAMINATIONS.

DURING the sitting held in Munich on the 8th September 1912, a cord-like structure was seen on the medium's dress. As already reported, it left behind on the dress a patch 9 inches long and 2 or 3 inches broad, which is reproduced in the illustration accompanying the report of the sitting (Fig. 114). In addition, the breast portion of the dress, which had been quite clean before the sitting, was found to have some smaller white spots on it. The material so obtained was handed over to the chemical laboratory of Messrs Schwalm, Munich, for examination.

The expert opinion on this material is as follows :—

On the 9th inst. you handed to me for examination a black dress having some matter deposited on the outside in various places.

Physical Structure of Deposit.—The deposit consisted of long-drawn, narrow, twisted threads, and spots of a greyish-white colour.

Under a magnifying glass it was found to be a dried mass resembling a secretion.

Manner of Preparation.—At suitable places the substance was separated from the dress, and observed partly in water, and partly after colouring with iodine solution, dilute solution of methylene blue, hæmalum, and dilute carbolic fuchsine and embedding it in glycerined gelatine.

Microscopic Structure.—Preparation I. in water. The microscopic image shows conglomerates of colourless, lamellar, cohesive bodies, without a definite structure. There are also single laminæ of various forms, polygonal, oval, etc. These resemble human epithelium, but exhibit no nuclei.

Preparation II. coloured with Lugol's iodine solution and embedded in glycerined gelatine. Same microscopic appearance as No. I.

Preparation III. coloured with hæmalum. The microscopic image shows the finest veil-like lamellæ, some of them broken up into fibres, but otherwise without a definite structure. No nuclei are to be seen (Figs. 160, 161, 162).

Preparation IV. coloured with methylene blue and embedded in glycerined gelatine. The microscopic image consists partly of conglomerates, partly of diffused bodies of various forms resembling epithelium (polygonal, round, spindle-shaped), with nuclei in some places. Also conglomerates of structures showing a cellular constitution, and resembling vegetable cells. Those admixtures which do not occur in the human body might be derived from the air or from the black stuff of the dress.

In the sitting of 11th September 1912 I succeeded in catching a small amount of the liquid matter in a porcelain dish.

The analysis, again carried out in the Schwalm laboratory, is as follows :—

On the 12th inst. you handed to me some material for examination which was at the bottom of a porcelain dish.

One portion of the material was examined physico-microscopically, and another physico-chemically.

I. PHYSICO-MICROSCOPIC EXAMINATION.

Physical Observation.—The material forms a grey, veil-like, moist film.

Mode of Preparation.—Transfer preparations were made of the ground deposit embedded in glycerined gelatine, some of the preparations being previously stained with iodine solution, hæmalum, dilute methylene blue solution, or dilute carbolic fuchsine.

Result of Microscopic Examination (Figs. 163, 164, 165).

Preparation I. embedded in glycerined gelatine. The microscope shows colourless, diffused bodies resembling epithelium, some of which show nuclei, and can then be identified with human epithelium. There are numerous bacterial threads. Also small groups of bacterial spores and fibrous vegetable remains.

MICROPHOTOGRAPHS
ENLARGED 160 TIMES
(MADE BY DR. STEIN).

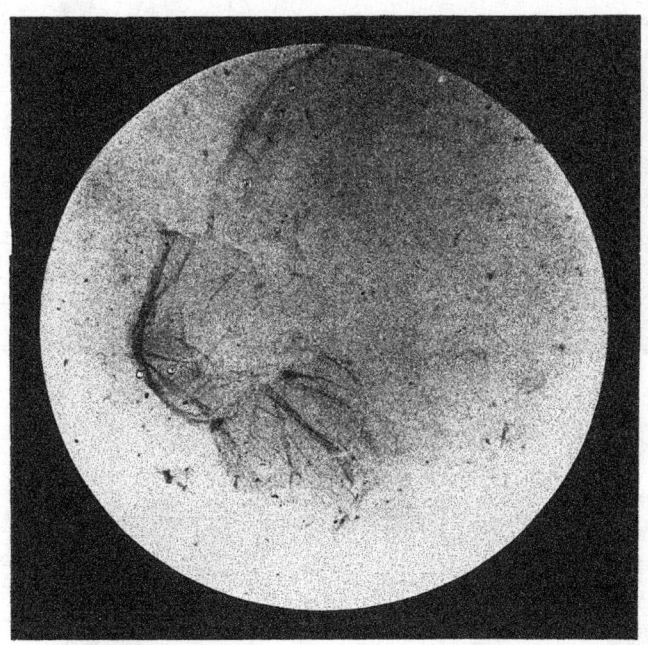

FIG. 160. PREPARATION 3A. VEIL-LIKE LAMELLA BROKEN UP INTO FIBRES, NONDESCRIPT STRUCTURE

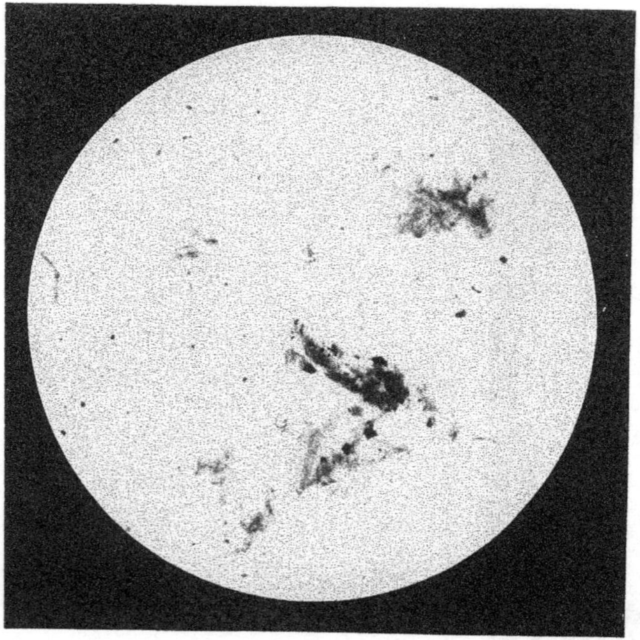

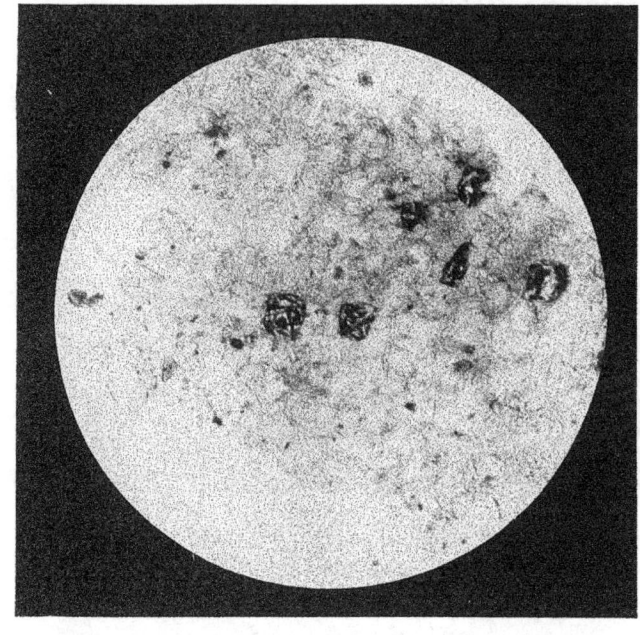

Fig. 161. Sitting of 8 September, 1912. Preparation same as 3A. The black spots are accidental admixtures.

Fig. 162. Sitting of 8 September, 1912. Preparation 3C. Sod-like structures with polygonal cells, revealing vegetable parenchyma. The black spots are accidental admixtures.

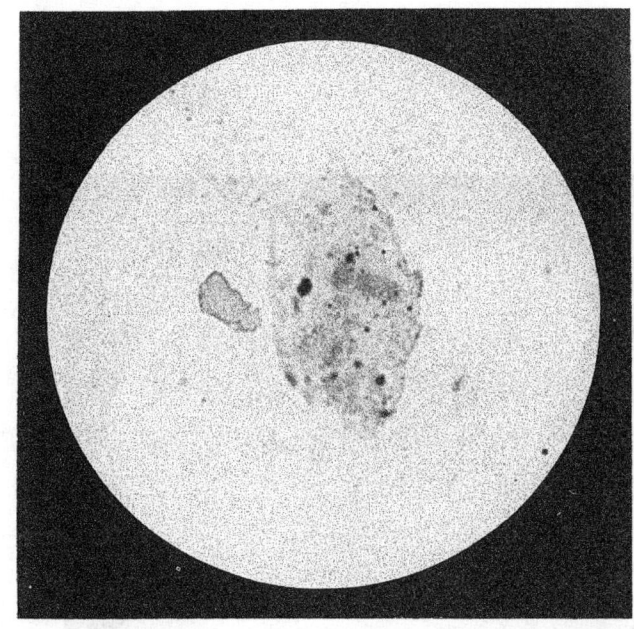

Fig. 164. Sitting of 11 September, 1911. Epithelioid body with distinctly darker body (nucleus ?), enlarged 200 times.

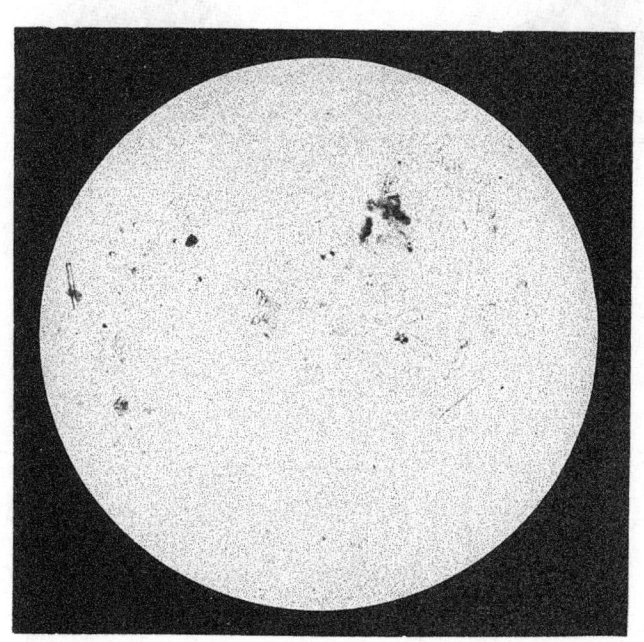

Fig. 163. Sitting of 11 September, 1911. Delicate conglomerate of epithelioid bodies and crystalline admixtures, enlarged 160 times.

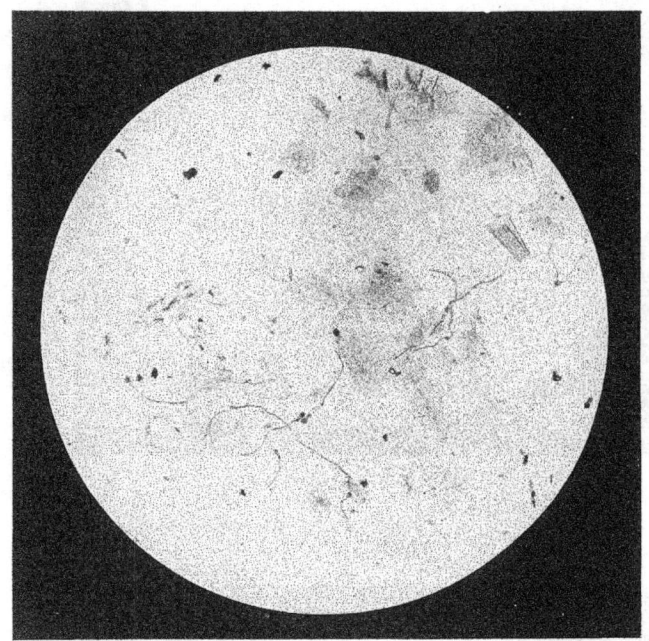

FIG 165   SITTING OF 11 SEPTEMBER, 1912   NUMEROUS EPITHELIOID BODIES WITHOUT NUCLEI   ALSO GROWING BACTERIAL SPORES.

RESULT OF THE MICROSCOPIC EXAMINATIONS

Preparation II. stained with hæmatoxylin (nuclear staining) and embedded in glycerined gelatine. Same result as No. 1, except that the epithelium bodies, bacterial fibres, and vegetable remains occur in greater numbers.

Preparation III. stained with methylene blue and embedded in glycerined gelatine. Same as II.

Preparation IV. stained with carbolic fuchsine and embedded in glycerined gelatine. Same as III.

II. PHYSICO-CHEMICAL EXAMINATION.

A portion of the material was collected on platinum foil, dried, and weighed.

Physical Condition of the Material and its Ashes.—The material is of a brownish-black colour, and weighs 0·002 gramme. On ignition, the substance carbonises and smells distinctly of burnt horn. A pure white ash remained, which weighed 0·0006 gramme.

Chemical Composition of the Ashes.—In the ashes are found: sodium chloride and calcium phosphate. The dark colour of the material is evidently due to dust (or to a pigment ?).

The process of combustion indicates the presence of nitrogen, as in albuminous bodies.

In the same sitting (11th September) spots remained on the medium's dress after contact with the teleplastic substance, which also was analysed in the Schwalm laboratory. The report on this is as follows:—

Physical Condition of the Deposit.—Part of the deposit consisted of a patch the size of a hand, and another part of long-drawn, curved streaks and spots of a whitish-grey colour. Examination with a magnifying glass showed a dried mass resembling a secretion. There were also white conglomerate specks embedded in the mass.

Preparation.—At suitable places the deposit was detached from the dress and embedded in glycerined gelatine, some of it after staining with iodine solution, hæmatoxylin, dilute methylene blue, and dilute carbolic fuchsine.

In the folds of the dress, inside, minute transparent scales were found

MICROSCOPIC RESULT.

Preparation (*a*). Shows conglomerates containing starch granules.

Preparation (*b*). Shows a tangle of colourless (with a few dark blue) cotton threads and wood-fibre products. Among them there are numerous colourless lamellar bodies without definite structure, some of them showing forms characteristic of human epithelium. No nuclei can be found. (Fig. 166.)

Preparation (*c*), from inside of dress. The microscope shows small groups and isolated colourless, epithelioid, coherent, unnucleated bodies without definite structure. Also starch grains here and there.

Preparation (*d*). Shows colourless filmy conglomerates with fine unsymmetrical cross-hatching.

Preparation (*e*). Shows colourless conglomerates of epithelioid coherent bodies of indefinite form. At their rims polygonal shapes are found in some places. No definite structure recognisable. No nuclei.

The starch granules mentioned in the above report may be derived from face-powder used by Eva C. In the dressing-room there was a powder-box on the washhand stand. The question has also been raised whether the cell detritus might be derived from a secretion of the mammary glands. This must be answered in the negative. In colostrum we find fatty cells having the appearance of alveolar epithelium with fatty degeneration. They occur in the company of small round fat globules.

Four further microscopic preparations were obtained by the author in the Paris sitting of 18th November 1912, and were examined in the Antoine Hospital in Paris. The result is as follows:—

(1) Large quantities of cell detritus and cell nuclei.
(2) Large, clear, and well-isolated plate epithelium cells in conjunction with various microbes.

(3) Mucus-like substance with cell detritus and numerous microbes.
(4) Some wool threads (from dress).

The origin of the cells, whether from the mouth or the vagina, cannot be determined.

Preparations (1) and (2) were sent later (4th December) to the Schwalm laboratory for a further examination, with the following result (Figs. 167 and 168):—

Preparation (1), coloured red. The microscope shows conglomerates of epithelioid bodies of irregular shape, probably embedded in mucus-like substance. Nuclear structures are recognisable in a few cases. The epithelioid bodies are mostly decomposing, though a few are intact.

Preparation (2), stained blue. The microscope shows mucoid, formless masses, and dispersed among them numerous unnucleated, polygonal, epithelioid structures, with many nucleated ones; the latter are sometimes so well defined that they can be termed epithelium cells. There are also isolated cotton threads and fungoid threads.

The liquids obtained on 27th November 1912 could not be preserved, owing to incorrect treatment. The preparations made eight days later from this evaporated residue showed nothing remarkable.

Only one of them showed coarsely made, formless structures with irregular markings, consisting of roundish elongated meshes. This shows some hæmorrhagic staining, and gives the impression of a thickened fragment of epidermis. Perhaps there is here an epidermis scale removed by scratching.

In judging the above material we must first eliminate the accidental admixtures derived from the air and from the cotton dress, like fibrous vegetable remains, bacterial spores, starch grains, dust particles, and other impurities. Only those elements which occur in all the preparations are significant. These include cell detritus and epithelium cells, with or without nuclei, finest veils, lamellæ, either intact or dissolving into fibres, filmy aggregates, isolated fat grains and mucus.

The combustion process shows the organic origin of the residues, but, in addition, the microscopic results obtained in Paris and Munich do not permit the slightest doubt that we have to do with organic, i.e., originally *living matter*.

Without wishing to draw far-reaching conclusions from this fact, it does speak against the supposed use of textile products, of paper, rubber objects, etc., for the artificial presentation of the phenomena and of the automobile substance observed.

As regards the probable origin of the material, such epithelial bodies and their products of disintegration would be normally looked for in the female genital system and in the mouth and gullet.

The genital origin would in this case presuppose the penetration of the organic material through the black tricot and the black cotton dress, i.e., through a double layer of textile fabric. In the cases dealt with the tights were free from spots. That the genitals can give rise to the phenomena in question is already proved by observations. But the microscopic observations do not show a single leucocyte, such as always accompanies vaginal epithelia, nor Döderlein's vaginal bacillus and other characteristic bodies. The lamellar veils shown in the microphotographs do not occur in vaginal secretions, so that the vaginal origin is very improbable.

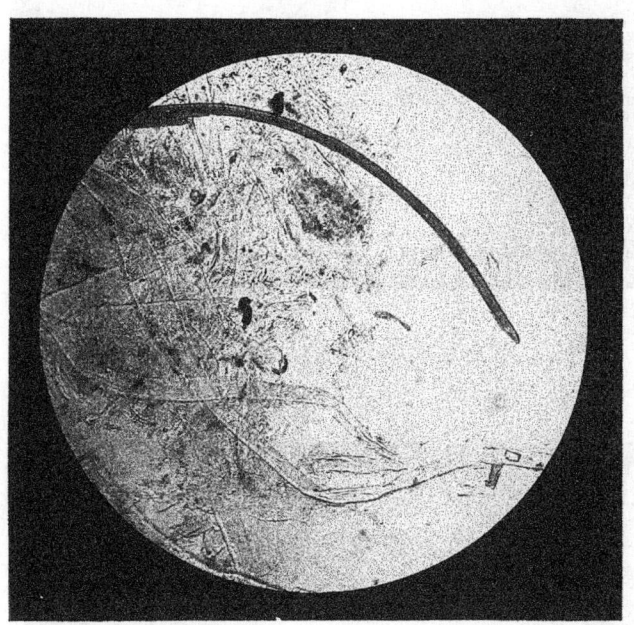

Fig. 166. Preparation (B). SITTING OF 11 SEPTEMBER, 1911.

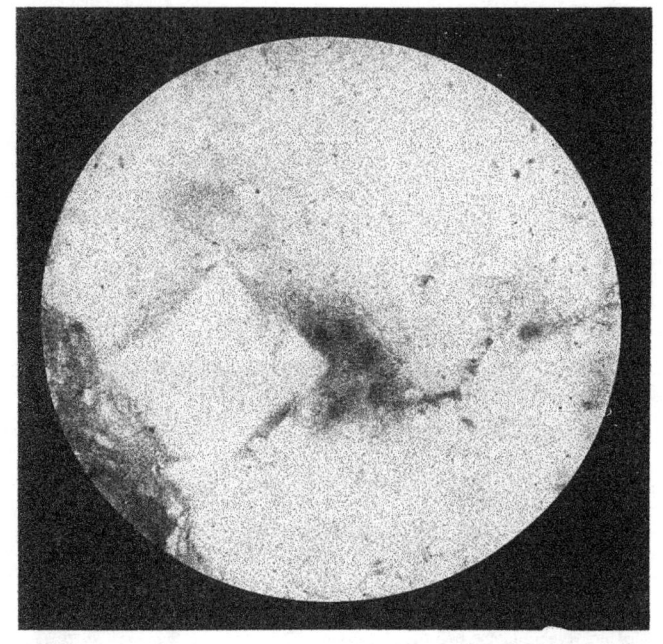

Fig. 168. Same. The lighter rectangle is accidental.

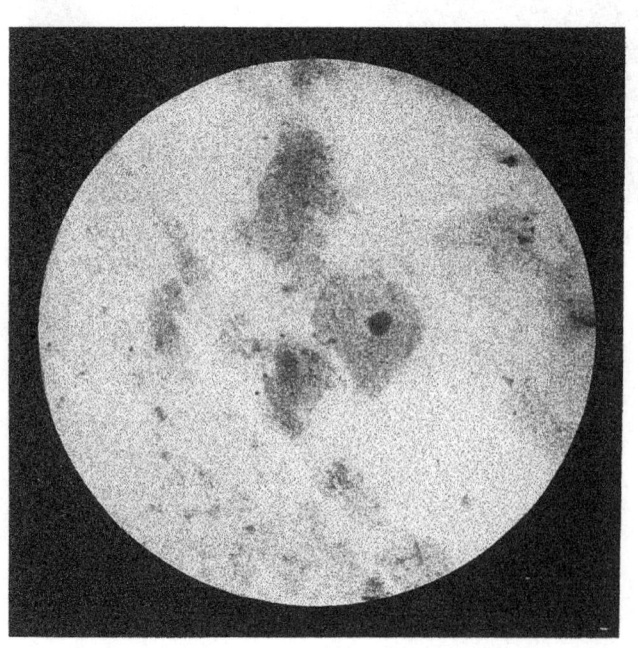

Fig. 167. Preparation 2. Sitting of 18 November, 1912

RESULT OF THE MICROSCOPIC EXAMINATIONS

As regards the mouth and pharynx, we may recollect that in one case, in Bayonne, sputum was traced, in conjunction with other cell products. Human saliva, as secreted by the three large glands, the parotid, submaxillary, and sublingual, as well as the smaller glands in the mouth epithelium, is a light blue, odourless, viscid, " stringy " liquid, which, when allowed to stand, separates into a transparent upper layer and a dull whitish-yellow layer, the latter consisting of mucus flocculi, salivary corpuscles, and buccal epithelium. The latter are mostly polygonal, and have a considerable size. There are also red blood corpuscles, leucocytes, fat droplets, common bacilli, and other micro-organisms and bacteria. The most important and ever-present constituent are the saliva corpuscles, which resemble leucocytes, but are larger and show a granulated protoplasm.

Now, the material collected by us has a certain resemblance to saliva, while liquid. It is colourless, covered by a mouse-grey film, " stringy," viscid, and odourless. The light blue colour is absent; on standing the liquid evaporates, leaving a dry residue (cell detritus) instead of separating into a yellowish layer, like saliva.

This shows already that our liquid matter is not saliva.

Out of all the microscopic preparations there is no case in which saliva corpuscles were shown to be present. White and red corpuscles were also absent, and so were the micro-organisms and bacteria characteristic of the mouth, like *leptothrix* and *sarcina*.

The supposition that the cellular tissues and filmy veils of the material examined originate in the mucous membrane and pharynx is contradicted by the total absence of the blood corpuscles, bacteria, and saliva corpuscles characteristic of that origin.

We must also take into account that even in air breathed out from the mouth we find such admixtures, and can nearly always detect their presence, as is shown by the microscopic preparations of precipitates on telephone diaphragms.

Thus the absence in our microscopic preparations of products characteristic of the mucous membrane of the mouth and pharynx tells against regarding these membranes as the origin of the teleplastic tissues. If these were only detritus of the mouth they would certainly contain salivary corpuscles; we can, therefore, exclude this possibility with some certainty. All the same, the material can originate in the mouth, as has often been observed and photographed, but its development must be independent of the mucous membrane, and the building up of the tissue cannot depend on the mouth itself. During expulsion from the mouth it might easily take some secretion from the mouth with it, so that a microscopic proof of such an admixture would have no connection with the real process of development. This may explain the results obtained in the Bayonne laboratory.

Very probably the formation of the substance, which appears in the sittings as liquid material, and also as amorphous material, or filmy net-like and veil-like material in the form of shreds, wisps, threads, and cords, in large or small packets, is an organised tissue which easily decomposes—a sort of transitory matter which originates in the organism in a manner unknown to us, possesses unknown biological functions, and formative possibilities, and is evidently peculiarly dependent on the psychic influence of the medium. Thus the appearance shown in Figs. 127, 129, and 135 corresponds to organic bodies both in its structure and its grouping, and recalls placental and mesenteric structures. Complicated functions of motion (growth and involution) and sensation (reaction to touch) were observed in them. The constituents of the veil-like and tissue-like creations also resemble fundamental shapes of the organic world in the branching and in the joining of their fibres (Fig. 154).

But the investigations hitherto made do not suffice for any definite indications concerning the structure, composition, or function of this substance.

At present we can only assert that such a self-moving, formative material can develop outside the body, and that during its disappearance it often leaves behind cell detritus, which permits us in conjunction with other observations to draw conclusions regarding its morphological composition. On account of its body-forming property we can compare the fundamental substance with structureless plasma. By plasma we mean the formative substance, or organic material, which is the vehicle of vital processes. Now, since all the changes of the substance observed by us take place outside the medium's organism, first on her skin, then on the clothed body, and finally separated from it, the name *teleplasm* is appropriate, once we admit the actuality of the substance.

The cell detritus which remained behind and was collected by us is not an accidental admixture with the teleplasm. This is shown by the manner in which it was obtained and the absence of the characteristic elements of the bodily orifices from which such products might be derived.

As regards the structure of the teleplasm, we only know this: that within it, or about it, we find conglomerates of bodies resembling epithelium, real plate epithelium with nuclei, veil-like filmy structures, coherent lamellar bodies without structure, as well as fat globules and mucus. If we abstain from any detailed indications concerning the composition and function of teleplasma, we may yet assert two definite facts :—

(1) In teleplasm, or associated with it, we find substances of organic origin, various cell forms, which leave behind cell detritus.
(2) The mobile material observed, which seems to represent the fundamental substance of the phenomena, does not consist of india rubber or any other artificial product by which its existence could be fraudulently represented.

For substances of this kind can never decompose into cell detritus, or leave a residue of such.

PHENOMENA WITH STANISLAVA P.

INTRODUCTION.

THE Polish medium, Stanislava P., at the author's invitation, placed herself at his disposal in Munich for a series of sittings extending from 29th September 1912 to 21st February 1913. The mediumship of this nineteen-year-old girl, who was employed as a cashier in a business at Warsaw, was discovered a year before and developed by Mr S. at Warsaw in a series of sittings.

In her eighteenth year Stanislava P. experienced in her room a telepathic hallucination by the optical appearance of her friend Sophie, of the same age, who, as it was afterwards found, had unexpectedly died at that moment. This experience directed attention to her mediumistic faculty, and suggested experiments with Stanislava in conformity with the spiritistic tradition. After this, the personification "Sophie" played the leading part in the manifestations.

Stanislava P. came of a good family, but lost her parents at an early age, and was adopted by a gardener. Up to her tenth year she remained illiterate, and when, at eighteen years, she took part in the sittings for the first time, she could not yet read or write perfectly. She showed, in accordance with her degree of education, a very limited comprehension of the necessary conditions of these experiments, only consenting to them with reluctance, to oblige her benefactor, and in order to earn her living. In her case, there is a great æsthetic awkwardness and a lack of disposition towards plastic art, and this is clearly seen in her materialised products. "Spiritism" she did not know even by name, when the first experiments were made with her, thus any assumption relating to a possible training in conjuring are devoid of every foundation.

On the other hand, it should be mentioned that Stanislava P. created the most favourable impression on the persons whom she met in Warsaw and Munich by her modest, simple, and amiable character. But her excessively developed modesty, her great timidity, and emotional disposition rendered the application of rigid experimental conditions difficult. Any new method of control she regarded as an aspersion upon her honesty, and this was often followed by emotional excitement, tears, sleepless nights, and negative sittings. She did not permit an examination of her naked body by the author or any other male person, whereas she had no objection to the presence of ladies while she undressed and put on the séance costume (tights and apron dress, as in the case of Eva C.). For this reason ladies had to be admitted to the sittings. After her return, a lady physician sent the author a virginity certificate concerning the medium.

The arrangement of the experiments required, from the beginning, a delicate adaptation to the peculiarities of her character, but especially a discreet consideration for her well-developed sense of female honour and modesty, if positive results were to be achieved at all. Finally, we must not forget that in Stanislava P. we have a young novice whose mediumistic career, hardly a year old, cannot be compared with the experience and education of Eva C., extending over nearly ten years. For that reason, conditions which could be applied, after four years, to Eva C., as the result of long and laborious training, could not be immediately applied to Stanislava. Under these circumstances, some of the phenomena presented by this mediumistic debutante are less evidential and convincing than the manifestations of Eva C. Yet there has never been any indication justifying the suspicion that she had introduced fabrics, veils, hands, gloves, etc., into the cabinet in any form. Before every sitting Stanislava usually undressed completely in the presence of a lady, and put on the séance costume which was prescribed by the author, consisting of tights with a black apron tunic. The two articles of apparel were not sewn together, as even if that had been done it might have been maintained that the medium could touch her skin, so long as she had the use of her hands. The medium's condition and history exclude the use of the vagina as a hiding place, but so long as the character of the phenomena is such that they cannot be imitated under the same conditions, such objections may be disregarded in any case.

During the second series of experiments in Munich, June to August 1913, we often used a black tricot for the whole body which had only to be closed down the back. A veil securely sewn to the neck of the garment covered the whole head, and was closed with ribbons at the neck (Fig. 169). Along the slit on the back, and on the veil, there were a large number of black rings through which a string was drawn. The knot was sealed with a lead seal. If we also take into account that the hands were contained in white or black sacks of veiling sewn to the sleeves, one must admit that it is altogether impossible to smuggle objects for a fraudulent purpose out of this prison enclosing the whole body. Besides, the material of the tricot is sufficiently transparent to show the whole surface anatomy and the main shades of the epidermis. Since the cabinet was also strictly searched beforehand, we may assume that under these conditions it would be an absolute impossibility to produce previously hidden objects, and to manipulate them through the delicate veils with the hands. The practical results achieved by this method may be considered as of equal value to those obtained by Eva C Of the whole photographic results obtained with Stanislava P., only those are here communicated which are of interest for the present work on account of their agreement with those of the Paris meetings.

Sittings in January and February 1913 (Munich).

SITTING WITH STANISLAVA P. ON THE 25TH JANUARY 1913.

Present.—Privatdozent Dr E., Freiherr von Gleichen-Russwurm (author) with his wife, Herr von Kaiser (painter), a Pole who acted as interpreter, the author and his wife.

Séance Room.—Cabinet and cameras as during the Munich sittings with Eva C.

Illumination.—As in August 1912, but the illumination of a hundred

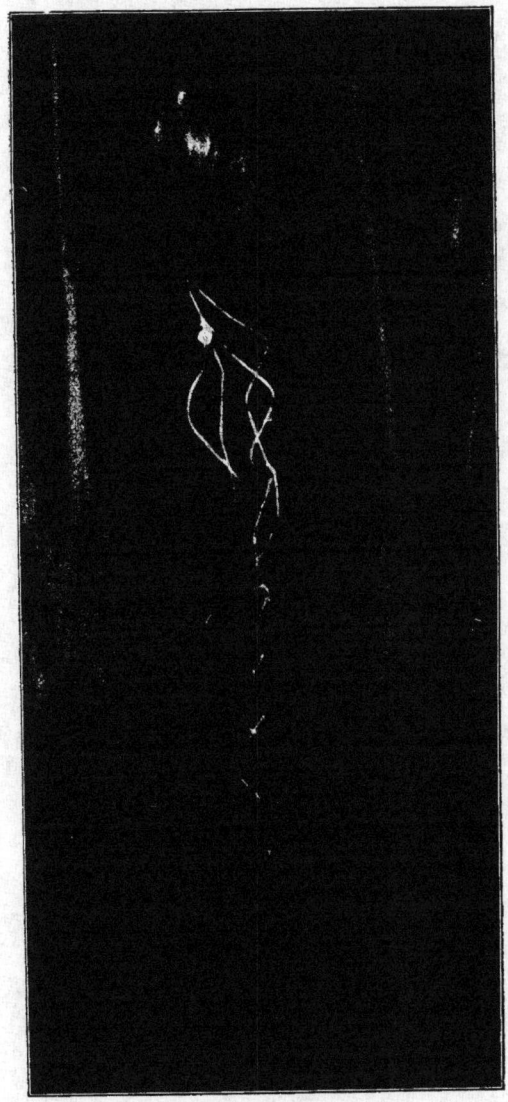

FIG. 169 FASTENING OF THE COSTUME WORN BY STANISLAVA P IN THE SITTINGS FROM 23 JUNE TO 1 JULY, 1913.

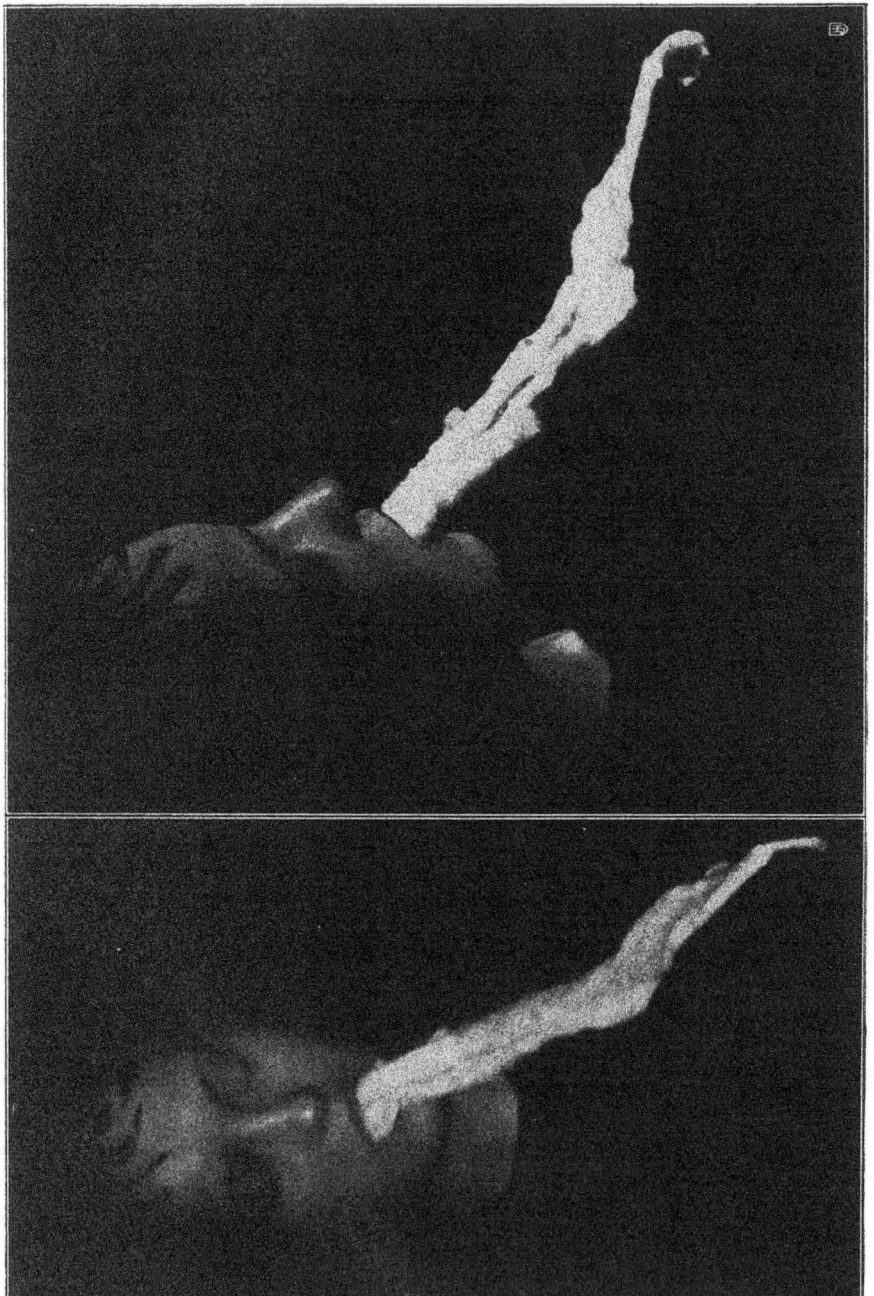

FIG. 170. AUTHOR'S FLASHLIGHT PHOTOGRAPHS, 25 JANUARY, 1913.

candle-power was too bright, and, as a rule, we had to switch off four lamps, so that only a thirty-five candle-power red bulb gave light, yet the room was sufficiently bright. The sitters sat 5 to 7 feet in front of the curtain.

Initial Control and Dress.—Before every sitting the young girl went into a separate room accompanied by the author's wife or some other lady. Here she undressed completely and put on the séance costume (exactly like Eva C.), so that, under the tricot and the dress, there was only her naked body (no shoes). Her own dress remained in the room referred to, and was sometimes examined without the medium's knowledge by the author. On account of the fine transparent material of the séance costume, an external examination sufficed to tell whether packets or veils were hidden anywhere. There was also an examination of the hair, done up in a braid, and of the ears, mouth, etc. This examination was carried out by Dr E. and the author.

It has been stated that hysterical persons, who have no reflex action of the soft palate, are able to use the inner nose passage as a hiding place. Apart from the pros and cons of such a far-fetched hypothesis, we must not lose sight of the fact that an obstruction of this passage renders the drawing of air into the nose impossible, and the author made the medium close her mouth and blow through each of her nostrils in turn. This regular test always gave a negative result. The access of air to the lungs through the nose was never stopped. After careful examination of the cabinet by Dr E., Stanislava entered the séance room (which she had not entered before), guided by Dr E. and the author, and took her place on the easy-chair in the cabinet.

Hypnotisation by the author: fixation, suggestion, and mesmeric passes. It should be mentioned that Stanislava, during this period, was hypnotised daily by the author, including the days when there were no sittings, so as to achieve by suggestion her favourable psychic adjustment. After barely half a minute, the medium fell into somnambulism, and remained in a state of passive hypnosis during the whole sitting. In contrast with Eva C., she hardly ever spoke during hypnosis, although she sometimes opened her eyes.

Course of the Sitting.—Commencement, 9 P.M. Only after the curtain had been closed did the other sitters enter the séance room and take their seats in the appointed places. Herr von Kaiser sat beside a musical box, which was kept going during the whole sitting, and attended to it, the medium having been accustomed to this by the Warsaw sittings.

Extinction of the white light. The sitters passed the time in conversation while the medium's hands were behind the curtain. A correspondence with the mediumistic forces was carried on by raps, which came from behind the curtain. These were not the subject of the investigation, so that it appears irrelevant whether they were produced automatically by the medium or telekinetically.

Of the occurrences observed during this sitting, it need only be mentioned that when the medium's hands opened the curtain a white wisp coming from her mouth was observed on her breast by all those present. The flash-light was turned on at the next exposure.

At the close of the sitting the author awakened the medium from a fairly deep hypnosis. Stanislava only recovered slowly. While she was still hypnotised, Dr E. and the author passed their hands over her whole body, and this was repeated when she awoke, but the examination of the medium and the cabinet was negative. On the breast of the dress, however, quite corresponding to the place at which the materialised structure had touched it, there was a white patch, about the size of half a crown, which on examination under the microscope in the form of ten preparations gave the following composition :—

In the first nine preparations examined there are cellular granulated structures, about the size and shape of white blood corpuscles, or mucus corpuscles,[1] and also bodies resembling epithelium without nuclei, and true epithelium. In Preparation No. 10 there were sharply defined nuclear aggregates of leucocytes and clearly marked epithelium.

The result of the examination of Preparation 10 justifies the assumption that the cellular granulated structures found in other preparations also represent leucocytes whose nuclei are concealed by the granulation, and that the unnucleated epithelioid bodies represent epithelium with its nuclei already decomposed.

As regards the origin of the material examined, its whole arrangement and composition, especially in Preparations 1 and 2, indicate sputum rather than anything else, since there are not only abundant leucocytes and mucus corpuscles, but also scale epithelia (squamous epithelium) as well as round epithelia with fatty degeneration (alveolar epithelia), as in Preparation 7, which fit into the scheme.

The elongated form of the leucocytes, which frequently occur in the viscous material, are characteristic of sputum.

On the other hand, the appearance of the spots on the black dress does not indicate dried sputum since the latter forms whitish, shiny pellicles, composed of innumerable small islets due to the air bubbles mixed with the sputum. The whitish spots examined were without lustre and showed no admixture of air bubbles.

Other origins (nose secretions would show characteristic epithelia) are excluded, since the spots were found on the breast of the tunic.

The successful photographic records (Fig. 170) show a broad compact irregularly formed mass about 20 to 22 inches long emerging from the open mouth of the medium and filling up its whole opening. This mass remains suspended ; it does not lie on the front of the dress. It seems composed along its whole length of two strips, which coalesce below, or are woven together. The longitudinal furrow on both pictures must be interpreted in that sense. The surface appears rough, irregularly formed, and somewhat resembling a wool product.

The great lightness of the substance is suggested by the fact that it does not sink but is suspended in the air, unless, indeed, it has a sufficiently rigid character, determined in its situation by the position of the mouth. Such a rough, shred-like character in materialised phenomena proceeding from the mouth is also seen in a number of photographs taken with Eva C., and the parallelism between the two mediums is worthy of notice.

Sitting of the 31st January 1913.

Present.—Mr and Mrs Schott, Miss Kolb, Colonel Pfülff, Dr E., von Kaiser, and the author.

The medium put on her séance costume in the presence of Mrs Schott and was examined by Dr E. and the author, and hypnotised as on

[1] These are often difficult to distinguish, especially in dried objects.

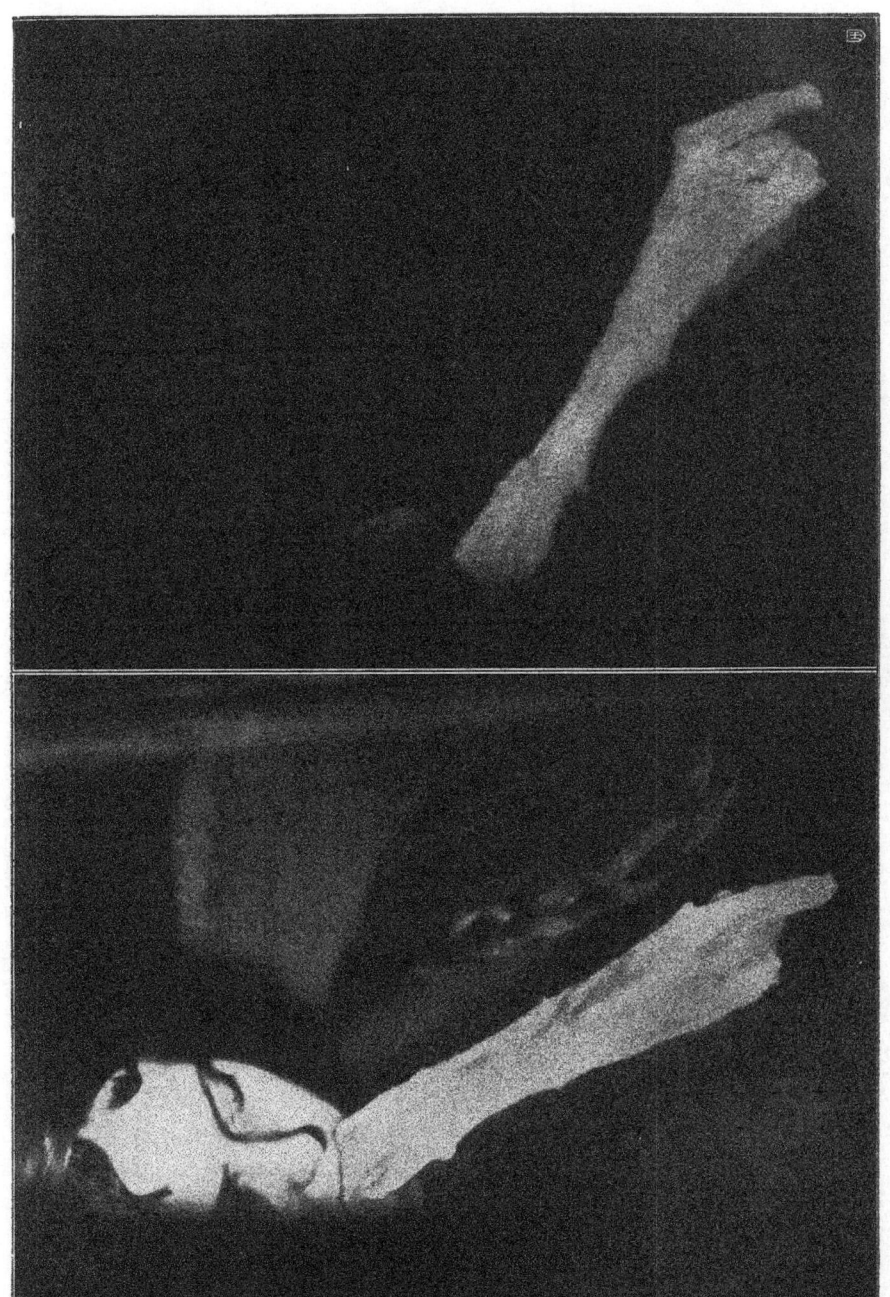

FIG. 171. AUTHOR'S FLASHLIGHT PHOTOGRAPHS OF 31 JANUARY, 1913.

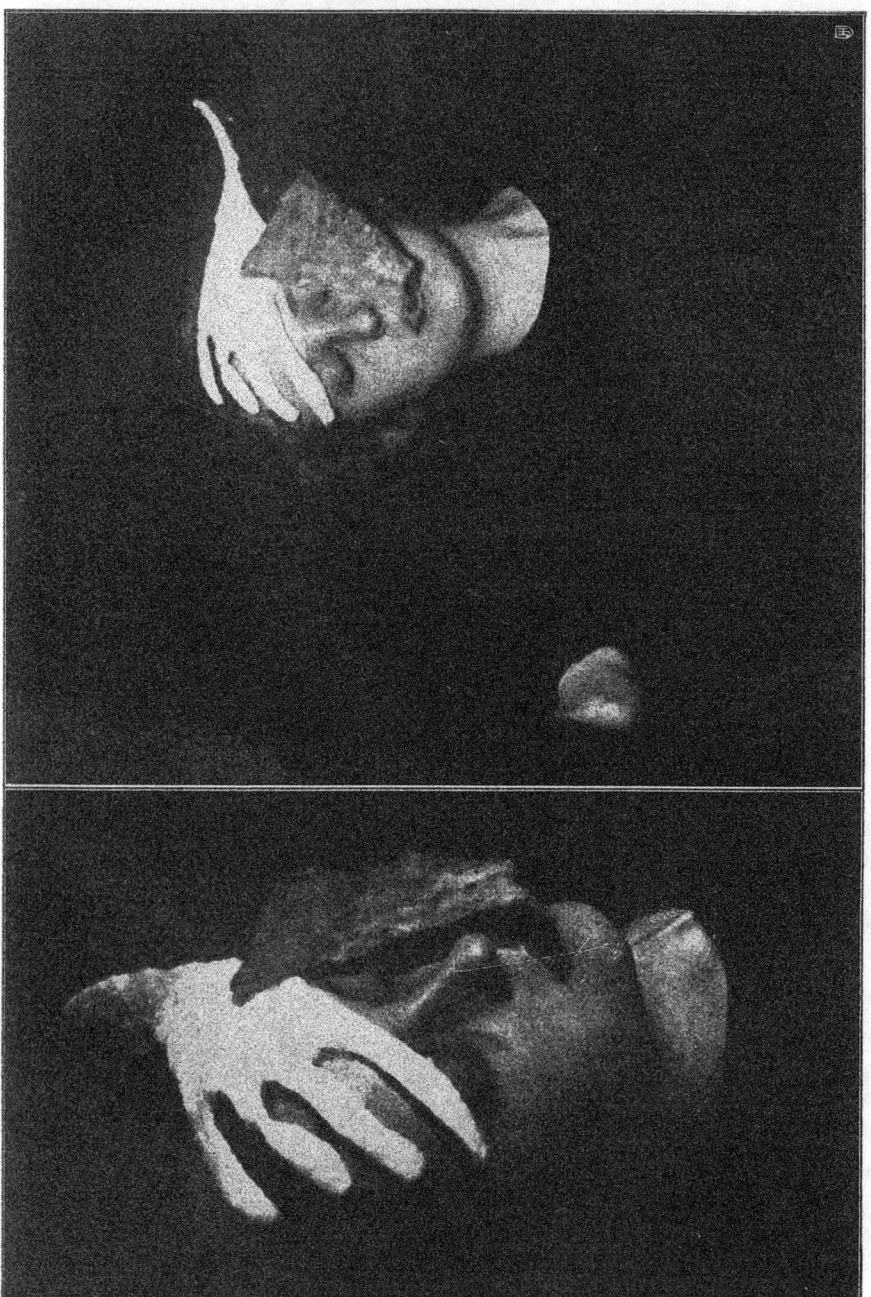

Fig. 172. Author's flashlight photographs of 15 February, 1913.

25th January. Illumination and experimental arrangements were the same as in that sitting.

After several occurrences of phenomena, not to be described here, the same long white materialisation proceeding from the mouth was observed as on 25th January. Some of the observers claimed to see, at the end of the strip, a hand with a stretched index finger. My wish to touch the structure and illuminate it with white electric light was refused. A flash-light photograph was taken, the curtain was closed, the phenomenon disappeared, and the sitting was continued. There were some further manifestations which have no connection with the mouth phenomena. The sitting was closed after lasting about an hour and a half. The final examination, as on 25th January, was negative.

As this day's photographs (Fig. 171) show, the structure developed from the mouth is essentially the same as that observed on the 25th January. There is a broad, thick, rough, and consistent white strand, resembling an arm, the fundamental structure of which, as shown by the enlargement, appears to be granular. No pattern of any organic or technical fabric is to be seen. The exterior surface is partly striped, irregular, and rough. At the end of the mass, which broadens below, there are three quite coarsely designed fingers, one of which, the index, is stretched, while the two others are bent. A fine and nearly transparent strip lies under the right external margin of the ribbon-like structure, as shown by the side view. This shape is also suspended, and does not touch the dress. Here, then, we find another parallel to the performances of Eva C. The product developed from the mouth, which is not veil-like, shows in both cases a tendency to form shapes such as hands and fingers.

Sitting of the 15th February 1913.

Present.—Mrs von S., who superintended the medium's dressing, Countess K., Dr E., von Kaiser, and the author.

Beginning, 5 P.M. Conditions, control, and plan of the sitting as before.

When a white surface became visible on her head, the author, with the medium's permission, turned on the flash-light. The sitting was closed after an hour's duration. Final examination negative.

On the photograph (Fig. 172) secured on 15th February the observer sees on the forehead of the somnambulist a white flat shape, with four projections, resembling a claw or a sketch of a hand of the most primitive form. The back of the hand ends pointedly in a stalk projecting into the dark space. The fourth member appears somewhat twisted about its own axis. On the enlarged side view one can see that the substance composing this structure has the same rough woolly character as the strip emerging from the mouth and described above. No sort of pattern is to be recognised, as there would be in the case of a woven fabric or wood-fibre product. The finger-shaped projections, corresponding to the size of an adult's fingers, follow the curvature of the forehead, curving round the temples, but stand off from the skin and cast shadows upon it. The projection corresponding to the left thumb is wanting, but a portion of the structure is held by a second triangular piece of dark material, which is also flat and emerges from the medium's mouth. The lowest pointed corner bends round and vanishes between the lips, filling up the half-open mouth. This dark substance also appears rough and fibrous.

The mediumistic products of the 25th and 31st January and of 15th February exhibit throughout a woolly character. With the help of wadding, one might perhaps produce similar pictures, but on further examination of the enlargements one does not anywhere find the characteristic fibrous composition of wadding. Besides, in manipulating wadding some fibres almost always adhere to the clothing, which could not be removed in the dark, and would have been found. Automatic motion is not found in any of the forms.

Considered objectively, the pictures make an unfavourable impression. Manipulation with the mouth might have been seen by Stanislava in the photographs of Eva C., and might have then been imitated. We must add that during the production of the phenomena the curtain was closed. If no other proofs were available for the mediumistic power of Stanislava P. we should have to arrive at an unfavourable judgment, in spite of the control being as strict as possible. We must not overlook the remarkable agreement of many details of observation of Stanislava P. with the phenomena produced by Eva C. Thus, the shred-like fibres and irregular fundamental character of the substance are similar with both mediums, so is the flat sketch-like impressionistic form of the structures, and, finally, the mode of occurrence by generation in an orifice of the body—in this case, the mouth. In any case, there seems to be an independent agreement in the results of both mediums, though the whole of the creations of Stanislava P. appear less perfect and could be more easily imitated.

The Polish medium, on her return journey, remained several days in Vienna, and in March 1913 she gave several sittings in a private house without the author's knowledge, who only learnt of this several months afterwards. The following extract is taken from a letter of a well-known Vienna physician, Dr Harter, with his permission :—

"Now I may tell you that at the first sitting I laughed! I sat mostly at the back. But during the second sitting I was puzzled, and since that time the Saul is become a Paul. This second sitting with Stanislava has had the result of totally reversing my former conception of life. All nature and all life for me has assumed a new aspect. I immediately threw myself with fiery zeal into the study of the literature of the subject, which at that time I had to pick up wherever I could get it. On one occasion I addressed my doubts to you by letter, and you were so kind as to give me really valuable hints, for which I am very grateful. Even to-day I thank the fate which by chance allowed me to see the little Polish girl, for I know to-day that I was an ignorant fool, and considered official science the beginning and end of wisdom. Now I am cured of that, although many scruples and doubts still assail me. In my occupation with this subject I found that which one loses in the exact sciences, namely, a belief in the soul."

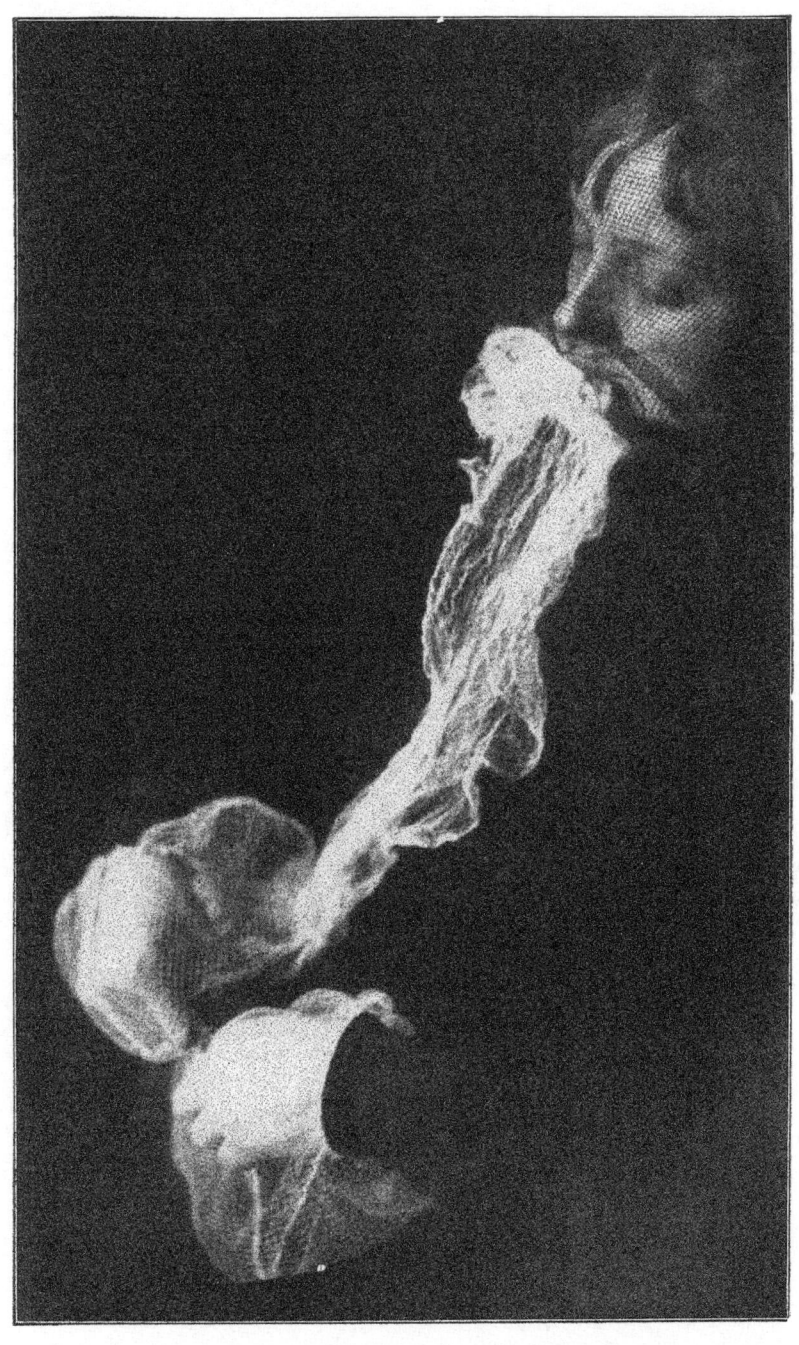

Fig. 173. Author's flashlight photograph, 23 June, 1913.

FIG. 174. AUTHOR'S FLASHLIGHT PHOTOGRAPH, 1 JULY, 1913.
FRONT VIEW.

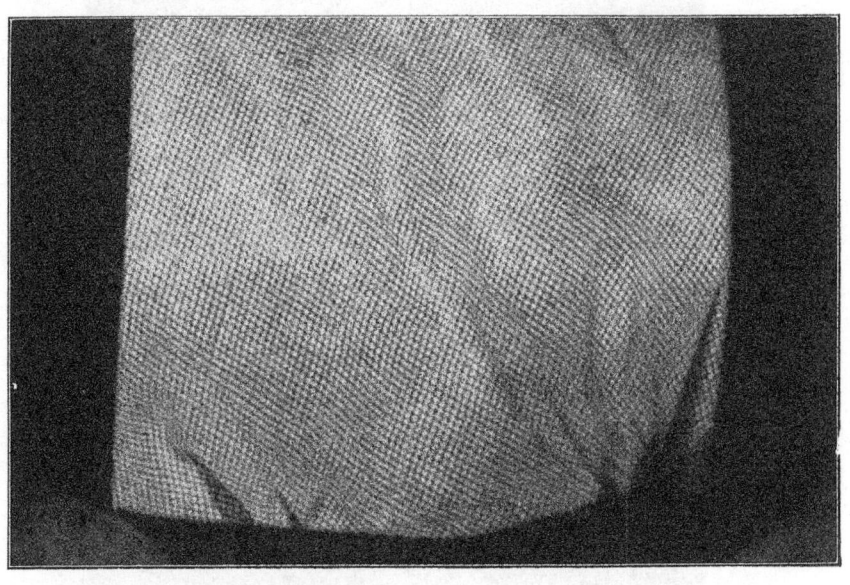

FIG. 175. CONDITION OF THE HEAD VEIL AFTER THE PHENOMENON OF FIG. 174.

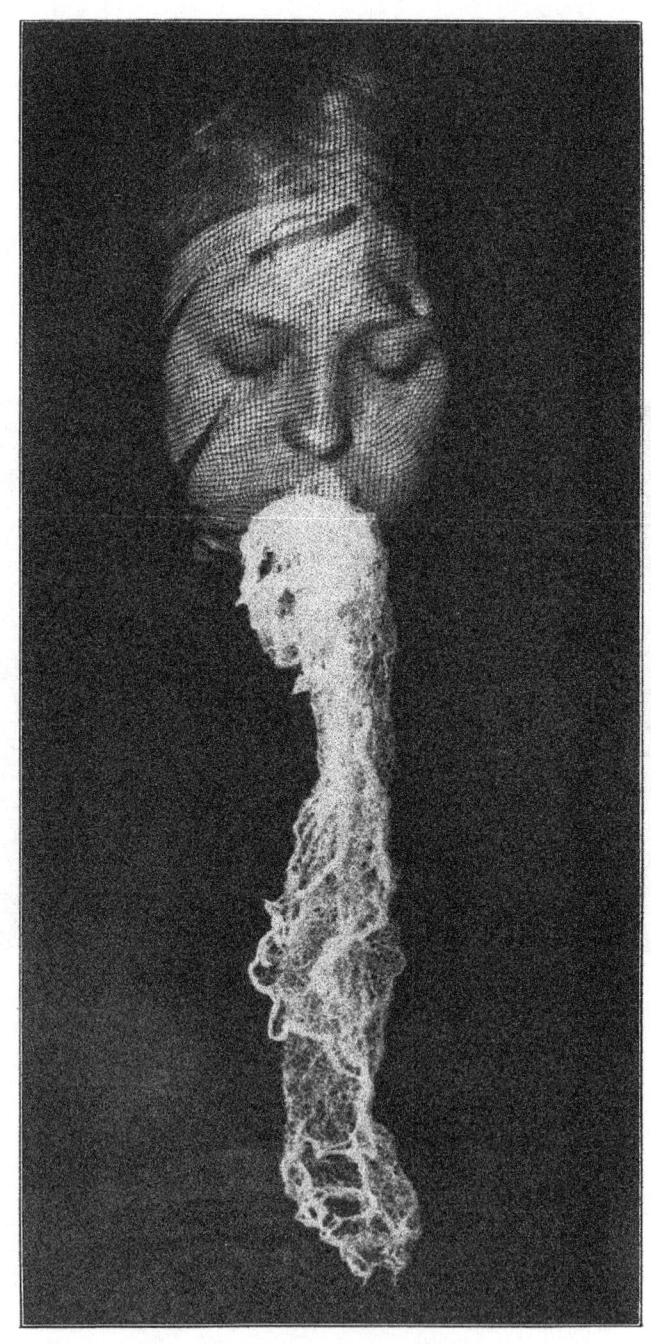

FIG 176. ENLARGEMENT OF FIG. 174.

Sittings of June and July 1913 (Munich).

SITTING OF THE 23RD JUNE 1913.

Present.—Herr von Kaiser, Herr Sch., Princess R., and the author.

Stanislava put on the whole tricot, with wide full bags for the hands, and a white veil covering over the head. The fastening of the head veil and the tricot were lead-sealed. All other conditions and control were as in the sittings of January and February 1913.

8.30 P.M. Hypnotisation by the author. Red light switched on, curtain closed. After about half an hour a long veil-like strip was shown, which came out of the medium's mouth and appeared to penetrate the veil. A flash-light photograph was taken. Sitting closed at 10 P.M. Final examination of the medium and cabinet negative. All the veils and lead seals intact.

The enlarged photograph (Fig. 173), taken from the left within the cabinet, shows the medium's head in a black veil, and her hands in white veils. From the mouth down to the left hand there extends a broad fibrous material passing through the veil, which at its upper end shows a thick bulge, and is marked by a transparent pattern which, in its branchings, recalls vegetable fibres rather than textiles. It is interesting to note the difference between the regular square thread structure of the white veil, covering the hands, and the marking of the mediumistic product. A piece of the black veil seems to be drawn back into the mouth by Stanislava, so that the process of the penetration of the veil is not clearly shown. For this reason the experiment was repeated under the same conditions, with the head veil drawn more tightly, and the suggestion was made not to draw it into the mouth. But the experiment, in any case, is evidential, since the medium had no materials at her disposal with which she could have brought about such a result, outside her dress.

SITTING OF THE 1ST JULY 1913.

Present.—Herr von Kaiser, Herr Sch., the author and his wife.

The sitters sat immediately in front of the curtain. Conditions, illumination, and hypnosis as on 23rd June 1913. The author's wife superintended the medium's toilet. She wore the whole tricot as on 23rd June. The white veil bags for the hands were replaced by black ones. The fastening of the head veil and tricot was lead-sealed.

After hypnosis had set in, it was suggested to the medium that she should repeat the experiment of 23rd June, so that we might be able to see the material both inside and outside the veil. The curtain was closed and a correspondence by raps took place.

After thirty minutes we again saw, extending from the mouth to the waist, a strip with a length of about 20 inches, and a width of 6 or 8 inches. A flash-light photograph was taken and the curtain was closed. The sitting came to an end, and the final examination was negative.

On the photograph, taken from the front (Figs. 174 and 175), the forms of the body are clearly marked out through the tricot. In this case, the veil was drawn more tightly over the face and showed fewer folds. The upper lip is covered by a white substance, which appears to penetrate the veil, broadening out on the outside. There is a remarkable difference from the drawing of the structure of 23rd June. While the former recalls vegetable fibres, the present photograph shows a structure of lace-work, of woollen threads of various sizes, with thickened edges (Fig. 176).

The views from the right and from the left (Figs. 177 and 178) corroborate these details, and hardly leave a doubt that the materialised substance, in a veil-like form, has penetrated the veil mask.

Fig. 175 shows the condition of the veil after the experiment, and particularly in the place where the penetration occurred. The conditions of attachment in the experiment of the 1st July did not allow any further possibility of a fraudulent production of these phenomena. They form an interesting analogy with the experiments of Eva C. on 16th May 1913.

Sittings of the 25th June and 13th July 1913.

Conditions, illumination, and plan of the sitting as before. Professor B. and the author undertook the initial and final examinations of the medium and the cabinet on 25th June, and Dr C. (physician) and the author on 13th July.

In these sittings the veil phenomenon already mentioned was again produced. The curtain was only opened after the material had been formed.

On both evenings we succeeded in working the kinematograph for several minutes. These were the first occasions on which this had been done. The film taken on the first evening comprises about 360 pictures, and that on 13th July over 400. The two films in Figs. 179 and 180 show the recession of the material into the mouth, and the second film also shows the broadening and narrowing of the substance. On 30th July some photographs were taken with a portion of the matter still attached to the mouth, and finally the mouth was shown after the material had disappeared. The changes, visible on Fig. 180, might not suffice for the proof of an independent inner motion of the substance, however remarkable they may be. That the changes in the volume are produced by motions of the head is hardly suggested by the kinematograph. The objection will no doubt be raised that Stanislava probably drew the veil-like substance with her tongue into her mouth, and then swallowed it.

It is not denied that this is physiologically possible, but such an explanation would, in any case, assume an occurrence experienced only in a few rare cases by specialists in digestive diseases. The mere proof by photography of such a fact in the case of the medium would be a novel achievement worthy of mention for this reason alone. In any case, in both sittings the mouth was examined after the phenomenon had disappeared, without any remnants being found. Although this occurrence is not, by itself, evidential, as regards the disappearance and change in volume of the substance, the success of the kinematographic record of a mediumistic materialisation phenomenon represents such a considerable progress in method that, for this reason alone, the publication of some selected pictures of the series in both films should not be

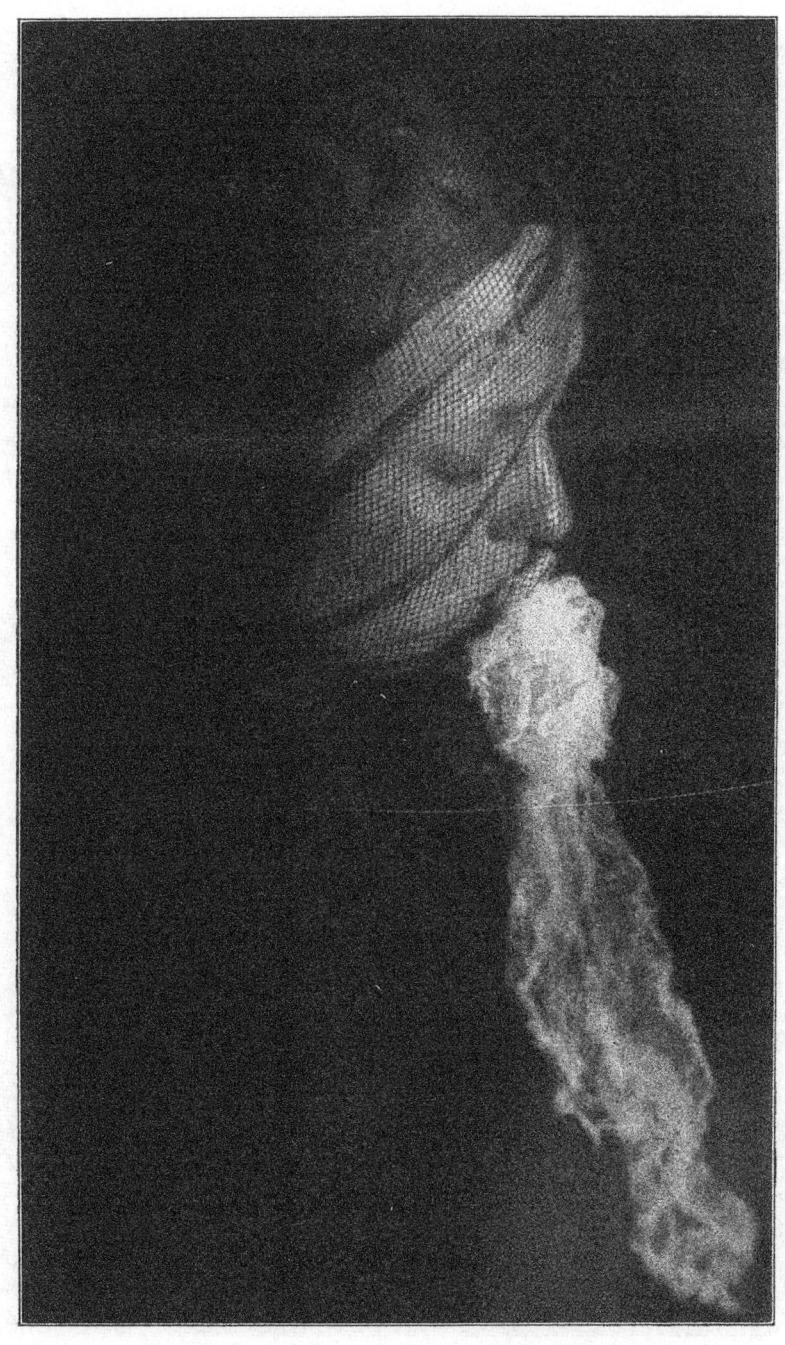

FIG. 177. SIDE VIEW FROM WITHIN THE CABINET. (*Right.*)

Fig. 178. Side view from within the cabinet. (*Left.*)

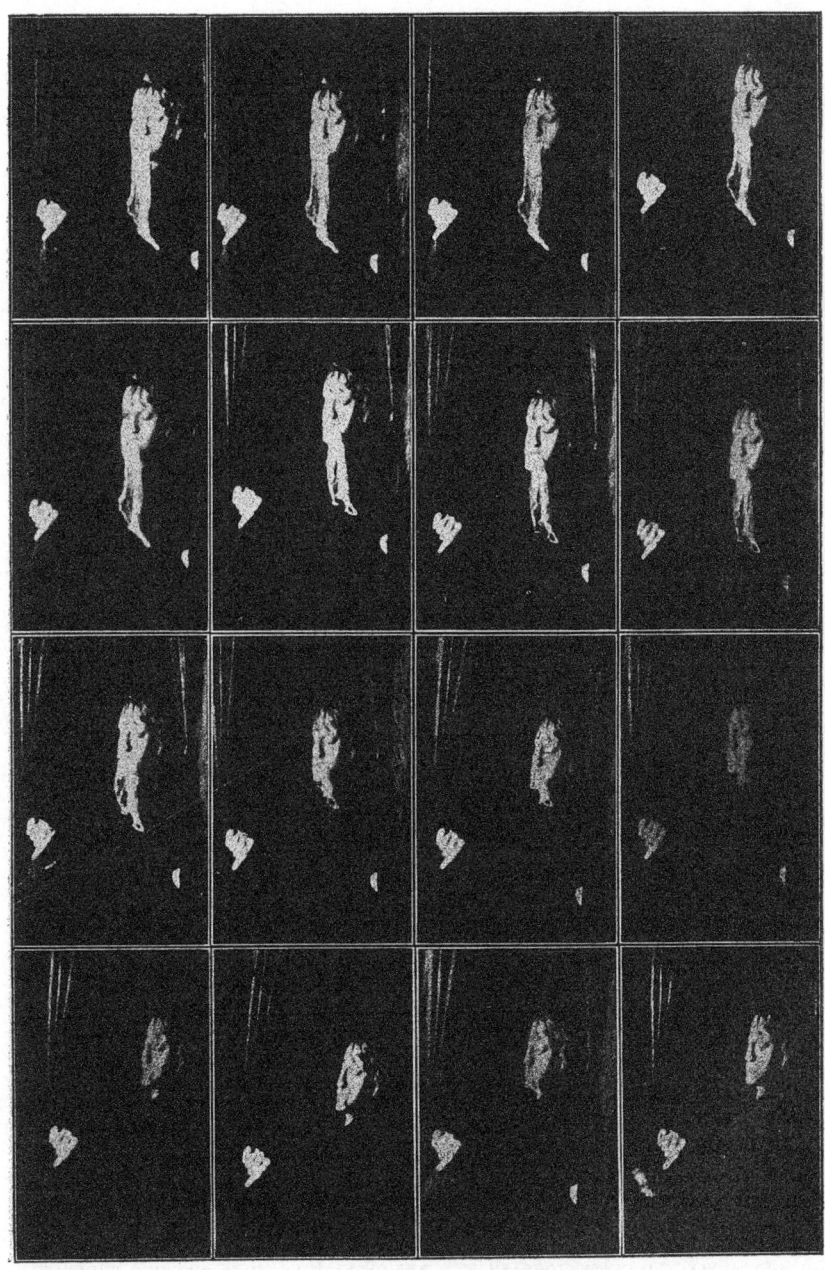

FIG. 179. SELECTED CINEMATOGRAPH PICTURES OF 25 JUNE, 1913, SHOWING ABSORPTION OF THE SUBSTANCE INTO THE MOUTH.

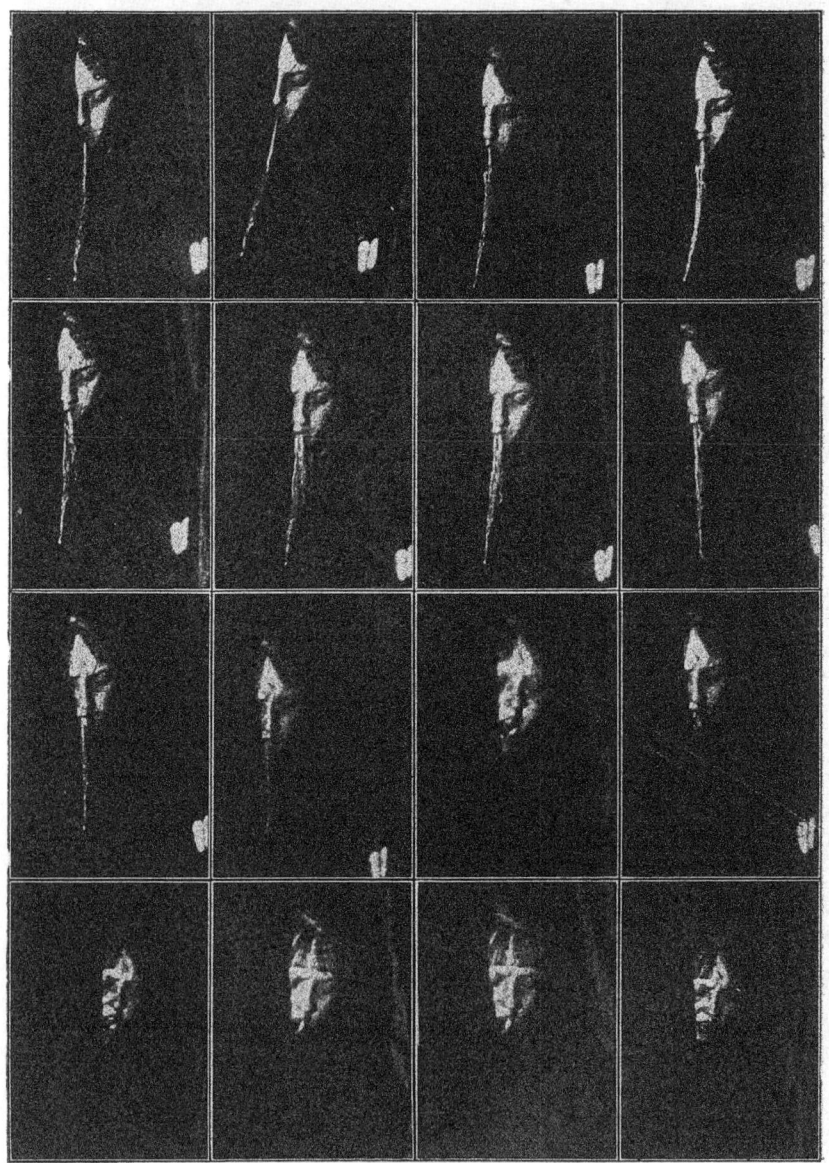

Fig 180. Selected cinematograph pictures of 13 July, 1913, showing widening and narrowing of the substance, and its recession into the mouth.

omitted. The investigator must in all his work state the truth, without considering whether it corresponds to his expectations or not.

RESULTS OF THE OBSERVATIONS.

THE proof of the mediumistic faculty in Stanislava P. is not only found in her materialisation phenomena, but also in certain telekinetic actions spontaneously occurring, in her case, in daylight, as the author has several times had occasion to observe. If one only judged by the appearance of the products exposed in the sittings, which partly resembled large flat men's leather gloves, or compact woolly masses up to the size of a forearm, or veil materials of fairly coarse structure, the decision would not be in her favour. Besides, the structures produced by her are all coarse and imperfect in their form.

Now, it has already been pointed out by Colonel Peter [1] that, during materialisation phenomena, the apparel, *i.e.*, the dress materials, produced and partly used for clothing the phantoms, give the strongest handle for the criticism advanced by sceptics, as soon as it is shown that they resemble terrestrial materials, or are composed of them. Peter has shown, by careful examination of such cloth samples as the finest crêpe, which were obtained from phantoms of different mediums under conditions excluding fraud, that they do not differ in any way from materials produced by the weaving loom. The creation of such materials is not more wonderful than the materialisation of living members, so that, in judging this point, we always come back to the conditions of production.

The initial and final examination of the bodily surface regularly carried out with Stanislava P., the wearing of a special séance costume, and the large volume of the material represented by the photographs, speak against the possibility of hiding them on or about her body. This also disposes of the objection of a scientific witness whose only reason for refusing to vouch for the genuineness of the phenomena was that the medium did not give him permission for a gynæcological examination.

Quite apart from this question, the genuineness of the mediumistic performances can be vouched for by the character of the phenomena themselves.

Thus, with Stanislava P. the author could, on several occasions, and under conditions excluding such manipulations as are referred to by Ochorowicz, in his essay on " Involuntary Production of Unconscious Fraud," observe a structure resembling a hand, which carried out movements, and grasped and threw away objects held out to it. In this case, the medium's hands are visible, holding the curtain, her feet and knees were in their place, as was proved by the author during the phenomenon, by touching her knees several times, and her head was also visible in the red light. The author sat immediately in front of the curtain, and again and again verified the entire inactivity of the medium's limbs during the investigation. Under the same evidential conditions (immobile, visible body of the medium) a handkerchief held out by the author into the back of the cabinet was grasped and drawn away with

[1] Joseph Peter, *Die Gewandung der Phantome* (the dress of phantoms), *Zentralblatt für Okkultismus*, July 1902.

considerable force, as was a handkerchief laid on the hands in the medium's lap in another sitting, while her head was visible. These examples suffice to show the evidential character of certain phenomena in themselves.

In the suspicions cast upon all mediums, even now, and in the attempts at negative explanations, we find performances assumed which have not been successfully accomplished under the same conditions even by the cleverest conjurors, and which in themselves require a proof of their possibility as manual tricks. That many phenomena, especially among those presented by mediumistic beginners of undeveloped power, can be imitated, is not to be denied, especially if the experimental conditions are not carefully chosen. But does this circumstance alone suffice to support a serious imputation of fraud ? Surely not.

The objections should be further tested in other sittings, and proved facts should take the place of mere suspicions and vague possibilities.

In the photographs of the sittings of Stanislava P. we may distinguish two groups, those of January and February 1913 and those of June and July 1913. The former shows, in four pictures, a fairly long white substance emerging from the mouth, and in two other pictures flat, badly-drawn hand-shapes. The substance used for these seems to be the same in all three cases. In the second group, including the kinematograph reproductions, the mouth is again the origin of the long veil-like substance which hangs down her breast and penetrates the tulle veil covering her head.

In the first veil photograph the material shows the structure of unravelled vegetable fibres, while the fundamental structure in the second experiment shows a resemblance to irregular distorted crochet work in wool threads. Although this point cannot be decided from the kinematograph pictures, on account of their smallness and indistinctness, we appear to have to deal with a structure resembling vegetable fibre. In neither case do we find the characteristic marking of the squarely arranged threads of purchasable silk veils. The conditions of the veil phenomenon excluded the possibility of fraudulent production. Like Eva C., Stanislava P. produces flat forms resembling sketchy hands. The emergence of the material from the mouth, and its disappearance into it, which was also observed in the case of Eva C. under evidential conditions, was found again with Stanislava P., and even recorded by the kinematograph. We also find remarkable analogies between the two mediums in the bizarre and irregular formation of the structures, and in the veil-like, fibrous condition of the material produced.

RETROSPECT.

NEGATIVE POINTS AND THE HYPOTHESIS OF FRAUD.

THE study and comparison of the illustrations published in this work will no doubt give rise to objections of all sorts, especially if the experimental arrangements described in the records of the sittings are not taken into account, *i.e.*, if it is assumed that, in spite of four years of effort, and in spite of every care, the observers were the victims of elaborate fraudulent manipulations. It is true that the consistent execution of such manipulations for so long a time would be from the conjuring point of view a most formidable and astounding performance, which would offer new psychological points of view concerning possibilities of deception and errors of observation, which have not been hitherto known to the same extent.

Even from this point of view, the publication of all the experiments is justified, as it would contribute an informing chapter to the subject of superstition and magic.

What is first noticed, during a superficial examination of the pictures, is their extraordinarily improbable appearance. Most of the products and objects photographed recall well-known objects familiar from our own observations. Thus the amorphous substance often resembles bunches and fibres of unravelled wool or cotton, as, for instance, in the photograph of 13th March 1911. The fingers, resembling pseudopods, or ribbons, as well as the hand-shapes seen in the years 1911-12, are mostly flat, and have the appearance of stencils cut out of paper in the semblance of gloves, as, *e.g.*, the hand lying on Eva's shoulder taken in the same sitting. The finished products visible on Eva's body, which clothe her head and breast, cover her face, or later are used for the decoration of the mediumistically produced faces and heads, resemble fabrics of silk or cotton, or handkerchiefs and napkins. To this we must add that the margins are often turned in and apparently hemmed, and that the fundamental design appears to correspond to the pattern of fine hand embroidery in lace and linen. Also, we even notice the use of threads, recalling linen threads, of twine and ribbon-like shreds, which may even be looped and tied round the objects and used for suspending them (Figs. 58, 123, 130, 148, and 158).

Some of the materials have even a skin-like, hairy quality, and give the optical impression of tanned leather, with spotted shading. On the 17th and 20th May 1912, solid bodies, in the shape of a slipper, appeared, and in another sitting a structure appeared which resembled a long, empty, woman's white glove.

It is certainly asking a great deal of common sense to believe that all these things, familiar in our daily life, owe their existence to a mediumistic creative process of a totally unknown nature; that they are generated from an invisible substance derived from the medium's organism, and that, after a fugitive earthly existence, they again dissolve and are reabsorbed by that same organism. It is surely simpler and more natural to assume that these objects are somehow at the medium's disposal, and were smuggled in, in spite of our control, than that they are fugitive forms of transitory matter of psycho-physical emanation.

The problem becomes more complicated if we study the face and head pictures, which come in fragments or isolated, flat, or mask-like forms, mostly in a drapery of veiling or cloth. In spite of an extraordinary vivacity of expression in many portraits, neither the observer nor the student of the picture ever get the impression that we have to do with real, living, though incomplete forms. The pictorial, mask-like, diagrammatic character predominates. In contrast with other observers, the author has never been able to perceive separate motions of the mouth or the eyes in these faces. Mme. Bisson claims sometimes to have observed motions of the eyes. On the other hand, the flat and plastic hand-shapes often proved their mobility by the grasping of objects and by various touchings of the sitters. The flat, pictorial, sketch-like appearance of the heads, which often appear as if cut out, and therefore with sharp edges, must, on a superficial examination, give rise to suspicion. Among possible foundations we might consider, in this connection, the finest sorts of paper, as well as fabrics of silk and linen. Thus we find, in the face profiles photographed by the author on 15th August 1912, that the portrait ends backwards in a broad, flat, and obviously stiff band, which, by its consistency, gives an obvious impression of paper. This seems to have been repaired in one place by laying, or sticking on, a semicircular sheet (Fig. 113). Such a composition is also indicated by the ridges and furrows of the folds, which are clearly recognised and fit into each other. On the other hand, the face of a young woman, reproduced in Fig. 103, is surely drawn on a soft textile foundation, as is shown by the side and back views (Figs. 104 and 105).

The pictorial character is also clearly seen in the portrait of M. Bisson (Fig. 92), which looks like a blown charcoal or tone drawing. The sketchiness, hastiness, inaccuracy, and imperfection of particular portions prove, apart from the clearly recognisable strokes, that we have to do with a product of draughtsmanship, or something similar. A photographic reproduction from life would not show distortions, such as we see here. Male portraits in Figs. 136, 143, and 149 show the draughtsman's technique at the first glance, and corroborate the observations made on the " Bisson " portrait. Only in one of the pictures (the phantom reproduced on Fig. 146) does the ground show a regular pattern resembling a textile fabric or linen. It is remarkable that this kind of artistic technique is much less marked in the female portraits than in the male portraits. If one were still inclined to doubt that these pictures were produced by some (mysterious ?) graphic method, we need only refer to the photograph in Fig. 119, where we find, on a horizontal strip, the printed words " Le Miroir." This example shows that both the letters and the features are produced by a hitherto unknown graphic technique.

Criticism directed especially towards the consideration of the negative points could bring forward even more formidable objections, by pointing out the folded, furrowed, torn, and crumpled appearance of many of the products. This quality may be consistently traced through the majority of mediumistic creations. It is found not only in the flat pictorial representations, but also in the plastically developed fragments and masks, in the flat hand-shapes, and even in the unformed material emanations. That this peculiarity is not quite so regular as one might expect, is due to the frequent lack of definition in the photographs themselves. Even if the cameras are focused on a particular point, the objects, during their short exposure and rapid motion, are often photographed at another place, which accounts for the lack of distinctness of many pictures. It is mostly in the faces that the torn and furrowed appearance is presented. That such furrows can traverse the length of the whole phantom is shown by an analysis of the photographic results of the 23rd February and 8th June 1913. In this connection one should examine the following illustrations : Figs. 64, 81, 88, 89, 95, 97, 100, 101, 108, 109, 111, 113, 115, 123, 124, 125, 131, 136, 138, 143, 149, and 159.

The flat hand, lying on the medium's lap, photographed on the 11th August 1911, shows round folds, while the finger projections, on other pictures, appear twisted and bent in.

The creases are the more clearly marked the more the basis (paper ?) is consistent and flat. But the rents, fissures, and furrows occur even in the semi-soft, compact patches, resembling sculpture. The optical impression of a furrow or fold is sometimes produced by regularly shaped pieces stuck on (clearly seen in Fig. 149), and we even sometimes get the impression as if some faces had been composed like a mosaic of several pieces (Fig. 132). The strokes of the drawing are sometimes indistinguishable from fissures, and produce the same optical impression.

The furrows and creases are almost always in geometrical form, usually parallel, crossed, and rectangular. Some pictures seem to be unfolded from a regularly folded packet. Out of the two pictures quoted as examples, we find on one side prominent creases, with partly-bent corners, which when produced in a straight line correspond to the furrows.

These positive and negative parts, which fit together, are separated by a third furrow, crossing them at right angles in a vertical direction, as in the case of a sheet of paper folded double and square, and subsequently unfolded. In Fig. 113 the same process is evident, so that a fold towards the outside and top is always matched by another towards the inside and downwards. Nothing can be said against the conclusion that we have here to deal with unfolded sheets showing traces of a geometrically arranged folding.

In some portraits as, for instance, that in Fig. 149, we have lines at considerable distances, and we also find by suitable magnification of some head pictures numerous small crumplings, proceeding like rays from a point, or irregularly, *i.e.*, fine folds going outward and inward, as would be seen during the smoothing out of fabrics or papers, which have been crumpled into balls. It is all the more remarkable that such traces cannot be found on other portrait photographs by examining their enlargements with a high magnifying power or by studying the stereoscopic transparencies, *i.e.*, in the female face of Fig. 122.

In view of these observations, it may be taken for granted that portraits folded up and unfolded in the sittings, and consisting of a basis resembling cardboard or paper, are shown in some of the sittings. The author was able to prepare a paper model from Fig. 136 and to fold it, in the folds shown in the photograph, in such a manner that the various folded portions fitted accurately together.

To the negative character of facts of this kind we must add the proof that, in some of the sittings, images were attached to the curtain with pins, as described in detail in the reports of the Munich sittings.

As early as 21st May 1912 fragments of faces and head images appeared at the left curtain, and at first were higher than Eva's head. A whole series of pictures, from May till August 1912, were exposed in Paris and Munich at about the same part of the curtain. Since in

Munich we operated with a newly-prepared cabinet, it was easy to discover pin-holes, and they were regularly found at the places where the pictures were exposed by rolling up the curtain. A pin was found after the departure of the medium on the under side of the left arm-rest. Stanislava P. also, in one case, attached the end of a materialised veil substance coming from her mouth very awkwardly to the curtain with a pin.

The co-operation of the hands of the medium Eva C. was proved by the photographic record of 9th August 1912. The medium holds the mask-like head fragment with the left hand (to which she had, indeed, drawn attention herself in the sitting), and, in the place of her left hand, there is a mass of white substance on her lap. It is quite conceivable that, in the red light, this mass might have been misinterpreted and taken for the medium's left hand. Already, in the experiments at St Jean de Luz, on one occasion it had been proved photographically that a flat white hand structure lay on her knee in the place of her right hand, while the latter held a piece of substance out of the curtain, but without any recognisable resemblance of the material with the medium's hand. Finally, at several sittings, the author observed the co-operation of the medium's hands, and noted this on each occasion in his records.

As a result of this observation, a change in the experimental arrangement was made in October 1912, so that from this time forward the medium's hands remained for the whole sitting outside the curtain, or at the curtain, visible and tangible. Yet the phenomena occurred as before, but the fixation of structures at the curtain was no longer observed. In some cases the pictures were attached to the medium's hair (Fig. 142), as when the female picture appeared at the sitting of 30th November 1912 (with the exclusion of any manual co-operation by Eva's hands) on the medium's head. After it had been photographed, the author permitted the withdrawal of the hands behind the curtain for the rest of the sitting. Thereupon (Fig. 123) the same image appeared at the level of Eva's head, and suspended by a thread which itself was attached to a horizontal cord connecting the medium's hair with the curtain. A similar mode of fastening is shown in the picture of 25th November 1911, in which a fairly broad, twisted band passes from Eva's head to the curtain. To this is suspended a cloth, showing several parallel creases, like a handkerchief folded and pressed and then unfolded. In both cases the fixation is obviously done with the help of the hands.

Besides the leaning of the pictures against the head, other modes of attachment were observed. Thus, in some cases, the threads which hold the object seem to be stuck to the black satin of the curtain, or the back wall, with the help of the mysterious material. In any case, some white and fairly wide spots were found in these places, and show the same structure as those microscopically examined.

It has also been suggested that some suspension arrangements, attached to the roof of the cabinet, might have been used for moving the images up and down, by means of fine threads attached to them. This would presuppose the attachment of nails, rings, and other apparatus to the roof of the cabinet, in the Paris and Munich séance rooms, *i.e.*, some preparations before the sitting, but neither in Paris nor in Munich did Eva C. enter the séance room except during the sitting itself. The height of the cabinet in Paris was 9 feet, and in Munich $8\frac{1}{2}$ feet.

The medium would then have to get up on the chair (without attracting the attention of the sitters, sitting within a couple of feet of her), in order to attach some fitting to the roof of the cabinet during the sitting itself. In the first place, such a complicated manipulation could not be carried out at all without attracting attention. Secondly, some traces would remain in the cabinet; and, thirdly, she would have to have the necessary tools about her, as well as the objects serving for the representations of the phenomena, in spite of the initial and final examination; and, finally, the two or three cameras in the cabinet, and perhaps also those in front of the curtain, would show on the negatives such threads connected with the images. Even if they could not be seen on simple prints, the sharply defined stereoscopic images on glass, and the enlargement of the original negatives, must have revealed this mechanism of fraud. The author maintains that in the arrangement adopted in the sittings such coarse manœuvres could not possibly have escaped discovery.

As regards the activity of the medium's hands during production of the phenomena, it is proved, by the author's repeated observations, and also objectively by photography, that Eva C. used her hands in various cases to expose the objects already produced in a manner most favourable to the observer, to fix them to her head, to the curtain or to the back wall; in short, to improve the materialisation phenomena. The use of a pin, or of the medium's own hand, in place of which a flat hand-formation or a white strip of substance was laid down, may be interpreted as attempts at the fraudulent representation of non-existent things, although we must also take into account the medium's undoubted hypnotic condition, and her wish to intensify the optical impressions on the observers. Under such circumstances we cannot be surprised that the disappearance of the medium's hands behind the curtain was often objected to by the observers, and we are probably not wrong in assuming that, in many cases, the hands played a part in the arrangement of heads, in their distribution and position, without being discovered. On the other hand, the suggestion that the artistic products, such as hands, face forms, masks, and drawings had been formed, during the sitting itself, with the help of the hands, is excluded by the extremely complicated character of the artistic representations.

It has also been repeatedly alleged that objects concealed in the orifices of the body (small packets, etc.), had been brought out by hand in the dark, unfolded, and then exposed as phenomena.

A very natural suggestion which, however, cannot be maintained on account of the careful initial, and final, examination of the medium, the variability, size, and character of the objects in question, and also because when the help of the hands was excluded by new experimental arrangements (hands held by the observers, or visibility of the hands in front of the curtain during the whole sitting), the same phenomena occurred as before. Finally, the disposal, packing up, and concealment of the objects used would meet with unsurmountable difficulties, especially if we take into account the time and circumstances in which these manipulations would have to take place, *i.e.*, sometimes in one second.

The four years' observations give no support whatever to the suggestion that the hands played any part at all in the real genesis and disappearance of the phenomena, though they may have had a part in the arrangement and the disposal of the objects and images, once they were mediumistically produced.

As is shown by several photographic records, and by several observations, especially during the first part of the sittings, Eva C. exposed her head and body, clad in materials and veils, to the red light on several occasions, apparently with the object of producing on the observers the impression of a phantom. The somnambulist, in this case, used materials mediumistically produced, and acted in good faith, in this sense, that the genesis and disappearance of these materials in these sittings constituted the phenomenon in question, as may be clearly seen from the records.

She never spoke during these representations, nor did she show any action pointing towards dramatic representation of any type of personality. If, therefore, we assume and admit that nothing but mediumistically produced materials were exhibited on the medium's body, we can hardly speak of a fraudulent intention in the hypnotic condition, but simply of a wish of the medium to drape herself, and to produce, in the form of a "transfiguration," an impressive demonstration of her power. But whatever we may think of this, the consciousness of fraud was absent in her state of deep trance. If, in this case, observers with spiritistic tendencies had regarded the masked medium as a "spirit," the sitters alone were responsible for this error, and not the instinctively acting medium herself. That this transition stage of transfiguration is observed in nearly all materialisations has already been mentioned in the introduction.

After a study of the pictures and the records, one might also raise the objection that on several occasions the same images, types and objects were exhibited by the medium in various sittings, and one might conclude that such objects were permanently in existence. But a detailed examination of the material points to other conclusions, for in no case could the identity of type be proved in the case of several appearances, separated by intervals of time. This we recognised in the male face photographed by Bourdet on 11th September 1911, the structure resembling a death-mask, which was photographed by the author on 5th November 1911. But while Bourdet's negative shows a flat development, the author's photographs show an incomplete, distinctly modelled, and therefore plastically formed, face, although there could be no doubt that the same model was used for the two kinds of artistic representation.

The same observation applies to that group of female heads designated by the medium as "Berthe." In this connection one should examine the pictures of 30th December 1911 and 7th June 1912 (Figs. 60 and 64). In spite of their great similarity, which again suggests different works after the same model, or after the same memory image, the photographed objects are really different, as is shown by a comparative study. Even the head pictures, taken at the same sitting, at an interval of from five to seven minutes, show distinct differences in development, in the opening of the eyes and in the facial expression, quite apart from the change in the decorative arrangements. In the portraits of the type "Bisson" at various ages, we have on the 1st June quite a different front view from that of the 21st June 1912, in which the left supraorbital region appears modelled, whereas the Munich negatives (Figs. 100 and

101), in half profile, only show a faint resemblance to the original. In the portrait produced on the 6th March 1913 one finds certain features in the build of the forehead, in the eyes, and in the cut of the full beard, which make it a matter for discussion whether this creation was inspired by the original model or not. It appears impossible to attain such different effects with a single picture model, made for fraudulent purposes.

In the torn female profile, photographed by Mme. Bisson on 30th December 1912 (Fig. 125), we undoubtedly find the same features as in the author's photograph of 10th September 1912 (Fig. 115). The lines of the forehead and mouth are the same in both cases, though the projection of the nose appears somewhat longer on the 30th December 1912; but in Fig. 125 the limit of the hair is quite different, quite apart from the doubling or the unjustifiable prolongation of the whole structure downwards, which is absent in Fig. 115. We have again the same process. The similarities in the profile, in the gaze, and in the whole arrangement, point back towards the same original, but surely one could not, by using the objects shown in Fig. 115, produce a picture looking like Fig. 125.

The differences in the four photographs of the phantom have already been sufficiently pointed out in the records of the sittings. The greatest resemblance is between the two appearances photographed on 23rd February and 19th May 1913. But the mere comparison of the left eye in the two pictures shows considerable differences in the more oval form, the high light and the appearance of the pupil on Fig. 157. Besides, the face (the upper part of which stands out in relief) and the whole build of the body seem to be broader in the phantom photographed by the author in May 1913 than in that photographed by Mme. Bisson in February. With the same model one could not have produced four such different pictures, whereas in four different sittings the same personification was always produced, with differences resembling differences of memory.

From these examples, which could easily be multiplied, it is evident that the repeated use of the same originals for the production of the phenomena, as far as we can judge from the photographs, is out of the question.

A further ground for suspicion might be found in the repeatedly observed noises (like the rustling of silk or rubbed paper), and also the diversion of the attention from the activity of the medium, by the conversation of the sitters desired by Eva.

The first-named occurrence was often observed, while the medium's hands were excluded from participation, by the experimental arrangement. It is therefore independent of Eva's manual assistance, and must be regarded as a subsidiary accompaniment of the phenomena.

As regards the diversion of the attention, one must remember the common experience that a too intense concentration of attention on the medium herself may hinder her activity. Possibly there is here a remnant of spiritistic tradition which should be eliminated. As against this objection, the author may point out a large number of phenomena set down in the records, which took place, from beginning to end, before the eyes of the sitters, *i.e.*, under rigid control. In any case, talking does not hinder the concentration of the attention upon the mediumistic processes, but might contribute to exercise a soothing influence upon the excited nervous system of the producing medium.

Among the most frequent objections to materialisation phenomena, such as those described in the present work, we have the assertion that the medium fraudulently uses prepared artificial sheets covered with pictorial representations and pressed into an infinitesimal volume, these sheets consisting of the finest veiling or of shagreened Japanese paper. Such products, according to this view, can be compressed to the size of a pea, and can be so hidden about the body that even a rigorous initial and final examination is unable to discover them.

In order to examine the technical possibility of such a trick, the author procured from the largest Berlin firm for this branch of industry a yard of the finest obtainable chiffon veiling and a yard of the finest silk veiling, and through another big firm samples of the thinnest existing sorts of paper (*e.g.*, grey Japanese paper prepared from rags without chlorine, etc.), and made several test experiments with these.

As regards the compression of such veiling having an area of one square yard, the smallest circumference within which such a packet can be compressed is 6 inches. That corresponds to about the size of a small apple. But even by using smaller quantities, we should, in any case, get the size of a walnut. Pellets the size of a pea, on the other hand, are much too small to yield sufficient material for the average size of the phenomena.

Now, packets of this size, and of even smaller volume, would certainly have been discovered during the initial or final control. And, further, none of these substances are sufficiently consistent to allow themselves to be sufficiently smoothed out and put up like disks, as, for instance, the head image (Fig. 120). Finally the traces of crumpling are, as a rule, different from the traces shown on Fig. 149. In particular, a fairly thick paper would have been required for the image shown on Fig. 120. While some of the pictures show an extremely fine basis, which suggests the use of fine material, others, as shown by the photographs from behind and above, are very voluminous, and have a distinct thickness (*see* Fig. 93). The materials used for a portion of the drapery of the Bisson portrait have a thickness of 4 or 5 inches. Fine paper and veiling materials are so transparent that this quality would immediately be evident on the negative. One may compare the veil photographs of the Polish medium Stanislava P. in this connection. Finally, it may be doubted whether graphic sketches of heads, on such material, are even approximately similar to the appearance of the portraits reproduced. And there is no doubt that the enlarged negatives of the veiling would show the regular structure of the woven, or hand-worked, pattern. In silk veils this pattern is square. The direction of the threads would have been apparent, in any case. In the same way the characteristic structure of the wood fibre would be evident in the case of paper. The appearance of a whole series of phantoms, the sculptural modelling of mask-like heads, and of more massive compositions, could not be explained by this hypothesis, which only applies to a small number of photographs. Only in a single case, viz., in the second phantom photograph by Mme. Bisson, of 24th March 1913, does the fabric show a regular pattern comparable with fairly coarse canvas. It is certain that the substance was neither silk nor paper.

Concerning the suggested swallowing and bringing up of such packets by a sort of rumination, all that is necessary has already been said at the end of the report of the Munich sittings. The enclosing of the head in a veil, as practised later, also refutes this assumption (Fig. 154).

The hypothesis of the fraudulent use of paper, or veiling, cannot be maintained, if we take into account the whole of the photographic material reproduced in this work. But the fact remains that in some of the pictures there is a distinct similarity of the material basis of the production to veiling materials, paper and canvas.

Even if there is an appearance of fraud, the assumption of its actual existence is not necessarily justified. The author may here refer to his arguments used in discussing the phenomena of Linda Gazerra, in which he said: "If we see before us some materialisation product like the shape of a white flat hand, the picture of a head, or white materials, we are obliged, by instinctive association, to think of analogous pictures from the world of our own experience. The white hand shows an unmistakable similarity with a shape cut out of paper, the portrait-like character of the head reminds us of an enlarged photograph, and the material fabric recalls the idea of veiling or finest Indian silk.

"No doubt one could produce similar impressions with the help of such objects. But, on the other hand, the mysterious character of the psycho-dynamic phenomena consists just in the variety of possibilities and causal actions, so that they can produce upon us visual impressions, which have the greatest similarity with things from the world as we know it. The unknown force, of a possibly psychic origin, as soon as it wishes to present or materialise things for our senses, uses a picture language known to us in order to be at all intelligible. Any one who has had the opportunity, as the author had with Eva C., to observe with what unheard-of facility, in contrast with ordinary physics and biology, materialised fabrics and structures alter their condition, form and character, when the mediumistic power is at all great; how they disappear in the fraction of a second, *i.e.*, cease to be optically perceptible to us, will surely not be surprised to find, in the photographic rendering of teleplastic products, many similarities to known forms, besides some really surprising and apparently novel products.

"The suspicious appearance of a mediumistic photograph is not sufficient proof of production by fraudulent manœuvres, and, generally speaking, the whole use of the photographic art has no significance except in conjunction with an accurate record of the experimental conditions."

If the play of a natural law, unknown to us, consisted in presenting to us optical images which are sometimes flat, sometimes plastic, sometimes coarse, and sometimes equipped with the finest detail; having all the appearances of life on one occasion, and none of these on another occasion, we should have to accommodate ourselves to the fact, however strange it might appear in a given case. So long as the effective forces are entirely unknown to us, as they are to-day, we have no right to reject any phenomenon simply because its flat appearance, or its similarity with veiling, paper, or canvas does not agree with the assumptions of our usual thought, that is to say, with our preconceived opinion.

If we disregard these considerations, as well as the contents of the records, and the most careful control, we must admit that the purely objective consideration of a number of the pictures reproduced indicates fraud, particularly the flat appearance of many of the photographs which appear cut out, the canvas or paper-like consistency of the basis in some cases, the hand-shapes looking as if they were cut out, the regular foldings and creases on numerous images, the occurrence of cords, loops and threads or shreds of material, recalling spread handkerchiefs, the pictorial, or graphic, character of the documents (such as the printing on Fig. 119), and the amateurish and sketchy treatment of some of them.

The counter proof to these considerations is given by the mode of production of the photographs (simultaneous exposures on five to seven cameras, within and without the cabinet), by the rigorous initial and final examinations, by the dress of the medium, by the sittings with the nude medium, by the occurrence of curious forms and fragments which cannot easily be produced by commercially obtainable figures, by the numerous plastic products, by the artistic character of certain portraits, which cannot be imitated in this way, by the repeated photography of features of deceased persons recognised by their families, by the growth and recession of the teleplastic phenomena, by their movements, proved evidentially through the sense organs (*e.g.*, materialised hands which make touches or grasp objects, etc.), by the lightning-like appearance and disappearance of the phenomena, while the medium's body is visible and motionless, and, finally, by a class of phenomena which cannot at all be imitated artificially, as, for instance, the creation of an amorphous, living and moving substance, leaving a residue of decomposition products of organised matter, and the penetration of the substance produced through textile fabrics and veils (*see* Figs. 152 and 153). To this we must add the progressive development, advancing from simple to complex performances, the elementary character of the forms and phenomena, and the consideration that a fraud, which would require at least a laboratory for producing the most varied assortment of pictures and utensils, and would presuppose the use of considerable sums of money for procuring them, could hardly have been practised for four years, in spite of the constantly varying and continuously intensified precautions and photographic methods, and could not have been carried out without the slightest failure, in the face of the acumen of numerous learned observers. Also, the improvised character of the momentary teleplastic creations speaks against a prepared manipulation of artistic illustrations, masks and similar objects, whose exposure on the negatives would have produced quite different pictures, and would have been easily recognised.

Finally, we must take exception to the comparison of our observations with the results of conjuring. Neither the twenty-six-year-old Eva C., nor the twenty-year-old Stanislava P., have any relation to that art, which surely requires thorough instruction and practice. The whole life of these two girls, their course of education, and their interests are known, and are clearly accessible to the observer. Every conjuror requires the use of his hands, but a very large number of phenomena, especially with Eva C., occurred after the use of her hands had been eliminated, as they were either held by the observers during the phenomena, or remained visible grasping the curtain.

Such objections are inadmissible so long as nobody has succeeded in producing the same performances, under strictly equal experimental conditions, by conjuring, for which one would have to offer very high remuneration.

When, in the end, all the objections applying to the medium's person are exhausted, so that the appearances cannot be explained by reference to the medium alone, common sense, driven into a corner, always has recourse to the theory of accomplices. Servants and persons not taking part in the sittings are excluded at once by the conditions (repeated change of abode and locality). In the sittings with Eva C., as already mentioned, suspicion used to centre on her protectress, Mme. Bisson. Now, as already pointed out, the phenomena are not conditioned by her presence; they had already occurred for four years with Eva, before Mme. Bisson made her acquaintance. Besides, this question has been examined, in Munich and Paris, by critical savants, during the sittings themselves, and they decided that there was no justification for any suspicion directed against the lady in question. Finally, in the case of the Polish medium Stanislava P., some of the phenomena were produced, as in the case of Eva C., although the two mediums were not acquainted with each other, and have nothing in common. Therefore the hypothesis of accomplices is also untenable. Whether the counter arguments enumerated in this chapter are strong enough to exclude the possibility of fraud, as the author considers they are, the reader must decide for himself.

Undoubtedly, in a question of such importance as is represented by the problem of mediumistic materialisation, all objections are justifiable, and every conceivable precaution is necessary to exclude every possibility of production, except that by mediumistic power.

ARTISTIC AND TECHNICAL OPINIONS.

PROFESSOR ALBERT VON KELLER, several of whose works relate to occult and mediumistic problems (*e.g., The Awakening of Jairus' Daughter, The Somnambulist, The Witch's Sleep, A Portrait of Eusapia Paladino, Studies of the Dream Dancer, Madeleine G.*, and other pictures), kindly placed the following expert opinion on the artistic significance of the photographs published in this book, at the author's disposal :—

" The pictures comprised in the first group (Figs. 27, 31, 45, 72, 74, 75, 77, and 78), which all show a white material about the body of the medium, sketchy, flat hand-forms, or more or less developed finger fragments, seem to me to give some information concerning the entirely elementary character of the formative material. The substance itself gives the impression of a fluctuating natural creation of an entirely organic character, but, in spite of this, it is not without a certain grandeur of design.

" An interesting example of this fact is shown by Fig. 148, for, apart from the plastic development of the finely-drawn finger, it shows a character in the ribbon of material holding it, such as it would be impossible to produce on the loom. The remarkable lines of this shred-like substance remind me of the play of forms in cast lead. On Fig. 133 the two finger fragments on the hair surprise us by their fine plastic anatomy.

"In the face and head fragments (Group II.) I see a strong development of the artistic impulse towards the production of the forms in question. The front view of the image produced on 1st November 1911 (Figs. 47 and 48) resembles the head of an ape, but the full profile already assumes the aspect of a human face and is plastically developed.

"The same plastic development in low relief is shown by all the photographs of this group (Figs. 49, 50, 51, 73, 76, 79 and 80). In Figs. 82 and 83 the formative process, evidently in the course of forming a head, seems to have been interrupted by the photographic exposure.

"The condition of the material in this group is yielding, soft, and fluctuating. It never shows a paper-like character, and shows that the veil materials are formed from it, as are the face forms. This transition is clearly seen in Figs. 82 and 83.

"The climax of artistic completion is shown in some female heads of the next group. Thus the creation shown in Fig. 56 is of unsurpassed beauty in form, drawing and composition, such as only the work of a master can show. We have, in these remarkable performances (especially in Figs. 55, 56, 60, 61, 62 and 63), the direct impression of life, seen through the temperament of a great artist. Fig. 62 is remarkable for its classic profile and for the admirably successful expression.

"The plastic modelling is proved by the differences in the photographs from various points of view. This applies particularly to the photographs in Figs. 55 and 56. The fluctuating condition of the ground substance, and its capacity for development, are shown by the remarkable change in expression, and in the position of the head, on comparing several photographs taken of the same object within a few minutes of each other.

"In my opinion, we have to deal with several stages of development. The impression of perfect plastic development is also made by the charming female face of Fig. 94, which reaches the same level of beauty. The unity of style in this group of heads (particularly those in Figs. 55, 56, and 94, and the female head photographed by Mme. Bisson, Figs. 90 and 91) indicates that the same artistic individuality has created all these products. Sometimes the same type seems to be intended, although the differences are too great for identification.

"Perhaps we have to deal with several attempts to render the same model, which each time is interpreted differently. As the terrestrial artist is constantly engaged in struggling with his material, so in this case there are many indications of great difficulties in the treatment of the teleplastic material.

"The reproductions in Figs. 103 to 108, 115, 116, and 120 to 123, do not attain the same artistic level as those above mentioned. They are flat and pictorial, and evidently the products of reminiscences of pictures. But, even in these, the intensity of expression is well marked, and governs the design. Great artistic force is shown by Figs. 115 and 122.

"The male portraits in Figs. 95, 136, 140, 142 and 143 indicate an unusual artistic intelligence, and show technical refinements of drawing such as can only be executed by great artists. This is specially noticeable in Fig. 149. As regards the extraordinarily remarkable appearances on the naked body of the medium (Figs. 127, 129 and 135), these are evidently elementary chance products of nature having an organic character. I do not know of any substance, produced mechanically, or manually, with which similar forms could be made. They give a convincing impression of natural creations, generated in a mysterious manner.

" On comparing Figs. 135 and 148, the equality and agreement in the elementary form, which is also found in other pictures, is very evident. It shows that, again and again, the same mysterious creative process is in operation, which follows its own laws, and is indicated by a distinct style.

" The forms of this group are otherwise only found in the vegetable or mineral kingdoms, in sea-weed, in trees, in lava, in molten metal, and in living organisms. Such lines do not occur in artificial or artistic products. They are the peculiarities of the spontaneous creations of nature.

" To say another word about the four phantom pictures, I can only corroborate that the four representations of the same type show quite notable differences, and cannot, therefore, be produced from the same model. The high lights on the eyes in Figs. 157 and 159 do not look drawn, but look like real high lights, although, otherwise, these whole figures do look like drawings.

" To sum up my own judgment, it appears to me that the uniform elementary character of the material, as seen in so many pictures, both formed and unformed, seems to indicate that creations of such a remarkable kind cannot be produced artificially by fraud. In this case, the fluctuating condition of the fundamental substance, its stages of development, and the soft rounding of the portraits, which is also seen in several sketches, can hardly be imitated. The artistic performances, seen in Eva's productions, are of very various levels, from the highest artistic power down to an amateurish awkwardness. Certain head formations are so convincing, by their originality and their mysterious composition, that they cannot be compared with the works of human technique, and seem to be elementary natural creations of chance."

Herr Fritz Müller, Manager of the Graphic Art Works of Hamböck, by whom the whole of the reproductions for this work were carried out, is well qualified to express a technical opinion, by his long experience in the subject of photo-chemistry and methods of reproduction, as well as his preparation of the photographic originals in this book for autotype. His opinion is as follows :—

" According to your wish, I certify with pleasure that the photographic negatives of the present work were obtained in a manner technically free from objection, that is to say, the negatives were taken at one exposure, without subsequent illumination, or any kind of manipulation. The photographic copies have not been retouched or subjected to any other manual treatment, as I have had occasion to observe in preparing the blocks for the photographs.

" The appearance presented by the photographs lacks all characteristics denoting paper or fabrics prepared manually or mechanically. The masses rather resemble vegetable and animal forms. That some of the appearances are plastically developed is clearly seen from the photographs, taken from the right, or left, and from in front. The mass itself seems fluctuating and easily changeable in its form, for photographs taken in short succession show differences of outline. What the mass consists of, I cannot say, since I have not come across similar materials in my practice.

"A peculiarity lies also in the transition between the material and the plastic forms. The latter must be in relief because, when the light falls from the left, the shadows, both of the medium's head and of the phenomena, are on the right, but another portion of the forms represented gives an impression of flat drawn sketches. If these were art publications previously existing, and arranged in the sitting for photographic exposure, there would be some indications of the direction of the illumination in which the originals were produced, and these would probably be in contradiction to the direction of the illumination in the sitting; but in the material submitted no such contradiction can be traced. Besides, the remarkable softness and rounding of a large portion of the products speaks against the use of sketches or enlarged photographs, which would come out much harder on negatives, and are easily recognised in other ways.

"I should also like to point out that the basis of one of the phantom pictures shows the characteristics of canvas, and that the high lights in the eyes are, in some of the photographs, real—that is to say, not drawn. I do not consider myself competent to judge of the artistic technique expressed in the pictures or the frequent fissures and folds."

METHOD OF OBSERVATION AND DEVELOPMENT OF TELEPLASTIC STRUCTURES.

THE occurrences observed with Eva C. during a period of four years all belong to the same class.

They always consisted of the appearance of definite material aggregates, substances, forms and objects, under various experimental conditions which were arranged with the object of excluding conscious, or unconscious, fraudulent co-operation by the medium, and also designed to assist the production of the phenomena by providing the *milieu* found by experience to be required (cabinet and red light). In order to record the extremely fugitive, visible effects of the psycho-dynamic processes, whose nature is still quite unknown, in a manner independent of the testimony of the senses, photography was used as freely as possible. In the first year, 1909, the arrangements for flash-light photographs were so imperfect that only a small number of exposures were successful. In order to fill up this gap several situations observed were drawn by the painter Gampenrieder. At the end of the fourth year seven to nine cameras, inside and outside the cabinet, were ready to record the results of the materialisation process from all sides. This procedure itself excluded any manipulation with prepared plates. The author himself inserted the plates, selected the moment for igniting the flash-light, and usually only photographed that which had been previously seen. The development of the negatives was carried out in his presence. No retouchings, corrections, or changes have been made,

DEVELOPMENT OF TELEPLASTIC STRUCTURES

with the exception of the photographs taken with the naked medium, where the sex characteristics were obliterated, as the medium had made this a condition for her permission to publish them. The assumption of hallucination is entirely disposed of by the photographic plates, and the latter afford a valuable corroboration of visual impressions. During the whole period not a single sitting was held in the dark, and the red light was strengthened more and more until, in July 1912, six lamps, totalling one hundred candle-power, illuminated the room.

The greatest care was taken throughout to have a thorough initial and final examination of the medium. This included a search extending over the whole skin, and sometimes into all the bodily orifices. Eva's costume in the sittings consisted of knitted tights, with an apron tunic closed down the back. Before each sitting Mme. Bisson sewed up the back, the wrists, and the junction of the tights with the dress. In May 1913 Eva, at the desire of the Paris physicians, put on a tricot in one piece, closing only down the back, and her head was also covered with a veil, sewn on to the neck.

Not one of the observers, during these four years, has ever found on the medium's body, or in the séance costume, anything which could have been used for the fraudulent production of the phenomena. The importance of this negative result can hardly be emphasised too strongly. The author was a witness to the thorough performance of this task on no less than 180 occasions. *The honesty of the medium is therefore not a probability, but a certainty placed beyond all question.* She has never introduced any objects into the cabinet with which she could have fraudulently represented the teleplastic products.

The various séance rooms, in different houses, had no secret passages or trap-doors, and were regularly examined, both before and after every sitting, by the savants who took part in the sittings. The séance room was locked so that no servants had access to it. The number of sitters, at first rather large, was reduced more and more, so that during the last years it was only rarely that more than four persons were present. Many important sittings took place in the presence of Mme. Bisson and the author only.

During the last years the phenomena could often be illuminated by the sitters with red or white electric torches. In some sittings the curtains were not closed at all, and the phenomena were often observed from beginning to end, while the medium's body was motionless and visible. There were also a large number of sittings with the naked medium, only attended by Mme. Bisson, and two attended by the author.

On reviewing the experimental arrangements and records, one must admit that everything was done, that was within the power of the observers, to exclude fraud and self-deception. But it may be objected that nobody made an attempt to grasp the material and solve the question by force. In answer to this, it must be stated that *such an attempted exposure, made at Munich, was a failure.* The phantom on the left of the medium disappeared entirely. Dr Kafka did not succeed in grasping the brown or grey piece of substance on the left of the medium's neck. The only consequences were some profound fainting fits, several days of illness, and an instinctive timidity of the medium, which lasted for six months, and had a very unfavourable effect on the sittings. On a few occasions Mme. Bisson did grasp some of the materialisation, but it dissolved in her hand, while the attempt to grasp it produced violent pains in the medium. In the sitting of 15th November 1910, the author grasped a piece of material which had given a blow on his right hand, but the mass wriggled out of his hand like a snake, while Eva screamed with pain. If we also take into account that the phenomena often appeared with lightning-like rapidity, and might disappear in the fraction of a second, we must reckon with the fact that these transitory structures do not hold out under our physical contact, and that the suggested procedure, while yielding no success to the observer, has grave consequences for the medium. In any case, the material does not seem to withstand the light, but appears to liquefy very easily, or even to evaporate. Many experiments in this direction gave material in a liquid state or in the form of residues on the medium's dress, which contained cell detritus. The few cases in which more permanent material was obtained (hair, etc.) are too isolated to affect the general conclusion.

Assuming the actuality of the phenomena, we may next endeavour to describe their evolution. The first stage is the appearance of a mobile substance, near the body of the medium. We may call it the stage of *teleplastic evolution.* The substance appears diffuse and cloudy, like a fine smoke of white or grey colour. On further condensation it becomes white, and transforms itself into amorphous coagulated masses or packets, or assumes the structure of the finest web-like filmy veils, which may develop into compact organic fabrics or conglomerates. Sometimes the veil-like forms are doubled at the margin, so that the first impression is that of a stitched hem. The veils never show the characteristic square thread-work of real veils. There is something inconstant and irregular in all these formations, and sometimes the morphological structure is different in the centre and at the rims. All observers, who have touched this filmy grey substance with their hands, agree in describing it as cool, sticky, and rather heavy, as well as endowed with a motion of its own. The sensation may be compared with that produced on the skin by a living reptile.

The existence of this material with the properties described has lately been proved to be the primordial phenomenon for telekinetic processes (raps, levitations, etc.) by the British investigator, Dr W. J. Crawford, of Belfast, who felt the substance on the occasion of the levitation of a table, which he traced to an invisible lever proceeding from a point near the medium's feet towards the under surface of the table. He says that the material felt cold, sticky, and like the skin of a reptile. This indicates that the material foundation of the telekinetic phenomena is the same as that of the teleplastic phenomena, only with the difference that in telekinetics it is not yet condensed into visibility, and therefore represents a preliminary grade of the aggregate used in teleplastics. Crawford finds, in this organic matter, a thread-like structure, which is usually invisible, but is capable of carrying out motions of its own and of becoming the conductor of psychic impulses. I have also succeeded, in the case of the free levitation of a small object, by the approach of the hands (with the Polish medium Stanislava

Tomezyk), in photographing such invisible threads on stereoscopic pictures, an experiment which was first performed in Warsaw by Ochorowicz. The magnification of the thread images shows an organic structure, and the absence of all marks of the loom.

The teleplastic substances condensed into the filmy veil show elasticity, like that of rubber, and change their volume, length, and shape while the medium is motionless. The pieces look like torn shreds of fabrics, or like ribbons, strings, or long fibres, or again like low organisms. They are usually connected with the medium's head by a long extensible cord. The mass seems to pass freely through the lighter materials of the dress, penetrating them, perhaps, in a vaporous form, and subsequently condensing in the form of grey flakes.

In the next stage, that of development or evolution, the teleplastic substance grows before the eyes of the sitters, and sometimes in a very short time (ten to forty seconds). We could even watch the process of growth. At first a reddish spot, the size of a pea, was seen on the dress, which grew into a strip about 46 inches long, or into some other more compact form, while the medium's body remained at rest. When this growth took place on the dress, no visible connection with the body could be perceived. We also succeeded on various occasions in watching the evolution from the mouth. It was always accompanied by a very intensive co-operation of the respiratory organs of the medium. The substance has first the appearance of smoke, and streams from the mouth with strong expirations, afterwards assuming a vaporous, or veil-like, appearance. The impression would be the same if the medium were to blow the finest muslin veiling out of her mouth. On 17th May 1910 the author observed this process fairly accurately while kneeling beside the medium in the cabinet. The exhaled mass is very light. It seems at first to float in the air, and only sinks gradually while it condenses. On touching it the finger has the impression of destroying a spider's web. Similar observations were made in the case of Stanislava P. (*see* Fig. 170).

The material produced by Eva C. shows movements of various kinds. After separation from the body, these movements may become independent. Such independent motion was observed by two observers on the medium's naked body. The movements are slowly undulating, sometimes in zigzag, or in wavy lines, comparable with the creeping of a snake, or the progress of a jelly-like material, over a flat surface.

The stage of recession, or involution, often takes the form of a sudden jerk towards the body of the medium, which reabsorbs the substance. This could never be observed in detail, on account of its rapidity.

The recession can also take the form of a simple optical disappearance. This may happen in the fraction of a second, and leaves no trace anywhere about the medium or the cabinet. Such disappearances often took place when the medium was frightened, when the flash-light was turned on, or after unexpected noises, like the fire-alarm of 25th November 1909.

The reappearances of such objects were often as sudden as the disappearances, as was shown by numerous examples. The stage of teleplastic metamorphosis is just as mysterious as the simple movements. We have here the production of distinct parts, from a uniform formative substance. The flat white viscous material, visible to the eye, puts forth excrescences and projections of an elementary character, resembling leaves. This process is not, indeed, more wonderful than the replacement of the head of an annelid worm, after it has been twelve times cut off, or the new formations in planarians, crustaceans, and salamanders. In order to indicate their peculiar character, they are called " pseudopods " in the records. Besides these projections, we also find more differentiated forms, like sketchy fingers and hands. Finally, there are quite a number of hand-shapes, shown in the collection of photographs, which seem white and flat, as if cut out of paper. But the examination of enlarged photographs of these very suspicious-looking forms has never revealed the characteristic structure of paper, or of wood-fibre products, but show a granular ground substance. The use of paper for these forms is therefore excluded. Besides, in some of the negatives, this substance gives the impression of being semi-liquid and soft, as it sinks in and adapts itself to its support. (*See* Photograph, 11th August 1911.)

These sketchy hands, lacking all external detail, also grow without any connection with the primitive teleplasm, lie on the medium's shoulder, on her head, under a heap of veiling, etc., and disappear as spontaneously as they are formed. In one case, the author watched such a formation on the medium's shoulder quite closely, and timed it. It disappeared after exactly forty seconds.

The results recorded in this work concerning teleplastic hand-shapes are corroborated by the experience of other authors. Thus, Crookes speaks of hand-forms condensed from clouds. With the medium Carancini a whole flat hand was photographed. We also find in the work of Imoda, among very convincing hand-shapes, a number of flat, glove-like, and undeveloped formations of this kind. Finally, Delanne, who has much experience in this subject, mentions that these fluidic hands often give the impression of inflated gloves : " The hands and fingers do not always appear solid as in living people, sometimes they resemble a cloud, which has been partly condensed into a hand."

The same white sketchy hand-forms were seen with the Polish medium Stanislava P. (Fig. 172). The author endeavoured to imitate this class of phenomena with the help of white gloves, but the pictures looked quite different, and do not contribute anything to the elucidation of this problem.

But not only rough forms of hands, lacking all elements of life, were seen, but sometimes the external contours of arms and human limbs, these sometimes having all the plastic characteristics of human organs. On a few occasions, organs true to life—one could almost say living—especially hands (fingers with nails), could be perceived simultaneously by sight, touch, and hearing, while the medium's hands were kept motionless. These organs showed their living character by grasping objects held out to them, by various movements, by digging their nails into the skin of our hands, while they could not possibly be mistaken for the hands of the medium (*see* Sitting of 18th November 1910, where a hand provided with three finger-stumps pressed its nails into the back of the author's hand). The same imperfections in the development of materialised forms were shown by the medium Eusapia Paladino. Thus the author recollects having seen an arm stump with three fingers during the Munich sittings with that medium. In other ways, also, the experiences with Eva C. show many correspondences with the phenomena of Eusapia. The symptoms of mediumistic labour and its muscular accompaniments were found in both persons. The same utterances of pain, the same moaning and pressing, the same effort of will, when, for instance, the materialised limb is to touch one of those present, or to carry out definite actions. Perhaps, even when the teleplastic organ, or fragment, is apparently separated from the medium's body, there may be a connection with it by invisible threads, which transmit nerve impulses outward or inward. We must, at least, assume, in view of the results of 16th May 1913, that the movement of the suspended finger observed by Dr Bourbon was transmitted by the cord-like connection with the medium, which apparently consisted of organised matter. In general, the completely developed vital aggregates seem to have an animal nature. They are the bearers of kinetic energies, they sometimes, by means of an entirely unknown mechanism, produce motor effects, which resemble the effects of human limbs, and they are subject to the influence of the unconscious psychic activity of the medium. Perhaps, also, the mental activity of the sitters has some effect.

HEAD FRAGMENTS, FACES AND PHANTOMS.

THE last, and perhaps most interesting series of observations and photographic records in this work concerns the appearance and reproduction of distinctly marked faces, heads and whole figures in the form of fragments, mask-like forms, and pictorially and artistically produced portraits. These objects are sometimes sketchy and incomplete, as if surprised by the light during development, sometimes plastically developed; or, again, drawings on a soft, flat basis, and are fastened either to some part of the medium's body, to the curtains, or to the back of the cabinet (excepting the freely suspended picture of 10th September 1912). The majority of them are picturesquely draped with grey or black veils, or with some solid fabrics which, in some cases, conceal portions of the face.

In none of these forms have the independent movements of living organisms been observed or clearly proved to take place, although some heads give the impression of being taken from nature, while others appear to be images representing objects seen and retained by the memory. The general impression made by the comparative study of these mediumistic products is that there is a distinct tendency to represent, with the most varied artistic means, the essential features of certain types of faces in the teleplastic material provided, *i.e.*, to materialise them. In a considerable number of these representations (Figs. 62, 63, 68, 92, 108, 116, 122, and 149) the vivacity of the expression, their impressionistic and elementary character, and the softness of the outlines, are noted with some surprise, while others look more conventional and wooden (*see* Figs. 63, 112, and 115). While the former presuppose certain artistic talents, some of the latter appear amateurish.

Possibly the many disproportions of parts in the faces, the remarkable distortions, displacements, and bendings, as well as the imperfections and faults of execution, may be due to the manner of production and to the quality of the basis, which is sometimes soft and pulpy, and sometimes flat and resistant. The decorative veil-like ornaments, sometimes very cleverly arranged, appear to coalesce with the heads as if originating in the same primitive ground substance, thus increasing the peculiar softness of the structure and composition. According to the opinion of artistic and technical experts, the same impression cannot be obtained with purchasable masks, or pictures provided with veiling, since these would always look hard, and, on an enlarged picture of this kind, the origin of the preparations could easily be recognised.

The homogeneous character of the creations also appears in the flowing transition from the flat to the plastic, as seen in Figs. 65, 95, 106, 122, 137, and 157. Faces drawn on a flat surface show real hair of beard, or head, in the shape of a short-haired substance, apparently laid on, of which Fig. 137 gives an interesting example, on studying this stereoscopic transparency in a bright light. Or a twisted piece of fabric, laid over the forehead, represents the bridge of the nose, and, at its lower end, assumes the real form of a nose.

The question of the plastic development of the images shown is best judged by the distribution of shadows, the comparison of front views and side views, and the study of the parallax effects presented by stereoscopic photographs. That the material is not only plastic, but capable of change and development, is proved by the differences observed in photographs of the same object taken in rapid succession. Thus, on 30th December 1911, and on 7th June 1912, we succeeded in photographing the same female face twice, at intervals of a few minutes. In both cases we find not only a considerable advance in the poise of the head, in outline and in expression, but the second picture also shows a higher grade of development, thus indicating progress in the process of materialisation. The use of prepared sheets of drawings, or enlarged photographs, is also rendered very improbable by the distribution of the light and shade, which would have to correspond with the direction of the light at the sitting itself. But on none of the photographs obtained are there any shadows inconsistent with the actual direction of the magnesium light. Nor could the medium prepare for this particular incidence. In Paris, two flash-light apparatus were placed on different sides of the room, and she could not know which was about to be used. It may be regarded, as a general rule, that the exposure of a completed head image is preceded by a state of development. During this stage there are exhibitions of white conglomerates, films, and veils, which begin at the mouth, or in the medium's lap, and change their place, while the medium's hands are controlled. The mysterious intelligence, which appears to be concerned in this preparatory work, evidently wishes to make face and head types optically visible, but requires a certain time for doing so, which may amount to as much as an hour. Sometimes several heads are shown simultaneously, the maximum number observed by the author being three. The single exhibition of a finished image is usually very short, and never longer than several seconds. In the meantime the images retire into the dark, to emerge again shortly afterwards, as if by magic. On several occasions the cabinet and the medium were searched after such a disappearance, without finding anything.

The personal impression of the rapid appearances and disappearances is as if the light illuminating the object were suddenly switched on or switched off. As a rule, the later exposures show a higher development and a greater finish in the objects than the earlier ones. This is especially the case as regards the plastic development of the objects.

The stages in the development of head forms may be divided into three :—

    No. 1. Production of elementary material in the form of white conglomerates, wisps, and shreds.

    No. 2. Development of flat pictorial portraits on a soft and flat basis.

    No. 3. Formation of a plastic relief of certain portions of the face, and, in the hairy portions, up to complete sculptural modelling.

The material is sometimes self-luminous, as is shown by the photographs of 7th June 1911 and 21st August 1911, as well as by the cloud seen on 23rd February 1913. Mme. Bisson observed this luminosity as the preliminary stage in the development of the phantom on 8th June 1913.

The question as to what is preserved, during the disappearance and reappearance of a given image, is not easily answered. The differences observed, for instance, in the four portraits of M. Bisson indicate a process something like that by which an artist makes four independent pictures from the same model. It is remarkable that practice appears to make such reproductions easier, the medium being less exhausted by the later productions than by the earlier ones. It sometimes happens that the later exhibitions of a given image show less clearness and detail than earlier ones. This may be at the end of a sitting, when the medium is exhausted. The process of disintegration may be instantaneous, or it may, like the process of formation, take place in stages. The author's observations of 30th November 1912 (Figs. 123 and 124) show that an intact and completely developed female face may shrivel up and show parallel fissures, such as are also shown in earlier stages of development.

Such a process of involution was once observed by Mme. Bisson on the naked body of the medium. The process of indentation and fusion plays a great part in embryonic development, and, as Hæckel pointed out, in his *General Morphology of Organisms*, there is no hard and fast separation between the building of regular crystals and that of organic structures, so that geometrical forms are ultimately the foundation of both.

A frequent accompaniment of the more elaborate materialisation processes is found in the small particles, or aggregates, of teleplastic matter which are found on the skin, the clothing, or in the neighbourhood of the medium, having no apparent connection with the main materialisation. Thus, on 15th November 1910, the tips of the left index and middle fingers are enveloped in an extremely fine veil-like fabric. Smaller subsidiary materialisations occurred on 5th November 1911, 20th April 1912, and 30th August 1912. If Eva's performances consisted of fraudulent manoeuvres, with objects smuggled in, in spite of the control, the production of these smaller things, which can only be made visible by enlargement, or by special photographic processes, is quite unexplained, whereas, if we have to deal with an unknown formative process, such by-products may very well arise. The fact that the teleplastic matter leaves behind traces mostly of a liquid or semi-liquid character eliminates many hypotheses based upon fraud or hallucination, and must also profoundly influence our ideas of its fundamental character.

It is too early to formulate hypotheses, but whatever may be the laws and forces governing materialisations, the medium's *psyche* must be brought in as a determining, or, at least, as a contributing, factor. Eva herself has no artistic talent or education ; nor does she show any desire to visit Art Collections, or otherwise develop her own artistic sense. Mme Bisson, on the other hand, being a practical artist, must have exerted a profound influence on the medium by her authoritative suggestions. Without knowing it, Mme. Bisson must have played a very important part in the genesis of the psycho-physical images recorded. Mme. Bisson was often able to obtain materialisations of a special character by suggestion, and sometimes, at the end of a séance, when the medium was tired and wished to close the sitting, she secured the repetition of a phenomenon by energetic suggestions.

Eva knew M. Bisson when he was about sixty. The portrait shown on the 1st June 1912 corresponds to his appearance at thirty-eight. This suggests the materialisation of a memory image of Mme. Bisson, and so does the production of the portrait of her nephew. The production was facilitated by Eva having seen both these persons. It would be quite out of place to conclude, from the materialisation of the features of these persons, that the spiritistic view should be adopted. The spiritistic view is also weakened by the undoubted influence of the ideas prevailing among the sitters upon the products of materialisation. The phenomena obtained with Eva C. may be considered as the products of a still unexplained ideoplastic capacity of the mediumistic constitution.

The materialisation process consists of two factors, one of which is the simple spontaneous secretion and formation of a material of a transitory character, while the other is the utilisation of this material for the production of forms, images, and living organs. The emanation of the teleplastic ground substance is the first requisite for the ideoplastic process.

The foregoing purely hypothetical hints are only made for the purpose of taking the facts observed and recorded in this book out of the region of the marvellous, and of spiritistic faith, into the region of natural law, and to indicate the direction in which, perhaps, a possible explanation may be found.

Thus, for the unprejudiced investigator, the medium is not only the unconscious producer of phantasms, but is the physiological source of material for making them visible, as well as the formative power in the phenomena. While the inspiration and the genesis of the mediumistic processes appear to proceed in many cases from the somnambulic or subliminal consciousness, suggestively influenced by the memory images of the persons taking part in the sittings.

CONCLUSION.

In a comparative survey of the whole of the teleplastic productions of the medium Eva C., we are struck by their variety and the wealth of forms which mark these creations. This is not only shown in the fantastic lines and in the extraordinary appearance of the simple products and fragments of organs which, as already pointed out by Professor von Keller, resemble the play of natural forces found among creatures which are half animal and half vegetable, as well as among corals and stalactites; but is also seen in the tendency towards harmonious completeness, artistic composition, and vivacity of expression in the faces and phantom forms.

This æsthetic impulse towards formation and spatial expression corresponds to the fundamental tendency of nature, which ever produces new forms and shapes, while bearing within itself its own laws and conditions.

The observation of the phenomena in the photographic records from various sides leaves no doubt of the fragmentary character of that which is represented, especially where we see the reproduction of human creatures and members. The materialisation usually ends in the optically perceptible portion of that which is exposed to the light. Thus, in the profile images, the half of the face not visible to the observer is usually lacking. Never was a back of a head attached to a face modelled in relief. The stereoscopic transparencies, when carefully studied, show holes and black spots where, perhaps, a right eye ought to be. On the full phantoms the feet are wanting, and the position of a hand is only very roughly indicated. We can, therefore, with the material at our disposal, lay down a general law that a *continuation of the materialisation of organic parts, beyond the field of vision of the observers, is non-existent.*

While in a real living being the plastic anatomy is developed in all directions, in the observations here described only the visible portions are finished and brought into view, and these are limited to the most necessary means of expression. It is true that in the shadow of the curtains we find stalk-like projections and connections for the forms and faces, but we never find such organs and parts as would be found in living organisms as necessary supplements. Here we have undoubtedly an intention of the creative force, working with limited means and possibilities, so that there is only the production of fugitive material, a more or less well-developed impression of form fragments, with the object of producing a definite impression on the eye of the beholder. This raises the important question whether the whole materialisation process has not hitherto been misunderstood and falsely interpreted by exaggerating the analogy of these teleplastic productions of mediumship with living organisms under the influence of the "spirit" hypothesis. In discussing this question, it should be mentioned that the scanty material hitherto published, in the way of photographs of this kind, contains no contradiction of the experiences gained through Eva C. The elucidation of this important point must be reserved for future research.

If we attempt to analyse the simplest teleplastic processes, there are numerous questions which we cannot answer at present.

Are the changes in the living substance, called teleplasm, produced by known mechanical or physical forces?

Does the teleplastic material resemble the most primitive living substance by consisting of a colloidal and a crystalloidal solution, such as is described by Thomas Graham, as the fundamental property of living matter?

Do active mechanical agents, with the help of fine membranes, produce assimilation and dissimilation in teleplasm as in protoplasm, thus accounting for the phenomenon of growth?

Are its spontaneous movements and changes of form comparable with the movements of the *amœba*, which projects pseudopods through its structureless mass, and thus creeps across the field of the microscope?

Do the processes of materialisation mean the transitory formation, the fugitive and evanescent building-up, of multicellular organs and organisms, whose existence, as in all higher creatures, is conditioned by motion, nutrition, growth and reproduction?

Does the rational, positivist point of view apply to the materialisation problem at all?

Even the conception of vitalism, or biological energy, gives no real explanation. A description is no explanation. Science reveals causal connections, and shows changes to be the effects of definite causes, but the way in which the effect results from the cause remains unknown. " The falling stone in this sense is a miracle to us, for we do not know how the earth manages to attract the stone. Neither do we know what are the energies whose effects we perceive."[1]

But all the daily miracles around us fulfil definite laws within a distinct region of nature, while the phenomena described in this book seem to lie outside them, since, at present, we are unable to find any connecting link with known laws. They therefore offer a large field to the craze for the marvellous and to mystical fancy.

Considering the abysmal contradiction between the physical processes of mediumship and the results of the exact sciences, it is natural for serious investigators to assume that the mediums conjure up a world of spirits by means of painted sheets of paper, rather than that we have to do with a definite region of fact. For science is not yet sufficiently advanced to assimilate, without an effort, these new, improbable, and yet authentic results of observation. But that is no reason to consider this region of fact as devoid of interest. Perhaps some investigator will arise, sooner or later, who will find it worth while to concern himself seriously with the mediumistic problem, and to re-examine the contents of this book.

Let us hope he may find many valuable hints for his own studies.

But will he succeed in bringing these strange riddles nearer solution and satisfy our thirst for knowledge? Or will he, like all investigators who have hitherto tried to raise the veil, have to conclude his work with the words " We do not know," and perhaps ask again the old question raised by Kepler: " Is it possible that the whole visible world is but the outer shell of an invisible world of forces? "

[1] Carl Jentsch, *Ostwald und die Mystik*. *Der Tag*, 1911.

Part II.

OBSERVATIONS 1913-1919.

INTRODUCTION.

" Conflict is the father of all things."—HERACLITUS.

WHEN Du Moncel, on 11th March 1878, first exhibited to the French Academy of Sciences the phonograph, a savant, named Bouillaud, took him by the throat and called him a swindler and a ventriloquist. This happened in the presence of Camille Flammarion. According to some savants, the medium Eva C. produced some of the materialisation phenomena described in Part I. fraudulently with the muscles of the stomach and œsophagus.

But since the rumination hypothesis would only apply to a few of the phenomena, the medium would have to be a snake-charmer and first-rate conjuror as well, and would be wiser to exhibit her art on the stage instead of leading a simple and retired life.

Even should the medium possess all these talents, they would not suffice to explain the facts observed by the author.

Yet the criticism advanced in the daily and scientific press prefers to deny these facts and to regard the author as the victim of a deception extending over four years.

The objections put forward in the press and in pamphlets could not be answered as they came, since it was often necessary to deal with some of them, such as those concerning the use of illustrations from *Le Miroir*, by means of new experiments, and to obtain expert opinions.

The world war which broke out in 1914 interrupted the investigations and discussions for several years. Yet even during the war a few stray accounts of further tests appeared, till, in 1918, Dr Geley published his comprehensive and favourable observations.

The material published after the issue of the first German edition, with some chapters from the author's *Kampf um die Materialisations Phænomene* ("Controversy concerning Materialisation Phenomena"), is comprised in the present Part II., and forms an important supplement to the original volume.

In addition, some analogous experiences with other mediums are briefly cited, so that the reader now not only gets a survey of the ten years' work with Eva C., but is shown that such phenomena are not so rare as one might expect, and that they show great similarities in their occurrence and development.

The illustrations in this Part II., in so far as they are not repeated from Part I., are made by Messrs Hamböck at Munich. For the reproductions from *Le Miroir* the original pages have been used.

Finally, the author takes much pleasure in thanking Colonel Peter and Prof. Urban for their co-operation in this work.

THE RUMINATION HYPOTHESIS.

THE special gift of Eva C. lies, as already mentioned, in the region of teleplastics or materialisation. The only possible objection which can be made is that the materialisation products are, in some way, fraudulently smuggled into the séance room. The business of the control is, therefore, the comparatively simple one of preventing the medium from bringing in objects for exhibition, or having them passed to her by an accomplice. The result of the control has been consistently negative, and therefore favourable to the medium.

This must be specially emphasised since the Munich observers, who doubted the genuineness of the phenomena, had to admit that " nobody can find any material which might be used in these materialisations, either before or after the sitting."

Being thus driven into a corner, the need for an explanation takes refuge in the rumination hypothesis, which asserts that the stomach, or the gullet, may be used as hiding-places for the images and objects produced, and assumes that the medium is an expert in the rumination process.

One of the supporters of this theory, now advanced for the first time in the history of mediumistic phenomena, describes the process as follows : " It is quite simply (!) done like this : Pictures are drawn, painted, or photographically reproduced on chiffon gauze, after the dressing has been removed in hot water. These pictures are then cut out along their contours. The same can be done with gold-beaters' skin, which has the advantage of being unaffected by moisture (saliva and gastric juices). It is also very thin, and therefore occupies a small space when folded. It is soft, noiseless, and shows no traces of folding, crumpling, or rolling. Such things are swallowed before the experiment. Among other things there are rubber gloves, such as are used for operations, objects cut out in the shape of hands, formless shreds of animal mesentery, as well as catgut, and the like, which can be inflated. All these can be swallowed into the same human stomach.

" The investigator, of course, cannot find these things by inspection, nor even by means of X-rays. They can only be discovered by the stomach-pump. The medium, either tied up or held by the hands during the sitting, brings up these things noiselessly behind the curtain and unfolds them with the hands, or her mouth, on her knees, which are drawn up for this purpose under her chin. The medium then suspends these things with her hands or her mouth at the curtain by means of

THE RUMINATION HYPOTHESIS

small hooks attached to the preparations (twisted pins). These hooks are turned inwards before swallowing, so as to produce no injury. The suspensions of these hooks can be traced by pin-holes actually found in the curtain. The removal of the materialisations is also affected by the hands or the mouth. When the flash-light is turned on the medium regularly simulates a strong nervous shock, makes convulsive defensive movements, frees her hands from control, and closes the curtain as if for defence. Then, behind the closed curtain, the medium swallows the objects, after hastily crumpling them up into a small compass. Agility is not witchcraft, but a matter of practice."

The final stage in this fraudulent manipulation is imagined by the critic to be as follows: "The materialisations are then vomited at home, or if they keep lying in the stomach, because they have perhaps unfolded themselves, they are removed, in a natural way, by means of mashed potatoes or stewed plums."

The process here described therefore presupposes: Painted or drawn images on gold-beaters' skin, chiffon gauze, paper, or some textile fabric, to which twisted pins or small hooks are attached, and for the other experiments the smuggling of shreds of mesentery, or the guts of cats or lambs, the repeated closing of the curtain, and rising from the chair for the purpose of fastening these things to the curtain, which is supposed to be done exclusively with the mouth, and finally—"mashed potatoes and stewed plums!"

The presence of prepared images is contradicted by the technical opinion given by the Manager of the Hamböck Institute of Graphic Art. The structures resemble animal and vegetable forms, and show no marks indicating manual work or manufactured fabrics. For this and other reasons stated in the report, we cannot be dealing with prepared images. (*See* also the discussion at the end of Munich Sittings.)

The production by rumination cannot be assumed in the case of a whole extensive group of phenomena, in which odd forms and fragments of members and faces are generated before the eyes of the observers, without the participation of the medium's mouth or respiratory organs, while her body is motionless (knees immobile, hands under visible control, or held by the observers, and head visible in a red light of about one hundred candle-power). In these conditions the materialisations have been observed to execute automatic movements (changes of shape and of place). Nor can the instantaneous appearance and disappearance of the structures be explained in this way. The development of a forearm and hand out of a white patch in front of the medium's feet (Fig. 26), the pressing of fingers provided with nails into the back of the author's hand, three times in succession, while the medium's hands were held and her body was visible and motionless (Fig. 22), the luminosity of the material in the dark (Fig. 141), are all examples which tell against this theory. More than half the observations are excluded from discussion in connection with the rumination hypothesis by the fact that they had no connection with the mouth.

It has, indeed, been proved, partly by photography, in another large class of experiments, that the substance often emerges from the mouth and disappears in the same way, and that, therefore, the organs of respiration and digestion may be concerned in the production of the transitory material, but one cannot see how solid and plastic objects, the size of human faces, could be swallowed and brought up again, out of the stomach, without attracting attention. The help of the knees and hands is eliminated by the new control introduced in November 1912 (hands held, or visible, during the whole sitting), and also by a large number of previous experiments.

That flat substances can be withdrawn from their envelopes, spread out, smoothed, set up, folded up again, and compressed into a given small volume, and all in one or two seconds, is an assertion which, in itself, requires proof.

In the sitting of 9th May 1913 the medium Eva C. was completely sewn into a tricot garment in one piece, which only left her hands free. Her head was enveloped in a veil, sewn on to the neck of the garment all round, and her hands remained visible in the light during the whole sitting, and took no part. The materialisation phenomenon, as shown by the photograph, Fig. 150, developed outside this cage, which enclosed her whole body, and could not, therefore, have been produced by rumination, unless we assume that the substance penetrated the veil. Such a penetration could be photographically proved under the same rigid conditions in the case of two different mediums. The process by which the material penetrated through the meshes of the veil has no connection with the act of rumination, and in this, as well as in previous occurrences, other hypotheses must be brought forward for an explanation.

Finally, rumination presupposes an abnormal functioning of the stomach and gullet, as well as the dilatation of the walls of the stomach. In the two mediums with whom the author experimented (girls of twenty-six and nineteen respectively) such pathological peculiarities are not found, nor could they have been hidden from observation for four years. There are no indications pointing in that direction.

It has also been objected that the medium can always prepare herself behind the closed curtain, so that there is always a possibility of making materialisations appear without any apparent participation by the mouth.

This objection also does not apply. Hands and feet remained visible even when the curtain was closed. In a number of sittings the materialisation process even commenced during hypnotisation, and the author had hardly time to open the cameras. In the sitting of 17th May 1910, which also began with an open curtain, the author sat by the medium in the cabinet and observed the evolution out of Eva's mouth of a flocculent substance, which in no way corresponded to the supposed scheme of rumination. The production of complete head images often took place so quickly after hypnosis (*e.g.*, 1st June 1912) that the fraudulent technique required for rumination was rendered impossible owing to the shortness of the time available.

On 1st June 1910 the phenomena were observed with an open curtain. At the sitting of 28th October 1910 the curtain was open from the beginning. Further records of curtains being open will be found in the reports of 3rd November and 28th December 1910, 7th June and 16th August 1911, and 11th September 1912.

Although the above arguments, which could easily be multiplied, dispose of the hypothesis of the rumination of swallowed objects, that hypothesis was further investigated in a sitting on 26th November 1913 in Paris. The initial and final examination of the medium (mouth, nose, and hair, as well as a gynæcological examination), of the séance costume and the cabinet, conducted by the Paris physician, Dr Bourbon, and the author, were negative. M. Bourdet and Mme. Bisson were also present. Eva C. dined at seven o'clock. The sitting commenced at 8.45 P.M. in a feeble white light. Hands and knees were visibly inactive during the whole sitting. The medium did not leave her chair in the cabinet for a moment. The curtains were open while the phenomenon took place.

Between 9 P.M. and 9.10 P.M., without the help of the hands or knees, a flowing white substance emerged from the medium's mouth, which was inclined towards the left. It was about 20 inches long and 8 inches broad. It lay on the breast of the dress, spread out, and formed a white head-like disk, with a face profile turned to the right, and of life size. Even after the flash-light was ignited the curtain remained wide open. At the same moment the author illuminated the structure with an electric torch, and found that it formed a folded strip, which receded slowly into the medium's mouth, and remained visible until the sitting closed at 9.20 P.M.

While in the state of hypnosis, the medium rose from her chair and took an emetic tendered to her by the author (1 gramme ipecacuanha and ½ gramme tartar emetic), was completely undressed while standing half in and half out of the cabinet, and examined in detail by the author and Dr Bourbon, who took charge of the séance costume, and also examined it carefully. The final examination of the cabinet and chair gave no result. Dressed in a dressing-gown, Eva C. was then laid on a couch in the room, and was not left unobserved for a moment. After two further doses of the same strength, vomiting set in at 9.30 P.M., which brought up the contents of the stomach. The quantity was about a pint, and was taken charge of by the author, who did not give it out of his hands until he handed it over to the Masselin Laboratory in Paris for analysis. The vomit was brown in colour, and besides the wafers taken with the powders there was no trace of any white substance such as observed by us. The detailed report of the Laboratory in question, dated 29th November 1913, closes with the words: "The final result of the examination shows that the vomit consisted exclusively of food products and the emetics, and contained fragments of meat, fruit, and vegetables, probably mushrooms, which were found in pieces of considerable size. The rest of the contents consisted of food in an advanced state of digestion. There was not the slightest trace of a body whose appearance or histological structure gave the impression of a foreign body, or of a substance not used for nutrition, and, in particular, there was no trace of paper or chiffon." Although this experiment is a sufficient refutation of the rumination hypothesis, Eva C. announced her readiness to submit on another occasion to the process of stomach rinsing. A record was made of the sitting, and was signed by all those present. The above procedure may be taken as a definite proof of the inadequacy of the rumination hypothesis to explain the phenomena observed to develop from Eva's mouth. So long as images like those published in this book have not been brought up by rumination, correctly exposed, and disposed of in the same way, without the use of the hands or knees, and so long as a technique assumed by the critics is not proved to be possible by evidential experiments, this attempted explanation must be considered as an hypothesis itself requiring proof.

EXPERT OPINION ON THE FRAUDULENT USE OF CERTAIN MATERIALS FOR PRODUCING TELEPLASTIC IMAGES.

ALTHOUGH the proper movements of the formations and their shapes tell against the rumination hypothesis, Colonel Peter has made experiments on the use of delicate fabrics for deceptive purposes.

His opinion is as follows :—

"No. I. ' Crumpled and folded papers.'—I drew some heads with chalk and charcoal on the finest tissue papers, fixed them and folded them up in small pellets or rolls, which could easily be concealed in the mouth. I then went into a dark room, in order to fix the paper head to a black curtain. At once I came up against a great difficulty. It was not at all easy to unfold the moist pellet in the dark. The paper tore in several places, although I used every care. Then I did not know which was the right side for exposure. When I had succeeded, after patient labour, in sticking up the head, I was faced with new difficulties. The paper always collapsed and folded up again. Finally, I had to use four or five pins. At last the ' phenomenon ' stuck. Then I turned on the light and found that I had pinned the head upside down ! It is quite unthinkable that all this delicate and difficult work should be done in a short time in the dark by any person. The assertion that the medium does it when her hands are free for a moment, or even with her mouth, is absurd. The images show their mode of production; the thousands of small folds or rents do not allow of the production of a single smooth surface, as shown in nearly all the pictures in Dr von Schrenck's book. The first comparison shows that the phenomena cannot be produced in this way.

" No. 2. ' Gold-beaters' skin.'—I doubt if any one who considers this a suitable material for the fraud in question has ever seen gold-beaters' skin, for when I had acquired a piece the size of a human head, I saw at once that, on account of its yellowish-grey colour and its transparency, it was quite unsuitable. A drawing in charcoal or the like is hardly visible when the skin is put on a dark curtain. I had to put it on top of a white tissue paper. In spite of the double layer the head could be folded into a very small compass. The unfolding and attachment of the picture in the dark room was attended by the same difficulties as before.

" The flash-light photograph (Fig. 181) immediately betrays the origin of the ' phenomenon.' One sees at once that there is no plastic development. The thin white foundation is recognisable throughout. Shadows are lacking, or are wrongly distributed. The crumpling and folding into a small compass distorted the face, especially the eyes, nose and mouth. It is evident that the phenomena described cannot be reproduced with gold-beaters' skin.

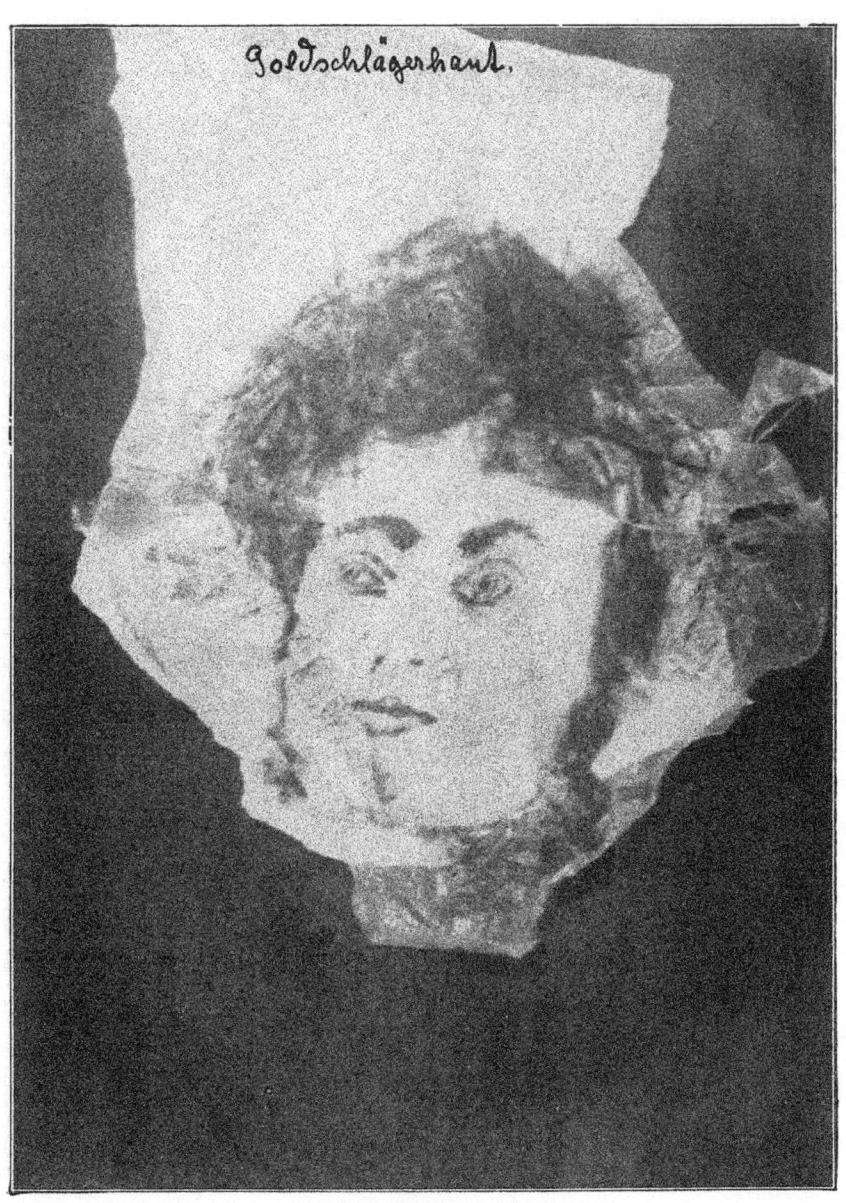

FIG. 181. IMITATION ON GOLD BEATERS' SKIN.

FIG. 182. IMITATION ON CHIFFON.

" No. 3. ' Pieces of Chiffon,' even strongly compressed, occupy more space. The drawing of a life-sized human head on this material could not be concealed in the mouth. If one has got hold of the packet in the dark, the difficulty is here not the unfolding, but the sticking up. It requires several pins.

" The picture (Fig. 182) shows the work of the loom, especially at the margins, and the folds distort the features. The conclusion is that the fraud cannot be carried out with chiffon.

" For the methods Nos . 1 to 3, it must be assumed that the medium herself can draw, which is known not to be the case ; or that she has an able assistant who provides the images for the phenomena. If the critic says that ' artists have given the private opinion that the images are at no higher artistic level than typical heads on cigar boxes, or in fashion journals,' we can only reply that their judgment must be subordinated to that of an authority like Professor von Keller.

" No. 4. ' Images are taken from the illustrated journal *Le Miroir* and gone over with charcoal, chalk, etc., in such a way that the origin is no longer recognisable.'

" A simple practical experiment shows that this assertion cannot be substantiated. The picture in the flash-light shows a lack of contrast. The folds of the paper are easily recognised.

" *General Conclusion.*—The pictures and fragments obtained by Dr von Schrenck in the sittings with Eva C. cannot be produced with paper or by masks of the materials suggested."

Besides the rumination hypothesis, our opponents have advanced a number of unverifiable assertions, consisting largely of gossip and slander, against the medium and her protectress. These assertions are composed of alleged facts which on close examination turn out to be quite unfounded, unjustified assumptions or allegations due to the negative, subjective predisposition of the critic.

It is fairly well known that every publication about mediumistic phenomena is followed, after a brief interval, by a sensational report of an exposure. In view of the extreme readiness of many people to credit newspaper reports, it is not surprising that they are accepted in preference to observations which conflict with popular opinion and scientific orthodoxy. Such a typical development took place after the appearance of Richet's report, and also after the first publication of my work. A serious critic should take as the basis of his arguments, not the sensational reports of a newspaper, or second- or third-hand accounts, but only the authentic originals with their appended documents. In some cases a single encounter with the subject of our investigations is claimed as a qualification superior to years of study and experimental work. This is really to submit knowledge to the arbitrament of ignorance. The expert is to acknowledge the layman as his judge! In spite of the general experience that the mediumistic phenomena " depend upon distinct physical and very delicate psychic conditions, that the experimental investigation requires much patience, knowledge and care, the lay mind retains the characteristic point of view that the phenomena must occur without a fulfilment of their natural conditions, on pain of denying them recognition." It is unfortunate that learned men, who see the phenomena for the first time, commit the error of supposing that their entry into the arena marks the beginning of the proper investigation of mediumistic phenomena. They disregard the copious literature and the many strictly scientific reports of their colleagues, such as the numerous unrefuted results obtained by eminent investigators with the medium Eusapia Paladino (the Italian savants, Morselli, Porro, Foà, Botazzi, and Luciani, as well as the report of the French Commission, edited by Professor Courtier). Nor do they take into consideration the many years of observation devoted by the author to the same medium. They demand that a judgment should be based upon the few positive sittings which they have themselves attended. Even if the author's results with the two mediums (which do not necessitate the spiritistic hypothesis) could be reduced to faulty observation and deception, such a considerable remnant of facts vouched for by other observers would remain, that, as Ostwald says, we should have to try to assimilate them.

FRONT PAGE ILLUSTRATIONS FROM THE JOURNAL *LE MIROIR*.

It was to be expected that the face and head images published in the works of the author and Mme. Bisson, appearing, as they do, in the form of isolated flat or mask-like forms, with or without a drapery of veils, should meet with severe criticism. As already discussed in detail in the chapter on negative points, a superficial examination of these photographs must, on account of their pictorial character and other resemblances to drawings sharply cut out, suggest fraud, unless the experimental conditions are taken into account, and this is, apparently, confirmed by the folded, crossed, torn and crumpled appearance of many of these productions.

This circumstance has been exploited by the Brothers Durville of Paris, owners of an institute for animal magnetism and massage, and proprietors of a book-selling and publishing business for the literature of the subject. In the journal *The Psychic Magazine*, founded by them on 1st January 1914, they published a series of articles directed against Mme. Bisson's book.

Their collaborator, Miss B. Barkley, claims to have identified a number of the head images produced by Eva C., and published in our works. She says, in No. I. of the magazine mentioned : " In Mme. Bisson's book there are no real materialisations, but only pictorial representations of faces. All these belong to well-known personages. The medium took her choice among the celebrities of the moment, contenting herself, in a childish manner, with defacing certain pictures by a few ridiculous and badly-placed retouchings." She continues : "Take, for instance, Figs. 119 to 121 " (in the author's work, Figs. 118 to 120), " which show the features of a woman. The inner camera registered on Fig. 112 " (the author's Fig. 119) " the word ' *Miroir*.' The medium therefore used the journal *Le Miroir* for her images. . . . Now, it is remarkable that the heads are nearly always the same size as that of the medium " (incorrect—author). " We have therefore to deal with fraud by the latter."

The lack of clearness in the above expressions concerning Figs. 118 to 120 produced, in the translation into German, the wrong impression that these belong to a single series of images produced at the same sitting, so that some critics have erroneously supposed that on one side of the exposed phenomenon the word ' *Miroir* ' was to be read, and, on the other, a female face was to be seen. This supposition is not supported by the photographic data. For the picture representing the side view from within the cabinet (Fig. 119), and containing the word '*Miroir*,' was produced in the sitting of 27th November 1912, and this isolated phenomenon had nothing to do with the head image (Fig. 120). The sitting of 29th November was negative as regards materialisations. It was only at the next experiment on 30th November 1912 that a well-developed female face (Fig. 120) could be photographed, standing on the medium's head The photographic results obtained on 27th and 30th November 1912 (Figs. 118, 119 and 120) are therefore quite independent of each other.

The heads of celebrities reproduced on the front pages of the journal *Le Miroir* are a little below life-size, and are all in black and white autotype.

Miss Barkley's allegations were taken up by the *Neue Wiener Tageblatt*, and elaborated as follows " Miss Eva prepared the heads before every séance, and endeavoured to make them unrecognisable. A clean-shaven face was decorated with a beard. Grey hairs became black curls, a broad forehead was made into a narrow one. But, in spite of all her endeavours, she could not obliterate certain characteristic lines. I (Miss Barkley) eliminated the disguises and reproduced the originals from the ghost pictures. There is, first of all, a picture of M. Poincaré. The hair of the President of the Republic has been altered and blackened, and his face has been lengthened, but all the other characteristic lines of his face remained. In a similar manner I have established the identity of all the other ghosts. I find among them the heads of President Wilson, of Paul Deschanel, the King of Bulgaria, and several eminent actresses of the Comédie Française."

According to the same journal, on 30th December 1913 the medium is supposed to have photographed every picture after these retouching operations. The journal then adds: " A tall ghost in white drapery was Ferdinand of Bulgaria, only thinner. And another ghost is the beautiful actress Mona Delza, only deprived of her beautiful hair and of her eyebrows."

The Parisian daily *Le Matin* did not allow such an opportunity for a sensation to escape, and published a whole series of articles (15th, 26th, 27th and 29th December 1913 and 2nd, 3rd, 5th and 8th January 1913) centring round Miss Barkley's alleged discovery.

Before proceeding to a strict examination of the material brought forward by Miss Barkley to support her serious accusation, I may refer to some explanatory remarks regarding these pictures published in Part I. It seems, in the first instance, to be faulty logic to derive a proof of fraud from the constitution of the materialised object, since there is always the possibility that such apparently suspicious substances may be produced by the medium under conditions excluding all fraud. In this connection I may refer to the discussion in the section on negative points and the hypothesis of fraud. The further question as to whether, in the sittings referred to, the conditions were so arranged that fraudulent manœuvres, enabling the medium to hide and smuggle in such pictures, were impossible, must be answered in the affirmative. In the sitting of 27th November 1912, in which the word " *Miroir* " was produced, both the cabinet (chair, walls, floor and curtains) and the medium's body (dressed only in tights and a black apron dress) were examined before and after the sitting. Eva C. was sewn into the dress at the waist, the back, the neck and the sleeves.

Still in the white light, and just before hypnosis, Eva's hands, being in front of the curtain, and holding both flaps, were laid on her knees, and remained there illuminated with the red light during the two hours of the sitting. At the extinction of the white light, Mme. Bisson held Eva's hands. The record was kept during the sitting, the times being correctly stated.

In this sitting also the medium's hands remained outside the curtain, visible in the red light (one hundred candle-power) until the close of the sitting, and could not have been used for the alleged unpacking and fastening of a disk-like structure on her hair, on the interior of which the word " *Miroir* " was printed.

Immediately on the ignition of the magnesium light at 10.42 P.M., the phenomenon disappeared without a trace. The final examination of the medium and the cabinet was negative. How could this absolute disappearance take place in the fraction of a second ? The author, by the way, closes the account of this sitting with the words: " I can at present form no opinion concerning this curious result."

The picture which Miss Barkley describes as resembling President Poincaré was taken by the author at the sitting of 6th March 1913. Before this, as before every other sitting, the cabinet and the chair were examined. (*See* report of the Sitting of 6th March 1913.)

The second photograph taken during this sitting is reproduced in Figs. 142 and 143, and is supposed to resemble President Poincaré, as regards the shape of the tie ! The first picture during the same sitting shows a self-luminous materialisation.

Let us assume for the moment that Miss Barkley is right. How would the medium have been able to hide the *Miroir* reproduction, to unravel it, to expose it on her head, and to make it disappear without a trace ? The movements observed in the head when first seen gave the impression of a filmy substance and not of paper, and whence the accompanying phenomena ? and what is the connection between the self-luminous neuroblastic structure and the picture from *Le Miroir* ? Is it rationally thinkable that, amidst the most puzzling phenomena which are sometimes exhibited even on the medium's naked body, suddenly a *Miroir* reproduction should appear ? That is not only improbable, considering the course of the sitting, but is impossible on account of the experimental conditions observed during this sitting.

The materialisation identified with President Wilson (Fig. 136) was taken by Mme. Bisson alone, whereas the one provided with the three warts, also identified with President Poincaré (Fig. 149), was obtained

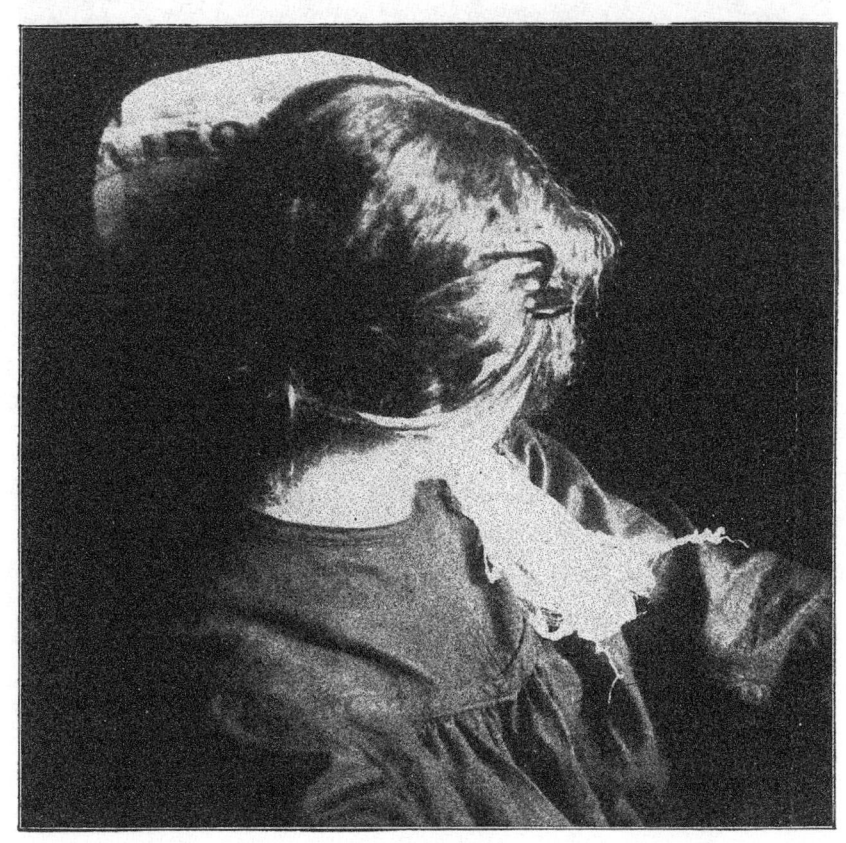

FIG. 183. AUTHOR'S PHOTOGRAPH OF 27 NOVEMBER, 1912, ENLARGED. (FIG. 119 REPEATED)

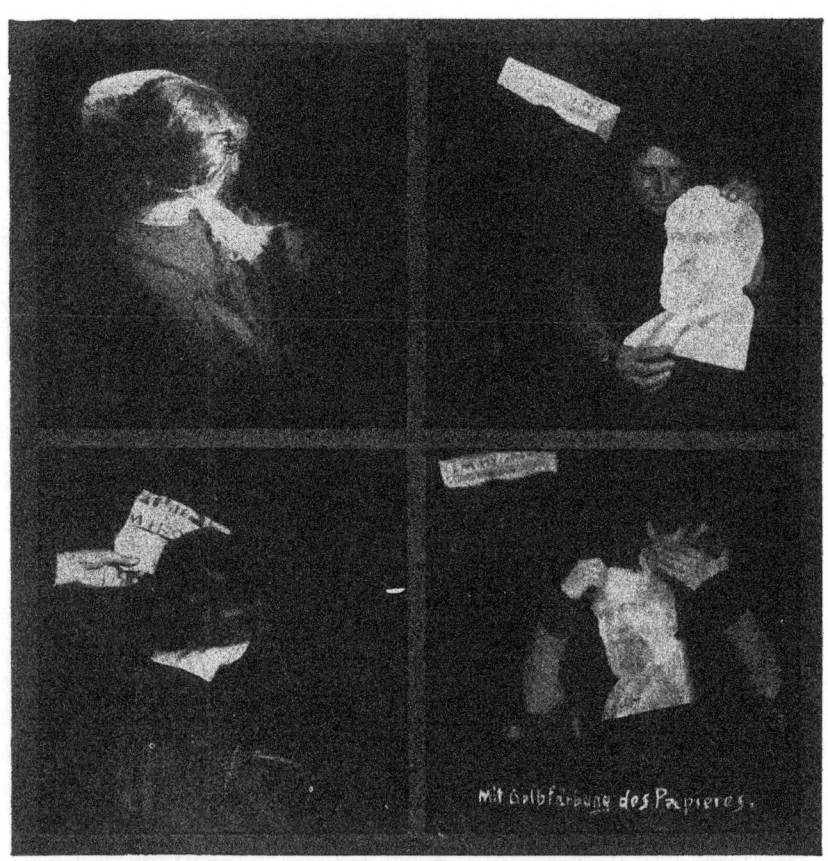

FIG. 184. TOP LEFT. SEE FIG. 183. BOTTOM LEFT: AUTHOR'S ATTEMPT TO IMITATE FIG 183 BY EXPOSING THE TITLE PAGE OF "MIROIR" AGAINST EVA C TOP AND BOTTOM RIGHT: IMITATION EXPERIMENTS WITH TITLE OF "MIROIR" AND PORTRAIT OF PRESIDENT POINCARE, BY DR HAUBERRISSER PHOTOGRAPHIC CONDITIONS THE SAME AS AT THE SITTINGS.

in the presence of the Paris physician Dr Bourbon, while the medium's head was entirely sewn up in a veil, and while her hands remained visible outside the curtain during the whole sitting.

Miss Barkley now owes us a proof that under such conditions a *Miroir* picture could be exposed.

Miss Barkley's assertion that our books contain no true materialisations, but only pictorial representations of heads and faces, can surely only mean portraits reproduced on a flat surface. But in answer to this we may refer to the arguments brought forward on page 280, Part I.

All these careful individual observations, the regular recurrence of the same process of development and disappearance, and especially the plasticity of many faces, as proved by mathematical and stereoscopic considerations, cannot be brought into harmony with Miss Barkley's hypothesis, which, in any case, is based only on very few appearances. Although the conditions of the control at the sitting of 27th November 1912, in which the word *Miroir* was produced, excluded fraudulent manipulation, so that the phenomena obtained must be declared to be genuine, I shall yet examine the objections of the critics who utter the suspicion that the heading of the journal *Le Miroir* might have been exposed in this case (Fig. 183).

In order to examine this question independently, the author made test experiments with two title-pages of *Le Miroir* of the year 1912, reconstructing the photographic conditions of the sittings (Fig. 184).

In all cases, as shown by the expert opinion of Dr Hauberrisser, the type comes out much too weak in comparison with the strong development of the original letters on our negative. Now, we could hardly assume that the colour and shape of the letters could be increased by any transfer process, especially when the original is printed. On the contrary, such a reproduction always shows a diminution of the colour contrast in comparison with the original. Now, if we wished to assume that Eva had strengthened the letters by hand, she would have been wiser to draw the letters herself to begin with. That would have been much simpler than the very lengthy process described by the critics. Besides, any manual retouching would be easily traced in the considerable enlargement of a transparency. We may therefore assert, on the basis of the expert tests, that in print both the original *Miroir* title-page and a reduced reproduction thereof, when photographed under the original conditions, yield other and very much weaker pictures than those shown by the strongly marked letters of the phenomenon itself.

Neither the original print of the *Miroir*, nor any copy of the same, technically produced, can, therefore, have been exposed on that occasion. Hence the genesis of these letters is none other than the process by which pictorial materialisations products are generated. We have, therefore, the two following facts: (1) With an exposure of headings of the journal *Le Miroir* we cannot produce a negative such as is shown in Fig. 119; (2) the shade and form of the letters does not differ materially from the productions of the printers' press.

The presence of the article "*Le*" indicates some connection with the journal *Le Miroir*, and it is not probable that there is some other connection, such as an advertisement in another paper.

As regards the similarities described by Miss Barkley (Fig. 95, Deschanel; Fig. 108, Mme. Leconte; Fig. 116, Mme. Faber; Fig. 120, Mona Delza; Fig. 136, President Wilson; Fig. 138, Ferdinand of Bulgaria; Figs. 143 and 149, President Poincaré), these so-called identifications, by their grotesque exaggeration, constitute a first-class journalistic bluff, which reduces itself to the correspondence of certain details in only three pictures, *i.e.*, Figs. 136, 143 and 149. All the rest belong to the region of arbitrary guesswork. Correspondences in certain features, lines and directions of gaze can, in any case, be easily discovered. One need only examine illustrated journals from this point of view, and one will find astonishing similarities where there is no connection between the two objects compared. Besides, a chance similarity of type is very frequently found in external form, pose and expression. That is easily explained, since organisms, such as human beings, have developed according to the same morphological principles, and have a certain sameness in that development. Nothing is easier, for instance, than to discover two entirely similar noses in two people not related to each other; or to find similar collars and ties on different men. But if we go as far as Miss Barkley, then, finally, every comparison can be permitted, for every human being has two legs, one nose, two eyes, and two ears. He moves according to definite rules; he is dressed according to the fashion of the day, which suppresses all individuality. Thus, between any two male individuals, certain qualities and correspondences can always be found.

An interesting example is furnished by Fig. 108, obtained as a third flash-light photograph at the sitting of 5th August 1912 in Munich. Now, the alleged *Miroir* original of this photograph (Figs. 185 and 186), the portrait of the actress Mme. Leconte, appeared on 4th August 1912 in Paris.

We may regard it as impossible that Eva C. could have seen this journal only twenty-four hours afterwards, on the 5th August, in Munich, and could have altered it and used it for fraudulent purposes. In judging of this point, we must take into account the fact that this photograph shows, in itself, a transformation, since Fig. 103, the first photograph of 5th August 1912, shows the same type of face with less elaboration. In both cases we have to do with the same model. This is shown by a comparative study of the expression, the build of the nose, forehead and eye-sockets, and the fabric ornamentation. The flash-light photographs are not rigid drawings on an unchanging surface, but show a flowing variation, with a change of numerous details. Besides, the dissimilarity of all details in the *Miroir* picture (Fig. 185) is almost as great as it can be, compared with Fig. 186, although we may recognise a distant similarity in the formation of the head.

The picture which is supposed to represent Mona Delza (Figs. 122 and 188) did not appear in the *Miroir* at all, but in the *Journal Femina* of April 1912, below life-size, and could be obtained commercially only in a small size through Felix & Cie, Paris (Fig. 187). How this picture, redrawn life-size, could be exposed as Fig. 120 of this work, has not been indicated by Miss Barkley. She contented herself with adopting the fraud hypothesis, without a shade of similarity or a particle of evidence.

The comparison of Fig. 140 with the King of Bulgaria, whose portrait

FIG 185 PORTRAIT OF MME LECONTE
TITLE PAGE OF "MIROIR," PARIS
4 AUGUST, 1912.

FIG. 186. AUTHOR'S THIRD PHOTOGRAPH, MUNICH, 5 AUGUST, 1912. (FIG. 108 ABOVE.)

FIG 187. PORTRAIT OF THE ACTRESS MONNA DELZA, PUBLISHED IN "FEMINA" APRIL 1912.

FIG 188. AUTHOR'S FLASHLIGHT PHOTOGRAPH OF 30 NOVEMBER, 1912. (REPRODUCTION OF FIG. 122.)

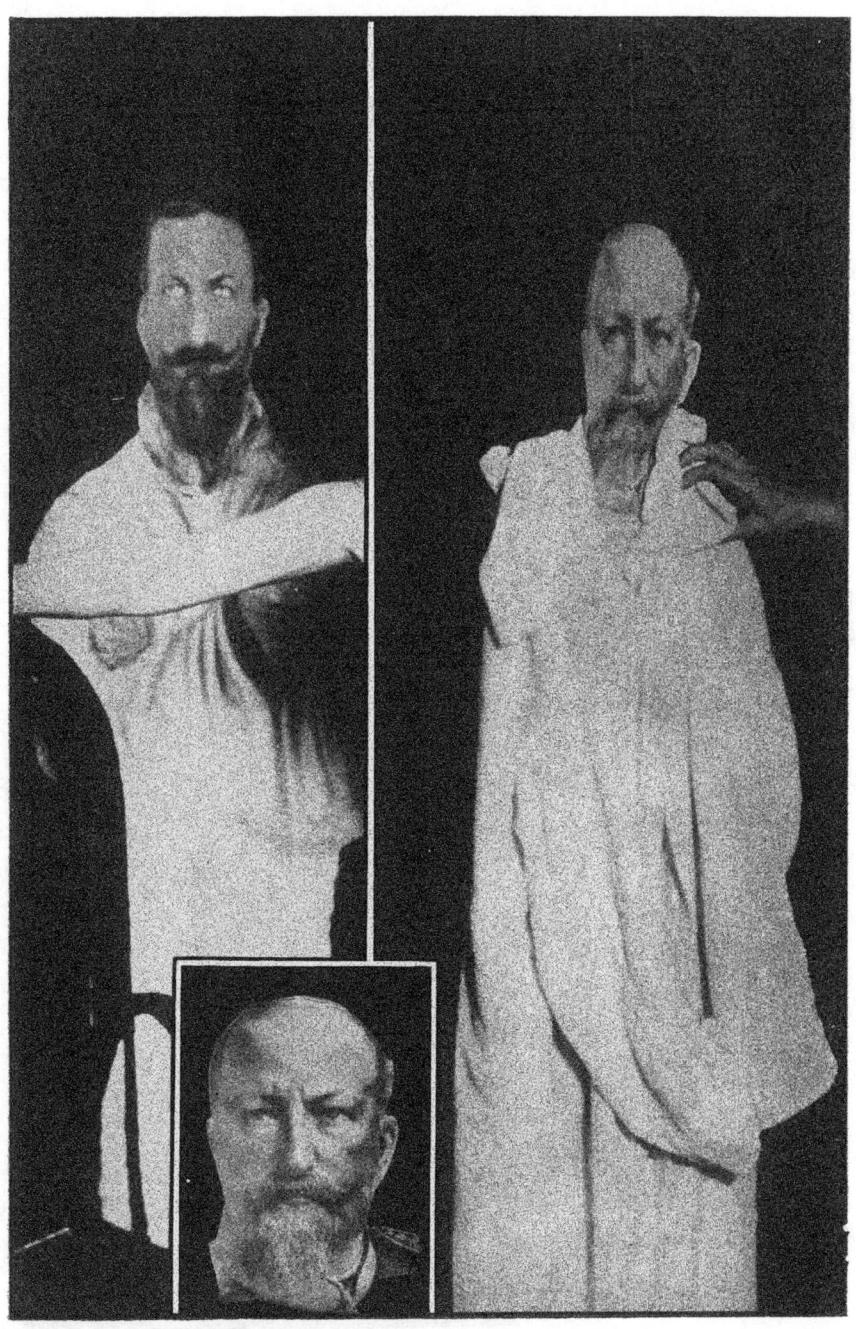

FIG 189 LEFT PHANTOM PHOTOGRAPHED IN THE SITTING OF 13 FEBRUARY, 1913 (FIG. 140 ABOVE) RIGHT PORTRAIT OF THE KING OF BULGARIA FROM "MIROIR" WITH WHITE MANTLE TO RESEMBLE PHANTOM BELOW KING'S HEAD ENLARGED.

PORTRAIT OF M. DESCHANEL
M TITLE PAGE OF "MIROIR"

FIG. 191. PHOTOGRAPH OF 24 JUNE, 1912. (FIG. 95 ABOVE.)

Fig. 192. Photograph of 2 May, 1912. (Fig. 149.)

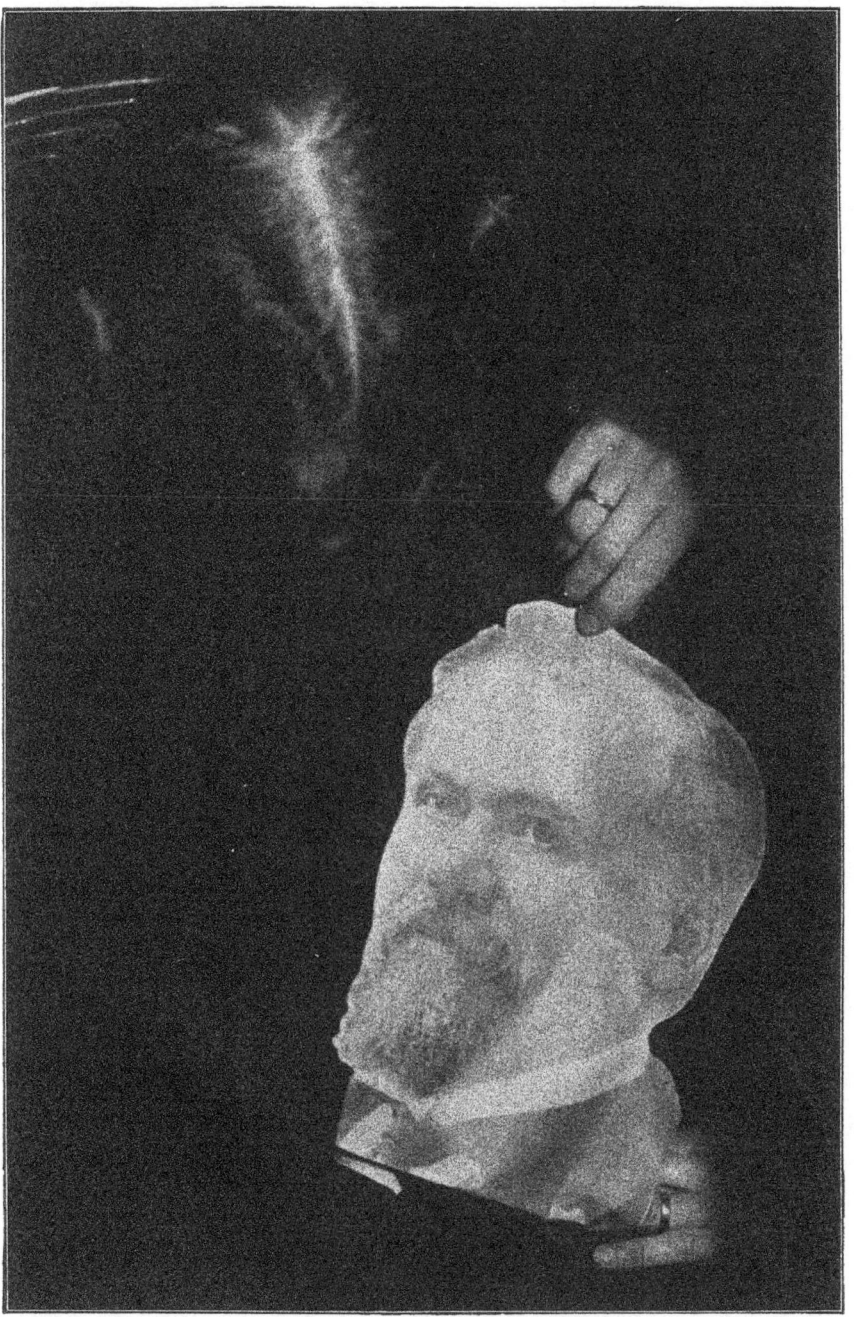

FIG. 193 PRESIDENT POINCARÉ'S PORTRAIT CUT FROM "MIROIR" AND PHOTOGRAPHED BY AUTHOR WITH EVA, UNDER PHOTOGRAPHIC CONDITIONS, AS AT THE SITTINGS

was made as similar to the phantom as possible by means of a bathing wrap (Fig. 189), is also entirely devoid of foundation. It appears from a letter from an Italian correspondent, that he finds the greatest resemblance between the phantom and a deceased relative of his. While Dr von Gulat, in Frau von Kemnitz' pamphlet, asserts that it resembles the author. Perhaps there will be a few more identifications!

In comparing Fig. 191 with the head of the politician Deschanel (Fig. 190), there is only the direction of the gaze to go upon. All the other lines and features are entirely different.

The examples quoted suffice to reduce Miss Barkley's arbitrary constructions *ad absurdum*.

In another picture, Fig. 192 (Fig. 149), the comparison with the face of President Poincaré, Fig. 193, reduces itself to a similarity of the three pimples on the left fold of the cheek. The development of the left nostril is similar in both, but not the same, since it forms a greater elevation on the phenomenon picture. All the other lines—the whole build of the face, the eyes, and the gaze—are quite different in the two pictures. Furthermore, the expression, in the phenomenon pictures, is particularly lively, and much more marked than in the *Miroir* original, which could hardly be expected in a secondary reproduction. In addition, the stereoscopic photographs show distinctly that the hair on the phenomenon consists of actual hair. Also, the size of the two pictures, compared by taking one part—say the nose—as a unit, is so different that no amount of redrawing could have enabled any one to use the *Miroir* picture as the foundation for the alleged transformation.

As regards the three pimples, the fold joining the nose and cheek are specially favoured positions for such growths. Thus, the late M. Alex. Bisson had three pimples exactly in the same spots. We might, therefore, assert with the same show of reason that his portrait had been used as a model.

When the publications in the *Matin* gave rise to the suspicion that for the above-named mediumistic picture portraits from the journal *Miroir* had been redrawn and fraudulently used, the author went to Paris, cut the heads in question out of the numbers of the *Miroir*, and photographed these on the medium's body, with the help of the photographer Barenne, in the séance room, under photographic conditions precisely the same as those of the sittings, in order to decide whether autotype prints could have been exposed by the medium at all. But, as shown by the agreement of the expert opinions of the Paris and Munich photographers, in all these tests the *Miroir* pictures came out uniformly so feeble, and so devoid of vivacity and relief, and markedly less defined than the reproductions shown in this work, that, for this reason alone, Miss Barkley's hypothesis is untenable.

In particular, the photograph of the head of President Wilson, as seen in the reproduction of our test experiment, is immediately recognised as a reproduction, since on the left shoulder and the breast of the coat, as well as on the lip, eyelid, and moustache, the marks of the process plate can be seen with a magnifying glass, and betray the process of reproduction. It is altogether an impossibility entirely to eliminate these marks of the process plate by manual treatment; nor can the grain of the photographic plate be relied upon to obliterate the dots of the Meisenbach screen. Considering the large number of illustrations, the origin would be betrayed somewhere. In some places the autotype tonings would be retraced, as in Fig. 19, where even the structure of the medium's skin is seen, that being a proof of the sharpness of the photography. The screen used for the figures in the *Miroir* shows four points per millimetre, and is therefore fairly coarse and easily recognised. We must, indeed, in judging of the phenomenon photographs, take into account that the simple exposures do not show the plastic character of the fabrics and veils added to the portraits, and may thus give rise to errors, since these veilings almost always show some kind of pattern (moiré structure), which could easily be mistaken for the screen pattern. As regards the composition of the draped mediumistic heads, the stereoscopic photographs are decisive. By manual treatment the screen pattern, particularly the half-tones, cannot be entirely obliterated, while any painting over the pattern would be immediately recognised with the naked eye. The phenomenon pictures reproduced, if obtained from art publications, would have to show a moiré structure in the photographs as reproduced, owing to the interference of the double pattern, but that is not the case.

This is another reason for saying that prepared *Miroir* reproductions cannot have been exposed as materialisation phenomena.

Of particular interest is a comparison of Fig. 143 with the same *Miroir* portrait of President Poincaré. One remarks the same cross striping and the same distribution of light and shade on the long ends of the two ties; while the upper loop of the phenomenon is short and broad, and only shows one cross fold. Poincaré's tie is provided with a longer knot and several cross folds. There are other distinct and obvious differences, especially in the narrower end of the tie, which, in the phenomenon, appears torn off, and ends a few millimetres below the knot. There are also distinct differences in the opening of the waistcoat and coat, as well as the length of the beard. It is certain that no exposure of the Poincaré original, in spite of the similarity of some details, would give an image of the neck portion equal to that of the phenomenon.

Careful measurement also shows that the phenomenon head is large in proportion to the dimensions of the tie, and that no exposure, even after working up details, will give the phenomenon picture of 6th March 1913. Such difficulties may also have occurred to the person who wrote the attack in the *Matin* of 26th December 1913, in which great emphasis is laid on the similarities in the two ties, for in presenting the two portraits the phenomenon picture was changed almost beyond recognition. The lines of the eye were strengthened, the tie was darkened and redrawn, so that now both the ends run into the knot. Also, a wing of the collar, which is not in the original, was added. The collar of the coat was changed, the tie was lengthened, and the folds of the coat collar were modified. In this way, of course, any degree of similarity can be artificially produced.

The illustrations Figs. 194 and 195 show the accuracy of these observations. It was unfortunate that the whole attack on the illustrations in the works of Mme. Bisson and the author was based upon

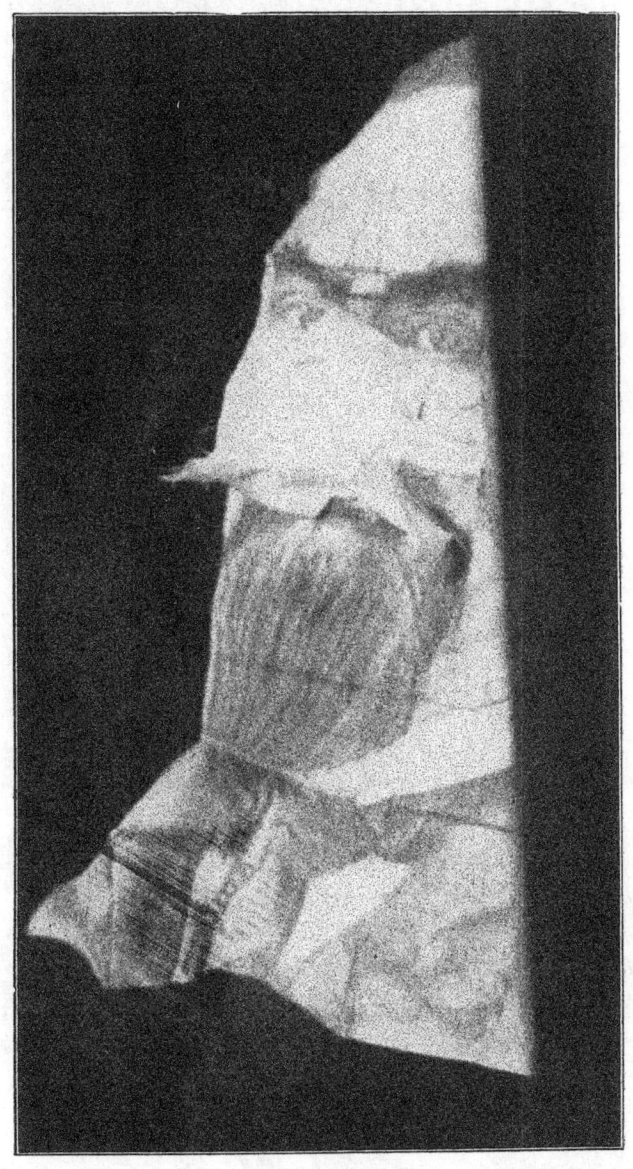

FIG. 194   PHOTOGRAPH TAKEN 6 MARCH, 1913   (FIG 143 ABOVE.)

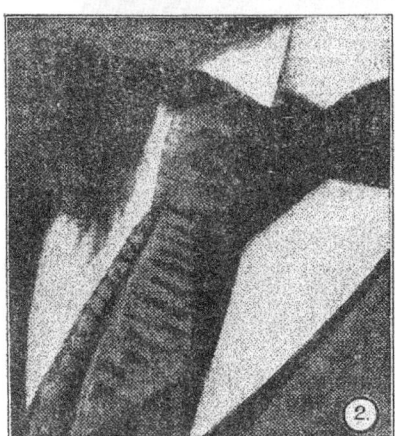 

Fig 195 Top President Poincaré, as published by "Miroir" Bottom left: Manipulated tie and shirt-front from the phantom (Fig 194) published by "Matin" 26 December, 1913 Bottom right Collar and tie from above portrait, published by "Matin" of 26 December, 1913

this picture, which had been worked up in favour of the hypothesis of fraud, and was largely quoted in the German and foreign press. None of the critics seem to have considered it worth while to verify the assertions in the *Matin* by comparison with the originals in our books.

Another important point in comparing the autotype pictures of the materialisations is that the medium, in our photographs, always shows the same photographic exposure as the products, even when the latter are pictorial, and this is not the case with prepared illustrations or drawings, as is shown by the following opinions :—

Opinion of the Photographer, Barenne (Paris).

" I, the undersigned, hereby declare that for four years I developed the photographic plates handed to me by Dr von Schrenck Notzing, and derived from the sittings with Eva C., at the residence of Mme. Bisson. Dr von Schrenck has always been present at the development of the negatives.

" It has been asserted that the medium used portrait heads published in the journal *Le Miroir*.

" In order to refute this accusation, Dr von Schrenck called on me, and on Friday, 9th January 1914, we made test experiments in Mme. Bisson's flat, by attaching the portrait heads in question to the medium, seated in the cabinet, or asking her to hold them. For this purpose we had cut out first the portrait of President Poincaré (Fig. 193) ; secondly, that of President Wilson ; thirdly, that of the King of Bulgaria (Fig. 189, right) ; and fourthly, that of Mme. Lecomte. All these portraits had appeared in the *Miroir*. Besides these, a test photograph of the heading of the journal *Le Miroir* was made, when held against Eva's hair (Fig. 184).

" We endeavoured to take these photographs under precisely the same conditions as the photographs of the original sittings. Immediately on developing the plates I found that the development met with extraordinary difficulties, which had never been encountered in the negatives obtained with Eva C. The impression made by the photographed pictures is feeble and lifeless. The pictures came out too light in tone, and were veiled on the negative.

" I had to employ a special process to obtain detail on the cut-out heads, while preserving the life-like character of the medium's head. Such an expedient had not been necessary during the four years of work with the mediumistic plates. On the contrary, the expressiveness of the materialisation on the plate was always in right relation with the clearness of the medium's features. I must also remark that the slightest correction with the retouching pencil of the faces reproduced would have been recognised immediately on development. Every photographer would say the same, just as every photographer can confirm that the fundamental substance of the materialisations of Eva C. gives no impression of paper.

" We may, therefore, assert with absolute certainty that the medium cannot have used the reproductions in question.

" (Signed) Barenne, *Photographer*,

" Paris, 11*th January* 1914. " Rue Duret, 27 *bis*."

Opinion of the Photographer, Albert Halse (Paris).

"For the last two years Mme. Bisson has handed me photographic plates for development without any further details. The negatives excited my interest to a great extent. Anxious to obtain an explanation, I enlarged the pictures on the negatives until the medium had the dimensions of a giantess. Whenever I had any doubts with regard to the objects represented, I employed this means of satisfying my thirst for knowledge. A very strict examination of the materialisations, thus enlarged, always brought me back to the conviction that it was not a case of deception. Later, Mme. Bisson also asked me to produce enlargements of various pictures. Now it has been maintained that these photographs were produced with cuttings from journals. Such an assumption is only consistent with a very superficial examination. No photographer, familiar with photographic technique, would make such an assertion, since he has at his disposal more scientific methods of control than a simple examination with a magnifying glass. As regards the supposition that the negatives themselves were fraudulently produced, one may assert the absolute contrary with a clear conscience. Since the photographic methods, now generally known, are practised even by amateur photographers, any one can recognise, with ease and certainty, whether or not these negatives have been retouched. The repairing of small unexpected injuries to the pictures was abstained from in order to be able to say quite definitely that even the slightest correction had never been applied. At Mme. Bisson's request, I photographed some of these illustrations for comparison. The pictures look different from the photographed phenomena of materialisation, for the latter appear on the negative quite distinctly and clearly during development as if they were objects in relief, while the former, under the same conditions, appear grey, flat and indistinct.

" (Signed) ALBERT HALSE.
" Paris, *January* 1914."

Opinion of Dr Georg Hauberrisser (Munich).

" MUNICH, 15*th January* 1914.
" I was commissioned by Dr Freiherr von Schrenck Notzing to ascertain whether pictures, cut out of the journal *Le Miroir*, and worked upon by hand, could have been used for representing the materialisation phenomena. I am convinced that, in spite of several agreements in detail (tie, eye-glass, pimples), cut-out pictures could not have been used in their original condition. As every photographer knows, the time required for a black and white picture is only from one quarter to one-eighth of the time required for persons and other things. If, therefore, the head of the medium is correctly exposed, a picture from the *Miroir* would be nearly white, owing to over-exposure, and would only appear very feebly drawn.

" By a practical experiment, in which all conditions were, as far as possible, the same as at the sittings (same flash-light, powder in same

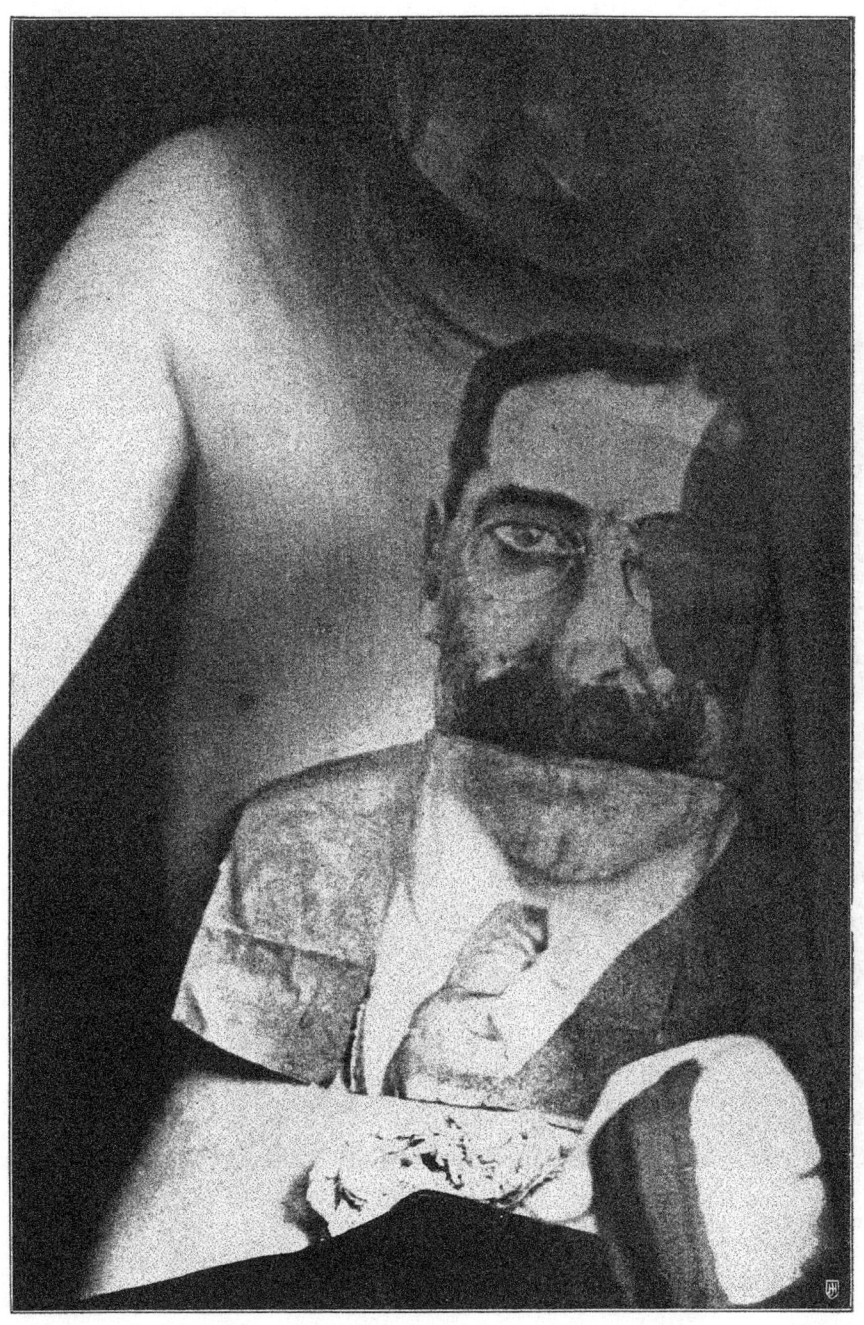

FIG. 196   MME. BISSON'S PHOTOGRAPH OF 19 JANUARY, 1913   (FIG 136 ABOVE.)

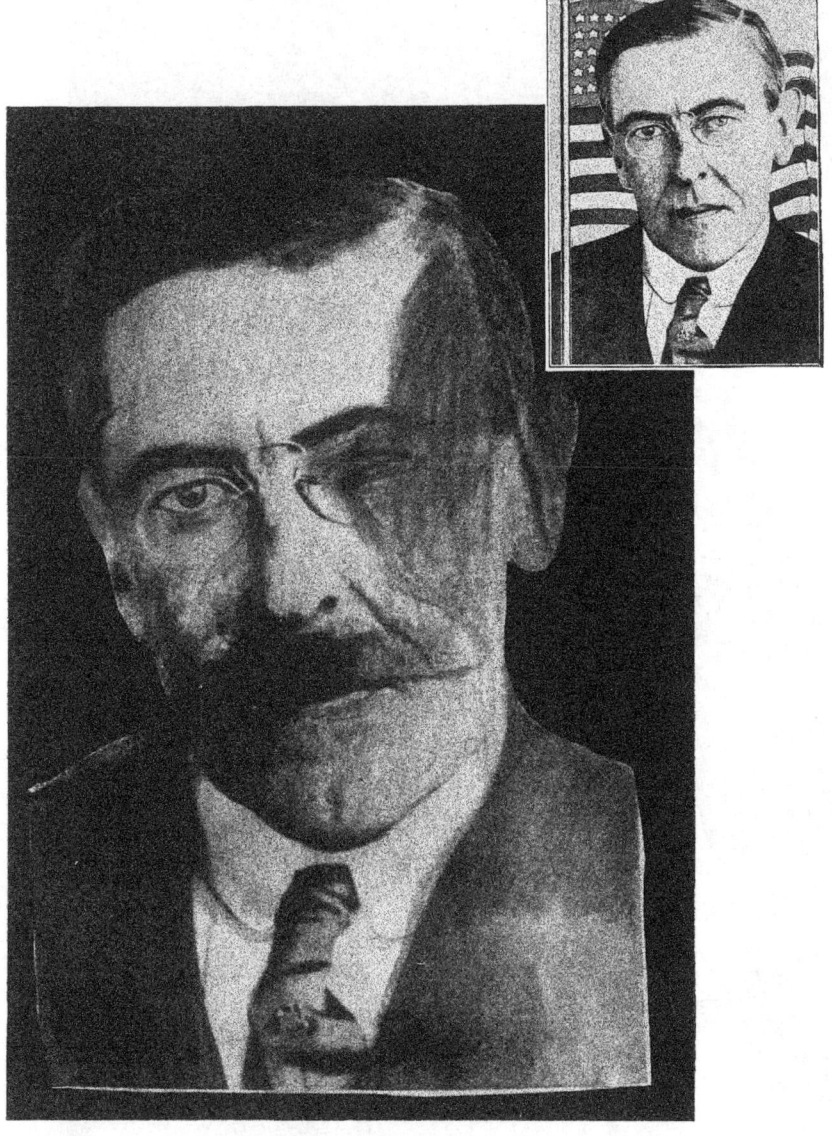

FIG 197 RIGHT CORNER PRESIDENT WILSON'S PORTRAIT FROM "MIROIR" NO 34, 1912 BELOW: THE SAME, ARTISTICALLY TREATED TO RESEMBLE FIG. 196

quantity, same distance, black background, same opening of diaphragm, same plates and sensitiveness, similar development, and other treatment of the negatives), a head cut out of the *Miroir* was, indeed, obtained, nearly white, with only very slight definition, something like a relief in plaster of Paris, while the phenomena, in Dr von Schrenck's originals, show strong definition, and about the same brightness as the medium's head. The title of the journal *Le Miroir*, when photographed under the same conditions, also only appears feeble, while, in Dr von Schrenck's photograph, the letters are clearly marked.

"Heads cut out of the *Miroir* can, under the same conditions, only have been used by colouring the paper with a non-actinic colour (brown, red, or yellow) and strengthening the drawing by hand in nearly all its parts. The cut-out heads could be obtained with the same clearness as the materialisation phenomena, if the exposure were reduced some sixteen to thirty times, but in this case the experimental photographic conditions would be quite different from those applied by Dr von Schrenck Notzing.

"(Signed) Dr GEORG HAUBERRISSER,
" *Photo-Chemist*."

Opinion of Professor Hermann Urban (Munich).

"DR. VON SCHRENCK NOTZING handed to me, on 12th January 1914, No. 34 of the French journal *Le Miroir*, on the front page of which was found a portrait of President Wilson. He also gave me a greatly enlarged photograph of a male portrait reproduced as Fig. 136 of the *Phenomena of Materialisation*. The problem was to ascertain whether this portrait could have been produced by changing, or working-up, President Wilson's head, as was maintained in the *Psychic Magazine* of 1st January 1914. On a superficial examination of the two pictures, there certainly appear to be some correspondences or similarities of detail, which suggest a discussion of the assumption, and giving rise to some suspicion.

"Both pictures (Figs. 196 and 197) show the same form, the same shading, and the same lines of collar and tie. But exact measurements, with a scale, show that the lines in the materialisation photograph run differently from those in the Wilson portrait, especially on the right-hand edge of the tie. In the picture of the phenomenon, the tie on the right is more round and bunchy. The coat collar of the phenomenon is also more vertical and stretched than in the Wilson portrait. The tie itself shows an agreement in both pictures, as regards drawing, especially in the shading and folds. The right-hand portion of the shirt and coat collar also corresponds to the *Miroir* reproduction.

"While Wilson's head is bent to the right and is pointed below, the head of Fig. 196 is placed quite straight on the shoulders and does not taper below, having a broader jaw down from the cheek-bone. The middle of the lips is also displaced towards the right, which is not the case in the Wilson portrait. That this displacement, which only affects the head and not the basis, could have been produced by the method of photography, seems to me impossible, for the whole picture would have to give a distorted impression, which is not the case, as is particularly evident from the regular forehead and eye portion. In painting, there is usually a numerical proportion, the line passing vertically through the centre of the face, being divided into three approximately equal parts, which are—first, forehead down to the root of the nose; second, root to tip of nose; third, tip of the nose to the point of the chin. Now, if the Wilson portrait had been changed by drawing and then exposed, these constant proportions would also have to agree, both in the phantom reproduction and in the *Miroir* original.

"The height of the forehead fits nearly three times in the vertical middle line in Wilson's portrait, while, in the phantom photograph, the same ratio is over three and a half, the forehead being too low in comparison with the lower portion of the head, the chin being rather short. If the Wilson portrait had been used, it is difficult to say why, in Fig. 196, the head stands vertically on the neck, or perhaps somewhat bent backwards, which makes the chin project, while in the *Miroir* picture the head is bent forward, with a slight turn towards the right. The result is that, in the *Miroir* picture, the forehead is nearer the camera and the chin seems to recede, while in the phenomenon picture the lower half of the head projects, and the forehead is slightly further away from the camera, which may account for the short forehead. If a horizontal line is drawn over President Wilson's eyebrows and touching them, the ear is a trifle below this line, on account of the head being bent forward. If the same is done in the phenomenon portrait, the ear is rather lower, which indicates either a bending backwards or an entirely upright position. That is a point determined by the proportions of the lines, and cannot be affected by redrawing, without entirely displacing the axis of the phenomenon head. The objection that the forehead had been cut short is disposed of by the fact that the typical position of the head would not be affected, even if the forehead were raised.

"At first sight the right eye is apparently the same in both pictures, and the upper line of the eye-glass passes in the same direction, but a further examination shows that the eye in the *Miroir* picture is straight when a diameter is drawn through the corner of the eye, while the same ratio, applied to the phenomenon head, shows a slight inclination to this line, the outer corner being higher (Mongolian eye).

"Furthermore, the drawing of the eye-glass, in the phenomenon picture, is a displaced oval, while in Wilson's case the outline of the eye-glass shows the regularity and accuracy of a photograph. The differences in the eyebrows, and the line of the hair, need not be dealt with in detail, since such changes could be produced with a chalk pencil, as Miss Barkley suggests.

"I have tried to convert the Wilson portrait into a copy of the phenomenon picture with a charcoal pencil, but it was impossible to alter the position of the head, which shows at once that this picture cannot have been used fraudulently for the phenomenon picture. It also appears to be impossible to hide the marking of the half-tone screen by drawing, especially in the light and middle tones, while, in the enlargement of the phenomenon head, I discovered no indications of the half-tone screen, as would have been the case if the Wilson portrait had been drawn over and thereafter exposed.

" Neither could I transform the chin into the characteristic shape of the phenomenon image, because one could only obliterate the line of the chin by erasure, a process which is not only fatal to thin paper, but which would also dispose of the half-tone marks, and that would be immediately discovered in a photograph. Such significant marks of the half-tone screen are not found in the original, although, in the reproductions of the phantom picture in the book, they are easily recognised. It follows that the marks of the half-tone screen cannot be hidden at all, and betray themselves with absolute certainty.

" To this must be added that the enlargement of the original negative handed over to me is nearly double the size of the reproduction of this negative in the book itself (with visible screen marks). Screen marks would, therefore, have to be more characteristic and visible with the naked eye, while they are actually not even seen with a magnifying glass.

" The phenomenon image recalls a typical soft charcoal or chalk drawing, and therefore suggested a charcoal drawing. The latter cannot show the screen structure throughout. That could only be obtained by liquid painting, superimposed gouache or water-colour. This is contradicted by the characteristic appearance of the phenomenon picture, which recalls pencil drawing, or stump technique, and not painting, which, indeed, would present extraordinary difficulties on bad paper. It would also show the marks of the brush, which would have to be used with thick paint, in order to produce a complete covering up of the half-tone screen pattern.

" If the Wilson portrait from the *Miroir*, modified by drawing, had been used for the phenomenon picture shown in Fig. 136, it would show screen marks, while the technique used for producing the changes would betray itself by a dozen characteristics.

" It would also be impossible to obliterate the differences between the two heads, as to their position, their proportions, and the several details of the face.

" It follows, with absolute certainty, from these considerations, that the portrait of President Wilson, shown in the *Miroir*, No. 34, 1912, could not have been made into the phenomenon picture, Fig. 136, by any artistic manipulation, in spite of some striking similarities.

" (Signed) HERMANN URBAN.

" Munich, 14*th January* 1914."

In connection with Professor Urban's Opinion, it should be pointed out that, in President Wilson's portrait, the tie is tied with a pin, the head of which is evidently engraved with a coat of arms. This is absent in Fig. 196, and although Miss Barkley indicates a slight shading on the latter, which might represent that object, it is too far on the right-hand side.

The whole of the similarities with the *Miroir* pictures, of which so much has been made in the Press, reduce themselves to the following four points :—

    1. The agreement of certain details of Fig. 196 with the Wilson portrait.

    2. A partial resemblance of the tie marks of Fig. 194 with the portrait of President Poincaré.

3. In the three pimples characteristic of that face, shown in the head of Fig. 192; and
4. In the occurrence of the letters *Miroir*.

As no explanation is forthcoming based upon fraudulent manipulation by the medium, and as it is impossible that either the originals of the *Miroir* pictures, or manually altered copies of them, could have been exposed to produce the photographs in question, we must look for some other explanation, based upon the origin of the teleplastic creations.

The teleplastic creations are so closely connected with the psychic condition of the medium that Morselli compared them with materialised dream images. This view regards the products as ephemeral, externalised precipitates of the medium's psychic impressions and reminiscences. That the phenomena in many cases realise the thoughts of the medium may be considered as established. I need only recall the repeated occurrences of hands as suggested by the sitters, and other fulfilments of their wishes. Such a process may also account for the projection of memory images of deceased persons, such as M. Alexandre Bisson and Mme. Bisson's nephew; also the production of an image resembling Leonardo da Vinci's "Mona Lisa," which was so greatly talked about when it was stolen from the Louvre. Here, again, we have no slavish replica, but an impressionistic representation of the style in which the picture was painted. The results of this process, which may be called ideo-plastics, are closely connected with the psychic life of the medium, with her storage of memories, and with the intensity of dominant ideas.

Optical, or visual, images appear to play the chief part in the case of Eva C. Now, it is well known that the clearness of memory may rise to an abnormal level in the case of hysterical persons (hypermnesia). Thus, some slight event of youth, or an entirely lost language, can be revived under abnormal conditions, such as somnambulism or some diseases.

As Offner points out,[1] painters like Vernet, Doré, and Makart were able to paint accurate representations of objects and persons after seeing them once. Of the philosopher Seneca, it is said that he could recite three thousand words accurately after hearing them once, and that he could repeat two hundred verses in the reverse order. A deceased relative of the author was able to reproduce a speech verbatim which he had once heard ten years before. The sharpness of memory, in such abnormal cases, is sufficiently illustrated by these examples, and may be compared to the sharp definition of a photographic plate.

The occurrence of cryptomnesia, or the recalling of a former memory image which had never entered the normal consciousness, is quite an ordinary occurrence with hypnotised persons and somnambulists. Thus, the important nucleus of a thing, or the chief points of a picture, can be completely forgotten, while some unessential detail (in our case, the form and marking of a tie, the position of three pimples, the shape of a prominent print, and certain lines and types of face) may be reproduced most accurately, and may occur in a new connection as an independent psychic performance. This may explain the speaking in

[1] Offner, Gedachtnis, *Handbuch der Naturwissenschaften*, Vol. 4.

foreign languages (glossolalia). That the cryptomnesic pictures may lead to the most remarkable and complicated combinations in the trance condition is shown by Flournoy's studies on the " Martian " language of Helène Smith.

Cases have been known, both among painters and musicians, in which cryptomnesic performances were regarded by the artists as their own independent creations, although they could be shown to be identical with works of old masters. In mediumistic phenomena we may have a combination of ideoplastics with cryptomnesia, and such a combination may account for the observed coincidences in the case of the *Miroir* portraits, which were exhibited in nearly all the newspaper shops in Paris. If we suppose that the medium saw the *Miroir* number of 17th November 1912 with Wilson's portrait, within a few days of its publication, and had received a strong optical impression of the title-page, with the word "*Miroir*" at the head, and of the features of President Wilson, it is easily understood that on the 27th November she produced the word "*Miroir*," and later, on the 9th January, the type which contained cryptomnesic reminiscences of the tie markings and collar, and some facial lines from this visual memory. For the production of a word by the ideoplastic process and that of a picture is the same process of creation, and the former is only remarkable because it was observed only once in the course of four years.

In the case of other details, like the three pimples (Fig. 149), it is possible that an independent teleplastic creation may contain cryptomnesic elements, which are embodied in it. Such intermixtures are already well known in the purely psychic region, and have ceased to be wondered at. The literature of occultism contains a number of parallel cases. Thus, in a sitting held by Richet with Linda Gazerra, an angel head, by Rubens, was apparently the model for an ideo-plastic reproduction.

Morselli draws attention to the fact that such forms, in the first instance, are developed in two dimensions, and therefore show a flat appearance. He says: " Sometimes they even give the impression of being cut out of cardboard, while in other cases their margins are undefined." It is only on further development that stereoplastic forms are produced, consisting of fragments of limbs, hands, arms, faces, heads, up to the formation of a whole identity. The above considerations dispose of the objections raised by Miss Barkley, as far as they are concerned with the possible fraudulent use of the *Miroir* portraits.

The result of the examination of these objections may be summarised as follows :—

1. Even if the alleged agreement between certain portrait heads, reproduced on the title-pages of the journal *Le Miroir*, and certain phantom pictures were greater than it is, yet, in consideration of the experimental conditions of the sittings, a deception due to the smuggling in of prepared art journals, and their exposure in the places of the ideo-plastic images, is quite excluded.
2. The alleged similarity of the portraits produced by autotype in the journal *Le Miroir* is confined to the single occurrence of

the title heading "*Miroir*" and the similarity of a few details in the portraits of Presidents Wilson and Poincaré to those in the phantom pictures of 19th January, 6th March, and 2nd May 1913.
3. The journal *Le Matin* published, as a basis of its attack of 26th December 1913, an illustration from the work of Mme. Bisson, which had been manipulated and retouched by hand, in order to make it resemble President Poincaré.
4. Expert opinions are unanimous in saying that, if the author's photographic conditions are strictly observed, neither the original pictures from the *Miroir*, nor any worked-up copies thereof, could have been exposed at the sittings so as to produce the author's published photographs.
5. The occurrence of certain details derived from the title-pages of *Le Miroir* in the phenomenon of the sittings of 2nd November 1912 and of 19th January, 6th March, and 2nd May 1913, is explained by the cryptomnesic function of memory, such as is often observed in the somnambulistic condition. Reminiscences of former visual impressions and fragments of dream images coalesce unconsciously with the ideoplastic creations to form an unified presentation, which may be so misinterpreted as to give rise to suspicion.

Sittings with Eva C. in November and December 1913 and January 1914 (Paris).

THE criticisms and attacks following upon the publication of the German and French editions of our records induced us to make new experiments with Eva C. as a further test of the objections raised. Some records of the observational material thus obtained will be communicated here.

The sittings took place in the room described at No. 33 Rue Georges Sand, which was used in May and June 1912. Since, for the first, photography was not to be used, a dim white light was employed. On the right, beside the cabinet, a screen was placed, and behind this there hung a fifty candle-power electric lamp, attached to the pendent, and draped with a dark blue rather transparent cloth, which did not perceptibly alter the colour of the light. The degree of brightness obtained in this manner enabled us to make more accurate observations than with the red light. Print of a medium size could be easily read, and the record could be kept during the sitting. The eye was less easily fatigued, and the objects, upon which it was concentrated, appeared brighter.

The cloth covering of the chair was removed at the end of December, and also the red electric lamp in the cabinet, for the suspicion had been uttered that the electric lamp, hanging at the back of the cabinet 7 feet above the floor, and possibly the cloth covering of the arm-rests, might be used by the medium as hiding-places. During the sittings about to be described, the medium regularly wore a tricot covering her whole body, closing down the back, and provided with sleeves and stockings, all in one piece. Over this she put on the apron dress already used in previous sittings, and was then sewn up at the neck and sleeves, before every sitting. The initial and final examination of the medium, cabinet, and chair took place in the same way as in May and June 1913. A gynæcological examination was unnecessary, partly on account of the manner of dressing, and also because the medium could never use her hands during the sitting. The hands were always at the curtain, holding the two flaps, and resting on her knees. Eva crossed her arms from time to time to avoid fatigue, but the forearms were never withdrawn, so that every objection, based on the supposed participation of her hands, is eliminated. Her feet and knees remain in the same position, corresponding to her sitting posture. Eva C. did not rise from her chair once, but remained in a sitting position during the whole of the observations. The records were kept (as they have been since 1912) with an exact indication of the time, and are here quoted in an abridged form.

Sitting of the 7th November 1913.

Present.—Dr Bourbon, Mme. Bisson, and the author.
Condition.—As above described.
9 P.M. Hypnotisation by Mme. Bisson in thirty seconds. Hands visible during the whole sitting, sometimes held by Mme. Bisson, sitting in front. The curtain was hardly ever closed. This enabled us to be sure that at—
9.45 P.M., the white patch, visible in the medium's lap, did not come out of her mouth. The substance grew before our eyes to the size of a human forearm.
9.50 P.M. The strip becomes wider, appears to have mobility of its own, takes up a position on the right shoulder in the shape of a flat white disk, the size of a head, and disappears upwards towards the right before our eyes (not into the medium's mouth).
10.10 P.M. Further efforts, without result.
10.45 P.M. Close of the sitting. Final examination negative. The movements took place without movement of the hands, and while the medium's head was motionless and visible.

Sitting of the 13th November 1913.

Present.—Mme. Bisson and the author.
All conditions as on 7th November.
8.55 P.M. Hypnotisation of the medium by Mme. Bisson. The opening of the curtain was about 12 or 14 inches half way up, from the beginning of the sitting, so that one could look into the cabinet to the right and to the left. The hands were under constant control visibly holding the curtains, and I touched them from time to time. We sat immediately in front of the curtain. The medium never rose from her chair.
9.5 P.M. Eva suddenly opened the curtain at her right hand, and I saw, on the left against the back wall, about 4 feet above the floor, a flat life-sized male portrait, with neck and face turned forwards. It had a sharp outline, but did not seem sufficiently clearly developed in its details. The curtain was opened wider (without being ever com-

pletely closed), and the formation showed itself several times, giving the impression of a white marble relief.

9.7 P.M. With an open curtain, and the medium's body motionless, the portrait, quite separate from her body, and about 28 inches away from her head, disappeared before our eyes into the black background, as if it had lost its own luminosity. An accurate observation showed that it had not fallen down, nor was it in any way withdrawn by the medium.

9.10 P.M. On the medium's breast we saw a broad mass, about 16 inches long, hanging from her mouth. The medium turned her head to the left. The mass disappeared from our eyes, and was not seen again.

9.35 P.M. Close of the sitting. Final examination negative. The appearance of the white portrait might be regarded as a hallucination, if it were not for the fact that for four years we always corroborated, by photography, the reality of the objects seen, so that such an objection cannot be maintained. In any case, the accurate observation of the disappearance of a portrait, the size of a medallion, in a few seconds, corroborates numerous observations of this kind, and similar kinds, described before.

Sitting of the 26th November 1913.

This was described in the chapter on the rumination hypothesis.

Sitting of the 8th December 1913,

Present.—Dr Bourbon, Mme. Bisson, and the author.

All conditions as in previous sittings.

6.5 P.M. Hypnotisation. The curtain remained open from the beginning of the sitting. The hands were constantly visible and under control, and were not withdrawn for an instant.

6.45 P.M. The medium takes off the tricot because it is uncomfortable, and is only clothed in the apron dress. During the change the medium's hands were strictly watched.

6.48 P.M. Loud whimpering. The medium opens and closes the curtain with her constantly visible hands. On the left upper arm and breast we see a bulky white mass.

6.55 P.M. We see a life-sized male head on her breast, covering it entirely. It gives the impression of a strong pictorial representation on a skin-like basis. The full beard is especially clear. The head resembles that of the whole phantom. It disappears before our eyes while the curtain is open, without being absorbed by the mouth, and again as if its luminosity had ceased. The hands did not move during the occurrence, and Eva's head also remained motionless. The drawing of the face was black on a white ground.

7.5 P.M. Close of the sitting. Final examination negative.

A few days before the author's return, on the 7th January, Mme. Bisson, in a sitting alone with Eva, again observed the phantom seen by the author on 8th December. She turned on the red light and

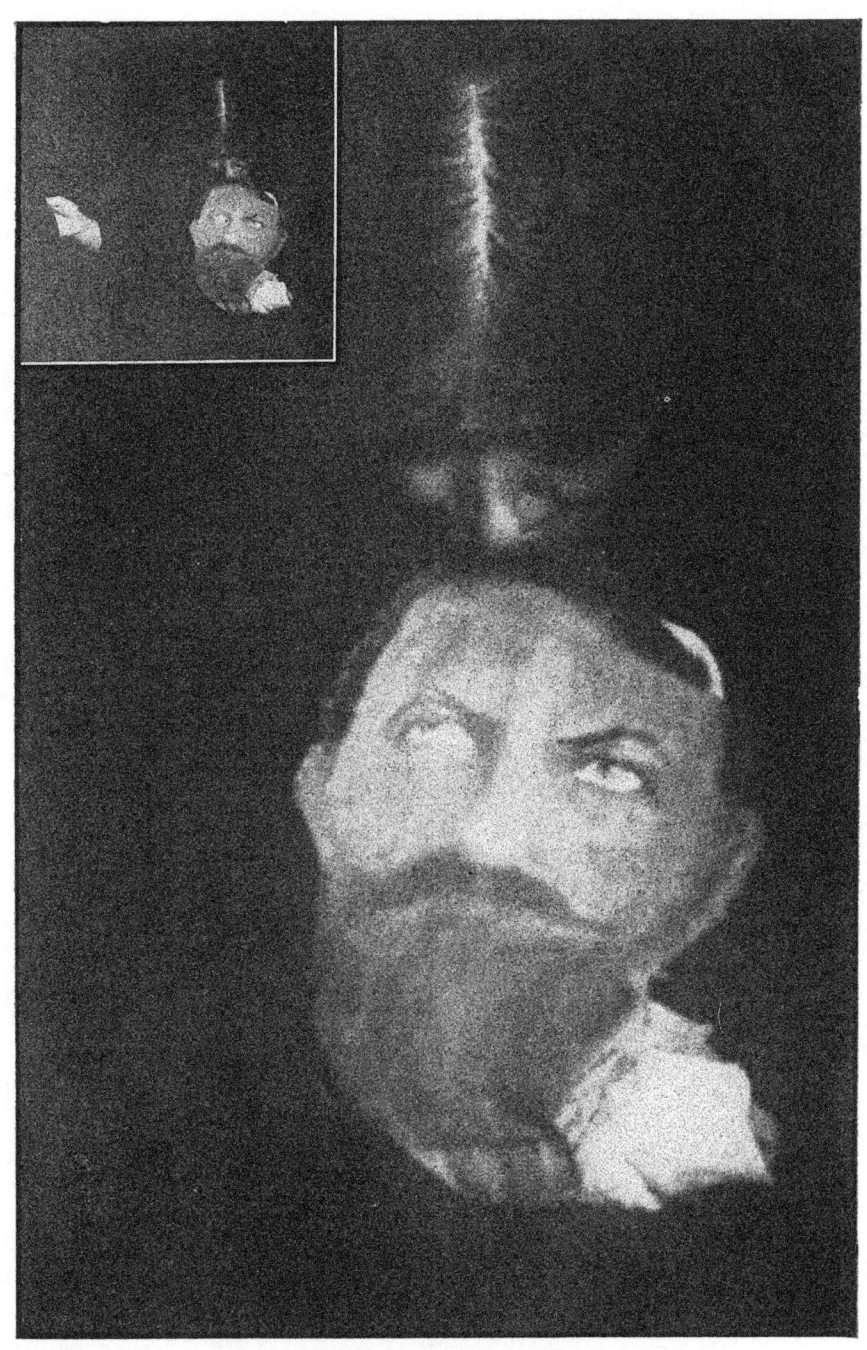

Fig 198 Mme Bisson's photograph of 7 January, 1914.

then ignited the magnesium apparatus. In this experiment, also, the medium's hands were always visible and excluded from participation. The photographic result (Fig. 198) completely corroborates the author's observation of the 8th December 1913.

We see the same phantom head as was photographed four times previously (23rd February, 24th March, 19th May, and 8th June 1913), so that this is the fifth independent representafion of the same kind of face. While the position of the eyes recalls the photograph of 19th May, the drawing of the moustache is more stretched out, as in the earlier photographs. The proportions of the face make it shorter and broader. The forehead especially is lower, the line of the hair being specially drawn down on the left side. The full beard is shorter and differently shaped from that in the previous photographs. A foreshortening of the whole face is also quite possible, owing to the somewhat inclined position of the structure in the medium's lap. The head is supported on the left by Eva's hand, and is evidently pressed down by the chin. The product does not show any rents or folds anywhere, the base presenting a homogeneous textile character. The impression itself is so vivacious, plastic, and sharp that the use of a black and white drawing is immediately excluded. Paper is also excluded, owing to the soft fibrous margins of the picture.

A comparison with the *Miroir* portrait of the King of Bulgaria shows a totally different structure of face in the two objects. The eyes in the *Miroir* reproduction give quite a dead impression compared with the phenomenon, quite apart from the different position of the eyeballs, and other deviations. The photograph of this head was obtained after the chief attacks had already been published.

Sitting of the 9th January 1914.

Present.—Mme. Bisson and the author.

Conditions as in November 1913. Chair without covering, no red lamp in the cabinet, reduced white illumination. Medium's hands visibly controlled during the whole sitting, so that their co-operation in the phenomena was excluded. Sometimes they were held by me—for instance, at the moment when Mme. Bisson opened the camera and switched on the red light. Clothing—whole tricot and dress.

9.11 P.M. Hypnotisation by Mme. Bisson. Curtains nearly always open. Only at a few moments were the flaps drawn together more tightly, while the hands always remained outside the curtains. There was no change of hands, which would enable one hand to hold the curtain while the other was withdrawn into the dark.

10.3 P.M. A greyish-white patch appears on Eva's breast. Again, we have the impression of a skin-like substance on which a profile was drawn. I approached my hand carefully to the structure and touched the head image with my right forefinger. It gave the sensation of a very fine slimy skin, and through it I could feel the stuff of the dress.

10.5 P.M. Red light switched on.

10.6 P.M. Curtain wide open, flash-light ignited. Eva's hands at the moment of the flash-light remained at the open curtain, and, at the same moment, I quickly touched her breast with my right hand, but only felt the dress. Everything disappeared without a trace, and without the participation of the hands or the head, nor could anything be found of the picture in the cabinet.

10.8 P.M. Another plate is inserted.

10.10 P.M. The same image appears on the breast, the medium's hands being in the same position as before, but the image is less distinct and paler. As during the first appearance, the substance this time also shows a striped structure.

10.11 P.M. A second photograph. Probably less distinct than before, owing to the magnesium smoke in the room. The image immediately disappeared with the flash-light, and without any change in the position of the medium's hands, head, or body.

10.28 P.M. Close of the sitting. Final examination of medium, cabinet and chair negative.

When Eva rose from her chair the author put a question to her as to whence the materialisation had come, since, on this day, the mouth had been out of action. She replied, " The neck." I then found that the neck, under the hair-line, was covered with a thin layer of a viscous substance. I immediately took two glass slides and obtained some of this substance for microscopic examination. Eva undressed completely in the author's presence, put on her dressing-gown, and went to bed in the somnambulistic condition. No residues of the phenomenon were found on the dress. The microscopic examination of the preparations, treated with iodine, showed numerous plate epithelia, with distinct nuclei embedded in a viscous substance. The second preparation showed numerous bacteria in the form of rods and diplococcus. The epithelia in question resembled those found in a mucous membrane, and did not give a horny impression. This result agrees with the findings previously enumerated, but we must not exclude the possibility that in scraping the neck some cells of the epidermis may have got on to the glass slide.

The photographs (Figs. 199 and 200) of the sitting of 9th January 1914 completely corroborate the visual observations. The first photograph shows a male face, rather over life-size, on an apparently compact fabric, with vertical stripes, the quality of which gives no impression of paper. All the margins are torn, and the structure resembles a coarse, but strongly characterised, sketch on a flat ground. We remark the strongly curved form of the nose, the slanting nostrils, and the peculiar form of the eye. Several deep creases, at the neck and on the forehead, prove a soft basis. The position of the mouth is only marked by a shadow. The moustache is broad, short and drooping.

The second photograph, taken five minutes after the first, shows the whole silhouette of the head, which, in comparison with the head of the medium (who, in both cases, appears to press the formation with her chin against her breast), is over life-size. At the forehead the head is bent round, and this reveals the soft thin fabric. In this case the ear is distinctly drawn. The most remarkable change, in comparison with the first photograph, is in the shape of the moustache, which is no longer short and drooping, but reaches to the middle of the cheek in a broad wavy line. The deep black vertical shadow, which in Fig. 199 cuts off

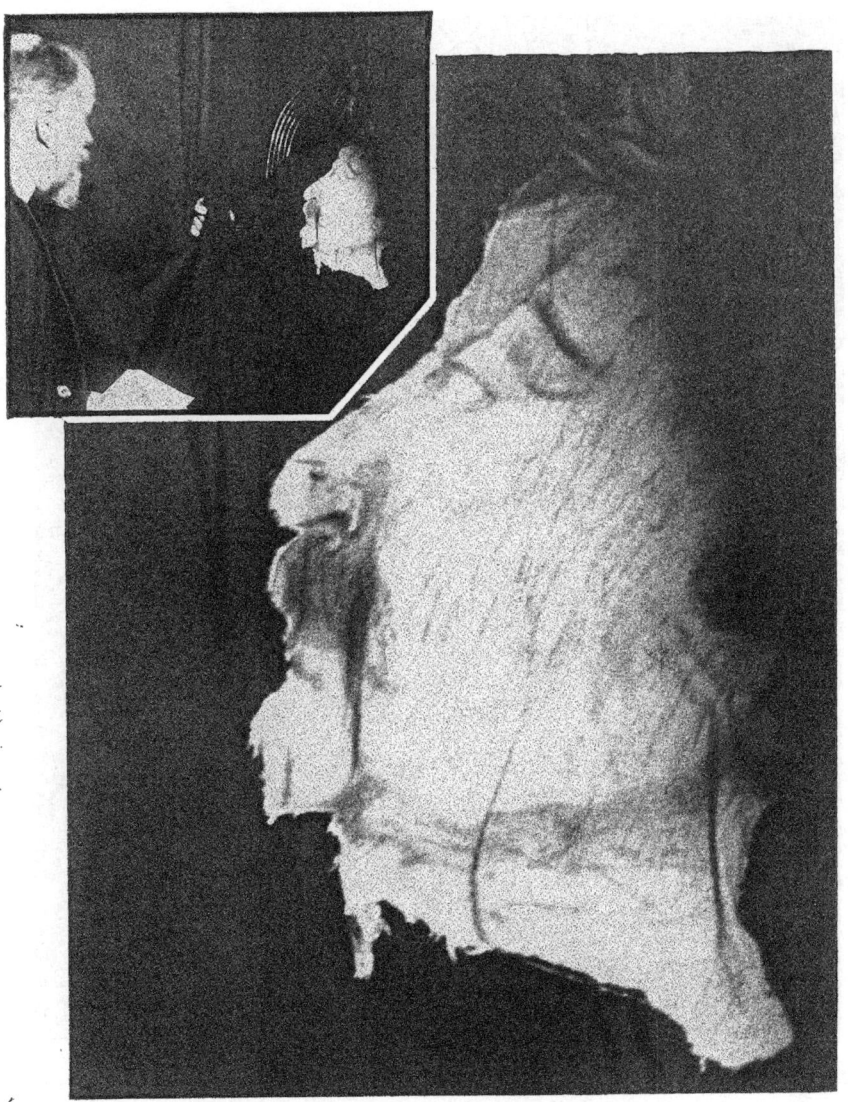

Fig. 199 Author's first flashlight photograph of 9 January, 1914.

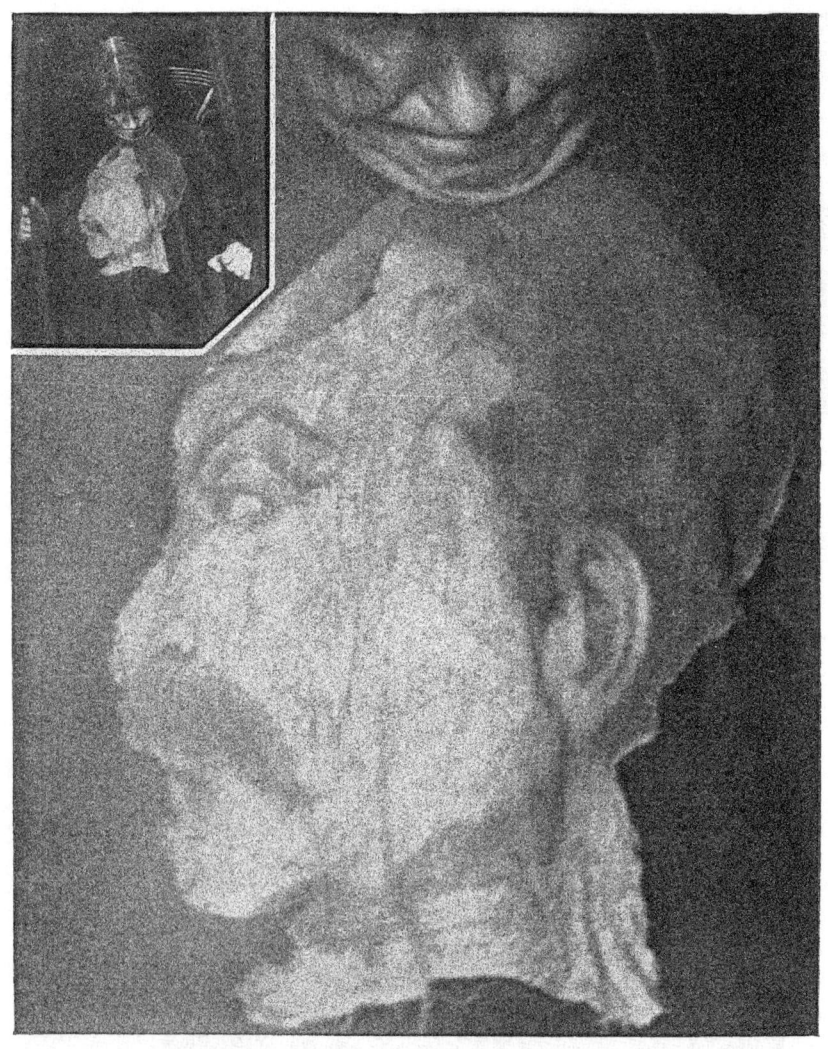

Fig. 200. Author's second flashlight photograph, five minutes after Fig. 199.

the moustache at the corner of the mouth, has disappeared. The outline of the chin is rounder, and distinctly changed in comparison with Fig. 199. The vertical folds and irregularities of the first photograph have remained, and serve to identify the two pictures.

That we have here no previously arranged art journal sheet goes without saying, but the changes in the outline, and in the drawing of the moustache, betray again the fluctuating and variable character of these teleplastic products, a point which weighs heavily against the hypothesis of fraud, for how is it possible to transform the drawing and shape of the same product in this manner in five minutes ? The transformation process of materialised products, as already pointed out, is one of the strongest proofs for their authenticity. To this we must add the extinction of the phantom pictures, which has frequently been observed, while the medium was motionless in a reduced white light, and could not have used her hands or her mouth. These new observations by the author, together with those of other witnesses, confirm the facts observed in other sittings, and eliminate the hypothesis of fraudulent manipulation.

Sittings with Eva C. in May and June 1914 (Paris).

Experimental Conditions.

In April 1914 Mme. Bisson moved to No. 1, Rue de La Muette (fifth floor). Here she arranged the séance room in the manner described before, so that the cabinet stood detached, and could be inspected from both sides. The wall of the room forming the back of the cabinet was part of the lift well. The frame of the cabinet was made of simple smooth laths, to which the black lining was attached by nails.

The medium's chair consisted of simple black bamboo and wood laths. A white electric lamp of thirty-two candle-power hung behind a screen, and its brightness was reduced by some dark cloth. The illumination was bright enough to read print easily.

The observers took their places immediately in front of the cabinet, Mme. Bisson, as a rule, on Seat 2 (*see* Diagram).

Red light was arranged for, but was not used, since there was no intention of continuing the photographic records. The séance room was always locked. It was unlocked regularly by one of the observers before the sitting, and during the sitting it was kept locked from the inside.

The roof of the cabinet was $8\frac{1}{2}$ feet high. The author could not touch it without mounting on a chair. Before and after each sitting the cabinet was closely examined, as was the chair, but always with a negative result.

Initial Control of the Medium.

The séance costume worn by Eva C. consisted of a black cotton tricot of one piece, laced up the back from the waist to the neck, so that the whole body was covered by it except the hands and the head. Over this tricot she put on the black apron dress described on several previous occasions, which was sewn up at the neck and the sleeves while it remained open behind. In all the sittings these two articles of clothing were closely examined in Eva's absence by the sitters, sometimes with the help of an electric lamp. The costume remained in the hands of one of the observers until it was put on by the medium.

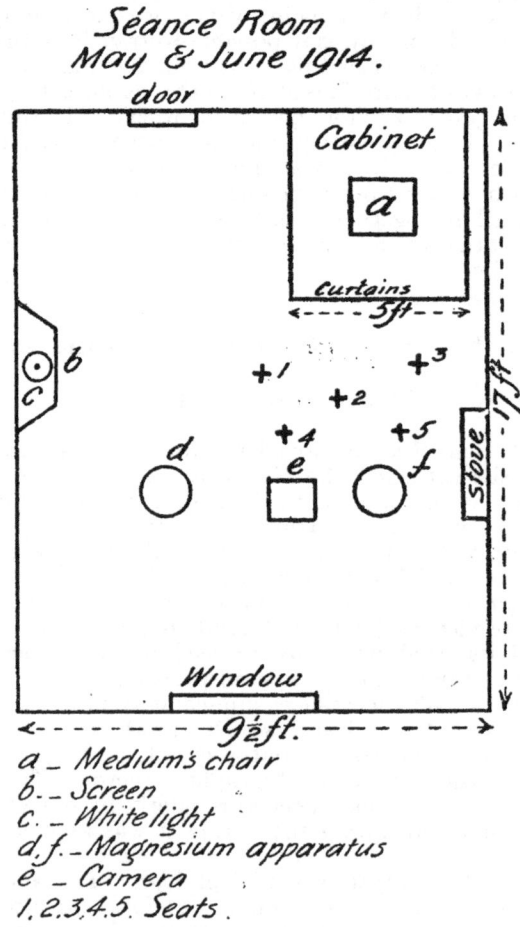

a — Medium's chair
b. — Screen
c. — White light
d, f. — Magnesium apparatus
e — Camera
1, 2, 3, 4, 5. Seats.

DIAGRAM VIII.

Eva entered the séance room wearing nothing but a blue dressing-gown, and accompanied by Mme. Bisson. She then put on the tricot and dress in the presence of the sitters, who closely watched all her movements. Then Mme. Bisson closed and sewed up the dress as described. The medium's mouth was then closely examined by means of a spatula, to which an electric lamp was attached. The ears were examined, and she was made to blow through each nostril in turn. The medium's hair was taken down, and after the combs had been removed, nothing suspicious was found. The neck and wrist fastenings were then examined once more. Only after the observers had declared that Eva C. had nothing suspicious about her body was she allowed to enter the cabinet, and take her seat.

HYPNOTISATION.

Two of the observers present then took their seats in places 1 and 3, Mme. Bisson sitting between them in place 2. She takes the medium's thumbs and hypnotises her by fixation in about thirty seconds, whereupon the medium subsides into the chair. The main illumination over the chimney is then extinguished, the lamp behind the screen being left on. The difference of illumination does not dazzle the eyes.

The medium's hands were not withdrawn for an instant behind the curtains in the sittings about to be described. They remained the whole time visible to the gaze of those present outside the curtain, and either lying on the medium's knees, holding the curtain themselves, or grasped by the sitters in places 1 and 3. This excludes all attempts at explanations which presuppose the participation of Eva's hands.

During the productions the curtains above the visible hands were occasionally closed by one of those present with a simple clip, in order to cut off the light. During the demonstration itself Eva C. opens and closes the curtains with her hands, which remain always visible.

OTHER CONDITIONS OF CONTROL.

Mme. Bisson never entered the cabinet during the sittings about to be described, but, in a few cases, one of the men present (a savant or journalist), entered the cabinet in order to lay his hands on Eva's head and neck. There was no singing or formation of chains. Quiet conversation was carried on, but attention was not diverted from the control for an instant.

The persons sitting next to the curtain could, at any time, touch Eva's hands, so as to satisfy themselves that they were the warm living hands of a human being, and not wax imitations. When they wished to do so, they could also take hold of the medium's hands and hold them, so that some of the phenomena took place while the medium's hands were being held. Sometimes the medium seized Mme. Bisson's hands ostensibly to gather force.

ILLUMINATION OF THE TELEPLASTIC PRODUCTS WITH ELECTRIC LAMPS.

On account of the fugitive character of the materialisation phenomena, the visual impression is often not sufficiently precise to discern any details. In order to remedy this defect an electric hand-lamp was connected to the supply circuit by means of a flexible cord. It could be made to shine with a red, green, or white light. On such occasions one of those present undertook the duty of illuminating the phenomenon for a few seconds, which enabled those sitting behind to see it distinctly.

FINAL CONTROL.

At the close of every sitting Eva C., still in the somnambulic condition, rose from the arm-chair, stepped in front of the curtain, and was again examined as during the initial control, but in the reverse order. Her mouth was illuminated, and her hair, ears and hands examined. Then, in our presence, the seams were undone, the tricot and dress were taken off, and remained in the hands of the observers. The medium was then dressed in her dressing-gown and went to bed, still in the somnambulic condition. The cabinet, chair and séance costume were then finally examined, always with a negative result. All the records quoted below were made by the author, during the sittings.

SITTING OF THE 15TH MAY 1914.

Present.—Henriques Philippe (contributor to the *Monde Illustré*), Mr Crawford (British savant), Van Eck, Dumoir van Twick (Secretary of the Society for Psychical Studies, The Hague), also two ladies, Mme. Bisson and the author.

Arrangements and control as described. Van Twick took the place to Mme. Bisson's right, Mr Crawford the place on her left, while the author sat behind in the third row.

9.14 P.M. Hypnotisation of the medium by Mme. Bisson.
9.30 P.M. Pains and muscular efforts. Hands always visible.
9.55 P.M. Mediumistic labour. Mme. Bisson closes the curtain above the medium's hands.
10.9 P.M. Strong suggestions towards materialisation.
10.25 P.M. Eva opens the curtain. A triangular grey mass, about 10 inches long, lies on her left shoulder. The product was illuminated by a red torch, and disappeared under the eyes of those present. The author, from his seat, could not observe any details, but the men sitting in front declared that they observed the transformation of the piece into stripes, which had a motion of their own.
10.45 P.M. The skin-like substance becomes visible on Eva's breast. I distinctly recognise, on this surface, the profile of a male portrait, life-size. The hair appeared to be genuine and the ear was clearly shown, though the picture appeared distorted. Illuminated with a red torch, the phenomenon disappeared before the eyes of those present, in a fraction of a second, while the medium's body remained motionless. Eva immediately bent forward out of the cabinet and allowed us to touch her head and breast. Her hands had not changed their position. The sitting closed. The final examination was negative, but the dress showed traces of viscous moisture at the neck.

SITTING OF THE 19TH MAY 1914.

Present.—Mr W. B. Yeats (London), Dr G. Montalescot (physician), M. Nicolle (of the *Annales*), Countess W., Mme. Bisson, and the author.

Yeats sits on the left, Montalescot to the right of Mme. Bisson, and the author in the third row.

9.4 P.M. Hypnotisation. Eva's hands visible during the whole sitting.
9.32 P.M. Mediumistic labour. Accelerated respiration. Whimpering and gasping.

9.45 P.M. On Eva's left shoulder a white luminous material becomes visible.

9.55 P.M. The teleplastic mass changes its position. It assumes a square form, 10 inches long and 8 inches wide, lies on the medium's breast, and resembles a serviette. Repeated illumination with the electric torch clearly shows a picture in the state of development.

10.5 P.M. During the next illumination the author has the distinct impression of a stiff white lace fabric, closely resembling the fabric materialised from the mouth of the Polish medium Stanislava P., on the occasion of the kinematograph record.

10.8 P.M. A new exposure of a few seconds shows a skin-like surface, with the front view of the face of an old woman. All those present confirmed this observation. Those sitting closer maintain that the nose was plastically developed.

10.30 P.M. Close of the sitting. Final control negative.

The next morning Mme. Bisson communicated the following by letter: " After you had left, I went into Eva's bedroom, and found her still in the critical condition. I took her back into the séance room, and had most interesting manifestations. The image of an old woman showed itself about twenty times, and I believe I recognised in her my deceased mother. I succeeded on this occasion in photographing two heads, one of a man and one of the woman. Eva fainted away, and I took her to bed."

SITTING OF THE 22ND MAY 1914.

Present.—Mr E. N. Bennett (formerly Fellow of Hertford College, Oxford, and M.P.; a member of the Council of the Society for Psychical Research, London), W. B. Yeats, Commandant Romain, Mme. Bisson, and the author.

Bennett sat to the right, Yeats to the left, of Mme. Bisson. The author in the second row.

Eva's disposition was rather unfavourable.

9.10 P.M. Hypnotisation.

9.55 P.M. Bennett holds both Eva's hands, and seems to notice on her left shoulder a piece of white material.

9.59 P.M. Bennett observed a materialisation process in the medium's lap.

10.5 P.M. On the medium's thighs, in various places, small luminous strips and points appear for a few seconds, and disappear before the eyes of the sitters.

10.9 P.M. Strong crisis.

10.25 P.M. Cessation of the phenomena. Close of the sitting. Final examination negative.

SITTING OF THE 26TH MAY 1914.

Present.—Mr Yeats, Professor Courtier (Director of the Physiological Laboratory of the Sorbonne), M. and Mme. Faral, Mme. D., Mme. Bisson, and the author.

Initial control by Courtier and Yeats, as described in the introduction. Courtier sits at the curtain, on Mme. Bisson's right, Yeats on the left, and the author in the second row.

9.5 P.M. Hypnotisation. Eva's hands were always visible, and often held by Courtier.

9.40 P.M. Increased muscular efforts. "Cela vient." Eva is first comparatively quiet, then she screams with pain, as if under an operation.

9.42 P.M. Whitish luminous patches, and points of variable size, on the upper arm and dress. In order not to disturb the development, the curtains are closed with a clip above the hands, which are always visible in front of the curtain.

9.46 P.M. Increased excitement.

9.50 P.M. A phosphorescent strongly luminous mass in the shape of a pear-shaped pearl, about an inch long, forms on the medium's chest.

9.55 P.M. Eva's hands held by Courtier and Yeats. Courtier also takes the medium's feet between his own, while his left hand lies on the medium's knees. The curtain is quickly opened, and a white substance emerges from the medium's nose and mouth.

10.1 P.M. The mass assumes a flat, leaf-like shape, 8 or 10 inches square, and is now observed on the left breast and shoulder. The substance develops while hands and feet are held.

10.5 P.M. On opening the curtain, everything disappears. When the observers had satisfied themselves of the total disappearance, without movement of the medium, they release her hands

10.6 P.M. The hands are still at the curtain, and the white substance again becomes visible on the medium's breast, resembling, to the uninitiated, a handkerchief.

10.12 P.M. A pause.

10.15 P.M. At the next opening nothing is seen.

10.19 P.M. Renewed convulsive efforts, especially of the arms and the hands, which clutch the curtains. Eva pulls at the right-hand curtain, so that the curtain-rod hangs loose. The sitting is continued, while the medium utters cries of pain.

10.21 P.M. Renewed appearance of the white mass on the medium's chest. On Mme. Bisson illuminating it with a blue electric light, it immediately disappears. The blue lamp was then replaced by a red lamp.

10.29 P.M. The substance has the form of a long acute-angled triangle, about 10 inches in length, and lies on the medium's left breast. This mass also disappears on illuminating it with a red lamp.

10.30 P.M. Strong suggestion by those present in order to increase the phenomena. "Allez donc, donne bien," etc.

10.31 P.M. Courtier enters the cabinet and holds the medium's head with his hands, in order to soothe her. Eva's hands are constantly visible at the curtain.

10.32 P.M. While Courtier is still in the cabinet, the white substance appears on the medium's knees, and then disappears.

10.35 P.M. Courtier returns to his place.

10.37 P.M. Close of the sitting.

During the final control Courtier holds the medium's hands from the beginning. The result was negative. The dress at the left shoulder was moist, and showed numerous white spots.

Courtier declared to the author at the close of the sitting that after the series of ten sittings, at which he had been present, he had no doubt of the authenticity of the phenomena, and that there was no question of fraudulent manipulations or rumination.

SITTING OF THE 29TH MAY 1914.

Present.—M. Divoire (on the staff of the *Intransigeant*), Louis Gimiés and R. Guasco (on the staff of the journal *Opinion*), Henriques Philippe (on the staff of the *Monde Illustré*), Mme. D., Mme. Bisson, and the author.

9.7 P.M. Hypnotisation in thirty seconds.
9.30 P.M. Whimpering.
9.34 P.M. The medium says " Cela vient."
10.40 P.M. Nothing.
10.45 P.M. Divoire enters the cabinet and puts his hands on the medium's forehead and neck.
10.50 P.M. After Divoire has left the cabinet, small wisps of white material appear on the left shoulder.
10.51 P.M. Whimpering and mediumistic labour. A thread about 5 inches long, and apparently luminous, emerges from the mouth, and lies on her left breast.
10.55 P.M. Gasping respirations.
11 P.M. A piece of substance about an inch long appears on the left upper arm.
11.2 P.M. Everything has disappeared, though the hands were constantly visible.
11.10 P.M. Though Divoire enters the cabinet again, and tries to encourage the medium, the power to-day does not seem to suffice for strong materialisation.
11.55 P.M. Close of the sitting. Final examination negative.

SITTING OF THE 2ND JUNE 1914.

Present.—M. Philippe, M. and Mme. Grullu, Engineer Fauconnet and his wife, Comte Roger de Fontenay, Marquise de D., Mme. Bisson, and the author.

M. Fauconnet sat at Mme. Bisson's right, M. Grullu at the left, and the author in the second row near the fireplace.

9.5 P.M. Hypnotisation.
9.10 P.M. Moaning. Hands held by Grullu and Fauconnet.
9.15 P.M. " Cela vient." Strong whimpering.
9.22 P.M. A white substance becomes visible on the left shoulder.
9.25 to 9.30 P.M. Hands still held by the two men. The white mass, as shown at the next exposure, has formed into a broad surface extending across Eva's breast. The medium's hands hold the curtain.
9.32 P.M. Features are distinctly seen on the material, being a front view of a bearded male face, life-size, extending from the right shoulder to the left hip. It was illuminated twice with the red torch by Mme. Bisson, and once by Philippe. Repeated appearance and disappearance of the picture. The eyes are clearly directed upwards, and

the moustache is clearly visible. The flat portrait recalls the whole phantom previously described.

9.45 P.M. Philippe illuminates the product again.

9.50 P.M. Everything has disappeared. Close of the sitting. Final examination negative.

In a letter of 4th June, addressed to Mme. Bisson, Mme. Fauconnet confirms her own and her husband's impressions of the sitting of 2nd June as follows :—" In a good light I could see the following quite clearly : At first, on the left shoulder, and then on the breast and on the medium's right shoulder, a male face, on a flat surface, with beard and moustache. At the second illumination the eyes were distinctly seen. I observed, with special interest, the rapidity with which the whitish material disappeared and changed its place. Immediately after I had seen the face the medium again opened the curtains, and everything had disappeared without the slightest change in the control of the hands. The appearance of these materialisations is certainly most remarkable, and still disappointing. Why ? During the whole sitting the medium's hands never disappeared, and certainly not during the materialisations. The experimental arrangement of these sittings is beyond all criticism, even that of the most malignant opponents. I greatly appreciate the courage and energy which you devote to this thorny subject. But the present result should give you complete satisfaction by rewarding you for all your efforts, and give you the necessary enthusiasm to continue your studies."

Sitting of the 5th June 1914.

Present.—Giniés, Henriques Philippe, Professor Courtier, Mme. G., M. Gandara, Mme. Bisson, and the author.

Conditions and control as in previous sittings. Ginies sits on Mme. Bisson's left, and Courtier on the right.

9.15 P.M. Hypnosis.

10.12 P.M. First signs of a positive sitting. Hands always outside the curtain.

10.15 P.M. Whimpering and screaming.

10.17 P.M. Eva's hands held by Ginies and Courtier.

10.18 P.M. Large white flakes on the medium's left shoulder, which disappear again.

10.20 P.M. Courtier enters the cabinet and holds Eva's head, while Ginies holds both Eva's hands. Medium's pulse, 110. Strong convulsive muscular contractions in both arms. The author takes Courtier's place, and the medium grasps his hand, closing upon it like an iron clamp. Courtier touches the medium's neck and forehead.

10.28 P.M. Courtier resumes his seat. Eva holds the curtains with her hands.

10.40 P.M. Mediumistic labour.

10.42 to 10.45 P.M. A white mass is visible on Eva's face, giving the impression of a large white cloth, which appears to emerge from her mouth, cover the left half of her face, and hang down over her hair on to the left shoulder.

10.46 P.M. The substance, resembling a large white skin, has laid itself on Eva's breast.

10.50 to 10.55 P.M. Philippe twice shines the red electric light into the cabinet. The skin-like fabric hanging down from the left shoulder on to the medium's breast shows irregular shadings on its surface, but no recognisable features.

11 to 11.5 P.M. I twice illuminated the skin-like surface from above with a red torch, whereupon Courtier, the other observers and I agree in recognising a male portrait, again recalling the head of the whole phantom. It is the same as the head in the last sitting, but now resembles a crumpled mask. On illuminating the cabinet for the third time, the product has disappeared.

11.5 P.M. Courtier enters the cabinet, holds Eva's head, while her hands are held outside the curtain by Ginies, and in that position he sees a white piece of material on the medium's left shoulder, which falls into the medium's lap, before his eyes, and disappears. Courtier dictated these observations to the author.

11.10 P.M. Eva rose, stood in front of the cabinet, and was evidently under the impression that the end of her performances had come; but suddenly she called out " Cela revient," and returned to her seat. Her efforts were, however, fruitless, and at 11.12 the sitting closed, with a negative final examination. The left shoulder of dress and tricot, and some parts of the upper sleeve, showed a viscous moisture. During the inspection of the mouth I scraped the tongue with a spoon, and collected the product on a glass slide, for microscopic examination.

SITTING OF THE 9TH JUNE 1914.

Present.—Camille Flammarion (astronomer), whose lady secretary noted all his observations during the sitting; Dr L., M. de Vesme, Henriques Philippe, three ladies, Mme. Bisson, and the author.

Initial control by Flammarion and Dr L. (including an examination of the back of the cabinet from the outside). Dr L. sat on Mme. Bisson's left, Flammarion on the right, author in the second row.

9.9 P.M. Hypnotisation. Eva's hands remained visible during the whole sitting outside the curtain.

9.21 P.M. Eva: " Je sens quelque chose."

9.25 P.M. The materialisation process begins in the shape of small greyish-white flakes on Eva's breast.

9.40 P.M. On the left upper arm a piece of grey material appears about one-third of an inch broad and one inch long. Dr L. and the author now hold the medium's hands. The material grows and shrinks, and seems to phosphoresce. At Eva's request, Dr L. enters the cabinet and holds her forehead and neck. Under these conditions (with Eva's hands outside the curtain) the substance is visible on her left shoulder as a greyish-white patch.

10.6 P.M. Dr L. leaves the cabinet.

10.16 P.M. Eva's hands held by Dr L. and Flammarion. Mediumistic labour.

10.20 P.M. Under the same conditions, a fairly broad white band becomes visible on the left shoulder and hangs down over the upper arm. It may have been 8 inches long and 3 inches broad, and looked like a striped skin of whitish-grey colour.

10.21 P.M. The band falls into Eva's lap, while Dr L. and Flammarion still hold Eva's hands. Dr L. again enters the cabinet and sees a shred on her left shoulder, while Flammarion is holding both her hands.

10.25 P.M. L. resumes his seat.

10.30 P.M. A piece of white material again appears on the left shoulder, resembling a handkerchief spread out. It is about 8 inches wide and 12 inches long. Eva's hands are again held by L. and Flammarion.

10.35 P.M. The same control, while Mme. Bisson closes the curtain above Eva's hands.

10.40 P.M. The phenomenon shows again on the left upper arm, in the shape of a flake 2 or 3 inches long.

10.41 P.M. The same appearance is visible on the right upper arm, without any change in the control.

10.42 P.M. A packet of white material, half the size of a hand, lies on the right shoulder.

10.45 P.M. Close of the sitting. Final examination negative. Tricot and dress are moistened in the places where we saw the material, and some of the patches are already dry, leaving a grey crust. One has the impression that the material penetrates the tricot and dress in a liquid state.

Flammarion considers the phenomena evidential, and regards fraudulent manipulations as excluded by the method of control.

The following elements appeared remarkable to various observers: The change in the forms of the substance, which was sometimes leaf-shaped and sometimes kidney-shaped; the visible growth and displacement of the phenomena; the penetration through the medium's dress; and the liquid precipitate of the matter.

Result of the Observations.

C. de Vesme, Editor of the *Annales des Sciences Psychiques*, an observer well known for his critical acumen, published in those *Annales* in May, No. 14, his observations and impressions of his sittings with Mme. Bisson. They fully corroborate those of the author. We may quote some passages :—

" We know that nearly all persons who attended these sittings in Paris share my positive verdict on the phenomena. That was not the case in Munich, and that is not surprising. Similar experiences were had with Eusapia and other excellent mediums. The sittings succeed better in one *milieu* than in another, and since we have become acquainted with the mental disposition of the Munich gentlemen, from their publications in Germany and in Paris, we are prepared for anything.

" The impression produced on those who do not attend the sittings is mostly unfavourable. Why? Because they have no opportunity of convincing themselves of the reality of the phenomena; because they have only read the reviews and seen the photographs. Their attention concentrates itself chiefly upon those photographs, which create some suspicion, and it is just the latter which have been mostly published in the journals and discussed and interpreted in every possible way, while no attention has been paid to the good photographs.

" Mme. Bisson and Dr von Schrenck Notzing were quite aware of that, and they would, no doubt, have omitted these pictures from their books, if that had been an honourable proceeding. Just as it is expedient not to utter every truth, it might also have been expedient not to publish every photograph of genuine phenomena. But the authors were not guided by such considerations, for they knew, as all those who are really experienced in this subject know, that the admixture of apparent fraud (and sometimes of real fraud) is a mysterious and unpleasant accompaniment of mediumistic phenomena. The public at large is quite ignorant regarding these questions. It behaves just as it did seventy years ago, with regard to the phenomena of somnambulism. Some of the mediumistic photographs resemble certain faces in an illustrated journal, and a judgment is at once arrived at. That is the general rule. Simplicity itself becomes a detective."

Gabriel Delanne and L. Chevreuil, who had been present at a number of sittings, vouch for the genuineness of Eva's phenomena, in a series of articles in the *Revue du Spiritisme*, March to June 1914, waging a successful controversy against the Barkley-Durville attacks.

Dr Bourbon, who attended many of the sittings previously reported, publishes his testimony, based on eighteen months of personal observations at the Bissons' residence, in the *Annales* for 1914, and fully corroborates the genuineness of the phenomena. He fully describes the whole experimental arrangements, and shows the absurdity of the hypothesis of fraud, or of rumination. I shall confine myself to one of his observations, made in my absence:—

" In a sitting in July 1913, a grey substance appeared on the medium's shoulder and underwent various changes, sliding down on to her upper arm and breast, and carrying out a series of lively movements. At the same time a finger gradually formed in the region of the left groin, and showed some movement. Suddenly the substance mentioned fell upon the finger, quickly folded itself about it, and laid itself into the medium's lap, covering her thighs. The observation of the whole process was facilitated by the fact that Eva held the curtains wide open, and never attempted to close them, allowing her hands to rest outside the curtains on her knees." Dr Bourbon concludes as follows :—" At present we lack the means of classifying this kind of phenomena, which cannot be included in any class of known experiences. Photography can only prove the absence of collective hallucination. It tells us nothing about the changes, the development, the causation, or the essence, of these phenomena. It would be quite impossible to record much of what I have seen on the photographic plate; still less on the kinematograph."

If we consider that this testimony is that of an eminent French physician who has grown grey in his science, and is based upon a year and a half of observation, it should have greater weight than that of observers who only attended four or five sittings, modified their judgment subsequently, and finally appeared in public as opponents.

x

The peculiar origin and development of the teleplasm which precedes the final materialisation structure, and was also observed by Dr Bourbon as above, has recently been found in the case of other mediums, who gave results agreeing with the author's and Mme. Bisson's observations.

Thus two reliable experimenters, who compiled their records independently of each other, but whose investigations are still pending, inform the author that a young man of twenty-two, who is a medium, also exhibits materialisation phenomena resembling those of Eva C.: formation of an independently moving substance, which changes into shreds, cords, and patches, forms large disk-like surfaces, separates from the medium, and disappears without a trace or is reabsorbed. The materialisations become more distinct on forming a chain, as if the material were thus increased in quantity. The movements and changes of the formless material into a kind of shaking jelly, simple lumps, or veils and cords, agree closely with the changes of teleplasm in the case of Eva C. They observed in one sitting that a piece of material crept up the medium's body and disappeared in his mouth. The physiological accompaniments, such as moaning, are the same.

The experimental conditions seem to be even better than in the case of Eva C., for the young man is only clad in a black tricot, sits in front of the curtain during the whole sitting, and his hands are held by the experimenters. The illumination was partly by red light; but in the sitting of 4th August, which particularly showed the development of the teleplasm, the medium permitted the use of white lamp-light. In one case, the portrait of a young woman developed on the white material. The flash-light photograph in the author's possession closely resembles that obtained by Dr Imoda with the medium Linda Gazerra.

This is not the only confirmation. The Vienna physician, Dr Harter, who is known as an able and critical observer, reports that in the case of the medium Frau Fischer, he observed the formation of a flat face image, beside other materialised forms, while sitting 8 feet from the medium. If we add that another private circle of investigators succeeded in photographing a whole phantom with the same characteristics as observed by the author, one must admit that the probability that we have to deal with definite physical events, obeying laws of their own, at present unknown, is very great. And one can only hope that other experiments, impartially made with other mediums, may further confirm the accuracy of our observations with Eva.

The Editors of the journal *Opinion*, Gimés and Guasco, attended a series of sittings, and dealt with the whole of occultism in a series of articles. These observers also confirm the genuineness of Eva C.'s phenomena. Finally, M. Faral, a well-known author, in an article entitled " My Testimony Concerning Mme. Bisson's Experiments " (*Echo du Merveilleux*), 13th June 1914, gives his judgment in favour of the phenomena on the basis of six sittings. I may here quote a few passages from his report :—

" These experiments are conducted in a truly scientific spirit. Everything is done in a good light without chains, without songs, and without darkness. There is nothing suspicious, nothing mystical, such as we often see in the meetings of occultists. One gets the impression of serious scientific experiments. Participation in the sittings is an important supplement to the reading of the book on *Materialisations Phœnomene*. It is easily understood that this book leaves some doubts behind (*e.g.*, as regards the flat, paper-like, folded appearance of some of the images), but as soon as one has seen with one's own eyes how such materialisations are formed, no further doubt is possible. I myself noted the transparency of a phenomenon by observing through it details of the black dress worn by Eva. In the third sitting I could see the remarkable material called teleplasm for the first time. It appeared in the medium's lap in the shape of a small luminous sphere, the size of a nut, which grew visibly, disappeared in a few minutes, and then reappeared.

"This phenomenon took place at 20 inches from my eyes, and we could simultaneously observe the medium's feet and head. Her hands were motionless, and so were her feet. The control was as exact and perfect as possible. In the sitting of 5th May, after about forty-five minutes, a materialisation, the size of a human head, appeared on the medium's left breast and shoulder, showing a vague, flat, human profile of a dull white colour. This also appeared to be transparent. The phenomenon suddenly appeared, disappeared, and reappeared. When Mme. Bisson illuminated this face unexpectedly with an electric torch, the medium gave a little cry, and the materialisation immediately disappeared. During the phenomenon Eva remained quite motionless, only her sighs indicated that she suffered. Her hands were constantly visible from beginning to end.

"After the doubts which the reading of the book left in my mind, I have acquired a definite conviction on the basis of my own observations."

Faral also mentions the favourable impression made upon him by the medium, and concludes : " To the detractors of Mme. Bisson, I say, with the fullest conviction, ' You are on the wrong track.' I say it without any hope of convincing them, for people do not like to change an opinion once formed. But one must vividly regret that the first serious investigations of materialisation phenomena have been attacked —and with much vehemence and passion—by the very people whose duty it was to receive them with justice and sympathy."

It is not without interest to give a short list of the more important witnesses, drawn from every walk in life, who have taken part in the sittings, since the first publication of the *Materialisations Phœnomene*. During May and June 1914, thirty-three persons altogether took part in sittings at which the author was present. To these must be added observers from January to May 1914, so that since November 1913 there have been at least fifty or sixty. The witnesses already mentioned—Dr Bourbon (physician), Professor Charles Richet (physiologist), de Fontenay —as well as the authors, de Vesme, Delanne, and Chevreuil, have borne public testimony in favour of the genuineness of the phenomena in special articles and declarations. To these must be added the tests conducted by men of science, such as Professor Boirac (Rector of Dijon University), Professor Claparède (Zoologist of Geneva), Professor Courtier (Director of the Physiological Laboratory at the Sorbonne), Professor Bennett (formerly Professor of Philosophy at Cambridge), Professor Flammarion (Astronomer, of Paris), and the physicians Dr Potheau and Dr

Montalescot (who confirmed the genuineness of the phenomena in letters addressed to Mme. Bisson), Mr W. B. Yeats, Dr Kortsen (Psychologist of Copenhagen), and Van Twick of The Hague. Of representatives of the Press, the following have expressed themselves in favour of the reality of the phenomena : MM. Henriques Philippe, Divoire, Giniés, Guasco, R. Faral and Nicolle.

There is, therefore, a total of sixteen savants and six journalists who take the part of Mme. Bisson and her medium Eva C., as well as numerous responsible private persons, whereas the opponents consist of a few persons, some of whom did not attend a single sitting, while others, after a very few sittings (two to five) converted their originally favourable judgment afterwards into an unfavourable one.

It should be added that, at present, Eva C. is not the only person showing these peculiar materialisation phenomena. Independent observations by other investigators with new mediums will probably lead to a final solution of the teleplastic problem.

Reports of French Investigators 1916 (Paris).

SITTING OF THE 12TH FEBRUARY 1916.

Present.—Commandant Darget, R. de Fleurière, and Mme. Bisson.

Commandant Darget reports as follows :—

" I will say a few words about the precautions usually adopted by Mme. Bisson during the sittings. Close inspection of the séance room and the cabinet, and of the dress to be worn by the medium (black tricot, tights, and overall), as well as Eva's mouth and hair. Overall and tights were sewn together as to form one article of apparel without gaps. The medium then sits on an easy chair in the cabinet, with her hands resting on her knees. I hold her right hand, while M. de Fleuriere holds her left.

" An electric lamp with a strong white light is behind a screen during the whole sitting. The light is sufficient to see the medium and the hands of a watch clearly.

" After about twenty minutes small whitish flakes appear on the medium's black overall, and then disappear. Then, on the left shoulder, some material appears, very distinctly, against the black background on account of its luminous white colour. This material exhibits the outline of a human hand. This hand becomes more and more distinct, and moves the fingers. Then this well-developed hand moves over the medium's breast downwards, and remains for a moment on her lap. The size of the hand is that of a child of ten. At the urgent request of Mme. Bisson the small hand approaches the hands of the observers, touches them, and withdraws again. At Mme. Bisson's renewed request, the hand comes forward again and lays itself, without reserve, in my left hand. I was then invited to touch the phantom hand with my free right hand, and this gave me an opportunity of holding the materialised hand in both my own. I had the impression of a hand moistened by cold perspiration.

"Finally the hand withdrew gradually, though I did not particularly perceive the cessation of the contact. The hand melted away and disappeared, and I could not say at what precise moment it disappeared.

"At one instant my left hand, with the phantom hand in it, lay on the medium's right hand, and my own right was placed over the phantom hand, so that the four hands lay one over the other. During this time M. de Fleurière held the medium's left hand, and all this was perfectly visible. During the occurrence of these phenomena the medium was in the trance condition, and subsequently did not produce anything for a long time.

"Then a new and interesting manifestation occurred. The medium released her hands from those of the observers, and made the finger-tips of her two hands approach each other, and recede slowly several times. Gradually some white threads appeared before our eyes, joining the fingers of the two hands. While she continued these motions the threads became thicker and increased in number.

"Mme. Bisson asked Eva, next time the hands were rather far apart, to hold them steady, and she took a bundle of these threads into her right hand. I touched the substance with my right index finger, and had the impression of cool and damp material.

"When, at Mme. Bisson's request, I touched the threads extended between the fingers, I felt a slight resistance. The threads then gradually got thinner and thinner, and less numerous, until they entirely disappeared.

"As a last phenomenon, we observed the emergence of a white substance from her mouth. It hung down over her lower lip, and its colour contrasted with the red of the lips.

"The sitting began at nine and ended at ten. After the medium had undressed the final examination was carried out. On the dress a few places were moist. They corresponded with the points at which the substance had first appeared (chiefly at the left shoulder, where the hand had first formed itself).

"This kind of mediumship was unknown to me up to now, although I have been engaged in mediumistic research for forty-five years. I was all the more pleased to become acquainted with it. The productions of Eva C. are undoubtedly genuine, and only a malicious prejudice could doubt the reality of the occurrences. They enrich science as regards the physiological functions of the human body, a science which quarrels about hypotheses and theories, and has no knowledge of the forces in our bodies which transform organic material. It seems to me to be the duty of science to tackle this problem also. Claude Bernard wrote with justice: 'That which dominates life is neither chemistry, nor physics, nor anything of the kind, but the ideal principle of the life process.'

"The development of the materialised hand, the movement of its fingers, its approach and touch, in accordance with an expressed wish, give a stronger guarantee than the creeds of the various religions for the fact that we possess a soul, that it continues after death, and that it can manifest after death, by reassuming corporeal, visible, and palpable forms.

"It was not doubt as to the existence of such phenomena which took me to Mme. Bisson's sittings, for previously I had seen whole materialisations of deceased persons, as had also the great savants Crookes, Lombroso, and others, who had the courage to describe their experiences in public.

" The special characteristic of Eva C.'s phenomena is that, not only does she produce complete materialisations, but that she produces, step by step, the necessary teleplastic material, and forms it in successive stages."

The other witness of these occurrences, M. de Fleurière, a highly-placed French ecclesiastic, testifies as follows in a letter to the Editor of the *Annales des Sciences Psychiques* :—

" You ask for my testimony for, or against, the report communicated to me (Darget's). Very well. My conscience, my respect for the truth and the most elementary sense of honour, render it my duty to confirm, point by point, the report communicated to you. I had an opportunity of attending numerous sittings at Mme. Bisson's, and of observing really astounding phenomena, the genuineness of which is beyond all doubt. I intend shortly to publish the facts which I have myself seen, observed and controlled, with all the means of moral and material certainty, at the disposal of human investigation. Perhaps it is of interest to compare my report of the sitting of 12th February 1916 with that of Commandant Darget. For the agreement of both reports would enhance the interest, especially as they are the reports of two men who do not know each other, for I saw Commandant Darget for the first time at Mme. Bisson's, and have not seen him since the sitting, so that I had no opportunity to discuss my impressions with him. I append a short and hurried report :—

" ' After a relatively short period of waiting, some white patches, like drops of milk, appeared on the medium's breast, disappearing and reappearing. Shortly afterwards a white substance appeared on her left shoulder, and seemed to detach itself from her chin. It gradually assumed the shape of a hand, the outlines becoming more and more distinct. It was quite white and very fine, like the delicate hand of a child. It remained for a fairly long time, and we had sufficient time to study it, first on the medium's breast, and then on her knees. At Mme. Bisson's request, the small hand came nearer and stroked the hands of the observers, who held the medium's hands (Darget the right and I the left). After it had withdrawn a little, it appeared again, and laid itself in the hand of Commandant Darget, after which it allowed itself to be touched by Mme. Bisson and by me.

" ' After this Eva gave us an opportunity of observing further extraordinarily interesting phenomena. The medium, still in the trance condition, held her hands straight in front of our eyes, showed us transparent threads of substance emerging from her finger-tips, and connecting them, and drew them out, like a spinner draws a woollen thread, by increasing and diminishing the distance between her hands. We could touch this material, and it gave the impression of a moist, cool and somewhat resistant substance No doubt the materialised products are made of this elementary stuff. Slowly the threads became thinner and less numerous, and shortly afterwards we found that the medium's hands were again in their normal condition, and were as dry as our own.' "

Dr V. Gustave Geley (Paris) on his Observations with Eva C., 1918.

IN a Lecture[1] on "Supra-normal Physiology and the Phenomena of Ideoplastics," the well-known psychologist and physician, Dr Gustave Geley (Paris), deals with metapsychical phenomena, and especially their physiological aspects. In his view, our ignorance concerning this subject is due to our lack of knowledge of the original and essential laws of nature. Even normal physiology is full of riddles. Thus the whole mechanism of life, and the activity of the so-called functions, are still far from being clear. The constitution of the organism itself and everything connected with it—birth, growth, embryonic and post-embryonic development, the maintenance of the personality during life, and organic restitutions (in some animals this extends to the regeneration of limbs, and even of entrails)—are as many insoluble riddles, if we accept the scientific view of individuality, and regard these forms of activity as a complex of single elements and their functions. Why a complex of cells, by the fact of the association of its elements, should have this vital and individualising force, is an insoluble mystery. Equally unexplained is the repetition, in embryonic life, of stages traversed in the previous development of the race, of the series of metamorphoses which finally lead to complete forms, and therefore tend towards a definite end.

Among the mysterious processes of this kind we have, among certain insects, the stage of the chrysalis. Within the protective covering of the chrysalis (which shields the animal from light and other disturbing influences), the body of the insect is dematerialised. It dissolves into its constituents and forms a uniform mass, a homogeneous amorphous substance, in which the organic and specific differences more or less disappear. The muscles, the greater part of the viscera, and the nerves are reduced to the original primary substance—the basis of life. Then suddenly this substance organises itself, and a new materialisation takes place at its expense. The adult animal is quite different from the primitive larva. Facts are presented by supra-normal physiology analogous to the teleplastic structures produced by certain persons. Only here the physiological organisation transcends the limits of the organism, separates from it, and acts outside it (ecto-plastically). In this process also organic forms (or new representatives) are reconstituted from the ground substance.

Dr Geley studied materialisations in several mediums, but in his lecture he only refers to those observed in the case of Eva C. These results were obtained under control conditions,' which were completely satisfactory. They are less valuable for their transcendental character than for the accurate indications which they offer concerning the genesis and primordial character of materialisation. Geley continues as follows :

"Eva C. was educated and prepared for the investigations by Mme. Bisson. In the works published by this lady and Dr von Schrenck Notzing we find numerous particulars concerning the nature of materialisation.

[1] Lecture, on 28th January 1918, given in the large Medical Lecture Theatre of the Collège de France to the Members of the Psychological Institute.

"While Mme. Bisson's book represents a conscientious collection of facts, Dr von Schrenck Notzing's full treatise represents a scientific and complete investigation of the phenomena obtained with Eva C., carried out with great clearness and accuracy, and with an artistic understanding. It also contains experiments with another medium, whose gifts were quite similar to those of Eva C. Now I had the privilege of continuing these investigations, in conjunction with Mme. Bisson, for twelve months, with two sittings per week, which took place partly in her flat and partly (for three months) in my own laboratory."

Besides Dr Geley, more than a hundred scientific men, and especially physicians, had an opportunity of observing the same phenomena with Eva C., and he could only add his testimony to theirs. Finally, he succeeded in obtaining materialisation phenomena with new subjects, though they were more primitive than those presented by Eva C.

Dr Geley could see and touch the materialisations in question. The testimony of his senses was corroborated by registering instruments and by photography. He often followed the phenomenon from its origin to its end, for it formed and disappeared before his eyes.

"However unexpected," he continues, "however strange and impossible such manifestations seem to be, I have no longer the right to express any doubt as to their reality. Before I continue, I must testify that the medium, in my presence, always gave proofs of absolute honesty during the experiments. The intelligent resignation with which she submits to all conditions, and undergoes the really painful tests of her mediumship, deserves sincere recognition and gratitude on the part of all men of science worthy of the name."

Eva is brought, in the hypnotic state, to the stage in which she forgets her normal personality. Then she is made to sit in a black cabinet. The use of a black cabinet for materialisation has no other object than to withdraw the sleeping medium from the disturbing influences of her surroundings, and especially from the action of light. It thus becomes possible to maintain sufficient illumination in the séance room to observe the phenomena clearly.

Eva always remained partly outside the cabinet. Both her hands were outside the curtains, and a great security of observation was given by this control over her hands.

The phenomena set in after various intervals, sometimes very soon, sometimes very slowly, after an hour or more. They are always accompanied by painful sensations on the part of the medium. She sighs and groans, and recalls the condition of a woman in the act of parturition. These plaintive expressions attain a paroxysm at the moment when the phenomenon appears; they diminish, or cease, as soon as the materialisation is finished.

The phenomenon can be summarised as follows: A substance emanates from the body of the medium, it externalises itself, and is amorphous, or polymorphous, in the first instance. This substance takes various forms, but, in general, it shows more or less composite organs. We may distinguish (1) the substance as a substratum of materialisation; (2) its organised development. Its appearance is generally announced by the presence of fluid, white and luminous flakes of a size ranging from that of a pea to that of a five-franc piece, and distributed here and there over the medium's black dress, principally on the left side.

This manifestation is a premonitory phenomenon, which sometimes precedes the other phenomena by three-quarters of an hour, or an hour. Sometimes it is wanting, and it occasionally happens that no other manifestation follows.

The substance itself emanates from the whole body of the medium, but especially from the natural orifices and the extremities, from the top of the head, from the breasts, and the tips of the fingers. The most usual origin, which is most easily observed, is that from the mouth. We then see the substance externalising itself from the inner surface of the cheeks, from the gums, and from the roof of the mouth.

The substance occurs in various forms, sometimes as ductile dough, sometimes as a true protoplastic mass, sometimes in the form of numerous thin threads, sometimes as cords of various thicknesses, or in the form of narrow rigid rays, or as a broad band, as a membrane, as a fabric, or as a woven material, with indefinite and irregular outlines. The most curious appearance is presented by a widely expanded membrane, provided with fringes and rucks, and resembling in appearance a net.

The amount of externalised matter varies within wide limits. In some cases it completely envelops the medium as in a mantle. It may have three different colours—white, black, or grey. The white colour is the most frequent, perhaps, because it is the most easily observed. Sometimes the three colours appear simultaneously. The visibility of the substance varies a great deal, and it may slowly increase or decrease in succession. To the touch it gives various impressions. Sometimes it is moist and cold, sometimes viscous and sticky, more rarely dry and hard. The impression created depends on the shape. It appears soft and slightly elastic when it is expanded, and hard, knotty, or fibrous when it forms cords. Sometimes it produces the feeling of a spider's web passing over the observer's hand. The threads are both rigid and elastic.

The substance is mobile. Sometimes it moves slowly up or down, across the medium, on her shoulders, on her breast, or on her knees, with a creeping motion resembling a reptile.

Sometimes the movements are sudden and quick. The substance appears and disappears like lightning and is extraordinarily sensitive. Its sensitiveness is mixed up with the hyperæsthetic sensibility of the medium. Every touch produces a painful reaction in the medium. When the touch is moderately strong, or prolonged, the medium complains of a pain comparable with the pain produced by a shock to the normal body.

The substance is sensitive to light. Strong light, especially when sudden and unexpected, produces a painful disturbance in the subject. Yet nothing is more variable than the action of light. In some cases, the phenomena withstand full daylight. The magnesium flash-light acts like a sudden blow on the medium, but it is withstood, and flash-light photographs can be taken.

The substance has an intrinsic and irresistible tendency towards organisation. It does not remain long in the primitive condition. It often happens that the organisation is so rapid that the primordial substance does not appear at all. At other times one sees at the same time the amorphous substance, and some forms or structures, more or less completely embedded in it, *e.g.*, a thumb suspended in a fringe of the substance. One even sees heads and faces embedded in the material.

Dr Geley then proceeds to describe the structures formed. They are very various. Sometimes they are indefinite, non-organised structures, but most frequently they are organic formations, varying in their composition and completion. When the materialised organ is complete, it has the perfect appearance, and all the biological qualities, of a living organ. Fingers have been seen which were wonderfully modelled, including the nails; also complete hands, with bones and joints; a living brain-case, in which Dr Geley could touch the bones under thick hair. He also saw well-developed living human faces.

In many cases these structures were completely created and developed before his eyes from beginning to end. Thus Dr Geley was sometimes able to see fingers, projecting from the substance, which joined the fingers of the medium's hand. When Eva took away her hand the substance was pulled out, formed strong cords, and expanded, forming fringes resembling network. Finally, he saw in this network, in succession, the formation of some fingers, a hand, or a completely organised face. Sometimes such an organisation took place out of substance emerging from the mouth. Dr Geley gives the following case out of his note-book :—" A cord of white substance proceeds slowly from the mouth down to Eva's knees, having the thickness of about two fingers. This band assumes the most varied forms before our eyes. Sometimes it expands in the form of a membraneous fabric, with gaps and bulges. Sometimes it contracts and folds up, subsequently expanding and stretching out again. Here and there projections issue from the mass, a sort of pseudopods, and these sometimes take, for a few seconds, the form of fingers, or the elementary outline of a hand, subsequently returning back into the mass. Finally, the cord contracts into itself, extending again on Eva's knees. Its end rises in the air, leaves the medium, and approaches me. I then see that the end condenses itself in the form of a knot or terminal bud, and this again expands into a perfectly modelled hand. I touch this hand; it feels quite normal. I feel the bones and the fingers with the nails. This hand is then drawn back, becomes smaller, and vanishes at the end of the cord. The latter makes a few further motions, contracts, and then returns into the medium's mouth."

Often the substance proceeds from the surface of the medium's body, in an invisible and an impalpable state, no doubt through the meshes of the dress, and subsequently condenses. It is then found that a white patch has formed on the black tunic at the level of the shoulders, the breast, or the knee. This patch extends and assumes the outlines and moulding of a hand or a face. Whatever the formation may be, the phenomenon does not always remain in contact with the medium. It is often observed quite separated from her.

The following example is typical in this connection: " A head suddenly appears about 30 inches from the head of the medium, above her and on her right side. It is a human head of normal dimensions, well developed, and with the usual relief. The top of the skull and the forehead are completely materialised. The forehead is broad and high.

The hair is short and thick, and of a chestnut or black colour. Below the line of the eyebrows the design is vague, only the forehead and skull appearing clearly. The head disappears for a moment behind the curtain, and then reappears in the same condition, but the face, imperfectly materialised, is covered with a white mask. I extend my hand, and pass my fingers through the bushy hair, and touch the bones of the skull. The next moment everything has disappeared."

The structures, therefore, show a certain independence. The materialised organs are not without vitality, and are alive, in the biological sense. Thus a well-developed hand has the functional capacities of a normal hand. I have often been touched by a hand, or grasped by fingers.

Well-developed organic formations, having the full appearance of life, are rather rare with Eva. Often there are imperfect formations, flat and without relief, or sometimes partly flat and partly in relief. Geley, in some cases, saw a hand or face which was flat, but which subsequently assumed a third dimension before his eyes. The dimensions of the imperfect formations are sometimes smaller than in nature, and the structures are really miniatures.

" Dr von Schrenck Notzing," continues Geley, " observed, with the help of stereoscopic cameras and by means of cameras mounted in the cabinet on one side, that the back of the materialisations consisted of a mass of amorphous substance, that the organic form was lacking, and sometimes showed empty spaces. I was able to confirm this fact. The phantom formations often show defects, faults and gaps in their newly-formed organs."

There are all kinds of transitions between the perfect and imperfect organic structures, and the change from one to the other, as already mentioned, often occurs under the eyes of the observer. Besides these formations, a curious species of structures must, according to Geley, be considered. They are not organs, but rather imitations thereof, more or less successful, and more or less magnified. They are true phantoms. Thus we may observe : Phantoms of fingers having nothing of such an organ, except the general form, no warmth, no flexibility, no joints ; phantoms of faces, which seem to be pictures cut out, or masks ; bundles of hair, attached to indefinite shapes, etc., etc. Such phantoms, properly so-called, whose metapsychic reality is undeniable (a very important point), have confused and bewildered many observers. " . . . One might say," exclaimed M. de Fontenay, " that a sort of malignant demon was making fun of the observers ! " In reality, according to Geley, these phantoms are easily (?) explained. They are produced, in his view, by a power of but slight metapsychic subtlety, which has inadequate means at its disposal, but does its best. It does not succeed, because its activity, taken out of the beaten track, does not possess the certainty, imparted to ordinary physiological acts, by the normal flow of biological processes. In order to understand what is here happening, it should be remarked that normal physiology often shows such false formations. Besides successful organic structures, there are monstrosities and irregular formations. In this respect, there is nothing more remarkable than the bizarre neoplasms and dermoid cysts, in which one finds hair, teeth, various organs, and more or less perfect embryonic structures. Just like normal physiology, super-normal physiology has both its successful products and its failures, its monstrosities, and its dermoid formations. A phenomenon, which is at least as remarkable as the appearance of the materialised forms, is their disappearance. This is sometimes instantaneous, or nearly so. In less than a second the structure disappears, although its presence has been previously verified by sight and touch.

In other cases the disappearance is gradual. We observe the return of the primitive substance and its absorption into the body of the medium in the reverse order in which it came. In other cases we observe that the disappearance takes place gradually, not by the absorption of the substance, but by a progressive diminution of its perceptible properties. Thus the visibility of the structure slowly decreases, its outlines become fainter, and are finally extinguished.

During the whole time of the materialisation phenomenon the product formed is in obvious physiological and psychical connection with the medium. The physiological connection is sometimes perceptible in the form of a thin cord joining the structure with the medium, which might be compared with the umbilical cord joining the embryo to its parent. Even if this cord is not visible the physiological *rapport* is always close. Every impression received through the teleplasm reacts upon the medium and *vice versa*. The sensation reflex of the structure coalesces with that of the medium; in a word, everything proves that the teleplasm is the partly externalised medium herself.

Dr Geley here only speaks from the physiological point of view, without considering the psychological side, and continues: " Both normal and super-normal physiology tend to establish the unity of the organic substance. In our experiments we have observed, above all, that a uniform amorphous substance externalises itself from the medium's body, and gives rise to the various ideoplastic forms. We have seen how this uniform substance organised and transformed itself under our eyes. We have seen a hand emerging from the mass of the substance; a white mass developed into a face. We have seen how, in a few moments, the form of a head was replaced by the shape of a hand. By the concurrent testimony of sight and touch we have followed the transition of the amorphous unorganised substance into an organically developed structure which had temporarily all the attributes of life—a complete formation, so to speak, in flesh and blood.

" We have watched the disappearance of these formations as they sank back into primitive substance, and have even observed how, in an instant, they were absorbed into the body of the medium. In supra-normal physiology there are no different organic substrata for the various substances as, *e.g.*, a bone substance, a muscular, visceral, or nervous substance; it is simply, then, a single substance, the basis and substratum of organic life.

" In normal physiology it is exactly the same, but it is not so obvious. In some cases it appears quite clear that the phenomenon which takes place in the black séance cabinet, takes place also, as already mentioned, in the chrysalis of the insect. The dissolution of tissues reduces a large proportion of the organs, and their various parts, to a single substance, that substance which is destined to materialise the organs and the various parts of the adult form. We, therefore, have the same manifestation in both physiologies."

Geley discusses the completion of the unit of the organic substance, which applies to supra-normal as well as to normal physiology. It appears to Geley to be the most important point in the biological problem. He also assumes a dynamism which organises, centralises, and directs.

Hyslop, in his article on " Super-normal Physiology and the Phenomena of Ideoplastics " (*Jour. Am. Soc. for Psych. Res.*, May 1919), recognises Geley's method as truly scientific, but questions the justification of his somewhat arbitrary division.

A classification is not an explanation. A one-sided biological conception of the materialisation phenomena is insufficient, for the process not only includes formations of an organic character, but textile products (veils, etc.), with the external signs of manufacture by machinery, as well as certain unorganic materials. We must also consider the action of entirely unknown physiological laws, in such things as the appearance and disappearance of objects and pictures, and the telekinetic phenomena. Whether the ideoplastic hypothesis will turn out to be fruitful and sufficient cannot as yet be decided. But all authors who recognise the reality of the materialisation phenomena agree with Geley that, as Hegel says, the idea, the spirit, must be regarded as the ultimate source from which all the phenomena flow.

To illustrate his argument, Dr Geley reproduces a number of photographs of materialisation phenomena with Eva C., obtained in 1918. These interesting photographs were obtained with the co-operation of Mme. Bisson, M. Calmette (General Inspector of Paris Hospitals), and Jules Courtier (Professor of Physiological Psychology at the Sorbonne). The first two pictures demonstrate the amorphous substance which developed under Geley's eyes. The other pictures give representations of faces and heads developing out of this substance. Their production was accurately observed from the beginning to the end while the curtain was fully opened. Some of them were formed from a solid cord of matter emerging from the medium, or from a nebulous substance, the condensation of which could be observed. Considerable amounts of the original cord, and the primary matter, remained on the fully materialised structures. Geley convinced himself by the eye, by the touch, and by stereoscopic photographs, of the three-dimensional character of these formations.

Various faces show, in their size and in their physiognomy, great analogies, as well as differences, from one sitting to the next, or even in the same sitting. The degree of completion varies probably on account of imperfect materialisation. The rudiments of the substance, according to Geley, indicate a metapsychic embryology of considerable importance for the genesis of the product. The better the forms are materialised, the greater is their independence. They move about Eva C., or show themselves in natural size, giving an impression of remarkable vivacity, and sometimes of great beauty, as they appear at the opening of the curtain. The usual precautions were carried out in Dr Geley's laboratory in a very strict manner. Eva C. was undressed on entering the séance room in the presence of Dr Geley and Mme. Bisson. She then put on the séance costume, which was sewn up the back. Her hair and mouth were examined by Dr Geley, or one of his collaborators. Eva C. then took her seat on the wicker chair in the cabinet. *Her hands were always visible, and were held outside the curtains.* There was always sufficient light in the séance room.

Geley concludes his lecture with the words, " I do not say, ' there was no fraud during these sittings ' ; but I say, ' the possibility of fraud was altogether excluded.' I cannot repeat it too often : the materialisations were always produced before my eyes, and I observed the whole genesis and development with my own eyes."

With Dr Geley's permission, the author here reproduces ten photographs (Figs. 201-210) from his collection, which show the complete *agreement* of the author's results with these further results, obtained five years afterwards, in different circumstances, and under probably even more rigid conditions. The creative and formative power is the same in both series of observations, and exhibits the peculiarities characteristic of the productions of Eva C. There are expressive female faces, draped with veil-like fabrics, and fragments of teleplasm. The cleverly arranged decorative elements combine to form an artistic total impression intended for the observer. The faults of proportion in the faces, the indentations, the sketchiness and incompletion of the execution ; in short, the technique of production, has remained the same in every point as in the case of the author's results. Rents, breaks and cracks, such as have been alleged by critics as evidence of fraud, are also present in Geley's pictures, and are particularly well shown in the enlarged reproduction of the teleplastic female face (Fig. 210), in the cross lines of the lower portion, which also shows the character of a material resembling paper. We have here, both in the positive and negative sense, identical results forming an extremely valuable corroboration of the accuracy of the author's own investigations.

The biological significance of the " primordial " substance, the ideoplastic development of organic and organised forms, of human limbs, heads, and imitations of these, are sufficiently dealt with in the first part of this work. The same may be said of their teleplastic evolution and involution, and the chemical and microscopic investigations in connection with them. But this is not intended to detract from the great progress represented by Dr Geley's investigations.

We must also point out that the observations with Eva C. are not unique, in spite of the sporadic occurrence of mediumship. Thus Professor Enrique Morselli, in his work *Psychology and Spiritism*, gives some clear representations of phantom formations obtained with Eusapia Paladino, which also give the impression of being incomplete and imperfect, some showing nebulosity and vague outlines, while others are flat without any density, wrapped in veils, and very luminous. In his book Morselli warns against admitting intruders with their " impertinent and arrogant judgment unsupported by any previous study."

Similar experiences are reported by Madeleine Lacombe (*Ann. Sc. Psychiques*, 1918 and 1919) in her letters to Camille Flammarion in connection with the private medium, the Countess Castelvicz, in Lisbon. Here again the phantoms began as luminous, transparent, and subsequently condensing clouds. They were only partly materialised at first, and, in addition to formations true to life, they show also mask-like and sketchy types. The phantom of a nun (Fig. 211) is flat, in spite of the very vivid expression of the face. The face is veiled, and the upper

Fig. 201. Teleplasm emerging from the hands.

Fig. 202. Emergence of the substance from mouth and nose.

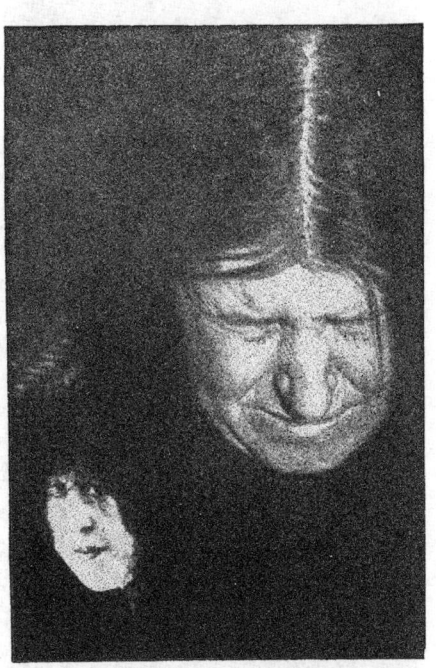

Fig. 203. Face developed from a nebulous mass at the medium's right shoulder. Lips modelled in an otherwise plat face.

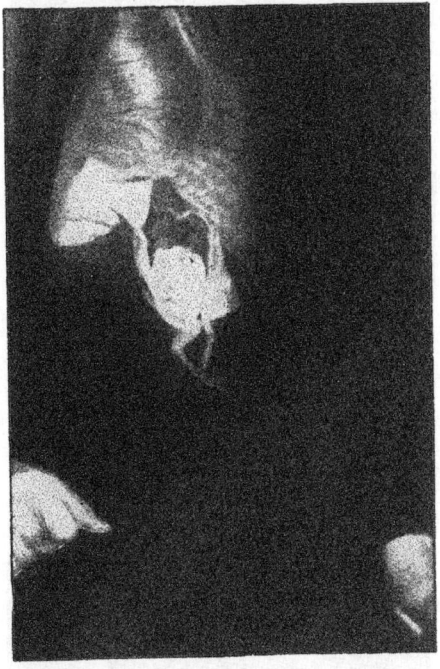

Fig. 204. Face and veil seen to develop from a cloud.

FIG. 205 HEAD SAME AS FIG 204, MORE HIGHLY MATERIALISED

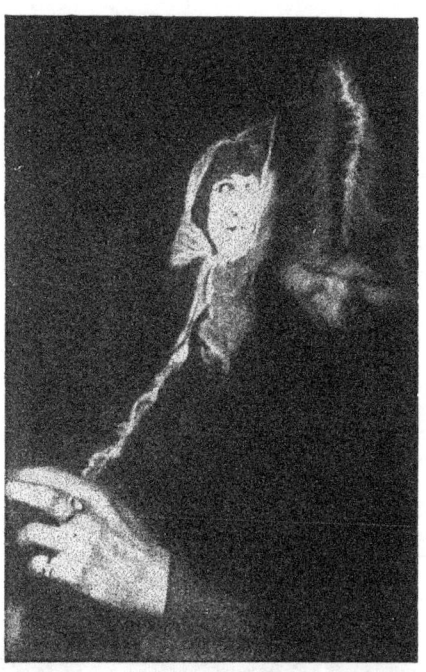

FIG. 206. THE SAME FACE, ON THE MEDIUM'S RIGHT.

FIG 207 THE SAME FACE IN ANOTHER POSITION, PARTLY COVERED BY THE HEAD OF AN OBSERVER.

FIG. 208. THE SAME, DEMATERIALISING.

body is draped with a white fabric. It is remarkable, in this figure that the whole right side, including the right ear, shoulder, and arm, is entirely wanting, as if this part had been torn off a life-sized portrait. The margin of the phantom on the right side shows an irregular structure, tears, fragments, and threads, somewhat resembling a torn piece of paper. This recalls the structure of the phantom (Fig. 157), which shows a pencilled character in the design of the mantle, and also fibres and threads in its outer margin. In spite of the entirely independent genesis of these two phantoms, the creative agency seems to have worked according to the same scheme. Similar analogies are obtained in pictures of mediums of widely different nationalities. Thus, the author observed in the case of a boy of sixteen, the son of a workman living near the frontier of Upper Bavaria, in a sitting on 16th October 1919, that the substance emerged from his mouth in the form of a self-luminous cloudy ribbon, and this ribbon expanded near the shoulders and enveloped the upper body in a white mass. With the same medium, the representative of the author, who was himself prevented from attending the séance, observed, on the 8th November 1919, at a distance of about 18 inches, a sort of thick fog rising behind the medium in the cabinet. The fog descended on to the boy's head, and finally extended, like a cloth, over his whole face. After some six or eight seconds the apparition changed itself altogether and disappeared at the medium's neck. Later, the author also observed the genesis of a finely-drawn left female hand out of a strongly luminous white, cloud-like substance, emanating from the same medium. These analogies, with previous observations, might be carried much further, from the author's own experience, but for the present he wishes to confine himself to a hasty glance at the photographic material which has been placed in his hands during the last few years by various private circles. Stricter conditions than those covering the sittings with Eva C. could hardly be expected, but their absence need not reduce the accuracy of the observations, in spite of the possibility of errors, since the persons furnishing the accounts are reliable investigators, whose only interest is the service of truth.

Fig. 212 shows a materialisation in its initial stage in the case of a Dutch landed proprietress, who acted as a medium in a private circle, and who placed some photographs at the author's disposal. This photograph recalls that published by Aksakof in his work *Animism and Spiritism*, Vol. II., Plate 1. The next two pictures (Figs. 213 and 214) concern a young Pole from Galicia, with whom the author held a sitting under unfavourable conditions, with a negative result. A Galician Mining Director was a witness of numerous mediumistic phenomena obtained with him, and took some photographs of the teleplastic substance, which developed about the body of the young man in the form of amorphous material, or white fabrics, and lay on the back of the chair, or on his head. Although the author must leave the responsibility for the genuineness of the phenomena on the shoulders of his correspondent, whom he knows to be trustworthy, the analogy with Eva's earlier phenomena is so striking as to give a considerable interest to this photograph, which was obtained before the results with Eva C. were known. The next four photographs are furnished by the same person, and concern a Polish girl in the service of a land agent (Figs. 215, 216, 217 and 218). In this case the substance lies on the face like a grey rag, or projects irregularly from the neck opening, or the mouth. Here again we have striking analogies with Eva C. and Stanislava P. (Figs. 32, 158, 170, 172 and 176).

The next photograph (Fig. 219) shows a large mass of flocculent substance, behind which the head of a phantom is visible. Some stereoscopic pictures of the sittings with Eva C. show the same kind of material, resembling torn cotton, as does an additional photograph of Stanislava P. (Fig. 220), taken by Mr. L., of Warsaw. On the two photographs obtained by the author on 26th October 1919 we see the sixteen-year-old Willy S. opening the curtain with one hand and holding a planchette in the other (Fig. 221), supported by a drawing-board on the boy's knees. A large mass of white substance covers the right shoulder and upper arm, like a white napkin, and is fastened at the neck. The second picture (Fig. 222) shows a white substance on the head covered with large solid strips of a dark colour. The third and fourth photographs (Figs. 223 and 224) show various formations of teleplasm, and the fifth (Fig. 225) shows a primitive face, like that of a snow-man. A comparative survey of the observational material of the last ten years with Eva C., and similar experiences with the medium Stanislava P., as well as with subjects of quite different nationalities (Portugal, Galicia, Italy, Poland and Germany), when clearly examined, does not admit of any doubt concerning the actual, though sporadic, occurrence of the teleplastic faculty in a number of individuals who, quite independently of each other (both in time and space), are capable of producing the same class of phenomena. It is obvious that the teleplastic appearances follow a distinct (biological?) sequence, which covers not only the simpler formations as illustrated, but also more complicated organic and organised bodies, fragments, types, and diagrammatic imitations. However wonderful these phenomena may appear to be, they depend upon a biological mechanism hitherto unexplored; upon a system of forces working with a certain, almost monotonous, uniformity, which is again clearly connected with the most elementary facts of the problem of life.

CONCLUSION.

IF we have a right to expect from every investigator, who takes responsibility for the observations he describes, the qualities of veracity and conscientiousness, as well as a strict objectivity, this requirement applies in an even higher degree to the critic who undertakes publicly to deny the facts stated, and to represent them as the products of error, of inaccurate observation, and of fraud.

It goes without saying that, in the first instance, only such investigators come into the question as have made a special study of the subject, and who possess sufficient experience of their own, and a knowledge of the literature of the subject.

Judgments of savants who are only familiar with other regions of knowledge, and who are not familiar with the matter to be criticised, have no weight, not to speak of laymen. Thus, a botanist will not presume to judge concerning astronomy. " According to the principles of unprejudiced investigation, nobody has the right to doubt the reality

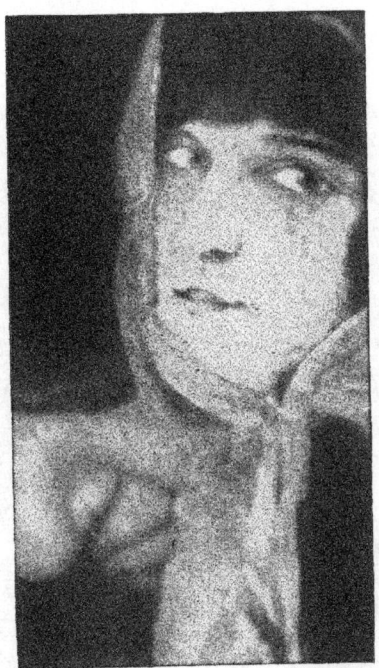

FIG 209. HEAD, SAME AS FIG. 208, BEFORE DEMATERIALISATION, IN ANOTHER POSITION, AND ENLARGED.

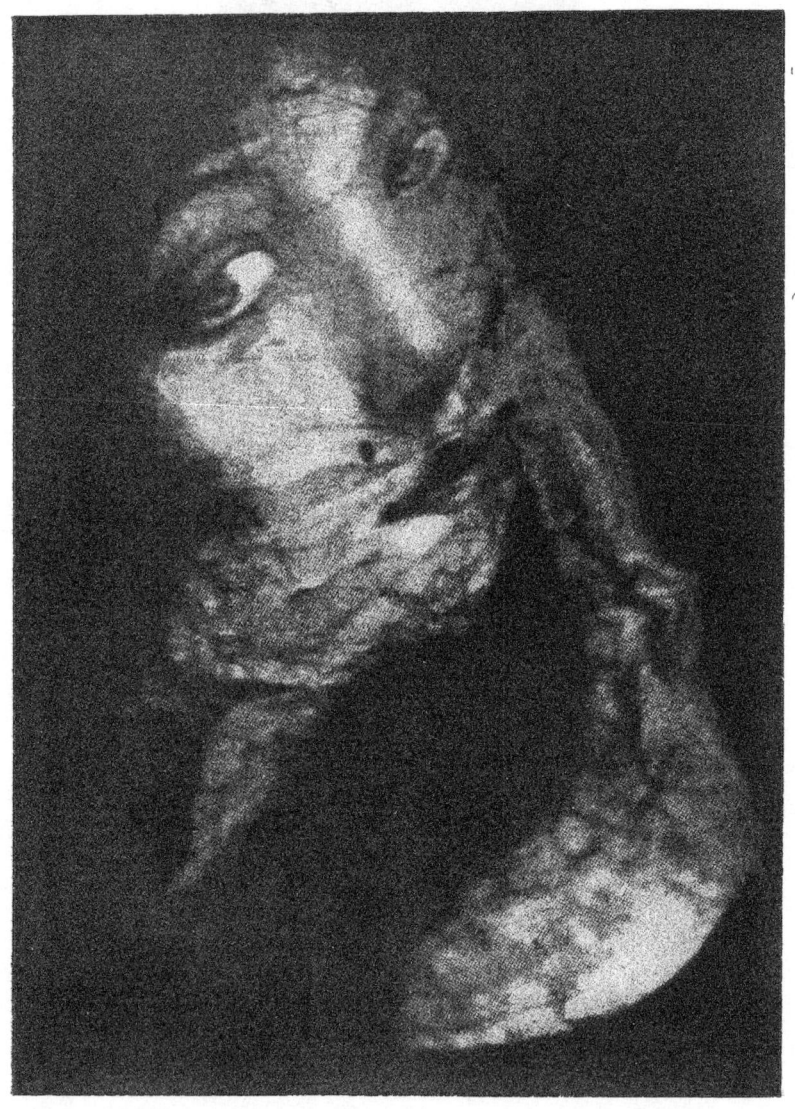

Fig. 210 This head (enlarged) was seen to form from a mass emerging from Eva's mouth. The upper half of the face is more materialised than the lower. Numerous rents and folds.

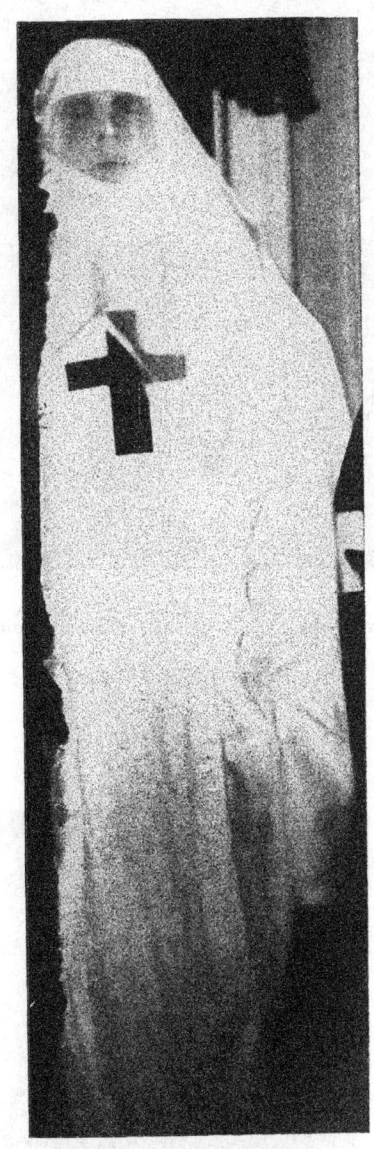

FIG. 211. PHANTOM OF A NUN, TAKEN BY MME. LACOMBE.

Fig. 212 Initial stage of materialisation in the form of a cloud Dutch medium.

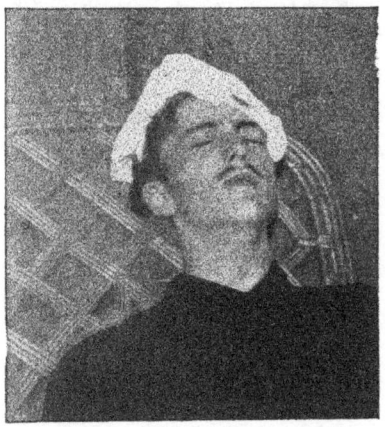

Fig 213 Teleplastic substance on the head of a young Pole in a trance.

FIG. 214. TELEPLASM ON THE LEFT BREAST OF THE YOUNG POLE. PAINED EXPRESSION ON FACE.

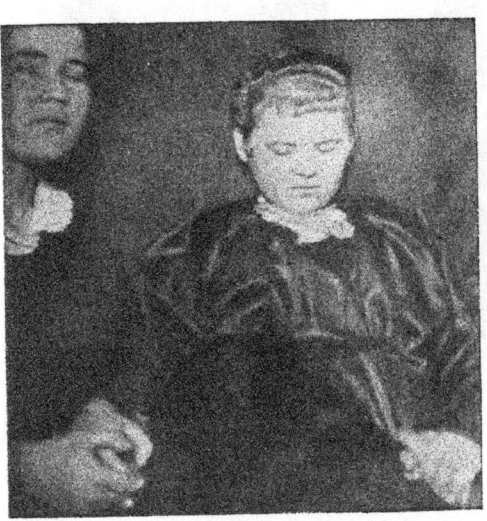

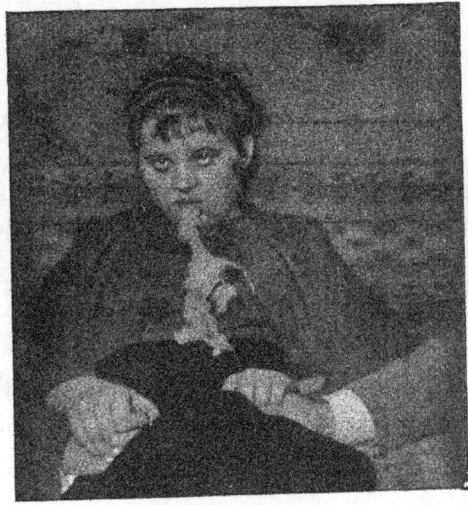

FIG. 215. TELEPLASM AT THE NECK OF A GALICIAN GIRL.

FIG 216 TELEPLASM EMERGING FROM THE MOUTH OF THE SAME MEDIUM.

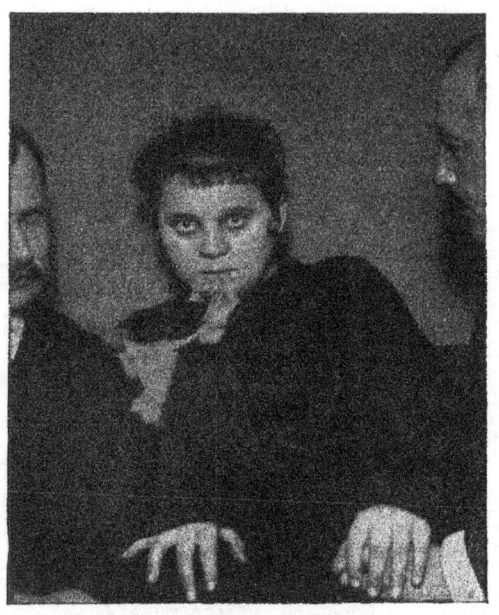

FIG 217. ANOTHER CASE RESEMBLING FIG 214

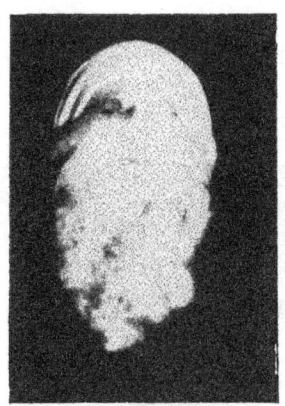

FIG 219 PHANTOM HEAD FROM THE SITTING OF MME. LACOMBE LOWER PART OF THE FACE, AS WELL AS THE NECK, COVERED WITH TELEPLASTIC MATTER

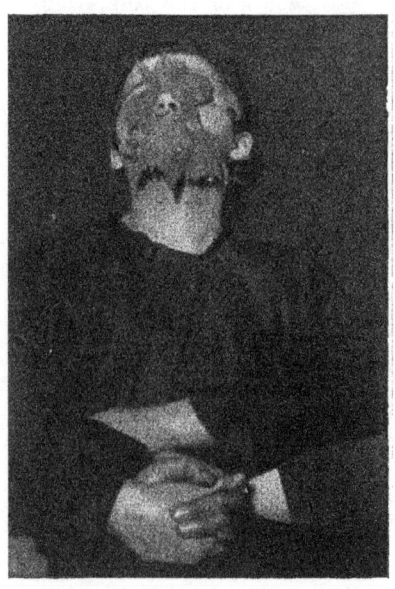

FIG. 218. TELEPLASM COVERING THE FACE OF THE GALICIAN MEDIUM

FIG. 220. TELEPLASTIC MATTER IN FORM OF A VEIL ON THE BREAST OF THE POLISH MEDIUM, STANISLAVA P (WARSAW PHOTOGRAPH.)

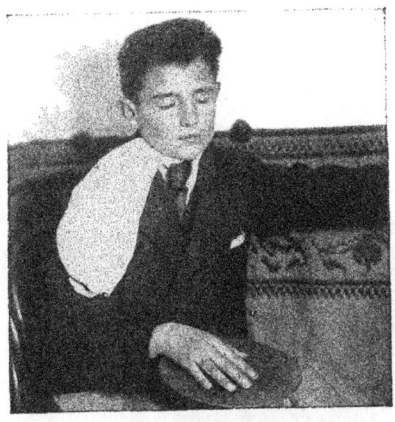

FIG. 221. TELEPLASTIC FABRIC ON THE RIGHT SHOULDER AND ARM OF THE 16 YEAR OLD AUSTRIAN MEDIUM, WILLY S (AUTHOR'S PHOTOGRAPH.)

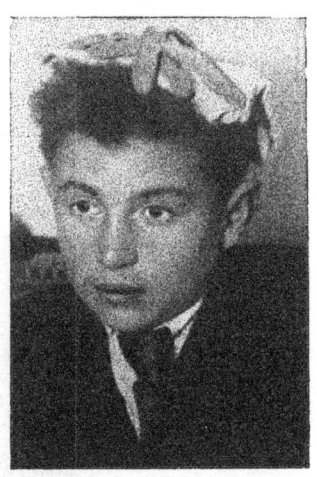

FIG 222 GREY AND WHITE FRAGMENTS ON THE HEAD OF WILLY S. (AUTHOR'S PHOTOGRAPH)

FIG. 223. TELEPLASTIC MATERIAL ON THE CHEST OF WILLY S. (AUTHOR'S PHOTOGRAPH)

FIG 224 PRIMITIVE HAND AT EAR OF WILLY S , WITH TELEPLASTIC MATTER ON RIGHT SHOULDER. (PHOTOGRAPH OF AUTHOR'S COLLABORATOR K..

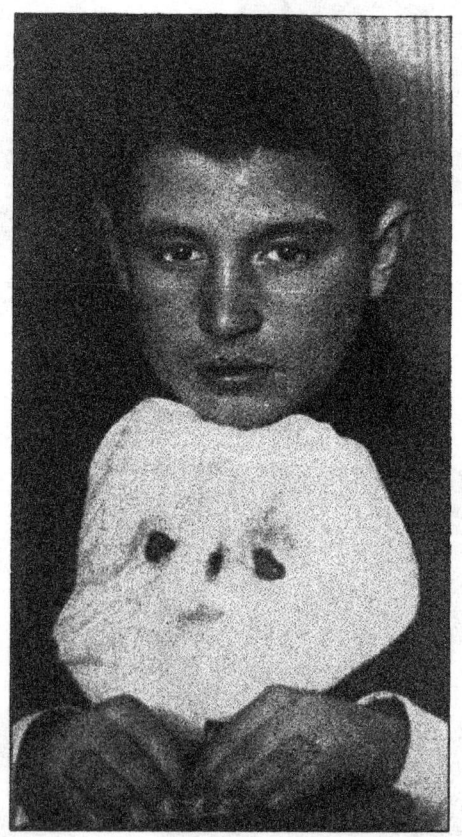

FIG. 225 PRIMITIVE FACE, WITH HOLES, RENTS, AND FOLDS ON THE TELEPLASTIC FOUNDATION. WILLY S. (PHOTOGRAPH TAKEN BY THE AUTHOR'S COLLABORATOR K.)

CONCLUSION

of conscientiously observed facts, or to deny them, until he has himself repeated the experiments in question " (Logothetti).

The unbridled criticism which has been let loose upon the work *Materialisations Phœnomene* shows the very opposite to the obvious postulate mentioned above, and it outrages the right of free investigation. Thus the medium was simply denounced as a conjurer, and the author's investigations as a comedy of fraud. Although nobody was obliged to believe the facts related, or to occupy himself with them, the Kemnitz pamphlet, written by two medical authors, offered a welcome means, at the right moment, to fight and condemn the author's unwelcome observations, which contradict the dominant mechanistic view of the universe.

Detailed investigation of our opponents' assertions, or even a comparison of their contents with the records of the sittings, has hardly been carried out in a single case.

A careful examination of the objections and arguments brought forward by our opponents has shown their baselessness. The first objection was the rumination hypothesis. To put the ruminant Wittig, without further ado, on the same level as the medium, is a logical somersault. It is only when the ruminator has produced the same phenomena under the same conditions that he can be discussed at all. But, up to now, the connection between the two is entirely lacking.

To this must be added the circumstance that these assertions have been carefully tested by us, by means of pictorial experiments on goldbeaters' skin, chiffon, tissue paper, etc. But the results are not at all to be compared with the phantom pictures, quite apart from the absolute impossibility of carrying out, without the use of the hands, the unfolding of the pictures, their fixation, folding up, and the other manipulations required. If, therefore, our opponents wish to establish this objection, they must first of all procure pictures, some of them mask-like, *i.e.*, plastically formed faces with hair, which approach those published in the book, in artistic quality and general appearance, and which, with the same photographic exposure, appear as clearly on the negative as the medium's head itself. That is the first supposition. The second requirement would be the packing and hiding of such packets in the stomach or the gullet. That there must also be small hooks or bent pins, our opponents admit themselves. But then the medium would always risk bodily injury in swallowing such things, for such packets might accidentally release themselves from the packing, under the influence of the liquid contents of the stomach or the intestine, and could involve very dangerous, or even fatal, consequences.

During the process of emergence the knees and hands are quite excluded, and the medium must not rise from the chair. All the manipulations, like folding, fixing to the curtain, folding up, have to be carried out exclusively with the mouth and the tongue. As soon as our opponents are in a position to bring forward a ruminator who can perform all these things, exactly in the manner described, and with the same speed as Eva C., and lead to the production of photographs showing the same appearance as those published in this book, only then can the discussion of rumination be continued. Until then, we must claim the liberty of denying the so-called possibility advanced by our opponents, for only in a purely experimental way, and not by a fight about words on quite wrong premises, or by pure assumptions and hypotheses, can the truth be determined.

The author and his friends have carefully gone over the objections raised, both that of rumination and that of the copying of the *Miroir* reproductions, by conducting further experiments with the medium. They have a right to expect the same painstaking accuracy from their opponents, and it goes without saying that the existing records of the sittings must serve as a model of the experimental conditions. For we must not take details out of the context of the sitting and use them for an attack, or for assertions which cannot be substantiated by the records, *e.g.*, the withdrawal of the hands, the domination of the medium, the hiding of objects in the seat of the chair, or the regular closing of the curtains before the occurrence of the phenomena.

We must also protest against entirely baseless rumours, reports of detective bureaus, or low gossip (Richet case, Algiers) being presented to the reader as proved facts. Such a procedure, as well as the introduction of personal bias into the discussion, is inconsistent with the duty of both parties in a purely scientific discussion, and diverts the attention to minor matters which only have a remote connection, or no connection at all, with the main question of the genuineness and the origin of the mediumistic phenomena.

After the numerous diversions of the Kemnitz-Gulat pamphlet, the author declines, for the future, any such pointless word-battles as have, for instance, been carried on in the daily press, though he is ready, at any time, to examine any facts obtained by his opponents under the conditions of his own experiments, and communicated without animosity. For along the path of theoretical and polemical discussion, which is not bound by the rules of parliamentary politeness, and in which we miss the personal esteem of the opponent, we can hardly expect to obtain a solution of the mediumistic riddle. Only new series of unprejudiced experiments from both points of view can clear the situation. It goes without saying that the right of criticism is not to be limited in any way, for it is a necessary condition of the acquisition of knowledge.

As regards the result of the tests, whether *Miroir* pictures, artistically manipulated, were exposed as phantom pictures, it has been shown that the agreements in certain details cannot be explained by fraud. The dissimilarity between the phantom pictures and all the supposed models, as regards the build of the face, the expression, and the whole form of the heads, is so great that one is not justified in making the new objection that these models had been copied to produce the mediumistic images. For, in this case, there should be similarities, above all in the expression, and in the proportions of the faces, but these are entirely absent.

Finally, the more recent observations made by the author and other savants with the medium Eva C. have yielded nothing that could justify the opponents' objections, and the independent determinations of one of Italy's greatest savants show that similar materialisation phenomena were observed in another medium (Eusapia Paladino).

After the appearance of the first German edition of the *Materialisations Phænomene* (end of 1913), the author had an opportunity, during November and December 1913, and January, May and June 1914, of minutely dealing with critical objections by means of the series of sittings already

CONCLUSION

reported. None of the objections turned out to be valid; nor could any of them even suggest an improvement in the method of observation.

Other observers belonging to the first period (1909 to 1913) gradually emerged into publicity with observations of their own. Among them Guillaume de Fontenay (*Ann. Sc. Psych.*, March 1914), who deals with the experimental arrangement, with the objections raised, with the hypothesis of conjuring, and the ideoplastic theory, and who, finally, fully corroborates the accuracy of the author's observations. In the course of a lecture he also demonstrated his measurements of relative proportions in the photographed materialisation images, as compared with certain portrait heads from the journal *Le Miroir*. This re-examination, made quite independently of the author, arrives at the same result, viz., that reproductions from the *Miroir* could not have been fraudulently used by Eva C., since the relative proportions of the features do not correspond to the alleged models, as well as for other reasons.

Since the same savant took a number of photographs during the sittings with Mme. Bisson, he placed the following letter at our disposal for publication :—

"PARIS, 18*th January* 1914.

"DEAR HERR VON SCHRENCK NOTZING,

"In reply to your letter of 16th January 1914, I can repeat and emphasise my former declaration. Neither you nor I are infallible, and no physicist or any other observer is free from error. It would, therefore, be childish to assert that we could not have been deceived. But, as far as I am concerned, I feel justified in stating that I cannot understand how it would have been possible to deceive us.

"The various ideas which were instinctively suggested (hidden papers, hands of leather, rubber, or gold-beaters' skin, as well as other means of deception), cannot be fitted into the phenomena observed. Even if we assume the rumination hypothesis, it could only be applied to a limited class of phenomena, and would therefore be insufficient. Both you and Mme. Bisson have given your testimony. I gladly add mine as requested, and I consider that it is now the duty of your opponents to prove by deeds, and not by words, that we have been deceived, and how we have been deceived. I await the result of this counter-proof with interest and curiosity.

"Yours, etc.,
"G. DE FONTENAY."

Opponents have sought to find matter for suspicion in the sense of a disavowal of the author, and of metapsychic matters, in the lack of any testimony of the Paris physiologist Charles Richet (discoverer of Anaphylaxis), who took part in several sittings, and had already published a report on his own experiences in Algiers. Professor Richet has kindly explained his attitude in the following letter, addressed to the author :—

"MY DEAR FRIEND,

"I am surprised and annoyed that any one should have attributed to me any sort of contempt, indifference, or opposition with regard to the experiments conducted by you with so much zeal, sincerity, intelligence, and tireless energy, and with results which have not disappointed your four years' work. Occupied as I was with work of a different kind, I could not take part in these experiments as I should have wished. But the little I have seen suffices to enable me to say that every possible precaution was taken.

"As regards my former experiments in Algiers with Eva C., I do not withdraw a single word. Here I follow the example of the great and noble savant William Crookes, who, a short time ago, said, 'I do not withdraw anything of what I have said.'

"Criticism there must be; it is a condition of science itself. The truth must appear in its full beauty, but that will not happen through the agency of incompetent and ignorant persons, who have seen nothing, controlled nothing, examined nothing; who have not even carefully read the accounts of the sittings. But it must come through savants who have really worked, who have experimented without cessation, and who prefer truth to probability. Man is so made that he does not want to accept truth if it does not appear probable, and it is certainly not our fault if the metapsychic region shows so many improbabilities and contradictions.

"Therefore, courage, my dear friend! *Laboremus!*
"Yours sincerely,
"PARIS, 10th June 1914.   "CHARLES RICHET."

Towards the end of the first ten years of observations the well-known Paris psychologist, Dr Gustave Geley, published his essay on "La Physiologie dite Supra-Normale et les Phenomènes d'Idéo-Plastie" which not only acknowledged the correctness of all our previous determinations in every detail, on the basis of his own observations, but also attempted to link materialisation phenomena with physiological, biological, and philosophical considerations.

The importance of Geley's work consists not only in the continuation of the methodical observation of these phenomena, as first elaborated by the author and Mme. Bisson, for the region of materialisation, not only in the systematic treatment of the collection of facts, but especially in the attempt to find its place in the circle of natural phenomena, and in the proof that the reality of such phenomena is one of the strongest arguments against a materialistic and mechanical view of the universe. Even though in discussing details of this work, especially the theoretical deductions, one cannot always agree with the author, one cannot deny the great merit of Geley in applying a new stimulus to these researches. His reports produce an impression that the long years of schooling undergone by the medium have made the phenomena more capable of resistance, and more accessible to scientific treatment, than they were before the war. Thus Geley was able to observe some manifestations uninterruptedly from their genesis to their disappearance. This alone involves an enormous progress in method, which disposes of all suspicion directed against the medium, and eliminates explanations based upon the fraud hypothesis. The perceptions, by sight and touch, were made more objective by registering apparatus and photography.

It is true that, concerning the phenomena themselves, we get nothing new. All that he brings forward had been described and observed by the author and Mme. Bisson many years earlier. Much, indeed, had been examined by us in greater detail, though, as regards theoretical interpretations of this extraordinarily difficult subject, we imposed upon ourselves much greater reserve.